GREAT JEWS IN MUSIC

GREAT JEWS
IN MUSIC

by

DARRYL LYMAN

 Jonathan David Publishers, Inc.
Middle Village, New York 11379

4087

GREAT JEWS IN MUSIC

Copyright © 1986

by

Darryl Lyman

No part of this book may be reproduced in any form without
the prior written consent of the publisher. Address all inquiries to:

Jonathan David Publishers, Inc.
68-22 Eliot Avenue
Middle Village, New York 11379

1989 1988 1987 1986
10 9 8 7 6 5 4 3 2 1

Library of Congress Cataloging-in-Publication Data

Lyman, Darryl, 1944-
  Great Jews in music.

  Includes index.
  1. Musicians, Jewish—Biography. I. Title.
ML385.L95   1986   780′.92′2 [B]   85-27510
ISBN 0-8246-0315-X

Book design by Arlene Schleifer Goldberg

Printed in the United States of America

4087

To my mother,
IDA LYMAN
(née WANDELL)

Photograph Credits

Acknowledgments and thanks are due to the following institutions and persons for having kindly permitted their photographs to be used in this book:

Academy of Motion Picture Arts and Sciences—pages 21, 24, 35 (photo by John Miehle), 50, 73, 95 (photo by Robert W. Coburn), 183.

American Jewish Archives—pages 47, 90, 178, 231.

Arnold Schoenberg Institute—page 189.

Austrian Press and Information Service, New York—pages 122, 190, 293, 298.

Avidom, Menahem—page 304.

Bar-Illan, David—page 32 (photo by Peter Kaplan).

Bob Dylan Office—page 64.

Boston Symphony Orchestra—pages 38, 41 (photo by Whitestone Photo), 53, 67, 108, 109, 113 (photo by Walter H. Scott), 147, 153, 193, 212.

Brooklyn Philharmonic Orchestra—page 70.

Carson Office—pages 37, 143 (photo by Dennis Wile), 292 (photo by Roger Greenawalt).

Chicago Symphony Orchestra—pages 31, 115, 165, 175, 208, 223, 235, 274, 287.

Cincinnati Symphony Orchestra—page 288.

Columbia Artists Management, Inc.—pages 68 (photo by Paul J. Hoeffler), 112 (photo by Christian Steiner), 131, 233 (photo by Christian Steiner), 256 (photo by Christian Steiner).

Dimitroff, Lucienne Bloch—page 45 (photo by Boychuk Studio).

German Information Center—pages 102, 129, 136, 237, 241, 261, 273, 277.

Glass, Philip—page 75 (photo by Jack Mitchell).

Gould, Morton—page 79.

Harrison/Parrott, Ltd.—page 26.

Herbert H. Breslin, Inc.—page 158 (photo by Newey).

ICM Artists, Ltd.—pages 177 (photo by Christian Steiner), 214, 215.

International Musician—pages 28, 77, 88, 93, 106 (photo by Press Department, New York Philharmonic), 111 (photo by Lipnitzki), 126 (photo by John Reggero), 170, 199, 206.

Israel Philharmonic Orchestra—pages 92, 141, 157.

Kipnis, Igor—pages 98, 100.

Los Angeles Philharmonic—pages 226 (photo by Allan Dean Walker), 227.

Minnesota Orchestra—page 62.

Musical America—pages 42, 55, 83, 104, 117, 139, 151, 185, 195, 197, 210.

Peerce, Alice K.—page 154 (photo by Martin Reichenthal).

Pittsburgh Symphony Orchestra—page 162.

Rochberg, George and Gene—page 169 (photo by Bachrach).

Rochester Philharmonic Orchestra—page 57 (photo by Levi).

Royal College of Music (London)—pages 148 (photo by Fritz Luckhardt), 180.

Saint Louis Symphony Orchestra—page 268.

Saint Paul Chamber Orchestra—page 250.

San Francisco Opera—pages 99, 135, 155, 156, 166 (photo by Carolyn Mason Jones), 167 (photo by Ron Scherl), 202 (photo by Carolyn Mason Jones), 203 (photo by Carolyn Mason Jones), 204 (photo by David Powers), 216, 229 (photo by Carolyn Mason Jones), 230, 238, 239 (photo by Robert Lackenbach), 283 (photo by Morton Photographs).

Schneider, Alexander—page 187.

Seattle Symphony—page 69.

Shaw Concerts, Inc.—pages 144, 224, 225, 260, 276 (photo by Christian Steiner), 286 (photo by Christian Steiner), 291, 306 (photo by Alex Von Koettlitz), 307 (top left), 307 (bottom right), 308, 310, 312.

Shirley Kirshbaum and Associates—page 249 (photo by Christian Steiner).

Shuman Associates, Inc.—pages 61 (photo by Diana Michener), 309 (photo by Jack Mitchell).

Streisand, Barbra—page 219.

Styne, Jule—page 221.

Tal, Josef—page 311 (photo copyrighted by Aliza Auerbach).

Teicher, Louis—page 295.

courtesy of University of Southern California School of Music—pages 81, 160, 259.

Weiner, Sarah Naomi—pages 244, 248.

Wolpe, Hilda—page 246.

Young Concert Artists, Inc.—page 303 (photo by Christian Steiner).

Contents

Major Biographies

Thumbnail Sketches

8

Israeli Music Figures

9

10

Acknowledgments

I would like to thank Alfred J. Kolatch of Jonathan David Publishers, Inc., for his help in establishing the general shape of this book and for his patience in waiting for its completion.

My principal starting point for finding Jews in music was the "Musicians" entry in the *Encyclopaedia Judaica* (Jerusalem: Keter Publishing House, Ltd., 1972). My main reference sources for music matters were *The New Grove Dictionary of Music and Musicians,* edited by Stanley Sadie (London: Macmillan Publishers, Ltd., 1980), and the seventh edition of *Baker's Biographical Dictionary of Musicians,* revised by Nicolas Slonimsky (New York City: Schirmer Books, 1984). I culled biographical facts from hundreds of books (especially biographies and autobiographies), newspaper and magazine articles, and press kits sent out by artists' agents.

Special thanks go to Sarah Naomi Weiner, who provided me with valuable information about, and photographs of, her late husband, Lazar Weiner, and her son Yehudi Wyner.

Extraordinary efforts to supply me with photographs were put in by Shirley Fleming, editor of *Musical America;* Annemarie (Woletz) Franco, assistant editor of *International Musician;* Uta Hoffmann, photo librarian of the German Information Center; Krista Lewis of the Austrian Press and Information Service; Lesley Ann Ploof of the promotion office of the Boston Symphony Orchestra; and Robert M. Robb of the public-relations department of the San Francisco Opera.

I would also like to thank the following people for helping me in my search for biographical materials and photographs: Evan Alboum of the publicity department of Shaw Concerts, Inc.; June August, director of public information of the University of Southern California (USC) School of Music; Menahem Avidom; David Bar-Illan; David A. Blakiston, Jr., publicity-materials director of Columbia Artists Management, Inc.; Lucy Breaks, promotion manager of the Philharmonia Orchestra of London; Nancy B. Calocerinos, director of marketing of the Rochester Philharmonic Orchestra; Hattie Clark of Columbia Artists Management, Inc.; Lydia Colley of Harrison/Parrott, Ltd.; Robert Cushman, photograph curator of the Academy of Motion Picture Arts and Sciences; David Diamond; Misha Dichter; Lucienne Bloch Dimitroff of the Ernest Bloch Society; Jackie Durra, production assistant of the Brooklyn Philharmonic Orchestra; Philip Glass; Morton Gould; Susan Hurrell of the Department of Portraits of the Royal College of Music in London; Mimi Keller, public-relations manager of the Seattle Symphony; Igor Kipnis; Jerry McBride, acting archivist of the Arnold Schoenberg Institute; Nathalie McCance of the Department of Portraits of the Royal College of Music in London; Kevin J. Martin, media director of the Saint Louis Symphony Orchestra; Angelina Marx; Deborah L. Meth of ICM Artists, Ltd.; Alice K. Peerce; George and Gene Rochberg; D'Arcy Rohan of International Production Associates, Inc.; Ellen Romberg of the public-relations department of the Chicago Symphony Orchestra; Jeff Rosen of the Bob Dylan Office; Alexander Schneider; Lawrence Schoenberg; Rob Selden of the Carson Office; Nancy Sells, public-relations secretary of the Minnesota Orchestra; Constance Shuman of Shuman Associates, Inc.; Paul Sperry; Jonathan Stern of the public-relations department of the Chicago Symphony Orchestra; Barbra Streisand; Jule Styne; Henryk Szeryng; Josef Tal; Louis Teicher; William Thomson, dean of the USC School of Music; Hilda Wolpe; and Fannie Zelcer, archivist of the American Jewish Archives.

Introduction

Music is one of the areas in which Jews have traditionally excelled. When I was a music student in college, my amazement at the number of famous Jewish musicians grew almost daily as I discovered ever more of them.

As a theory-composition major, I gradually collected information about Jewish composers and about the diverse, subtle ways in which their careers and non-Jewish music had been affected by their ethnic heritage. Later I expanded the collection to include great Jews in all areas of music.

This book culminates that research. The purpose of *Great Jews in Music* is not to prove that Jews are supermusical, nor is it to present a history or analysis of Jewish music. It fulfills, I hope, a need, expressed to me by many Jews and non-Jews, for an up-to-date single-volume biographical guide to Jews involved in a wide range of sacred, classical, and popular music spheres. The principal earlier works along these lines, Gdal Saleski's *Famous Musicians of Jewish Origin* (1949) and Artur Holde's *Jews in Music* (1959), have very little material on popular music.

It is perfectly natural that many members of a long-oppressed people, such as the Jews, would be interested in the outstanding achievements of others in the group. Youths, in particular, look to those achievers for inspiration, while older Jews can gain a deeper and broader cultural awareness. It is also clear from my communications with non-Jews that many of them are fascinated by, and want to read about, the magnitude of the Jewish contribution to the entire spectrum of music.

But *Great Jews in Music* covers more than just professional careers. It also explores the triumphs and tragedies of human beings who happen to be Jewish musicians.

For many centuries musicians in the Diaspora had only two primary roles available: cantor and klezmer (an entertainment instrumentalist, often itinerant and usually poor, who specialized in playing at weddings and bar mitzvahs). Entry into the non-Jewish music world was extremely difficult and rare. Perhaps the most notable achievement before the year 1800 was that of the seventeenth-century composer Salamone Rossi, whose works were historically important for both the Jewish and the non-Jewish communities.

In the nineteenth century many parts of western and central Europe granted Jews a certain degree of emancipation, including the right to enter various professions and the right to reside outside the ghettos. To facilitate their assimilation into non-Jewish culture, many Jews left their faith either tacitly or through formal baptism into Christianity. In some cases the baptism was performed in childhood at the instigation of the parents. The composer Felix Mendelssohn became a Christian in that manner. In other cases an adult converted merely to obtain a certain professional post in a location where Jews were unofficially but routinely excluded. Such was the case with the conductor-composer Gustav Mahler in Vienna.

Assimilation took another form as well. The emancipation helped to propel the Jewish Reform movement, which remodeled synagogal music along the lines of non-Jewish church-music and art-music practices. The great Viennese cantor Salomon Sulzer was among the leaders in that endeavor.

Through assimilation many talented musicians were able to emerge from the ghettos. Jewish singers, conductors, and musicologists tended to spring from cantorial and rabbinical backgrounds, while most instrumentalists and popular composers inherited the klezmer tradition. Symphonic composers and piano virtuosos often came from nonmusical backgrounds.

Even the less emancipated eastern European Jews benefited from the new social conditions in the western areas. The nineteenth-century rise of the middle class in Europe created a huge market for international musical interpreters, that is, for traveling virtuosos. Many of those virtuosos came from the Russian Jewish Pale (the limited parts of Russia, mainly in the Ukraine, where Jews were permitted to live). Russian Jews, rooted in a universal philosophy and ambitious for liberation, readily developed their folk-music tradition into concert-hall virtuosity. Their specialty was the fiddle, and from their ranks came such outstanding violinists as Mischa Elman, Jascha Heifetz, Nathan Milstein, Alexander Schneider, and Efrem Zimbalist. Innumerable others were born in Russia but left as infants (such as Isaac Stern) or were born elsewhere of Russian immigrants (such as Yehudi Menuhin).

Of course, the emancipation did not end the hostility toward Jews. In his pamphlet *Das Judenthum in der Musik* ("Judaism in Music"; 1850, revised 1869), the vicious anti-Semite Richard Wagner, blinded and deafened by his paranoid belief that Jews were behind the early negative reception to his music, led the chorus of those who claimed that Jews, such as Felix Mendelssohn and Giacomo Meyerbeer, were, precisely because they were Jews, incapable of profundity. In his essay "Erkenne dich selbst" ("Know Thyself," 1881), Wagner praised the Russian massacres of Jews and suggested that the Germans should do likewise. Cosima Wagner, his wife, once quoted him as uttering the following "vehement jest": "All Jews should be burned!"

Fifty years later came Adolf Hitler. In March 1936 the once respectable German magazine *Die Musik* ("Music"), by then an official organ of the Nazis, issued a number featuring anti-Semitic articles along with pictures of the Jewish composers Mendelssohn, Meyerbeer, Gustav Mahler, Jacques Offenbach, Arnold Schoenberg, and others, retouched to make the facial expressions appear sinister. Set in bold type were quotations from Hitler, such as "The Jew possesses no culture-building power whatsoever."

The Nazis drove countless Jewish musicians out of Europe and banned performances of works by Jewish composers. However, in the late 1930s the Nazis made a terrifying discovery: the nineteenth-century Johann Strauss family of Vienna—the most famous waltz composers in history and the very symbols of Austro-German culture—were of Jewish origin! Johann Strauss I, whose great grandfather was a Hungarian Jew named Wolf Strauss, tried to keep the family's Jewish past a secret. He succeeded so well that it was not till generations later that the fact was discovered by a handful of people. But in 1939, German cultural officials, having already lost many other popular Jewish composers and fearful of losing the Strauss family, falsified the parish register of Saint Stephan's Church in Vienna so that no one would know about the family's origin. Hence, it was not till well after World War II, when the Hitler influence was buried, that the public became aware of the Strausses' Jewish connection.

Wagner and Hitler, of course, represented extremes. But they and their like tended to fuel the growing Zionist movement, which had developed partly out of the emancipation and assimilation movements of western and central Europe and even more out of the opposite circumstances in eastern Europe. Hence, the first phases of emigration to Palestine in the early twentieth century came mostly from eastern Europe.

Likewise the first generation of composers dedicated to a modern Jewish national music were eastern Europeans, especially Russians, such as Joel Engel. However, the first great symphonic composer to come out of the nationalist movement was Ernest Bloch, a Swiss. At about the same time, scholars, notably Abraham Zvi Idelsohn, began to study the theory and history of Jewish music.

In modern times Jews have profoundly enriched literally every aspect of music: religious, secular; Zionist, cosmopolitan; classical, popular; creative, performance, scholarly. Besides the artists already mentioned, the list contains the symphonic composers Aaron Copland and William Schuman, the popular-song composers Irving Berlin and George Gershwin, the pianists Arthur Rubinstein and Artur Schnabel, the violinists Itzhak Perlman and Pinchas Zukerman, the cellists Gregor Piatigorsky and Leonard Rose, the opera stars Jan Peerce and Beverly Sills, the conductors Leonard Bernstein and Arthur Fiedler, the jazzmen Benny Goodman and Harry James, the prerock popular singers Al Jolson and Sophie Tucker, the contemporary vocalists Bob Dylan and Barbra Streisand, and a host of others of equal stature.

In selecting musicians for entry in this book, I had to face the familiar question, Who is a Jew? Many reference sources include people whose Jewish connections were extremely remote. In some cases the Jewish lines existed only as rumors. Even in recent times the non-Jewish composers Georges

Bizet, Maurice Ravel, and Camille Saint-Saëns have been listed as Jews. The rumor regarding Bizet was fed by the fact that he married a daughter of the Jewish composer Jacques Halévy. The confusion about Ravel stemmed partly from the similarity between his surname and that of some French Jews and partly from his friendships with many Jews. Popular belief had it that Saint-Saëns's mother was a Jew, a supposed proof being her hooked nose; but genealogical evidence shows no Jewish connection.

In this book, I have followed the definition established by Jewish law: a Jew is anyone who was born of a Jewish mother or who converted to Judaism. The fact that the person later defected and joined a Christian church would not matter; according to Jewish law the subject is still a Jew.

The above definition forces the exclusion of many musicians who have some Jewish elements in their backgrounds and who are often listed as Jews elsewhere. Examples include the conductor Josef Krips, the singer Olivia Newton-John, the film composer Max Steiner, and the pianist Paul Wittgenstein.

The opposite situation also occurs. That is, a person not generally listed as a Jew (and perhaps not regarded by himself or herself as a Jew) can technically be included here because of having a Jewish mother, as in the case of Risë Stevens.

Great Jews in Music is a compendium of about one hundred major biographies supplemented by an appendix of thumbnail sketches. There is no pretense here that all of the major biographees are "better" or "more popular" or "more historically important" musicians than all of the appendix subjects. Rather, the primary aim in selecting the major biographees was to offer a representative variety of musical artists who reflect the widespread impact of Jews in music.

I hope that you, the reader, get as much enjoyment from reading the stories of these diverse and fascinating musical personalities as I did in researching and writing them.

DARRYL LYMAN

Whittier, California
June 1986

Note on Style

Dates and Abbreviations

Regarding dates in this book, the following rules, unless otherwise indicated in the text, apply:

DATES FOR	REPRESENT
compositions (except film scores)	completion
films (and film scores)	release
recordings	release
writings	publication

When explanations regarding dates are necessary, the following abbreviations are sometimes used:

comp. = composed
perf. = first performed
pub. = published
rel. = released

It should be noted here that in most cases a composition for the stage, such as an opera or a popular-theater musical, is dated according to its first major performance simply because that is the date traditionally, and sometimes solely, available. The date for an American musical, for example, generally refers to the Broadway opening, not to the earlier out-of-town performances.

Dating motion pictures is particularly difficult because of the problem of distinguishing dates of copyright, limited release, and general release. An example is *The Benny Goodman Story,* copyrighted and previewed in 1955 but generally released in 1956. The general-release date is the one given (or at least attempted to be given) here.

Recordings present problems similar to those of films. Again general-release dates are preferred.

Many of the biographees in this book were born in Russia before it adopted the Gregorian calendar shortly after the 1917 Revolution. Hence, the birth dates of those musicians are sometimes listed according to the old Julian calendar and sometimes revised to fit the modern Gregorian calendar (in which the date is pushed ahead by ten or more days). When such alternatives were available, the Gregorian was selected for use here.

Spellings

Regarding spellings of personal names, each subject's own practice is followed as closely as possible. For example, André Previn's works are regularly published with the acute accent in his first name. But Andre Kostelanetz's autobiography was published without an accent.

Certain compound words that various authorities spell open, hyphenated, or solid are here spelled solid, such as *folksong, foxtrot,* and *songplugger.* For consistency the word *theater* is stylized to that spelling throughout the book (except when the word is part of the title of a work, where the original spelling is used).

Foreign-Language Titles

Most foreign-language titles are given in their original languages. That procedure will provide a further degree of thoroughness to the readers' understanding of both the content and the ambience of each musician's career.

There are, however, three simple categories of exceptions to the above rule. All of them are practical, traditional stylizations that help to avoid unnecessary obstacles to a smoothly flowing text.

One category consists of generic titles, such as *First Symphony, Second String Quartet,* and *Violin Concerto.*

Another exception consists of a handful of famous works by non-Jews—pieces whose original, seldom-encountered foreign-language titles would provide no pertinent information for this book. Prime examples include Bach's *Goldberg Variations* and *St. Matthew Passion.*

The final category consists of transliterated titles, principally Russian, which, because of their unfamiliarity to most readers, are given in English only. Hebrew and Yiddish, however, are given in transliterated form before being translated into English, the assumption being that many readers of *Great Jews in Music* will have a special interest in those languages.

On its first occurrence in each biography, every foreign-language title is accompanied by an English translation (except, of course, when the title consists solely of an easily recognizable personal name). That procedure runs counter to traditional practice in some cases, such as the titles of famous operas in a context focused on the performances of a singer. But since this book is deliberately designed to be helpful to general readers, the extra translations have been incorporated.

Lists

Entries on major composers are followed by lists of some of their representative works. Entries on singers who record popular songs are followed by lists of some of their representative recordings.

These lists are not summaries of the artists' careers. The condensed biographies themselves serve as such summaries (including posts held, opera roles performed, and films appeared in). Rather, the lists, which are traditional additions to brief biographies of composers and popular-song recording artists, present new information to help show unique aspects of the artists' careers. For example, in many cases a song recorded by a popular-song performer is almost exclusively identified with that singer. On the other hand, classical performers naturally tend to record works from the same standard repertory. Therefore, lists of recordings by classical artists would not say anything unique about the performers. The greatness of such artists lies not in *what* they perform but in *how* they perform, and that quality is discussed in the biographies themselves.

For the purposes of this book, then, lists seem to be appropriate only for major composers and for popular-song performers. Any resulting differences in the lengths of various entries obviously have no bearing on the relative merits of the artists.

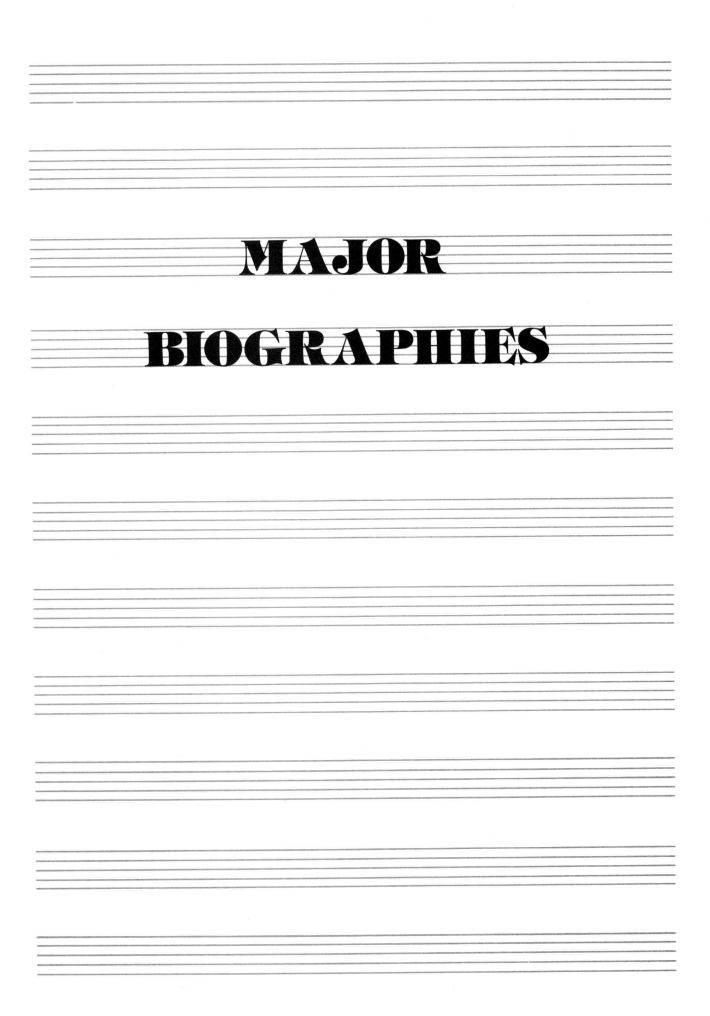

MAJOR BIOGRAPHIES

George Antheil
"Bad Boy" of Music
(1900-1959)

George Antheil, composer, was born in Trenton, New Jersey, on July 8, 1900. Of German descent, he was originally given the Germanic appellation Georg, but in his youth he Americanized his name by adding an *e* to it.

He studied piano, as well as theory and composition, for a number of years with Constantine von Sternberg, a former pupil of Franz Liszt. After graduating from Trenton High School near the end of World War I, Antheil joined the aviation branch of the United States Signal Corps. The war concluded before he could be sent into the fighting, but his involvement with airplanes and their noises had an effect on the sounds that he produced in some of his later compositions.

Released from the military, he returned to his studies with Sternberg. Soon, at Sternberg's suggestion, Antheil began to take composition lessons with the great Ernest Bloch. It was while he was with Bloch that Antheil wrote his first major work: the *First Symphony* (1922, revised 1923), the last movement of which was one of the earliest symphonic works to incorporate jazz elements.

During that same period, the early 1920s, he improved his piano technique under George Boyle at the Curtis Settlement School (the forerunner of the Curtis Institute of Music). In May 1922 Antheil went to Europe as a concert pianist.

In Europe he soon developed a reputation as an enfant terrible. Besides performing the traditional repertory (Bach, Mozart, Chopin), he distressed many auditors by playing modern works by Schoenberg, Stravinsky, and others. Even more disturbing to audiences were his own compositions, in which he presented, in his own words, "the anti-expressive, anti-romantic, coldly mechanistic aesthetic of the early twenties." He pounded out percussive, dissonant, rhythmically violent music in such piano works as his *Second Piano Sonata: The Airplane* (1921), *Jazz Sonata* (1922), *Sonata sauvage* ("Savage Sonata," 1923), and *Third Piano Sonata: Death of Machines* (1923). His concerts often provoked riots, the most famous being at the Théâtre des Champs-Elysées in Paris on October 4, 1923.

Despite his effect on general listeners, Antheil was befriended and championed by such eminent artists as the composer Erik Satie, the painter-sculptor Pablo Picasso, and the writers James Joyce, Ezra Pound, and William Butler Yeats. Pound wrote a book and numerous articles in praise of the young composer.

In 1923 Antheil began to compose a piece for which he sought a motion-picture accompaniment. The young American cameraman Dudley Murphy and the French painter Fernand Léger combined their efforts to create that movie, entitled *Ballet mécanique* ("Mechanical Ballet," 1924), a short work that was one of the earliest examples of abstract film. However, the music was never synchronized with the film (though they were played together in 1935, after the film and the music had gained reputations separately).

In 1925 Antheil finished a concert version of the *Ballet mécanique,* conceived for sixteen player pianos run electronically from a common control. He continued to revise and/or rescore the work in the years to come. The final version (1953) is scored for four pianos, recorded airplane-propeller sounds, electric bells, and various other percussion instruments.

The *Ballet mécanique* culminated the machine-influenced phase of Antheil's career. However, his pur-

(Courtesy of the Academy of Motion Picture Arts and Sciences)

pose in the work was not, as many have assumed, to imitate and glorify machines but, as he said, "to warn the age in which I was living of the simultaneous beauty and danger of its own unconscious mechanistic philosophy, aesthetic." It was also a technical experiment in which organization was created not by the traditional means of goal-directed tonal fluctuations but by simple blocks of time filled with, in Antheil's words, "musical abstractions and sound material. . . . I used time as Picasso might have used the blank spaces of his canvas." Thus, he did not hesitate to include long stretches of silence or repetition. Antheil's approach in the *Ballet mécanique* fore-shadowed many procedures that became common in experimental music more than twenty-five years later.

In 1925 Antheil married Boski Markus, niece of the Austrian writer Arthur Schnitzler. A political radical, Markus had barely escaped with her life when she fled from her native Hungary to Berlin, where Antheil met her in the early 1920s. He fell in love with her at first sight, though he had to struggle for some time to arrange a date with her through a third party. On that first date he surprised her by revealing a set of four-hand piano pieces already dedicated to her. Antheil and Markus immediately became inseparable companions. They had one child: Peter.

After the *Ballet mécanique*, Antheil turned to a more conservative, neoclassical idiom. His most important work in the late 1920s was the opera *Transatlantic* (1928), which centers on an American presidential election and presents a caricature of life in the United States. A highlight of the opera is an extended aria sung by the heroine while in her bathtub. When *Transatlantic* was premiered in Frankfort on the Main in 1930, it became probably the first American opera to have a major production in a foreign country.

After serving as assistant music director of the Berlin State Theater from 1928 to 1929, Antheil divided his time in the early 1930s between Europe and America. Among his major works during that period were the ballet-opera *Flight* (1930), on which Antheil had collaborated with his wife to create the story, and a set of piano preludes entitled *La femme 100 têtes* ("The Woman with a Hundred Heads," 1933), which musically illustrates a book of etchings by Max Ernst.

In 1933, after Hitler had come to power in Germany and after the money from a Guggenheim Fellowship had run out, Antheil returned to the United States and settled in New York City. There he was commissioned to write the ballet *Dreams* (1935) for the choreographer George Balanchine and a couple of film scores for the producers Ben Hecht and Charles MacArthur.

Moving to the Hollywood section of Los Angeles in 1936, Antheil composed background music for many films over the next twenty years. He scored the movies *The Plainsman* (1937), *We Were Strangers* (1949), *The Juggler* (1953), *The Pride and the Passion* (1957), and others.

Antheil expanded his interests into many nonmusical areas. He wrote books and articles on a wide variety of subjects, including the 1930 detective novel *Death in the Dark* (published under the pseudonym Stacey Bishop).

He studied the human glands, acted as a war analyst for the news media during World War II, and, with the actress Hedy Lamarr, invented a radio-directed torpedo that they patented in 1941. Antheil also wrote his auto-biography, *Bad Boy of Music* (1945), in which he emphasized his position as an enfant terrible, a role that he thoroughly enjoyed.

In his later years, however, the "bad boy" mellowed and often composed in classical forms and a post-romantic style. Lyricism, American folktune quotations, boogie-woogie rhythms, and a touch of his earlier dis-sonance characterize his post-World War II music. Among the best of his late works are the *First Serenade* for strings (1948), the *Fourth Piano Sonata* (1948), and the *Eight Fragments from Shelley* for chorus and piano (1951).

Despite his many activities and influential friends, Antheil lived most of his life in great financial hardship, constantly alternating between two conditions: doing a short-term commercial project (such as journalism and film work) to earn and save money, then living on that money while composing his serious music.

Antheil died in New York City on February 12, 1959. His wife, Boski, championed his music till her own death in 1978.

Selected works:

Stage

Transatlantic (opera; libretto, G. Antheil; 1928)
Fighting the Waves (incidental music, 1929)
Flight (ballet-opera; libretto, G. and B. Antheil; 1930)
Helen Retires (opera; libretto, J. Erskine; 1931)
Dreams (ballet, 1935)
Volpone (opera; libretto, A. Perry, after B. Jonson; 1952)
Capital of the World (ballet, 1952)
The Brothers (opera; libretto, G. Antheil; 1954)
Venus in Africa (opera; libretto, M. Dyne; 1954)
The Wish (opera; libretto, G. Antheil; 1954)

Films
(background scores)

Once in a Blue Moon (1936)
The Plainsman (1937)
Make Way for Tomorrow (1937)
Knock on Any Door (1949)
Tokyo Joe (1949)
We Were Strangers (1949)
In a Lonely Place (1950)
The Juggler (1953)
Dementia (1955)
Not as a Stranger (1955)
The Pride and the Passion (1957)

Orchestral

six symphonies (1922-50)
Ballet mécanique (1925, revised 1953)
A Jazz Symphony (1925, revised 1955)
Piano Concerto (1926)
Suite (1926)
Capriccio (1930)
Over the Plains (1945)

Violin Concerto (1946)
Autumn Song (1947)
First Serenade (strings, 1948)
Second Serenade (chamber orchestra, 1949)

Vocal

Songs of Experience (voice, piano; texts, W. Blake; 1948)
Eight Fragments from Shelley (chorus, piano; texts, P. Shelley; 1951)

Chamber

four violin sonatas (1923-48)
three string quartets (1924-48)

Piano

Fireworks and the Profane Waltzers (1919)
Second Piano Sonata: The Airplane (1921)
Jazz Sonata (1922)
Sonata sauvage (1923)
Third Piano Sonata: Death of Machines (1923)
La femme 100 têtes (1933)
Suite (1941)
Fourth Piano Sonata (1948)
Valentine Waltzes (1949)
Modern Sounds for Small Hands (1956, pub. 1969 as *Piano Pastels*)

Writing

Bad Boy of Music (1945)

Harold Arlen
America's Second Stephen Foster
(1905-1986)

Harold Arlen, composer, was born in Buffalo, New York, on February 15, 1905. His original name was Hyman Arluck, son of the celebrated cantor Samuel Arluck. (After his son became a famous composer, Samuel, by then the cantor at Temple Adath Yeshurun in Syracuse, New York, delighted his congregations by weaving Harold Arlen tunes, such as "Over the Rainbow," into the services.) Hyman grew up listening not only to live synagogal music but also to his father's record collection, which included cantorial music sung by Josef Rosenblatt and opera arias performed by other artists. Julius Arluck (later Jerry Arlen), Hyman's younger brother, grew up in the same surroundings and became a well-known theater conductor.

At the age of nine Hyman began to take piano lessons from local teachers. In his early teens he went to work as a pianist in a silent-movie theater; later he graduated to a larger movie house, where he played an organ. Through the rest of his teens he worked with several quasi-jazz bands as pianist, vocalist, and arranger.

His main interest at that time was in a singing career, though other musicians most admired his ability as an arranger. For example, while appearing in New York City with the Buffalodians, he made some arrangements for Fletcher Henderson's band.

Leaving the Buffalodians, young Arluck entered vaudeville in a single act, singing to his own piano accompaniment. But soon he tired of the singer's life of competitiveness and financial uncertainty.

By then, in his early twenties, he had already experimented with original composition, both songs and piano pieces. He wrote his earliest works under the name Harold Arluck, including the instrumental *Minor Gaff: Blues Fantasy* (in collaboration with Dick George), his first published composition (1926).

By 1928 he had changed his name to Harold Arlen. He arrived at the new surname by combining the first syllable of his original name, Arluck, and the sound of the second syllable of his mother's maiden name, Orlin.

In 1929 Arlen, after working for a while as a rehearsal pianist, finally found some financial security when he became a staff composer for the Tin Pan Alley publishing firm of Piantadosi, a subsidiary of Remick's. He soon teamed with the lyricist Ted Koehler and began to write songs for revues. Their first hit was "Get Happy" for the *9:15 Revue* (perf. 1930). But their most successful work was done for a now famous series of productions at the Cotton Club in New York City's Harlem district (1930-34). Those shows were highlighted by the classic songs "Between the Devil and the Deep Blue Sea" (1931) and "Stormy Weather" (1933).

During that period Arlen also wrote the memorable

23

"It's Only a Paper Moon" (lyrics, Billy Rose and E. Y. Harburg), originally introduced as "If You Believe in Me" in the Broadway play *The Great Magoo* (perf. 1932). Its great success came when it was retitled and inserted into the movie *Take a Chance* (1933). He wrote "I Gotta Right to Sing the Blues" (lyrics, Koehler) for the *Earl Carroll Vanities of 1932*, a Broadway revue.

One of the chorus girls in the 1932 edition of the *Vanities* was the extraordinarily beautiful Anya Taranda. Arlen immediately began a romance with her. One night five years later, in 1937, as he left her at her door, he handed her a note: "Dearest Anya, we're getting married tomorrow. 'Bout time, don't you think? All my love, H."

Anya became important in Arlen's creative life. When, for example, in 1939 he was commissioned by Meredith Willson to write an instrumental work for Willson's *Good News* radio show, Arlen thought of Anya. She had been studying ballet with Michel Fokine and was often asked to dance at parties. With both her and Willson in mind, Arlen composed his *American Minuet* (1939).

Anya was nearly always the first person to whom Arlen played his new melodies. He regarded her as his best and closest critic. A gifted artist, she also taught him how to paint.

After his early successes in revues, Arlen moved on to films and Broadway musicals, his primary lyricists being Ira Gershwin, E. Y. Harburg, and Johnny Mercer. Arlen's best-known song score for a movie is that for the sentimental fantasy *The Wizard of Oz* (1939), with "Over the Rainbow" (lyrics, Harburg), the song that shot Judy Garland to fame. *The Wizard of Oz*, besides having one of the most memorable collections of songs in the history of American popular music, was one of the first movies in which the songs were designed to be integral to the story and character development.

A completely different highlight in Arlen's film output is the comical "Lydia, the Tattooed Lady" (lyrics, Harburg), sung by the incomparable Groucho Marx in *At the Circus* (1939). Other Arlen movie songs include "Blues in the Night" (lyrics, Mercer) in the film of the same name (1941), "That Old Black Magic" (lyrics, Mercer) in *Star Spangled Rhythm* (1942), "Happiness Is a Thing Called Joe" (lyrics, Harburg) in *Cabin in the Sky* (1943), and "The Man That Got Away" (lyrics, Ira Gershwin) in *A Star Is Born* (1954).

Arlen's stage work includes *St. Louis Woman* (perf. 1946), with "Come Rain or Come Shine" (lyrics, Mercer); *House of Flowers* (perf. 1954), with "A Sleepin' Bee" (lyrics, Truman Capote and Harold Arlen); and *Free and Easy* (perf. 1959), a blues opera based on *St. Louis Woman*.

Though his name is not as widely known as some other popular-song composers (such as Irving Berlin and George Gershwin), Arlen has contributed as much of substantive value to American popular music as any other composer in history. Some of his songs from the 1930s ("Get Happy," "It's Only a Paper Moon," "Over the Rainbow") stand as unsurpassed reflections of the national mood during the Great Depression.

Harold Arlen

Many of his compositions blend the idioms of Tin Pan Alley and Afro-American music. Such tunes often draw on the style, if not the rigid form, of blues, as in "I Gotta Right to Sing the Blues," "Stormy Weather," and "Blues in the Night." Much of his work was written specifically for black performers, such as the early Cotton Club revues, the movie *Cabin in the Sky,* and the stage musicals *St. Louis Woman* (and its revision, *Free and Easy)* and *Jamaica* (perf. 1957). His efforts were among the first to help provide a mass commercial market for black entertainers. Musically knowledgeable observers have drawn a parallel between Arlen and Stephen Foster, both of whom, more than anyone else, had an uncanny ability to fuse Anglo-American and Afro-American elements into songs of genuine folklike quality and memorability.

But Arlen's gifts transcend any one kind of song. Among the most versatile of popular-song composers, he has written tunes as different from each other (and from the blues) as the cheerful "I Love a Parade" (lyrics, Koehler; 1931), the romantic "Let's Fall in Love" (lyrics, Koehler; 1934), the delightfully risqué "Lydia, the Tattooed Lady," and the hypnotic "That Old Black Magic." As for the fantasy *The Wizard of Oz*, it has been shown annually on TV since 1959 (its TV debut taking place in

1956), each new generation discovering afresh the sustained inspiration of the song score. And the film will undoubtedly continue to be shown and loved as long as there are people whose imaginations can leap "over the rainbow" and whose souls are gentle enough to appreciate the humor and humanity of one of America's true melodic masters.

Arlen died in New York City on April 23, 1986.

Selected works:

Stage

Earl Carroll Vanities of 1930 (lyrics, T. Koehler; perf. 1930)
Rhythmania (lyrics, T. Koehler; perf. 1931), including:
 "Between the Devil and the Deep Blue Sea"
 "Get Up, Get Out, Get under the Sun"
 "I Love a Parade"
Cotton Club Parade of 1932 (lyrics, T. Koehler; perf. 1932), including:
 "I've Got the World on a String"
Cotton Club Parade of 1933 (lyrics, T. Koehler; perf. 1933), including:
 "Stormy Weather"
Cotton Club Parade of 1934 (lyrics, T. Koehler; perf. 1934)
Life Begins at 8:40 (lyrics, I. Gershwin, E.Y. Harburg; perf. 1934)
Hooray for What? (lyrics, E. Y. Harburg; perf. 1937)
Bloomer Girl (lyrics, E. Y. Harburg; perf. 1944), including:
 "Evelina"
St. Louis Woman (lyrics, J. Mercer; perf. 1946), including:
 "Come Rain or Come Shine"
House of Flowers (lyrics, T. Capote, H. Arlen; perf. 1954), including:
 "A Sleepin' Bee"
Jamaica (lyrics, E. Y. Harburg; perf. 1957)
Saratoga (lyrics, J. Mercer; perf. 1959)
Free and Easy (revised version of *St. Louis Woman;* lyrics, J. Mercer, T. Koehler; perf. 1959)

Films
(song scores)

Let's Fall in Love (lyrics, T. Koehler; 1934), including:
 "Let's Fall in Love"
Strike Me Pink (lyrics, L. Brown; 1936)
The Singing Kid (lyrics, E. Y. Harburg; 1936)
Gold Diggers of 1937 (lyrics, E. Y. Harburg; 1936)
The Wizard of Oz (lyrics, E. Y. Harburg; 1939), including:
 "Ding-Dong! The Witch Is Dead"
 "If I Only Had a Brain/a Heart/the Nerve"
 "The Merry Old Land of Oz"
 "Over the Rainbow"
 "We're Off to See the Wizard"
At the Circus (lyrics, E. Y. Harburg; 1939), including:
 "Lydia, the Tattooed Lady"
Blues in the Night (lyrics, J. Mercer; 1941), including:
 "Blues in the Night"
 "This Time the Dream's on Me"
Star Spangled Rhythm (lyrics, J. Mercer; 1942), including:
 "That Old Black Magic"
Cabin in the Sky (lyrics, E. Y. Harburg; 1943), including:
 "Happiness Is a Thing Called Joe"
The Sky's the Limit (lyrics, J. Mercer; 1943), including:
 "One for My Baby"
Up in Arms (lyrics, T. Koehler; 1944)
Here Come the Waves (lyrics, J. Mercer; 1944), including:
 "Ac-cent-tchu-ate the Positive"
Casbah (lyrics, L. Robin; 1948), including:
 "For Every Man There's a Woman"
 "Hooray for Love"
The Farmer Takes a Wife (lyrics, D. Fields; 1953)
A Star Is Born (lyrics, I. Gershwin; 1954), including:
 "The Man That Got Away"
The Country Girl (lyrics, I. Gershwin; 1954)
Gay Purr-ee (lyrics, E. Y. Harburg; 1962)

Songs
(other than those for the above shows and films)

"Get Happy" (lyrics, T. Koehler; for the stage show *9:15 Revue,* perf. 1930)
"I Gotta Right to Sing the Blues" (lyrics, T. Koehler; for the stage show *Earl Carroll Vanities of 1932,* perf. 1932)
"It's Only a Paper Moon" (lyrics, E. Y. Harburg, B. Rose; for the film *Take a Chance,* 1933; originally "If You Believe in Me" for the play *The Great Magoo,* perf. 1932)
"Last Night When We Were Young" (lyrics, E. Y. Harburg; originally written for, but dropped from, the film *Metropolitan,* 1935, then issued as an independent song, 1936)
"Americanegro Suite" (lyrics, T. Koehler; 1940)
"I Could Go On Singing" (lyrics, E. Y. Harburg; for the film *I Could Go On Singing,* 1963)
"So Long, Big Time" (lyrics, D. Langdon; for the TV show *Twentieth Century,* 1964).

Instrumental

Minor Gaff: Blues Fantasy (piano, in collaboration with D. George, 1926)
Rhythmic Moments (piano, 1928)
Mood in Six Minutes (orchestrated by R. R. Bennett, 1935)
American Minuet (orchestra, 1939)

Vladimir Ashkenazy
Russian Pianist Who Outgrew
the Soviet System
(1937-   )

Vladimir Ashkenazy, pianist, was born in Gorki, the Soviet Union, on July 6, 1937. At an early age he used to listen to his father, an accompanist for variety shows, practice Russian popular music on the piano. Vladimir, too, wanted to play the piano, and when he was six he began to take lessons from a local teacher. Two years later, in 1945, young Ashkenazy enrolled at the Moscow Central Music School, where he studied piano with Anaida Sumbatian. He progressed very well, and in 1955 he won second prize in the Warsaw International Chopin Competition.

Also in 1955 Ashkenazy moved up from the Central Music School to the Moscow Conservatory and began piano studies with Lev Oborin. The following year he won first prize in the Queen Elisabeth International Piano Competition in Brussels, Belgium, just ahead of the American pianist John Browning. The Brussels victory led to a tour of Europe and, in 1958, the United States.

The year 1958 was also important to Ashkenazy's personal life. It was the year in which he met the lovely young Icelandic-born, British-bred pianist Thorunn Johannsdottir, who had gone to Moscow as an entrant in the International Tchaikovsky Piano Competition. Two years later she returned to become a student at the Moscow Conservatory. In 1961 Vladimir and Thorunn were married. They had five children: Vladimir, Nadia, Dimitri, Sonia, and Alexandria.

Ashkenazy graduated from the Moscow Conservatory in 1960. However, he got off to a bad start with the Soviet authorities in June 1960 when he attended the funeral of the Nobel Prize-winning poet-novelist Boris Pasternak (author of *Doctor Zhivago*), who was out of favor with the government. In tribute to the dead author, Ashkenazy assisted Sviatoslav Richter in playing a series of works on the upright piano in Pasternak's own home, an action not at all appreciated by the Soviet authorities.

Nevertheless, Ashkenazy was a brilliant young pianist, and the government urged him to enter the 1962 International Tchaikovsky Piano Competition in Moscow. He was reluctant to do so because he felt that competitions should be reserved for untested young pianists trying to prove themselves. Ashkenazy had already proven himself in many ways, especially by winning the Brussels competition. But the Soviet state is always anxious to win as many international competitions as possible because, according to Ashkenazy, the authorities "have to prove that their socialistic system is the best in the world; the 'book' says so, so they have to prove it in practice." Under pressure from the Soviet

authorities, he entered the Tchaikovsky Competition and shared first prize with John Ogdon, an English pianist.

Ashkenazy then began in earnest a successful international concertizing career. He made his second tour of the United States in the autumn of 1962. In early 1963 he toured Great Britain.

His wife went with him on the British tour, and she persuaded him to stay in England, where she had been reared and where her parents still lived. Ashkenazy was ready for such a move because he was tired of Soviet control over his life. The Soviet attitude is that the individual is valuable only to the extent that he is a contributing factor to the state. Therefore, the individual's activities have to be controlled so that he performs only those services that the state finds useful. Even musicians are

subjected to that bizarre, stifling philosophy. Ashkenazy has said that Russian musicians are trained and treated like athletes, so that the Soviet system "creates good musical sportsmen rather than great artists. They play well, but I don't think they say very much."

Ashkenazy's travels in the Western world had convinced him that only there could he find the peace of mind and freedom of expression for the fullest development of his art. He therefore defected from Russia in 1963 and lived in London till 1968. During those years he made numerous successful Western appearances.

In 1968 the Ashkenazy family moved to Iceland, partly because it was Thorunn's birthplace and partly because it could provide peace and solitude. In 1972 Ashkenazy became an Icelandic citizen.

However, it soon became evident that living in Iceland presented a serious geographical problem. As Ashkenazy's concerts increased (up to 130 performances a year), the few flights into and out of Iceland made it extremely difficult for him to be with his family. After ten years in Iceland, the Ashkenazys moved to Lucerne, Switzerland, which is much more accessible. He now spends as much time as possible at home with his family, and when the children are on vacation they often accompany their father on his concert trips.

Ashkenazy is widely regarded as the best of the younger Russian pianists. He combines a great intellectual understanding of music with a sincere expressiveness and a sensitivity to tone color. He has been particularly successful with Mozart, Scriabin, Rachmaninoff, and Prokofiev.

Ashkenazy has performed much chamber music. Among his partners have been the cellist Jacqueline du Pré and the violinists Itzhak Perlman and Pinchas Zukerman. In recent years Ashkenazy has also turned to conducting, establishing a particularly close association with the London Philharmonia Orchestra.

Burt Bacharach

Composer of
Sophisticated Popular Songs
(1928-   )

Burt Bacharach, composer, was born in Kansas City, Missouri, on May 12, 1928. In the early 1930s his family moved to New York City, where Burt grew up in the Forest Hills section of the borough of Queens. He was a lonely child because he was shorter than his peers (though he eventually grew to nearly six feet in height), because he was a Jew in a Catholic neighborhood, and because he was forced by his mother to practice the piano while the other boys played sports. Ultimately, however, it was music—through his performing with a dance band at Forest Hills High School—that helped Burt to snap out of his loneliness.

After graduating from high school, he played boogie-woogie and bop piano in nightclubs, on United Service Organizations (USO) tours of army hospitals, and elsewhere. He also formally studied music at McGill University in Montreal, Canada; the Mannes School of Music and the New School for Social Research, both in New York City; and the Music Academy of the West in Santa Barbara, California. Among his composition teachers were Henry Cowell, Bohuslav Martinu, and Darius Milhaud.

Most of Bacharach's studies were in art music, and for a time he considered becoming a composer in that field. But when he saw the financial struggles of serious composers, he opted for popular music. During the late 1940s he made his first, though unsuccessful, efforts at songwriting.

In 1950 Bacharach was drafted into the army, where he spent the next two years. During his tour of duty, he worked as a pianist and arranger at various army bases. While performing such work in Germany, he met the singer Vic Damone. In 1952, after being released from the army, Bacharach became Damone's piano accompanist. Over the next several years, he went on to accompany a number of other singers, including the

Ames Brothers, Polly Bergen, Georgia Gibbs, Joel Grey, Steve Lawrence, and Paula Stewart. Bacharach wedded Stewart in the late 1950s, but the marriage ended in divorce after only a few years.

As an accompanist Bacharach became dismayed at the poor material available, and he decided for the first time to begin songwriting in earnest. During his first year (1956-57), his efforts were unsuccessful, and he continued to support himself by accompanying singers. Then, in 1957, he met the lyricist Hal David in the offices of the Paramount Music Corporation. They teamed up and immediately came out with two successful songs: "Magic Moments" and "The Story of My Life."

Through Hal David, Bacharach met Mack David, Hal's older brother and a longtime lyricist for Hollywood movies. With Mack David, Bacharach wrote the title song for the 1958 movie *The Blob* (though their work was uncredited on the screen), one of the earliest title songs in a rock-'n'-roll idiom. The pair also wrote "Hot Spell," inspired by, but not used in, the 1958 movie of the same name.

From 1958 to 1961 Bacharach reduced his songwriting while he toured the United States and Europe as piano accompanist for Marlene Dietrich. In 1960, however, he took time to write, with the lyricist Bob Hilliard, "Mexican Divorce" for the Drifters. The song was recorded with a background supplied by the Gospelaires, the leader of whom was Dionne Warwick. When Bacharach heard Warwick, he knew that he wanted to write for her: "What emotion I could get away with!" he said about the prospect of composing for the young singer.

Beginning in 1962 Bacharach and Hal David, with principal interpretations by Dionne Warwick, came out with a string of hits that dominated the American popular-music scene for the next decade. Bacharach and David became the most celebrated songwriting team since Richard Rodgers and Oscar Hammerstein II began to collaborate in the early 1940s.

Among the outstanding independent Bacharach-David songs in the 1960s were "Don't Make Me Over" (1962), "Anyone Who Had a Heart" (1963), "Close to You" (1963), "Any Old Time of the Day" (1964), "What the World Needs Now Is Love" (1965), and "Do You Know the Way to San Jose?" (1967). The team also wrote title songs for films, including those for *What's New, Pussycat?* (1965), *After the Fox* (1966), and *Alfie* (1966). Nontitle songs written for movies were highlighted by "The Look of Love" in *Casino Royale* (1967) and "Raindrops Keep Fallin' on My Head" in *Butch Cassidy and the Sundance Kid* (1969). Bacharach and David also wrote songs inspired by, but not used in, films, such as "Wives and Lovers: Hey, Little Girl" after the movie *Wives and Lovers* (1963) and "A House Is Not a Home" after the film of the same name (1964).

In 1965, with *What's New, Pussycat?*, Bacharach began to compose complete background scores for movies. They were highlighted by *Butch Cassidy and the Sundance Kid,* which has a delightful waltzlike main theme in addition to the song "Raindrops Keep Fallin' on

Burt Bacharach

My Head." He also wrote the complete song score for the film musical *Lost Horizon* (1973).

In 1968 Bacharach and David supplied the songs for the extremely successful Broadway musical *Promises, Promises* (with Neil Simon's book based on the 1960 movie *The Apartment).* The hits of the show were the title song and "I'll Never Fall in Love Again."

Since the late 1960s Bacharach has appeared many times in TV specials, nightclubs, and theaters as singer-pianist-conductor of his own music, which he himself skillfully arranges and orchestrates. His handsome features and charming, natural manner have made him a pop-culture figure even beyond his role as a composer.

He has sung his songs on a number of albums. His recordings include *Reach Out* (1967), *Make It Easy on Yourself* (1969), *Burt Bacharach's Greatest Hits* (1974), *Futures* (1977), and *Woman* (1979).

With Paul Anka supplying the lyrics, Bacharach composed the song score for the film musical *Together?* (1980). He then wrote the background scores for the movies *Arthur* (1981) and *Night Shift* (1982). For *Arthur* he collaborated with Peter Allen, Christopher Cross, and Carole Bayer Sager to supply the film with a title song.

Bacharach's compositions are arguably the most professional, sophisticated music to appear by a newcomer on the popular scene (as distinct from the late works of earlier giants, notably Richard Rodgers) since the beginning of the rock era in the mid-1950s. He has borrowed elements from bop, rock, soul, progressive jazz, Tin Pan Alley, Latin American music, and other styles; but he has synthesized them in such a way that the result is a uniquely Bacharach sound. Characteristic features include complex rhythms and unusual accents, boldly original harmonic progressions, and unconventional but memorable melodic patterns that often leap about with a naturalness that only an exceptionally gifted melodist can achieve. In addition, Bacharach, perhaps more than any other popular-song composer, has been responsible for the recent development of flexible phrasing, in which phrase lengths often vary from the traditional four or eight measures. He is probably the finest craftsman among active popular-song composers in America.

Bacharach's second marriage, in 1965, was to the actress Angie Dickinson. They had one child: Lea. The separate careers of Bacharach and Dickinson often kept them apart. But when there was a conflict in their schedules, she was usually the one who made adjustments because of her high regard for his work. "I almost respect Burt more than I love him," she once said. "His music . . . is so much more important to the world than anything I can ever do." Nevertheless, the marriage finally ended in divorce in 1982.

Later in 1982 Bacharach married the lyricist-singer Carole Bayer Sager, with whom he had collaborated on the title song for the movie *Arthur*. They have continued to work together, notably on "That's What Friends Are For" (1982), which, through Dionne Warwick's recording, became one of the top hits of 1986.

Selected works:

Stage

Promises, Promises (lyrics, H. David; perf. 1968), including:
"I'll Never Fall in Love Again"
"Promises, Promises"
"Whoever You Are, I Love You"

Films
(background scores and song scores)

What's New, Pussycat? (background score and songs, including title song; lyrics, H. David; 1965)
After the Fox (background score and title song; lyrics, H. David; 1966)
Casino Royale (background score and song "The Look of Love"; lyrics, H. David; 1967)
Butch Cassidy and the Sundance Kid (background score and song "Raindrops Keep Fallin' on My Head"; lyrics, H. David; 1969)
Lost Horizon (song score; lyrics, H. David; 1973)
Together? (song score; lyrics, P. Anka; 1980)
Arthur (background score; title song, "Arthur's Theme: Best That You Can Do," in collaboration with Peter Allen, Christopher Cross, Carole Bayer Sager; 1981)
Night Shift (background score, 1982)

Films
(title songs only)

"The Blob" (lyrics, M. David; for the film *The Blob*, 1958)
"Love in a Goldfish Bowl" (lyrics, H. David; for the film *Love in a Goldfish Bowl*, 1961)
"Forever My Love" (lyrics, H. David; for the film *Forever My Love*, 1962)
"Send Me No Flowers" (lyrics, H. David; for the film *Send Me No Flowers*, 1964)
"Alfie" (lyrics, H. David; for the film *Alfie*, 1966)
"Promise Her Anything" (lyrics, H. David; for the film *Promise Her Anything*, 1966)

Songs
(other than those for the above show and films)

"Magic Moments" (lyrics, H. David; 1957)
"The Story of My Life" (lyrics, H. David; 1957)
"Hot Spell" (lyrics, M. David; 1958; inspired by the film *Hot Spell*, 1958)
"Don't Make Me Over" (lyrics, H. David; 1962)
"The Man Who Shot Liberty Valence" (lyrics, H. David; 1962; inspired by the film *The Man Who Shot Liberty Valence*, 1962)
"Only Love Can Break a Heart" (lyrics, H. David; 1962)
"Anyone Who Had a Heart" (lyrics, H. David; 1963)
"Blue on Blue" (lyrics, H. David; 1963)
"Close to You" (lyrics, H. David; 1963)
"Walk On By" (lyrics, H. David; 1963)
"Wishin' and Hopin'" (lyrics, H. David; 1963)
"Wives and Lovers: Hey, Little Girl" (lyrics, H. David; 1963; inspired by the film *Wives and Lovers*, 1963)
"A House Is Not a Home" (lyrics, H. David; 1964; inspired by the film *A House Is Not a Home*, 1964)
"Any Old Time of the Day" (lyrics, H. David; 1964)
"Don't Go Breakin' My Heart" (lyrics, H. David; 1965)
"What the World Needs Now Is Love" (lyrics, H. David; 1965)
"Do You Know the Way to San Jose?" (lyrics, H. David; 1967)
"One Less Bell to Answer" (lyrics, H. David; 1967)
"The Green Grass Starts to Grow" (lyrics, H. David; 1970)
"That's What Friends Are For" (lyrics, C.B. Sager, B. Bacharach; 1982)
"Finder of Lost Loves" (lyrics, C.B. Sager; 1984)

Daniel Barenboim

Master of "the Eternity of Feeling" in Music

(1942-   )

Daniel Barenboim, pianist and conductor, was born in Buenos Aires, Argentina, on November 15, 1942. His parents, Argentine natives of Russian extraction, were piano teachers. At the age of four Daniel began to study the violin, but he soon changed to the piano, taking lessons first from his mother and then from his father. Daniel never had another formal instructor in piano.

At seven he gave his first public recital, in Buenos Aires. The audience demanded numerous encores, but after the seventh encore young Barenboim turned to his listeners and apologetically announced that he had run out of music to play.

Many international musical celebrities visiting Buenos Aires became guests at the Barenboims' home. One visitor was the conductor Igor Markevitch, who urged them to take Daniel to the famed summer music classes in Salzburg, Austria, where Markevitch was an instructor.

The Barenboims accepted Markevitch's suggestion and traveled with the nine-year-old Daniel to Salzburg, where he performed so well at the Mozarteum that he was allowed to play a keyboard instrument that had once belonged to Mozart, the first person so honored in twenty-five years. He also observed Markevitch's conducting class.

In 1952 the family settled in Israel. The following year Daniel made his major debut, as piano soloist with the Israel Philharmonic Orchestra.

Young Barenboim returned to Salzburg in the summers of 1954 and 1955. He studied conducting with Markevitch, chamber music with Enrico Mainardi, and piano literature with Edwin Fischer. From 1954 to 1956 Barenboim studied theory and composition in Paris with Nadia Boulanger on a scholarship from the America-Israel Cultural Foundation, the first granted to an Israeli for music studies in Europe. In 1956 he became the youngest student ever to receive a master's degree in music from the Saint Cecilia Academy in Rome. In the summer of 1956 he studied conducting with Carlo Zecchi at the Chigiana Academy in Siena, Italy.

Barenboim concertized extensively even while he was still a student. Besides giving solo recitals, he debuted in Paris in 1955 with the orchestra of the Paris Conservatory conducted by André Cluytens, in London in 1956 with the Philharmonia Orchestra under the baton of Josef Krips, and in New York City in 1957 with the Symphony of the Air conducted by Leopold Stokowski. His American debut was arranged by the impresario Sol Hurok, to whom Barenboim had been introduced by the

pianist Arthur Rubinstein. Hurok later set up more American appearances by the young pianist. (Barenboim kept a close association with the Hurok management and its successors till the late 1970s, when he no longer had time for American tours.)

In his late teens Barenboim experienced a crisis in his career. No longer a child prodigy and not yet a mature artist, he was seldom engaged to perform. In 1960 the crisis was resolved when the city of Tel Aviv invited him to play the complete cycle of Beethoven sonatas. He was also asked to return the following year for a series of Mozart recitals.

The year 1962 brought another turning point in his life: the beginning of his conducting career. After making some conducting experiments in Israel, he went on a tour of Australia, where he conducted full-scale professional orchestras for the first time.

During the next few years Barenboim continued to appear frequently as a piano soloist, notably with the Berlin Philharmonic Orchestra from 1963 to 1965 and with the New York Philharmonic in 1964. But by the mid-1960s he had begun to turn more seriously toward conducting, especially by forming a close and long association with the English Chamber Orchestra, which he conducted not only from the podium but also frequently from the keyboard. London became the headquarters for his international career.

Early in 1967 Barenboim met the English cellist Jacqueline du Pré at a party in the London home of a mutual friend. Du Pré, shy and insecure except when she was at the cello, became so flustered at meeting the energetic and confident Barenboim that she immediately began to play for the party. Barenboim also performed, and they quickly fell in love. That spring they announced their engagement to be married the following September. Meanwhile, each had a busy concert schedule to follow.

However, their plans were interrupted by the Arab-Israeli Six-Day War in June 1967. Barenboim and du Pré canceled all of their scheduled concerts so that they could hurry to Israel and perform for the Israelis, both military and civilian. On June 15, 1967, a few days after the end of the war and as soon as du Pré had completed her conversion to Judaism, they were married in Jerusalem. That night they performed with the Israel Philharmonic Orchestra in Tel Aviv, the bride playing the Schumann *Cello Concerto* while the groom conducted. In July and August they toured North America with the same orchestra.

Their careers blossomed, and they tried to coordi-

nate their schedules so that they could be together as much as possible, sometimes for joint appearances. Their love and marriage were often compared with the famous nineteenth-century romance of Robert and Clara Schumann. The Barenboims' London home became the social center for a group of outstanding musicians often referred to as the Barenboim Gang, including such contemporaries as the pianist Vladimir Ashkenazy, the conductor Zubin Mehta, and the violinists Itzhak Perlman and Pinchas Zukerman, as well as such older masters as the baritone Dietrich Fischer-Dieskau, the pianist Arthur Rubinstein, and the violinist Isaac Stern. Barenboim often surprised his wife by taking friends to the Barenboim home with little or no notice, including, at least once, an entire orchestra. Du Pré, whom Barenboim nicknamed Smiley, took it all in stride.

In 1973 that bright musical world was suddenly darkened when it became known that du Pré had developed multiple sclerosis, a disease that involves the deterioration of the central nervous system and is virtually incurable and often fatal. Her career ended, she began a life centered on physical therapy at home. No longer able to play music together, du Pré and Barenboim learned how to talk about music, and he arranged his schedule to be with her in London whenever he could.

Meanwhile, Barenboim's career progressed rapidly. He first conducted a symphony orchestra in Europe when he led the New Philharmonia in London in 1967. The same year, he toured the United States with the Israel Philharmonic, usually playing concertos but occasionally conducting. In 1968 he made his New York City conducting debut by leading the visiting London Symphony Orchestra, substituting at the last minute for the ailing István Kertész. In 1969 he guest-conducted the Berlin Philharmonic, followed by the New York Philharmonic in 1970.

Since 1970 he has appeared on the podium numerous times with many of the major orchestras in America (most often with the Chicago Symphony Orchestra), as well as with the London Philharmonic and the Orchestra of Paris, of which he has been music director and principal conductor since 1975—his first permanent post as a conductor. During his roughly twenty weeks a year with the Paris orchestra, Barenboim became accustomed to commuting between Paris and London to be home virtually every weekend with his stricken wife. In 1973, at the Edinburgh Festival, he debuted as an opera conductor, with Mozart's *Don Giovanni*.

Barenboim is widely regarded as one of the leading conductors of music from the classical and romantic periods. His repertory also includes Bach, Elgar (to whom Barenboim is particularly attracted), and others. He has conducted with many leading soloists, such as the pianists Clifford Curzon and Arthur Rubinstein and the violinist Isaac Stern. Barenboim greatly admires, and has learned much from, the recordings of the late conductor Wilhelm Furtwängler, with whom he has been compared because of his free, expressive interpretations.

31

As a piano soloist, Barenboim had a remarkably varied and mature repertory when he was a teenager, including twentieth-century music. But in recent years he has limited his solo work to Mozart, Beethoven, Chopin, and Brahms. He has attained an outstanding pianistic virtuosity despite his small hands (appended to a 5′6″ frame).

As a piano accompanist, he has performed with such outstanding soloists as the singers Janet Baker and Dietrich Fischer-Dieskau. Among his chamber-music partners have been the violinists Itzhak Perlman and Pinchas Zukerman, and, of course, his cellist wife.

Besides being blessed with musical talent and an incredible memory, Barenboim is extremely articulate, dynamic (hence his leadership of the Barenboim Gang), and intelligent (speaking six languages fluently—English, French, German, Hebrew, Italian, and Spanish). His approach to music tends to be logical and analytical, yet his ultimate goal is to vitalize the intellectually derived sonic information into a kind of transcendent musical and human experience: "The power of music," he has said, "is precisely that of expressing the eternity of feeling, not transient or subjective emotion." At such expression, Barenboim is a present-day master.

David Bar-Illan
"Among the Greatest of the Great"
(1930-   )

David Bar-Illan, pianist, was born in Haifa, Palestine (now Israel), on February 7, 1930. He studied at the Haifa Music Institute, and in 1946 he debuted by appearing as soloist with the Palestine Broadcasting Service Orchestra. After graduating from the Haifa Music Institute, he became a scholarship student at the Juilliard School of Music in New York City in 1947.

In 1948 he interrupted his schooling and returned to Israel to serve in its army during the War of Independence. Stationed in Galilee, he often went to his Haifa home to practice the piano during lulls in the fighting.

In 1949 he returned to Juilliard, where he studied piano with Rosina Lhevinne. He graduated from Juilliard in 1950 and then studied theory and composition under Felix Salzer at the Mannes School (later College) of Music (1951-53), at the same time privately studying piano with several teachers, including Abram Chasins.

In 1953 Bar-Illan began his concert career in earnest by appearing at London's Wigmore Hall. The following year he gave his first American concerts, including his Carnegie Hall debut in New York City.

His first major appearance on the international scene came in Israel in 1959 when he performed as soloist with the Israel Philharmonic under Dimitri Mitropoulos. On Mitropoulos's urging, Leonard Bernstein engaged Bar-Illan for performances with the New York Philharmonic

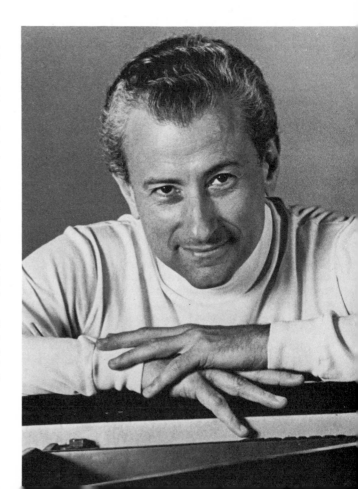

in 1960. During the following season Bar-Illan made his first appearance with the Berlin Philharmonic, under Karl Boehm, soon followed by a sensationally successful performance of the Liszt *First Piano Concerto* with the Amsterdam Concertgebouw Orchestra under Bernard Haitink, which solidified Bar-Illan's international reputation.

Since then he has appeared with almost all of the major orchestras in Europe and the United States. He has also made annual sold-out recital tours of Europe, the United States, Canada, South America, and Israel. Bar-Illan was accorded the honor of giving the first piano recital at the John F. Kennedy Center for the Performing Arts in Washington, D.C.

He gave the world premieres of Robert Starer's *Second* and *Third* piano concertos, the former with the Israel Philharmonic under the baton of Dimitri Mitropoulos in 1959 and the latter with the Baltimore Symphony conducted by Sergiu Comissiona in 1975. Bar-Illan has also performed other contemporary works, notably Leonard Bernstein's *The Age of Anxiety.* But his reper-

tory is centered on the works of nineteenth-century romantics, especially Liszt.

Bar-Illan possesses an outstanding technique, a flexible musicianship, and a profound intellect. An Amsterdam critic hailed him as "among the greatest of the great."

Bar-Illan has a broad range of interests, including mathematics, history, and archeology. He has published articles on psychology and music in several major American periodicals.

Formerly an artist-in-residence at Southern Methodist University, Bar-Illan, since 1975, has held a similar post at the College Conservatory of Music of the University of Cincinnati.

In the mid-1950s he married Willetta Warberg. In the late 1960s that marriage ended in divorce and he wedded Beverly Slater. He has three children: Kim, Daniela, and Jeremy.

When not on tour, Bar-Illan, who became a naturalized American citizen in 1967, makes his home in New York City and in Haifa.

Irving Berlin

America's Most Successful
Popular-Song Composer
(1888-   )

Irving Berlin, composer, was born in Temun, Russia, on May 11, 1888. His original name was Israel Baline, son of Moses Baline, cantor in the local synagogue. When Israel was only four years old, a pogrom took place and the Balines' tiny home was burned beyond use. Moses then led his family to the United States, arriving in 1893 and settling in the poverty-stricken Lower East Side of the borough of Manhattan in New York City. Unable to find a job as a cantor, Moses worked as a supervisor in a kosher slaughterhouse. But he regularly took little Israel to a synagogue and taught the boy to sing Jewish melodies.

In 1896 Moses died, and the eight-year-old Israel immediately quit school and got a job selling newspapers to help support his mother and his siblings. But music

was already in his blood: he had soaked up not only his father's synagogal melodies but also songs of all kinds (including Italian and Yiddish) that he had heard in the streets. Thus, at fourteen he tried street singing and was so electrified by having pennies tossed to him that he was hooked on show business forever.

For the next two years he worked primarily as a singer on an irregular basis in various Bowery saloons, though he did have one prolonged stint as a songplugger planted as a member of the audience at Tony Pastor's famous Music Hall.

At sixteen he finally got a permanent job, as a singing waiter at Pelham's Café in Chinatown. While at Pelham's, Izzy, as Israel was known to his friends, wrote the lyrics to his first published song, "Marie from Sunny

Italy" (1907), with music by the café's pianist, Nick Nicholson (listed as M. Nicholson on the sheet music). A printer's error on the sheet music of that song gave credit for the words to "I. Berlin." The young man liked the name and adopted it.

By 1908 he had become a singing waiter at a bar owned by the one-time boxing champion Jimmy Kelly. There Berlin began to experiment with adding tunes to his lyrics. But since he could not then (or ever in the future) read music, he had friends jot down the melodies that he hummed.

Later in 1908 he became a staff lyricist for Ted Snyder's Tin Pan Alley music-publishing firm, where for the first time he called himself Irving Berlin. He won the job by presenting the company with his "Dorando," which became the first published song having both words and music by Berlin. However, his new job required him to write lyrics for which others, usually Snyder himself, supplied the tunes. In 1910 he made his stage debut by appearing in the Broadway revue *Up and down Broadway,* singing songs on which he had collaborated.

Soon, however, Berlin decided that he did not want to be dependent on others for the music in his songs. He learned to improvise melodies on the piano, but both then and later he could play only in the key of F-sharp major. To produce other tonalities, he adjusted a specially built lever under the keyboard; thus, while he continued to play in the key of F-sharp, the sounds that emitted were in the adjusted tonalities. Trained musicians wrote down the melodies for him (a procedure that he continued to follow for the rest of his career).

In 1910, using his special piano mechanism, Berlin created a tune destined to become his first classic. However, for one year the melody failed several times to attract significant attention. Then, in 1911, he added words to the tune and created "Alexander's Ragtime Band." Soon an international success, the song became the theme for a new style of social dance and the most popular of the many Tin Pan Alley ragtime songs. Though not, strictly speaking, true ragtime music, "Alexander's Ragtime Band" had an energetic, swinging quality that changed American popular song forever. (Not long after it came out, thirteen-year-old George Gershwin pointed to the song and told his teacher, "This is the kind of music *I* want to write.") Influenced by his piano's new mechanism for instantly changing tonalities, Berlin created in "Alexander's Ragtime Band" one of the earliest Tin Pan Alley songs having a verse and a refrain in different keys.

In the same year, 1911, he produced "Everybody's Doin' It Now," which popularized another new dance, known as the turkey trot. During that period, Berlin also began to make a serious mark on Broadway, where he contributed songs to the 1910 and 1911 editions of the *Ziegfeld Follies* revue. The 1910 show featured Fanny Brice singing Berlin's "Goodbye, Becky Cohen" in her Broadway debut.

In February 1912 Berlin married Dorothy Goetz, sister of E. Ray Goetz, who had supplied lyrics for a few of Berlin's melodies. But she contracted typhoid during their honeymoon in Cuba and died in New York City in July of that year. Berlin wrote "When I Lost You" (1912), his first real ballad, in her memory.

In 1914 he finally hit Broadway with his first complete score, for the revue *Watch Your Step.* The show featured the Broadway debut of the dancers Vernon and Irene Castle, who made Berlin's lilting "Syncopated Walk" famous. The outstanding song of the revue was "Play a Simple Melody," Berlin's first duet.

During World War I Berlin was inducted into the army, where he became a sergeant in the infantry. There he wrote, organized, and starred in the all-soldier revue *Yip, Yip, Yaphank* (perf. 1918), with the song "Oh, How I Hate to Get Up in the Morning." One patriotic song written for the show was withdrawn by Berlin himself. "It seemed a little like gilding the lily to have soldiers sing it," he said. The song, which he filed away for the next twenty years, was "God Bless America." (In 1938, with war clouds again on the horizon, the singer Kate Smith asked Berlin for a patriotic song. He gave her a revised version of "God Bless America," which thereafter became closely identified with Smith and which soon became a second national anthem. Berlin assigned all royalties from the song to the Boy Scouts and Girl Scouts of America.)

Released from the army in 1919, Berlin soon formed his own publishing company, having just withdrawn from a publishing partnership established several years earlier with Henry Waterson and Ted Snyder. The company, called Irving Berlin, Inc. (later the Irving Berlin Music Corporation), provided him with a vast fortune from the sale of both his own songs and those of others.

Also in 1919 Berlin began to supply material once again for the *Ziegfeld Follies.* The hit of that show was "A Pretty Girl Is like a Melody," which became the theme song for subsequent editions of the *Follies.*

In 1921 Berlin, with Sam H. Harris as partner, built the Music Box Theater. There Berlin presented four consecutive annual editions of *The Music Box Revue* (perf. 1921-24), which featured his own songs.

In 1924 Berlin met and began to court Ellin Mackay, daughter of Clarence Mackay, a wealthy, snobbish, Catholic, anti-Semitic businessman. The father firmly opposed his daughter's relationship with Berlin on both religious and social grounds. Nevertheless, she continued to see the songwriter.

During the courtship, Berlin wrote the song score for his first Broadway musical comedy: *The Cocoanuts* (perf. 1925), starring the Marx Brothers. One of the songs that he wrote for the show was rejected by George S. Kaufman, the book author. Shortly thereafter, in January 1926, Berlin married Ellin and gave her the song (including the copyright and all future royalties) as a wedding present. It turned out to be one of his biggest hits: "Always." He later said, " 'Always' was a love song I wrote because I had fallen in love."

The romance and elopement of the East Sider Irving Berlin and the socialite Ellin Mackay was one of the most widely publicized events of the 1920s. But the young couple weathered the storms from the badgering press and the angry Mr. Mackay to live happily thereafter.

34

Irving Berlin

They had three children who survived to adulthood: Mary, Linda, and Elizabeth. A fourth child, a boy, died in infancy in 1928. Mary's birth inspired one of Berlin's most beautiful tunes: "Russian Lullaby" (1927).

Breaking precedent, Berlin was contracted to write the complete score for the 1927 edition of the *Ziegfeld Follies*. Each previous edition of the famous annual revue had consisted of songs by several composers. The most successful song from the 1927 show was "Shaking the Blues Away."

The already incredibly successful Berlin then went on to write a long string of hits in every major area open to him. Among his later revues was *As Thousands Cheer* (perf. 1933), with "Easter Parade" (a flop in 1917 under the title "Smile and Show Your Dimple"). His musical comedies were topped by *Annie Get Your Gun* (perf. 1946), with "There's No Business like Show Business," and *Call Me Madam* (perf. 1950), both starring Ethel Merman.

Some of Berlin's best work was written for films, where his songs were linked especially with Fred Astaire, Bing Crosby, Ethel Merman, and Ginger Rogers. Several of Berlin's films were adaptations of his Broadway shows, and others were stories that incorporated old Berlin songs. But among the movies for which he wrote all or much new material were *Top Hat* (1935), *Carefree* (1938), and *Holiday Inn* (1942), the last including "White Christmas."

In the 1950s Berlin's inspiration finally began to taper off. Some of his notable later songs were "Israel" (1959), a tribute to the nation for which he had a deep emotional attachment; "One-Man Woman" (1963); and "An Old-fashioned Wedding" (1966), interpolated into a revival of *Annie Get Your Gun*.

In 1973 Berlin donated his upright piano—the one fitted with a special mechanism to effect modulations—to the Smithsonian Institution.

Probably the most successful American popular-song writer ever, Berlin was also the most versatile. His hits included tender love songs and snappy ragtime tunes, sophisticated fare and simple ditties, sentimental ballads and rousing showstoppers. He absorbed every significant musical trend around him and, in his own works, fused those elements into a fresh, original, uniquely American kind of commercial music. Berlin can justifiably be called the most comprehensively representative composer in the history of American popular song. Jerome Kern said of him: "Berlin has no place in American music. He *is* American music."

Still alive in his late nineties, Berlin has been a living legend for over seventy years.

Selected works:

(lyrics and music by Berlin unless otherwise stated)

Stage

Watch Your Step (perf. 1914), including:
  "Play a Simple Melody"
  "Syncopated Walk"
Stop! Look! Listen! (perf. 1915), including:

  "The Girl on the Magazine Cover"
Yip, Yip, Yaphank (perf. 1918), including:
  "Mandy"
  "Oh, How I Hate to Get Up in the Morning"
The Music Box Revue (perf. 1921, 1922, 1923, 1924), including:
  "Say It with Music" (1921)
The Cocoanuts (perf. 1925)
Ziegfeld Follies of 1927 (perf. 1927), including:
  "Shaking the Blues Away"
Face the Music (perf. 1932), including:
  "Let's Have Another Cup of Coffee"
  "Soft Lights and Sweet Music"
As Thousands Cheer (perf. 1933), including:
  "Easter Parade" (originally "Smile and Show Your Dimple," 1917)
Louisiana Purchase (perf. 1940)
This Is the Army (perf. 1942)
Annie Get Your Gun (perf. 1946), including:
  "Anything You Can Do I Can Do Better"
  "Doin' What Comes Natur'lly"
  "The Girl That I Marry"
  "There's No Business like Show Business"
Call Me Madam (perf. 1950), including:
  "They Like Ike" (title later adapted to become the famous political slogan "I Like Ike")
  "You're Just in Love"
Mr. President (perf. 1962)

Films
(song scores)

Puttin' On the Ritz (1930), including:
  "Puttin' On the Ritz"
Top Hat (1935), including:
  "Cheek to Cheek"
  "The Piccolino"
  "Top Hat, White Tie, and Tails"
Follow the Fleet (1936)
On the Avenue (1937)
Carefree (1938) including:
  "The Night Is Filled with Music"
Holiday Inn (1942), including:
  "White Christmas"
White Christmas (1954), including:
  "Count Your Blessings Instead of Sheep"

Songs
(other than those for the above shows and films)

"Marie from Sunny Italy" (music, M. Nicholson; 1907)
"Doranda" (1908)
"Sadie Salome, Go Home" (music, E. Leslie; 1909)
"Goodbye, Becky Cohen" (for the stage show *Ziegfeld Follies of 1910*, perf. 1910)
"Alexander's Ragtime Band" (1911)
"Everybody's Doin' It Now" (1911)
"When I Lost You" (1912)
"God Bless America" (dropped from the stage show *Yip, Yip, Yaphank*, perf. 1918; revised 1938)
"A Pretty Girl Is like a Melody" (for the stage show *Ziegfeld Follies of 1919*, perf. 1919)
"You'd Be Surprised" (for the stage show *Ziegfeld Follies of 1919*, perf. 1919)
"Always" (dropped from the stage show *The Cocoanuts*, perf. 1925)
"Remember" (1925)
"Blue Skies" (interpolated into the stage show *Betsy*, perf. 1926)
"Russian Lullaby" (1927)
"The Song Is Ended" (1927)
"How Deep Is the Ocean?" (1932)
"Sayonara" (title song for the film *Sayonara*, 1957; originally written in 1953 as "Sayonara, Sayonara")
"Israel" (1959)
"One-Man Woman" (1963)
"An Old-fashioned Wedding" (interpolated into a revival of the stage show *Annie Get Your Gun*, perf. 1966)

Leonard Bernstein

The Preeminent Musical Personality
in the World Today

(1918-)

Leonard Bernstein, the first internationally known musician wholly a product of American schooling, plays a unique dual role in today's world of music. On the one hand, he functions as a respected leader among art-music connoisseurs. On the other hand, he serves as a cultlike figure enjoying a level of popularity with the general public usually reserved for movie stars and rock musicians. As an immensely gifted conductor, a skilled composer of both art and popular music, an excellent pianist, an articulate writer about music and other subjects, and an inspirational teacher and TV commentator, Bernstein—Lenny, as he is affectionately known to friends and admirers—has been probably the most consistently dominant personality on the world's music scene since the 1950s. For many, he virtually symbolizes music.

Bernstein was born of Russian immigrants in Lawrence, Massachusetts, on August 25, 1918. While being raised in Boston (his mother had gone to Lawrence to be with her parents during the delivery), Lenny was victimized by serious bouts with chronic asthma, which made him a sickly, introverted, unhappy boy. But in school he already showed signs of the intelligence that marked him as a gifted child. He had few musical experiences, though he was attracted by the Hasidic tunes sung by his father at home and by the liturgical music of the family's Conservative synagogue, Temple Mishkan Tefila. When Lenny was ten, a relative who was moving out of state left her piano with the Bernsteins. Lenny immediately fell in love with the instrument and soon begged to have lessons. After a year of elementary work with a local teacher, Frieda Karp, he studied for about two years with Susan Williams at the New England Conservatory of Music.

However, his businessman father, Samuel (originally Shmuel) Bernstein, strongly opposed Lenny's total absorption in music. "Stop that damn piano!" the elder Bernstein shouted nightly at his son. Samuel feared that the boy would end up like a klezmer, an impoverished, wandering musician who specialized in weddings and bar mitzvahs in eastern Europe. But Lenny's mother, Jennie Bernstein (originally Charna Resnick), had a more romantic spirit and encouraged him, partly because as a child in Russia she had often trailed after klezmorim, listening to their lovely music.

Because Samuel refused to pay for the lessons at the New England Conservatory, Lenny began to earn his own money by playing in pickup dance bands and giving elementary piano lessons. Soon, with a saxophonist and a drummer, he formed a trio that played at weddings and

bar mitzvahs. Samuel shuddered; his klezmer nightmare seemed to be coming true. (Later, however, after Lenny had become successful, Samuel was genuinely proud of him.)

In his early teens Lenny felt the need for a drastic change in his piano studies. Susan Williams had forced him to hold his hands in an unnatural, paralyzing way. He

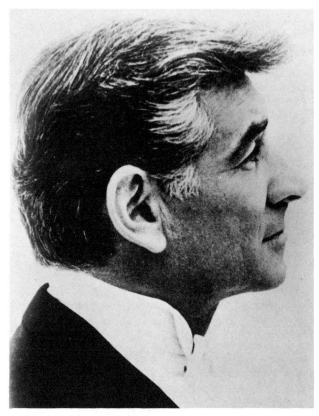

Leonard Bernstein

auditioned for Heinrich Gebhard, the most famous piano teacher in Boston, and was assigned by the master to his finest assistant, Helen Coates, with occasional lessons from Gebhard himself. Coates (who would later become Bernstein's longtime secretary) allowed her student's innate musicality to blossom.

In 1935 Bernstein graduated from Boston Latin School and entered Harvard University, where he studied with a number of teachers, notably Walter Piston (advanced harmony and fugue) and Edward Burlingame Hill (orchestration). Meanwhile, during his first year or so at Harvard, Bernstein continued his private piano lessons with Coates, switching thereafter to Gebhard.

Also during his Harvard years, Bernstein made three off-campus friendships that profoundly affected his life and career. In his sophomore year he was extremely excited by a concert in which the Boston Symphony Orchestra was guest-conducted by Dimitri Mitropoulos. Soon afterward Bernstein met Mitropoulos, who quickly discovered the young man's incredible musicality and encouraged him to become a conductor.

In his junior year Bernstein met Aaron Copland, America's leading composer, during a visit to New York City. Soon they were fast friends, and Copland became the closest thing to a composition teacher that Bernstein ever had. Their close personal and professional relationship still endures, nearly fifty years later.

The third of his three important new friendships began during his last year at Harvard. Bernstein directed a student production of Marc Blitzstein's musical play *The Cradle Will Rock,* which the composer witnessed and praised. Bernstein and Blitzstein developed a lifelong friendship, not only because of their professional respect for each other but also because of their mutual interest in progressive social and political ideas.

After graduating from Harvard in 1939, Bernstein spent the summer in New York City but could not find a steady job. He returned to Boston, on the verge of having to enter his father's business, a hair-supplies company. But in a last desperate bid for a music career, Bernstein returned to New York City and told his plight to Mitropoulos, who arranged for the young man to audition for Fritz Reiner at the Curtis Institute of Music in Philadelphia, where he could receive the intense musical training that he needed. Reiner, impressed by the audition, accepted Bernstein and arranged a scholarship for him.

For two years (1939-41) Bernstein attended the Curtis Institute, where he studied conducting with Reiner, piano with Isabella Vengerova, and orchestration with Randall Thompson. During his first term, Bernstein was asked by Reiner to conduct the Curtis Institute Orchestra in a public performance of Thompson's *Second Symphony.* On that occasion Bernstein discovered his true calling, for, as he later recalled, it "seemed the most natural thing in the world for me to be conducting."

In the summers of 1940 and 1941 Bernstein further studied conducting under Serge Koussevitzky at the newly established Berkshire Music Center on the Tanglewood estate near Lenox, Massachusetts. While Reiner taught in an intellectual, analytical way, with an emphasis on technique, Koussevitzky's method was exactly the opposite: instinctive and inspirational, with an emphasis on the essence and spirit of the music. Bernstein found value in both methods, and he combined them to help form his own approach to conducting.

After graduating from the Curtis Institute in 1941, Bernstein again fell into a period with no career prospects. His attempt to become a private piano teacher failed when the United States entry into World War II took attention away from the arts. He could not even join the war effort, being 4-F because of his chronic asthma. In the summer of 1942 he got a boost when Koussevitzky, with whom he soon developed one of his closest personal relationships, asked Bernstein to be his assistant at Tanglewood. (After Koussevitzky died in 1951 Bernstein was given a pair of the master's cuff links, which Bernstein began to wear at all of his concerts, kissing them before going onstage.) But that autumn Bernstein was back in limbo again.

He went to New York City, where he went through a miserable period that he has called "my Valley Forge." He worked at a number of miscellaneous jobs, such as vocal coach, rehearsal pianist, and piano teacher. His immediate financial worries were alleviated when he was hired by a music publisher to perform such tasks as making piano arrangements of popular songs and transcribing improvisations by jazz performers—all done under the pseudonym Lenny Amber (*Bernstein* being the German word for "amber").

Then came the turning point in his career. On August 25, 1943, his twenty-fifth birthday, he was asked by Artur Rodzinski to become assistant conductor of the prestigious New York Philharmonic, of which Rodzinski was the newly appointed music director. On November 14, 1943, replacing the ill guest conductor Bruno Walter, Bernstein, on only a few hours' notice and with no time for rehearsals, made a spectacular debut by leading the orchestra in a program that began with Schumann's *Manfred Overture;* continued with the world premiere of Miklós Rózsa's *Theme, Variations, and Finale;* followed with Richard Strauss's *Don Quixote;* and concluded with Wagner's "Prelude" to *Die Meistersinger* ("The Mastersingers"). The live audience, the critics, and, because the concert was nationally broadcast over the radio, the entire country immediately acclaimed Bernstein as a major conductor.

Soon he was given more opportunities to conduct the New York Philharmonic, as well as to guest-conduct most of America's other leading symphony orchestras. However, his rising reputation as both a conductor and a composer (his *First Symphony: Jeremiah* was enthusiastically received in several major American cities in early 1944) pushed the Philharmonic's music director, Rodzinski, out of the limelight. Already an unstable soul, Rodzinski, in a fit of jealousy, physically attacked Bernstein and attempted to strangle him in a dressing room. Bernstein, partly to end the organization's backstage tension and partly to broaden his own conducting activity, resigned from the New York Philharmonic in 1944, after only one season.

He then headed the New York City Symphony Orchestra (1945-48), served as a member of the faculty at the Berkshire Music Center (1948-55, succeeding Koussevitzky as head of the conducting department, 1951-55, and maintaining a later association as an adviser), taught at Brandeis University (1951-56), and returned to the New York Philharmonic, coconducting it with Mitropoulos (1957-58) and then leading it as music director and chief conductor (1958-69)—the first American-born musician to hold that important post. When he resigned from the Philharmonic in 1969 (to devote more time to composition and other projects), he was appointed laureate conductor for life. He has subsequently returned to lead the orchestra many times, notably on an American bicentennial tour in the United States and Europe in 1976.

Since the mid-1940s Bernstein has guest-conducted major orchestras not only in America but also in Europe. Showing his versatility, he has often appeared, with the New York Philharmonic and other orchestras, as pianist-conductor in both standard and modern piano concertos. He has also conducted opera at the New York Metropolitan Opera, the Vienna State Opera, and La Scala in Milan, where his appearance in 1953 marked the first time that an American-born conductor had performed at La Scala during the regular season.

In 1947 Bernstein began his long and close association with the ensemble then known as the Palestine Symphony Orchestra but since 1948 called the Israel Philharmonic Orchestra. In late 1948 he led the Israel Philharmonic in a series of concerts in Tel Aviv, Jerusalem, and other cities in the newly formed state of Israel, often appearing as pianist-conductor. Since Israel was then involved in open warfare with the Arabs, Bernstein and the orchestra frequently performed near war zones. On more than one occasion their music was accompanied by the sounds of exploding shells. Besides giving his formal concerts on the tour, Bernstein often stopped in at military camps and hospitals to entertain the troops with his piano playing.

When the Israel Philharmonic made its first tour of the United States, in early 1951, Bernstein and Koussevitzky shared the conducting duties. (After Koussevitzky's death later that year, Bernstein helped to create the Koussevitzky music collection at the National Library in Jerusalem.) Since then Bernstein has led the orchestra many times in Israel, America, and Europe. One of the most memorable performances took place on July 9, 1967, a month after the Israelis' remarkable victory over the vastly more numerous surrounding Arabs in the Six-Day War. The concert was held on Mount Scopus, on the northeastern side of Jerusalem, where Bernstein led the Israel Philharmonic in a program featuring music by two Jews: Mendelssohn's *Violin Concerto* (Isaac Stern, soloist) and Mahler's *Second Symphony,* popularly known as the *Resurrection Symphony* (performed to symbolize Israel's rebirth), with the final chorus specially translated to be sung in Hebrew.

Because of his complete absorption in the music while he is conducting, Bernstein tends, perhaps more than any other conductor of his time, to use his entire body for expressive purposes. Thus, he has been criticized by some lazy commentators for, in his own words, "the acrobatics, the big gestures, the dramatic leaps." Careful observers, however, recognize Bernstein's "choreography" as being merely surface manifestations—the physical spillover—of a deep and genuine emotional involvement through which he nevertheless generates, and conveys to the orchestra, entirely functional musical information.

Bernstein conducts a broad repertory, but he is particularly noted for his exciting performances of Beethoven and the romantics, especially Mahler. In 1967 Bernstein became the first conductor ever to release recordings of all nine Mahler symphonies as a single unit.

However, Bernstein has long been devoted to the cause of modern music—a devotion made even more intense by his association with Koussevitzky, who was perhaps the most important proponent of new music in the twentieth century. As early in his career as 1946, when he was with the New York City Symphony, Bernstein conducted the world premiere of a work by another composer: his friend Blitzstein's *The Airborne Symphony.* While guest-conducting the Boston Symphony Orchestra, Bernstein led the first performances of such major works as David Diamond's *Fourth Symphony* in 1948 and Olivier Messiaen's *Turangalîla* ("Love Song") *Symphony* in 1949. With the New York Philharmonic, Bernstein introduced a great many works, including Charles Ives's *Second Symphony* in 1951 (composed fifty years earlier!), Gunther Schuller's *Spectra* in 1960, Lukas Foss's *Time Cycle* in 1960, Diamond's *Eighth Symphony* in 1961, Copland's *Connotations* in 1962,

William Schuman's *Eighth Symphony* in 1962, Hans Werner Henze's *Fifth Symphony* in 1963, Carlos Chávez's *Sixth Symphony* in 1964, and Milton Babbitt's *Relata II* in 1969.

Bernstein's incredible energy led him to expand his roles as conductor and teacher, an expansion that also resulted in his first books. In an effort to explain music without the usual silly extramusical interpretations and at the same time without excessive musical jargon, he made many national TV appearances on the *Omnibus* series (1954-58), beginning with a now famous program in late 1954, in which he discussed the musical structure of the first movement of Beethoven's *Fifth Symphony* in a fresh, exciting way and with everyday language. Some of his most memorable appearances took place during his commenting and conducting for the nationally televised New York Philharmonic Young People's Concerts (1958-72). Through his TV appearances, he virtually introduced great music to millions of new listeners. In fact, Bernstein was probably the first, and has unquestionably been the most effective, conductor to exploit TV. He has continued to make numerous TV appearances in recent years, including some magnificent performances with the Vienna Philharmonic, taped in Vienna and then televised in the United States, notably the eleven-part series *Bernstein, Beethoven* (1981-82).

Most of Bernstein's books have been directly related to his educational activity, both on TV and in the classroom. His TV scripts form the core of his first three books: *The Joy of Music* (1959), *Leonard Bernstein's Young People's Concerts for Reading and Listening* (1962, revised 1970), and *The Infinite Variety of Music* (1966). *The Unanswered Question: Six Talks at Harvard* (1976) is a publication of his lectures as the 1972-73 Charles Eliot Norton Professor of Poetry at Harvard; they were also taped for TV use by the Public Broadcasting Service (PBS). Miscellaneous writings by Bernstein from his childhood through 1980 constitute *Findings* (1982).

A man of broad intellectual and social interests, Bernstein has also applied an inclusive approach to his compositions. Depending on the various moods and concepts that he wants to evoke at any given moment, he will use widely varying techniques and styles, sometimes in close juxtaposition within a single piece. He has been particularly influenced by Stravinsky, Copland, and Shostakovich, as well as by Richard Strauss, Mahler, Berg, and Hindemith. Other influences include Brahms, jazz, Jewish cantillation, Tin Pan Alley, and the twelve-tone technique (though always only briefly within a solidly tonal context).

Bernstein is especially fond of an unusual chain-reaction compositional device in which a musical idea evolves through successive stages into new ideas, as in the linguistic parallel *cat-cot-cog-dog*. He used the device for the first time in his *Second Symphony: The Age of Anxiety* (1949). In his background score for the movie *On the Waterfront* (1954), he gradually and ingeniously transmuted a barbaric percussion fugato into a lyric love theme.

Bernstein's first major work, written shortly after he had graduated from the Curtis Institute, was the *Clarinet Sonata* (1942). It combines Hindemithian neoclassicism with elements of jazz.

Soon, however, he turned to the theater, for which he had a particular love and flair. His first ballet, *Fancy Free* (1944), composed in a sophisticated jazz idiom, was so successful that he used the same scenario (three sailors on shore leave pursuing girls in New York City) as the basis for his first Broadway musical: *On the Town* (perf. 1944). He later brought American popular musical theater to an unprecedented level of sophistication in his *West Side Story* (perf. 1957), in which he combined Latin American rhythms, big-band and cool jazz, and expressive love songs. Other dramatic works include *Trouble in Tahiti* (perf. 1952), a one-act opera on his own libretto satirizing suburban life; *Candide* (perf. 1956), a comic operetta based on Voltaire's satire; *Mass* (perf. 1971), a theater piece composed for the opening of the John F. Kennedy Center for the Performing Arts, Washington, D.C.; *Dybbuk* (1974, now entitled *Dybbuk Variations)*, a ballet based on a Yiddish play by Shloime Ansky about exorcism in a Hasidic community in eastern Europe; and *A Quiet Place* (perf. 1983), a sequel to *Trouble in Tahiti*.

Bernstein has also, of course, written many orchestral works, most of them naturally given their world premieres under his baton. Several of them reflect his Jewish background. (Samuel Bernstein came from a long line of scholar-rabbis and, though opposed to his son's pursuit of a music career, actively promoted Lenny's love for Jewish studies.) An intense racial feeling pervades his *First Symphony: Jeremiah* for mezzo-soprano and orchestra (1942), evoked partly by the quotation of a couple of Hebrew melodies but mostly, in Bernstein's words, by the music's "emotional quality." The spirit of Jewish liturgical cantillation is especially well captured in the third movement, "Lamentation," sung in Hebrew.

Also based on his religious studies are the *Third Symphony: Kaddish* ("Holy") for orchestra, chorus, boys' chorus, speaker, and soprano (1963) and the *Chichester Psalms* for chorus, boy soloist, and orchestra (1965). In the *Third Symphony* an existential sense of despair in the spoken text by the composer is juxtaposed to the Jewish prayer of mourning. In the *Chichester Psalms* a spirit of simple optimism prevails.

Bernstein's famous *Second Symphony* is subtitled *The Age of Anxiety*, after the W. H. Auden poem of the same name. Like the poem, the music is, in the composer's own explanation, "a record of our difficult and problematical search for faith." Other orchestral works include *Serenade* (1954, inspired by Plato's *Symposium)*, *Songfest* (1977), and *Divertimento for Orchestra* (1980). *Halil* ("Flute," 1981) is for flute, string orchestra, and percussion and is dedicated to the memory of an Israeli soldier killed in action.

In 1946 Bernstein became engaged to Felicia Montealegre Cohn, who had been born in Costa Rica but reared in Chile. Her father, Roy Cohn, was an American Jew who had settled in South America; her mother, the former Clemencia Montealegre, was a Latin American Catholic. Originally hoping to become a concert pianist,

Felicia had studied the piano under the great Chilean pianist Claudio Arrau (who introduced her to Bernstein) after her arrival in the United States. But when she realized that her true talent was acting, she became a leading lady, under the name Felicia Montealegre, in the New York theater and on American TV.

In 1947, by mutual agreement, Lenny and Felicia called off their engagement, feeling that they were not yet ready for marriage. But in 1951 they reunited; and in September of that year, immediately after she had formally converted to Judaism, they were married in Temple Mishkan Tefila. They had three children: Jamie, Alexander, and Nina. When Felicia died in 1978, Bernstein established three scholarships in her name: one each at Columbia University, New York University, and the Juilliard School of Music.

Bernstein is one of the few remaining influential composers who conceive of music as a social and moral force. He believes that the artist's approach to solving the problems of our time has to begin with Keats's famous equation: "Beauty is truth, truth beauty." But Bernstein further believes that today "our sense of truth must be interdisciplinary, and our sense of beauty must be expansive, even eclectic" (hence, perhaps, his compositional style). A strong and vocal proponent of social progress and opponent of the nuclear-arms race, he feels that music, along with the other arts, can have a profound and positive effect on the world's problems by generating, through its heartfelt beauty and truth, "the big dreams" that "can break down self-interest [and] reinforce us against moral deterioration."

Leonard Bernstein

Selected works:

Dramatic

Fancy Free (ballet, 1944)
On the Town (musical comedy; lyrics, B. Comden, A. Green, L. Bernstein; perf. 1944), including:
  "New York, New York"
Facsimile (ballet, 1946)
Trouble in Tahiti (opera; libretto, L. Bernstein; perf. 1952)
Wonderful Town (musical comedy; lyrics, B. Comden, A. Green; perf. 1953)
On the Waterfront (film, background score; 1954)
Candide (comic operetta; lyrics, R. Wilbur, J. La Touche, D. Parker, L. Hellman, L. Bernstein; perf. 1956) (new version: lyrics, R. Wilbur, J. La Touche, S. Sondheim, L. Bernstein; perf. 1973)
West Side Story (musical; lyrics, S. Sondheim; perf. 1957), including:
  "I Feel Pretty"
  "Maria"
  "Tonight"
Mass (theater piece; singers, players, dancers, orchestra; text, liturgy of the Roman Mass; additional texts, S. Schwartz, L. Bernstein; perf. 1971)
Dybbuk Variations (originally *Dybbuk,* ballet, 1974)
A Quiet Place (opera; sequel to *Trouble in Tahiti;* libretto, S. Wadsworth; perf. 1983)

Orchestral

First Symphony: Jeremiah (mezzo-soprano, orchestra; third-movement text, Bible; 1942)
Second Symphony: The Age of Anxiety (piano, orchestra; 1949)

Serenade (violin, string orchestra, harp, percussion; 1954)
Third Symphony: Kaddish (orchestra, chorus, boys' chorus, speaker, soprano; text, Jewish liturgy; speaker's text, L. Bernstein; 1963, revised 1977)
Chichester Psalms (chorus, boy soloist, orchestra; text, Bible; 1965)
Songfest (six singers, orchestra; texts, various American poets; 1977)
Divertimento for Orchestra (1980)
Halil (nocturne for flute, string orchestra, percussion; 1981)

Vocal

I Hate Music (five songs; soprano, piano; texts, L. Bernstein; 1943)
Hashkivenu ("Cause Us to Lie Down"; cantorial tenor, chorus, organ; text, Jewish liturgy; 1945)
Yigdal ("May He Be Magnified"; chorus, piano; text, Jewish liturgical hymn, after Maimonides; 1950)

Chamber

Clarinet Sonata (1942)
Brass Music (1948)
Shivaree (double brass ensemble, percussion; 1969)

Piano

Seven Anniversaries (1943)
Four Anniversaries (1948)
Five Anniversaries (1954)

Writings

The Joy of Music (1959)
Leonard Bernstein's Young People's Concerts for Reading and Listening (1962, revised 1970)
The Infinite Variety of Music (1966)
The Unanswered Question: Six Talks at Harvard (1976)
Findings (1982)

Marc Blitzstein

Creator of a New
American Musical-Theater Idiom
(1905-1964)

Marc Blitzstein, composer, was born in Philadelphia, Pennsylvania, on March 2, 1905. A genuine child prodigy, he began to play the piano by ear at the age of three and soon afterward took his first lessons. Two years later he played in public, and at seven he began to compose.

At sixteen Blitzstein entered the University of Pennsylvania, where he continued both his musical and his academic training. After failing a physical-education class, he lost his scholarship and dropped out of the university. But that episode proved to be a blessing in disguise because he then turned his full attention to music. In 1922 he received an award as a pianist from the Philharmonic Society of Philadelphia, and the following year he began to study piano with Alexander Siloti in New York City. In 1924 he enrolled at the new Curtis

Institute of Music in Philadelphia, studying composition there with Rosario Scalero.

In 1926 he performed as piano soloist with the Philadelphia Orchestra under Henry Hadley. Later that year Blitzstein went to Europe, where he studied composition with Nadia Boulanger in Paris (1926) and Arnold Schoenberg in Berlin (1927).

Returning to the United States, Blitzstein made his first major appearance as a composer-pianist, playing his own *Piano Sonata* (1927), in late 1928 in New York City. At the same time he began his important career as a music critic for several periodicals. Later he also lectured at women's clubs, colleges, and the New School for Social Research in New York City.

After another trip to Europe, Blitzstein returned to America and in the early 1930s went through a change in his attitude toward composition. His music up to then had been mostly abstract instrumental works in a severely dissonant neoclassical idiom. But he gradually became disenchanted with such music, regarding it as irrelevant in the real world of the twentieth century.

He found his true metier when he began to adapt to the American stage the socially conscious musical play that had been cultivated in Germany in the 1920s by Kurt Weill, Ernst Krenek, and others. Blitzstein himself wrote the librettos for most of his dramatic works. For example, he based his choral opera *The Condemned* (1932) on the real-life ordeal of the anarchists Nicola Sacco and Bartolomeo Vanzetti, who were tried and executed for a 1920 theft and murder.

In 1933 Blitzstein married Eva Goldbeck, daughter of the opera singer Lina Abarbanell and the writer Edward Goldbeck. A politically leftist writer, Eva influenced Blitzstein to write for the mass public rather than for sophisticated audiences. In some of her work, she analyzed the role of music in various socially significant stage pieces, but she died in 1936, before her husband created his own most important contributions to that genre.

Among the other influences on Blitzstein were the composer Hanns Eisler and the dramatist Bertolt Brecht, both of whom subscribed to the idea of "art for society's sake." In 1935, for example, Blitzstein witnessed Brecht's *Die Mutter* ("The Mother") in an English version with music by Eisler.

Later Blitzstein wrote a song about a streetwalker and performed it for Brecht, who thereupon suggested that the young composer expand that idea into an examination of other kinds of prostitution. The result was Blitzstein's famous play in music *The Cradle Will Rock*. It was while he was working on *The Cradle Will Rock* that his wife became ill and died in the middle of 1936. For the next few months he devoted himself to the work as a form of emotional release.

Partly opera, partly musical comedy, and partly revue, *The Cradle Will Rock* is an assault on those who sell out their convictions to the establishment and on capitalists who attempt to stop labor movements. It had originated as part of the Works Progress Administration's Federal Theater Project. But when government authorities realized the controversial nature of the work they withdrew their support and even padlocked the New York City theater where the premiere was scheduled to take place in 1937. When the players and the audience arrived, they were led by Blitzstein, Orson Welles (the show's director), and John Houseman (the producer) to another house, rented to them at the last minute. Since the musicians had been forbidden by their union to participate, Blitzstein played the score on the piano alone, while the cast performed in their everyday clothes. Since then, *The Cradle Will Rock* has often been performed without costumes or scenery and with a solo piano accompaniment as a homage to the original production.

Blitzstein continued working for the next several years in the same vein. *I've Got the Tune* (1937) is a radio musical about a composer's gradually coming to political awareness. He composed, in collaboration with Virgil Thomson, the background score for the anti-Fascist film *The Spanish Earth* (1937). The opera *No for an Answer* (1940) focuses on the personal tragedies of immigrant citizens. And he wrote the background score for a portrayal of the Ku Klux Klan in the movie *Native Land* (1942).

Blitzstein's change to the theater of sociopolitical agitation and propaganda was accompanied by a change in his musical style. He moderated his dissonance, though he continued to use it liberally. And he began to use traditional melodic shapes—often flavored with elements of jazz, blues, or popular tunes—and put them into standard song forms, including the twelve-measure blues and the thirty-two-measure commercial song. His rhythms brilliantly captured the flavor of American vernacular speech. The result was a unique blend of contemporary classical idioms and the American popular musical theater.

In 1942 Blitzstein enlisted in the United States Army Air Forces, where he served throughout the rest of World War II. During that period, he composed works in favor of the Allied cause. He wrote the symphonic poem *Freedom Morning* (1943) for tenor, men's chorus (originally consisting of black troops), and orchestra. *The Airborne Symphony* (1946, begun in 1944) was commissioned by the Eighth Air Force.

Immediately after the war Blitzstein began to compose his most ambitious dramatic work: the opera with spoken dialogue *Regina* (1948). Based on Lillian Hellman's famous play *The Little Foxes, Regina* is a strong indictment of capitalistic greed and power hunger.

In 1949 Blitzstein left the Communist party, of which he had been a member since 1938. Nevertheless, for the rest of his life he continued to function as a social critic, as in the musical plays *Reuben, Reuben* (1955) and *Juno* (1959), the latter based on Sean O'Casey's play *Juno and the Paycock*. However, the post-World War II work that gained Blitzstein his greatest fame was his brilliant, slangy English adaptation of Brecht's German lyrics for Weill's 1928 musical play *Die Dreigroschenoper* ("The Threepenny Opera"), which enjoyed many years of success after its initial production in 1952.

In 1960 the Ford Foundation wanted to commission an American opera, and the Metropolitan Opera Association recommended Blitzstein. To fulfill the commission, he chose to continue a dramatic composition that he had already begun: *Sacco and Vanzetti*, which returned to the subject matter of his 1932 work *The Condemned*.

In 1962-63, while still working on *Sacco and Vanzetti*, Blitzstein served as playwright-in-residence at Bennington College in Vermont. There he met, and became friends with, the writer Bernard Malamud. Setting aside his large opera, Blitzstein began to set two of Malamud's short stories to music: *The Magic Barrel* and *Idiots First*. The latter is a deeply emotional work especially notable for its sensitive setting of the speech rhythms of Yiddish-American English.

However, before he could finish those three dramatic works, Blitzstein went for a vacation to Martinique, an island in the West Indies. There he was savagely beaten, apparently while being robbed by a group of men with whom he had had a political argument in a bar. He died of brain damage in Fort-de-France, Martinique, the following day, January 22, 1964.

Blitzstein is difficult to categorize because he refused to restrict himself to any single approach to dramatic composition. While *Regina,* for example, is not quite a traditional opera, *Reuben, Reuben* is not quite a traditional Broadway musical.

What he did most of all, though, was to develop the first convincing American musical-theater idiom that utilized both contemporary musical language (popular and classical) and vernacular speech style. Blitzstein's work, including his social awareness, paved the way for Leonard Bernstein (as in *Trouble in Tahiti* and *West Side Story*), Stephen Sondheim (as in *Sweeney Todd*), and others.

Selected works:

Dramatic

Triple Sec (opera-farce; libretto, R. Jeans; 1928)
Cain (ballet, 1930)
The Harpies (opera; libretto, M. Blitzstein; 1931)
The Condemned (choral opera; libretto, M. Blitzstein; 1932)
The Cradle Will Rock (play in music; libretto, M. Blitzstein; 1937)
I've Got the Tune (radio song-play; libretto, M. Blitzstein; 1937)
Julius Caesar (incidental music, 1937)
The Spanish Earth (film, background score; in collaboration with Virgil Thomson; 1937)
No for an Answer (opera; libretto, M. Blitzstein; 1940)
Labor for Victory (radio series; texts, M. Blitzstein; 1942)

Native Land (film, background score; 1942)
Androcles and the Lion (incidental music, 1946)
Another Part of the Forest (incidental music, 1946)
Regina (opera; libretto, M. Blitzstein, after L. Hellman; 1948)
Reuben, Reuben (musical play; lyrics, M. Blitzstein; 1955)
Juno (musical play; lyrics, M. Blitzstein; 1959)
Toys in the Attic (incidental music, 1960)
Sacco and Vanzetti (opera; libretto, M. Blitzstein; incomplete)
The Magic Barrel (opera; libretto, M. Blitzstein, after B. Malamud; incomplete)
Idiots First (opera; libretto, M. Blitzstein, after B. Malamud; incomplete)

Orchestral

Sarabande (1926)
Piano Concerto (1931)
Freedom Morning (symphonic poem; tenor, men's chorus, orchestra; 1943)

Vocal

songs (voice, piano; texts, M. Blitzstein, English and American poets; 1925-60)
The Airborne Symphony (tenor, bass, narrator, men's chorus, orchestra; text, M. Blitzstein; 1946)

Chamber

String Quartet (1930)
Serenade (string quartet, 1932)
Discourse (clarinet, cello, piano; 1933)

Piano

Piano Sonata (1927)
Piano Percussion Music (1929)
Scherzo (1930)
Suite (1933)

Ernest Bloch
First Great Composer of Modern Jewish National Music
(1880-1959)

Ernest Bloch, composer, evolved his personal style through a mystical identification with the Hebraic spirit. "It is the Jewish soul that interests me," he said, "the complex, glowing, agitated soul that I feel vibrating throughout the Bible" and "that I strive to hear in myself and to translate in my music."

He was born in Geneva, Switzerland, on July 24, 1880. His father, a clock merchant, loved to sing Jewish liturgical songs but wanted his boy to become a shop-keeper, not a musician. However, when Ernest was eleven years old, he wrote out a vow to become a musician, placed it under a mound of rocks, and built a ritual fire around it. The son's determination was so great that the father finally relented.

In Geneva young Bloch studied violin with Louis Rey and theory with Emile Jaques—Dalcroze from 1894 to 1897. Bloch composed several immature works during that period, notably the *Symphonie orientale* ("Oriental Symphony"), in an undisciplined, hyperromantic style.

He then went to Brussels, where he studied violin with the celebrated Eugène Ysaÿe and composition with

François Rasse from 1897 to 1899. Bloch completed his studies by working on composition with Ivan Knorr at the Hoch Conservatory in Frankfort on the Main (1899-1901), who taught Bloch to think independently, and privately with Ludwig Thuille in Munich (1901-1903).

In Munich he completed his first major composition, the Richard Strauss-like *Symphony in C-sharp Minor* (1902), and in 1903 he took it to Paris. After a year of failing to get a hearing, he returned discouraged to Geneva and entered his father's clock business.

In 1904 Bloch married the pianist Margarethe Schneider, whom he had met as a fellow student at the Hoch Conservatory in 1900. They often performed duets together. The Blochs had three children: one son, Ivan (an engineer), and two daughters, the younger being Lucienne (a painter) and the older being Suzanne (a noted lutanist and scholar specializing in early music).

For the next several years Bloch continued to work in his father's clock shop, while composing in his spare time. He derived his *Hiver-Printemps* ("Winter-Spring," 1905) from the impressionistic style of Claude Debussy,

poèmes juifs ("Three Jewish Poems") for orchestra (1913), *Israel Symphony* (inspired by the liturgy for Yom Kippur) for solo voices and orchestra (1916), and *Schelomo* ("Solomon," a rhapsodic portrait of King Solomon) for cello and orchestra (1916). Thus began what came to be known as Bloch's Jewish Cycle of compositions, through which he became the leader of the twentieth-century movement to create a Jewish national music.

Bloch explained his purpose: "I am a Jew. I aspire to write Jewish music . . . because it is the only way in which I can produce music of vitality—if I can do such a thing at all." The works in his Jewish Cycle are highly emotionally charged reflections of the history and culture of the Jewish people. However, Bloch seldom quoted authentic Hebrew melodies. Instead, he absorbed, and created new material from, intervallic and rhythmic patterns characteristic of Jewish liturgical and secular music. For example, some of his melodic leaps and repeated-note patterns evoke the call of the shofar (a trumpetlike instrument made from a ram's horn), which has been sounded during Jewish high religious observances since ancient times. Bloch's passages in free-flowing rhythms are suggestive of much Jewish chant, and his frequent accents on the last or penultimate beats of measures have analogies in the Hebrew language.

In 1916 Bloch came to the United States as conductor for the dancer Maude Allen and her company. Stranded when the troupe went bankrupt, he nearly starved during the next few months.

In 1917 he began to teach at the David Mannes School of Music in New York City. During the next few years, his music received important performances by various ensembles, sometimes with Bloch himself as conductor. His reputation as a "Jewish" composer grew rapidly.

In 1920 he was appointed director of the Cleveland Institute of Music, where his advanced ideas about education (such as dropping examinations and textbooks in favor of direct musical experience) created tension between him and his superiors. In 1925 he was forced to resign. Bloch then became director of the San Francisco Conservatory, where he remained till 1930. Among his students in America were George Antheil, Isadore Freed, Frederick Jacobi, Douglas Moore, Quincy Porter, Bernard Rogers, and Roger Sessions—all of whom Bloch taught to follow their individual artistic inclinations.

In 1924 Bloch became a naturalized American citizen; and in a spirit of patriotism he wrote *America* for chorus and orchestra (1927), which won a prize from the magazine *Musical America* and increased his fame immensely. However, the work (which quotes American folk and composed tunes) was uncharacteristic of his music written in the 1920s, which turned to a neoclassical style utilizing seventeenth- and eighteenth-century forms and gestures but modern rhythms and dissonances. Notable works from that period include the *First Violin Sonata* (1920); the *First Piano Quintet* (1923), which uses quarter-tone intervals in the first and last movements; and the *First Concerto Grosso* (1925), written by Bloch as a model of neoclassicism for his Cleveland students.

whom Bloch had met in Paris. Bloch's most important composition before 1910 was *Macbeth,* an opera that he finished in 1909. It shows the influence of postromantic and impressionistic elements.

The world premiere of *Macbeth* took place in 1910 at the Opéra-Comique in Paris. The eminent French musicologist Romain Rolland was so impressed by that performance that he traveled to Geneva to meet the composer. Outraged to see Bloch wasting his time with routine business matters, Rolland became a zealous propagandist for the young man's art and persuaded Bloch to devote himself entirely to music.

Leaving the clock business, Bloch taught composition and lectured on aesthetics at the Geneva Conservatory from 1911 to 1915. He continued to compose in his spare time, but with a change in style. Pulling away from his earlier Germanic postromanticism and French impressionism, he began to create works more overtly Jewish in content and subject matter, such as *Trois*

A grant from a wealthy San Francisco music lover enabled Bloch to retire from teaching in 1930 and devote himself to composition. Moving back to Europe, he lived primarily in Switzerland during the 1930s and once again poured out a series of epic Jewish compositions. The most important work was the *Avodath hakodesh* ("Sacred Service") for baritone, chorus, and orchestra (1933), the Sabbath morning service with a Hebrew text based on the liturgy according to the American Union prayer book. Bloch's *Avodath hakodesh* synthesizes the Ashkenazic (central and eastern European Jewish) and the Gregorian (medieval Christian) musical traditions with modern techniques to produce one of the great monuments in synagogal music. The work has received concert performances in many countries.

Because of the rise of Nazism in Europe and because of his desire to retain hs American citizenship, Bloch returned to the United States in 1938. In the early 1940s he settled in Agate Beach, Oregon, where he lived for the rest of his life. However, during the succeeding summers (till his retirement in 1952), he taught composition at the University of California, Berkeley.

Bloch virtually ceased to write overtly Jewish works in his late years, though he frequently composed in the rhapsodic manner and with some of the intervallic and rhythmic characteristics of his Hebrew music. His late works summarize the various influences in his career. The *Concerto symphonique* ("Symphonic Concerto," 1948), for example, is neoromantic, while the *Second Concerto Grosso* (1952) is neoclassical and the *Sinfonia breve* ("Short Symphony," 1952), with its postromantic extension of chromaticism into near-atonality, is expressionistic. As he grew older, Bloch tended to write more chamber music, including several string quartets, the *Second Piano Quintet* (1957), and two suites for unaccompanied violin (commissioned by Yehudi Menuhin, 1958).

In 1958 Bloch had unsuccessful cancer surgery, and he died in Portland, Oregon, on July 15, 1959. In the spring of 1968 the Ernest Bloch Society was established in the United States, largely through the efforts of Bloch's three children. Suzanne Bloch, with Irene Heskes, published *Ernest Bloch, Creative Spirit: A Program Source Book* (1976).

Selected works:

Opera

Macbeth (libretto, E. Fleg, after W. Shakespeare; comp. 1909, perf. 1910)

Orchestral

Symphony in C-sharp Minor (1902)
Hiver-Printemps (1905)
Trois poèmes juifs (1913)
Schelomo (cello, orchestra; 1916)
First Concerto Grosso (strings, piano; 1925)
Helvetia ("Switzerland," 1929)
Voice in the Wilderness (orchestra, cello; 1936)
Evocations (1937)
Violin Concerto (1938)
Suite symphonique ("Symphonic Suite," 1944)
Concerto symphonique (piano, orchestra; 1948)
Suite hébraïque ("Hebraic Suite"; viola [or violin], orchestra; 1951)
Second Concerto Grosso (strings, string quartet; 1952)
Sinfonia breve (1952)
Symphony in E-flat Major (1955)

Vocal

Prelude and Two Psalms (soprano, orchestra; texts, Bible; 1914)
Psalm 22 (alto [or baritone], orchestra; text, Bible; 1914)
Israel Symphony (five vocal soloists, orchestra; 1916)
America (chorus, orchestra; text, E. Bloch; 1927)
Avodath hakodesh (baritone, chorus, orchestra; text, Jewish liturgy; 1933)

Chamber

five string quartets (1916-56)
two violin sonatas (1920, 1924)
Baal shem ("Master of the Divine Name"; violin, piano; 1923, orchestrated 1939)
two piano quintets (1923, 1957)
From Jewish Life (cello, piano; 1924)
Méditation hébraïque ("Hebraic Meditation"; cello, piano; 1924)
Prelude (string quartet, 1925)
Two Pieces (viola, piano; 1951)
three suites for solo cello (1956-57)
two suites for solo violin (1958)
Suite (viola, 1958)

Piano

Four Circus Pieces (1922)
In the Night (1922)
Poems of the Sea (1922)
Piano Sonata (1935)
Visions and Prophecies (1936)

Fanny Brice

Queen of the Comic Song

(1891-1951)

Fanny Brice, singer and comedienne, was born in New York City, New York, on October 29, 1891. Her original name was Fannie Borach. While growing up in various sections of New York City, including Brooklyn, she learned the European accents that she later used in her humorous dialect songs. Her parents were saloon owners, and as a tiny tot she began to accumulate show-business experience when her father, Charles Borach (a happy-go-lucky gambler known as Pinochle Charlie), encouraged her to sing for his customers. Later she earned pennies by singing with neighborhood boys in backyards and poolrooms.

At thirteen Fannie won an amateur-night contest at Keeney's, a Brooklyn theater, with her seriocomic singing of "When You Know You're Not Forgotten by the Girl You Can't Forget." She earned ten dollars for winning the contest, plus three dollars tossed to the stage by the audience.

Fannie went to school only sporadically. "I ran away from every school I ever went to," she admitted, "or if I didn't I was thrown out." By the time she turned fourteen, she had already quit school for good, having decided to enter show business full time.

Soon she was averaging thirty dollars a week in amateur-night prize money. It was during that period that she changed her name to Fannie (later Fanny) Brice, after John Brice, a friend of her mother's. The entertainer said that she changed her name because she was tired of having her real name punned by friends, as in "More-Ache" and "Bore-Act."

At fifteen she was hired as a chorus girl for a Broadway show, George M. Cohan's revue *The Talk of New York*. Cohan fired her during rehearsals when he found out that she could not dance. Though thus ignominiously dismissed from her first professional job, Brice immediately bounced back and got a job for the 1906-1907 season touring Pennsylvania in a show called *A Royal Slave*, in which she played the part of an alligator.

Her first big break as a singer came in *Transatlantic Burlesque* (1910) in New York City and on the road. Also in 1910, while touring in the burlesque show *The College Girl*, Brice impulsively married Frank White, a Springfield, Massachusetts, barber. The marriage was soon annulled on the grounds that she was underage.

While Brice was with *The College Girl*, the young composer Irving Berlin gave her one of his songs, "Sadie Salome, Go Home" (lyrics by Berlin, music by Edgar Leslie), a takeoff on opera. Berlin suggested that she sing it with a Yiddish accent. She did, and thus began her career as a singer of Yiddish-type comic songs. Her performances made a tremendous impact on audiences, among whom was the great Broadway producer Florenz Ziegfeld, who quickly signed her for the 1910 edition of the *Ziegfeld Follies* revue.

For the *Follies*, Brice persuaded the songwriters Joe Jordan and Will Marion Cook to write the ballad "Lovie Joe" for her. The coproducer of the show, Abe Erlanger, fired her when he heard her sing the word *more* with the standard burlesque pronunciation *mo'*. Ziegfeld, however, intervened, and she remained. Brice's instincts were correct, and she stopped the show with her singing of "Lovie Joe" in the *Follies*, receiving, it is said, twelve encores on opening night. In the same production, Brice sang "Goodbye, Becky Cohen" by Irving Berlin (words and music), also associated with his first *Follies*. Brice went on to appear in many of the annual *Follies* shows throughout the 1910s and early 1920s, specializing in humorous songs and skits in which she frankly made a virtue of her plainness.

In 1918 she married the gambler Jules W. ("Nick") Arnstein (also known by several other names). She remained loyal to him through his costly court battles and through his imprisonment in Sing Sing for fraud (1915-17) before their wedding and in Leavenworth, Kansas, for theft (1924-25) during their marriage. But she finally divorced him in 1927 for infidelity. Their two children, Frances and William, were raised by servants while she worked. Brice's own parents had separated when she was a child, and she learned from her mother, who went into the real-estate business, how to be an independent woman. But Brice missed having a family life. "I didn't want my daughter to have a career," she said. "Because if a woman has a career, she misses an awful lot. . . . If you have a career, then the career is your life."

Meanwhile, her own career flourished. Besides appearing in the *Follies,* she worked in other shows throughout the 1910s, including the Broadway musical comedy *The Honeymoon Express* in 1913 and a vaudeville act in London in 1914.

In 1921 Ziegfeld handed her an English-language version, "My Man," of the French torch song "Mon homme." Till then she had been purely a comic singer, but Ziegfeld saw the parallel between the subject matter of the ballad and Brice's unhappy marriage to Arnstein. "Do you think you can make them cry?" he asked as he gave her the song. "I think you can," he answered himself. She did make audiences cry, and it became the song with which she was most closely identified. (On November 21, 1927, in her first public appearance after her divorce from Arnstein, she stood silent for fifteen minutes onstage in the Palace Theater, refusing audience demands for the song.)

After the 1923 *Follies,* Brice appeared in *The Music Box Revue* (1924) and toured in vaudeville (1925-26). Then came her only stage failure, a serious dramatic role in David Belasco's production of Willard Mack's *Fanny* (1926), a story unrelated to the star's own life. She soon returned to her natural genre of the musical comedy by appearing in *Fioretta* (1929).

In 1929 Brice married the Broadway producer Billy Rose (originally William Samuel Rosenberg). Soon she was featured in two of his shows: *Sweet and Low* (1930) and *Crazy Quilt* (1931). But she reached the zenith of her stage career in the 1934 and 1936 editions of the *Ziegfeld Follies.* In 1938 she divorced Rose for (as with Arnstein) infidelity.

Brice displayed a large and varied repertory of material in her stage work. Both as a singer and as an actress, she gained special renown for her devastating mimicry. Her vocal techniques included her satiric "concert-room vocalizing," her broadly humorous specialties (such as "I'm an Indian"), and her custom-tailored ballads (such as "I Should Worry," "Rose of Washington Square," and

"Second Hand Rose"). As an actress-clown, she was famed for her lampoons of fan dancers, tap dancers, lady evangelists, and silent-screen vamps. Her comic performances of *The Dying Swan* ballet and of modern dance were hilarious, as were her burlesque of Camille (with W. C. Fields as the maid) and her Yiddish-dialect monologues. But Brice was never cruel; she always poked fun with sensitivity and human understanding.

She made six movies, the first being *My Man* (1928), in which she sang not only the title song but also "I'd Rather Be Blue," the most popular song that she introduced in films. Her other movies were *Night Club* (1929), *Be Yourself!* (1930), *The Great Ziegfeld* (1936), *Everybody Sing* (1938), and *Ziegfeld Follies* (1946). Brice, however, was never really comfortable in movies. Her ethnic humor found its best home in the theaters of burlesque and vaudeville.

She did, however, influence the films of others. She brought a $750,000 defamation suit against Twentieth Century-Fox for the 1939 film *Rose of Washington Square* because of its use of her life story without her permission. The suit was settled out of court, Brice receiving $30,000 in December 1940. Many years later Barbra Streisand made her greatest impact by sensitively portraying Brice in the Broadway musical *Funny Girl* (1964) and in its movie adaptation in 1968, as well as in a film sequel, *Funny Lady* (1974).

Radio proved to be a good medium for Brice's talents. In 1932 she performed as a straight singer with George Olsen's orchestra in a short-lived radio series. But she became best known to millions of listeners for her creation of the impish little-girl character Baby Snooks. Brice had invented the character, based on the real-life child star Baby Peggy, as part of her vaudeville act in 1912. At a party in 1921 Brice revived the character to perform the burlesque song "Poor Pauline" as a six-year-old child might sing it. Baby Snooks then appeared on the stage in *Sweet and Low* in 1930, as well as in the 1934 and 1936 editions of the *Ziegfeld Follies.* Also in 1936 the precocious brat was introduced to radio listeners on *The Ziegfeld Follies of the Air.* She then made regular appearances on *Good News* from 1937 to 1940, when the program changed its name to *Maxwell House Coffee Time,* where she remained a fixture for the next several years. In 1944 the enfant terrible was given her own radio series, *The Baby Snooks Show,* which remained on the air for the rest of Brice's life.

As Baby Snooks became increasingly established as an individual entity, Brice almost completely abandoned her natural voice in public, preferring to speak in Snooks's mischievous-little-girl tones. In interviews the entertainer often referred to "Schnooks" as if the child were a real person.

In her own real life, Brice was interested in far more than just show business. She was an art collector, an oil painter, a dress designer (she designed the costumes for *Crazy Quilt),* and a gifted interior decorator (she decorated the homes of Eddie Cantor, Ira Gershwin, Dinah Shore, and others).

Brice had red hair, green eyes, and a large mouth.

Her nose-straightening surgery in August 1923 received wide publicity.

At the age of fifty-nine she had a massive cerebral hemorrhage at her home in Beverly Hills, California. She died five days later, on May 29, 1951. Brice left the bulk of her $2 million estate to her two children.

Selected recordings:

Singles

"I Don't Know Whether to Do It or Not" (1916, Columbia)
"Second Hand Rose" (1921, Victor)
"My Man" (1921, Victor)
"I'm an Indian" (1921, Victor)
"I'd Rather Be Blue" (1928, Victor)
"When a Woman Loves a Man" (1930, Victor)

Eddie Cantor
King of the Comic Song
(1892-1964)

Eddie Cantor, singer and comedian, was born of Russian immigrants in New York City, New York, on January 31, 1892. His poverty-stricken parents died when he was a toddler, his mother in 1893 and his father, an unemployed violinist, a year later. The orphan, originally named Isidore Itzkowitz, was raised on the Lower East Side of the borough of Manhattan in New York City by his maternal grandmother, Esther Kantrowitz, a warmhearted, giving woman who became the dominant influence in forming his character.

She was also responsible, inadvertently, for his eventual name and career. When the school registrar asked for the six-year-old's name, Esther, who spoke no English (only Yiddish, Polish, and Russian), became confused and started to give her own name, Kantrowitz, but never finished it. The registrar wrote down "Isidore Kanter." Later the boy himself changed the spelling to Cantor. Still later he changed the Isidore to Eddie because his girlfriend, Ida Tobias, liked the name Eddie.

As an excellent mimic, Grandma Esther gave Cantor the idea of performing for others. His sentimental recitations kept him in school for several years after he had stopped earning passing grades. And he often sang and performed comic impersonations for his friends, sometimes combining the two skills, as when he pretended to be Anna Held singing "I Just Can't Make My Eyes Behave."

After he left school at the age of thirteen, Cantor failed at several odd jobs. Then he and a friend formed a variety act that performed at weddings, club socials, and amateur theatricals. At the Clinton Music Hall in 1907, Cantor and his partner made their first appearance on a real stage, falling flat because they spoke in English, not realizing that they were in a Yiddish theater. The following year Cantor, on his own, entered an amateur contest as a comic impersonator at a Bowery theater and won five dollars, plus several dollars in coins tossed to the stage.

After playing more amateur nights with his comedy-dialect routines, Cantor got a job with a touring burlesque show, his first professional engagement. When the tour folded four weeks later, he became a singing waiter in a Coney Island saloon. The pianist at the saloon became one of Cantor's best friends, as well as one of the world's greatest entertainers. His name was Jimmy Durante.

In 1909 Cantor was hired as a comedian on a small vaudeville circuit. There he was praised for his ability to repeat the same act in various ethnic accents, including one in blackface. He continued his blackface role from 1910 to 1912 as an assistant to the comedy juggling team of Bedini and Arthur. The trio burlesqued and parodied the famous stars of the day. Cantor's big step forward came when he was allowed to sing Irving Berlin's "Ragtime Violin" as part of the act. He was so nervous at the first performance that he pranced quickly up and down the stage, clapping his hands and rolling his eyes as he sang. Those actions later became his trademarks.

From 1912 to 1914 Cantor toured with Gus Edwards's

Kid Kabaret revue, which featured a number of talented youngsters. One of them was George Jessel, who, like Durante, was destined to become a famous entertainer and one of Cantor's best friends. (Cantor's close friends later included such stars as Irving Berlin, Fanny Brice, W. C. Fields, Al Jolson, and Will Rogers.)

In 1914 Cantor married Ida Tobias. He had met her in 1905, when he was only thirteen, and she encouraged him through his early struggles. Their marriage was widely regarded as one of the most harmonious in show business. It also became one of the best-known marriages because Cantor later incorporated numerous anecdotes about his wife and five daughters (Marjorie, Natalie, Edna, Marilyn, and Janet) in his routines. He adopted "Ida, Sweet As Apple Cider" as his theme song.

The Cantors went to London for their honeymoon in 1914. There, in the revue *Not Likely,* Cantor scored his first major success. Till then he had relied on imitations and dialects. In *Not Likely* he sang and performed comedy routines as himself. The English press gave him his first real notices.

Back in the United States later in 1914, Cantor renewed his vaudeville work as a comedian and singer in blackface—but, perhaps for the first time by any blackface performer, without dialect and without comedy clothes. In 1916 he appeared in his first musical: the Los Angeles production of *Canary Cottage.*

From Los Angeles he went back to New York City for twenty-seven weeks in Florenz Ziegfeld's supper club, the Midnight Frolic. That engagement led to Cantor's Broadway debut in the *Ziegfeld Follies of 1917,* followed by the 1918 and 1919 editions of the show.

But when Cantor helped to lead an Actors' Equity Association strike that briefly shut down all Broadway shows during the run of the *Follies of 1919,* Ziegfeld felt betrayed and he dropped the young star from the following year's show. Cantor immediately went to work for the Schuberts, Ziegfeld's rival impresarios, and appeared in two revues: *The Midnight Rounders* (1920) and *Make It Snappy* (1922).

Then Ziegfeld, not wanting a valuable asset to get away from him, reestablished his association with Cantor and backed him in the musical comedy *Kid Boots* (1923), which turned out to be one of Cantor's greatest hits. In the *Ziegfeld Follies of 1927* Cantor broke precedent by being the only star in the whole revue. That show was followed by the musical comedy *Whoopee* (1928). His last stage work was in *Banjo Eyes* (1941), the title coming from his nickname, which referred to his wide, expressive eyes.

In his stage appearances, Cantor did some of his routines with, and some without, blackface. As with many other white entertainers of the time, such as Al Jolson and Sophie Tucker, Cantor's use of blackface was intended not as a racial slur but simply as a theatrical convention that helped performers overcome inhibitions; then, with their confidence built, they could come out from behind the "mask" and perform without the black makeup.

The development of movies with sound in the late 1920s doomed vaudeville and hurt the live theater in general. Cantor quickly jumped into the new medium. His first film appearance was in a silent-movie version of *Kid Boots* (1926). Among his musical talkies were *Glorifying the American Girl* (1929), a film version of *Whoopee* (1930), *Palmy Days* (1931), *The Kid from Spain* (1932), *Roman Scandals* (1933), *Kid Millions* (1934), *Ali Baba Goes to Town* (1937), *Thank Your Lucky Stars* (1943), *Show Business* (1944), and *If You Knew Susie* (1948). He appeared briefly in, and sang for the music track of, the biopic *The Eddie Cantor Story* (1953), in which he was portrayed by Keefe Brasselle.

Despite his success in movies, Cantor actually reached the peak of his popularity in radio. After a few minor appearances during the 1920s, he made his first

(Courtesy of the Academy of Motion Picture Arts and Sciences)

Eddie Cantor

real impact on Rudy Vallee's *Fleischmann Hour* in February 1931. In September of that year Cantor took over as host of *The Chase and Sanborn Hour,* which soon developed the alternate title *The Eddie Cantor Show.* He had his own radio variety show, under various titles, almost continuously for the next two decades. Cantor, beginning in 1932, pioneered the use of live-audience response on radio, where studio visitors had previously been admonished to remain silent.

Besides offering his own vigor, sentimentality, and comedic instinct on his radio programs, Cantor provided audiences with such new talents as the comedian Harry Einstein (famous as Parkyakarkus) and the singers Bobby Breen, Deanna Durbin, and Dinah Shore. When he hired Thelma Carpenter for a season, it was the first time that a female black singer had been on radio for other than just a guest appearance. (In 1949 Cantor helped to get Eddie Fisher's career under way by taking the young singer on a live tour.)

In 1950, at Cantor's own suggestion, the National Broadcasting Company (NBC) established the TV series *The Colgate Comedy Hour,* in which Cantor and other comedians rotated in hosting their own variety programs. *The Eddie Cantor Show* was part of that series, which lasted several seasons. In 1955 he hosted *The Eddie Cantor Comedy Theater,* another variety show. After that he made guest appearances on many TV programs.

Cantor's singing success was due to his unique manner of performing lighthearted songs with an irresistible cheerfulness, a dignified yet boyish charm, and a sincere human warmth. He was closely identified with a number of songs besides his theme ("Ida, Sweet As Apple Cider"), including "Ain't She Sweet?" "Dinah," "If You Knew Susie Like I Know Susie," "Ma, He's Making Eyes at Me," "Makin' Whoopee," "Margie" (inspired by his daughter Marjorie; lyrics by Benny Davis, music by Con Conrad and J. Russel Robinson), "Yes, We Have No Bananas," and "You'd Be Surprised." Cantor himself provided lyrics for several songs, notably "There's Nothing Too Good for My Baby" (collaborators, Benny Davis and Harry Akst), which he introduced in the movie *Palmy Days.*

He was extremely active in raising funds for many causes. In 1920 he began to give benefits for Surprise Lake Camp for underprivileged youngsters. The project was especially dear to him because it was while he him-self was at the camp in his own childhood that he had first realized what a great morale boost such kindness can give to people living in bleak circumstances. In the late 1930s he helped to raise money for sending refugee children, whose parents had been killed or interned by the Nazis, to Palestine. He raised hundreds of millions of dollars for other causes, including hospitals, veterans, Catholic and Protestant projects, and the United Jewish Appeal. Much of his work was done for the state of Israel, where he was affectionately referred to in Yiddish as the *schnorrer* ("beggar"). When President Franklin D. Roosevelt asked Cantor to organize a drive to raise money for fighting infantile paralysis, the entertainer suggested a plan in which each donor would be asked for only ten cents, calling it a "march of dimes." Roosevelt immediately adopted that slogan for the program. When Dr. Jonas Salk developed his polio vaccine in the 1950s, the money had come from the March of Dimes.

Cantor wrote several books, including the autobiographical *My Life Is in Your Hands* (with David Freeman, 1928) and *Take My Life* (with Jane Kesner Ardmore, 1957). *As I Remember Them* (1963) is a book of recollections.

After a 1952 heart attack, Cantor was forced into semiretirement. In 1962 his life changed even more drastically with the death of his beloved Ida. His own death, in the Hollywood section of Los Angeles, California, came on October 10, 1964.

Selected recordings:

Singles

"The Modern Maiden's Prayer" (1917, Aeolian Vocalion)
"You'd Be Surprised" (1919, Emerson)
"Margie" (1920, Emerson)
"If You Knew Susie" (1925, Columbia)
"Makin' Whoopee" (1928, Victor)
"There's Nothing Too Good for My Baby" (1931, Victor)
"Alexander's Ragtime Band" (1938, Decca)
"If You Knew Susie Like I Know Susie" (1939, Columbia)
"Yes, Sir, That's My Baby" (1941, Decca)
"They Go Wild, Simply Wild, over Me" (1941, Decca)
"We're Having a Baby, My Baby and Me" (1942, Decca)

Album

The Eddie Cantor Story (1954, Capitol)

Aaron Copland
Symbol of American Music
(1900-   )

Aaron Copland, the first internationally renowned composer of music with an "American" accent, was born of Russian immigrants in New York City, New York, on November 14, 1900. His father's original name was Harris Kaplan. When Harris stopped over in England to earn money for the rest of his passage from Russia to the United States, a British immigration official mistakenly transcribed the name as Copland, a spelling that Harris kept permanently. In America, Harris Copland opened his own department store and became president of Beth Israel Anshei Emes, the oldest synagogue in the borough of Brooklyn.

Aaron, the fifth and youngest child in the family, was exposed to many early musical experiences, especially violin playing, piano playing, and singing by various members of the family. At Jewish weddings, Aaron heard mostly American dance music, such as ragtime and waltzes, along with an occasional Jewish dance. At the family's Conservative synagogue, the cantor's music consisted of pure, unaccompanied Jewish melody handed down for generations. (Copland, however, has written very little music based on Jewish sources.)

After taking some piano lessons from an older sister, Copland studied piano with Leopold Wolfsohn. Beginning in 1917, and especially after graduating from Boys' High School in Brooklyn in 1918, he intensified his private music studies, including advanced piano work with Victor Wittgenstein and Clarence Adler.

Meanwhile, he studied theory and composition with Rubin Goldmark. Goldmark's Germanic conservatism only served to increase young Copland's leanings toward the forbidden fruit of modernistic non-Germanic composers, such as the Frenchmen Claude Debussy and Maurice Ravel, and the Russians Modest Mussorgsky and Alexander Scriabin. Copland soon learned to turn in to Goldmark only routine academic exercises. He kept his more exciting work to himself. One of the fresh compositions that he wrote during that period is the little piano piece *The Cat and the Mouse,* which contains some spicy dissonances; written in 1920, it is Copland's earliest composition to retain some currency in the standard repertory.

During his student years in New York City, Copland missed the companionship of other students. Aaron Schaffer, a literary friend who was studying in Paris, wrote to Copland about the intellectual and artistic life in the French city. Soon Copland decided to continue his studies in France.

In 1921 he enrolled at the new American Conservatory in Fontainebleau, near Paris. It was the only music school that he ever attended, and he stayed only three months. He was bored with the conventional, routine assignments demanded by Paul Vidal, his composition teacher. But on the faculty was a brilliant young teacher of harmony and orchestration: Nadia Boulanger. Copland followed her to Paris and privately studied composition with her from 1921 to 1924. He recruited others and became the first in a long line of important American composers to study with Boulanger, including Roy Harris, Walter Piston, Virgil Thomson, Quincy Porter, Marc Blitzstein, and Elliott Carter.

Copland has described his studies with Boulanger as the most important musical experiences of his life. Her general enthusiasm and her interest in contemporary music (especially that of Igor Stravinsky) spilled over to Copland. Most important of all, she inspired him with confidence in his own creative powers.

Copland returned to the United States in 1924, fortunately at a time when there was a great deal of money available for the creative arts. He was helped by private patronage, fellowships, commissions, and prizes. For example, in 1925 and 1926 he was awarded the first Guggenheim Fellowships given to a composer.

Copland resolved to break the bonds of European influence on American music. He wanted American music to form its own character, just as French and Russian music had done in opposition to the long-dominant German style. As his first step in that direction, Copland immediately incorporated jazz into his scores. He began with his *Symphony for Organ and Orchestra* (1924), which Boulanger, an organist, introduced during her American tour in early 1925. Later he revised that work to form his *First Symphony* (1928), without organ. But the highlight of Copland's jazz-related works of the 1920s is his exciting *Piano Concerto* (1926). During that period he became the first composer of distinctly American qualities (based especially on a fresh kind of rhythmic vigor) to win international recognition.

Copland, however, did not simply carry barroom jazz into the concert hall. He synthesized American jazz and the modern European musical techniques of Stravinsky and others. Yet the result was, from the very beginning, colored with Copland's personal mode of expression— grandiose, dramatic, and tragic.

In the late 1920s Copland entered a transitional phase in his music. The works from that period still contain jazz elements, yet they also point forward to a more abstract style. The climax of the transition is the outstanding *Symphonic Ode* for orchestra (1929). Some observers have found in the *Symphonic Ode* a "Jewish" spirit, not with respect to material, since there are no Jewish themes in the work, but to a "prophetic" quality created by profound, speechlike musical utterances cast in a mold of tragic grandeur. The same quality can be found in many of his earlier and later compositions as well.

In the early 1930s Copland was influenced by a new national mood. The Great Depression had brought a sense of disillusionment and a retreat from the careless extravagance of the jazzy 1920s. Copland's reaction was to write music that has been characterized as objective, austere, and abstract (that is, music consisting of rigorous intellectual development of little musical cells, rather than straightforward expositions of jazz motives or traditional melodies). An early sign of that approaching style is in his *Vitebsk: Study on a Jewish Theme* for piano trio (1928). The *Piano Variations* (1930) and the *Statements* for orchestra (1935) highlight Copland's "abstract" phase.

He then decided to expand his audience by trying to express his musical thoughts "in the simplest possible terms." To do so, he turned to folksong. It is the music from the "folk" period of his career that has brought Copland his greatest fame.

He began by using Mexican folk materials in his orchestral piece *El salón méxico* ("The Mexican Salon," 1936). Copland, of course, did not simply string together preexisting tunes; he molded the materials to his own personality, adapting them to his own unique harmonic and rhythmic gestures. He went on to apply the same procedure to works pertaining to the United States, using cowboy songs, New England and Quaker hymns, and original material that reflects the spirit of such folk sources. His most popular folk-related works are the ballets *Billy the Kid* (1938), *Rodeo* (1942), and *Appalachian Spring* (1944).

Composing movie music was another step that Copland took to reach a broader audience. He established new high standards in background scores, which had previously consisted almost entirely of rehashed nineteenth-century romanticism. Copland showed how to use modern techniques while still providing memora-

ble melodies and powerful underscoring of the dramatic action. He composed outstanding scores for *Our Town* (1940), *The Red Pony* (1949), and *The Heiress* (1949).

Other highlights during that period include *A Lincoln Portrait* for speaker and orchestra (1942), *Fanfare for the Common Man* for brass and percussion (1942), and *Clarinet Concerto* (1948), which contains some jazz elements and which he dedicated to the jazz clarinetist Benny Goodman. The beautiful *Third Symphony* (1946) merges Copland's folk style with his earlier abstract manner.

Beginning with his *Piano Quartet* (1950), Copland adopted a personalized use of the twelve-tone technique. He continued that line in his complex *Piano Fantasy* (1957) and in his orchestral works *Connotations* (1962) and *Inscape* (1967).

Since the late 1950s, Copland has turned his attention from composing to conducting. He has traveled the world and conducted his own music with many great orchestras, such as the Boston Symphony.

Besides presenting the world with his own compositions, Copland has played a leading role in bringing widespread attention to the entire modern American school of music. With Roger Sessions he organized the Copland-Sessions Concerts (1928-31) in New York City, which featured the works of American composers. In 1932 he helped to inaugurate the festivals of American music at Yaddo, in Saratoga Springs, New York. And in addition to his formal activities with the League of Composers and the American Composers' Alliance, he has always been generous with his informal help and advice to other, especially younger, American composers.

Copland has also been active as a teacher and writer. He lectured general audiences on music at the New School for Social Research in New York City (1927-37) and taught young musicians during the summer-school sessions at the Berkshire Music Center at Tanglewood, near Lenox, Massachusetts (1940-65). During 1951-52 he gave the Charles Eliot Norton lectures at Harvard, the first American composer to have that honor. Copland published his Norton lectures in his book *Music and Imagination* (1952). He has also published music-appreciation books for a general audience.

Unmarried, Copland is a simple, unassuming, urbane man who enjoys traveling, reading, and maintaining many friendships. One of his most enduring friendships has been with the conductor Leonard Bernstein, who performs Copland's works with a special warmth and understanding.

Selected works:

Operas

The Second Hurricane (libretto, E. Denby; 1936)
The Tender Land (libretto, H. Everett, after E. Johns; 1954, revised 1955)

Ballets

Billy the Kid (1938)
Rodeo (1942)
Appalachian Spring (chamber orchestra, 1944; full orchestra, 1945)

Films
(background scores)

Of Mice and Men (1939)
Our Town (1940)
The North Star (1943)
The Red Pony (1949)
The Heiress (1949)
Something Wild (1961)

Orchestral

Music for the Theatre (1925)
Piano Concerto (1926)
First Symphony (1928; from *Symphony for Organ and Orchestra*, 1924)
Symphonic Ode (1929, revised 1955)
Short Symphony (1933)
Statements (1935)
El salón méxico (1936)
A Lincoln Portrait (speaker, orchestra; 1942)
Fanfare for the Common Man (brass, percussion; 1942)
Third Symphony (1946)
Clarinet Concerto (1948)
Connotations (1962)
Inscape (1967)

Songs

Twelve Poems of Emily Dickinson (voice, piano; texts, E. Dickinson; 1950)

Chamber

Vitebsk: Study on a Jewish Theme (piano trio, 1928)
Piano Quartet (1950)
Nonet (strings, 1960)
Duo (flute, piano; 1971)

Piano

The Cat and the Mouse (1920)
Piano Variations (1930)
Piano Sonata (1941)
Piano Fantasy (1957)
Proclamation (1982; orchestrated by Phillip Ramey, 1985)

Writings

What to Listen for in Music (1939; second edition, 1957)
Our New Music (1941; revised and enlarged, as *The New Music, 1900-1960,* 1968)
Music and Imagination (1952)
Copland on Music (1960)

Sammy Davis, Jr.
Complete Entertainer
(1925-   )

Sammy Davis, Jr., singer and all-around entertainer, was born of a Baptist father and Roman
Catholic mother in the Harlem section of New York City,
New York, on December 8, 1925. His father was the lead
dancer, and his mother a top chorus girl, in Will Mastin's
vaudeville troupe. The boy's paternal grandmother took
care of him in Harlem while his parents traveled with the
show. When he was two years old, his parents separated
and his father took him to join the Will Mastin players. At
first little Sammy performed only as a silent prop, bringing laughter by mugging the actions of other performers.
Later he learned to sing and dance in the show.

At the age of seven he won the title role in the two-reel
movie *Rufus Jones for President* (1933), which starred
Ethel Waters and was filmed in the borough of Brooklyn
in New York City. Soon afterward he made another film,
Seasoned Greetings (1933), with Charlie Chaplin, Jr.,
and Chaplin's mother, Lita Grey, who wanted to adopt
Sammy and take him to the Hollywood section of Los
Angeles, California, to make him a movie star. But the
Davis family decided to stay together.

In 1934 vaudeville was in the early stages of its de-
mise, brought about largely by competition from talking
movies. Will Mastin, a close friend of the Davis family,
had to reduce his troupe down to just himself, Sammy
Davis, Sr., and Sammy Davis, Jr. The child had already
become the main attraction, and the new group was
called Will Mastin's Gang, Featuring Little Sammy. After
other name changes, the group was eventually billed as
the Will Mastin Trio, Featuring Sammy Davis, Jr. In the
late 1930s and early 1940s, the trio worked across the
United States and Canada numerous times. During that
period Sammy met the legendary tap dancer Bill ("Bojangles") Robinson and the young singer Frank Sinatra.

World War II came, and when Sammy turned eighteen he was drafted into the army. During basic training,
young Davis, a black, experienced, for the first time in his
life, blatant, brutal racial prejudice. Then he was transferred into Special Services, where he did shows in
camps across the country.

After the war, Sammy rejoined the Will Mastin Trio.
But vaudeville was dead, and the act went through some
lean years, playing nightclubs in various cities. Young
Davis constantly worked on developing new skills to
freshen up the act, which soon became a showcase for
him, while the two older men tap-danced and soft-shoed
in the background. Besides broadening his singing and
dancing repertory, he played various instruments and
did impressions of singers and screen stars.

In 1947-48 they toured in a show starring Mickey

Rooney, from whom Sammy learned much about live
performing. Within the next few years the trio, because
of young Davis's growing talent and reputation, began to
receive big-time engagements, notably on Eddie Cantor's TV show *The Colgate Comedy Hour*. They also
performed at the famed Copacabana nightclub in New
York City, which a few years earlier had refused, on
racial grounds, to allow Sammy even to enter the
building.

Then, in November 1954, while driving from Las
Vegas to Los Angeles, Sammy was in a horrible automobile accident, as a result of which he lost his left eye. One
of his visitors during his hospital stay was Eddie Cantor,

who earlier had given Davis a mezuzah (a holy Hebrew charm) as a gift and whose depth of understanding in this crisis favorably impressed the young man. Sammy was also visited in the hospital by a rabbi, who was making routine rounds.

After he left the hospital young Davis began to study Judaism seriously. He saw the affinity between the Jews and the blacks as oppressed peoples. Within months his conversion to Judaism was psychologically complete, the formal ceremony coming a few years later, in 1958.

Meanwhile, he made his show-business comeback. Wearing an eye patch (later a glass eye), he performed successful engagements at major American nightclubs. In fact, the publicity surrounding his accident actually increased the demand for the Will Mastin Trio.

In 1956 they hit Broadway with *Mr. Wonderful,* a musical play written especially for Sammy, about a young black nightclub entertainer who becomes successful by virtue of his talent and will in the face of strong racial opposition. The production itself was widely criticized, but the show lasted over a year because of the versatile power of young Davis himself.

Soon after *Mr. Wonderful* the trio broke up, both Mastin and Sammy Davis, Sr., retiring. But the career of Sammy Davis, Jr., skyrocketed. Besides continuing as a major attraction in nightclubs, he went back to Broadway for the musical *Golden Boy* (1964) and the one-man show *Sammy* (1974). He also starred in *Stop the World—I Want to Get Off* (1978) at the New York State Theater in Lincoln Center.

Davis has been active in movies as well. Perhaps his most memorable film role was Sportin' Life in George Gershwin's black opera *Porgy and Bess* (1959). Davis went on to perform in such movie musicals as *Pepe* (1960), *Robin and the Seven Hoods* (1964), *A Man Called Adam* (1966), *Sweet Charity* (1969), and *Sammy Stops the World* (1978). He became a member of a famous Hollywood group of entertainers and friends called the Rat Pack or the Clan, led by Frank Sinatra.

Davis has made numerous TV guest appearances. He has also hosted his own TV variety specials and series, notably the series *Sammy and Company* (1975-77).

Davis has recorded dozens of singles and albums. His most successful singles include "That Old Black Magic" (1955), "What Kind of Fool Am I?" (1962), and "The Candy Man" (1972). Among his albums are *Just for Lovers* (1955), *I've Gotta Be Me* (1969), and *Sammy*

Davis, Jr.: A Live Performance of His Greatest Hits (1977), including "Mr. Bojangles."

However, Davis has never claimed to be trained and polished in his singing. His success as a singer comes through his energetic style, flexible voice, vocal carrying power, and ability to project the essence of a song in a unique way. Singing is only one aspect of Davis's entertainment repertory. Singer, dancer, actor, comedian, impressionist—he is one of the last great examples of the "complete entertainer" nurtured in vaudeville.

Davis has had three marriages. In the late 1950s he wedded Loray White, a black dancer; but they were divorced after only one year together. Shortly thereafter he married the white Swedish actress May Britt. They had a natural daughter (Tracey) and two adopted sons (Mark and Geoff). Because of their racially mixed marriage, Davis and Britt were subjected to many ugly remarks and incidents. That marriage, too, ended in divorce. Since 1970 he has been married to Altovise Gore, another black dancer.

Davis is the author of the autobiographical books *Yes, I Can: The Story of Sammy Davis, Jr.* (with Jane and Burt Boyar, 1965) and *Hollywood in a Suitcase* (1980).

Selected recordings:

Singles

"Hey There" (1954, Decca)
"Something's Gotta Give" (1955, Decca)
"Love Me or Leave Me" (1955, Decca)
"That Old Black Magic" (1955, Decca)
"What Kind of Fool Am I?" (1962, Reprise)
"The Shelter of Your Arms" (1964, Reprise)
"I've Gotta Be Me" (1968, Reprise)
"The Candy Man" (1972, MGM)

with Frank Sinatra:

"Me and My Shadow" (1962, Reprise)

Albums

Just for Lovers (1955, Decca)
"What Kind of Fool Am I?" and Other Showstoppers (1962, Reprise)
The Shelter of Your Arms (1964, Reprise)
I've Gotta Be Me (1969, Reprise)
Now (1972, MGM)
Sammy Davis, Jr.: A Live Performance of His Greatest Hits (1977, Warner Bros.)

David Diamond
Composer Who Has Blended Neoclassicism and Romanticism
(1915-   )

David Diamond, composer, was born in Rochester, New York, on July 9, 1915. His family was too poor to buy music lessons for him, but at the age of seven he borrowed a friend's violin and taught himself to play the instrument. Soon he invented a method of notation to write down his own melodies.

In 1927 the family, no longer able to maintain its own residence, moved to Cleveland, Ohio, to live with relatives. There Diamond began his formal music study by taking lessons from André de Ribaupierre, a Swiss musician who arranged for the boy to enter the Cleveland Institute of Music, which Diamond attended from 1927 to 1929.

The family then returned to Rochester, where in 1930 Diamond entered the Eastman School of Music on a scholarship and studied violin with Effie Knauss and composition with Bernard Rogers. During that time Diamond was still a student at Benjamin Franklin High School. After he graduated from high school in 1933, he intensified his studies at Eastman. However, he became dissatisfied with the Eastman curriculum, and in 1934 he went to New York City, where he studied composition with Roger Sessions.

In 1936 a private patron enabled Diamond to go to Paris, France, to finish a ballet, *Tom* (1936), in collaboration with the choreographer Leonide Massine. While there Diamond composed *Psalm* (1936), his first successful orchestral piece. The following two summers, 1937 and 1938, he returned to France to study composition with Nadia Boulanger at the American Conservatory in Fontainebleau. His contacts in France with such men as the author André Gide and the composers Maurice Ravel, Albert Roussel, and Igor Stravinsky broadened his artistic and philosophical thinking.

Early in his career Diamond worked occasionally as a violinist in radio and theater orchestras. But his subsistence through the years has come mostly from a wide variety of grants, awards, and commissions, with periodic positions as a teacher.

In the 1940s he lived principally in the United States. But in 1951 he was appointed Fulbright Professor at the University of Rome in Italy, a post that he held till 1952. In 1953 he settled in Florence, Italy, where he remained till 1965, with periodic visits to the United States.

On a couple of those visits Diamond taught at the University of Buffalo (1961 and 1963). In 1965 he returned to America on a more permanent basis, at first for the purpose of taking part in a series of activities celebrating his fiftieth birthday, during which he conducted the New York Philharmonic, the Rochester Philharmonic, and other orchestras. He then served as chairman of the composition department at the Manhattan School of Music in New York City (1965-67), followed by various posts at the University of Colorado in Boulder (1970), the American Academy in Rome (1971-72), and the Juilliard School of Music (since 1973). He has continued to receive important grants and commissions, including a Rockefeller Foundation grant in 1983.

Symphonies, string quartets, and songs form the core of Diamond's large and varied output. His style blends a neoclassical tightness of form (including sonata-

allegro movements, as well as masterful fugues and sets of variations) with a romantically tinged lyricism and melodic grace. The whole is set in a moderately dissonant texture, expressed through brilliant orchestration, and marked by strong rhythms that are often inspired by folklike patterns.

Many of his most popular pieces are early works, including the *Rounds* for string orchestra (1944) and the incidental music to Shakespeare's *Romeo and Juliet* (1947). Such works were written in a clearly tonal, diatonic-modal framework. But beginning in the 1950s Diamond turned to a more chromatic, complex manner of expression, occasionally even adopting a modified version of the dodecaphonic method, as in *The World of Paul Klee* (1957), which is a symphonic suite consisting of impressions of four Klee paintings.

However, the basic personal characteristics of his earlier style have remained intact throughout his career. His later works include *Second Overture: A Buoyant Music* for orchestra (1970), *Piano Quintet* (1972), and *A Roust* for piano (1980).

Of Jewish inspiration is the sacred service *Mizmor l'David* ("Song of David") for tenor, chorus, and orchestra (1951, commissioned by the Park Avenue Synagogue of New York City).

A bachelor, Diamond enjoys many nonmusical activities, especially painting. He is also a skilled student of numerous languages.

Selected works:

Dramatic

Tom (ballet, 1936)
Romeo and Juliet (incidental music, 1947)
Anna Lucasta (film, background score; 1949)
The Rose Tattoo (incidental music, 1951)

Orchestral

Psalm (1936)
three violin concertos (1936, 1947, 1967)
Cello Concerto (1938)
Concerto (chamber orchestra, 1940)
eight symphonies (1941-60)
Rounds (string orchestra, 1944)
The Enormous Room (symphonic poem, 1948)
Piano Concerto (1950)
The World of Paul Klee (symphonic suite, 1957)
Second Overture: A Buoyant Music (1970)
Flute Concerto (perf. 1986)

Vocal

Mizmor l'David (tenor, chorus, orchestra [or organ]; text, Bible; 1951)
This Sacred Ground (baritone, chorus, children's chorus, orchestra; text, A. Lincoln; 1962)
A Secular Cantata (vocal soloists, chorus, small orchestra; text, J. Agee; perf. 1977)
many songs and song cycles

Chamber

Cello Sonata (1938)
ten string quartets (1940-68)
Violin Sonata (1946)
Quintet (clarinet, two violas, two cellos; 1950)
Woodwind Quintet (1958)
Nonet (three violins, three violas, three cellos; 1963)
Piano Quintet (1972)

Piano

Sonatina (1935)
Album for the Young (1946)
two sonatas (1947, 1972)
Then and Now (1962)
Alone at the Piano (1967)
A Roust (1980)

Neil Diamond
Pursuer of Beautiful Noise
(1941-   )

Neil Diamond, composer and singer, was born in New York City, New York, on January 24, 1941. He grew up in the borough of Brooklyn, and there, at the age of ten, he began to sing in the streets with a group of youths called the Memphis Backstreet Boys. Passersby would toss money to the youngsters. At thirteen he ran away from home and traveled to the Midwest, where he formed a folk group, the Roadrunners, and performed at coffeehouses.

At fifteen Diamond returned to Brooklyn. He attended Erasmus Hall High School, where one of his classmates was the future singing star Barbra Streisand (with whom he later recorded a duet of his song "You Don't Bring Me Flowers," 1978). Diamond spent most of his spare time with music, occasionally getting singing jobs. He wrote his first song at sixteen and discovered that songwriting was a good way to try to overcome his general lack of self-esteem.

Later, while attending New York University as a premedical student, he became a songplugger, trying to get other people's records played by radio disc jockeys. In 1962 he dropped out of college in his senior year to become a staff songwriter for Sunbeam Music Company, creating material, usually on order, for other performers. Unsuccessful at that, he was in and out of other publishing offices for the next few years.

In 1965 Diamond struck out on his own. He rented an office (where he lived as well as worked), bought a used upright piano, and wrote songs (words and music) that he sent out to various performers. He supported himself during that time by playing one-night stands at Greenwich Village coffeehouses.

Soon his luck began to change when some of his songs were successfully recorded by others. Jay and the Americans recorded Diamond's "Sunday and Me" (1965), while the Monkees came out with his "I'm a Believer" (1966) and "A Little Bit Me, a Little Bit You" (1967).

In 1966 he finally got a chance to record his own songs. His first single, "Solitary Man" (1966), was moderately successful. But his reputation as a major figure was really established with his next recording, "Cherry, Cherry" (1966). After recording such other hits as "Sweet Caroline" (1969), "Holly Holy" (1969), and "Cracklin' Rosie" (1970), Diamond found himself performing in front of packed audiences on American and world tours.

From the beginning of his career, Diamond has shown a stylistic versatility. His works cover the categories of folk, folk-rock, gospel, and country-rock. His 1970 album *Tap Root Manuscript* includes a composition entitled "The African Trilogy," which tries to depict the three main stages in life (birth, maturity, and death) through rhythmic forms derived from gospel music and African melodies. *Beautiful Noise,* a 1976 album, is a virtual history of Tin Pan Alley, with Diamond songs written in most of the basic pop styles of the twentieth century.

Diamond composed the songs and recorded the music track for the movie *Jonathan Livingston Seagull* (1973). He also sang on the music track of the 1980 remake of *The Jazz Singer,* in which he made his movie-acting debut. In the latter film, Diamond plays the role of Yussel, assistant to his cantor father in a New York City synagogue. Yussel forsakes his roots for a new life as a Los Angeles recording artist but eventually returns to replace his father. Diamond sings both traditional Jewish melodies and his own original songs in the movie. He felt closely identified with his role because, as he said, "there were so many connections between it and me" (particularly the Jewish and musical contexts, and the inner conflict between the desire for worldly success and the quest for deeper values). While working on the film, Diamond gave Yiddish lessons to Laurence Olivier, who played Yussel's father.)

In spite of his success, Diamond found it difficult to rid himself of an early personal problem: lack of self-esteem. He finally sought help through psychoanalysis, which helped him come to terms with his own individuality. "After years of working with a psychiatrist," he said, "I have finally forgiven myself for not being Beethoven."

Diamond is soft-spoken and does not socialize easily, though he is now more relaxed than he was before his psychoanalysis. His home life is vital to him. He lives with his wife, Marcia (whom he married in the late 1960s), and his two sons, Jesse and Micah. By an earlier marriage, he had two daughters, Marjorie and Elyn, who live with their remarried mother but often visit Diamond during holidays.

Jesse is one of his father's toughest critics. In 1982 Diamond made a demo tape of the single "Heartlight," which was inspired by the film *E.T.* Hoping the song would appeal especially to youngsters, Diamond sent the tape to Jesse, who was away at a New England summer camp. Buoyed by Jesse's enthusiastic approval, Diamond issued the single and the follow-up album *Heartlight* (1982), both of which became tremendously successful.

Selected recordings:

Singles

"Cherry, Cherry" (1966, Bang)
"Girl, You'll Be a Woman Soon" (1967, Bang)
"Sweet Caroline" (1969, MCA)
"Holly Holy" (1969, MCA)
"Cracklin' Rosie" (1970, MCA)
"I Am . . . I Said" (1971, MCA)
"Song Sung Blue" (1972, MCA)
"Longfellow Serenade" (1974, Columbia)
"Love on the Rocks" (1980, Capitol)
"Hello Again" (1981, Capitol)
"America" (1981, Capitol)
"Heartlight" (1982, Columbia)
"Headed for the Future" (1986, Columbia)

with Barbra Streisand:
"You Don't Bring Me Flowers" (1978, Columbia)

Albums

The Feel of Neil Diamond (1966, Bang)
Just for You (1967, Bang)
Touching You, Touching Me (1969, MCA)
Sweet Caroline (1969, MCA)
Shilo (1970, Bang)
Tap Root Manuscript (1970, MCA)
Do It (1971, Bang)
Hot August Night (1972, MCA)
Jonathan Livingston Seagull (1973, Columbia)
Double Gold (1973, Bang)
His Twelve Greatest Hits (1974, MCA)
Beautiful Noise (1976, Columbia)
Love at the Greek (1977, Columbia)
I'm Glad You're Here with Me Tonight (1977, Columbia)
You Don't Bring Me Flowers (1978, Columbia)
September Morn (1979, Columbia)
The Jazz Singer (1980, Capitol)
On the Way to the Sky (1981, Columbia)
Yesterday's Songs (1981, Columbia)
Heartlight (1982, Columbia)
Primitive (1984, Columbia)
Headed for the Future (1986, Columbia)

Misha Dichter

Pianist Who Combines
Virtuosity and Emotional Appeal
(1945-   )

Misha Dichter, pianist, was born in Shanghai, China, on September 27, 1945. His parents, of Polish origin, had stopped off in Shanghai on their way to the United States. In 1947 they finally arrived in Los Angeles, California, where Misha began to take piano lessons at the age of six. In 1953 he became a naturalized American citizen.

He studied with several teachers in California, the most important being Aube Tzerko, a former Artur Schnabel pupil. From the age of twelve to the age of eighteen, Dichter was with Tzerko. During that time, in 1961, Dichter won first prize in a competition sponsored by the Music Educators National Conference, Western Division. The award brought him his first appearance with an orchestra, a performance of Rachmaninoff's *Second Piano Concerto* at the Santa Monica Civic Auditorium.

Dichter graduated from Beverly Hills High School in 1963. He then enrolled at the University of California in Los Angeles (UCLA), majoring in English. He attended UCLA for only two semesters (1963-64); but during that time he won the Atwater Kent Award in piano and was soloist with various local orchestras, notably the Los Angeles Philharmonic at a Symphonies for Youth Concert.

In June 1964 Dichter attended a Los Angeles master class held by the famed piano teacher Rosina Lhevinne, who urged him to transfer to the Juilliard School of Music in New York City, where she was on the staff. After receiving a scholarship, he did transfer to Juilliard, where Lhevinne guided his technical and musical development in the Russian tradition. He graduated in 1968.

In 1966, while still a student at Juilliard, Dichter launched his career by winning second prize in the pres-

tigious International Tchaikovsky Piano Competition in Moscow, the Soviet Union. His fiery temperament and effortless technique made him immediately popular with the Russian public, and he won tremendous applause at his concerts in Moscow after the competition.

Returning to the United States, Dichter made his major American debut in August 1966 in a concert with the Boston Symphony Orchestra, Erich Leinsdorf conducting, during the Berkshire Music Festival at Tanglewood, near Lenox, Massachusetts. The event was telecast nationally. That appearance soon brought Dichter engagements with numerous other American orchestras, including the New York Philharmonic under the baton of Leonard Bernstein.

The following year, 1967, Dichter appeared in London with the New Philharmonia Orchestra. In 1969 the Soviet Minister of Culture invited Dichter to the Soviet Union for his first major tour of that country. The tour was extremely successful, and he has since been reinvited for further concerts there.

His repertory extends from Mozart through early twentieth-century composers. He has little interest in the works of contemporary composers because he feels that their works require too many hours of preparation for too few expressive possibilities. Dichter has a good command of pianistic virtuosity, but he prefers to subordinate that aspect of his playing to the higher goals of meticulous musicianship and emotional appeal.

Dichter's wife is the former Cipa Glazman, a Brazilian-born pianist whom he met while they were both students at Juilliard. They were married in January 1968 with the impresario Sol Hurok as best man. The Dichters have two children: Gabriel and Alexander. The boys were purposely introduced to classical music through recordings, not lessons, when they were tiny tots. Misha and Cipa wanted the children's first encounters with music to be experiences of beauty and joy, not work.

Misha and Cipa, however, do work at music, and Cipa often joins him for duo-piano performances. Since their debut together in 1972 they have appeared in numerous recitals and orchestral concerts in America and Europe.

Misha himself regularly appears in recital and with major orchestras in the United States and abroad, performing over one hundred times a year. He has also been frequently seen on national TV.

Antal Doráti
Outstanding Trainer of Orchestras
(1906-   )

Antal Doráti, conductor, was born in Budapest, Hungary, on April 9, 1906. His father, Sándor Doráti, was a violinist at the Budapest Opera. His mother, Margit Doráti (née Kunwald), was a remarkable, though untrained, pianist. When Antal was five, he began to receive piano lessons, first from his mother and then from a local teacher. At the same time he learned the cello so that he could play chamber music at home with other family members.

At fourteen young Doráti entered the Franz Liszt Academy in Budapest, where his principal teachers were Leó Weiner (chamber music) and Zoltán Kodály (theory and composition). Doráti was also influenced, though

never formally taught, by the great composer-pianist Béla Bartók, who was on the faculty at the academy.

In 1924 Doráti graduated from the Liszt Academy and became a coach at the Budapest Opera, where he remained till 1928. He then spent one year as an assistant to the conductor Fritz Busch at the Dresden Opera (1928-29).

During the late 1920s Doráti met the beautiful Klári Kórody when she was a member of an audience of young ladies whom he was lecturing about opera. Antal and Klári soon fell in love, but her father, a wealthy banker-businessman, cautioned them to put off marriage till Antal had more financial security. Doráti quickly found a job as principal conductor of opera in Münster, married Klári in 1929, and, after a honeymoon in Italy, took up his first position of leadership.

After three seasons in Münster (1929-32) Doráti went to Paris and joined the Russian Ballet of Monte Carlo. He helped to conduct the Russian Ballet on its tours from 1933 to 1938, when the company split into two wings, Doráti opting to go with the one called the Original Russian Ballet (1938-41).

In 1941, while World War II was ravaging Europe, Doráti immigrated to the United States; and in 1947 he became a naturalized American citizen. His first post in his new homeland was as conductor of the Ballet Theater (later called the American Ballet Theater) in New York City (1941-44).

In 1945 he began to earn his reputation as an outstanding trainer of orchestras. In that year he formed the new Dallas Symphony Orchestra, which he led till 1949. He rapidly built the orchestra into a fine ensemble and gave it added prestige by conducting it in the world premieres of Hindemith's *Symphonia serena* ("Serene Symphony") in 1947 and William Schuman's *Sixth Symphony* in 1949.

Then he took over the Minneapolis Symphony Orchestra (now known as the Minnesota Orchestra), and during his tenure there (1949-60) he turned it into one of the world's finest ensembles and established its international reputation through a number of recordings. He also continued his policy of presenting significant world premieres, including Bartók's *Viola Concerto* in 1949, Walter Piston's *Fourth Symphony* in 1951, Ernst Toch's *Fourth Symphony* in 1957, Gunther Schuller's *Seven Studies on Themes of Paul Klee* in 1959, and Roger Sessions's *Fourth Symphony* in 1960.

During the 1940s and 1950s he made many guest appearances in Europe, particularly with the London Symphony Orchestra (with which he debuted in 1946), whose later standards his performances greatly influenced. He also developed a close association with the Hungarian refugee orchestra, known as the Philharmonia Hungarica, on its formation in 1957.

In 1962 Doráti began to appear regularly as conductor of the British Broadcasting Corporation (BBC) Symphony Orchestra, of which he formally served as principal conductor from 1963 to 1966. There followed an eight-year period as head of the Stockholm Philharmonic (1966-74).

While he was in Stockholm, Doráti's marriage, which had produced one child (Antonia), dissolved. In 1968 he formed a new union, with the Austrian pianist Ilse von Alpenheim, whom he had socially met in 1959 and had performed in a concert with two years later. In 1971 Antal and Ilse married. They have made a number of recordings together.

Doráti first visited Israel in 1960, when he conducted the London Symphony there. Shortly afterward, still in 1960, he conducted the Israel Philharmonic. He returned to Israel every season for ten consecutive years, but since 1970 he has appeared there less frequently.

From 1970 to 1977 Doráti led the National Symphony Orchestra of Washington, D.C., which he conducted in the opening concert at Kennedy Center in 1971. With that orchestra he also conducted the world premiere of Schuman's *The Young Dead Soldiers,* as well as the first performance of Schuman's *Tenth Symphony,* both in 1976.

Doráti's last two regular posts to date were with the Royal Philharmonic Orchestra of London (nonofficially from 1974, officially 1975-78) and the Detroit Symphony Orchestra (1977-81).

Since 1981 he has spent more time on composition, which has occupied him off and on for many years. His works, in a mildly modern but melodious style, include chamber pieces but center on orchestral compositions, such as the *Symphony* (perf. 1960), the *Piano Concerto* (perf. 1975), and the *Cello Concerto* (perf. 1976).

His conducting style is marked by a rigorous sense of rhythm and a remarkable ear for orchestral color. Doráti wrote the autobiographical book *Notes of Seven Decades* (1979, revised 1981).

Bob Dylan

Freewheelin' Musician

(1941-   )

Bob Dylan has been one of the most influential figures in modern American popular music. A singer and songwriter (lyrics and music), he rose to lead the folk movement with his social-protest songs in the early 1960s and then went on to spark the merging of folk, rock, and country music still going on in the 1980s.

He was born in Duluth, Minnesota, on May 24, 1941. His original name was Robert Allen Zimmerman. He taught himself the guitar, the piano, and the harmonica. During high school and a brief stay at the University of Minnesota (1959-60), he performed in coffeehouses. While he was at the university, he began to use the name Bob Dylan, after the poet Dylan Thomas (a change that became legal in 1962).

By early 1961 he was performing in coffeehouses in New York City's Greenwich Village. He was musically influenced by the folksinger Woody Guthrie and his followers, such as Pete Seeger. Dylan himself sang in a speech-song style with a harsh, nasal voice. Times were hard, and he often rode the subways just to have a place to sleep and keep warm. In April 1961 he began to attract attention while performing at Gerde's Folk City. Later that year he recorded his first album, *Bob Dylan,* which was released early in 1962.

Dylan's recording career can be viewed as consisting of four evolutionary stages. The first was his folk period. He began, in the album *Bob Dylan,* by showing that he was an original interpreter of traditional folk material. But then he came out with a succession of original songs that caught the mood of American youth and became anthems for the civil-rights and social-protest movements. *The Freewheelin' Bob Dylan* (1963) is highlighted

Bob Dylan

by "Blowin' in the Wind," which, especially through the recording made by Peter, Paul, and Mary, created a Dylan cult. *The Times They Are A-changin'* (1964) contains many topical and protest songs, including the title song.

At the Newport Folk Festival in the summer of 1965, Dylan performed with an electric guitar and a rock-band accompaniment. Enraged folk purists nearly booed him off the stage. But he went on to spearhead a folk-rock fusion. The album *Bringing It All Back Home* (1965) includes "Mr. Tambourine Man," an abstract ballad.

Highway 61 Revisited (1965) has "Like a Rolling Stone," a condensed expression of the social revolution of the 1960s.

In 1966 Dylan was in a motorcycle accident. During the 1½ years of his recovery, he created *The Basement Tapes*, which, however, he did not release for another decade.

When Dylan reemerged in 1968, he surprised everyone by presenting yet a third stage in his work (following his folk and folk-rock stages). His lyrics became more tranquil and personal, as opposed to the urgent social messages in his earlier songs. In his music, he showed a country-rock fusion. Those elements are evident in the albums *John Wesley Harding* (1968), *Nashville Skyline* (1969), and *Pat Garrett and Billy the Kid* (1973), the last being derived from the music track of a movie in which Dylan had acted.

The fourth stage in Dylan's career has been one of merging all of the earlier elements, as well as some new ones. His work has covered a wide range of subject matter and musical styles. In *Before the Flood* (1974) he reinterprets old material in new ways. *Desire* (1975) presents an overview of the major themes in Dylan's previous work, including social protest (as in "Hurricane") and romance (as in "Sara"). *Street Legal* (1978) incorporates Latin rock, reggae, and soul. During this period Dylan also wrote, starred in, and directed the film *Renaldo and Clara* (1978); the nearly four-hour movie includes about fifty songs in concert footage.

Dylan's inner life, like his musical style, has been subject to evolutionary changes. For most of his career, he had seemed to be indifferent to religious matters, including his own Jewish heritage. But in 1979, in his album *Slow Train Coming,* he revealed that he had been converted to fundamentalist Christianity. The same viewpoint dominates his next two albums: *Saved* (1980) and *Shot of Love* (1981).

Then, in 1982, Dylan renounced his conversion and committed himself to Judaism. He has recently been linked with the conservative Lubavitch movement, a Hasidic sect based in the Brooklyn section of New York City.

Infidels (1983) is widely regarded as his best work in many years. Religion and politics are touched on, but the main theme of *Infidels* is sadness—of broken hearts and dreams, of middle age.

In 1965 Dylan married the former model Sara Lowndes (originally Shirley Noznisky), to whom he was drawn by their mutual interest in Oriental thought. Sara brought with her a daughter, Maria, by a previous marriage. The Dylans had four more children: Jesse, Anna, Seth, and Samuel.

Bob and Sara divorced in 1977, but he has retained a deep interest in the children's activities. In June 1983 he attended the ceremonies for Maria's graduation (as a

history major) from Macalester College in St. Paul, Minnesota. In September 1983 he participated in Jesse's bar mitzvah, held at the Western Wall in Jerusalem.

At Maria's graduation, Dylan was seen in public with his ex-wife, Sara, for the first time since their divorce. Previously, however, Sara had appeared with him in his 1978 film *Renaldo and Clara*. Also in the film was the singer Joan Baez, with whom Dylan had been romantically involved in the early 1960s.

Selected recordings:

Singles

"Like a Rolling Stone" (1965, Columbia)
"Positively Fourth Street" (1965, Columbia)
"Rainy Day Women #12 and 35" (1966, Columbia)
"Lay, Lady, Lay" (1969, Columbia)
"Knockin' on Heaven's Door" (1973, Columbia)
"Gotta Serve Somebody" (1979, Columbia)

Albums

Bob Dylan (1962, Columbia)
The Freewheelin' Bob Dylan (1963, Columbia)
The Times They Are A-changin' (1964, Columbia)
Another Side of Bob Dylan (1965, Columbia)
Bringing It All Back Home (1965, Columbia)
Highway 61 Revisited (1965, Columbia)
Blonde on Blonde (1966, Columbia)
Bob Dylan's Greatest Hits (1967, Columbia)
John Wesley Harding (1968, Columbia)
Nashville Skyline (1969, Columbia)
New Morning (1970, Columbia)
Bob Dylan's Greatest Hits, Vol. 2 (1971, Columbia)
Pat Garrett and Billy the Kid (1973, Columbia)
Planet Waves (1974, Asylum)
Before the Flood (1974, Asylum)
The Basement Tapes (1975, Columbia)
Desire (1975, Columbia)
Hard Rain (1976, Columbia)
Street Legal (1978, Columbia)
Slow Train Coming (1979, Columbia)
Saved (1980, Columbia)
Shot of Love (1981, Columbia)
Infidels (1983, Columbia)
Empire Burlesque (1985, Columbia)
Biograph (1985, Columbia)

Arthur Fiedler

Mr. Pops
(1894-1979)

Arthur Fiedler, one of the most colorful conductors of the twentieth century, won worldwide renown for his special ability to blend classical and popular music on his programs. Born of Austrian immigrants in Boston, Massachusetts, on December 17, 1894, he came from a line of Fiedlers (*Fiedler* is an old form of German meaning "fiddler") who had been musicians for generations, his great-grandfather, grandfather, and father all being violinists, as were his father's two brothers. Arthur, too, learned to play the violin, his first teacher being his father, Emanuel. For a long time, however, Arthur had only a casual interest in music.

In 1910 Emanuel, who was European to the core and never became an American citizen, returned with his family to his native Austria, settling in Vienna. Soon, however, the family moved to the musically livelier city of Berlin, Germany.

When the sixteen-year-old Arthur told his family that he had no interest in obtaining a university education, Emanuel suggested that Arthur try a career in business, whereupon the youth went to work as an office boy for a German women's magazine; but he hated the job and left it after three months. Emanuel took his son aside and said that with college and business rejected, there seemed to be only one thing left: "Would you like to try music?" Arthur, who had continued his violin practice and whose magazine work had introduced him to the exciting musical activity in Berlin, said, "All right. I'll give that a try."

In 1911 he began to study at the Royal Academy of Music in Berlin. He studied violin with Willy Hess (a former concertmaster of the Boston Symphony Orchestra), conducting with Arno Kleffel, and chamber music with the famed composer Ernst von Dohnányi. Soon he began to earn money by playing the violin in cafés and with various orchestras. In the summer of 1913 he played for six weeks in an orchestra conducted by Johann Strauss III. During his third year (1913-14) at the Royal Academy, he was given a chance to conduct a professional orchestra, largely made up of military musicians. From that time on, Fiedler devoted himself to becoming a conductor.

He continued his studies at the Royal Academy into 1915. Then, on May 7, 1915, the British liner *Lusitania* was sunk by a German U-boat, killing 128 Americans on board. It appeared that the United States would now be drawn into World War I against the Germans. Arthur Fiedler returned to America, while the rest of the family remained in Berlin.

In September 1915 he joined the Boston Symphony Orchestra, where his father had long been a member and where one of his uncles was still a violinist. Arthur began in the second-violin section but was moved during the 1916-17 season to the viola section, where he remained for many years.

In 1924 he was asked to become the conductor of the MacDowell Club, an orchestra of students, amateurs, and semiprofessionals. His conducting appetite whetted, Fiedler hired twenty-two of his Boston Symphony Orchestra colleagues to form his own little orchestra, the Boston Sinfonietta. The group, later often called the Arthur Fiedler Sinfonietta, gave its first concert on October 30, 1925. Its program, like all future Arthur Fiedler concerts, was a balance between light music and standard symphonic fare.

In 1929 he established a series of free outdoor summer symphony concerts on the Esplanade, near the banks of the Charles River in Boston. The first concert was held on July 4, 1929. Fiedler conducted members of the Boston Symphony Orchestra, beginning the program with John Philip Sousa's *Stars and Stripes Forever,* a work with which Fiedler eventually became closely identified in the public mind. The first season was a tremendous success, and the concerts have continued every summer to the present. The July 4, 1976, Esplanade concert celebrating America's bicentennial was heard by a live audience of four hundred thousand people, as well as by millions on radio and TV.

In 1930 he was appointed conductor of the Boston Pops Orchestra, the eighteenth musician and the first American to hold that position. The Pops, founded in 1885, was at low ebb. But Fiedler's forceful personality and broad approach (with each program consisting of classical, semiclassical, and popular music) turned the orchestra into one of the most successful in the world. He stayed with the organization for the rest of his life, nearly fifty years, and attained worldwide renown as Mr. Pops.

Fiedler always overworked himself. During the early and middle 1930s, he spent every October through April playing the viola in the Boston Symphony Orchestra and conducting his Sinfonietta. Every spring, he conducted the Boston Pops, followed in the summer by the Esplanade concerts. In addition, he managed to conduct several other groups during the year. As a result, in 1939 he had a heart attack. In succeeding years he had several more heart attacks, but he never really slowed down. Throughout the rest of his long career, he went on many nationwide tours with the Boston Pops and often guest-conducted with orchestras in the United States, Europe, and elsewhere, including Israel.

Handsome, urbane, and charming, Fiedler was long known in Boston as a ladies' man. One of his early romances was with the famous actress Jeanne Eagels, once called "the Yankee Bernhardt," whom Fiedler met in 1919 and saw off and on for several years.

At the age of forty-seven he finally married Ellen Bottomley, who came from a socially elite Boston family. But the marriage had many obstacles to overcome. The first was Ellen's mother (her father had died when she was eleven), who objected to Fiedler because of his many affairs with other women and because of the difference in their ages, Fiedler being nearly twenty years Ellen's senior.

Perhaps the most serious obstacle to their marriage was the conflict between Ellen's Catholicism and Fiedler's Jewish heritage. At the request of Catholic authorities and for the sake of Ellen's beliefs, Fiedler signed a document agreeing to raise his children as Catholics. (He later told a friend that he had signed it because at his age he did not expect to have children anyway.) But when he was asked to renounce Judaism and promise never to practice it, Fiedler, though not a religious man, refused, partly because he did, in fact, firmly regard himself as a Jew and partly because he was fiercely independent and resented being forced to make such a commitment. Later a formal document of consent was granted by the pope's emissary in Washington, D.C., allowing the marriage to take place without Fiedler's having to renounce his faith.

By now, Mrs. Bottomley was willing to allow the marriage. The next problem came from Fiedler's family, who had returned from Europe to live in Boston again. The Fiedlers, though never before particularly strict about their Judaism, refused to attend the Catholic wedding. They compromised by agreeing to go to the reception after the ceremony.

The wedding finally took place in January 1942 at Boston's Cathedral of the Holy Cross. Because Fiedler was Jewish, the cathedral itself was barred to them, and the event was held in the rectory. While Ellen knelt for the various blessings, Fiedler defiantly stood next to her with his arms folded.

Arthur and Ellen formed quite a contrast. She was deeply religious; he was not. She was outgoing and warm; he was suspicious of others. Furthermore, he was an unabashed male chauvinist. Ellen, with her patience and good humor, asserted her independence by playfully disparaging him and his views. She once called him "this dear little devil."

They had three children: Johanna, Deborah, and Peter. Because Johanna was born on Yom Kippur, she was nicknamed Yommie (later Yummie because of the New England way of pronouncing o). Fiedler, whose life revolved around his music, paid little attention to the children when they were small; he especially avoided their religious activities, including Communions and confirmations. (At the same time, he did not affiliate himself with a synagogue.) All of the children learned musical

instruments: Johanna (Yummie) the viola, Deborah the cello, and Peter the piano and organ. But Fiedler seldom heard them, partly because they were afraid to play for such an august maestro.

However, as the children grew older, Fiedler developed closer ties with them. Peter said of his father that "beneath the gruffness, . . . there was a very tender person, with deep tender feelings, not only for his own family, but for all people, all mankind, and I think he transmitted this every day of his life through his music."

Fiedler was a stoic, seemingly unaffected by joy, grief, pleasure, or pain; and he seldom displayed open affection. Yet he was an extremely colorful and generous man. During the Davy Crockett craze of the 1950s, he wore a coonskin cap while conducting. In the 1960s every time he conducted an arrangement of the Beatles song "I Want to Hold Your Hand," he put on a Beatle wig. Never refusing a request if he could possibly help it, he appeared for innumerable causes and with all sorts of groups, even high-school bands. He spent an entire evening at a disco dance hall to raise money for an orphanage and conducted an all-Jewish symphony to raise emergency funds for Israel.

Fiedler was a fire buff. He collected helmets, fire-chief badges, and replicas of fire engines. On his seventy-fifth birthday, he received the gift of a 1937 Ford fire engine from Ellen. Nearly four hundred fire departments throughout the world made him an honorary fire chief.

He was also made an honorary chief of the Otoe Indians in Oklahoma. They called him the Maker of Sweet Music.

Fiedler ultimately died of his chronic heart trouble on July 10, 1979, in Boston.

Leon Fleisher
Outstanding Pianist and Conductor
(1928-   )

Leon Fleisher, pianist and conductor, was born in San Francisco, California, on July 23, 1928. His father, a native of Russia, was a fashion designer. His mother, a native of Poland, had been a teacher of singing before her marriage. She was extremely ambitious for her children; and as soon as four-year-old Leon sat down at the piano, she became determined to make him one of the world's greatest pianists.

For the next five years he took lessons from local teachers. By the time he was seven he had already shown signs of being a genuine child prodigy; and his parents, as Fleisher himself later admitted, decided to exploit him. In 1935 he made his first public appearance, a recital in San Francisco. Two years later he performed as soloist with the San Francisco Federal Symphony Orchestra.

The great pianist Artur Schnabel heard the nine-year-old Fleisher play and was so impressed that he ignored his own rule against teaching child prodigies and took the boy as a pupil. Fleisher studied with Schnabel for ten years, first in Tremezzo (on the shores of Lake Como in Italy) and then, after the outbreak of World War II, in New York City.

During his years with Schnabel, Fleisher began to receive offers to perform with major orchestras. In 1942 he played the Liszt *Second Piano Concerto* with the San Francisco Symphony Orchestra under Pierre Monteux, and the following year the Brahms *First Piano Concerto* with the same accompaniment. Monteux called the fifteen-year-old Fleisher "the pianistic find of the century." In 1944 Fleisher performed the Brahms work again, with the New York Philharmonic under Monteux.

When Fleisher ended his studies with Schnabel in 1948, the young pianist decided to take two years off to, as he put it, "bum around." Being a child prodigy had been "a painful experience" because he was deprived of normal boyhood activities. Now he simply felt that he had to get away from it all for a while.

By 1950, however, he had resumed his intensive practicing. In 1952 he won the Queen Elisabeth International Piano Competition in Brussels, Belgium, the first American to win a major European competition. That victory marked the beginning of his international career, and he soon set out on a series of concert appearances throughout Europe. Over the next few years he became one of the most traveled pianists in the world, regularly giving concerts in Europe, the United States, Canada, and Latin America. In 1958 he was among the American artists asked to represent the United States at the Brussels World's Fair. His pianistic career continued to flourish into the mid-1960s.

Fleisher combined intellectual power and warmth of feeling in his playing. He concentrated on the standard classical and romantic repertory. But he also performed contemporary works, notably in 1963 when, with the composer conducting the Seattle Symphony, Fleisher played the solo part in Leon Kirchner's *Second Piano Concerto,* a work that Fleisher had commissioned with a grant from the Ford Foundation.

However, in 1964 he began to experience a tingling sensation, followed by a cramping of the fingers, in his right hand. Audiences and critics, unaware of his problem, were baffled by the flaws suddenly appearing in his performances. By 1965 the hand was completely unable to play; and within a few years Fleisher, a right-hander, could barely use it to sign his name. Doctors could not

determine the cause of, or find an immediate cure for, the painful muscular problem, which some medical experts have come to label carpal-tunnel syndrome.

After an initial period of despair, Fleisher courageously went to work learning piano compositions for left hand alone. That repertory consists largely of pieces written for Paul Wittgenstein (a pianist who lost his right arm in World War I) by such composers as Ravel, Prokofiev, and Britten. Fleisher soon proved that he could concertize as musically with one hand as with two.

But he was not satisfied with the limited range offered by the left-hand piano literature, and his thoughts turned to conducting. He recalled that at the age of eleven he had once asked Monteux to be allowed to conduct an orchestra. But the wise and witty older man replied: "Once you get the stick in your hand, you'll never want to let it go." Fleisher was now ready to take that chance.

In 1967 he cofounded the Theater Chamber Players in Washington, D.C., whose programs he began to conduct. In 1970 he led the New York Chamber Orchestra's Mostly Mozart Festival at Philharmonic Hall in Lincoln Center. Also in 1970 he became music director of the Annapolis Symphony, a post that he held for many years

but finally relinquished because of other commitments. He served as associate conductor of the Baltimore Symphony (1973-78) and has guest-conducted many other major American orchestras.

Through the years, Fleisher has faithfully carried out his doctors' instructions, undergoing three kinds of therapy for his hand: electrical techniques, biofeedback, and muscle strengthening. Finally, in September 1982, he returned to the two-handed piano repertory by playing, before a nationwide TV audience, a concert with the Baltimore Symphony under Sergiu Comissiona. Soon, however, it was discovered that he needed more therapy, and he went back to playing left-hand pieces.

Another sphere of interest for Fleisher is teaching. Since 1959 he has been on the faculty of the Peabody Institute in Baltimore. His pupils have included André Watts and Lorin Hollander.

Fleisher married Dorothy Druzinsky in 1951 and with her had three children: Deborah, Richard, and Leah. They were divorced in 1962, and later that year he married Risselle Rosenthal, a former dancer. His second marriage produced two children: Paula and Julian.

Lukas Foss

Experimentalist

(1922-   )

Lukas Foss, composer and conductor, was born in Berlin, Germany, on August 15, 1922. His surname at birth was Fuchs, but the entire family later changed it to Foss. Fortunate enough to have cultivated parents (his father being a professor of philosophy and his mother a painter), he was exposed to classical music at an early age. He received an accordion when he was hardly more than a toddler, and at seven he began serious piano and theory lessons in Berlin with Julius Goldstein (also known as Julius Herford).

After the rise of Nazism in Germany in the early 1930s, the family moved to Paris, where young Foss studied piano with Lazare Lévy, composition with Noël Gallon, orchestration with Felix Wolfes, and flute and chamber music with Marcel Moyse. In Paris, Foss developed his first interest in modern music, particularly that of Paul Hindemith.

In 1932 the family moved from Paris to the United States, where Foss became a naturalized citizen in 1942. He enrolled at the Curtis Institute of Music in Philadelphia and there studied piano with Isabella Vengerova, composition with Rosario Scalero, and conducting with Fritz Reiner. Foss graduated from Curtis in 1940, took composition lessons as a special student under Hindemith at Yale University (1940-41), and during the same period studied conducting under Serge Koussevitzky at the summer sessions of the Berkshire Music Center at Tanglewood, near Lenox, Massachusetts.

In 1945 Foss became the youngest composer ever to win a Guggenheim Fellowship. However, his early reputation was made primarily as a dazzling pianist, becoming, for example, pianist for the Boston Symphony Orchestra in 1944. In 1950 he resigned that post to spend two years composing in Rome. Returning from Italy, Foss made a number of appearances as pianist and conductor.

In 1953 he was appointed professor of composition at the University of California in Los Angeles (UCLA), where he remained till 1962. During his years at UCLA, Foss brought to a culmination the first of the two main periods in his development as a composer. His early work can be described as generally neoclassical, with special leanings toward Hindemith and Stravinsky. Yet his basically romantic nature prompted him to express his neoclassicism in a more lyric, grandiloquent manner than his models did. Notable among his works from that period are the *Symphony in G* (1945); the *First String Quartet* (1947); various choral works, including the biblical *Song of Songs* (1947) and *Psalms* (1956) and the nonbiblical *Parable of Death* (1952); the *Second Piano Concerto* (1951), with which he first established his international reputation by performing the work himself in Venice, Italy; and the orchestral *Symphony of Chorales* (1958), based on the music of Bach.

In an understandable effort to take root in his adopted land, Foss wrote some compositions having an element of American popularism, much in the manner of Aaron Copland. *The Prairie* (1944), for example, is a choral work based on a Carl Sandburg poem, while *The Jumping Frog of Calaveras County* (1950) is an opera based on Mark Twain's celebrated tale.

In 1956 Foss began to experiment with ensemble improvisation, primarily for the benefit of his UCLA students. The following year he founded the Improvisation Chamber Ensemble at UCLA and outlined what he called "system and chance music," a type of controlled improvisation. At that time Foss's own music entered a transitional phase (1957-62) during which he began to apply those new principles, as in the *Concerto* for five improvising instruments (1960).

After leaving UCLA in 1962, Foss became totally committed to the cause of new, especially experimental, music—both his own and that of others. He abandoned tonality and fixed forms in favor of serialism, aleatoricism, and graphic notation. For example, *Elytres* ("Elytra") for a small ensemble (1964) has a score containing on every page certain basic materials from which the players select different extracts for each performance. In the *Concert for Cello and Orchestra* (1966) the soloist plays in competition with a prerecorded tape of cello music. Unusual sonorities are sometimes employed, as in the *Baroque Variations* for orchestra (1967), where a percussionist uses a hammer to smash a bottle in a bag. *M.A.P.* ("Men at Play," 1970) is a multimedia piece involving five instrumentalists, electronic tapes, and quasi-dramatic visual elements supplied by the musicians. Foss's *Solo Observed* for a small ensemble (1982) is an example of musical minimalism.

Meanwhile, Foss also established a career as a conductor. In 1963 he was appointed conductor and music director of the Buffalo Philharmonic Orchestra. In his first year at Buffalo he founded the Center for Creative and Performing Arts, which he has continued to direct ever since. Foss proved to be an excellent conductor of Bach and Mozart, but he also programmed numerous works by such modernists as John Cage and Karlheinz Stockhausen. Many concertgoers were annoyed by the new works, and Foss finally resigned from the Buffalo Philharmonic in 1970.

After serving on the faculty of Harvard for a year (1970-71), Foss took over as conductor and music director of the Brooklyn Philharmonia (now the Brooklyn Philharmonic Symphony Orchestra) in 1971, a post that he still holds. He also led the Jerusalem Symphony Orchestra from 1972 to 1976, and since 1981 he has been conductor and music director of the Milwaukee Symphony Orchestra. In addition, he has guest-conducted many orchestras in the United States and Europe. Everywhere he goes, he champions the cause of new music.

Foss married Cornelia Brendel, a sculptor and painter, in the early 1950s. They had two children: Christopher and Eliza.

Selected works:

Stage

Gift of the Magi (ballet, 1945)
The Jumping Frog of Calaveras County (opera; libretto, J. Karsavina, after M. Twain; 1950)

Orchestral

Symphony in G (1945)
Second Piano Concerto (1951, revised 1953)
Symphony of Chorales (1958)
Concert for Cello and Orchestra (1966)
Baroque Variations (1967)
Geod (abbreviation of *Geodesic,* 1969)
Orpheus (1974)
Percussion Concerto (1975)
Exeunt (1982)

Vocal

The Prairie (vocal soloists, chorus, orchestra; text, C. Sandburg; 1944)
Song of Songs (soprano, orchestra; text, Bible; 1947)
Adon olam ("Lord of the Universe"; cantor, chorus, organ; text, Hebrew hymn; 1947)
Song of Anguish (baritone, orchestra; text, after Bible; 1950)
Parable of Death (speaker, tenor, vocal soloists, orchestra; text, R. M. Rilke; 1952)
Psalms (chorus, orchestra [or two pianos]; text, Bible; 1956)
Time Cycle (soprano, orchestra; texts, several authors; 1960)
American Cantata (soprano, tenor, two speakers, chorus, orchestra; text, A. Sachs, L. Foss, others; 1976, revised 1977)

Chamber

First String Quartet (1947)
Concerto (five improvising instruments, 1960)
Elytres (flute, two violins, ensemble; 1964)
Paradigm (ensemble, 1968)
Waves (ensemble, 1969)
M.A.P. (five instrumentalists, tapes; 1970)
The Cave of the Winds (wind quintet, 1972)
Quartet Plus (narrator, double string quartet; 1977)
Solo Observed (piano, cello, organ, percussion; 1982)

Piano

Four Two-voiced Inventions (1938)
Grotesque Dance (1938)
Passacaglia (1940)

Art Garfunkel
See Paul Simon and Art Garfunkel

George Gershwin
Symphonic Composer from
Tin Pan Alley
(1898-1937)

George Gershwin, one of the most naturally gifted of all American composers, was an enormously successful commercial-song writer who eventually became best known for his use of popular and jazz elements in serious symphonic works. He was born of Russian immigrants in the borough of Brooklyn, New York City, New York, on September 26, 1898. His birth certificate lists him as "Jacob Gershwine." His father's original name was Moishe Gershovitz, but he adopted the Americanized spelling Morris Gershvin. The "Gershwine" on the birth certificate is a misspelling. The "Jacob" however, was Gershwin's legal given name, though the family always called him George. He changed the spelling of his surname from Gershvin to Gershwin when he became a professional musician, the other members of his immediate family quickly following suit.

Gershwin grew up in a poor Jewish section of the borough of Manhattan's Lower East Side. As a child, he excelled at street sports. But he had little exposure to music till 1910, when his family bought a used upright piano for George's older brother, Ira (later to gain fame as a lyricist, while the youngest of the family's three brothers, Arthur, followed George as a popular-song composer). Soon, however, Ira gave up the piano, and George quickly learned the instrument. In 1912, unsatisfied with the lessons he had received from neighborhood teachers, Gershwin began to study with the well-known Charles Hambitzer, who improved Gershwin's piano technique and stimulated his interest in the music of the masters, especially Chopin, Liszt, and Debussy. Gershwin, however, always preferred popular music and jazz. He later briefly studied theory, harmony, counterpoint, and orchestration with a number of teachers, notably Edward Kilenyi, Rubin Goldmark, Henry Cowell, Wallingford Riegger, and Joseph Schillinger. But he never attained more than a rudimentary knowledge of such subjects, and even his music-reading ability was limited.

During his summer vacation from school in 1913, Gershwin was hired as a pianist, playing popular pieces, at a summer resort in the Catskill Mountains. In May 1914 he left high school for good to become a pianist and songplugger at Remick's, a New York City music publisher; only fifteen years old, he was one of the youngest pianists in Tin Pan Alley, the center for popular music in the nation.

In his spare time from Remick's, Gershwin frequented the National Theater on Second Avenue to learn as much as he could about the Yiddish musical theater. His interest was not ethnic (the Gershwins were little involved with Jewish customs) but practical: composing for the Yiddish theater offered financial security. However, Gershwin's career soon moved ahead in Tin Pan Alley and on Broadway, and he never composed anything explicitly for the Yiddish theater. (In 1929 he signed a contract to compose a Jewish opera, *The Dybbuk*, for the Metropolitan Opera; but the plan fell through when the rights to the play were lost.)

In 1916 Gershwin played one of his songs, "When You Want 'Em, You Can't Get 'Em; When You've Got 'Em, You Don't Want 'Em," for the renowned entertainer Sophie Tucker. She liked it and recommended it to the publisher Harry Von Tilzer. Thus, in March 1916, at the age of seventeen, Gershwin had his first published song. During the next few years, he worked as an accompanist for solo vocalists and as a rehearsal pianist on Broadway. Meanwhile, he continued to compose, occasionally contributing individual songs to other composers' Broadway shows. Besides making important contacts with publishers and performers, he met such composers as Victor Herbert, Irving Berlin, and Jerome Kern (Gershwin's idol).

The big breakthrough in Gershwin's career came in 1919 when he composed the complete score for the Broadway musical comedy *La, La, Lucille*. In the same year, he also wrote his first hit song: "Swanee." The song made little impact till Gershwin happened to play the tune for Al Jolson at a party. Jolson loved the song and made it famous through his stage performances (interpolating it into his show *Sinbad)* and through his classic 1920 recording for Columbia Records. With his fame rising, Gershwin went on to score a number of Broadway shows in the early 1920s, including the 1920 through 1924 annual editions of *George White's Scandals*.

An important advance in Gershwin's career came in early 1924. The bandleader Paul Whiteman had asked Gershwin to write an extended composition for a concert whose purpose was to display jazz as a serious art form. Gershwin responded with what has become his best-known work: the *Rhapsody in Blue*. He composed the piece for jazz band and piano, the jazz-band music being laid out as a piano score. At the now famous Aeolian Hall concert of February 12, 1924, Gershwin played the piano solo while Whiteman conducted an orchestral accompaniment prepared by Ferde Grofé (Whiteman's arranger) from Gershwin's jazz-band piano score. However, neither Gershwin nor Grofé initiated the now familiar opening clarinet wail (in which the instrument slowly ascends by sliding through the pitches

George Gershwin (left) and Ira Gershwin (right)

instead of playing each tone distinctly—an effect that is usually referred to as a glissando but that, strictly speaking, is actually a portamento). Gershwin had written an ordinary seventeen-note scalar run in his piano score, and Grofé (perhaps at Gershwin's suggestion) had given the line to the clarinet. But at one of the rehearsals, Ross Gorman, Whiteman's virtuoso clarinetist, played the wail as a joke. Gershwin, however, liked the sound and asked Gorman to perform it that way at the concert. The wail became part of the published score. Gershwin claimed to have orchestrated all of his own later symphonic works, but he may have had assistance, especially from his teacher-friend Joseph Schillinger.

Gershwin went on to create a number of other pieces in which he attempted to merge the classical tradition with elements from jazz, Tin Pan Alley, and Broadway. Among such compositions are the *Concerto in F* for piano and orchestra (1925), the *Preludes for Piano* (1926), and the orchestral tone poem *An American in Paris* (1928).

Meanwhile, throughout the 1920s and 1930s, Gershwin composed the scores for a series of successful stage shows and musical films. From 1924 on, nearly all of his vocal music was composed to lyrics by his brother Ira. They wrote "Fascinating Rhythm" for the musical comedy *Lady, Be Good!* (perf. 1924) and "'S Wonderful" for *Funny Face* (perf. 1927). *Girl Crazy* (perf. 1930) introduced Ethel Merman to the Broadway stage; her rendition of "I Got Rhythm" in the show made the song famous and made her an overnight star. The well-known "Embraceable You" was written by the Gershwins for the same show.

Gershwin made his first trip to the Hollywood section of Los Angeles, California, in 1930 and soon began to compose for movies. Among his song scores are those for the films *Shall We Dance* (1937), *A Damsel in Distress* (1937), and *The Goldwyn Follies* (1938).

His most ambitious, and perhaps his best, work is the black opera *Porgy and Bess* (perf. 1935). For the libretto, DuBose Heyward adapted his own play about the crippled beggar Porgy and the poor blacks of Charleston, South Carolina. To soak up the proper atmosphere, Gershwin lived on a small island near Charleston during the summer of 1934 while composing the first part of the opera. He observed the lifestyle, vocal music, and speech of the local blacks. Among the songs in *Porgy and Bess* are "It Ain't Necessarily So" and "Summertime."

Gershwin often played his own works in public, but he avoided the classics because he felt that his training was inadequate. He was particularly brilliant at improvising variations on his own tunes.

Gershwin wrote his songs quickly and easily, improvising at the piano. His longer, more serious works were composed in basically the same style as the songs, with the addition in the concert pieces of some gestures borrowed from nineteenth-century romanticism, especially the music of Liszt.

Not generally recognized is the fact that Gershwin's music has a number of characteristics that resemble Jewish prayer chants and secular tunes. One such trait is the recurring prominence of the melodic interval of a minor third, as in the second of the three *Preludes for Piano*, "Funny Face" from *Funny Face*, "Wintergreen for President" from *Of Thee I Sing* (perf. 1931), and "It Ain't Necessarily So" from *Porgy and Bess*. His song "'S Wonderful" from *Funny Face* opens with minor-third motives that appear to be a direct borrowing from the song "Noach's teive" ("Noah's Ark"), a number from the Yiddish operetta *Akeidas Izchok* ("The Sacrifice of Isaac") by Abraham Goldfaden.

Some of Gershwin's melodies also exhibit the expressive speechlike traits of synagogal chant, as in the repeated tones (corresponding to the chanting tones of Jewish cantillation) in "My One and Only" from *Funny Face*. "In the Mandarin's Orchid Garden" (1929), Gershwin's only art song, displays similar characteristics.

Another resemblance with traditional Jewish music is in Gershwin's melodies that echo the frailachs, lively Jewish folkdance tunes. The reiterated, stepwise mannerisms of such tunes can be found, for example, in Gershwin's "Seventeen and Twenty-one" from *Strike Up the Band* (1927 version).

Gershwin himself, however, never discussed the Jewish elements in his music, and their use may have been entirely unconscious. At any rate, his true musical base was the American secular scene—Tin Pan Alley, Broadway, and jazz.

His lifestyle also reflected secular American values. Never married, Gershwin associated with high-income, elite circles; and he was often romantically linked with film stars, such as Simone Simon and Paulette Goddard. In 1926 he started his collection of contemporary art; in 1927 he began to paint as a hobby, eventually spending nearly half his time with it. He worked hard; he played hard.

In June 1937 Gershwin began to experience headaches and dizzy spells. He grew weaker, and on July 9 he fell into a deep coma. By July 10, it was realized that he had a brain tumor. An operation was performed the next day, but he never regained consciousness. He died in Los Angeles, California, on July 11, 1937, at the age of thirty-eight.

Selected works:

Stage

La, La, Lucille (lyrics, A. Jackson, B. G. De Sylva; perf. 1919)
George White's Scandals of 1920 (lyrics, A. Jackson; perf. 1920)
George White's Scandals of 1921 (lyrics, A. Jackson; perf. 1921)
George White's Scandals of 1922 (lyrics, B. G. De Sylva, E. R. Goetz; perf. 1922), including:
  "I'll Build a Stairway to Paradise" (lyrics, B. G. De Sylva, A. Francis [pseudonym of I. Gershwin])
George White's Scandals of 1923 (lyrics, B. G. De Sylva, E. R. Goetz, B. MacDonald; perf. 1923)
George White's Scandals of 1924 (lyrics, B. G. De Sylva; perf. 1924), including:
  "Somebody Loves Me" (B. G. De Sylva, B. MacDonald)
Lady, Be Good! (lyrics, I. Gershwin; perf. 1924), including:
  "Fascinating Rhythm"
  "Oh, Lady, Be Good!"
Tip-Toes (lyrics, I. Gershwin; perf. 1925), including:
  "That Certain Feeling"
Oh, Kay! (lyrics, I. Gershwin; perf. 1926), including:
  "Clap Yo' Hands"
  "Do, Do, Do"
  "Someone to Watch Over Me"
Funny Face (lyrics, I. Gershwin; perf. 1927), including:
  "Funny Face"
  "He Loves and She Loves"
  "My One and Only"
  "'S Wonderful"
Rosalie (lyrics, I. Gershwin, P. G. Wodehouse; supplementary music, S. Romberg; perf. 1928), including:
  "How Long Has This Been Going On?" (lyrics, I. Gershwin; previously dropped from the Gershwins' stage show *Funny Face*, perf. 1927)
Show Girl (lyrics, I. Gershwin, G. Kahn; perf. 1929), including:
  "Liza"
Strike Up the Band (lyrics, I. Gershwin; perf. 1930, revised version of the 1927 stage show of the same name), including:
  "I've Got a Crush on You" (previously used in the Gershwins' stage show *Treasure Girl*, perf. 1928)
  "Strike Up the Band" (from the 1927 show, revised in 1936 to "Strike Up the Band for U.C.L.A.")
Girl Crazy (lyrics, I. Gershwin; perf. 1930), including:
  "Bidin' My Time"
  "But Not for Me"
  "Embraceable You"
  "I Got Rhythm"
Of Thee I Sing (lyrics, I. Gershwin; perf. 1931), including:
  "Of Thee I Sing"
  "Who Cares?"
  "Wintergreen for President"

Porgy and Bess (lyrics, I. Gershwin, D. Heyward; perf. 1935), including:
  "Bess, You Is My Woman"
  "I Got Plenty o' Nuttin'"
  "It Ain't Necessarily So"
  "Summertime"
  "A Woman Is a Sometime Thing"

Films
(song scores)

Delicious (lyrics, I. Gershwin; 1931)
Shall We Dance (lyrics, I. Gershwin; 1937), including:
  "Let's Call the Whole Thing Off"
  "Shall We Dance"
  "They Can't Take That Away from Me"
A Damsel in Distress (lyrics, I. Gershwin; 1937), including:
  "A Foggy Day"
  "Nice Work If You Can Get It"
The Goldwyn Follies (lyrics, I. Gershwin; 1938), including:
  "Love Is Here to Stay"
  "Love Walked In"

Songs
(other than those for the above shows and films)

"When You Want 'Em, You Can't Get 'Em; When You Got 'Em, You Don't Want 'Em" (lyrics, M. Roth; pub. 1916)
"Swanee" (lyrics, I. Caesar; for the stage show *Capitol Revue,* perf. 1919)
"The Man I Love" (lyrics, I. Gershwin; dropped from the Gershwins' stage show *Lady, Be Good!,* perf. 1924)
"Seventeen and Twenty-one" (lyrics, I. Gershwin; for the Gershwins' stage show *Strike Up the Band,* perf. 1927)
"In the Mandarin's Orchid Garden" (lyrics, I. Gershwin; dropped from the Gershwins' stage show *Show Girl,* perf. 1929)

Instrumental

Rhapsody in Blue (jazz band, piano; 1924)
Concerto in F (piano, orchestra; 1925)
Preludes for Piano (1926)
An American in Paris (orchestra, 1928)
Second Rhapsody (orchestra, piano; 1931)
Cuban Overture (orchestra, 1932)

Philip Glass
Unique, Influential Composer
(1937-   )

Philip Glass, composer, was born in Baltimore, Maryland, on January 31, 1937. At the age of eight he began to study flute at the Peabody Conservatory. Several years later he took up the piccolo as well and played both instruments in local orchestras.

In 1952, at the age of only fifteen, Glass enrolled at the University of Chicago, where he studied mathematics and philosophy. During his years in Chicago, he began to compose atonal pieces patterned after the works of Schoenberg, Berg, and Webern.

Soon after graduating from the University of Chicago (B.A., 1956), Glass entered the Juilliard School of Music in New York City, where he studied with the composers Vincent Persichetti and William Bergsma. Glass's own works at that time turned toward a Coplandesque American idiom.

He graduated from Juilliard (M.S., 1962) and then spent two years (1962-64) in Pittsburgh under a Ford Foundation grant, composing works for high-school bands as part of a training program for promising young composers.

In 1964 Glass went to Paris to study harmony and counterpoint with the renowned Nadia Boulanger. But while he was there, his growing dissatisfaction with his own music reached a culminating point. "I found twelve-tone music ugly and didactic," he later admitted, "and I didn't care for French or German or any other kind of 'school.' " Glass wanted to write music that had "a sense of community," that is, music that captured the spirit of the times for a general audience—a quality that seemed to him to be lacking in the main currents of modern Western art music. Yet he did not want to shift completely over to commercial popular music.

Finally, in the winter of 1965-66 in Paris, a new direction was revealed to him when he met the famed Indian sitarist Ravi Shankar, whose music Glass was notating for a film soundtrack. Glass soon began to study Indian and other Eastern music.

In that pursuit, he hitchhiked to Spain and then down to North Africa. There he composed music for an American troupe of traveling actors and actresses, one of whom, JoAnne Akalaitis, he married. Glass, with his wife, traveled across North Africa, through the Middle East, and into Asia, studying indigenous music all along the way.

In 1967 Glass returned to the United States and settled in New York City. Scrapping his entire earlier output, he rejected the Western modernist techniques of atonality, serialism, and aleatoricism. Instead, he began to construct works that combined Eastern and selected traditional and moderately modern Western elements.

In 1968 he founded the Philip Glass Ensemble, consisting of players on a variety of electronic devices and electrically amplified keyboards and wind instruments. He soon became a leader in the musical wing of the artistic movement known as minimalism, in which the aim is to achieve maximum effects with minimum means.

However, the late 1960s and early 1970s were rough for him financially. He lived partly on foundation money and grants from private individuals, but he also had to work as a furniture mover, cabdriver, and plumber.

Eventually his audience grew, and his ensemble has successfully toured the United States and Europe many times. In 1972 he established his own record company: Chatham Square Productions. His Town Hall debut came in 1974 and his initial Carnegie Hall appearance in 1978.

The ensemble performs Glass's own music, which is generally characterized by harmonic stasis, melodic repetition, complex Eastern-based rhythms, and (like Indian music) extraordinary, mystic-consciousness-inducing length. His highly original sonorities have profoundly influenced the sounds of many different kinds of music, both serious and popular.

His early instrumental pieces range from those for one performer, such as *Two Pages* (1969), to those for a fairly large ensemble, such as *Another Look at Harmony* (1974). His mature style is well displayed in his hypnotic background score for the documentary film *Koyaanisqatsi* ("Life out of Balance," 1982) and in his multimedia piece *The Photographer: Far from the Truth* (1983).

In recent years Glass has produced a series of important operas, principally *Einstein on the Beach* (perf. 1976), *Satyagraha* ("Truth and Firmness," perf. 1980), and *Akhnaten* (perf. 1984). The first considers the effects of science on humankind. The second, based on the early life of Mahatma Gandhi, meditates on nonviolence. And the third explores the birth of monotheism.

Glass's first marriage ended in divorce, and in 1980 he wedded Luba Burtyk, an internist. That marriage, too, did not last. He has two children: Juliet and Zachary, both from his first marriage.

Though his abandonment of many fundamental aspects of both traditional and modernist Western music has created a heated controversy in the music community, Glass himself is shy, gentle, and reticent. His works speak for him.

Selected works:

Operas

Einstein on the Beach (libretto, P. Glass, R. Wilson; perf. 1976)
Satyagraha (libretto, C. de Jong, after the *Bhagavad-Gita* ["Song of the Blessed One"]; perf. 1980)
Akhnaten (libretto, P. Glass; perf. 1984)
The CIVIL WarS (libretto, R. Wilson; perf. 1984)

Others

One Plus One (solo performer on amplified tabletop, 1968)
Two Pages (one part, 1969)
Music in Fifths (two parts, 1969)
Music in Similar Motion (four parts, 1969)
Music with Changing Parts (six parts, 1970)
Music in Twelve Parts (1974)
Another Look at Harmony (ensemble, 1974)
Koyaanisqatsi (film, background score; 1982)
The Photographer: Far from the Truth (multimedia, 1983)

Benny Goodman
King of Swing
(1909-1986)

Benny (originally Benjamin) Goodman, jazz clarinetist and bandleader, was born of eastern European immigrants in Chicago, Illinois, on May 30, 1909. At the age of ten he began his musical training when he joined a special program at the Kehelah Jacob Synagogue. The officials at the synagogue put Benny on the clarinet, a light instrument, because he was the smallest of the three Goodman brothers who joined the program (the other two being given a tuba and a trumpet respectively). The following year he joined the band at Hull House, the Chicago settlement house founded by Jane Addams, where he took some lessons from the director of the band, James Sylvester. More important were two years of private lessons that he received (beginning when he was twelve and ending when he was fourteen) from Franz Schoepp, clarinetist for the Chicago Symphony Orchestra.

At the tender age of twelve Goodman made his professional debut by imitating the popular clarinetist-entertainer Ted Lewis at Central Park Theater in Chicago. After that, he played in various local dance bands, and at fourteen he left school to become a clarinetist on Lake Michigan excursion boats. During the next few years he performed with numerous jazz artists, notably the great cornetist Bix Beiderbecke.

In 1925 Goodman journeyed to Los Angeles and joined Ben Pollack's band as a soloist. Pollack had heard Goodman's Ted Lewis imitation several years before and now sent for the seasoned sixteen-year-old. While with Pollack, Goodman made his first solo recording, "He's the Last Word" (1926), which he cut under the influence of New Orleans clarinetists, especially Jimmy Noone. In 1928 the Pollack band went to New York City, where Goodman left Pollack the following year.

During the period 1929-34, Goodman worked as a leading freelance musician in New York City, building a reputation in theater orchestras, on radio, and through recordings. In 1933 he met John Hammond, a jazz critic and promoter, who helped Goodman assemble jazzmen, especially blacks, for recording dates. (Goodman later became the first major white bandleader to put blacks on his bandstand during live public performances.)

In 1934 Goodman formed his first permanent band and hired Deane Kincaide and Benny Carter, among others, to make arrangements for him. Carter's "Take My Word" (1934), with its masses of sound moving with the dexterity of an improvised solo, set the standard for a new era in jazz arrangements. Later in 1934 Goodman hired the black bandleader Fletcher Henderson to write new arrangements of traditional jazz numbers (such as

"King Porter Stomp"), as well as popular songs (such as "Sometimes I'm Happy"). To those arrangements, Goodman contributed a firm, no-nonsense approach to rehearsals; and under his direction the band became a model of ensemble discipline.

After a slow start, Goodman's band began to build an audience for itself and for a new, sophisticated kind of jazz. The band's performance in August 1935 at the Palomar Ballroom in Los Angeles is often cited as the beginning of the swing era, which was characterized by a move away from the unlimited individual expression of

early jazz and toward a technical brilliance in well-organized ensemble playing unheard of before. Solo improvisations, however, were still interpolated into the performances; and the band's popularity was enhanced by solo work from such outstanding jazz artists as the trumpeter Bunny Berigan, the drummer Gene Krupa, the pianist Jess Stacy, the vocalist Helen Ward, and, of course, Goodman himself—soon known as the King of Swing—on the clarinet. Later Goodman would use the talents of the trumpeters Ziggy Elman and Harry James; the pianists Fletcher Henderson and Mel Powell; the vocalists Dick Haymes, Peggy Lee, and Patti Page; and a vast array of others.

In the midst of his big-band innovations, Goodman decided to apply swing concepts to small ensembles as well. In 1935 he cut some records with the drummer Gene Krupa and the black pianist Teddy Wilson. The following spring the Benny Goodman Trio, consisting of those same three players, began to make widespread personal appearances. It was the first time that a black played jazz side by side in public with whites on an important national scale. Later that year the vibraphonist Lionel Hampton made the group a quartet, and in 1939 they became a sextet with the addition of the guitarist Charlie Christian and the string-bass player Arthur Bernstein. Thereafter Goodman's combos, from trios to septets (with many personnel changes) were an important part of his career and of the jazz scene in general.

The Goodman swing band reached its peak of popularity during the period 1936-39. In 1938 he took jazz to Carnegie Hall in New York City in a now famous concert that was recorded and that featured solos by his great sidemen Ziggy Elman, Lionel Hampton, Harry James, Gene Krupa, and others. Later he also took swing into other bastions of classical music, such as Symphony Hall in Boston and the Hollywood Bowl in Los Angeles, California.

During the 1940s Goodman broke up and re-formed his band several times. After World War II the big bands began to die out, and he established his last permanent band (his later bands being formed only for specific engagements) in 1948 with new personnel to play Chico O'Farrell's arrangements in the prevailing bop style. The following year he disbanded the group.

Besides giving concerts and making recordings, Goodman was active in the period up to 1950 in other outlets that increased his fame, namely, radio and movies. He was responsible for starting the popular *Let's Dance* radio program in 1934; and he regularly performed on other radio shows, such as *The Camel Caravan* (general name for a series of several different recurring variety shows, including *Benny Goodman's Swing School*, 1937-40), *Old Gold* (1941), and *The Victor Borge-Benny Goodman Show* (1946-47). Among the movies he appeared in were *The Big Broadcast of 1937* (1936), *Hollywood Hotel* (1937), *The Gang's All Here* (1943), and *A Song Is Born* (1948).

Goodman rose into a class of his own when, at the height of his popularity in jazz, he stepped into the world of art music and became the first great jazz musician to achieve success in the classical field. He recorded the Mozart *Clarinet Quintet* with the Budapest String Quartet in 1938, and in November of that year he appeared with the same group at Town Hall in New York City in his first public recital of classical music. Eventually he would appear as soloist with all of the leading American symphony orchestras and would perform and record works by Leonard Bernstein, Brahms, Debussy, Milhaud, Poulenc, Prokofiev, Stravinsky, Weber, and others. In 1949 Goodman, clearly showing the depth of his commitment to art music, began to study with the classical clarinetist Reginald Kell, from whom the jazzman learned new fingering techniques and a new embouchure.

Goodman was responsible for the births of three important classical works. In 1938 he commissioned Béla Bartók's *Contrasts* for clarinet, piano, and violin, which was given its world premiere by Goodman (with Bartók at the piano and Joseph Szigeti at the violin) in 1939. Later he commissioned clarinet concertos from Aaron Copland and Paul Hindemith, both of which Goodman premiered in 1950.

From 1950 to 1955 Goodman continued to record, but his live appearances were reduced to occasional performances. Then a sudden resurgence of interest in him resulted from the biopic *The Benny Goodman Story* (1956), in which Goodman was portrayed by Steve Allen and for which Goodman recorded the clarinet part on the music track. He began to form a variety of ensembles for numerous special purposes, including a Far East tour in 1956-57, the TV show *Swing into Spring* in 1958 and 1959, and a tour of the Soviet Union in 1962 (with the first jazz band allowed into that country). In recent years he has established a pattern of performing jazz in the first half of each concert and classical music in the second half.

During the period of Goodman's greatest impact, the 1930s and 1940s, he was an important figure in several ways. As a jazz clarinetist, he had no peer in technique and style; his flawless solo improvisations set the standards of excellence for his instrument. As a bandleader, he established the unprecedented policy of converting jazz numbers and popular songs into a brilliant kind of ensemble playing, thus ushering in the new era of swing; he also founded and directed the most important musical groups of the period. As an enlightened man, he contributed to social progress by becoming the first major white bandleader to integrate his ensemble with blacks for public performances. He was also the first white bandleader to successfully adopt a genuine jazz style (as distinct from the simplified versions of jazz in earlier white groups). Goodman's efforts broadened the audience for, and brought a new level of recognition to, jazz.

When his skill in classical music and his gentlemanly character are added to his accomplishments in jazz, Goodman must be regarded as one of the towering musicians of his time and as one of the world's genuine treasures.

Goodman married Alice Duckworth (née Hammond), sister of his friend John Hammond, in 1942. The Goodmans had two children: Rachel and Benjie.

Goodman died in New York City on June 13, 1986.

Morton Gould

Popular Native American
Concert Composer

(1913-   )

Morton Gould, composer and conductor, was born in New York City, New York, on December 10, 1913. He began improvising at the piano when he was four years old. At six he composed *Just Six,* a waltz that was published.

Gould entered the New York Institute of Musical Art (later called the Juilliard School of Music) when he was eight. Later he studied at the New York University

School of Music, completing his courses there at the age of fifteen. His principal teachers were Abby Whiteside (piano), who helped to spark Gould's interest in jazz, and Vincent Jones (theory and composition).

Gould concertized extensively as a child-prodigy pianist and composer, performing on the stage (including vaudeville) and over the radio. At seventeen he joined the staff of the Radio City Music Hall in New York City, a year later obtaining a position with the National Broadcasting Company (NBC) as a radio pianist. At twenty-one he became conductor and arranger of his own weekly light orchestral radio show: *Music for Today.* After about nine years with that series he went on to direct other radio music shows.

For those radio programs and for general concert use Gould wrote many light orchestral works of his own, drawing on American subject matter and American folk, jazz, and composed styles. Gould himself characterized his compositions as being "an integration and crystallization of influences in our native musical scene." Among his early orchestral works were three *American Symphonettes* (1933, 1935, 1937), *Chorale and Fugue in Jazz* (1936), *Spirituals* (1941), and *Lincoln Legend* (1942). His *American Salute* (1947), an arrangement of Patrick Gilmore's song "When Johnny Comes Marching Home," became one of the most frequently played contemporary orchestral pieces in America.

By the late 1940s Gould, with Aaron Copland and George Gershwin, had become one of the three most popular native American concert composers. He had his own touring orchestra, his own recording studio, and his own publishing company (which came to be known as Lawson-Gould Music Publishers, Inc., in New York City).

Besides composing his concert works, Gould successfully entered the realm of musical comedy with *Billion Dollar Baby* (perf. 1945) and ballet with *Fall River Legend* (1947). His background film scores include those for *Delightfully Dangerous* (1945) and *Cinerama Holiday* (1955), and his music for TV productions is highlighted by his work on the miniseries *Holocaust* (1978).

Gould has guest-conducted many major orchestras in America and elsewhere. Among his foreign debut tours were those in Europe (1966), Australia (1977), Japan (1979), and Israel (1981).

Through the years, particularly since the 1950s, Gould has supplemented his popular works with compositions in which he explored deeper levels of technique and expression, as in his first four symphonies (1943-52)

and his twelve-tone-influenced *Dialogues* for piano and strings (1958).

Gould's utilization of American popular elements has continued in such works as the *American Ballads* (1976) and the *Symphony of Spirituals* (1976), both written in honor of the American bicentennial. His recent compositions include the *Burchfield Gallery* for orchestra (1981) and the *Cello Suite* (1982).

Gould married Shirley Bank in 1944. They had two daughters (Deborah and Abby) and two sons (David and Eric).

Selected works:

Musical Comedies

Billion Dollar Baby (lyrics, B. Comden, A. Green; perf. 1945)
Arms and the Girl (lyrics, D. Fields; perf. 1950)

Ballets

Fall River Legend (1947)
Fiesta (1957)

Films
(background scores)

Delightfully Dangerous (1945)
Cinerama Holiday (1955)
Windjammer (1958)
Holocaust (TV, 1978)

Orchestral

three *American Symphonettes* (1933, 1935, 1937)
Chorale and Fugue in Jazz (1936)
Piano Concerto (1937)
Violin Concerto (1938)
Foster Gallery (1940)
Latin-American Symphonette (1941)
Spirituals (1941)
Lincoln Legend (1942)
Cowboy Rhapsody (1942)
American Concertette (1943)
four symphonies (1943-52)
Interplay (piano, orchestra; 1943)
Concerto for Orchestra (1945)
Minstrel Show (1946)
American Salute (1947)
Philharmonic Waltzes (1948)
Americana (1950)
Dialogues (piano, strings; 1958)
Festive Music (1965)
Vivaldi Gallery (string quartet, orchestra; 1968)
Soundings (1969)
American Ballads (1976)
Symphony of Spirituals (1976)
Cheers (1979)
Burchfield Gallery (1981)
Celebration '81 (1981)
Housewarming (1982)

Band

Symphony for Band (1952)
Inventions (four pianos, brass, percussion; 1953)
Derivations (clarinet, band; 1956)

Others

chamber music
piano pieces

Jascha Heifetz

King of Violinists

(1901-   )

Jascha Heifetz, violinist, was born in Vilnius, Lithuania (now in the Soviet Union), on February 2, 1901. At the age of three he began to take violin lessons from his father, a professional violinist who played in a local orchestra. When Jascha was four, his father, astonished at the boy's rapid progress, took him to study with the noted teacher Elias Malkin at the Royal School of Music in Vilnius. By the time he was five, Jascha had already become one of the best students in the school, and at six he could play Mendelssohn's difficult *Violin Concerto*.

In 1910 Jascha was accepted at the Saint Petersburg Conservatory. The elder Heifetz went along to watch over the boy. To avoid the ban against Jews other than

conservatory students living in Saint Petersburg (the city of the czar), Jascha's middle-aged father also enrolled at the conservatory. After a brief period of taking lessons with an assistant teacher, Jascha began to study with the famous Leopold Auer.

In 1911, in Saint Petersburg, young Heifetz made his official concert debut, followed by a spectacularly successful first appearance in Berlin at the Academy of Music in 1912. The latter performance induced the well-known conductor Arthur Nikisch to invite the youth to play Tchaikovsky's *Violin Concerto* with the Berlin Philharmonic Orchestra later that year.

Soon Heifetz was playing in many Russian cities, where the enthusiasm for his performances sometimes became so great that he needed a police escort to get home. He began to tour Europe as well.

By his early teens Heifetz had already attained a technical mastery so complete that he could devote his energy to developing interpretative skills almost unbelievable in one so young. He was widely hailed as the greatest violinist of his time.

On October 27, 1917, during the height of the Russian Revolution, Heifetz made his American debut with an appearance at Carnegie Hall in New York City. During intermission at that concert the violinist Mischa Elman, a former child prodigy himself, remarked to the pianist Leopold Godowsky that the hall seemed hot, to which the sharp-witted Godowsky replied, "Not for pianists." Soon Heifetz settled in the United States, becoming a naturalized American citizen in 1925.

In the 1920s and 1930s he toured widely and often. His travels took him to, among other places, England in 1920, Australia in 1921, the Far East in 1923, Palestine in 1926, and, in an emotional return to his homeland, the Soviet Union in 1934. On his Palestine tour, he donated his fees for the purchase of a concert hall in Tel Aviv.

During World War II Heifetz gave concerts for American servicemen in North Africa and the Mediterranean theater. In 1947 he took a sabbatical, during which he rested and reassessed his repertory and technique. In 1949 he returned to great public acclaim.

During the 1950s and 1960s he continued to concertize, but much less frequently than before. In 1953 he was slightly injured when an extremist Jewish youth in Jerusalem viciously struck Heifetz on the right arm with an iron bar after the violinist had performed a sonata by Richard Strauss, a composer objectionable to many Israelis because of his associations with Nazism. Nevertheless, Heifetz continued to perform for Israeli causes, both in Israel and with the Israel Philharmonic Orchestra on its tours of the United States (notably in the Hollywood Bowl after the Six-Day War in 1967).

Heifetz blended well with others in chamber music, such as the cellist Emanuel Feuermann and the violist William Primrose. In 1949 he was part of what *Life* magazine called "the Million Dollar Trio," consisting of Heifetz, the pianist Arthur Rubinstein, and the cellist Gregor Piatigorsky. In the early 1960s Heifetz and Piatigorsky began their long series of famous Heifetz-Piatigorsky Concerts in Los Angeles, in which Heifetz performed with Piatigorsky and others.

The name Heifetz has long been synonymous with violinistic perfection. His performances have become the standard by which other violinists are measured. With an almost immobile stance, he stressed musical technique, not musical exhibitionism. He held the violin very high and far back, with his face turned toward his left-hand fingers. His right elbow was held unusually high because of his almost exaggerated Russian-style grip of the bow (in which the center joint of the index finger is pressed against the bow stick, a method that Heifetz learned from Auer). Heifetz produced a powerful tone with an intense (but not sentimental) vibrato, a transparent texture, and a well-balanced sense of phrasing.

He was criticized for being impersonal and detached. That criticism probably evolved partly from his intense, unsmiling appearance (even while acknowledging applause) and partly from his tendency to present a given work with a single, ideal approach at each performance, whereas many musicians and music lovers prefer that an artist vary his approach during different performances. But Heifetz, by searching for perfection, also strove for universality—a lofty and honorable goal. Furthermore, he played with a concentration, a boldness, and a musical understanding that could have come only from one who was personally and deeply involved with the music.

Besides performing the standard classical and romantic repertory, Heifetz actively promoted new music. For example, he performed the world premieres of violin concertos by Mario Castelnuovo-Tedesco in 1933, William Walton in 1939, Louis Gruenberg in 1944, and Erich Wolfgang Korngold in 1947—all of which Heifetz had commissioned.

Heifetz himself made numerous violin transcriptions, the most famous being that of the Romanian composer Grigoraş Dinicu's *Hora staccato*. Among Heifetz's other activities were appearances in the commercial movies *They Shall Have Music* (1939), in which he had an extended speaking role in addition to his playing, and *Carnegie Hall* (1947), in which he only performed.

Heifetz's two marriages were unsuccessful. In 1928 he wedded Florence Vidor, a former movie actress. They had two children: Josepha and Robert. Their marriage ended in divorce in 1945. In 1947 he married Frances Spiegelberg. With her he had one child: Joseph. In 1963 that marriage, too, ended in divorce.

After the failure of his second marriage, Heifetz made fewer and fewer public apperances, finally settling into what many have called a "reclusive" existence, in which he avoids public events.

Since the early 1960s he has taught master classes at the University of Southern California (USC), where a Heifetz chair in music was established in 1975 with Heifetz himself as its first occupant. One of his students was Eugene Fodor. Some of Heifetz's classes were filmed and shown on educational TV. His last public performance was in 1972, a recorded concert in Los Angeles for the benefit of a scholarship fund at USC.

In 1981 he refused offers of a public celebration of his eightieth birthday. Shortly afterward he underwent an unsuccessful shoulder operation, and he now plays with great difficulty.

In spite of Heifetz's rejection of a public ceremony on his eightieth birthday, the event did not go unnoticed. On February 2, 1981, the outstanding young violinist Itzhak Perlman gave a concert at Alice Tully Hall in New York City. At one point he faced the audience and announced that it was Heifetz's eightieth birthday, referring to the older master as "the greatest violinist that ever lived."

Myra Hess
Patriotic Pianist
(1890-1965)

Myra Hess, pianist, was born in Hampstead (in an area now in Kilburn), near London, England, on February 25, 1890. Her original name was Julia Myra Hess, but from the age of three she was always called Myra. Later she said that she would have preferred the name Julia.

She showed early signs of musical aptitude by picking out tunes on the piano before she had reached the age of five, when she began to take lessons from local teachers. At seven she entered the Guildhall School of Music and Drama in London; at eight she began to play in public; and at thirteen she earned a scholarship to London's Royal Academy of Music, where she studied piano with the famous pedagogue Tobias Matthay.

Hess graduated from the Royal Academy in 1907 and later that year, at Queen's Hall in London, made her concert debut, performing, among other works, Beethoven's *Fourth Piano Concerto* with Thomas Beecham conducting the New Symphony Orchestra. In early 1908, at Aeolian Hall in London, she gave her first major solo recital.

Recognition, however, came slowly, especially in

England. For more than a decade she gave only occasional performances, meanwhile earning a living as a teacher and continuing to practice diligently.

An important step in building her reputation came in 1912 when she appeared as a guest soloist with the Concertgebouw Orchestra in Amsterdam, Willem Mengelberg conducting. In 1922 she gave a New York City recital that marked the real beginning of her musical maturity. After her success in New York City, she received more general acceptance in Europe. In the United States, however, she always remained a special favorite, and she toured America extensively throughout the 1920s and 1930s.

Then came World War II. At first Hess joined the Women's Voluntary Service in London and helped to evacuate children from the city. But she soon became preoccupied with another concern. The war had caused all of London's concert halls to be closed. Hess, feeling that wartime England needed music, instituted a series of daily lunchtime concerts at London's National Gallery (whose art works had been removed for their safety). She expressed her purpose in this way: "I want to keep this little oasis of peace going in the heart of London, and although we may be a small community, the principle of not being deterred by these evil forces is important."

Besides boosting morale, the wartime concerts raised money to help needy musicians. Audience members paid a small admission charge, but the performers—even the most famous—were given only a token payment. Some of the profits were donated to the Musicians' Benevolent Fund for young and little-known musicians. The rest of the profits were put into a reserve account.

Hess herself began the series with a solo recital in the autumn of 1939. Later other performers, both soloists and ensembles, participated in a variety of concerts, especially of chamber music. Hess, who appeared more often than any other performer, not only never took a fee but also, to support London and the concerts, gave up opportunities to make large sums of money in America.

Besides playing at the National Gallery Concerts, she made appearances all over England and frequently performed on radio for the British Broadcasting Corporation (BBC). Throughout the most difficult periods of the war, including the Nazi air raids on London, she helped to keep music alive in England. The public soon developed a tremendous admiration and personal affection for her.

In 1941 Hess, in recognition of her wartime public service, was awarded the highest honor that the nation could bestow on a woman: King George VI made her a Dame Commander of the Order of the British Empire.

To widespread regret, the National Gallery Concerts were ended in April 1946 because with the coming of peace the art collection was returned to the gallery for public view. Hess revealed the extent of her own feelings about the concerts: "If I had died the day peace was declared, I would have felt my life's work was complete."

After the war she resumed her extensive concertizing and found that she was still extremely popular in America. During the 1950s she reached the zenith of her fame and artistry.

In 1960 Hess suffered a heart attack and the following year a stroke, which left her partially paralyzed. But she battled back and attempted to resume her career. Her last public appearance as a pianist, in October 1961 at the Royal Festival Hall in London, was in a concert commemorating the twenty-first anniversary of the end of the Battle of Britain in World War II. Her last performance was on a radio broadcast in January 1962. After that, a severe rheumatic condition prevented her from playing.

It had been a remarkable career. In her youth, Hess performed a large repertory, including much contemporary music and many virtuoso pieces that she played with great enthusiasm. Later she restricted herself to an older, less flashy repertory: the works of Bach, Domenico Scarlatti, the Viennese classicists (especially Mozart's and Beethoven's concertos), Schumann, Chopin, Franck, Brahms, Grieg, and Debussy. Hess was greatly admired for her poetic sensibility, as well as her thoughtfulness and humor. She made numerous piano transcriptions of baroque music, notably of Bach's *Cantata 147* setting of the chorale tune known today as "Jesu, Joy of Man's Desiring," which she brought to worldwide popularity.

Hess never married. "I'm afraid I would be too earnest about marriage," she explained, "and in this business there is only one thing one can be really earnest about. That is playing the piano. One sacrifices a great deal, but there are compensations."

After her retirement in 1962 Hess, dejected at being unable to play the piano, went into virtual seclusion at her home in London. She died of multiple ailments in London on November 25, 1965.

Vladimir Horowitz
King of Piano Virtuosos
(1904-   )

Vladimir Horowitz, pianist, was born in Berdichev, the Ukraine (now in the Soviet Union), on October 1, 1904. His original name was Vladimir Gorovitz. Soon after his birth his family moved to the nearby city of Kiev, where there were greater economic opportunities despite the occasional Jewish deportations and the constant threat of pogroms, which decimated Kiev's Jewish sections in 1881 and 1905.

To protect themselves, the Gorovitzes deemphasized their Jewishness, religious observances, for example, never being held in the home. Nevertheless, baby Vladimir was nearly killed when the windows of the Gorovitz apartment were shattered by bullets during the 1905 pogrom.

In Kiev the Gorovitzes lived on a street happily named Music Lane, where indeed the family made a great deal of music. Vladimir's mother, Sophie, was a fine amateur pianist who gave all four of her children their first piano lessons. The oldest child, Regina, became an accomplished pianist. Also musical, though less talented than their sister, were Vladimir's older brothers: Jacob (pianist) and George (violinist).

Vladimir's father, Simeon, was a businessman who had only a rudimentary knowledge of music, but Simeon's mother had been an excellent pianist, encouraged, it was said, by the great Anton Rubinstein. Simeon's brother, Alexander, was the first professional musician in the family; he was a pianist-teacher who by 1904 had become director of the music school in Kharkov. For many years Alexander Gorovitz showed great interest in the training of his talented nephew Vladimir.

At the age of three Vladimir regularly observed his mother giving piano lessons to his sister, Regina. Once, while tapping on a windowpane in imitation of his mother's keyboard technique, be became so excited that he pushed his hands through the windowpane, breaking the glass and cutting his hands. When he was six, he began his own lessons with his mother, who encouraged the boy to familiarize himself with a wide variety of music.

He was not a prodigy, but by 1912 he had shown so much promise that his parents decided to enroll him at the Kiev Conservatory. There he studied piano with Vladimir Puchalsky, Sergei Tarnowsky, and Felix Blumenfeld. Blumenfeld passed along to young Vladimir Gorovitz the virile, romantic style of playing that Blumenfeld himself had learned from his own teacher, Anton Rubinstein, the revered father of all Russian piano virtuosos.

During his student years in Kiev, Vladimir wanted above all to be a composer, particularly in emulation of Sergei Rachmaninoff, his idol. But when the Bolsheviks took control of Kiev in 1920, his father's business was confiscated and the family's personal possessions were stolen or destroyed; even the Gorovitz piano was thrown through the window and into the street. To earn money for the family, Vladimir gave up his dreams of composition and turned to the concert stage.

In the autumn of 1921, in Kharkov, he made his formal debut, a recital arranged by Alexander Gorovitz, his uncle. Playing to a sparse audience, Vladimir nevertheless received a tremendous ovation.

Soon he was concertizing in Moscow and other cities in the Soviet Union (of which the Ukraine became a part in 1923). During that time he broadened his circle of musical acquaintances, the closest of whom came to be the outstanding young violinist Nathan Milstein, whom he met in late 1921.

By 1925 Vladimir had attained great success in the Soviet Union, but at the same time his resolve to leave the country had become fixed. Sick of the restrictions in the Soviet state, he dreamed of living and concertizing in the West.

He would be leaving behind a shattered family. His brother Jacob, a budding pianist himself, had been drafted and killed during the Russian Revolution. George, his other brother, committed suicide in 1925. Their parents, shaken by a steady stream of griefs, became emotionally unstable. Regina, who played well enough to give chamber-music concerts with Vladimir and Milstein, was the stablest member of the family (including Vladimir); but after having an unsuccessful marriage, she was left with a small daughter to raise. Sacrificing her career to care for her parents, remaining brother, and child, Regina nevertheless hoped that one day Vladimir would send for her so that she could join him as an artist abroad. But the invitation never came, and her hopes for a European career were never realized.

Obtaining a six-month visa on the pretext of wanting to study with Artur Schnabel in Germany, Vladimir stuffed extra money into his shoes (no one being allowed to leave the country with more than the equivalent of five hundred dollars) and left the Soviet Union for good in late 1925. Other than one visit with his father outside Russia in the 1930s, the break with his family was also permanent.

He soon arrived in Berlin, where, under the name Vladimir Horowitz, he debuted in January 1926. He was so nervous at his first recital that he played poorly. The night before his second recital, he was given an injection that helped him to relax and sleep. That recital and later performances in Berlin were successful.

However, the big break in Horowitz's career came in February 1926 in the city of Hamburg. Replacing at the last minute an ailing pianist, Horowitz performed the Tchaikovsky *First Piano Concerto* with the Hamburg Philharmonic conducted by Eugen Pabst. The response was overwhelmingly favorable, and the young pianist soon began to receive offers for future concerts throughout Europe. For the next couple of years the number of Horowitz's fans grew rapidly, though he was sometimes taken to task by critics for putting technique and acrobatic display ahead of musical and poetic ideas.

In January 1928 Horowitz arrived in New York City, and his first wish was to meet the Russian pianist-composer Sergei Rachmaninoff, the "musical god" of Horowitz's youth. Within two days the meeting took place, at which Horowitz played the older man's *Third Piano Concerto* while the composer accompanied on another piano. Later Rachmaninoff said, "Until I heard Horowitz, I did not realize the possibilities of the piano!" His *Third Piano Concerto* became a Horowitz trademark.

On January 12, 1928, Horowitz made his American debut by playing Tchaikovsky's *First Piano Concerto* at Carnegie Hall in New York City. That performance became a classic battle between a conductor and a soloist with different ideas regarding musical interpretation. The conductor was the self-absorbed Thomas Beecham, and his slow tempos irritated Horowitz, who, as the soloist, traditionally had the right to choose tempos. Finally losing his patience, Horowitz cut loose during the last movement and finished almost a full measure ahead of the orchestra. As in Europe, the critics gave Horowitz both great praise for his virtuosity and severe criticism for his lack of complete musicality.

He gave many more performances in America, including, on February 20, 1928, his first American solo recital, again at Carnegie Hall. The public completely adored Horowitz, not only because of his onstage pyrotechnics but also because of his offstage color, such as his coy demeanor with the press, his childlike delight in receiving attention, and his wearing of bright red and pink shirts. In America, for the first time in his career, Horowitz became financially solvent.

He continued to concertize extensively in Europe and America for the next several years, including chamber-music appearances with the violinist Nathan Milstein and the cellist Gregor Piatigorsky.

In the spring of 1933 in New York City, Horowitz met the famed conductor Arturo Toscanini, who led the New York Philharmonic while the pianist played the Beethoven *Emperor Concerto*. In December of that year Horowitz wedded Toscanini's daughter Wanda, a marriage that surprised the virtuoso's friends and associates because of his known homosexual inclinations. It was widely assumed that he took the step partly to put stability into his home life and partly to form a personal link with Toscanini, whom Horowitz revered.

Wanda, for her part, was an iron-willed young woman who had inherited her father's violent temper. In Horowitz, she saw a glamorous musician with whom she could travel and be independent of her father. Yet, in a sense, her role with both men was the same: she acted as a sort of mother figure who protected, cared for, and shared in the successes of the men she loved.

The Horowitzes had one child, Sonia, with whom the father had an aloof relationship. (When she died in early 1975, at the age of forty, Horowitz reacted in a detached manner. "He draws an iron curtain around himself," explained Wanda. "He doesn't let unpleasantness touch him.")

In 1936 Horowitz went into the first of his three famous "retirements" from the concert stage. Numerous factors contributed to his withdrawal, including his contraction of phlebitis, his need to reflect on how his artistic growth had been limited by an emphasis on technique, his tension created by his new family responsiblities, and his inner turmoil at the fate of his parents in the Soviet Union (his mother having died of peritonitis after an unattended case of appendicitis, and his father having died in a prison camp, to which he had been sent on the apparent and bizarre charge that the poor mentally deteriorated man was—because he spoke fluent German and French—a spy!). Horowitz spent much of the next two years in Switzerland.

In late 1938 he returned to the stage in a series of European recitals, playing with new self-confidence and enthusiasm. However, he avoided appearing in the Fascist countries of Germany and Italy.

In late 1939 the Horowitzes settled in the United States, where he remained to concertize extensively during World War II and to become a naturalized citizen in 1942. Among his most important performances during the war were his presentations of the American premieres of three piano sonatas by the Soviet composer Sergei Prokofiev: the *Sixth* in 1942, the *Seventh* in 1944, and the *Eighth* in 1945. The composer had specifically requested that the difficult works be given their American premieres by Horowitz, who enjoyed the technical challenges of the sonatas.

The only America piano composer who appealed to Horowitz was the romantic Samuel Barber. The pianist gave the world premieres of Barber's *Excursions* in 1945 and *Piano Sonata* in 1949.

In the spring of 1953 Horowitz entered a second, more serious period of retirement, caused by physical and nervous exhaustion. In the early 1960s his mental depression was successfully treated with electroshock therapy at Columbia Presbyterian Hospital in New York City. The retirement lasted twelve years, during which time he did, however, make some recordings.

His historic, emotional return to the concert stage came on May 9, 1965, in a recital at Carnegie Hall. For the next few years he continued to give recitals.

Then, after a recital in the autumn of 1969, he ceased public activity once again. The main reason, he said, was to protect his health. As with his second retirement, he continued to make recordings during his third.

After more electroshock treatments in late 1973, he felt well enough to return to the stage with a recital in Cleveland on May 12, 1974. He explained why he came out of retirement: "I don't want to be a legend. I am not a ghost but a real live human being." His first major reappearance was a recital at the Metropolitan Opera House on November 17, 1974. Horowitz felt rejuvenated: "Now I take no more retirements."

He gave numerous recitals in the United States over the next few years. The climax of his return came in a series of events connected with the fiftieth anniversary of his American debut. His golden jubilee received immense newspaper and magazine coverage, and Horowitz was thrilled to be the subject of a TV interview by Mike Wallace on the *Sixty Minutes* show that was telecast on December 26, 1977. On January 8, 1978, Horowitz gave the anniversary concert itself, playing Rachmaninoff's *Third Piano Concerto* with Eugene Ormandy conducting the New York Philharmonic in Carnegie Hall. (The date should have been January 12, but Horowitz preferred to play on a Sunday.) It was his first concert with an orchestra since his silver jubilee in America twenty-five years earlier. On February 26, 1978, he gave a recital that was radiocast live (and later telecast) from the White House, President Carter introducing Horowitz as a "national treasure." On September 24, 1978, Horowitz played the Rachmaninoff *Third Piano Concerto* again, with Zubin Mehta and the New York Philharmonic, a concert that was telecast live to the nation. During the course of these events, Horowitz became a media celebrity.

In 1981 Horowitz reappeared for a recital at the Metropolitan Opera House. And in 1982 he made his first European tour since 1951, saying that he would continue to play as long as he felt "the devil and the angel within." He took his Steinway piano, his private cook, his favorite piano tuner, and his wife with him on the tour.

In 1986 he visited Russia for the first time since 1925. On April 20 he gave a triumphant Moscow recital, which was nationally telecast in the United States.

Horowitz had mixed results in his piano teaching, for which he was not temperamentally suited. Among his pupils were Gary Graffman and Byron Janis.

Horowitz is renowned primarily as a brilliant technician, possibly the greatest in piano history. He can play with great speed and force, and with extraordinary control of articulation and dynamics. He firmly believes in the nineteenth-century romantic tradition of freedom of expression during performance: the player's interpretation is essentially an independent activity, not necessarily an exact duplication of the composer's printed ideas (though he is more careful with certain composers—notably Beethoven—than with others). He is heard to best advantage in the romantic virtuoso works of Liszt and Rachmaninoff, as well as in his own dazzling transcriptions of John Philip Sousa's march *The Stars and Stripes Forever* and of themes from Bizet's *Carmen*. Among modern compositions, the lyrical sonatas of Scriabin and the virtuoso pieces of Prokofiev also provide showcases for Horowitz's incredible pianistic powers.

Harry James
Man with the Sweet-sounding Trumpet
(1916-83)

Harry James, jazz trumpeter and bandleader, was born in Albany, Georgia, on March 15, 1916. His father, Everette, led the band in the Mighty Haag Circus, where his mother, Maybelle, was an aerialist. As a tiny tot Harry entered the circus, one of his big acts being a dive through a flaming hoop while balancing a glass of water on his head. When he was six, an illness ended the athletic phase of his circus career.

Soon, however, he was playing the drums in his father's circus band. At about the age of ten he switched to the trumpet, learning the instrument from his father.

The boy studied the trumpet by playing classical music, but the literature was so small that he turned to the popular field. When Everette took over the first (main) band for the Christy Brothers Circus, he let Harry conduct the second band.

At fourteen Harry won a statewide contest for trumpeters in Texas, to which his family had recently moved. Thus encouraged, young James soon became a professional and played with several dance bands throughout the Southwest.

His first big break came when he was hired for Ben

Harry James

ground of soft string sonorities. At theaters and elsewhere, teenagers still clamored to hear his hot music; but at hotels and nightclubs and in recordings—the areas where he received his most enduring support—he found more success with his sweet manner. Soon he had one of the best-known swing ensembles in the big-band era, eventually using such individual talents as the singer Frank Sinatra and the drummer Buddy Rich.

James utilized a broad repertory, from blues and boogie-woogie to Viennese waltzes. His biggest hits tended to come from his nonjazz solos, notably "You Made Me Love You," a recording of which first brought him to national attention in the early 1940s. Other tunes with which he became identified included "Carnival in Venice," "The Flight of the Bumblebee," "I've Heard That Song Before," and "Velvet Moon."

James made his movie debut as a member of the Goodman band in *Hollywood Hotel* (1937). He later appeared on his own in the films *Springtime in the Rockies* (1942), *Two Girls and a Sailor* (1944), *Do You Love Me?* (1946), *Carnegie Hall* (1947), *The Benny Goodman Story* (1956), and *Ladies' Man* (1961). He also dubbed in the trumpet music in *Young Man with a Horn* (1950).

In the early 1950s James went into semiretirement in Los Angeles, making only occasional tours with his band. But after being featured in *The Benny Goodman Story*, he reorganized his group on a more permanent basis and toured Europe in 1957. At that time he began to place more emphasis on jazz in his performances than he had during the peak of his popularity in the 1940s.

From the 1960s on, he lived in Las Vegas, Nevada, but made frequent American and European tours, continuing to combine a commercial style with jazz.

James married Louise Tobin, a former Goodman vocalist, in 1935. They had two children: Harry and Timothy. After divorcing Tobin in 1943, James married the actress Betty Grable in the same year. James and Grable appeared together in the films *Springtime in the Rockies* and *Do You Love Me?* They had two children: Victoria and Jessica. After more than twenty years of having one of the most famous marriages in the entertainment business, James and Grable divorced in 1965. A brief marriage to showgirl Joan Boyd produced a son.

James died of cancer in Las Vegas on July 5, 1983.

Pollack's band in 1935. The following year James recorded his own "Peckin'." The great jazzman Benny Goodman heard the recording and hired James for the Goodman band in December 1936.

In 1939 James left Goodman and started his own band. Goodman himself lent money to James to help get the younger man started. After failing to get a following in hot jazz (marked by complex rhythms and expressive improvisations), James turned to a sweet style (marked by simpler rhythms and written-out arrangements) that featured his clear trumpet sounds against a rich back-

Al Jolson

Jazz Singer

(1886-1950)

Al Jolson, singer, was born sometime during the period 1880-86 in Srednike, Lithuania (now in the Soviet Union). Because no birth certificate was made out at the time, the exact date of his birth is not known. Later, however, Jolson himself selected May 26, 1886, as the birth date that he preferred. His original name was Asa Yoelson.

To escape the pogroms and generally repressive conditions in their homeland, Asa's mother, Naomi, decided that his father, Moses Yoelson, who was a rabbi-cantor and descendant of several consecutive generations of cantors, should travel to America to prepare the way for the rest of the family. With his face blackened to avoid detection in the dark of the night, Moses slipped out of Lithuania in the early 1890s. A few years later he sent for his family, who joined him in Washington, D.C., where he had obtained a post as a cantor.

After the death of his mother, when he was about ten, Asa came into constant conflict with his Orthodox father. Moses strictly upheld traditional Jewish views and practices, while Asa and his older brother, Hirsch, were lax in such observances. Moreover, though Moses taught both boys to sing, he hated popular music, while it was precisely American popular culture that most interested his sons. They sang in the streets to earn money from passersby and often ran away from home to try to break into show business. After Hirsch Americanized his given name to Harry, Asa followed suit by calling himself Al.

Al's first indoor musical job was singing "Rosie, You Are My Posie" in a Bowery restaurant, where his payment was a meal. At the Bijou Theater in Washington, he sang "Ida, Sweet As Apple Cider" from the audience as part of Eddie Leonard's act, later performing the same function there with "You Are My Jersey Lily" for the burlesque queen Jersey Lil. In 1899 he appeared on a stage for the first time, as an extra in the New York City presentation of the London Jewish epic *Children of the Ghetto*.

Having Americanized their surname to Joelson (a change initiated by Al), Al and Harry began touring in vaudeville as the Joelson Brothers in a comedy act called *The Hebrew and the Cadet*. Because Al's voice was changing, Harry sang while Al whistled. During the show-business slump following the assassination of President McKinley in 1901, the boys were laid off.

After a couple of years in burlesque, they returned to vaudeville in the comedy team Jolson, Palmer, and Jolson (a printer having suggested the change in spelling because two *Joelson*s were too long for their business card). The act, entitled *A Little of Everything*, was written by Ren Shields, lyricist of the classic song "In the Good Old Summertime." While doing that act, Al used blackface for the first time, finding that with a mask on he could perform with greater abandon.

The team lasted about three years, after which Al developed a solo act. In San Francisco, one week after the great 1906 earthquake there, he made his first significant appearance in his solo vaudeville routine. Performing in blackface, Jolson, a high baritone, sang popular songs with an impudent charm that soon proved to have broad appeal. His first great success, however, came when he performed as one of Lew Dockstader's Minstrels in New York City in 1909.

Jolson then began touring in vaudeville on his own again and perfected his technique as he went along. Cultivating a style of singing derived from Afro-American music and blackface minstrelsy, he characteristically performed with an intoned declamation that emphasized the text rather than the melodic line. Yet he was also noted for his melodic invention, often improvising whistled choruses in the manner of jazz instrumentalists. In fact, much of his routine was improvised. Besides performing his set numbers, he sang songs on request, sometimes whistled or broke into a buck and wing, and kept up a lively extemporaneous monologue consisting of anecdotes, homilies, and confessions.

In 1911 Jolson began to appear in Broadway shows, where he continued to utilize blackface for many years. His first Broadway appearance was in the revue *La belle Paree* ("Beautiful Paris," in which the composer Jerome Kern collaborated on his first complete score). Though not showing Jolson at his best, *La belle Paree* marked the beginning of his meteoric rise to the position of Broadway's greatest attraction. Later in 1911 *Vera Violetta* proved to be a better showcase for his talents.

In 1912 a runway was built into the orchestra area of the Winter Garden Theater for Jolson's use in the revue *The Whirl of Society,* in which he presented himself as the blackface character Gus. Jolson would use both the runway and the Gus character in several future shows.

In *The Honeymoon Express* (1913) Jolson employed for the first time two gestures that became his hallmark: falling to one knee and extending his arms in a pathetic appeal while singing. He performed those gestures while beseeching his mammy in "Down Where the Tennessee Flows." His original purpose, however, was not theatrical but practical: he was suffering from an ingrown toenail, and he went down to one knee to take pressure off the painful digit; his arms flew out as an instinctive compensation for the sudden immobility of his legs. But the favorable response of the audience induced him to keep the gestures as a regular feature in his act.

There followed numerous Broadway successes for Jolson, notably *Robinson Crusoe, Jr.* (1916), *Sinbad* (1918), and *Bombo* (1921). In *Sinbad* Jolson, on his own initiative, interpolated George Gershwin's previously unsuccessful song "Swanee," which quickly rose to immense popularity because of Jolson's snappy delivery. Besides "Swanee" and his highly personalized version of "My Mammy," other songs with which Jolson became closely identified included "April Showers," "California, Here I Come," "Rock-a-bye Your Baby with a Dixie Melody" (his favorite song), "Sonny Boy," and "Toot, Toot, Tootsie."

Most of the musicals starring Jolson had little plot interest. He was simply given the last segment of each show to work his magic and bring the entertainment to a climax.

In the late 1920s, after the successful *Big Boy* (1925), Jolson's popularity began to fade with the changing fashions in the theater public's taste. His last two major stage vehicles, *The Wonder Bar* (1931) and *Hold On to Your Hats* (1940), did not fare well.

Jolson, however, proved to be adaptable, and in the late 1920s he turned his attention from the stage to films. He debuted, in fact, in the first significant feature-length sound movie: *The Jazz Singer* (1927). Actually the film is not entirely in sound; it is for the most part a silent movie, with songs and bits of dialogue audible. The first spoken words in the film occur when Jolson, after singing "Dirty Hands, Dirty Face," says, "Wait a minute! Wait a minute! You ain't heard nothin' yet," and then introduces his next song, "Toot, Toot, Tootsie."

The Jazz Singer was originally a Broadway play in which the main character, Jakie Rabinowitz, was modeled after Jolson himself. Jakie is a cantor's son who runs away from home to become the jazz singer Jack Robin. When his father dies, Jack gives up his big chance on Broadway and goes home to take over his father's cantor duties at the synagogue. For the screen version, a final segment was added showing Jack singing in a Broadway musical entitled *The Jazz Singer*. George Jessel, the original Jakie Rabinowitz on Broadway, had been scheduled to take the screen role; but when he asked for too much money, he was replaced by Jolson.

Among Jolson's later films were *The Singing Fool* (1928), *Mammy* (1930), *Hallelujah, I'm a Bum* (1933), *Go into Your Dance* (1935), *The Singing Kid* (1936), *Swanee River* (1939), and *Rhapsody in Blue* (1945).

He was also a frequent performer on radio, both as the star of his own shows and as a guest on other programs. His first major entry into radio came in 1932 with the *Presenting Al Jolson* series. Four years later he teamed up with two comics, Martha Raye and Parkyakarkas (real name, Harry Einstein), on *The Lifebuoy Program,* a hit show for several years.

Jolson's popularity slipped again in the late 1930s and early 1940s. But the semibiographical movies *The Jolson Story* (1946) and *Jolson Sings Again* (1949) revived interest in him, and sales of his recordings suddenly shot up to the millions. He dubbed in the singing for Larry Parks (as Jolson) in the two films.

Jolson had four marriages. In 1906 he wedded Henrietta Keller, a chorus girl whom he had met in San Francisco; they divorced in 1919. He was then married to the Broadway dancer Alma Osborne, better known by the stage name Ethel Delmar, from 1922 to 1926, when they were divorced. His third marriage, beginning in 1928, was to the famed entertainer Ruby Keeler, star of both Broadway shows and film musicals (appearing with Jolson in *Go into Your Dance).* Al and Ruby adopted a son, whom they named Al Jolson, Jr.; but this marriage, too, was doomed, and they parted in 1939 and divorced in 1940. In 1945 he married Erle Chenault Galbraith, an X-ray technician and fan from Little Rock, Arkansas, with whom Jolson adopted another son (Asa) and, less formally, a daughter (Alicia).

Al Jolson

Jolson was generous with his time for benefit performances, particularly during wartime. He helped to sell World War I Liberty Bonds, and he performed on the United Service Organizations (USO) circuits during World War II and the Korean conflict. Having just returned from a Korean tour, Jolson was stopping over in San Francisco (where his solo career had begun) when he died of a heart attack on October 23, 1950.

His good friend George Jessel delivered the eulogy at Temple Israel in Los Angeles. The bulk of Jolson's estate, estimated at $4 million, was bequeathed to a number of institutions, including Jewish, Catholic, and Protestant charities.

Selected recordings:

Singles

"That Haunting Melody" (1911, Victor)
"You Made Me Love You" (1913, Columbia)
"Rock-a-bye Your Baby with a Dixie Melody" (1918, Columbia)

"Swanee" (1920, Columbia)
"April Showers" (1921, Columbia)
"Toot, Toot, Tootsie" (1922, Columbia)
"California, Here I Come" (1924, Brunswick)
"I'm Sitting on Top of the World" (1925, Brunswick)
"When the Red, Red Robin Comes Bob, Bob Bobbin' Along" (1926, Brunswick)
"My Mammy" (1928, Brunswick)
"Sonny Boy" (1928, Brunswick)
"The Cantor" (in Hebrew) (1932, Brunswick)
"Anniversary Song" (1946, Decca)
"Kol nidre" ("All the Vows," 1947, Decca)
"Cantor on the Sabbath" (1947, Decca)
"Chinatown, My Chinatown" (1949, Decca)
"Give My Regards to Broadway" (1949, Decca)
"Way Down Yonder in New Orleans" (1950, Decca)

with Bing Crosby:
"Alexander's Ragtime Band" (1947, Decca)

Albums

Al Jolson (volumes 1-3, 1946-48, Decca)
Jolson Sings Again (1949, Decca)
The Best of Jolson (1962, Decca)

Danny Kaye
Ambassador of Goodwill
(1913-   )

Danny Kaye, the internationally renowned singer, actor, comedian, and humanitarian, was born of Russian immigrants in New York City, New York, on January 18, 1913. His original name was David Daniel Kaminski (sometimes spelled Kominski or Kominsky).

He grew up in the Brownsville section of the borough of Brooklyn, the toughest district in all of New York City. Danny, or Duvidl, as his parents called him, survived by being the neighborhood entertainer, singing and clowning around. He always loved to make people laugh.

He attended Public School 149 and then Thomas Jefferson High School, where most of his energy went into sports, such as swimming and baseball. His work in the gym and on the athletic field helped to develop the strength, coordination, and sense of timing that he later applied to his vigorous stage and film routines.

Though his school grades were only average, Danny, encouraged by his mother, planned on a career as a physician. But when she died, the teenage boy began to change his plans. He felt that he should be making money for the household, like his two older brothers.

Soon he got a job as a messenger boy in the office of a dentist, Dr. Samuel Fine. The doctor's teenage daughter developed a crush on Danny, but he was so busy that he ran in and out of the office without even noticing her. One day Dr. Fine caught Danny making a sort of needle-point design on a piece of wood with a dental drill. The doctor fired the boy on the spot.

With a friend, Louis Eisen, Danny ran away from home and went to Florida, where they performed, like gypsy troubadours, for anyone who would listen to them, Danny singing to Louis's guitar accompaniment. Exhilarated, they soon returned home with several dollars' profit.

Danny Kaye conducting the Israel Philharmonic

Deciding not to go back to high school, Danny teamed up once again with Louis Eisen and performed a variety act at local private parties. They were well received, and their act was eventually broadcast over a small Brooklyn radio station, WBBC; but nothing further came of the experience.

Danny, desperate for money, temporarily turned away from show business, working as a soda jerk and then as an automobile appraiser for an insurance company. Like many people of great artistic talent, he found it impossible to focus his attention on such routine jobs, and he was fired from both of them.

In 1929, again with Louis Eisen, Danny went to work on the borscht circuit, the theaters and nightclubs associated with the Jewish summer camps and resort hotels in the Catskill Mountains of New York. There he combined the jobs of waiter, singer, actor, and comedian. His principal task was simply to keep the guests amused, which he often did by falling into the swimming pool—fully clothed, straw hat and all. In the language of the entertainment world, Danny was a toomler, a creator of tumult.

He continued to work as a toomler during the summers of 1930-32. However, he still had difficulty finding jobs during the rest of each year, and he had to live off his summer savings. In the summer of 1933 he finally got a job as a full-fledged member of the entertainment staff on the borscht circuit.

Also in 1933 he was asked to join the dancing team of Dave Harvey and Kathleen Young, forming a group called the Three Terpsichoreans. Opening night was in Utica, New York. Kaye, an inexperienced dancer, accidentally stumbled and fell during the performance. The audience began to laugh and applaud. Dave Harvey whispered to him, "They love it. Don't get up." Kaye, in a false whisper that could be heard throughout the auditorium, replied, "I can't get up. I've split my pants!" Kaye's clowning became a regular part of the act, which was hired by vaudeville theaters and burlesque shows.

In late 1933 the Terpsichoreans joined a revue troupe that worked its way westward across the United States and then sailed for the Orient in February 1934. By then Kaye was singing and monologizing in addition to dancing. To appeal to the non-English-speaking audiences of the Orient, Kaye learned to tell his stories in pantomime, to show emotions by making faces, and to entertain with scat singing, which consists of the expressive vocalizing of meaningless syllables with an occasional recognizable word for emphasis.

When the Oriental tour ended, Kaye found a number of minor engagements in the United States. For a while he toured with the famous fan dancer Sally Rand, holding her fans to assure that she was properly (that is, minimally) covered during her act. In 1938 he was hired for an important engagement at a London cabaret, but he failed to impress the British.

His career was stuck. He simply could not find the right material, especially songs, for his personality.

Then, in 1939, he went to the Keystone Theater on Fifty-second Street in New York City to see about a job. There, seated at the piano was an attractive brunette who looked vaguely familiar. She glanced up, smiled shyly, and said, "I know you, but I bet you don't remember me." It was Sylvia Fine, daughter of Dr. Samuel Fine. She was also the woman destined to change Danny Kaye's entire career and life.

They both got jobs that day, she as a pianist and songwriter and he as a performer, for *The Sunday Night Revue*. The show folded after only one night, but it was the beginning for Danny and Sylvia.

That summer they worked together again, putting on *The Straw Hat Revue* at Camp Tamiment, a Jewish resort camp in the Pocono Mountains of Pennsylvania. In the autumn the show made it to Broadway, where Kaye finally began to develop a significant reputation.

The new boost to his career can be traced directly to Sylvia Fine's sparkling melodies and absurd lyrics, perfectly tailored to showcase Kaye's personality and talent for dialect singing and for patter (humorous, rapid-fire) songs. There was, for instance, "Anatole of Paris," in which Kaye was a schizophrenic modiste with blue hair.

In early 1940 Danny and Sylvia were married. They had one child: Dena, who became a successful writer.

Later in 1940 Kaye was hired at the elite New York City nightclub La Martinique. After a shaky start, he was calmed down and technically advised by Sylvia. Soon he settled into a tremendously successful, now legendary, engagement. His biggest single song success was Sylvia's "Stanislavsky," in which Kaye, in Russian dialect, poked fun at the Soviet artists of the Moscow Theater, where students were taught to "become" inanimate objects.

Thereafter Sylvia continued to be the most important force in his career, not only writing much of his material but also serving as his personal coach and critic.

The playwright Moss Hart, after seeing Kaye at La Martinique, wrote a part for the young entertainer in the

Danny Kaye (right) with Laurie Ichino (left)

Kurt Weill musical *Lady in the Dark,* which reached Broadway in early 1941. Kaye brought the house down at every performance with his rendition of "Tschaikowsky," in which he rattled off the tongue-twisting names of about fifty Russian composers (strung together by Ira Gershwin) in the incredible time of only thirty-eight seconds.

After leaving *Lady in the Dark* in 1941, Kaye returned to La Martinique for another engagement. Later the same year he appeared in the Broadway musical *Let's Face It.*

When the United States entered World War II, Kaye tried to enlist for military service. But he was rejected by the army and the other branches because he had a sacroiliac problem. He thereupon aided the war effort by appearing at benefits and rallies to help sell war bonds and by performing at military camps and hospitals. He also appeared in United Service Organizations (USO) tours in Europe.

It was during the war that Kaye began to make movies, through which his talent became known worldwide. His first film was *Up in Arms* (1944), in which he starred with Dinah Shore. There followed a series of movies designed as vehicles for Kaye's unique comedic and musical versatility. Through the 1940s there were *Wonder Man* (1945), *The Kid from Brooklyn* (1946), *The Secret Life of Walter Mitty* (1947), *A Song Is Born* (1948), and *The Inspector General* (1949).

One of his most endearing performances came in his portrayal of the title role in the film *Hans Christian Andersen* (1952). He also sang in the movies *On the Riviera* (1951), *Knock on Wood* (1954), *White Christmas* (1954), *The Court Jester* (1956), *Merry Andrew* (1958), *The Five Pennies* (1959), *On the Double* (1961), *Pinocchio* (TV, 1976), and *Peter Pan* (TV, 1976).

Kaye has proven himself as a straight actor as well, notably in the films *Me and the Colonel* (1958), in which he plays a Jewish refugee fleeing 1940 France in the company of an anti-Semitic Polish colonel; *The Man from the Diners' Club* (1963); *The Madwoman of Chaillot* (1969); and *Skokie* (TV, 1981), in which he plays a Holocaust survivor confronting resurgent Nazism in contemporary America.

Kaye has also performed on radio (where he was one of the most popular personalities of the 1940s) and on TV. He had his own TV series, *The Danny Kaye Show* (1963-67); hosted *Danny Kaye's Look-in at the Metropolitan Opera* (1975), a children's program on how an opera is produced; appeared on *Live from Lincoln Center* (1981); and headed many other TV specials.

Also notable was his performance in the Broadway musical *Two by Two* (1970), based on the biblical story of Noah. But he has always preferred the freedom of concert appearances, where he can exercise his ability to improvise. Kaye, though he cannot read music, has frequently appeared on the podium with major orchestras, such as the Israel Philharmonic, conducting them with inspired hilarity.

He has maintained his interest in sports. In 1976 he became a founder and part owner of the Seattle Mariners professional baseball team. He sold his share in 1983.

But the dominant factor in his life for many years has been his work in behalf of the United Nations International Children's Emergency Fund (UNICEF). Since 1953 he has been UNICEF's official ambassador-at-large to the world's children. He has gone into remote areas of Europe, Asia, Africa, and Latin America to visit children who are undernourished, diseased, or orphaned by war. Exuding an obviously genuine affection for them, he entertains the children while teams of UNICEF workers administer medical and other aid.

In 1957 he hosted the TV program *The Secret Life of Danny Kaye,* in which he presented children of various countries to demonstrate the work of UNICEF. In 1983, while Kaye was recuperating from a successful heart bypass operation, UNICEF saluted him for his thirty years of service by naming him as an honorary delegate to the UNICEF Executive Board.

Fully recovered from his surgery, he continues to be active. In September 1985, for example, he comically conducted the Los Angeles Philharmonic Orchestra at the Hollywood Bowl in a benefit concert for a musicians' fund.

Because his humor is never unkind, is always solidly based in humility, is universal in appeal, and is channeled into helping the world's underprivileged children, Kaye is internationally recognized as one of humanity's greatest treasures and as an independent ambassador of goodwill to people everywhere.

Jerome Kern

Father of Modern
American Theater Music
(1885-1945)

Jerome Kern, composer, was born in New York City, New York, on January 27, 1885. His mother had a profound influence on his musical growth: she gave him piano lessons in his early youth, and for his tenth birthday she took him for his first attendance at a Broadway musical.

Two years later, in 1897, the family moved to Newark, New Jersey; and in 1899 he enrolled in Newark High School, where he was soon called on to play the piano and the organ at school assemblies. In 1901 he composed music for, and performed in, a school musical show. The following year he wrote the score for a musical staged by the Newark Yacht Club. Flushed with the local success of his creative efforts, Kern dropped out of high school to devote himself to a career in music.

His first step, common among aspiring American composers of the period, was to travel to Germany for music lessons. He studied in a small town near Heidelberg (though he never specified where or with whom) for a few months in mid-1902. Returning to New York City, he composed a light piano piece entitled *At the Casino*, which, in September 1902, became his first published work. Later in 1902 he enrolled at the New York College of Music, where he studied piano with Albert von Doenhoff, counterpoint with Austin Pierce, and harmony and composition with Paolo Gallico and Alexander Lambert. However, his stay there was brief.

In 1903 Kern began to receive opportunities to interpolate his songs into the stage works of other composers. Most of the shows for which he provided interpolated songs were foreign (especially British) operettas adapted for American audiences, such as *Mr. Wix of Wickham* (perf. 1904). *The Earl and the Girl* (perf. 1905) included Kern's most memorable early song: "How'd You Like to Spoon with Me?" He eventually became the leading composer of interpolated songs in the history of American musical theater.

On December 31, 1907, Kern's mother—who had been his teacher, spokesperson, and friend—died. For the rest of his life, in memory of his mother, he declined all invitations to New Year's Eve parties. His father, a prominent businessman, died the following year.

In 1909 Kern, on a short vacation, was in the village of Walton, England, and happened to go into a pub-hotel named the Swan, where he met Eva Leale, daughter of the managers of the establishment. During his stay in England he returned to the Swan several times to see Eva. He broke down her reserve by playing the piano for

her. "I had never heard such piano-playing in my life," she later recalled, "and as he played I would float off into another world." She admired Kern's "How'd You Like to Spoon with Me?" but refused to believe that he had written the music till he showed her the sheet music with his name on it.

Kern returned to New York City and began to send letters to Eva. Her father insisted on reading both Kern's letters and her replies, but she soon found a way to slip in extra little notes before her letters were mailed. Deeply touched by the notes, Kern, in one of his letters, formally

(Courtesy of the Academy of Motion Picture Arts and Sciences)

asked Mr. Leale for Eva's hand in marriage. The ceremony took place in Walton in October 1910, and the Kerns soon settled in America.

Kern—Jerry to Eva and his friends—and Eva made an interesting contrast. He was city bred, impish, and sometimes authoritarian. She was village bred, retiring, and usually submissive. Moreover, he was an American Anglophile, while the English Eva became an ardent American. But the marriage was a happy one, helped along by Eva's warmth and intelligence. They had one child, Elizabeth, who was always referred to as Betty.

By World War I Kern had interpolated more than one hundred songs into thirty shows. The most historically important such song was "They Didn't Believe Me," interpolated into the New York City version of the British musical *The Girl from Utah* (perf. 1914). The song is universally cited as the one that established the basic character of all modern American musical-theater songs. It is more musically sophisticated than earlier American theater tunes, yet it also avoids the typical European flavor in the music of such well-schooled American operetta composers as Victor Herbert. Kern became the acknowledged father and master of a new kind of music, one that was imitated by virtually all of the great American theater composers who followed him.

After revolutionizing the musical content of individual theater songs, he proceeded to revolutionize the musical structure of entire shows. He had already been given opportunities to compose complete scores of his own. In 1911 he collaborated with Frank Tours on the music for the revue *La belle Paree* ("Beautiful Paris," in which Al Jolson made his Broadway debut). In 1912 he composed the first complete score of his own, for *The Red Petticoat* (originally called *Look Who's Here)*. But his first real success came in 1915 when he began to compose a series of history-making musicals for the little Princess Theater in New York City. In *Nobody Home* (perf. 1915) and *Very Good, Eddie* (perf. 1915) he molded the songs to fit into the story and capture its flavor to a much greater degree than was common among the popular operettas and song-and-dance musicals of the day, which often stopped the story, if any, to perform irrelevant musical numbers. Kern continued to develop the principle of integration in the subsequent Princess Theater shows *Oh, Boy!* (perf. 1917) and *Oh, Lady! Lady!* (perf. 1918). His pioneering work influenced later composers, notably Richard Rodgers, who became famous for his supreme artistry in fusing music and story in his musicals.

However, Kern also composed traditional musical comedies as well, such as *Sally* (perf. 1920), with "Look for the Silver Lining"; *Sunny* (perf. 1925), with "Who?"; *Roberta* (perf. 1933), with "Smoke Gets in Your Eyes"; and *Very Warm for May* (perf. 1939), his last stage show, with "All the Things You Are."

His most famous and important production for the theater was another progressive work: *Show Boat* (perf. 1927). Often cited as the first modern American serious musical play, *Show Boat* was perhaps the most successful and influential Broadway musical ever produced. Working with his librettist, Oscar Hammerstein II, Kern wrote songs, including the classic "Ol' Man River," that

are integral to the atmosphere, the plot, and the characterizations. Furthermore, much of the action is accompanied by incidental (background) music of great emotional and dramatic value. For example, when the character Julie appears for the second time, the accompanying music foreshadows, even in the midst of a happy scene, her coming disaster. Throughout the score, themes referring to specific characters and concepts are quoted and developed in an almost operatic fashion. *Show Boat,* in fact, became the first musical to enter the repertory of a major opera company (New York City Opera, 1954).

But Kern's happiness over the success of *Show Boat* was lessened by a disturbing development at home. Eva, for no apparent cause, had suffered a nervous breakdown while *Show Boat* was still in the planning stage. Completely withdrawn from society, she was bedridden and under the care of nurses. Her condition made Kern realize that he had not given her enough attention in the past. After completing *Show Boat,* he curbed his work so that he could devote more time to his family. As a result, he and Eva grew closer together than ever.

A few years later they were at a house party in Nantucket, Massachusetts, when Kern was awakened by the warbling of a Cape Cod sparrow. Enchanted, he awoke Eva, and they listened together. Later he wrote down the birdsong and used it as the basis for "I've Told Every Little Star," which he used in *Music in the Air* (perf. 1932).

Many of Kern's Broadway shows were made into movies, and in his late years he composed numerous songs directly for films. His sophisticated music was particularly well suited to the suave singing style of Fred Astaire, as in the movies *Swing Time* (1936) and *You Were Never Lovelier* (1942). Among the highlights of his original film work are "The Way You Look Tonight" (*Swing Time), "The Last Time I Saw Paris" (Lady, Be Good,* 1941), and "Long Ago and Far Away" (*Cover Girl,* 1944).

On November 5, 1945, Kern suffered a cerebral hemorrhage. He was placed under an oxygen tent in a private room of a New York City hospital, and nearby rooms were given to Eva, Betty, and his lyricist-friends Oscar Hammerstein II and Dorothy Fields. His condition slowly deteriorated over the next week, and he lapsed into a coma. On November 11 Hammerstein sat down for a vigil at the composer's bedside. Remembering that Kern had a special fondness for "I've Told Every Little Star," Hammerstein lifted the oxygen tent and softly sang the song into the patient's ear. When he finished, he saw that Kern had died.

Kern is regarded by many as the greatest pure melodist in the history of American popular music. His elegant melodies are often characterized by a held note followed by a small group of quick notes (as in "Who?") or by subtle changes in the rhythm (as in "Look for the Silver Lining"). He was also one of the most prolific composers, having written over one thousand songs.

Though Kern was the first major American theater composer to turn away from European operetta, and though he adopted some elements of jazz in the 1920s, his graceful music seldom showed the raw emotions or swinging qualities found in the works of his younger American colleagues, such as George Gershwin, Richard Rodgers, and Harold Arlen. Thus, with respect to his musical style, Kern is properly regarded as a transitional figure.

But with respect to his role in creating the modern American musical play, Kern stands alone. By integrating the technical details and emotional flavor of his music with the demands of plot development and character motivation, he earned his place in history as the father of modern American theater music.

Selected works:

Stage

The Red Petticoat (lyrics, P. West; perf. 1912)
Nobody Home (lyrics, S. Greene, H. Reynolds [pseudonym of M. E. Rourke], H. B. Smith; perf. 1915)
Very Good, Eddie (lyrics, S. Greene; perf. 1915)
Oh, Boy! (lyrics, P. G. Wodehouse; perf. 1917), including:
  "Till the Clouds Roll By"
Leave It to Jane (lyrics, P. G. Wodehouse; perf. 1917), including:
  "The Siren's Song"
Oh, Lady! Lady! (lyrics, P. G. Wodehouse; perf. 1918)
Sally (lyrics, mostly C. Grey; perf. 1920), including:
  "Look for the Silver Lining" (lyrics, B. G. De Sylva; originally for Kern's stage show *Zip Goes a Million,* which folded in December 1919 before reaching New York City)
Sunny (lyrics, O. Hammerstein II, O. Harbach; perf. 1925), including:
  "Who?"
Show Boat (lyrics, O. Hammerstein II; perf. 1927), including:
  "Bill" (lyrics, P. G. Wodehouse; previously dropped from Kern's *Oh, Lady! Lady!,* perf. 1918)
  "Can't Help Lovin' Dat Man"
  "Make Believe"
  "Ol' Man River"
  "Why Do I Love You?"
Sweet Adeline (lyrics, O. Hammerstein II; perf. 1929), including:
  "Don't Ever Leave Me"
  "Here Am I"
  "Why Was I Born?"
The Cat and the Fiddle (lyrics, O. Harbach; perf. 1931), including:
  "The Night Was Made for Love"
  "She Didn't Say 'Yes' "
Music in the Air (lyrics, O. Hammerstein II; perf. 1932), including:
  "I've Told Every Little Star"
  "The Song Is You"
Roberta (lyrics, O. Harbach; perf. 1933), including:
  "Smoke Gets in Your Eyes"
Very Warm for May (lyrics, O. Hammerstein II; perf. 1939), including:
  "All the Things You Are"

Films
(song scores)

Swing Time (lyrics, D. Fields; 1936), including:
  "A Fine Romance"
  "The Way You Look Tonight"
High, Wide, and Handsome (lyrics, O. Hammerstein II; 1937)
One Night in the Tropics (lyrics, D. Fields; 1940)
You Were Never Lovelier (lyrics, J. Mercer; 1942), including:
  "Dearly Beloved"
  "I'm Old-fashioned"
  "You Were Never Lovelier"
Cover Girl (lyrics, I. Gershwin; 1944), including:
  "Long Ago and Far Away"
Can't Help Singing (lyrics, E. Y. Harburg; 1944)
Centennial Summer (lyrics, mostly L. Robin; 1946)

Songs
(other than those for the above shows and films)

"How'd You Like to Spoon with Me?" (lyrics, E. Laska; interpolated into the stage show *The Earl and the Girl,* perf. 1905)
"I Just Couldn't Do without You" (lyrics, P. West; interpolated into the stage show *The White Chrysanthemum,* perf. 1907)
"You're Here and I'm Here" (lyrics, H. B. Smith; written for *The Laughing Husband,* perf. 1914, but with that show's failure the song was switched to *The Marriage Market,* perf. 1913, with which the song is generally associated)
"They Didn't Believe Me" (lyrics, H. Reynolds [pseudonym of M. E. Rourke]; interpolated into the stage show *The Girl from Utah,* perf. 1914)
"The Last Time I Saw Paris" (lyrics, O. Hammerstein II; interpolated into the film *Lady, Be Good,* 1941)

Alexander Kipnis

Alexander Kipnis as Sarastro
in Mozart's *Die Zauberflöte*

Alexander Kipnis as Rocco
in Beethoven's *Fidelio*

Alexander Kipnis
Famed Bass
(1891-1978)

Alexander Kipnis, bass, was born in Zhitomir, the Ukraine (now in the Soviet Union), on February 13, 1891. His earliest music lessons were in trombone and double bass, and he graduated from the Warsaw Conservatory in 1912 with a major in conducting. Soon afterward he spent a tour of duty in the Russian army as a bandmaster.

Moving to Berlin, he studied singing under Ernst Grenzebach at the Klindworth-Scharwenka Conservatory. When World War I broke out, Kipnis was interned in Berlin as an enemy (Russian) alien. Soon released, he began his opera career in wartime Hamburg, later moving to Wiesbaden, where he sang for several years. Throughout the 1920s and into the early 1930s he sang opera regularly in Berlin.

Meanwhile, Kipnis also established himself at opera houses around the world, notably with the Chicago Civic Opera (1923-32). In the early 1930s he left Nazi Germany, settled in the United States, and became a naturalized American citizen. He then continued the worldwide recital tours that he had begun while living in Europe, and he performed with opera companies in San Francisco and elsewhere, including the Metropolitan Opera in New York City, where he closed his opera career in 1946. Thereafter he taught singing both privately and at various institutions, including the Juilliard School of Music in New York City and the Berkshire Music Center at Tanglewood, near Lenox, Massachusetts.

Kipnis was widely regarded as one of the great singers of the German opera repertory. His outstanding roles included Baron Ochs in Richard Strauss's *Der Rosenkavalier* ("The Knight of the Rose"), Rocco in Beethoven's *Fidelio,* and Sarastro in Mozart's *Die Zauberflöte* ("The Magic Flute"). But he was also a skilled interpreter of French, Italian, and Russian roles, particularly the lead in Mussorgsky's *Boris Godunov.* His recital repertory included lieder by Brahms, Schubert, Richard Strauss, and Hugo Wolf. Kipnis had a remarkable bass voice, renowned for its refinement, flexibility, wide range, and variety of tone color.

In 1925 Kipnis married Mildred Levy, daughter of the American concert pianist Heniot Levy. They had one child, Igor, who became one of the world's premier harpsichordists.

Alexander Kipnis died in Westport, Connecticut, on May 14, 1978.

**Alexander Kipnis as Baron Ochs in
Richard Strauss's *Der Rosenkavalier***

Igor Kipnis
Famed Harpsichordist
(1930-   )

Igor Kipnis, harpsichordist, was born in Berlin, Germany, on September 27, 1930. His father was the great bass Alexander Kipnis. After moving to the United States when he was a small child, Igor Kipnis took piano lessons from his materal grandfather, the concert pianist Heniot Levy. He then attended the Westport School of Music in Connecticut (1941-48), meanwhile often serving as piano accompanist for his father's pupils.

At Harvard University (1948-52) Randall Thompson's course on Handel induced young Kipnis to switch to the harpsichord. Later he was also influenced by the Boston organist and harpsichordist Melville Smith and by the British musicologist and harpsichordist Thurston Dart. However, Kipnis received only a few formal lessons on his new instrument, and those were given by Fernando Valenti.

After graduating from Harvard (B.A., 1952) Kipnis spent two years in the army. During that time, in 1953, he married Judith Robison, with whom he had a son, Jeremy. Returning to civilian life, he worked in New York City as a book salesman, a music director for a radio station, and an editorial adviser for Westminster Records.

In 1959 he made his debut as a professional harpsichordist, a radio performance on station WNYC in New York City. His recital debut, also in New York City, came in 1962.

Soon he began to perform in recital and as soloist with orchestras throughout the United States and Canada, followed by his initial appearances in Europe (1967), South America (1968), Israel (1969), Australia (1971), and the Soviet Union (1983). Besides playing the harpsichord, he has performed on the piano, the fortepiano (an eighteenth-century piano), and the clavichord.

Kipnis has a large, varied repertory, including music from every national school. Contemporary harpsichord music has been written for him by George Rochberg (Nach Bach ["After Bach"], premiered by Kipnis in 1967) and other major composers.

In his playing he stresses style and expression, though he possesses an outstanding technique as well. His performances of seventeenth- and eighteenth-century music are noted for their bold, imaginative ornamentation.

Kipnis has also participated in a wide variety of other music activities. He taught baroque performance practices at the Berkshire Music Center at Tanglewood, near Lenox, Massachusetts (summers, 1964-67), and served as associate professor of fine arts at Fairfield University in Connecticut (1971-75), where he later stayed as artist-in-residence (1975-77). Since 1974 he has presented an annual summer harpsichord workshop for the Festival Music Society of the Early Music Institute in Indianapolis, in addition to giving master classes at such institutions as Westminster Choir College, the Peabody Institute, and the Royal Northern College of Music in Manchester, England, where he was appointed visiting tutor in harpsichord and baroque music studies in 1982.

Kipnis is one of the artistic directors of the Connecticut Early Music Festival. (He makes his home in Redding, Connecticut.) A noted lecturer, critic, and writer for music periodicals, he also frequently appears on radio and TV. His work as editor includes *A First Harpsichord Book* (1970) and performing editions of various baroque works.

Otto Klemperer

Courageous Conductor
(1885-1973)

Otto Klemperer overcame terrible accidents and severe illnesses to become one of the great twentieth-century conductors. He was born in Breslau, Silesia (now Wrocław, Poland), on May 14, 1885. His father was a talented amateur singer, and his mother was a fine amateur pianist. When Otto was four, the family moved to Hamburg, where his mother soon began to give him piano lessons.

His formal study of music took place at the Hoch Conservatory in Frankfort on the Main (1901-1902), the Klindworth-Scharwenka Conservatory in Berlin (1902-1905), and the Stern Conservatory in Berlin (1905-1906). Klemperer's principal teachers were James Kwast (piano), Ivan Knorr (theory), Philipp Scharwenka (theory), and Hans Pfitzner (composition and conducting).

While still a student, Klemperer began his professional career by working as a pianist and piano accompanist. But his nervousness onstage was so great that he decided to change to conducting (where he could turn his back to the audience and be supported by the other performers).

In 1905 he assisted in a Berlin performance of Gustav Mahler's *Second Symphony,* conducting a special off-stage ensemble while Oskar Fried led the principal group onstage. The composer himself attended the concert and expressed pleasure with Klemperer's efforts.

The following year, as Fried's assistant at the New Theater in Berlin, Klemperer got his first chance to conduct before an audience when Fried, after arguing with a soprano, left his post. Conducting Offenbach's *Orphée aux enfers* ("Orpheus in the Underworld"), Klemperer made his formal debut in 1906, while still a student at the Stern Conservatory.

In 1907 Klemperer assisted Mahler himself in a performance of the latter's *Third Symphony* in Berlin. Witnessing the composer's rehearsals had an overwhelming impact on the aspiring conductor, and Mahler remained the dominant influence throughout Klemperer's life. Mahler, for his part, was impressed with Klemperer, especially after the latter played his own piano reduction of Mahler's *Second Symphony* for the composer's approval.

Later in 1907, with Mahler's written recommendation (a prized possession all of Klemperer's life), the young man obtained a post as assistant conductor at the German Opera House in Prague, where he remained till 1910. He then served as assistant conductor at the Hamburg Opera (1910-12), chief conductor at the Barmen Opera (1913-14), deputy music director (under Pfitzner) of the Strasbourg Opera (1914-17), and full music direc-

tor of the opera in Cologne (1917-24), where he also held his first symphony concerts.

In June 1919 Klemperer married Johanna Geissler, a soprano at the Cologne Opera. Having been converted just three months earlier to Roman Catholicism (on his own initiative, not simply for career advancement), Klemperer induced Johanna, a Lutheran, to formally adopt the Roman Catholic faith on the day of their wedding, which, however, was a civil ceremony. Klemperer's reserve was colorfully contrasted by Johanna's fiery temper and bohemian character; for example, she was surprised that he made no attempt to sleep with her before their marriage. She already had a daughter, Carla, and the Klemperers had two children of their own: Werner (an actor, notably in TV's *Hogan's Heroes)* and Lotte.

His fame spread rapidly throughout the 1920s, especially as music director of the Wiesbaden Opera (1924-27). He gained renown as one of the leading young German conductors of contemporary music and of less overtly emotional interpretations of the classics than was common among older conductors. With his new-age image, he was a natural choice in 1927 to be named director of a new branch of the Berlin State Opera, where his specific task would be to perform new and recent works, as well as older works in a nontraditional manner. The new branch was popularly called the Kroll Opera, after the Kroll Theater, in which the performances took place.

Klemperer boldly led the Kroll Opera in a great many exciting productions of contemporary dramatic works, such as Hindemith's *Cardillac,* Janáček's *Z mrtvého domu* ("From the House of the Dead"), Schoenberg's *Erwartung* ("Expectation"), and Stravinsky's *Oedipus rex* ("Oedipus the King"). He also conducted new and recent orchestral works in concerts at the theater. Economic distress and pressure from reactionaries caused the government to shut down the Kroll Opera in 1931.

Klemperer remained with the parent organization, the Berlin State Opera, till 1933. In that year he was rehearsing in Leipzig for a guest-conducting appearance at the Gewandhaus when he happened to lean back against the railing of the podium. The railing gave way (Klemperer being a large man, about 6'5" tall), and he fell several feet, striking his head on the floor. He received a severe concussion, was unconscious for hours, and was in bed for two days. Klemperer remained ill for several weeks; in fact, he never fully recovered, being troubled for the rest of his life with severe headaches and fainting spells.

In 1933 the Nazis came to power in Germany, and Klemperer, like others of Jewish birth, was attacked verbally by the press and physically by storm troopers. He fled to Vienna, to Switzerland, and then to the United States, where he served as principal conductor of the Los Angeles Philharmonic Orchestra (1933-39). With that ensemble he conducted the world premieres of Schoenberg's *Suite* for string orchestra in 1935, Joseph Achron's *Second Violin Concerto* in 1936, Toch's *Pinocchio* in 1936, and Bloch's *Voice in the Wilderness* in 1937.

Otto Klemperer

In 1939 Klemperer was subjected to another trauma: an operation, performed in Boston, to remove a brain tumor (unrelated to his 1933 fall). In the aftermath, his right side was paralyzed, and his career seemed to be over. But Klemperer fought back, performing painful exercises that brought life back into his limbs.

Managers and orchestras, however, hesitated to retain his services. Determined to resume his career, Klemperer, in 1940, began to conduct semiprofessional orchestras in the New York City area to prove that he could still perform. In the spring of 1941 he spent his savings to engage a symphony orchestra in a concert at Carnegie Hall. Though some critics praised his work as being more profound than his earlier conducting, no professional group would hire him.

Klemperer went into a state of deep mental depression, but eventually he pulled himself out of it and prepared for the next stage in his career. In 1946, after World War II had ended and cultural opportunities had begun to expand around the world, Klemperer returned to Europe, where he found guest-conducting assignments in Stockholm, Rome, and elsewhere.

In 1947 he was appointed music director of the Budapest Opera. A Budapest critic observed that Klemperer's face was "transformed" by paralysis and pain; yet "the tortured mouth breaks into a smile and the warm streams of music flow around the tragic profile."

Klemperer left Budapest in 1950 because of the Communist regime's restrictive policies regarding music. Later that year he went on a conducting tour of Australia. In 1951 he made his first guest-conducting appearance with the Philharmonia Orchestra of London. Finally the critics and the public were ready to accept him once again as a major conductor of international stature.

But it was not to be. In October 1951, having just arrived in Montreal for a conducting assignment, he fell down a flight of stairs in the airport and broke one of his hips. He spent the next year in a wheelchair, and his physicians told him that he would never again conduct.

Klemperer, however, did not believe it. He now began to use crutches to get to the podium, where he sat while conducting. (Later he would periodically be able to conduct while standing.)

In 1954 he conducted concerts and made recordings with the London Philharmonia Orchestra. Impressed, the management appointed him principal conductor of the orchestra in 1955.

However, in 1958 he was again victimized, this time by fire. Suffering third-degree burns in an accident, he was unable to work for a whole year. But Klemperer, as usual, recuperated, and in 1959 the officials of the London Philharmonia showed their faith in him by making his engagement as principal conductor a lifetime appointment. He also began to conduct opera at London's Covent Garden.

At the time of his London appointment in 1955, the seventy-year-old Klemperer entered the culminating phase in his remarkable career. Having in his late years turned increasingly to the classics, he came to be widely accepted during his London period as the world's most authoritative interpreter of the Austro-German repertory from Haydn to Mahler. He was praised for his power and intensity, his sense of heroic dimensions, and his grasp of musical architecture. Those qualities, of course, made him especially effective with Beethoven. But Klemperer's most important achievement was to reveal the full extent of his friend Mahler's genius by saving it from the earlier sentimental style of interpretation that had become prevalent. Klemperer celebrated his eighty-fifth birthday in May 1970 by leading a performance of Mahler's *Das Lied von der Erde* ("The Song of the Earth") with the New Philharmonia Orchestra (the ensemble having changed its name in 1964) in London. Reviewing that performance, a critic from the *Evening Standard* called Klemperer "the last of the titans."

Klemperer, having studied composition with Schoenberg in the mid-1930s when both men were in Los Angeles, wrote many works of his own, generally in a post-Mahlerian style. Among them were six symphonies, nine string quartets, and about one hundred songs. However, Klemperer himself destroyed much of his music. He also wrote his memoirs, *Minor Recollections* (1964).

In 1967 Klemperer left the Roman Catholic church and informally reverted to Judaism. In 1970 he went to Israel and asked for immigrant status. The government responded by granting him Israeli citizenship. From then on he divided his time between Israel and his home in Zurich, Switzerland, where he was attended to by his devoted daughter, Lotte (his wife having died in 1956). In 1972 he formally retired.

Klemperer died in his sleep at his Zurich home on July 6, 1973, and was buried in the city's Jewish cemetery.

Erich Wolfgang Korngold
One of the Last Great
Romantic Composers
(1897-1957)

Erich Wolfgang Korngold, composer, was born in Brünn, Moravia (now Brno, Czechoslovakia), on May 29, 1897. He was taught the fundamentals of music by his father, Julius Korngold, an eminent music critic, who moved his family to Vienna in 1901. A genuine child prodigy, young Korngold showed a gift for composition at the age of nine. At ten he played his cantata *Gold* (1907) on the piano for Gustav Mahler, who proclaimed the youngster a genius and recommended that he be sent for advanced study to the Austrian composer Alexander von Zemlinsky. Zemlinsky became Korngold's most influential teacher.

Korngold first attracted major attention when the public became aware of his *Piano Trio* (1909) and his pantomime *Der Schneemann* ("The Snowman," orchestrated by Zemlinsky), the latter of which caused a sensation when it was premiered at the Vienna Opera in 1910. Rumors flew that the works must have been ghostcomposed by some mature master—perhaps even Richard Strauss—not by a preteenager! However, Korngold

soon proved that his talent was genuine when he followed with the remarkable *Second Piano Sonata* (1910), which so impressed the great pianist Artur Schnabel that he played it all over Europe.

Already gaining a significant reputation, the fourteen-year-old Korngold was commissioned by Arthur Nikisch, director of the Gewandhaus Concerts in Leipzig, to compose an orchestral overture. The resulting work was the *Schauspiel Ouvertüre* ("Spectacle Overture," 1911), soon followed by his second orchestral composition, the *Sinfonietta* (1912). The fact that such works had been written by a mere adolescent filled Richard Strauss, as Strauss himself good-naturedly admitted, with "awe and fear." And Korngold's opera *Violanta* (perf. 1916) greatly impressed Puccini.

Korngold was widely said to resemble the young Mozart in precociousness, a comparison that had been hoped for by Julius Korngold when he gave his son the middle name Wolfgang (one of Mozart's given names). Of course, Korngold's gifts in no way matched Mozart's,

Erich Wolfgang Korngold

In 1934 the theatrical producer-director Max Reinhardt took Korngold to the Hollywood section of Los Angeles, California, to work on a film version of Shakespeare's *A Midsummer Night's Dream* (1935), for which Korngold arranged Felix Mendelssohn's incidental music to the play. Afterward Korngold stayed in Hollywood to create some of the most memorable of all film scores. His lush romantic style, superior craftsmanship, and dramatic flair (carried over from his operas) set him far above the other movie composers of his time and most of those who have followed. He scored each film not with bland background music but with a suitelike series of carefully constructed episodes. Suites arranged from his film scores attained independent popularity through recordings.

Korngold won special renown for his ability to compose colorful, exciting music for costume dramas and adventure stories, such as *Captain Blood* (1935), *Anthony Adverse (1936), The Adventures of Robin Hood* (1938), and *The Private Lives of Elizabeth and Essex* (1939). Among his other film scores were those for *Kings Row* (1942), *Between Two Worlds* (1944), *Of Human Bondage* (1946), and *Escape Me Never* (1947).

As the Nazi regime became more deeply entrenched in Europe and more openly barbaric in its designs, Korngold accommodated himself to the fact that he would have to stay in the United States; he became a naturalized American citizen in 1943. Of course, his film work provided him with a considerable income and made his new life comfortable. But he could not get used to the modern world's, especially the New World's, cultural scheme, in which movies dominated, while concerts and operas served a secondary role. He fondly remembered the genuine entertainment that he and others had derived from the exciting and enriching new music in early twentieth-century Vienna.

Consequently, after World War II, he nostalgically returned to composing absolute music. His most notable late works were the *Violin Concerto* (1945, commissioned by Jascha Heifetz), the *Cello Concerto* (1946), the *Symphonic Serenade* for string orchestra (perf. 1947), and the *Symphony in F-sharp Major* (1952).

However, during Korngold's last years and for some time after his death, his serious works suffered neglect and savage criticism, partly because his conservative style was out of favor and partly because his association with commercial movies caused many to dismiss him without a fair hearing. He died in Los Angeles, California, on November 29, 1957, widely regarded as a naturally gifted composer who never fulfilled his promise.

But in 1975 the New York City Opera revived Korngold's *Die tote Stadt* to capacity houses. And recordings of that work and the *Symphony in F-sharp Major* were received with great enthusiasm. His solid tonality, rich late-romantic harmony, sensuous orchestration, and eloquent melodies had come to be appreciated in their true light: the product of a gifted mind that created not for the sake of musical analysis but for the sake of musical expression. In that sense, Korngold *did* fulfill his promise.

but the youngster clearly showed exceptional talent and promise.

By 1920 Korngold had received many important public performances and had often appeared as conductor or pianist in his own works. His early fame reached its peak with the presentation of his opera *Die tote Stadt* ("The Dead City," perf. 1920), the libretto of which had been prepared by Korngold and his father (both under the pseudonym Paul Schott). It was produced to great acclaim throughout Europe and, in 1921, at the Metropolitan Opera House in New York City.

In 1924 Korngold married Luise von Sonnenthal, a granddaughter of the famous Viennese actor Adolf von Sonnenthal. They had two children: Ernest and George.

One of Korngold's most significant works of the 1920s was his *Piano Concerto for the Left Hand* (perf. 1923), commissioned by the one-armed pianist Paul Wittgenstein. Another composition that received great attention was his *First String Quartet* (perf. 1924).

By the end of the 1920s Korngold had proven himself to be one of the last great composers of the nineteenth-century Austro-German romantic tradition. He refused to make concessions to the fashionable styles of the modernists.

Stage

Der Schneemann (pantomime, perf. 1910)
Violanta (opera; libretto, H. Muller; perf. 1916)
Die tote Stadt (opera; libretto, P. Schott [pseudonym of E. W. and J. Korngold], after G. Rodenbach; perf. 1920)

Films
(background scores)

Captain Blood (1935)
Anthony Adverse (1936)
The Green Pastures (1936)
Another Dawn (1937)
The Prince and the Pauper (1937)
The Adventures of Robin Hood (1938)
Juarez (1939)
The Private Lives of Elizabeth and Essex (1939)
The Sea Hawk (1940)
The Sea Wolf (1941)
Kings Row (1942)
The Constant Nymph (1943)
Between Two Worlds (1944)

Deception (1946)
Of Human Bondage (1946)
Escape Me Never (1947)

Orchestral

Schauspiel Ouvertüre (1911)
Sinfonietta (1912)
Piano Concerto for the Left Hand (perf. 1923)
Violin Concerto (1945)
Cello Concerto (1946)
Symphonic Serenade (string orchestra, perf. 1947)
Symphony in F-sharp Major (1952)

Chamber

Piano Trio (1909)
String Sextet (1917)
First String Quartet (perf. 1924)
Second String Quartet (1935)

Piano

Second Piano Sonata (1910)
Third Piano Sonata (1931)

Andre Kostelanetz
Popularizer of Classical Music
(1901-1980)

Andre Kostelanetz, conductor, was born in Saint Petersburg, Russia (now Leningrad, the Soviet Union), on December 22, 1901. At the age of five he contracted scarlatina, and a young woman was brought into the house to care for him. One day, while he was lying in bed, he heard the nurse playing a Schubert impromptu on the piano. It was at that moment (partly because he had a crush on the nurse) that he first felt the desire to make music himself. Fortunately his parents were devotees of classical music (his father being an opera lover and his mother being an amateur pianist), and they often took him to operas and ballets. At the age of six he began to receive piano lessons from local teachers.

During the early (1917-18) stages of the Russian Revolution, Andre became separated from his parents and siblings. While living in Kislovodsk in 1918, Andre was out on an errand when he got detained by one of the warring factions. (He never knew if they were Reds or Whites.) Meanwhile, the rest of his family had escaped to Finland. Released unharmed, Andre soon obtained his first music job: vocal coach and assistant conductor of a newly formed opera company in Kislovodsk.

In 1919 he returned to his birthplace (which had been renamed Petrograd in 1914 and would become Leningrad in 1924). In 1920 he entered the city's music conservatory, where his most memorable lessons were in composition with Vasili Kalafati. At the same time, he became an accompanist-coach for the nearby Mariinsky Opera. One wintry day in January 1922 he went to the opera house and found a notice posted on the door: Opera Closed for Lack of Fuel. Disgusted, young Kostelanetz decided to leave Russia, whatever the risk.

In the newly formed Soviet Union, illegal emigration

Andre Kostelanetz

plied only with a strange look of misunderstanding. Years later Kostelanetz discovered that the perplexed student had been Richard Rodgers.

After his arrival in America, Kostelanetz worked for several years as an accompanist and vocal coach. In 1925 he met George Gershwin, whose compositions further inspired the Russian's growing interest in American popular music. Soon afterward Kostelanetz met Eugene Ormandy, conductor of the Capitol Theater Orchestra in New York City, from whom he took informal conducting lessons.

In 1930 he made the biggest leap of his career when he was named conductor of the Columbia Broadcasting System (CBS) Orchestra. Radio was still in its early, experimental stages; and Kostelanetz, deeply committed to the use of the medium to make good music available to millions of new listeners, pioneered methods of reaching the masses. His shows experimented with the use of new microphone techniques and other technical aspects of broadcasting. But he became best known for his programming innovations.

His first, and most controversial, procedure was to trim down many beloved classics so that they would fit into his limited air time. Many people objected to his tampering with such works. But in support of Kostelanetz's stated objective of popularizing the classics among the masses even if the works had to be shortened, the composer-author Deems Taylor said, "Better some than none." Kostelanetz also programmed semiclassical works, orchestrations of piano pieces, and, beginning in 1933, orchestral arrangements of tunes by such American popular-song composers as Jerome Kern, Cole Porter, and Richard Rodgers.

Toward the end of 1934 Kostelanetz auditioned the Metropolitan Opera star Lily Pons as a possible performer on his radio show. Reluctantly, he told her the truth: that her delicate coloratura soprano voice had deteriorated from abuse and that she needed rest and further study. With a remarkably mature attitude, Pons agreed. During the subsequent year that she devoted to recapturing her voice, Kostelanetz visited her to keep her spirits up. "By the end of that time," Kostelanetz later recalled, "two things were clear: her voice was on its way back to its full glory, and we were in love with each other."

Kostelanetz courted Pons for several years. When she went to the Hollywood section of Los Angeles, California, to appear in the film *I Dream Too Much* (1935), he made frequent flights from New York to California so that he could help her record the arias that she sang for the movie's soundtrack. She stayed in Hollywood for further film work, and he continued to fly out to visit her. During a two-year period he flew across the country virtually every week, in 1936 alone traveling 126,000 miles through the air.

Kostelanetz and Pons were married in 1938. They became one of the leading attractions in show business, and during World War II they were dubbed the First Family of Music when they made numerous joint appearances for the war effort, including overseas tours for the United Service Organizations (USO) in 1944.

(and no other kind was available) was a capital crime. Nevertheless, one dark night Kostelanetz, carrying his few worldly possessions in a single burlap bag, slipped into Poland.

In a Warsaw shoe store he happened to hear the shopkeeper playing a new, fascinating kind of music on a record player. Kostelanetz asked what it was. " 'Alexander's Ragtime Band,' " the man replied in English, "by Irving Berlin." It was a moment of musical revelation that Kostelanetz never forgot.

In September 1922 he arrived in New York City, where the other members of his family had settled. In 1928 he became a naturalized American citizen.

To learn English terminology for his profession, Kostelanetz attended a class in advanced music taught by Percy Goetschius at the Institute of Musical Art (later part of the Juilliard School of Music). One day after class he tried to test his new language skills by speaking in English to a nearby student. The other young man re-

In the 1940s Kostelanetz pulled away from broadcasting and turned toward recordings and live concerts, leading his own orchestra and guest-conducting elsewhere. One of his roles that he most treasured was that of being a catalyst for new works by major American composers, and he was proud of the wide variety of orchestral pieces that he had commissioned. He also thoroughly enjoyed conducting the world premieres of those works, including Aaron Copland's *Lincoln Portrait* with the Cincinnati Symphony Orchestra in 1942, Paul Creston's *Frontiers* with the Toronto Symphony Orchestra in 1943, Ezra Laderman's *Magic Prison* with the New York Philharmonic in 1967, and William Schuman's *Amaryllis* with the Philadelphia Orchestra in 1976.

In 1953 Kostelanetz established an important association with the New York Philharmonic, conducting a series of nonsubscription concerts. In 1963 he became principal conductor of the Philharmonic's spring concerts at Lincoln Center, a series called the Promenades.

Kostelanetz and Pons divorced in 1958, partly because their careers had pulled them apart and partly because she wanted to retire to southern California, while he wanted to stay active in New York City and elsewhere. Nevertheless, they remained close friends.

In 1960 he married Sara Gene Orcutt, a young medical technician and music lover. The marriage appeared to be successful, but one day ten years later she left and never returned. Kostelanetz had no children in either marriage.

Through the 1970s he continued to guest-conduct many of the world's major orchestras. One of his most memorable appearances was on an August evening in 1979 when a live audience of about 250,000 people heard him conduct the New York Philharmonic in Central Park.

While on a brief vacation in Port-au-Prince, Haiti, before a scheduled guest appearance in San Francisco, Kostelanetz died of a heart attack, after a bout with pneumonia, on January 13, 1980. He left behind an incomplete autobiography, which was finished by Gloria Hammond, his friend and collaborator, and published as *Echoes: Memoirs of Andre Kostelanetz* (1981).

Serge Koussevitzky
Conductor of New Music
(1874-1951)

Serge Koussevitzky was a great conductor who, by championing the works of modern composers, had a tremendous impact on twentieth-century music. He was born in Vyshni Volochek, near Tver (now Kalinin), Russia, on July 26, 1874.

Coming from a musical family, he received early piano lessons from his mother, while his father, a violin teacher and klezmer (Jewish instrumentalist who made a precarious living by playing at weddings, bar mitzvahs, and so on), provided him with basic information about stringed instruments. Serge also took lessons on various instruments, principally the cello, from a number of local musicians. Out of the same background an older brother, Adolf, developed a moderately successful career as a music teacher and conductor. Fabien Sevitzky (originally Fabien Koussevitzky), a well-known double-bass player and conductor, was Serge's nephew.

At fourteen Serge entered the Moscow Philharmonic Music School, choosing the double bass as his instrument because it was one of the few instruments, and the closest to the cello, for which scholarships were still available. His double-bass teacher was Joseph Rambousek.

In 1894 young Koussevitzky joined the double-bass section of the Bolshoi Theater Orchestra, and in 1896 he began to give solo recitals. He also wrote several works to supplement the small repertory for his instrument. Koussevitzky became one of the greatest double-bass virtuosos of his time, renowned for both his dexterity and his rich tone.

By 1902—the exact year is uncertain—Koussevitzky had married the dancer Nadezhda Galat, a member of the Bolshoi ballet corps. But while performing in Moscow drawing rooms, he met Natalya Ushkov, daughter of a

Serge Koussevitzky

as Prokofiev, Rachmaninoff, Scriabin, and Stravinsky. He also formed his own orchestra to propagate the music that he published or admired. He conducted, for example, the world premiere of Scriabin's *Prometheus* in 1911. In 1910, 1912, and 1914, he took his orchestra on riverboat concert tours of cities along the Volga River.

After the Russian Revolution of 1917, Koussevitzky was appointed director of the State Symphony (formerly Imperial) Orchestra. But life was miserable because his Russian holdings were confiscated and because he faced a tremendous amount of bureaucratic red tape in the pursuit of his art. In 1920, after getting official permission to fulfill a temporary conducting assignment in Europe, he and his wife left Russia with only the possessions that they could carry. They never returned.

The Koussevitzkys still had holdings outside the Soviet Union, so that their financial transition to a new life was fairly smooth. Settling near Paris, he created a new orchestra for his concerts and continued to be active as a publisher. He not only introduced the Parisians to contemporary Russian music but also promoted new works by French composers. Among his world premieres in France during this period, 1920-24, was that of Ravel's now famous orchestral transcription (commissioned by Koussevitzky) of Mussorgsky's piano work *Pictures at an Exhibition.*

In 1924 Koussevitzky moved to America as the newly appointed conductor of the Boston Symphony Orchestra, where he was to remain for the next twenty-five years. He overhauled the troubled orchestra and turned it into one of the great virtuoso ensembles in the world.

Koussevitzky had an enormous influence on cultivated music in America, and he was unsurpassed by any conductor in his influence specifically on new American music. As he had previously identified himself with living Russian and French composers, so he now enthusiastically championed contemporary American composers, such as Samuel Barber, Aaron Copland, George Gershwin, Roy Harris, Walter Piston, William Schuman, and Roger Sessions. Koussevitzky commissioned dozens of important new works and led the Boston Symphony Orchestra in their world premieres. Besides giving such premieres, he regularly conducted other compositions by contemporary Americans and Europeans.

To mark the fiftieth anniversary of the Boston Symphony Orchestra in 1931, Koussevitzky commissioned new works by the Americans Copland and Gershwin, the Europeans Hindemith and Ravel, and others. Among the commissioned works was Stravinsky's *Symphony of Psalms,* one of the great musical monuments of the twentieth century.

In the mid-1930s Koussevitzky began to conduct the Boston Symphony Orchestra at the annual summer Berkshire Music Festival. In 1938 the festival found its permanent home on the grounds of the former Tanglewood estate near Lenox, Massachusetts. In 1940 he established the Berkshire Music Center there as a summer school for music instruction and concerts. Koussevitzky directed the school and taught conducting (his pupils including Leonard Bernstein and Lukas Foss) till his death.

wealthy tea merchant. In 1905 he divorced his first wife and married Natalya, with whom he soon settled in Berlin, Germany.

Koussevitzky continued to give double-bass recitals, but simultaneously he began to prepare for a conducting career. In Germany he carefully observed the methods of professional conductors, such as Gustav Mahler, Felix Mottl, Richard Strauss, Felix Weingartner, and particularly Arthur Nikisch. With money from his wife's family, Koussevitzky engaged the student orchestra at the Berlin Academy of Music as, in effect, a rehearsal instrument. In early 1908 he made his conducting debut, presenting an all-Russian program with the Berlin Philharmonic Orchestra. Later that year he began his long association as guest conductor with the London Philharmonic Orchestra.

Returning to his homeland, Koussevitzky quickly became an important influence in the musical taste of the Russian public. In 1909, with Ushkov money, he founded a publishing house (known in the West as Editions russes de musique [Russian Editions of Music]) and issued works by such major contemporary Russian composers

Serge Koussevitzky conducting the Boston Symphony

In 1941 Koussevitzky became an American citizen. The following year his wife, Natalya, died. Soon afterward he set up the Koussevitzky Music Foundation as a permanent memorial to her, its funds to be used primarily for commissioning new works by composers of all nationalities. Among the early compositions thus encouraged into existence were Béla Bartók's *Concerto for Orchestra* (1943), Benjamin Britten's opera *Peter Grimes* (1945), Copland's *Third Symphony* (1946), Piston's *Third Symphony* (1947), and Olivier Messiaen's *Turangalîla* ("Love Song") *Symphony* (1948).

In his personal life Koussevitzky could be kind and warm. He developed, for example, a fatherly closeness with Leonard Bernstein that the latter still refers to with affection and gratitude.

As a conductor, however, Koussevitzky was egocentric and dictatorial, given to angry outbursts of verbal abuse toward his players during rehearsals. Yet he instilled into his orchestras a sense of discipline and an attention to detail that produced performances known for their colorful phrasing and high emotional intensity. His conductorial gifts were well suited to the twentieth-century works that he championed, but he seemed to be less comfortable with the eighteenth- and nineteenth-century standards.

In 1947 Koussevitzky married Olga Naoumoff, niece of his second wife, Natalya. Olga had lived with the Koussevitzkys since 1924.

In 1949 Koussevitzky retired from the Boston Symphony Orchestra. The following year he was persuaded by Leonard Bernstein to go to Israel and conduct a series of concerts with the Israel Philharmonic Orchestra. Assisted by Bernstein, Koussevitzky also directed the orchestra's first American tour (early 1951).

Koussevitzky died in Boston, Massachusetts, on June 4, 1951. He had donated his large library of music scores to the Hebrew University in Jerusalem, where a Koussevitzky Collection was established.

Wanda Landowska
Leader of the Harpsichord Revival
(1879-1959)

Wanda Landowska, harpsichordist and pianist, was born in Warsaw, Poland, on July 5, 1879. Her parents were Jews who converted to Catholicism. At the age of four she began to play the piano, and a few months later she gave her first public recital. From the beginning of her studies Wanda showed more interest in old music (especially that of Bach) than in the romantic pieces that appealed to most people of her time. Under her first teacher, she was allowed to play the old music. But her parents made her change to a teacher who put tight reins on her and insisted that she concentrate on dull exercises. Wanda made a secret vow, in writing, that when she grew up she would play the old music that she loved.

She had a number of piano teachers with each of whom she studied for only a short time. But the two teachers who had the greatest impact on her were Jan Kleczynski (early in her studies) and Aleksander Michalowski (later, at the Warsaw Conservatory), both of whom were Chopin specialists. While absorbing the general characteristics of romantic pianism from her teachers, Landowska nevertheless continued her interest in old music. After hearing her play Bach when she was in her early teens, the famed conductor Arthur Nikisch was so impressed that he nicknamed her Bacchante.

After graduating from the Warsaw Conservatory in 1896, Landowska moved to Berlin, where she studied composition with Heinrich Urban. In both Warsaw and Berlin she began to develop a reputation as a virtuoso pianist.

In 1900 Landowska went to Paris and married Henri Lew, who was a Polish journalist, actor, ethnographer, and authority on Hebrew folklore. At that time she began to devote herself seriously to the study of seventeenth- and eighteenth-century keyboard music, specifically to the authentic performance of such music on the harpsichord. Assisted by her husband, she went to libraries and museums to examine documents and old musical instruments.

In 1903, as part of her initial piano recital in Paris, Landowska performed some old music on a small, poorly reconstructed harpsichord, her first use of a harpsichord in public. She then began to give concert tours throughout Europe, playing both types of keyboard instruments.

She also wrote numerous articles to promote the results of her research on the interpretation of early keyboard music (the performing tradition of which had been distorted by romantic pianism) and to overcome the public and professional resistance to the harpsi-chord. With her husband she wrote *La musique ancienne* (1909; English, as *Music of the Past,* 1924), a book having the same purposes as the articles.

A great turning point in her career came in 1912: at the Breslau Bach Festival that year, Landowska introduced a new concert-sized, two-manual harpsichord built by the Pleyel piano firm according to her own specifications (based on her musicological research). In 1913 she began to teach a harpsichord class created for her at the Berlin Academy of Music.

During World War I Landowska and her husband were detained in Berlin as civil prisoners on parole. In 1919 Lew was killed in an automobile accident.

Landowska then went to Basel, Switzerland, where she played a harpsichord continuo in Bach's *St. Matthew Passion,* the first time since the composer's death (in 1750) that the harpsichord had been used in the work. She also gave master classes in Basel and elsewhere before returning to Paris.

In Paris she continued to teach and promote the harpsichord, and she resumed her concert tours. For example, in 1923 Landowska, taking four large Pleyel harpsichords with her, made the first of her many tours of the United States. She appeared as soloist with the Philadelphia Orchestra under the baton of Eugene Ormandy, at whose invitation she was making her first American visit.

In 1925 Landowska purchased a house in Saint-Leu-la-Forêt (just north of Paris), where she founded the School of Ancient Music and had a small concert hall built. The school attracted students from around the world; and the annual summer concerts (which began in 1927 and were held in the school's concert hall), with Landowska herself playing both as soloist and with her students, became increasingly famous. At a 1933 concert there, she gave the first twentieth-century complete harpsichord performance of Bach's *Goldberg Variations.* She also regularly played works by other early keyboard composers, such as Rameau, Handel, and Mozart. The pieces were played on replicas of instruments from the composers' own eras, manufactured under her supervision.

Inspired by Landowska, living composers began to write for the revived harpsichord. For example, Manuel de Falla dedicated to her his *Harpsichord Concerto,* which she premiered in 1926. And in 1929 she gave the first performance of Francis Poulenc's *Concert champêtre* ("Pastoral Concerto") for harpsichord and orchestra, also dedicated to Landowska. Both works were written in an appropriately neoclassical spirit.

When the German forces of World War II approached Paris in June 1940, Landowska had to abandon her home, her school, her large library, and her valuable collection of instruments. After more than a year as a refugee in Europe (mostly in the Pyrenees), she migrated to the United States in late 1941, taking with her a Pleyel harpsichord obtained through a loan from a former student.

In February 1942 Landowska made a spectacularly successful appearance at Town Hall in New York City, playing Bach's *Goldberg Variations*. Settling first in New York City and later (in 1947) in the rural setting of Lakeville, Connecticut, she continued to teach and concertize for a number of years.

Despite her interest in baroque and classical music, Landowska's own manner of playing was rooted in the romantic tradition that she learned in her youth. Even her typical concert appearance partook of romanticism: her short frame draped with a black flowing robe, her feet covered with velvet ballet slippers, and her dark hair falling over her shoulders. Her playing, in the romantic tradition, emphasized the spirit, not the letter, of the scores. But the liberties she took with the printed music were always aimed at underlining the true dramatic and emotional content.

Landowska established modern harpsichord technique, especially fingering. She emphasized a true legato and a variety of articulation, as well as the historically proper manner of realizing baroque ornaments, rhythms, and so on. When she played old music on the piano, she did so with special attention to the manner of transferring to the modern instrument with hammered strings (the piano) the tonal qualities characteristic of the eighteenth-century instrument with plucked strings (the harpsichord).

Landowska was one of the most influential musicians of the twentieth century. Through her teaching, writing, and performing, she helped to champion seventeenth- and eighteenth-century music and became the undisputed leader in the twentieth-century revival of the harpsichord. Many of her pupils became eminent harpsichordists and pianists, including Clifford Curzon, Alice Ehlers, and Sylvia Marlowe. Another pupil was the future Israeli musicologist Edith Gerson-Kiwi.

Selections of her extremely valuable writings were gathered into *Landowska on Music* (1965), edited by her disciple Denise Restout. One of Landowska's greatest achievements was to rescue Bach from the thick, romanticized piano transcriptions of his works by Franz Liszt, Carl Tausig, and others. Largely thanks to her, Bach is now usually performed in his original settings.

Landowska composed numerous works, including a *Hebrew Poem* for orchestra, a *Liberation Fanfare* for band (which commemorated the liberation of Paris and was played several times in New York City's Central Park), keyboard pieces, and songs. Most of her manuscripts were lost before they could be printed, but her cadenzas for keyboard concertos by Handel, Haydn, and Mozart were published.

Landowska died at her home in Lakeville, Connecticut, on August 16, 1959. The house is preserved as the Landowska Center, which functions both as a museum where her memorabilia are stored and as a school where her teachings are perpetuated.

Evelyn Lear

Brilliant Singing Actress and
Distinguished Concert Artist

(1928-   )

Evelyn Lear, soprano, was born in New York City, New York, on January 8, 1928. Her original name was Evelyn Shulman. She sprang from a musical family: her maternal grandfather, Zavel Kwartin, was a prominent cantor, while her mother sang professionally and her father was a devoted amateur musician.

She decided at a very early age that she would become a singer. Nevertheless, her first music studies were in piano and French horn, and as a teenager she played the latter instrument in an orchestra conducted by Leonard Bernstein at the Berkshire Music Center at Tanglewood, near Lenox, Massachusetts. She began her vocal studies at New York University when she was seventeen.

Also at seventeen she married Dr. Walter Lear, with whom she moved to Virginia. They had two children: Jan and Bonni.

During her early years of marriage, Evelyn Lear studied voice with John Wood in nearby Washington, D.C. She made numerous local appearances in nightclubs, in recitals, and especially on TV.

After seven years of marriage she divorced her husband and returned to New York City, where she studied at Hunter College of the City University of New York and at the Juilliard School of Music. At Juilliard she met the baritone Thomas Stewart, whom she married in 1955, retaining, however, the surname Lear for professional use.

Also in 1955 she made her New York City recital debut, an appearance at Town Hall. In 1957 she went to Berlin, Germany, for further study. There she made her professional opera debut in 1959. For the next several years she made concert and opera appearances at many major European theaters.

In 1965 Lear made her American opera debut, performing with the Kansas City (Missouri) Performing Arts Foundation. Soon she appeared with opera companies in San Francisco and Chicago. Since 1967 she has been a member of the Metropolitan Opera in New York City, her first role there being Lavinia in the world premiere of Marvin David Levy's *Mourning Becomes Electra*. She has also continued to appear with other major companies throughout the world, often performing in operas with her husband.

Lear, a brilliant singing actress, has sung a wide range of roles. Early in her opera career she proved herself in such roles as Cherubino in Mozart's *Le nozze di Figaro* ("The Marriage of Figaro") and Desdemona in Verdi's *Otello*. In 1972 she began to add heavier roles to her repertory, such as the title part in Puccini's *Tosca* and the Marschallin in Richard Strauss's *Der Rosenkavalier* ("The Knight of the Rose").

Lear has also been closely identified with many modern roles, particularly the title part in Alban Berg's *Lulu* and Marie in the same composer's *Wozzeck*. She has participated in several world premieres besides that of Levy's *Mourning Becomes Electra,* creating, among other roles, the title part in Giselher Klebe's *Alkmene* in Berlin in 1961 and the role of Madame Andrejewna in Rudolf Kelterborn's *Der Kirschgarten* ("The Cherry Garden") in Zurich in 1984.

Lear is in great demand as a soloist with the world's leading symphony orchestras. She is also a distinguished recitalist, singing in seven languages. A number of her appearances have been joint recitals with Thomas Stewart, her husband.

Lear possesses a warm, affecting voice and projects an intelligent understanding of her texts.

Erich Leinsdorf
Precisionist Conductor
(1912-   )

Erich Leinsdorf, conductor, was born in Vienna, Austria, on February 4, 1912. His original surname was Landauer. At the age of eight he began to take piano lessons with the wife of the famous composer Paul Pisk. After three years he switched to Paul Emerich, with whom he studied piano for five years. During that time he also studied theory with Paul Pisk himself.

Leinsdorf completed his formal music studies by attending the Vienna State Academy (1931-33). Meanwhile, he also functioned as rehearsal pianist (1932-34) for Anton von Webern's Choral Society of the Social Democratic Arts Council.

Not only a good pianist but also a quick learner with a remarkable memory, Leinsdorf attracted the attention of the great conductors Arturo Toscanini and Bruno Walter. From 1934 to 1937 Leinsdorf worked for both maestros in various capacities, notably as Walter's assistant conductor at the annual Salzburg Festivals (1934-37).

Leinsdorf's reputation as an outstanding musician grew rapidly, and in 1937 he was invited to the Metropolitan Opera in New York City as an assistant conductor. He made his Met debut early the following year, conducting Wagner's *Die Walküre* ("The Valkyrie"). Leinsdorf stayed at the Met till 1943, by which time he had already become a naturalized American citizen (1942).

His personal commitment to America deepened with his 1939 marriage to Anne Frohnknecht, daughter of an American mother and German father. The Leinsdorfs

had five children: David, Gregor, Joshua, Deborah, and Jennifer.

In 1943 Leinsdorf became conductor of the Cleveland Orchestra; but while he was serving in the army (1944), Cleveland made other plans. After a few years of guest-conducting with various orchestras, he led the Rochester Philharmonic (1947-55).

During the 1956-57 season Leinsdorf directed the New York City Opera, where his efforts to enliven the repertory and style were not well received. In 1957 he returned to the Met, where he conducted till 1962.

Leinsdorf then served as music director of the prestigious Boston Symphony Orchestra (1962-69). There he polished the technical finesse of the orchestra and tried to expand the repertory, as by presenting the world premieres of Samuel Barber's *Piano Concerto* in 1962 (at Lincoln Center, New York City), Ernst Toch's *Fifth Symphony* in 1964, and Elliott Carter's *Piano Concerto* in 1967.

In 1968 Leinsdorf divorced his first wife. Later that year he married the Uruguayan violinist Vera Graf, whose parents were of Hungarian origin.

Since he left the Boston Symphony in 1969, Leinsdorf has traveled as a guest conductor in Europe and the United States and has served as principal conductor of the West Berlin Radio Symphony Orchestra (1977-80). In 1976 he published his autobiography as *Cadenza: A Musical Career*. He also wrote the valuable book *The Composer's Advocate: A Radical Orthodoxy for Musicians* (1981).

Extremely intelligent and articulate, Leinsdorf tends to be methodical and thorough, rather than inspirational, in his conducting. He overcame his natural nervousness and restlessness through self-restraint. As a consequence, some critics have called his conducting mechanical and clinical, but he has always produced performances with excellent technical finish and precision. He is perhaps at his best in vocal works, such as Beethoven's *Fidelio* and Brahms's *Ein deutsches Requiem* ("A German Requiem").

James Levine

Leader of the Metropolitan Opera
(1943-   )

James Levine, conductor and pianist, was born in Cincinnati, Ohio, on June 23, 1943. The performing arts had long been an important part of his family's history. His maternal grandfather, Morris Goldstein, was a cantor and composer of liturgical music. James's mother, Helen Levine (née Goldstein) played ingenue roles on Broadway before her marriage. Lawrence Levine, James's father, was a violinist and (under the stage name Larry Lee) dance-band leader till his marriage, after which he entered the clothing business.

At the age of three James was already picking out melodies on the piano. At four he began to take piano lessons, which apparently helped him to overcome an early problem with stuttering. His parents often took him to local symphony concerts and opera performances, where he would sit with a score on his lap and conduct with a knitting needle. By the age of nine he was "producing" operas at home on a miniature puppet stage by playing recordings, singing along, and going through the motions of conducting. When he was ten, he made his debut as a piano soloist by playing Mendelssohn's *Second Piano Concerto* at a youth concert with the Cincinnati Symphony Orchestra under Thor Johnson. To celebrate his debut, his parents took him to New York City to attend a series of operas at the Metropolitan Opera House.

Soon afterward, young Levine began to study theory, score reading, repertory, and style with Walter Levin in Cincinnati. An important turning point in Levine's development came when he attended the Marlboro School of Music in the summer of 1956. Besides studying piano with Rudolf Serkin, he formed at Marlboro a permanent interest in chamber music. Even more important was the opportunity that he had at Marlboro to participate (mainly by conducting the backstage chorus) in a production of Mozart's opera *Così fan tutte* ("Thus Do All

Women"). From then on, Levine regarded conducting as a major objective in his career.

The following summer he went to the Aspen School of Music in Colorado to take piano lessons with Rosina Lhevinne, one of the most renowned piano teachers in the world. In 1961, after graduating from Walnut Hills High School in Cincinnati, he enrolled at the Juilliard School of Music in New York City. There he majored in conducting under Jean Morel and continued his piano studies with Lhevinne, who was on the Juilliard staff.

Levine's first summer at Aspen, in 1957, was followed by eight more consecutive summer sessions there. Besides taking piano lessons from Lhevinne, he studied conducting with Wolfgang Vacano. It was Vacano who gave Levine his first opportunity to conduct complete opera performances, beginning with Bizet's *Les pêcheurs de perles* ("The Pearl Fishers") in 1962.

During his final year at Juilliard, he participated in a young-conductors' workshop associated with the Peabody Conservatory of Music and the Baltimore Symphony Orchestra. He received instruction from Fausto Cleva, Max Rudolf, and Alfred Wallenstein. One of the judges in the project was the principal conductor of the Cleveland Orchestra, George Szell, through whom Levine joined that ensemble as an apprentice in 1964 and became an assistant conductor in 1965, the youngest assistant in the orchestra's history.

Working with Szell in Cleveland taught Levine how to operate a major orchestra on a daily basis. Szell also enriched Levine's knowledge of the Austro-German classics, an important factor because Morel, at Juilliard, had focused the young conductor primarily on the French repertory.

While with the Cleveland Orchestra (1964-70), Levine also broadened his musical experience through two other activities. One was to establish an orchestra program at the Cleveland Institute of Music. By the time he left Cleveland, he had built the student orchestra to the point where he could conduct public performances of works by such difficult moderns as Berg, Ligeti, Schoenberg, and Stravinsky. Levine also conducted a chamber orchestra and an opera orchestra at the institute.

Another extra activity during his Cleveland years was to help his colleague Robert Shaw (also an assistant conductor of the Cleveland Orchestra) to organize a summer music institute at the University of Oakland in Meadowbrook, near Detroit, Michigan. Levine taught students in the areas of orchestra, chamber, and opera. He also organized opera performances, using professionals as well as students.

By 1970 Levine had decided to leave Cleveland so that he could experiment with numerous orchestras before selecting one of them for the kind of long and close association that he regarded as ideal for his full development as a conductor. In June 1970 he made the first of his many guest-conducting appearances with the Philadelphia Orchestra. Later that summer he traveled to Cardiff, Wales, where he made his first appearances with a fully professional opera company, conducting the Welsh National Opera in Verdi's *Aïda* and Rossini's *Il barbiere di Siviglia* ("The Barber of Seville").

In the autumn of 1970 Levine conducted Puccini's *Tosca* in San Francisco. Soon he was making guest-conducting appearances with major orchestras in many American cities.

In the summer of 1971 Levine made three guest appearances that would greatly affect his future. In early June he debuted at the Metropolitan Opera by conducting *Tosca*. Later that month he appeared for the first time in the Chicago Symphony's Ravina Festival. And in July he conducted *Tosca* at the Greek Theater in Los Angeles.

The Greek Theater appearance quickly led to engagements with the Los Angeles Philharmonic, which, along with the Philadelphia Orchestra, Levine has subsequently guest-conducted more often than he has any other ensemble. His appearance at the Ravina Festival led to his appointment as the festival's music director in 1973.

However, the most important consequence of his summer assignments in 1971 was his spectacular showing at the Metropolitan Opera. After some more perfor-

mances at the Met in 1972, he was appointed its principal conductor in 1973 and its music director in 1976, wielding more artistic control, by contract, than any previous director of the company. The Met has become the long-term home base that Levine sought. National telecasts from the Metropolitan Opera House have made him a familiar figure to millions of TV viewers.

Noted for the vitality and architectonic clarity of his performances, Levine has explained his view of conducting as follows: "A conductor's job is to put before the public as perceptive an account of the composer's intentions as possible, as vital an account, as true an account." His large conducting repertory ranges from eighteenth-century classics to the works of such contemporary experimentalists as John Cage and Yannis Xenakis. However, he is especially renowned for his performances of the operas of Mozart and Verdi.

Levine has remained active as a pianist, especially in chamber ensembles. One of his favorite activities is to play concertos (particularly by Bach or Mozart) while conducting from the keyboard. He has also continued to expand his guest-conducting, notably by making his debut at the Bayreuth Festival in 1982.

In the 1970s Levine began his long-term relationship with the oboist Sue Thomson. During that time he attracted attention when he decorated his New York City apartment with Navajo rugs and dinosaur bones.

Josef Lhevinne

Pianist with a Prodigious Technique
(1874-1944)

Josef Lhevinne, pianist, was born in Orel, near Moscow, Russia, on December 13, 1874. (The original form of his surname would have been transliterated as "Levin" or "Levine." When he began to concertize in Western countries in his early twenties, he added, at the suggestion of his teacher Vassily Safonov, the *h* and the extra *n* to his surname to make it more unique and less Jewish. For many years he used the form "Lhévinne," but toward the end of his life the accent fell out of use.)

When he was about one year old, his family moved to Moscow, where his father, Arkady, worked as a professional trumpeter. At the age of four Josef began to take piano lessons with Nils Chrysander, a Swedish-born musician living in Moscow.

In 1885 Josef entered the Moscow Conservatory, where he studied piano with Vassily Safonov. Among Josef's fellow students at the conservatory were Sergei Rachmaninoff and Alexander Scriabin.

Young Lhevinne's progress was extremely rapid.

While still a student, he attracted the attention and praise of the great Russian musician Anton Rubinstein, who invited Lhevinne to publicly perform Beethoven's *Fifth Piano Concerto* with Rubinstein himself conducting the Moscow Symphony Orchestra.

In 1889 the nine-year-old pianist Rosina Bessie entered the Moscow Conservatory and began to study with Safonov. Lhevinne developed a close relationship with her during a period of time when he gave her substitute lessons for the ailing teacher.

After receiving a virtuoso diploma and a gold medal from the Moscow Conservatory in 1891, Lhevinne continued to deepen his musical knowledge through numerous private meetings with Rubinstein. During 1892 and 1893 Lhevinne also received musical advice from the legendary Russian composer Peter Tchaikovsky, particularly regarding the interpretation of the latter's *First Piano Concerto*.

Meanwhile, Lhevinne was earning a living through minor appearances as soloist, accompanist, and chamber-music player. But in 1895 he won the prestigious Rubinstein Prize, which launched him as a major touring artist in Russia and western Europe. However, his career was soon interrupted when he was forced into one year of military service.

In June 1898 Lhevinne wedded Rosina Bessie, thus beginning one of the most famous marriages in music history. Before the wedding could take place, Lhevinne had to undergo a formal religious conversion. The harassment of Jews was particularly intense at that time in Moscow, where Grand Duke Serge, in power since 1891, had vowed to "run every Jew out of town." For their own safety, the Bessie family, who were Jews, had been baptized into the Russian Orthodox church, and Lhevinne followed suit to marry Rosina. All of the conversions were mere expediencies. Josef and Rosina had only one religion: music. And both sets of parents were aloof from religion, though Josef's father boycotted the wedding because he disapproved of his son's baptism.

Just one week before the wedding, Rosina had graduated from the Moscow Conservatory, where she had shown every sign of being on her way to a brilliant future as a concert pianist. Instead, realizing that Josef had no talent for self-promotion, she devoted herself to supervising her husband's career for the rest of his life. She occasionally appeared with him in two-piano performances. They had two children: Constantine (later called Don) and Marianna.

In 1899 the Lhevinnes moved to Tiflis, where they gave their first two-piano performance and where Josef soon began to teach at the conservatory. In 1901 they moved to Berlin, where he increased his reputation as a concert artist. Returning to Moscow in 1902, he taught at

the conservatory till classes were disrupted by the revolution of 1905.

In January 1906 Lhevinne made his American debut with a concert at Carnegie Hall in New York City, playing Anton Rubinstein's *Fifth Piano Concerto* with the Russian Symphony Orchestra under the baton of Safonov. Lhevinne then concertized in other American cities.

Later in 1906 he returned to Europe, resigned his Moscow post, and soon settled in Wannsee, a suburb of Berlin, Germany. There he began to teach privately, assisted by his wife. He also made numerous concert tours of Europe and the United States till the outbreak of World War I in 1914. During the war the Lhevinnes were interned as enemy (Russian) aliens at their own villa and were greatly restricted in their ability to earn an income.

Distraught by that experience, the Lhevinnes moved to the United States in 1919 and soon became naturalized American citizens. At first they opened their own studio, many students being referred to them by the Juilliard Foundation. When the Juilliard Graduate School was founded in 1924, Josef joined the faculty, though Rosina often took his classes when he was on tour. In 1924 Josef published his *Basic Principles in Pianoforte Playing,* a collection of his previously printed essays (reprinted in 1972 with a foreword by his wife).

Soon after his move to the New World, he began to make annual concert tours of the United States and Latin America, as well as occasional tours of Europe. Some of his recitals included two-piano performances with his wife.

Lhevinne was ranked as one of the greatest virtuosos of his day. His few recordings (including works by Liszt and Debussy) show his prodigious technique. But he combined his brilliant virtuosity with a firm control of phrasing and tone color. Lhevinne was especially effective with the romantics, his Chopin performances being noted for their strong lines within a subtle rubato.

Lhevinne was a modest, noncompetitive man who, especially in his late years, would have made far fewer appearances than he did if his wife had not worked hard to promote his career. He died of a heart attack at his home in New York City on December 2, 1944. The following year Rosina was given Josef's former post at Juilliard, where she remained till her own death, in 1976.

Frank Loesser
Important Broadway Composer
(1920-69)

Frank Loesser, composer, was born in New York City, New York, on June 29, 1910. There was always music in the household: his father, Henry, was a German-born piano teacher (at one time an accompanist for the celebrated German soprano Lilli Lehmann); and Arthur Loesser, Frank's brother, became a concert pianist. The family was deeply devoted to intellectual pursuits and classical music. Frank, however, broke the mold, doing poorly in his schoolwork and leaning toward popular music. He learned to play the piano by ear, improvising his first tune ("The May Party") when he was six, and became proficient on the harmonica. But he showed no interest in the serious study of music, and he never took formal lessons.

Loesser left school in his late teens and for several years drifted through a series of odd jobs. At the same time, he began to write song lyrics for nightclub, vaudeville, and other purposes, with music by his childhood friend William Schuman, who later became one of America's outstanding symphonic composers. In 1931 one of their collaborations, "In Love with a Memory of You," became Loesser's first published song. Loesser continued to supply lyrics for several composers over the next few years without any major success. Beginning in 1934 he sometimes collaborated with composers on the tunes as well.

By 1935 he had joined Irving Actman as a songwriting team. They performed their own songs, in exchange for their dinners, every night at the Back Drop café in New York City. One evening Loesser sang all of his love songs directly to a tall, striking blonde in the audience. Later he learned that she was Lynn Garland (originally Mary

Blankenbaker), a local singer-actress. Within a year they were married.

In 1936 Loesser landed his first major assignment: writing the lyrics for *The Illustrators' Show*, a Broadway production. The show was not successful, but it led to a contract for him in the moviemaking world.

From 1936 to 1942 Loesser was in the Hollywood section of Los Angeles, California, supplying lyrics to several composers of movie songs. His first big hit was "The Moon of Manakoora" (music, Alfred Newman) for the film *The Hurricane* (1937). Even more memorable was his "Heart and Soul" (music, Hoagy Carmichael); it was originally written as an independent song in 1938 and then introduced in the early 1939 short film *A Song Is Born*. Another song from the period was the popular "Jingle, Jangle, Jingle" (music, Joseph J. Lilley) for the movie *The Forest Rangers* (1942).

Loesser, like other Americans, was shocked by the Japanese attack on Pearl Harbor on December 7, 1941. Inspired by a remark reputed to have been made by a chaplain during the height of the attack, Loesser created a song entitled "Praise the Lord and Pass the Ammunition" (1942). As had been his previous habit, he put a dummy tune of his own to the lyrics to test them before handing them over to a composer. But his friends liked not only his lyrics but also the tune and, in particular, the way that the words and the music complemented each other. Thus, he kept his own tune with the lyrics and created the first significant song that was completely his own.

After he released "Praise the Lord and Pass the Ammunition," Loesser enlisted in the army. He was assigned to write songs (words and music) for armed-services use, the profits of which went to the Army Emergency Relief. Loesser's "What Do You Do in the Infantry?" (1943) quickly attained tremendous popularity among both the foot soldiers themselves and the general populace. But his biggest wartime hit was "Rodger Young" (1945), a ballad based on the true story of an American infantry private who gave his life to save others on an island in the South Pacific and who was posthumously awarded the Congressional Medal of Honor. Loesser's wartime songs made him famous, and he was the most important young American songwriter to win his spurs during World War II.

After the war Loesser returned to Hollywood, where he worked as a lyricist-composer on several film musicals. *Neptune's Daughter* (1949) featured his song "Baby, It's Cold Outside." But the highlight of his film career, and undoubtedly one of the most richly melodious song scores in movie history, was his work on *Hans Christian Andersen* (1952), including "Thumbelina."

Broadway, however, was where Loesser reached his artistic peak. He began with *Where's Charley?* (perf. 1948), a musical version of the famed play *Charley's Aunt*.

His most important show was *Guys and Dolls* (perf. 1950), a landmark in the development of Broadway musical plays. Each song (lyrics and music by Loesser) provided essential impetus in defining the Damon Runyon characters and/or in contributing to the plot. The score included "A Bushel and a Peck," "Luck Be a Lady," and "Sit Down, You're Rockin' the Boat." However, the real attraction in the work was not the individual numbers but the cohesion of the book, lyrics, and music in the rich evocation of the New York City scene with its humor, romance, toughness, and tenderness.

Loesser's Broadway show *The Most Happy Fella* (perf. 1956) was special in at least three ways. First, it had an almost operatic dominance by the music, with over forty musical numbers and a minimum of dialogue. Loesser himself, however, referred to it as merely an "extended musical comedy." Second, it had two of his most popular songs: "Somebody, Somewhere" and "Standing on the Corner." Third, one of the stars of *The Most Happy Fella* became his second wife.

Her name was Jo Sullivan (originally Elizabeth Jacobs). Loesser, having divorced his first wife a few years earlier, married Sullivan in 1959.

His last major work was the satire *How to Succeed in Business without Really Trying* (perf. 1961). The most enduring song from the Broadway show is "I Believe in You."

Loesser was one of the few composers for the popular musical theater who wrote not only lyrics and melodies but also harmonies, overtures, transitional material, and other parts of the score usually left to professional arrangers. His inner need to be in control of all aspects of his work led him to open his own publishing company, the Frank Music Corporation, in 1958.

A nervous man, Loesser chain-smoked cigarettes. The result was early cancer and, at the age of only fifty-nine, death in New York City on July 28, 1969. Jo, his wife, continued to perform his songs in public.

Selected works:

(lyrics and music by Loesser unless otherwise stated)

Stage

The Illustrators' Show (music, I. Actman; perf. 1936)
Where's Charley? (perf. 1948), including:
  "My Darling, My Darling"
  "Once in Love with Amy"
Guys and Dolls (perf. 1950), including:
  "A Bushel and a Peck"
  "Guys and Dolls"
  "Luck Be a Lady"
  "Sit Down, You're Rockin' the Boat"
The Most Happy Fella (perf. 1956), including:
  "Somebody, Somewhere"
  "Standing on the Corner"
Greenwillow (perf. 1960)
How to Succeed in Business without Really Trying (perf. 1961),
  including:
  "I Believe in You"

Films
(song scores)

The Perils of Pauline (1947), including:
  "I Wish I Didn't Love You So"
Variety Girl (1947)
Neptune's Daughter (1949), including:
  "Baby, It's Cold Outside"
Let's Dance (1950)

119

Hans Christian Andersen (1952), including:
"Anywhere I Wander"
"Inchworm"
"No Two People"
"Thumbelina"
"Ugly Duckling"
"Wonderful Copenhagen"

Songs
(other than those for the above shows and films)

"The Moon of Manakoora" (music, A. Newman; for the film *The Hurricane*, 1937)

"Heart and Soul" (music, H. Carmichael; 1938)
"Jingle, Jangle, Jingle" (music, J. J. Lilley; for the film *The Forest Rangers*, 1942)
"Praise the Lord and Pass the Ammunition" (1942)
"What Do You Do in the Infantry?" (1943)
"The WAC Hymn" (1944)
"Rodger Young" (1945)
"Spring Will Be a Little Late This Year" (for the film *Christmas Holiday*, 1944)
"What Are You Doing New Year's Eve?" (1947)
"On a Slow Boat to China" (1948)

Frederick Loewe
Composer of Musical-Theater Classics
(1901-   )

Frederick Loewe (né Löwe), composer, was born of Viennese parents in Berlin, Germany, on June 10, 1901. His father was the well-known operetta tenor Edmund Löwe. The waltzes and songs in the European (especially Viennese) operettas of the time greatly influenced Frederick's musical tastes. He wrote numerous such songs as a youth, some of which his father sang in variety theaters throughout Europe. One of Frederick's songs became a major commercial success: "Kathrin, du hast die schönsten Beine von Berlin" ("Katherine, You Have the Most Beautiful Legs in Berlin," 1919).

However, Frederick's primary goal was to become a concert pianist. He studied in Berlin, where his most important piano teachers were Ferruccio Busoni and Eugène d'Albert, while he also studied composition for a year with Emil Nikolaus von Reznicek. Beginning in his early teens, Frederick performed as piano soloist with leading European symphony orchestras, including the Berlin Philharmonic. His career as a European pianist reached its peak when he won the prestigious Holländer Medal in 1923.

The following year he moved to the United States and settled in New York City. After a Town Hall recital that attracted little attention, young Loewe turned to commercial music, working, for example, as a nightclub pianist in Greenwich Village.

Discouraged at the lack of progress in his music career, he entered a several-year period of doing odd jobs. At various locations on the East Coast, he worked as a bus boy in a cafeteria, a horseback-riding instructor, and even a professional boxer (winning his first eight fights but being clobbered in his ninth—and final—bout). He then tried his luck out West, where he punched cows, prospected for gold, and carried mail on horseback.

Returning to the East, Loewe was hired as a pianist on a boat running between Miami and Havana, entertaining Prohibition-era passengers determined to get liquor even if they had to travel to Cuba for it. Later, during the early 1930s, he found a steady job as a pianist in a German beer hall in New York City.

In the mid-1930s Loewe, still dissatisfied with his lot as a pianist, began once again to write popular songs. He placed some in Broadway productions, notably "A Waltz Was Born in Vienna," with lyrics by Earle Crooker, interpolated into *The Illustrators' Show* (perf. 1936). Then, again with Crooker's lyrics, Loewe composed the song score for the musical comedy *Salute to Spring*, staged in Saint Louis in 1937. That show led to an opportunity to write a Broadway musical: Loewe and Crooker's *Great Lady* (perf. 1938). Both shows were unsuccessful, one problem being that Loewe's music was still too much in the style of the old Viennese operettas, by the late 1930s no longer in fashion in America.

For the next several years Loewe performed minor musical chores, such as playing the piano in restaurants. In 1942 he attempted to revive his concert career with a recital at Carnegie Hall in New York City. But again he had little success.

Nevertheless, 1942 proved to be the year in which his luck finally began to change for the better. He was offered a chance to restage his *Salute to Spring* if he would quickly revise it, including the lyrics. But he did not have a lyricist at that time and did not know how to find one. However, he happened to be a member of the Lambs Club in New York City, which put on an annual Lambs Gambols musical show with lyrics most recently supplied by another member, a radio writer named Alan J. Lerner. Loewe, running short on time and spotting Lerner one day at the Lambs Club, impulsively walked up and asked him if he would be interested in doing some songwriting. Lerner, whose own career was also stalled, immediately said yes. Thus, in August 1942, was casually formed a lifelong friendship and one of the most important professional partnerships in the history of the American musical theater.

Their first work together was the revision of *Salute to Spring*, which was renamed *Life of the Party* and staged in Detroit late in 1942. The team reached Broadway with the musical comedy *What's Up?* (perf. 1943), followed by *The Day before Spring* (perf. 1945). Their first three collaborations were undistinguished; but the shows did reveal an increasing originality in their songs, Loewe gradually becoming more Americanized in his musical style.

The first great Lerner and Loewe musical was *Brigadoon* (perf. 1947). It contains songs of a dramatic poignancy rare in the popular musical theater, as in "Almost like Being in Love."

Paint Your Wagon (perf. 1951) is a Gold Rush musical that draws on American folk life, dance, and musical styles. "They Call the Wind Maria" is one of the show's colorful songs.

The team's next, and most famous, musical was *My Fair Lady* (perf. 1956), based on George Bernard Shaw's play *Pygmalion*. It concerns the efforts of Professor Henry Higgins, a philologist and phoneticist, to turn an uneducated waif, the flower seller Liza Doolittle, into a lady by improving her speech. *My Fair Lady* has been highly praised for its integration of a distinctive song score with an unusually strong plot. Among the many memorable songs from the show are "I Could Have Danced All Night" and "On the Street Where You Live."

Camelot (perf. 1960), the final Lerner and Loewe musical for the stage, was another huge success, though it suffered some criticism because of inevitable comparisons with their masterpiece, *My Fair Lady*. The most famous song from the show is "If Ever I Would Leave You." Based on the Arthurian legend, *Camelot,* for many Americans, came to symbolize an ideal society most nearly attained during the presidency of John F. Kennedy, who loved to listen to a recording of the musical and who was assassinated when the show was at the height of its popularity. Near the end of the reprise of the song "Camelot" comes the phrase "one brief shining moment," which became synonymous with the brevity and the climate of intellectuality, culture, and idealism of Kennedy's administration (1961-63). (Lerner, who had been one of Kennedy's classmates at Choate and Harvard, was so emotionally stunned by the new meanings attached to his work that he was never again able to attend a performance of *Camelot*.)

Besides having their four major stage musicals filmed, Lerner and Loewe wrote original song scores for two other movies. *Gigi* (1958), a comedy about a teenage girl being trained to become a courtesan in 1900 Paris, has an appropriately light, French-flavored score. *The Little Prince* (1974), based on Antoine de Saint-Exupéry's allegorical fantasy, has the lovely song "Little Prince." But Loewe's score was marred by the director, who changed tempos, deleted phrases, and performed other acts of musical insensitivity. After that experience Loewe went into permanent retirement.

Loewe's music is noted for its liveliness. Even his most lyrical passages are generally in a quick tempo, with short, memorable phrases and simple, reiterated patterns.

Loewe, known as Fritz to his friends, was married in 1931 to the Viennese-born Ernestine Zwerleine, daughter of a European architect. She was manager of the Hattie Carnegie fashion enterprises. The Loewes separated in 1957.

Selected works:

Stage

Salute to Spring (lyrics, E. Crooker; perf. 1937)
Great Lady (lyrics, E. Crooker; perf. 1938)
Life of the Party (revision of *Salute to Spring*; lyrics, A. J. Lerner; perf. 1942)
What's Up? (lyrics, A. J. Lerner; perf. 1943), including:
  "You've Got a Hold on Me"
The Day before Spring (lyrics, A. J. Lerner; perf. 1945)
Brigadoon (lyrics, A. J. Lerner; perf. 1947), including:
  "Almost like Being in Love"
Paint Your Wagon (lyrics, A. J. Lerner; perf. 1951), including:
  "I Talk to the Trees"
  "They Call the Wind Maria"
My Fair Lady (lyrics, A. J. Lerner; perf. 1956), including:
  "Get Me to the Church on Time"
  "I Could Have Danced All Night"
  "I've Grown Accustomed to Her Face"
  "On the Street Where You Live"
  "The Rain in Spain"
  "With a Little Bit of Luck"
  "Wouldn't It Be Loverly?"
Camelot (lyrics, A. J. Lerner; perf. 1960), including:
  "Camelot"
  "If Ever I Would Leave You"

Films
(song scores)

Gigi (lyrics, A. J. Lerner; 1958), including:
  "Gigi"
  "I Remember It Well"
  "Thank Heaven for Little Girls"
The Little Prince (lyrics, A. J. Lerner; 1974), including:
  "Little Prince"

Song
(other than those for the above shows and films)

"A Waltz Was Born in Vienna" (lyrics, E. Crooker; for the stage work *The Illustrators' Show*, perf. 1936)

Gustav Mahler
Fiery Romantic at the Crossroads
(1860-1911)

Gustav Mahler was best known to his contemporaries as an important and unconventional conductor. Today, however, he is remembered chiefly as one of the last great composers in the Austro-German tradition.

He was born in Austrian-ruled Kalischt, Bohemia (now Kaliště, Czechoslovakia), on July 7, 1860, and raised in Iglau, Moravia, where he was exposed to folk, military, popular, and art music of various types, all of which he would later draw on while constructing his symphonic masterpieces. His father, a businessman who owned a distillery and several taverns, recognized Gustav's talent and hired a succession of local musicians to give the boy lessons in piano and theory. Making rapid progress, young Mahler gave his first public recital in 1870.

In 1875 he enrolled at the Vienna Conservatory, where he studied piano with Julius Epstein, harmony with Robert Fuchs, and composition with Franz Krenn. While he was at the conservatory, his main interest turned from performance to composition, in which he graduated in 1878.

Mahler's lifelong intellectual interests were now blossoming. From 1877 to 1880 he attended classes in historical and philosophical subjects at the University of Vienna.

Meanwhile, after his graduation from the conservatory, Mahler worked as a music teacher and began to compose his first important work, the cantata *Das klagende Lied* ("The Song of Lament"). It was finished in 1880 (though, like many of his works, it would be subsequently revised).

Also in 1880 Mahler began the slow climb from small theaters to large opera houses as a conductor. In the summer of that year, he conducted operetta at a small theater in the town of Hall, in Upper Austria. The following summer he conducted a more interesting repertory in Laibach. In early 1883 he went to Olmütz, where the company was in a depressed artistic condition. Mahler's authoritarian attitude upset some performers, but he raised the theater's musical standards.

Having attracted attention at Olmütz, Mahler was given the position of music and chorus director at Kassel, which he held from 1883 to 1885. He was praised for his precision and enthusiasm, but he was criticized for his excessive bodily movements and unconventional tempos.

While at Kassel, Mahler fell in love with one of the singers. The emotional heightening of that unhappy romance generated the composition of Mahler's first masterpiece, the song cycle *Lieder eines fahrenden Gesellen* ("Songs of a Wayfarer"), completed in January 1885. The texts, by Mahler himself, focus on the rejected lover wandering alone over the face of the earth.

Mahler, as would become typical of his career, could not get along with his superiors at Kassel. He left on July 1, 1885.

Later that month he took a position at the German Opera in Prague. There, for the first time, he was allowed to conduct the works with which he came to be most closely associated: the operas of Gluck, Mozart, Beethoven, and Wagner. He was praised and criticized as he

had been at Kassel; and again he conflicted with his superior, the director. But Mahler's primary objective, as always, was the technically flawless presentation of opera, regardless of what conventions he broke or whose feelings he hurt along the way. His conducting work was characterized by his search for precision, clarity, and faithfulness to the spirit of each original score.

In July 1886 Mahler went to Leipzig, where he conducted a large, well-equipped orchestra and company. His performance there of a Wagner opera in early 1887 firmly established him among the critics and the public as a major artist.

In Leipzig, Mahler met Carl von Weber, grandson of the great composer Carl Maria von Weber. Mahler fell in love with Weber's wife and, in the nineteenth-century romantic tradition, composed music to express his sense of hopeless yearning. The results, in 1887, were a symphonic poem (eventually his *First Symphony*) and the beginning of what came to be his *Second Symphony*.

In 1887 Mahler also discovered the musical potential of *Des Knaben Wunderhorn* ("The Youth's Magic Horn"), a collection of German folk poetry. It provided him with almost all of the texts for his vocal works during the next fourteen years.

Early in 1888 he met the composers Peter Tchaikovsky and Richard Strauss. Mahler and Strauss remained close friends for the rest of Mahler's life. In May 1888 Mahler argued with the Leipzig stage manager and resigned his post.

He then served as director of the Royal Opera in Budapest (1888-91), his first major position. The Royal Opera was modern and well equipped. But as so often happened in his career, Mahler inherited a company in a depressed state: it operated at a financial loss, performed a limited repertory, and had poor artistic discipline. There was also a rising voice against foreign-language opera and in favor of a Hungarian national opera.

Mahler faced the Budapest challenge at a time of great personal sadness. The year 1888 saw the deaths of his father, his mother, and one of his sisters. And in 1889 the Budapest public reacted unfavorably to a performance of the innovative symphonic poem that later became his *First Symphony*.

Nevertheless, Mahler, with his accustomed energy and intelligence, attacked the problems at the Royal Opera. He arranged for operas to be performed in the Hungarian language; and he formed ensembles consisting, as much as possible, of native singers. He also enlarged the local repertory, including the addition of new Italian operas. Most of all, he created an atmosphere of artistic discipline.

In December 1890 Mahler presented a new production of Mozart's *Don Giovanni*. In the audience was the great Johannes Brahms, who, wheedled by friends into attending the opera, had earlier said that he had never heard a proper performance of Mozart's masterpiece. But at intermission Brahms went backstage, embraced Mahler, and expressed great admiration for the production.

In 1891 Mahler discovered that he would soon have a new superior, who planned to take over the artistic control of the Royal Opera. Mahler, of course, soon resigned, leaving a company that was now operating at a profit and performing an enlarged repertory with much higher artistic standards. He had done little composing, however, during his Budapest years.

His next stop was Hamburg, where he conducted opera from 1891 to 1897. In the spring of 1891 he conducted up to nineteen operas a month. During his Hamburg years he established the work pattern that he kept for the rest of his life: composing short scores during the summer, while revising and orchestrating them during the theater season. He finished the *Second Symphony* in 1894 and the *Third Symphony* in 1896. The premiere of the *Second Symphony*, in Berlin, on December 13, 1895, was Mahler's first great public success as a composer.

Mahler began to develop an international reputation, making a tour in early 1897 of Moscow, Munich, and Budapest. His compositions were increasingly performed.

Mahler was now ready for the most important step forward in his career: a conducting post in Vienna. He began negotiations with Viennese officials, and he was enthusiastically recommended by Brahms. But there was an obstacle—his Jewish origin.

Mahler realized that under the prevailing social climate in Vienna, the appointment of a Jew to a high musical position was nearly impossible. Thus, on February 23, 1897, he accepted baptism into the Catholic faith. Though raised as an Orthodox Jew, Mahler as an adult apparently did not practice Judaism, nor did he subsequently practice Christianity. His writings indicate that he inclined toward a pantheistic mysticism. Mahler said of his baptism that "this action, which I took from an instinct of self-preservation and which I was fully disposed to take, cost me a great deal," a reference to the anguish he felt at being pressured into renouncing his heritage. Later in 1897 he was appointed head of the Vienna Opera, the most important musical position in the Austrian Empire.

Mahler's ten-year (1897-1907) tenure as director of the Vienna Opera is still regarded as a legendary golden era for that institution. He built the Vienna Opera into the premiere company in Europe, controlling almost every aspect of many outstanding and memorable productions. Inheriting a Viennese public with frivolous operatic tastes, Mahler, with his ideals and energy, taught that same public to revere Gluck, Mozart, and Beethoven, as well as to listen to uncut versions of Wagner's lengthy operas.

Mahler's summer vacations became very productive during his Vienna years. His output included five huge symphonies, the *Fourth* (1900) to the *Eighth* (1906).

Mahler was not interested in teaching music or being the leader of a group. Nevertheless, young radical Viennese composers tended to gather around him. Among them were Schoenberg, Webern, and Berg.

In 1901 Mahler met and fell in love with Alma Schindler, daughter of an Austrian landscape painter and herself a very intelligent student of musical composition. They were married in 1902 and had two children: Maria and Anna. In Mahler's *Sixth Symphony* (1904) he created musical portraits of his family, his wife being characterized by, in Alma's words, "the great soaring theme" in the second subject of the first movement and the girls by the second (scherzo) movement, which represents, according to Alma, "the arhythmic games of the two little children, tottering in zigzags over the sand."

In many of life's little problems, Mahler relied on his wife almost as a little boy depends on his mother. Once he had a toothache, but he was not sure which tooth was hurting. She found it for him and then sat in the waiting room while he was in the dentist's office. "Suddenly the door flew open," she later recalled, "and Mahler called out: 'Alma dear, which tooth is it actually that's aching?' He was astonished when everyone laughed."

Despite such apparent signs of blissful domesticity, the marriage was a troubled one. Mahler, who required that everything be arranged around his own creative work, insisted that Alma give up composition. In her memoirs (*Gustav Mahler: Memories and Letters,* 1946), Alma expressed the deep hurt and sense of frustration that she experienced by not being allowed to write her own music. She also justifiably felt that he neglected her "in his fanatical concentration on his own life."

However, Alma was not wholly without responsibility for Mahler's preoccupation with his art. She once said to him, "All I love in a man is his achievement. The greater his achievement, the more I love him." Mahler replied, "You mean if anyone came along who could do more than I—" Alma: "I'd have to love him."

Their marital problems were exacerbated by the difference in their ages (Alma being about nineteen years younger) and by the conflict between their personalities (the middle-aged and morose Mahler having settled into his own private world of musical struggles, while the youthful and vivacious Alma was much more outgoing).

In 1910, after Alma had finally convinced her husband of the seriousness of their situation, Mahler went to Sigmund Freud to be psychoanalyzed. Mahler the intellectual surprised Freud by showing a firm grasp of the principles of psychoanalysis. Through Freud, Mahler gained insight not only into his marital problems but also into his creative personality. He rediscovered the depth of his love for Alma and expressed it through his touching messages to her in the 1910 manuscript of his sketches for the *Tenth Symphony:* "To live for you! To die for you! Almschi!"

Meanwhile, Mahler's career had taken another turn. In spite of his achievements in Vienna, a campaign was mounted against him, led by the anti-Semitic Viennese press. His appointment at the Vienna Opera had been accomplished largely by its suddenness, before any opposition had had time to form. But through the years, the forces against him became increasingly more open. He was finally forced to resign in December 1907.

The year 1907 had earlier brought him two other traumatic events. In the summer, his daughter Maria, whom he adored, died of scarlet fever. Soon afterward it was discovered that Mahler himself suffered from a heart ailment.

In 1908 and 1909 Mahler conducted at the Metropolitan Opera in New York City. It was an unhappy experience. For one thing, friction developed between Mahler and the management when the Italian conductor Arturo Toscanini was brought in and given preferential treatment. Moreover, Mahler's recent traumas had had a drastic effect on his attitude toward life and art. The Metropolitan was exactly the opposite of what he had always striven for; it focused on stars, not on an integrated ensemble. But unlike the Mahler of old, he gave in. For example, he agreed to cuts in Wagner. He also allowed indifferent performances.

Mahler did, however, continue to compose at a heated pace, finishing in 1909 *Das Lied von der Erde* ("The Song of the Earth") and the *Ninth Symphony.* Though Mahler himself regarded *Das Lied von der Erde* as a symphony for voices and orchestra, he superstitiously avoided labeling it his *Ninth* (which, in fact, it was) because the other work would then have become his *Tenth.* He cited such examples as Beethoven and Bruckner to show that other great romantic symphonists had died before they could complete their tenth symphonies. After Mahler finished his *Ninth* (actually his *Tenth),* he thought that he had cheated fate; and while composing his next symphony, which he labeled the *Tenth,* he said, "Now the danger is past."

In 1909 Mahler canceled his contract with the Metropolitan and accepted the conductorship of the New York Philharmonic, where his unhappiness increased. When members of the board complained about his programming (which often featured modern composers, such as Debussy), Alma publicly defended him. "In Vienna my husband was all-powerful," she told the press. "Even the Emperor did not dictate to him, but in New York he had ten ladies ordering him around like a puppet."

In 1910 Mahler began sketches for his *Tenth Symphony.* But he did not live to complete it; his trick on fate did not work. In early 1911, while engaged in another New York Philharmonic season, he fell ill with a bacterial infection. Returning to Vienna, he died on May 18, 1911.

It took many years following Mahler's death for his music to gain wide acceptance. But interest grew, particularly in the 1960s. From today's perspective Mahler can be seen as an important transitional composer. He both sums up the nineteenth-century romantic tradition and, in his late work, reflects new twentieth-century concerns.

Mahler's romantic attitude can be seen in one of his own statements: "To write a symphony is, for me, to construct a world." Mahler, in his musical world, combined the sophisticated and the simple in an attempt to breathe vitality into the disintegrating tradition of nineteenth-century romanticism. Much of his music consists of a mosaic of such diverse and romantic elements as long lyric melodic lines, rich harmony, colorful orchestration, folk tunes, popular dance rhythms, nature painting (such as birdcalls), chorales, military marches, funeral marches, parody, and passages that have been described as spooky, mysterious, and grotesque. In spite of such diversity, Mahler's music always bears the stamp of his own unique personality.

The line of great Austro-German symphonists, beginning with Haydn and continuing through Mozart, Beethoven, Schubert, Bruckner, and Brahms, ended with Mahler. But Mahler pointed toward the future in his last completed works, *Das Lied von der Erde* and the *Ninth Symphony,* which were written after his traumatic year of 1907. His earlier lush textures now became clearer and more austere, with an orchestral style largely based on counterpoint. His chamberlike textures anticipated what came to be common twentieth-century practice. Mahler also foreshadowed the twentieth century's weakening or rejection of the traditional sense of tonality.

Thus, even while emotionally trying to preserve the tradition, Mahler was artistically compelled to pull away from it. He felt the same sense of rootlessness in his personal life: "I am thrice homeless. As a Bohemian born in Austria. As an Austrian among Germans. And as a Jew throughout the world." The tension created by those artistic and personal conflicts pervades Mahler's music, in which he projects a sense of unrest and nostalgia.

Selected works:

Symphonies

First Symphony (1888, revised 1896)
Second Symphony (voices, orchestra; fourth-movement text, *Des Knaben Wunderhorn;* fifth-movement text, F. Klopstock, G. Mahler; 1894, revised 1903)
Third Symphony (voices, orchestra; fourth-movement text, F. Nietzsche; fifth-movement text, *Des Knaben Wunderhorn;* 1896, revised 1906)
Fourth Symphony (soprano, orchestra; fourth-movement text, *Des Knaben Wunderhorn;* 1900, revised 1910)
Fifth Symphony (1902)
Sixth Symphony (1904, revised 1906)
Seventh Symphony (1905)
Eighth Symphony (voices, orchestra; part-one text, *Veni creator spiritus;* part-two text, J. W. von Goethe; 1906)
Ninth Symphony (1909)
Tenth Symphony (incomplete, 1910)

Vocal

Das klagende Lied (cantata; voices, orchestra; text, G. Mahler; 1880, revised 1893 and 1899)
Lieder und Gesänge ("Songs and Chants"; voice, piano; texts, various authors; 1890)
Lieder eines fahrenden Gesellen (song cycle; voice, orchestra [or piano]; texts, G. Mahler; 1885, revised 1896)
Des Knaben Wunderhorn (group of songs; voice, orchestra [or piano]; texts, *Des Knaben Wunderhorn;* 1898)
Kindertotenlieder ("Songs on the Death of Children"; voice, orchestra; texts, F. Rückert; 1904)
Das Lied von der Erde (song cycle; voices, orchestra; texts, H. Bethge; 1909)

Barry Manilow
Musician with a Human Element
(1946-   )

Barry Manilow, singer and composer, was born in New York City, New York, on June 17, 1946. He learned to play the accordion at the age of eleven and the piano at thirteen. Later he studied at the New York College of Music.

Manilow then worked in the mailroom of the Columbia Broadcasting System (CBS) TV network, meanwhile attending classes at the Juilliard School of Music. At CBS he eventually became the film editor of *The Late Show,* for which he arranged a new musical theme. In the late 1960s he left CBS, and soon he had opportunities to serve as music director for the WCBS-TV series *Callback* and for Ed Sullivan Productions. In 1970 he arranged old songs by other composers and wrote new ones himself for the off-Broadway production *The Drunkard.*

However, in the late 1960s and early 1970s Manilow advanced his career primarily by writing jingles and singing them in radio and TV commercials for such products as Dr. Pepper, Kentucky Fried Chicken, Pepsi-Cola,

Barry Manilow

to be released while he was on tour with Midler in 1973. His recording company arranged for him to push the album by opening the second act of Midler's stage show. "I was totally convinced that Bette's audience was going to kill me," he admitted. But he was well received. Soon he came to be best known for his awkward gestures onstage and for the appealing catch in his voice.

His first hit single was "Mandy" (1974), which he then put on his next album, *Barry Manilow II* (1974). His popular "Could It Be Magic?" (1975) is a melancholy love song based on a Chopin prelude.

Manilow began to tour on his own, backed by various groups—in 1975 and 1976, for example, by the female trio Lady Flash. In 1977 and 1978 he made two highly successful TV specials. Also in 1977 he came out with the album *Barry Manilow Live,* which features his "Very Strange Medley," a collection of his old commercial jingles.

Manilow's most avid fans appear to be British. In 1982 half a million people applied for the 21,500 seats that were available for his five concerts at the Royal Albert Hall in London, England. In a September 1983 concert at Blenheim Palace, sixty-five miles north of London, he drew the largest live audience of his career—forty thousand.

Manilow's musical style can be described as middle-of-the-road romantic pop. It is often based on his singing his own sentimental tunes (and partly his own lyrics) against a hard-rock background. However, his album *2:00 AM, Paradise Café* (1984) introduced a new, mellow, jazz-flavored quality into his repertory.

Manilow himself attributes his success to "the big emotional element" in his work. "I try to be human and natural on records. . . . You can hear me spitting. You can hear me making mistakes. . . . There's a more human element in a song if my voice cracks or if you can hear me sighing."

Tall and lean, with large blue puppylike eyes, Manilow is easygoing and talkative, with a self-deprecating sense of humor. Known for his quiet, well-mannered lifestyle, he enjoys watching TV and going to scary movies.

Manilow is psychologically healthier than many others in show business and does not worry about his public image. "I'm just not sensational," he says. "If I'm boring, then I'm boring. . . . But I'm not unhappy! I'm having a fabulous time."

Manilow's one-year marriage to his high-school sweetheart ended in divorce in 1968. He then developed a long-term relationship with Linda Allen, but they split up in 1982. "I'm married to my work," he says. "My children are my songs."

Spaghettios, and State Farm Insurance. He became best known, however, for singing the "You Deserve a Break Today" jingle for McDonald's (which Manilow himself did not write).

In 1972 he was subbing for the house pianist at Continental Baths in New York City when Bette Midler made one of her celebrated appearances there. Manilow soon joined Midler's entourage as a producer-arranger.

His own first album, *Barry Manilow,* was scheduled

Selected recordings:

Singles

"Mandy" (1974, Bell)
"It's a Miracle" (1975, Arista)
"Could It Be Magic?" (1975, Arista)
"I Write the Songs" (1975, Arista)
"Tryin' to Get the Feeling Again" (1976, Arista)
"Weekend in New England" (1976, Arista)

126

"Looks Like We Made It" (1977, Arista)
"Can't Smile without You" (1978, Arista)
"Copacabana" (1978, Arista)
"Somewhere in the Night" (1979, Arista)
"Ships" (1979, Arista)
"I Made It through the Rain" (1980, Arista)
"Somewhere down the Road" (1982, Arista)

Albums

Barry Manilow (1973, Arista)

Barry Manilow II (1974, Arista)
Tryin' to Get the Feeling (1975, Arista)
This One's for You (1976, Arista)
Barry Manilow Live (1977, Arista)
Barry Manilow's Greatest Hits (1978, Arista)
One Voice (1979, Arista)
Barry (1980, Arista)
If I Should Love Again (1981, Arista)
Barry Manilow: Greatest Hits, Volume 2 (1983, Arista)
2:00 AM, Paradise Café (1984, Arista)

Felix Mendelssohn
One of the Most Gifted Musicians of the Nineteenth Century
(1809-1847)

Felix (originally Jakob Ludwig Felix) Mendelssohn, composer, was born in Hamburg, Germany, on February 3, 1809. His paternal grandfather was Moses Mendelssohn, an important philosopher of the Enlightenment and a leader of the movement for Jewish freedom. Felix's father, Abraham, became a wealthy banker and provided a comfortable, cultured life for his children. Music was important to all of Felix's siblings: his older sister, Fanny (a pianist); his younger sister, Rebecka (a singer); and his younger brother, Paul (a cellist, for whom Felix wrote his *Second Cello Sonata* in 1843).

When Felix was two years old, the family moved from Hamburg to Berlin. The following year, 1812, the emancipation edict was issued in Prussia, granting Jews most of the rights of citizenship. But conversion to Christianity was still required to attain true civil equality. Thus, in 1816, when Felix was seven, Abraham and his wife, Lea (daughter of wealthy Berlin Jews), had their children baptized into the Lutheran church. Abraham, whose early exposure to his father's rationalist philosophy had made him somewhat of a religious skeptic, later explained his practical action in a letter to Fanny: "We have educated all of you in the Christian faith because that is the creed of most civilized people and it contains no precept that could lead you away from virtue." Despite the conversion, the sensitive Felix suffered much from anti-Semitism, including at least one stoning. Berlin was a hotbed of such prejudice, and Felix gradually came to detest the city.

In 1822, when Abraham and Lea themselves converted to Christianity, they and their children took the dual surname Mendelssohn Bartholdy (without a hyphen, which was adopted later by Paul's descendants). The latter appellation was borrowed from Lea's brother, originally named Jakob Salomon, who had changed his surname to Bartholdy after purchasing a Berlin garden formerly owned by someone of that name.

Later, when Felix began to earn an international reputation, his father urged him to drop the name Mendelssohn altogether ("If Mendelssohn is your name, you are ipso facto a Jew") and become simply Felix Bartholdy. But Felix refused—not, however, out of a desire to emphasize his Jewish origin. On the contrary, he considered himself a Protestant, largely because of his deep commitment to the musical heritage of Bach. The simple fact was that, because of his famous grandfather, people preferred to call him Mendelssohn, under which name he scored his early successes. He therefore saw to it that the world knew him as Felix Mendelssohn, though many of his works were published under the name Felix Mendelssohn Bartholdy.

Felix was educated privately at his Berlin home, at first by his parents and later by a succession of teachers in many fields. He wrote poetry and became skillful at drawing and painting. His earliest music lessons, on the piano, were given by his mother. Then, after a few months of lessons in Paris with Marie Bigot, he returned to Berlin and began to take lessons from his principal piano teacher, Ludwig Berger, who had studied with Muzio Clementi and John Field. From Clementi, Berger had learned precision; and from Field, a singing quality. Berger passed both traits on to his pupil Felix. At a small private concert in 1818, the nine-year-old Felix made his first appearance as a pianist. He also received some lessons from the celebrated pianist Ignaz Moscheles when the latter visited the Mendelssohn home in 1824.

After briefly studying the violin with Carl Wilhelm Henning, young Mendelssohn developed great skill on that instrument under Eduard Rietz. Eventually he also learned the viola and the cello. In 1819 he began to train his voice at the Berlin Singing Academy.

Mendelssohn took theory and composition lessons from Adolf Bernhard Marx, who led the boy into the study of Beethoven. But Mendelssohn's most important theory and composition teacher was Carl Friedrich Zelter, director of the Berlin Singing Academy. Zelter encouraged his pupil to study old music, particularly Bach.

Mendelssohn's earliest extant compositions date from 1820, when he was eleven years old. Written under the influence of Bach's counterpoint and Mozart's classical idiom, the works up to 1825 reveal an increasing technical mastery and evolving personal style. The young composer's artistic growth was helped immensely by the wealth of his father, who hired large ensembles of musicians to perform his son's works, including symphonies and comic operas, under Felix's own direction in the family home.

Late in 1821 Zelter took his young protégé to Weimar to meet the great German author Goethe, a personal friend of Zelter's. It was the first of several visits with Goethe during the years 1821-30. Goethe proved to be a powerful influence in Mendelssohn's life, the elder man's literary works exemplifying the classical sense of form and aristocracy of expression that came to be echoed in the younger man's music.

The Mendelssohns' home developed into the most important salon in Berlin. It was the site of numerous theatrical performances, literary readings, and concerts that often featured Felix's music. Guests included famous people of music, philosophy (notably Hegel), science, theater, and other fields.

Such a rich cultural atmosphere nurtured young Mendelssohn's natural gifts into an early blossoming. Stimulated by some lines from Goethe's *Faust,* Mendelssohn, in 1825, wrote his *String Octet,* which showed for the first time his full individual maturity. The following year he composed what is still his most popular work: the overture to Shakespeare's play *A Midsummer Night's Dream.* No one in the history of music, not even Mozart, has written such gloriously inspired and finished music at the tender ages of sixteen and seventeen.

In 1827 Mendelssohn entered the University of Berlin and briefly studied general subjects, including aesthetics under Hegel. Two years later, in March 1829, Mendelssohn conducted a revival of Bach's *St. Matthew Passion* at the Berlin Singing Academy, the first performance of the work since the composer's death in 1750 and the event that ushered in the modern realization of Bach's true stature.

The following month, April 1829, Mendelssohn, because his parents felt that traveling was essential for a complete education, embarked on a series of visits to leading European music capitals. During that period of extensive traveling, which lasted into 1835, he frequently appeared as pianist and conductor, sometimes performing his own works.

A number of his compositions were directly affected by his travels. For example, his 1829 visit to Edinburgh generated the first ideas for his *Third* (or *Scottish*) *Symphony* (1842). In the same year, 1829, a stormy steamship crossing to the Hebrides (islands off the west coast of Scotland) and a visit to the famous cave there inspired his concert overture *Die Hebriden* ("The Hebrides," 1830), also called *Fingals Höhle* ("Fingal's Cave"). An 1830 visit to Italy occasioned the beginning of his *Fourth (Italian) Symphony* (1833).

From 1833 to 1835 Mendelssohn spent most of his time in provincial Düsseldorf as the town's music director. He directed Catholic church music, organized concerts, and conducted operas. In addition, he arranged several Handel oratorios for performance, an activity that inspired the composition of his own Handel-like oratorio *St. Paul* (1836). During the years 1829-35 he also wrote many of his early poetic little piano pieces called *Lieder ohne Worte* ("Songs without Words").

In 1835 Mendelssohn was asked to take over the Gewandhaus Concerts in Leipzig. He jumped at the opportunity to rise from the sleepy village of Düsseldorf to a major city—especially since Leipzig had been the home of his idol, Bach. The years that Mendelssohn spent in Leipzig (1835-47) as conductor, music organizer, and performer were the most significant period of his life.

He revolutionized orchestral playing. Previously orchestras had been directed by one of the performers, usually the first violinist. Mendelssohn was among the first independent, baton-wielding conductors in the modern sense, and he trained the Gewandhaus Orchestra into one of the most precise ensembles of the era.

His work as a music organizer in Leipzig was also revolutionary. Before he arrived, the most frequently played composers had been minor, now-forgotten figures. But he cultivated his audiences' musical appreciation by programming the finest music available, both old and new. He made Mozart and Beethoven the backbone of his repertory, followed by Bach, Handel, Haydn, and Weber. One of the most important musical events of the era was the world premiere of Schubert's *Ninth (Great) Symphony,* conducted by Mendelssohn in 1839, eleven years after the composer's death. He also encouraged, with performances, such living composers as Frédéric Chopin, Ferdinand David, Niels Gade, Ferdinand Hiller, Franz Liszt, and, above all, Robert Schumann. Mendelssohn developed a close friendship with Schumann and his wife, the remarkable pianist Clara Wieck, whom Schumann married in 1840.

Not only important composers but also eminent performers were attracted to the Gewandhaus Concerts under Mendelssohn. He invited such soloists as the pianists Franz Liszt, Ignaz Moscheles, Anton Rubinstein, Clara Schumann (née Wieck), and Sigismond Thalberg;

the violinist Joseph Joachim; and the singer Jenny Lind. Mendelssohn himself performed as a pianist and organist.

Moreover, he did away with the customary variety programs and began to organize concerts in the modern fashion: an overture, a large-scale work, a concerto or another large-scale work, and a shorter piece. He refused to go along with the tradition of separating the movements of a symphony by inserting lighter forms of music.

His innovations at the Leipzig Gewandhaus—training the orchestra into a precision unit, playing important old works as well as significant new ones, recruiting outstanding performers, and organizing well-structured programs—laid the groundwork for modern symphonic organizations and concerts.

During his Leipzig years, Mendelssohn went through great changes in his personal life. In November 1835 he was shattered by the death of his father. Feeling a sudden and unwonted loneliness, he deliberately set out to find a wife. The following summer, in Frankfort on the Main, he met Cécile Jeanrenaud, daughter of a deceased Calvinist pastor. She put happiness back into his life: "Because of Cécile I am once again merry and glad and as carefree as I have not been since I left my parental home." They married in March 1837, after which their relationship grew even more ardent. Both of them found the separations during Felix's travels to be almost unbearable. They had five children: Karl, Marie, Paul, Felix (who died in childhood), and Lili, none of whom was musically gifted.

Cécile was a cultured woman, particularly fond of reading Goethe. But she was utterly unmusical. It was his sister Fanny, an excellent pianist, to whom Mendelssohn always turned for musical discussion and advice. Fanny married the artist Wilhelm Hensel, who painted an excellent portrait of Felix.

While retaining his connection with the Gewandhaus Concerts, he performed other major musical functions. In 1841 he was asked by Friedrich Wilhelm IV, king of Prussia, to take charge of an expanded program of musical activities in Berlin. One of Mendelssohn's duties was to compose incidental music for plays, including Shakespeare's *A Midsummer Night's Dream* (1842). In some of his pieces for that work he used themes from the overture that he had written sixteen years earlier. The music is particularly remarkable for having so thoroughly captured an English spirit. In fact, Mendelssohn was an Anglophile; and in his numerous visits to England, that nation fully returned his affection.

Discouraged by a lack of cooperation from his superiors in Berlin, Mendelssohn finally withdrew from his post there in 1844. Meanwhile, however, in 1843 he had become the first director of the newly established Leipzig Conservatory, where he again proved to be successful at organization. He formed a faculty that included Ferdinand David (violin), the important music theorist Moritz Hauptmann (harmony and counterpoint), Robert Schumann (piano and composition), and Mendelssohn himself (piano, later also composition). Within a few years they were joined by other outstanding musicians, such as the pianists Ignaz Moscheles and Clara Schumann.

In May 1847 Mendelssohn's sister Fanny suddenly died. He composed his last great work, the deeply moving F-minor *Sixth String Quartet* (1847), as a memorial for Fanny.

Already having shown signs of increasing weakness before his sister's death, Mendelssohn could not recover from the emotional and physical draining that he suffered when he lost her. After a series of strokes, he died in Leipzig on November 4, 1847, at the age of only thirty-eight. He was buried in Berlin, next to Fanny.

Mendelssohn's music is a very personal blend of romantic and classical elements. Living during a period

Felix Mendelssohn as painted by Wilhelm Hensel, Mendelssohn's brother-in-law

of growing romanticism, he often adopted the romantics' use of literature and other extramusical stimuli to inspire compositions. He was strongly influenced in that direction by Hegel, who held that even instrumental music should not only have its own abstract structure but also express something, however indeterminate. Yet, influenced by his father's conservatism, Goethe's classicism, and his own inclinations, Mendelssohn wrote music that, despite the romantic extramusical references, displays the techniques, forms, clarity, elegance, and grace of eighteenth-century classical and preclassical music.

By his midteens he had already absorbed the romantic and classical aspects of his creative nature and developed his own personal characteristics as well, such as small-scale rhythmic figures, melodies that incorporate a variety of motives, and flexibility in the use of traditional forms. The *String Octet* exemplifies all of the above characteristics, as do the incidental music to *A Midsummer Night's Dream,* the *Italian* and *Scottish* symphonies, and many others.

The course of Mendelssohn's music and reputation since his death has not been a smooth one. In the second half of the nineteenth century, the inappropriate application of romantic performance techniques (such as exaggerated fluctuations in tempo and phrasing) led to a sentimentalizing, and thus misunderstanding, of his music. At the same time, he was demeaned and his music was devalued at every opportunity by anti-Semites, led by the vicious Richard Wagner, who claimed that Mendelssohn, as a Jew, was incapable of creating music that moved the heart and soul. Fifty years later came Adolf Hitler, who not only attempted to annihilate all living Jews but also suppressed the cultural heritage from earlier Jews, including Mendelssohn. In 1936 the Nazis destroyed the famous statue of Mendelssohn that had stood in front of the Gewandhaus in Leipzig since 1892.

Since the defeat of the Nazis in World War II, Mendelssohn has risen in stature throughout the Western world. Research has led to more appropriate, classically oriented interpretations of his music, and he can now be accurately assessed as one of the greatest composers and most influential musicians of the nineteenth century.

Selected works:

Stage

Antigone (incidental music, 1841)
A Midsummer Night's Dream (incidental music, 1842)

Orchestral

A Midsummer Night's Dream (concert overture, 1826)
Meeresstille und glückliche Fahrt ("Calm Sea and Prosperous Voyage," concert overture, 1828)
Die Hebriden (or *Fingals Höhle;* concert overture; 1830, revised 1832; based on an 1829 version entitled *Die einsame Insel* ["The Lonely Island"])
First Piano Concerto (1831)
Fifth (Reformation) Symphony (1832)
Fourth (Italian) Symphony (1833)
Rondo brillant (piano, orchestra; 1834)
Second Piano Concerto (1837)
Ruy Blas (concert overture, 1839)
Third (Scottish) Symphony (1842)
Violin Concerto (1844)

Vocal

Die erste Walpurgisnacht ("The First Walpurgis Night"; cantata; text, J. W. von Goethe; 1832, revised 1843)
St. Paul (oratorio; text, J. Schubring, after the Bible; 1836)
Elijah (oratorio; text, J. Schubring, after the Bible; 1846)
choral songs
psalms
sacred cantatas
solo songs

Chamber

Sextet (violin, two violas, cello, double bass, piano; 1824)
Octet (four violins, two violas, two cellos; 1825)
Third, Fourth, and *Fifth* string quartets (1838)
First Piano Trio (1839)
Second Cello Sonata (1843)
Second Piano Trio (1845)

Piano

Rondo capriccioso ("Capricious Rondo," 1824)
Capriccio ("Caprice," 1825)
Lieder ohne Worte (many sets, 1830-45)
Variations sérieuses ("Serious Variations," 1841)

Yehudi Menuhin
Violinist and Humanitarian
(1916-   )

Yehudi Menuhin, violinist, was born of Russian immigrants in New York City, New York, on April 22, 1916. His father had originally transliterated the family name as "Mnuchin" before settling on the present spelling. Early in his parents' marriage, while looking for a place to live, they were shown a New York City apartment by the landlady, who, in ignorance of the young couple's background, tried to clinch the bargain by saying, "And you'll be glad to know I don't take Jews." Bitter at discovering in the New World the same hostility that drove them out of the Old, they found another apartment and vowed to give their children names that would proudly proclaim their heritage to everyone. Hence, the

first child, a boy, was named after the Hebrew word meaning "Jew": Yĕhūdī.

When Yehudi was two years old, his parents moved to San Francisco, California, and soon began to take him to concerts of the San Francisco Symphony Orchestra, where the boy's attention focused on the concertmaster, Louis Persinger. Fascinated by Persinger's violin solos, Yehudi asked for, and received, a violin when he was four years old. After one year of lessons from a local teacher, Sigmund Anker, young Menuhin was accepted as a student by Persinger himself, who had studied with the famed Eugène Ysaÿe.

During the next couple of years Menuhin made some

minor public appearances, culminating in his formal debut in early 1924 when his performance of Charles-Auguste de Bériot's *Scène de ballet* ("Ballet Scene") was inserted into a San Francisco Symphony Orchestra concert at the Oakland Auditorium. The following year he performed with an orchestra for the first time (the Bériot work having been a nonorchestral piece) when he played Edouard Lalo's *Symphonie espagnole* ("Spanish Symphony") with the San Francisco Symphony under Alfred Hertz. Also in 1925 he gave his first full-length recital, in the Scottish Rite Hall in San Francisco. Then, in 1926, he went to New York City with Persinger as his accompanist and made his debut there in a recital at the Manhattan Opera House.

In early 1927, on his first trip to Europe, Menuhin made a sensational Paris debut and began to take lessons there from Georges Enesco. Back in the United States in late 1927, Menuhin played Beethoven's *Violin Concerto* with Fritz Busch conducting the New York Symphony Orchestra at Carnegie Hall in New York City. As a result of that concert Menuhin became an overnight world celebrity.

In 1928 he resumed his lessons with Persinger in San Francisco, made his first recordings, and started his first American tour. The following year he returned to Europe for further study with Enesco and with Adolf Busch (brother of Fritz Busch).

Menuhin debuted in Berlin in 1928 and in London in 1929. Throughout the 1930s he toured extensively in Europe and the United States. Highlights of that period included a recording and a concert performance (both in England, 1932) of Edward Elgar's *Violin Concerto* under the baton of the composer himself.

During World War II Menuhin gave over five hundred concerts for Allied troops in many theaters of war, and he was the first artist to appear in the reopened Paris Opéra immediately after the end of the German occupation in 1944. In July 1945, with the British composer-pianist Benjamin Britten as accompanist, Menuhin went to Germany to play for displaced people and survivors of the death camps. In November of that year he went to Moscow to help cement friendly relations between the peoples of Russia and America.

In 1947 Menuhin became the first Jewish artist to perform with the Berlin Philharmonic Orchestra under the conductor Wilhelm Furtwängler after the war. The violinist was much criticized, especially by Jewish communities, for appearing with Furtwängler, who had held his post during the Nazi regime. Menuhin, however, had acted partly out of his lifelong belief in the nobility of seeking conciliation rather than conflict, and partly out of his specific belief that Furtwängler had steered a middle course in which the conductor's main fault was in assuming that, in Menuhin's words, "the power of music" was "proof against contamination" by the Nazis.

Shortly after the Furtwängler performance, Menuhin went to Berlin's Deuppel Center, a camp for displaced people, mostly Jews. At first he was booed, hissed, and cursed. But after he explained why he was in Germany—to show that Jews would not imitate the hate-filled mentality of the Nazis and "to show how false was Hitler's caricature" of Jews—the people began to cheer him.

In 1950 Menuhin made the first of his many visits to Israel. He gave twenty-four recitals in twelve days. At first he sensed a tenseness toward him by the Israelis, but by the end of the tour they were offering only goodwill. However, further conflicts between Menuhin and some Israelis flared up in 1967 and 1974-75. After the Six-Day War in 1967, he gave concerts in Arab-speaking countries for the benefit of Arab refugees. In late 1974, after the general assembly of the United Nations Educational, Scientific, and Cultural Organization (UNESCO) had censured Israel for its treatment of Arabs, many Jewish musicians wanted the International Music Council (ICM, a subsidiary of UNESCO) to sever its connections with the parent body; and the Israeli ICM delegation itself issued a written statement censuring the UNESCO condemnation of Israel. Menuhin worked tirelessly for moderation and tolerance on both sides. The immediate problem was finally resolved—at least in the ICM ranks—and the Israelis retracted their statement of censure.

In further pursuit of his aim of international brotherhood, he made one of the earliest postwar concert tours of Japan by an American (1951). In 1952 he made his first visit to India and became fascinated by its yoga and its philosophy as well as its music. Soon he was bringing Indian musicians to the United States and was encouraging, and collaborating in, the performance of Indian music in Western culture; he has performed many times with the famed sitarist Ravi Shankar. Also, the efforts of Menuhin were largely responsible for the cultural exchange between the United States and the Soviet Union in 1955, accounting for the first American visit of the Soviet violinist David Oistrakh.

In 1959 Menuhin settled in London and began to diversify his musical activities. One of his major interests has been directing music festivals: the Bath Festival (1959-68), the Windsor Festival (1969-72), and the Gstaad (Switzerland) Festival (since 1956). In 1958 he formed a chamber orchestra for the purpose of recording Bach's *Brandenburg Concertos*. The group functioned so well that he took it to the Bath Festival a few months later and named it the Bath Festival Orchestra. Since 1968 the ensemble has performed under Menuhin's own name, with him as conductor or soloist-conductor. He has also guest-conducted many of the leading symphony orchestras in Europe and America.

In 1963 he founded a boarding school for musically talented children: the Yehudi Menuhin School of Music in the Kensington district of London. In 1964 he moved the school to the estate at Stoke d'Abernon, on the Surrey side of the city, where the institution is still active.

He has also fostered other educational facilities, has served as president of the Royal Philharmonic Orchestra since 1982, and has appeared regularly on British and American TV.

Menuhin is a world citizen with a wide range of non-musical interests. He actively supports well over two hundred organizations around the globe, including the America-Israel Society, the Anti-Apartheid Movement, the Fellowship of Reconciliation, the League of Non-Violence, and the Meals for Millions.

Menuhin has made numerous educational films on violin playing, and he supplied the violin music for the soundtrack of the commercial movie *The Magic Bow* (1946), supposedly a biopic of Paganini. In recent years he has turned to writing, including the books *Violin: Six Lessons with Yehudi Menuhin* (copyrighted 1971, published 1972), an instructional manual; *Theme and Variations* (1972), extremely lucid, thought-provoking essays on a variety of subjects; *Violin and Viola* (with William Primrose, 1976); *Unfinished Journey* (1977), an autobiography; and *The Music of Man* (with Curtis W. Davis, 1979), a music-appreciation book based on his TV series of the same name. He has also edited playing editions of works by Bartók, Mendelssohn, and Walton.

As a violinist, Menuhin is renowned for the purity of his style and for the nobility and depth of his interpretative power. However, he himself admits that he periodically rethinks the whole basis of his approach to violin technique. Thus, his artistic development has not followed a straight line but has jagged out of the traditional paths in search of ever broader musical and human values expressible through his violin.

He is widely regarded as being at his best in chamber music. Among his partners have been the violist Ernst Wallfisch, the cellists Pablo Casals and Mstislav Rostropovitch, and the pianists Vladimir Ashkenazy and Louis Kentner.

Menuhin's repertory covers a wide range. His favorites are Bach and Beethoven, though he regularly plays romantic and modern works as well, with Bartók high on his list of twentieth-century composers. However, Menuhin is also fond of playing light classics, especially Johann Strauss II and Offenbach.

Menuhin has greatly increased the modern repertory by commissioning works from composers. Among the numerous compositions written for him are unaccompanied violin sonatas by Bartók and Ross Lee Finney; suites for unaccompanied violin by Ernest Bloch; violin-piano sonatas by Paul Ben-Haim, William Walton, and Stanley Weiner; violin concertos by Easley Blackwood, Oedoen Partos, Malcolm Williamson, and others; and a concerto for violin and sitar by Alan Hovhaness. He has also championed much new music that he did not commission, including works by Bartók, Bloch, Britten, Enesco, Hindemith, Ravel, and many others.

Menuhin has had two marriages. In 1938 he wedded Nola Nicholas, daughter of a wealthy Australian industrialist. Her worldliness and his innocence caused a conflict from the very beginning, and they finally divorced in 1947 after having two children: Zamira and Krov. Later in 1947 he married Diana Gould, a ballerina and actress. They had two children: Gerard and Jeremy, the latter of whom has become a well-known pianist.

Menuhin has performed with many members of his family. His second wife, Diana, retired from the stage when she married, but she reemerged in 1969 in a comedy role in an English-language version of Mozart's *Der Schauspieldirektor* ("The Impresario," with the story rewritten by the British actor Robert Morley) at the Bath Festival, Menuhin conducting. Since then, with her husband's encouragement, she has gone on to do much acting and writing. Menuhin has performed numerous times, both as violinist and as conductor, with his son Jeremy at the piano. Menuhin's sister Hephzibah was an excellent pianist, and they often played sonatas together in public, beginning in the early 1930s. Her death in 1981 affected him deeply. In addition, he has performed with his other sister, Yaltah, also a pianist. In April 1966, at London's Royal Festival Hall, Mozart's *Triple Concerto* was played by pianists Hephzibah, Yaltah, and Jeremy, while Yehudi Menuhin conducted.

Robert Merrill

One of the Great Baritones of His Time

(1919-   )

Robert Merrill, baritone, was born of Polish immigrants in New York City, New York, on June 4, 1919. His original name was Moishe (sometimes anglicized as Morris) Miller. His father had been named Abraham Millstein in Poland. But at Ellis Island, while being processed for entry into the United States, he had difficulty in writing past the first four letters in his surname; an impatient official reached in and simply added an *e* and an *r*. Thus Abraham Millstein became Abraham Miller.

While Moishe's father worked as a sewing-machine operator in a clothing factory, his mother, Lotza (sometimes anglicized as Lillian), sang as a soprano at weddings and bar mitzvahs, as well as on local radio stations. But she was frustrated in her greater ambitions and decided to fulfill herself through the singing career of Moishe, whom she called "singer mine."

Moishe, though he loved to sing, was more interested in baseball. (In his late teens he played some semipro ball as a pitcher.) However, he agreed to study voice on the condition that he be allowed to sing like Bing Crosby, at that time the idol of American youth. Lotza wanted him to study opera, but she agreed (temporarily) to the condition: "So, singer mine," she said in her Polish-Yiddish accent, "we'll start with Pink Cruspy!"

She found an instructor to teach the boy "popular interpretation." Soon Moishe, in his early teens, was imitating all of the tricks of Crosby's crooning. It was not long before he had won a job singing Crosby songs at the same radio station, WFOX, where his mother sang. (After her son's career was well established, she stopped performing.) To keep his musical activities secret from his pals, he sang under the assumed name Merrill Miller.

But the radio work, though good experience, was nonpaying. It was during the depths of the Great Depression, and the sixteen-year-old Moishe had to take a job pushing a dress cart for his Uncle Abe on the streets of New York City. One day Moishe was passing the back of the Metropolitan Opera House and noticed that sets were being moved in. Pretending that the dresses on his rack were opera costumes, he sneaked into the Met. After he got inside, he hid in the dark and listened to Lawrence Tibbett and Lucrezia Bori sing a duet from Verdi's *La traviata* ("The Wayward Woman"), music that Moishe knew from his mother's records at home. It was a moment of revelation, and by the time that he was finally thrown out of the theater he had become completely stagestruck.

Soon after that he began to take serious vocal lessons with Samuel Margolis, who became his principal teacher.

When Moishe was eighteen, Margolis took him to see his first complete opera, a performance at the Met of Verdi's *Il trovatore* ("The Troubadour") with Richard Bonelli as Count di Luna. Moishe was "stunned" by Bonelli's performance, which changed the young man, in his own words, "from a confused, stagestruck kid to a true opera student."

Nevertheless, while studying opera, he entered show business to earn money. For the next several years, under the name Merrill Miller, he appeared at weddings, at bar mitzvahs, in synagogues (for Yom Kippur and Rosh Hashanah), on the borscht circuit (summer theaters and nightclubs associated with the Jewish resorts in the Catskills), on a radio program called *Serenade to America*, in a Jewish theater on Second Avenue, and elsewhere. He sang a wide variety of popular songs, making a special hit with the "Donkey Serenade." But he also performed opera arias, including the one that eventually became his trademark: the "Largo al factotum" ("Make Way for the Factotum") from Rossini's *Il barbiere di Siviglia* ("The Barber of Seville"). For Jewish audiences he translated into Yiddish, with his mother's help, such works as Rossini's "Largo al factotum" and Bizet's "Toreador Song" (the familiar name for the aria "Votre toast, je peux vous le rendre" ["For a Toast, Your Own Will Avail Me"]) from *Carmen*.

In 1944 he was scheduled to perform at a Red Cross benefit. At the rehearsal Mark Warnow, who conducted the *Hit Parade* and was slated to introduce Merrill Miller, turned to the young singer and said, "I can't stand your name, kid. . . . You look like a Bob to me." Thus Merrill Miller became Robert Merrill.

Also in 1944 Merrill made his opera debut, as Amonasro in a one-time performance of Verdi's *Aïda* staged in New Jersey by an independent company. The following year he won the Metropolitan Opera Auditions of the Air; and in late 1945 he made his Met debut, as the elder Germont in *La traviata*.

For the next several years he sang at the Met for his artistic fulfillment. But at the same time he continued his work in popular music both for the money (earning $2,000 a week on radio compared with $125 a week at the Met) and for the mass adulation that he craved at the time. Besides having his own radio program, *The Robert Merrill Show,* he was the star and host of radio's *Music America Loves Best*.

In 1946 the conductor Arturo Toscanini invited Merrill to sing the elder Germont in a National Broadcasting Company (NBC) Symphony Orchestra radio performance of *La traviata*. Merrill has described that invitation from the revered Toscanini as "perhaps the greatest moment of my life."

Also in 1946 Merrill appeared as the only singer at a service before both houses of Congress on the anniversary of President Franklin D. Roosevelt's death. He had earlier sung for the living President Roosevelt and would later perform for the next several presidents, having a particularly close relationship with President Truman, with whose daughter, Margaret, Merrill sang many duets while the president accompanied on the piano.

In 1951 Merrill missed the Metropolitan Opera's spring tour because he was making a movie at the time. In consequence, the Met's general manager, Rudolf Bing, dismissed Merrill from the company. The movie, *Aaron Slick from Punkin Crick* (1952), was a flop; and after making a public apology, he was reinstated by Bing in the spring of 1952.

Merrill became one of the most durable stars at the Met. In 1970 he celebrated the twenty-fifth anniversary of his Met debut, and in 1973 he became the first American to sing five hundred performances with the company. A few years later he left the Met.

During his Met years Merrill also made guest appearances at other opera houses, notably the San Francisco Opera; gave solo recitals; and performed in concerts with major orchestras. In 1970 he made his musical-theater debut, touring as Tevye in *Fiddler on the Roof*. Only occasionally, however, did he appear abroad. In 1975, for example, he made his London concert debut, and in the same year he toured Israel.

He has written two autobiographical books, *Once More from the Beginning* (with Sandford Dody, 1965) and *Between Acts: An Irreverent Look at Opera and Other Madness* (with Robert Saffron, 1976), as well as the novel *The Divas* (with Fred Jarvis, 1978).

Merrill was the preeminent baritone of his generation at the Met in terms of longevity, technical security, and natural beauty and resonance of voice. His repertory included all of the major French and Italian baritone roles, such as Amonasro in Verdi's *Aïda*, Escamillo in Bizet's *Carmen*, Figaro in Rossini's *Il barbiere di Siviglia*, the elder Germont in Verdi's *La traviata*, Iago in Verdi's *Otello*, and Rigoletto in Verdi's *Rigoletto*.

Merrill has long been closely associated with the New York Yankees baseball team, especially singing the national anthem at major events. In 1975 he sang in Saint Patrick's Cathedral in New York City during a memorial service for former Yankee manager Casey Stengel.

Merrill has had two marriages. In 1952, shortly after his return to the Met, he married Roberta Peters, another young star there. Soon, however, she left for the Hollywood section of Los Angeles to make a movie, and they were divorced later that year. But they remained good friends and since then have often appeared together in joint recitals.

Robert Merrill as the elder Germont in Verdi's *La traviata*

In 1954 he married Marion Machno, a young pianist and piano teacher. Even before they were married, Marion, instead of passively joining the general praise that he received from others around him, showed the honesty and devotion of a true friend by encouraging him to improve his performances through harder work and more careful listening to the other characters onstage: "I want you to be an *artist*, not just a singer," she told him. The Merrills had two children: David (who became a bass guitarist in a rock band) and Lizanne.

Giacomo Meyerbeer
Leader of French Grand Opera
(1791-1864)

Giacomo Meyerbeer, composer, was born in Vogelsdorf, near Berlin, Germany, on September 5, 1791. Originally named Jakob Liebmann Beer, he came from a family of wealthy merchants and bankers. His maternal grandfather was Liebmann Meyer Wulf (a businessman and highly respected leader of the Jewish community), whose middle name Jakob, early in his career, adopted to form the new surname Meyerbeer. The young composer also Italianized his first name to Giacomo.

In early childhood he was exposed to a rich cultural environment, the family home being a meeting place for many important figures in the arts, especially music. (Other members of the family also benefited from that atmosphere: his brother Wilhelm Beer became a well-known astronomer, while another brother, Michael

Beer, earned fame as a poet and playwright.) Jakob took some piano lessons from the famous Muzio Clementi when the latter was a guest in the Beer home. But the boy studied primarily with Franz Lauska, piano teacher to the royal princess.

In his early teens Jakob began to study theory and composition, first briefly with Carl Friedrich Zelter and then at greater length with Bernhard Anselm Weber. In 1810 young Meyerbeer's ballet-pantomime *Der Fischer und das Milchmädchen* ("The Fisherman and the Milkmaid") was performed in Berlin.

His progress was so great that Weber recommended him to Abbé Vogler, the leading music theorist in Germany. In the spring of 1810 the young musician traveled to Vogler's city, Darmstadt, where one of his fellow pupils was Carl Maria von Weber. During his nearly two years with Vogler, Meyerbeer made great progress as a pianist. He also composed many works, notably the opera *Jephtas Gelübde* ("Jephtha's Vow").

Meyerbeer, anxious to get his own career under way and tired of being overshadowed by his famous teacher, left Vogler near the end of 1811. Early the next year he moved to Munich and soon earned a reputation as a fine pianist. In December 1812 his *Jephtas Gelübde* was performed in Munich, followed in January 1813 by a production of his little comic opera *Wirth und Gast* ("Host and Guest") in Stuttgart.

Both works were poorly received. However, the second was soon accepted for production in Vienna. While traveling to that city, he learned that he had been named court composer to the grand duke of Hesse, a post secured for him by Vogler. The Vienna production of his opera was, as in Stuttgart, unsuccessful.

Meanwhile, his career as a pianist had been progressing well. But having been humbled by listening to the great pianist Johann Hummel, Meyerbeer put off his Vienna debut for several months to perfect his own technique. Finally reemerging, he quickly developed into one of the most renowned pianists in Europe. In late 1814 he went from Vienna to Paris, and in late 1815 to London.

However, he still felt that composing operas was his true vocation. Acting on Antonio Salieri's suggestion that a study of Italian melody would correct his heavy contrapuntal style, Meyerbeer traveled to Italy in early 1816 to spend a few months collecting and studying folksongs. But he found Italy so congenial that he stayed nine years, broken only by occasional visits to Germany and Austria.

Meyerbeer met numerous artists, librettists, and impresarios who gave him access to the Italian stage. He began with the monodrama *Gli amori di Teolinda* ("The Loves of Teolinda," perf. 1816) and then came out with six operas, beginning with *Romilda e Costanza* ("Romilda and Costanza," perf. 1817) and ending with *Il crociato in Egitto* ("The Crusader in Egypt," perf. 1824). The works were fabulously successful, and his popularity in Italy rivaled that of Rossini.

However, the reserve with which his Italian operas were met in Germany convinced Meyerbeer that instead of returning to his homeland, the next step in his career should be to go to Paris.

He arrived in the French capital in 1825, and thereafter Meyerbeer spent several months a year in Paris, but he never settled there permanently. A truly international figure—a German Jew who became famous with Italian operas and eventually wrote his best music to French words—Meyerbeer traveled incessantly: taking cures at health resorts, attending productions of his operas, and, above all, auditioning new singers (his habit being to tailor the music for all of his primary roles around the capabilities of specific performers).

He began his Paris career in 1825, with a production of his most successful Italian opera: *Il crociato in Egitto*. The following year he presented a revised, French-language version of another of his Italian operas: *Margherita d'Anjou* ("Margherita of Anjou").

His early years in France were marked by upheavals in his personal life. In 1825 his father unexpectedly died. The following year he married his cousin Minna Mosson, daughter of his mother's younger sister. They had two children: Eugénie and Alfred. But in 1827 and 1829 respectively, the children died in infancy, and Meyerbeer went into a period of deep depression.

But he fought his way back from grief by working out a method for a new kind of dramatic work. In 1831 he staged his first French opera, *Robert le diable* ("Robert the Devil"), followed in 1836 by *Les Huguenots* ("The Huguenots"). With those works Meyerbeer and his primary librettist, Eugène Scribe, firmly established the style for a kind of dramatic work that came to be known as grand opera, which evolved from the eighteenth-century heroic type. Grand opera was designed to appeal to the generally uncultured audiences of the middle class, who were new to the world of the high arts and went to the theater primarily in search of excitement and entertainment. As a result, grand operas are characterized by sentimentality, sensationalism, and spectacle, including many ballets, choruses, and noisy crowd scenes.

In 1839 Meyerbeer met Richard Wagner and gave him financial aid and valuable professional recommendations that paved the way for productions of Wagner's operas. But when Meyerbeer discovered that he was being criticized behind his back by Wagner, he dropped his support of the young man.

In 1842 a temporary liberalization of policy toward Jews allowed Meyerbeer to be appointed Prussian general music director. But, disgusted by a power struggle within the system, he left his duties and was finally dismissed in 1848.

However, the royal court itself retained his services as director for the rest of his life. For royal family occasions and official court entertainments, he composed many miscellaneous works, including several fackeltänze, or torch dances (German *Fackel* ["torch"]). He also wrote the opera *Ein Feldlager in Schlesien* ("A Camp in Silesia," perf. 1844).

In 1846 he provided incidental music for a production of the play *Struensee* by his brother Michael Beer. His next grand opera, *Le prophète* ("The Prophet," perf. 1849), brought him such fame that he became the first German musician ever to be decorated a Commander of the Legion of Honor (having earlier been made a Chevalier).

He also became one of the richest men in Europe. Journalists often asked Meyerbeer for loans, thus compromising their objectivity in writing about his music. A man who liked publicity, Meyerbeer virtually invented the modern press conference, including the use of refreshments.

His final grand opera, *L'africaine* ("The African Woman"), on which he had been working off and on since 1837, remained unfinished when he died in Paris on May 2, 1864. At Meyerbeer's own request François-Joseph Fétis made the final revisions of the opera, which was premiered a year after the composer's death.

Meyerbeer's operas have not held the stage well. Concentrating on spectacle and being a patchwork of Italian, French, and German elements, each opera—to a greater or less degree—lacks artistic unity and personal conviction. Nevertheless, Meyerbeer remains a significant figure on several counts. He was a dominant influence on grand opera for more than three decades. His experimental treatment of the orchestra influenced Verdi and other composers. He initiated the practice of using music research to help create a sense of historical authenticity in period operas, such as his study of sixteenth-century instrumental music for *Les Huguenots* and his use of the *Yigdal* (Hebrew, "May He Be Magnified," a liturgical hymn) in the same opera. And, of course, many individual passages in Meyerbeer's operas are of great dramatic and musical beauty.

Selected works:

Operas

Jephtas Gelübde (libretto, A. Schreiber; perf. 1812)
Wirth und Gast (libretto, J. G. Wohlbrück; perf. 1813)
Romilda e Costanza (libretto, G. Rossi; perf. 1817)
Margherita d'Anjou (libretto, F. Romani, after R. Pixérécourt; perf. 1820; revised, French, 1826)
Il crociato in Egitto (libretto, G. Rossi; perf. 1824)
Robert le diable (libretto, E. Scribe, G. Delavigne; perf. 1831)
Les Huguenots (libretto, E. Scribe, E. Deschamps; perf. 1836)
Ein Feldlager in Schlesien (libretto, E. Scribe, L. Rellstab, C. Birch-Pfeiffer; perf. 1844)
Le prophète (libretto, E. Scribe; perf. 1849)
L'africaine (libretto, E. Scribe, F.-J. Fétis; perf. 1865)

Other Stage

Der Fischer und das Milchmädchen (divertissement; libretto, E. Lauchery; perf. 1810)
Gli amori di Teolinda (monodrama; libretto, G. Rossi; perf. 1816)
Struensee (incidental music, perf. 1846)

Instrumental

four fackeltänze (military band, 1844-58)
orchestral marches

Vocal

choral works
songs

Bette Midler
Queen of Camp
(1945-   )

Known as "the Divine Miss M," the singer Bette Midler is famed for her unique song stylings and her lively (sometimes bizarre, as when she dresses as a hot dog or a female King Kong) stage shows.

She was born in Hawaii on December 1, 1945, not long after her parents had arrived from New Jersey. Her mother named the girl after the actress Bette Davis; but Mrs. Midler, like many other fans, mistakenly thought that Davis pronounced her first name "Bet" (instead of the correct "Bet-tē"). Thus, Bette Midler's given name has always been pronounced "Bet."

In Hawaii the Midlers were the only white people in a basically Oriental community. For psychological survival Bette pretended to be Portuguese because, as she later explained, "Portuguese people were accepted. Jews were not. I was an alien, a foreigner—even though I was born there."

Her sensitivity was increased by the fact that she was an overweight, plain-looking child. As she has put it, "I was an ugly, fat little Jewish girl with problems."

But she soon found a wonderful way to build her self-esteem: performing. In the first grade she won a prize for singing "Silent Night, Holy Night." After that, she was featured in many school and amateur productions. All during her youth, she dreamed of becoming a professional actress; and when she briefly attended the University of Hawaii, she studied drama.

In 1965 Midler got a bit part (as the seasick wife of a missionary) in the movie *Hawaii* (1966), which was being filmed on location. When the movie company traveled to Los Angeles to finish filming, she went with it. After the movie was completed, she moved to New York City to begin a stage career. She took miscellaneous jobs (hatcheck girl, typist, salesperson, go-go dancer) and landed a few minor roles in the theater. Finally, in 1966, one of those roles was in the immensely successful musical *Fiddler on the Roof*. She was with *Fiddler* for three years, working herself up from the chorus to one of the major roles.

It was while she was with *Fiddler* that she decided to concentrate on a career as a singer. She has said that the real catalyst for her vocal career was hearing Aretha Franklin's tribute to Dinah Washington, in which, according to Midler, Franklin "was singing but she was talking."

After getting some occasional singing jobs in Greenwich Village, Midler got her big break in 1970. She was hired as a singer at the Continental Baths, a Turkish bath for male homosexuals. Wearing platform shoes, toreador pants, strapless tops, and out-of-date costumes (she has called herself "the last of the truly tacky women"), Midler camped and strutted her way through a wide variety of novelty songs in front of an audience of men dressed in bath towels. The bizarre nature of her job led to requests for her to appear on the David Frost and Johnny Carson TV shows.

By 1972 Midler was being sought by leading clubs across the nation. Also in 1972 she came out with her first album, *The Divine Miss M.*

In 1973 Midler toured with her music director, Barry Manilow, a pianist whom she had met at the Continental Baths during a return engagement there in 1972. She did

not concertize or record during 1974. In 1975 she re-established herself with a cross-country tour that concluded with her Broadway performance in the successful revue *Clams on the Half Shell*.

Midler has shown versatility. Her repertory includes not only contemporary rock but also blues and various other stylings from the 1940s, 1950s, and 1960s.

She has also returned to her first love, acting, notably in the movies *The Rose* (1979) and *Divine Madness* (1980), the latter being a re-creation of her bawdy one-woman Broadway show of the same name. Midler also sang in both films.

Her versatility shows up in yet another facet of her career. She has written, to date, two books. *A View from a Broad* (1980) covers her adventures when she took her act on a world tour. *The Saga of Baby Divine* (1983) is a poetic fairy tale, ostensibly for children, about living life to the fullest.

In August 1983, while touring with her act *De Tour*, Midler fainted from overwork. Since then, she has stated that she may discontinue her singing activities and turn instead to the less demanding work of a stand-up comedienne.

In December 1984 Midler married Martin von Haselberg (alias Harry Kipper), a performing artist and commodities trader.

Selected recordings:

Singles

"Do You Want to Dance?" (1973, Atlantic)
"Boogie-Woogie Bugle Boy" (1973, Atlantic)
"The Rose" (1980, Atlantic)

Albums

The Divine Miss M (1972, Atlantic)
Bette Midler (1973, Atlantic)
Live at Last (1977, Atlantic)
The Rose (1979, Atlantic)
Divine Madness (1980, Atlantic)
No Frills (1983, Atlantic)

Darius Milhaud

Prolific French Composer
Identified with Polytonality
(1892-1974)

Darius Milhaud, composer, was born in Aix-en-Provence, France, on September 4, 1892. He was fortunate to have early cultural exposure from both parents, his mother having studied singing for many years in Paris, while his father was an able amateur pianist. By the age of four little Milhaud was playing piano duets with his father. At seven the boy began to play the violin and soon afterward started to compose.

In 1909 Milhaud went to Paris to attend the conservatory, where he studied violin with Henri Berthelier, harmony with Xavier Leroux, counterpoint with André Gédalge, orchestration with Paul Dukas, conducting with Vincent d'Indy, and composition with Charles-Marie Widor. Milhaud's artistic outlook was influenced by many writers and painters whom he met during his student years, especially Paul Claudel and Francis Jammes. Also at that time he began to travel widely, a lifelong habit even after he developed a severely disabling rheumatoid arthritis that eventually confined him to a wheelchair.

Milhaud composed a great deal of music while still a student. In 1915 he completed his most crucial early work: the incidental music to Claudel's play (after Aeschylus) *Les choëphores* ("The Libation Bearers"). In that music he established polytonality as his basic harmonic language, and his individual manner in using that device came to characterize almost all of his work. He was the first composer to exploit polytonality consistently.

When Claudel was appointed French minister to Brazil in 1916, he invited Milhaud to accompany him as his secretary. The nearly two years (early 1917 to late 1918) that they spent in South America made a lasting impression on the young composer, who soaked up the atmosphere and the native music. Among his works influenced by that stay are the ballet *L'homme et son désir* ("Man and His Desire," 1918) and the piano dance suites *Saudades do Brasil* ("Souvenirs of Brazil," 1921).

Returning to Paris, Milhaud joined a brilliant circle of writers (Cocteau, Apollinaire), artists (Picasso, Braque), and composers (Poulenc, Honegger). In 1920 the French critic Henri Collet coined the term *Les Six* ("The Six") to refer to Milhaud and five other young French composers actually having in common only their general reaction against both Germanic romanticism and French impressionism. Milhaud himself leaned toward a casual but sophisticated form of neoclassicism. At that time he had a reputation as an enfant terrible for his use of striking dissonances and unusual subject matter, as in the 1919 song cycle *Machines agricoles* ("Agricultural Machines," settings of farm-machinery descriptions in agricultural catalogs).

In 1920 Milhaud discovered jazz; and in 1922 he went on a tour of the United States, where he heard first-rate performances of such music. Inspired by his first experience of authentic black jazz in Harlem, he wrote the ballet *La création du monde* ("The Creation of the World," 1923), one of his most popular works.

Throughout the 1920s and 1930s Milhaud composed prolifically in a wide variety of genres, while touring extensively in Europe and elsewhere as a conductor and pianist.

During that time he bore with remarkable courage repeated attacks of crippling arthritis. In 1925 he married Madeleine Milhaud, his cousin. A devoted mate, she comforted him during his periods of severe pain and helped him with his wheelchair and cane when he traveled. She was also a gifted poet and actress, collaborating with him in a number of dramatic works, such as his opera *Médée* ("Medea"; comp. 1938, perf. 1939), for which she supplied the libretto.

The fall of France during World War II drove Milhaud, accompanied by his wife and son, Daniel (who later became a painter), out of the country. Arriving in the United States in 1940, he joined the faculty of Mills College in Oakland, California. From 1947 on, he divided his time between France, where he became a professor of composition at the Paris Conservatory, and the United States, where he taught at Mills College and other institutions, notably the summer school at Aspen, Colorado.

During those later years of his life, Milhaud continued to compose at an incredible pace, particularly considering his physical infirmity, which forced him into numerous bedridden periods of time. In 1952 he wrote the biblical opera *David* for the celebrations surrounding the three thousandth anniversary of Jerusalem as the capital of David's kingdom. During the composition of the work, he made a special trip to Israel to soak up the atmosphere. The opera was premiered, in a concert version, at the 1954 Festival of Israel in Jerusalem.

In 1971, when Milhaud was nearly eighty, poor health finally forced him to reduce his activities, whereupon he moved to Geneva, Switzerland. His last work was the cantata *Ani maamin, un chant perdu et retrouvé* ("I Believe, a Song Lost and Found," 1972), written for the

1973 Festival of Israel. He died in Geneva on June 22, 1974.

Milhaud was one of the twentieth century's most industrious composers, driven, at least in part, by a constant need to prove to himself that his creative powers were not limited by his illness.

He named the two main sources of his musical inspiration in the opening words of his autobiography *(Notes sans musique,* 1949; English, as *Notes without Music,* 1952): "I am a Frenchman from Provence, and by religion a Jew." Essentially a lyric composer, Milhaud, regardless of his subject matter or musical material, almost always evoked the Mediterranean spirit of his native region. Some of his works draw on actual folk or traditional melodies, as in the *Suite provençale* ("Provençal Suite") for orchestra (1936) and the *Suite française* ("French Suite") for brass band (1944). Many other works reflect the pastoral simplicity and directness of French folk-song, such as the *First String Quartet* (1912), the *First Piano Sonata* (1916), and the six chamber symphonies (1917-23).

For a number of his works, Milhaud drew on synagogal traditions (especially of his native region, the Comtat Venaissin). Intense emotion, particularly lamentation, characterize many of his Jewish compositions, such as the moving song cycle *Poèmes juifs* ("Jewish Poems," 1916), the *Liturgie comtadine* ("Comtadin Liturgy") for voice and instrumental accompaniment (1933), and the magnificent *Service sacré* ("Sacred Service") for voices and instrumental accompaniment (1947).

Among the other major influences on his music were New Orleans jazz *(La création du monde),* Latin American rhythms *(Saudades do Brasil),* and, of course, the device of polytonality. Yet in spite of those diverse elements—French tunes, Jewish emotion, jazz inflections, Latin American rhythms, polytonality—Milhaud's music is always couched in a style recognizably his own.

Darius Milhaud (seated)

Selected works:

Operas

La brebis égarée ("The Lost Sheep"; libretto, F. Jammes; comp. 1915, perf. 1923)
Christophe Colomb ("Christopher Columbus"; libretto, P. Claudel; comp. 1928, perf. 1930)
Médée (libretto, M. Milhaud; comp. 1938, perf. 1939)
Bolivar (libretto, M. Milhaud, J. Supervielle; comp. 1943, perf. 1950)
David (libretto, A. Lunel; comp. 1952, perf. 1954)
La mère coupable ("The Guilty Mother"; libretto, M. Milhaud, after P. Beaumarchais; comp. 1964, perf. 1965)

Other Dramatic

Les choëphores (incidental music, 1915)
L'homme et son désir (ballet, 1918)
Protée ("Proteus," incidental music, 1919)
La création du monde (ballet, 1923)
Espoir ("Hope"; film, background score; comp. 1939, rel. 1945)
The Private Affairs of Bel Ami (film, background score; 1947)
Saül ("Saul," incidental music, 1954)

Orchestral

six chamber symphonies (1917-23)
Suite provençale (1936)
Fourth Symphony (1947)
Fourth Piano Concerto (1949)
Eighth Symphony: Rhodanienne ("The Rhone," 1957)
Third Violin Concerto: Concert royal ("Royal Concert," 1958)
Tenth Symphony (1960)
Ode pour Jerusalem ("Ode for Jerusalem," 1972)

Brass Band

Suite française (1944)

Choral

Service sacré (baritone, reciter, chorus, orchestra [or organ]; text, Jewish liturgy; 1947)
Trois psaumes de David ("Three Psalms of David"; unaccompanied chorus; texts, Bible; 1954)
Pacem in terris ("Peace on Earth"; baritone, chorus, orchestra; text, Pope John XXIII; 1963)

Cantate de Job ("Job Cantata"; voice, chorus, organ; text, Bible; 1965)
Ani maamin, un chant perdu et retrouvé (cantata; soprano, four reciters, chorus, orchestra; text, E. Wiesel; 1972)

Solo Vocal

Poèmes juifs (voice, piano; 1916)
Machines agricoles (voice, seven instruments; 1919)
Catalogue de fleurs ("Catalog of Flowers"; text, L. Daudet; voice, piano [or seven instruments]; 1920)
Six chants populaires hébraïques ("Six Popular Hebrew Songs"; voice, piano [or orchestra]; 1925)
Liturgie comtadine (voice, piano [or small orchestra]; text, Jewish liturgy; 1933)
Couronne de gloire ("Crown of Glory"; voice, piano [or small instrumental ensemble]; text, A. Lunel [after three prayers in the liturgy of the Comtadin sect in Aix], S. B. Gabirol; 1940)

Chamber

eighteen string quartets (1912-50)

Piano

First Piano Sonata (1916)
Saudades do Brasil (1921)
Scaramouche (two pianos, 1937; after his incidental music to *Le médecin volant* ["The Flying Doctor"], 1937)
Carnaval à la Nouvelle-Orléans ("Carnival of New Orleans," two pianos, 1947)

Writings

Notes sur Erik Satie ("Notes on Erik Satie," 1946)
Notes sans musique (1949; revised and enlarged, as *Ma vie heureuse* ["My Happy Life"], 1974; English, as *Notes without Music*, 1952 in England, 1953 slightly enlarged edition in the United States)

Mitch Miller
Musical Phenomenon
(1911-   )

Mitch(ell) Miller has had an incredibly varied and successful career. He began as perhaps the finest classical oboist America has ever produced. Moving into the record business, he became the most innovative and sales-producing A-and-R (artists-and-repertory) man in history. Then, as a conductor of popular sing-along music, he rose to great fame through recording his own albums and hosting his own TV show. Today Miller appears as a symphony conductor with major orchestras throughout the United States and Canada.

He was born in Rochester, New York, on July 4, 1911. In his parents' home he heard much classical music through recordings played on a wind-up Victrola. His first instrument was piano. But at the age of eleven he started to play the oboe—simply because it was the only instrument left unclaimed when he went to join the local school's ensemble.

A couple of years later, after making rapid progress on the oboe, he became a scholarship student at the University of Rochester's Eastman School of Music. Soon after that he won the position of first oboist with the nearby Syracuse Symphony. Later, beginning while still a student at Eastman, he played with the Rochester Philharmonic (1930-33).

Shortly after graduating from Eastman (1932) Miller moved to New York City, where he worked as a freelance oboist in both classical ensembles and popular-music orchestras. In 1934 he toured with an orchestra put together by George Gershwin; they played Gershwin's symphonic works, such as the *Rhapsody in Blue,* with the composer himself at the piano. Ever since then Miller has been praised for his idiomatic interpretations of Gershwin. "I got my ideas from the man himself," he says. The following year (1935) he played in the orchestra during the original Broadway run of Gershwin's *Porgy and Bess.*

Miller then held the full-time position of oboe soloist with the orchestra of the Columbia Broadcasting System (CBS) from 1935 to 1947. His first oboe (as well as oboe d'amore and English horn) recordings date from that period. It was generally acknowledged that Miller produced a beauty of tone like no one else's. Critics variously described it as "rich," "voluptuous," "round without being oily."

In 1947 Miller was hired to produce some classical recordings for the then little-known Mercury Record Corporation. Soon he was put in charge of the company's popular artists and repertory. Mercury's sales skyrocketed. At about the same time he established the Little Golden Records, a children's line, with the same extraordinary results.

In 1950 he left Mercury to become head of the popular-music division at Columbia Records, where he stayed till 1961. His tenure there remains one of the industry's success legends. He introduced and promoted to world fame such singers as Tony Bennett, Rosemary Clooney, Vic Damone, Doris Day, Frankie Laine, Johnny Mathis, Patti Page, and Jerry Vale. In the process, he altered conventional recording methods, engaged new arrangers and gave them Miller ideas for harmonizations and orchestrations, and introduced new techniques of artificial reverberation and such unusual instruments as the harpsichord (played in a kind of barrelhouse style) and the French horn into pop-orchestra backgrounds.

While at Columbia Records, Miller hit on the idea of recording some sing-along albums of standards and nostalgic songs, conducted by himself, for American home consumption. The series, eventually a couple of dozen discs, sold more than twenty million copies, making Miller the largest-selling artist in the record business, a position that he held till 1976.

In the early 1960s he left Columbia Records and hosted the *Sing Along with Mitch* TV series, a tremendous hit for several seasons. After it left the air, he took his singers and orchestra on a number of tours as far away as Japan.

However, during the years that Miller was heavily involved with popular music, his heart still clung to his classical origin. When he was a pop-record producer, he was quoted as having said, "I wouldn't buy that stuff for myself. There's no real artistic satisfaction in this job. I satisfy my musical ego elsewhere."

Eventually, then, he turned to guest-conducting symphony orchestras. Besides regularly leading major American and Canadian orchestras, he has conducted in other lands, recently, for example, in Mexico City and at the Florence May Festival in Italy. His program format includes popular symphonic works and concertos, Broadway and movie selections, and sing-along tunes.

As successful in his new role as he was in his earlier ones, Miller has translated his popularity into a crusade to rescue symphony orchestras from financial peril. He accepts invitations from city after city to conduct fund-raising concerts.

While Miller was at the Eastman School of Music, he met Frances Alexander, a piano student from Quincy, Illinois. After a courtship conducted mostly by mail, they were married in 1935. They had three children: Andrea, Margaret, and Mitchell. All of the children work in the fine or literary arts.

Nathan Milstein

Fiery but Disciplined Violinist
(1904-   )

Nathan Milstein, violinist, was born in Odessa, the Ukraine (now in the Soviet Union), on December 31, 1904. When he was five years old, his mother, on the advice of a neighbor, bought a violin and pressured her "wild young Nathan" into playing the instrument in the hope that it would keep him out of mischief. After two years of lessons with a local teacher, Nathan entered the Odessa Conservatory, where he studied violin with Peter Stolyarsky till 1914. He made his concert debut at the age of ten, but he decided against a career as a child prodigy.

In 1916 young Milstein went to Saint Petersburg to study with the famous Leopold Auer at the conservatory there. Milstein's mother went with the boy; but because Jews other than conservatory students were not allowed to live in Saint Petersburg (the czar's city), she first had to go through considerable difficulty in getting the necessary special permission from the police.

Milstein's family suffered great hardship during and after the Russian Revolution of 1917. He soon began to give public performances so that he could provide the family with funds, and through 1925 he experienced a growing success in his Russian tours.

The most significant association that he developed during those years was with the brilliant young pianist Vladimir Horowitz. In the winter of 1921 Milstein went to the city of Kiev to give some recitals. After one of Milstein's performances, Horowitz and his sister, Regina (also a pianist), went backstage to introduce themselves and to invite Milstein to tea at their Kiev home. The

Horowitz family enjoyed the young violinist's company so much that they asked him to stay with them—first overnight, then indefinitely. He lived with the Horowitzes for the next three years, and during that time he toured in joint recitals with Vladimir and Regina. A typical program consisted of Milstein, accompanied by Regina, performing in the first half, while Vladimir, the star, took the second half.

In late 1925 Milstein received official permission to make a concert tour in Europe. The Soviets, of course, always gave (and still give) such permission for the sole purpose of showing off what the authorities believed to be the superiority of their political system. Milstein, like so many other freedom-loving Russians, took advantage of his European trip to defect to the West.

He spent several months receiving artistic advice from the Belgian violinist Eugène Ysaÿe in Brussels. The young Russian then went to Paris, where he joined Vladimir Horowitz, who had also used the ruse of a concert tour to defect from the Soviet Union. Milstein began to tour Europe extensively, often with Horowitz. Sometimes they were joined for trio concerts by the outstanding young cellist Gregor Piatigorsky, another recent Russian émigré.

In 1929 Milstein made his first tour of the United States. Throughout the 1930s his reputation grew as he made annual tours of Europe and gave frequent concerts in America and Canada.

With the outbreak of World War II Milstein settled in the United States, becoming a naturalized American citizen in 1942. In 1945 he married Thérèse Kauffman, with whom he had a daughter, Maria. When Milstein purchased a Stradivarius violin, he named it the Maria-Thérèse, after his daughter and wife.

After the war he resumed his European concert tours, eventually settling in London. In both Europe and America he has come to be regarded as one of the great musical figures of his time.

Through the 1930s Milstein was renowned primarily for his virtuosity. But beginning in the 1940s, his musicianship matured and he developed profoundly individual interpretative skills. Though he has the traditional fiery temperament of Russian violinists, he is perhaps the least "Russian" of that group because his instincts are so well disciplined by his intellect. He produces a classically pure line with a tone that is never distorted by excessive vibrato.

Milstein has made numerous violin arrangements and transcriptions and has composed some original works, notably the dazzlingly virtuosic *Paganiniana* (pub. 1954). He is also deeply interested in painting, politics, philosophy, and literature.

One of Milstein's most remarkable attributes is his longevity. Today, in his eighties, he still publicly performs with no discernable loss in his violinistic prowess.

Pierre Monteux
Genial Conductor
(1875-1964)

Pierre Monteux, conductor, was born in Paris, France, on April 4, 1875. He came from a family skilled in the performing arts. His mother was an excellent pianist, as was Marguerite, his sister. His brother Paul became a successful conductor of light music. And Henri, Pierre's most beloved sibling, had become one of France's greatest actors before he was murdered at the Buchenwald concentration camp during World War II. The Monteux family did not practice the Jewish religion, and Pierre eventually converted to Roman Catholicism.

As a child he heard Marguerite playing sonatas with the violinist Félix Bloch, their cousin. Pierre immediately decided to become a violinist, and at the age of six he began to take lessons with Bloch. After one year the lessons were taken over by Jules Dambé, conductor at the Opéra-Comique. At the age of nine Pierre entered the Paris Conservatory, where he remained for eleven years. After several years of preliminary study there, he received advanced violin lessons from Jean Pierre Maurin and Henri Berthelier.

Young Monteux quickly showed great professional promise during his student years. At twelve he was allowed to conduct his own polka at a charity ball. A few years later he became a violist at the Opéra-Comique (where, in 1902, he led the viola section at the world premiere of Debussy's opera *Pélleas et Mélisande* ["Pelléas and Mélisande"]). Soon afterward he began to play the viola for the Colonne Concerts and for the Geloso String Quartet, which performed a Brahms quartet in the great composer's presence and induced a warm compliment from him.

In 1896 Monteux graduated from the conservatory, and for the next several years he continued many of the musical activities that he had begun while a student. More and more, however, he focused his attention on conducting. In the years up to World War I, he conducted at the Colonne Concerts, the casino in Dieppe, the Paris Opéra, and the Opéra-Comique; and he led various orchestras in Berlin, London, Vienna, and elsewhere.

The year 1911 saw the great turning point in Monteux's life when the famed impresario Sergei Diaghilev appointed him principal conductor of the Russian Ballet, which Monteux subsequently led during the years 1911-14, 1916, and 1924.

In his post with the Russian Ballet, Monteux was destined to conduct some of the most spectacular and famous world premieres in twentieth-century music, notably Stravinsky's *Petrushka* in 1911, Ravel's *Daphnis et Chloé* ("Daphnis and Chloé") in 1912, Debussy's *Jeux* ("Games") in 1913, and Stravinsky's *Le sacre du printemps* ("The Rite of Spring") in 1913 and *Le rossignol* ("The Nightingale") in 1914. The premiere of *Le sacre du printemps,* at the Théâtre des Champs-Elysées in Paris, was one of the most violent events in music history. A conservative, anti-Stravinsky faction in the audience regarded the revolutionary score (as well as the paganistic subject matter) as a blasphemous attempt to destroy music as an art. They were opposed by an equally fierce pro-Stravinsky faction. People hissed, hooted, shouted, whistled, and even struck each other. The dancers could barely hear the music, yet Monteux courageously conducted to the final curtain. Stravinsky later said that he admired Monteux for being "as nerveless as a crocodile" during the ordeal.

Monteux enjoyed his years with the Russian Ballet, particularly because of the opportunity to be involved with new music. In early 1914 he furthered the cause of new music by organizing a series of concerts called the Popular Concerts (also known as the Monteux Concerts), which offered contemporary composers a chance to present their orchestral music to the public.

Later that year World War I began, and from August 1914 to September 1916 Monteux served as a private in the French infantry and fought in numerous battles. As part of the French propaganda effort to win American support, Diaghilev's Russian Ballet was scheduled to tour the United States in the autumn of 1916. The French War Ministry released Monteux from military duty and allowed him to join Diaghilev's company.

Early in the tour Monteux caused a considerable stir

when, for the Russian Ballet performance of October 9, 1916, at the Manhattan Opera House in New York City, he refused to conduct a ballet arrangement of Richard Strauss's *Till Eulenspiegels lustige Streiche* ("Till Eulenspiegel's Merry Pranks"), saying that he would not perform the work of a German enemy during wartime. The piece was conducted by a German, Anselm Goetzl, after which Monteux led the orchestra in the rest of the program, which consisted of Russian compositions.

Monteux's first performance with an American group took place when he led the New York Civic Orchestra in a concert during the summer of 1917. He then signed a three-year contract with the Metropolitan Opera, where he specialized in the French repertory, debuting with Gounod's *Faust* in November 1917.

The Met released Monteux from the last year of his contract when he was offered the conductorship of the Boston Symphony Orchestra, which he subsequently led from 1919 to 1924. Monteux rebuilt the slumping Boston Symphony into one of the world's truly great orchestras. He also instituted programs consisting of both classics and contemporary works, which thereafter characterized his programming in future posts with other orchestras as well.

With the Boston Symphony, Monteux conducted both American and world premieres of many important compositions, notably the world premieres of two American works: Charles T. Griffes's *The Pleasure Dome of Kubla Khan* in 1919 and Henry F. Gilbert's *Indian Sketches* in 1921. In November 1923 Monteux conducted the Boston Symphony in a concert featuring, at Monteux's insistence, the black tenor Roland Hayes, who thus became the first black soloist to perform with a major symphony orchestra in the United States. Critics generally praised Monteux's progressive programs and quiet professionalism, though audiences seemed less enthusiastic.

In 1924 Monteux returned to Europe, where he began a ten-year association with the Concertgebouw Orchestra of Amsterdam as assistant to Willem Mengelberg. While in the Netherlands, he also conducted operas for the Wagner Society.

In 1928 Monteux conducted the Philadelphia Orchestra when the group's regular conductor, the flamboyant Leopold Stokowski, went on a leave of absence. As in Boston, the audiences appreciated Monteux less than the critics did. He vowed never to return to the United States, where, as he quite justifiably said, "star-crazy" audiences were interested only in "slim, well-tailored conductors."

In 1929 Monteux took over the Symphonic Orchestra of Paris, which had been created the previous year and was now foundering. During Monteux's tenure (1929-38), he saved the orchestra and conducted many first performances, notably the world premiere of Prokofiev's *Third Symphony* in 1929. In 1932 he founded the Monteux School in Paris, where he coached young conductors.

In 1936 Monteux took another chance in the United States, accepting an appointment as principal conductor and music director with the San Francisco Symphony

Pierre Monteux

series and festivals to appeal to diverse audiences. San Franciscans adored him, and he remained till 1952.

Meanwhile, Monteux had established, in 1941, a summer school for young conductors at his American home in Hancock, Maine, an extension of his earlier teaching activities at the Monteux School in Paris. Among his pupils were Neville Marriner and André Previn. In 1942 Monteux became a naturalized American citizen.

After his retirement from the San Francisco Symphony in 1952, he made numerous guest-conducting appearances, most often with the Boston Symphony. He also returned to the Metropolitan Opera for two seasons beginning in 1954.

On April 4, 1955, Monteux celebrated his eightieth birthday by conducting the Boston Symphony in a concert that included Beethoven's *Fourth Piano Concerto,* for which Monteux had chosen as soloist his friend and protégé Leon Fleisher. After the intermission the conductor Charles Munch stepped to the podium and conducted two short works specially composed for Monteux's birthday, one each by Darius Milhaud and Igor Stravinsky (whose contribution, later published as *Greeting Prelude,* is based on the familiar "Happy Birthday to You" by Clayton F. Summy). One of the guests at the party following the concert was the black tenor Roland Hayes, who told the gathering: "Pierre Monteux gave me my chance at a time when it was not fashionable to give a Negro a chance, and because of his courage others of my race have followed into the concert world."

In 1960 Monteux celebrated his eighty-fifth birthday, again with the Boston Symphony, by conducting Beethoven's *Ninth Symphony.* His last appointment came in 1961, with the London Symphony Orchestra—a twenty-five-year contract though he was already in his eighties. In 1963, on the fiftieth anniversary of the famous Paris premiere of *Le sacre du printemps,* he conducted the work in London.

Monteux was one of the most gifted conductors of the twentieth century. His grasp of musical structure and his ear for sound quality were extraordinary. He could render powerful interpretations of the Austro-German composers Beethoven and Brahms, as well as of such diverse moderns as Debussy, Prokofiev, Ravel, and Stravinsky. And he was equally masterful in any sphere of conducting—opera, ballet, and symphony.

But many critics still feel that Monteux never received the public acclaim to which his abilities entitled him. His genial personality, his "Santa Claus" appearance (standing 5'5" and weighing 185 pounds), his unpretentious conducting style with minimum baton movements, and his instilling of discipline through quiet affection, not through noisy intimidation—all of these qualities misled audiences into underestimating his genius. His great personal warmth, however, was recognized by everyone, and he was often affectionately called Pierre or Papa.

Monteux was married three times. His first wife was a pianist from Bordeaux. His second was Germaine Benedictus, mother of his three children. His third was Doris Hodgkins, an American, whom he married in 1928. It was Doris's initiative that caused the Monteux School to be

Orchestra, which was financially and artistically bankrupt. Monteux rebuilt the orchestra, improved its musicianship, and raised it to an international level. He added to the orchestra's prestige by conducting it in the world premieres of works by important American composers, such as Ernest Bloch's *Evocations* in 1938, Roger Sessions's *Second Symphony* in 1947, and George Antheil's *Sixth Symphony* in 1949. He also programmed special founded in 1932. She published his life story as *It's All in the Music* (1965). Claude Monteux, Pierre's son, is a well-known American flutist and conductor.

In early 1964 Monteux conducted the Israel Philharmonic Orchestra in Israel. During his emotional visit to Jerusalem, Monteux, who had a special fondness for the music of Brahms, looked at the walls of the old city and said, "Well, I'm glad I play Brahms here!"

On April 1, 1964, while conducting Ravel's *Pavane*
pour une infante défunte ("Pavane for a Dead Princess") at a concert in Rome, Monteux had a fainting spell and fell backward off the podium and down several feet to the floor. He climbed back up and finished the program, including Debussy's *La Mer* ("The Sea"). He also tried to continue his tour, but he had to return, exhausted, to his home in Hancock, Maine, where, after experiencing several strokes, he died of a cerebral thrombosis on July 1, 1964.

Jacques Offenbach
King of Operetta
(1819-80)

Jacques Offenbach was one of the two (with Johann Strauss II) most significant composers of light music in the nineteenth century. His father, Isaac Juda Eberst, left his native town of Offenbach, Germany, as a young man and became an itinerant cantor in synagogues and a fiddler in cafés. People in other towns began to call him the Offenbacher, and soon he took Offenbach as his surname. In the early 1800s he finally married and settled in Cologne, where, besides being a cantor and a music teacher, he composed settings of the Psalms and the Jewish liturgy, among other works.

Jacques Offenbach, Isaac's second son and seventh of ten children, was born in Cologne on June 20, 1819, and was registered at birth with the first name of Jacob. Isaac began to teach Jacob the violin, but at the age of nine the boy switched to the cello and took lessons from local teachers. Soon Jacob was able to perform in a trio with his brother Julius (violin) and his sister Isabella (piano) in Cologne bars and restaurants.

In 1833 Isaac took Jacob and Julius to Paris for further study. Cologne being filled with anti-Semitism, Isaac selected Paris not only because it was a center of music but also because it was a center for freedom of thought, a place where Jews could feel at home. The city had already attracted such eminent Jews as the Halévy family, the composer Giacomo Meyerbeer, and the poet Heinrich Heine. Jacob Offenbach was enrolled at the Paris Conservatory and positions for him and his brother were found in a synagogue choir before their father returned to Cologne.

Jacob and Julius now began to call themselves Jacques and Jules. Jacques left the Paris Conservatory after one year and got a job playing cello in the orchestra of the Opéra-Comique in Paris. He finished his studies by taking private cello lessons with Louis Norbin and composition lessons with Jacques Halévy. Jacques Offenbach began to compose, and in the summers of 1836 and 1837 some of his waltzes were performed at the Turkish Garden by the conductor-composer Louis Jullien (a principal figure in the light music of the day) and his orchestra. One of the waltzes, *Rebecca*, is based on themes from fifteenth-century Jewish liturgical music.

Offenbach left the Opéra-Comique in 1838 and began to perform in Paris salons with the pianist Friedrich von Flotow, playing pieces for cello and piano jointly composed by the two performers. Through contacts made in the salons, Offenbach acquired music pupils and a commission to compose his first score for the stage, the vaudeville show *Pascal et Chambord* ("Pascal and Chambord"), which was produced in March 1839.

In the 1840s Offenbach continued his career as a cello virtuoso. He performed in Paris with the young pianist Anton Rubinstein in 1841, and in Cologne with the flamboyant pianist Franz Liszt in 1843.

Also in 1843 Offenbach dedicated a ballad entitled "A toi" ("For You") to Herminie d'Alcain, stepdaughter of Michael George Mitchell, an Englishman living in Paris. The composer had met Herminie at the Mitchells' salon, where his amusing conversation and entertaining musical performances charmed the teenage girl. Six months later he asked the Mitchells for permission to marry their daughter. They set two conditions before they would consent to the marriage: Offenbach had to prove his financial reliability by making a success of his upcoming visit to London, and he had to become a Catholic.

In May 1844 he went to England and was introduced to London audiences and presented to Queen Victoria by John Mitchell, a well-known London impresario and probably a relative of the Paris Mitchell. Offenbach performed at concerts with the young violinist Joseph Joachim, the famous composer-pianist Felix Mendelssohn, and others. The visit was a tremendous success, and Offenbach returned to Paris with plenty of money.

After conquering London and being baptized a Catholic, he married Herminie in August 1844. Later the Offenbachs became famous in the musical and theatrical world for their parties.

Meanwhile, however, Offenbach's career as a composer of light opera—his real ambition—was advancing very slowly. His efforts to get his stage works accepted by the Opéra-Comique were unsuccessful, and he had to arrange concerts of opera fragments to show his ability.

In 1850 he was appointed conductor at the Théâtre-Français in Paris. Herminie was relieved to have regular money coming in, and Offenbach was pleased to have assured performances of his incidental music to the (mostly spoken) plays produced at the theater. Nevertheless, he still had little success getting his principal stage works produced anywhere.

In 1855 he left the Théâtre-Français and opened his own musical theater in Paris, the Bouffes-Parisiens. The new theater featured short, one-act comic sketches by Offenbach himself, as well as light works by such composers as Adolphe Adam, Georges Bizet, and Charles Lecocq. Gradually Offenbach began to write more ambitious works, his first two-act production being *Orphée aux enfers* ("Orpheus in the Underworld," perf. 1858), the prototype of his later large-scale operettas.

In 1860 Offenbach's two-act ballet *Le papillon* ("The Butterfly") was produced at the prestigious Paris Opéra, and his three-act comic opera *Barkouf* (the name of a dog) was staged at the Opéra-Comique. Also in 1860 he became a naturalized French citizen.

Offenbach resigned as director of the Bouffes-Parisiens in 1862, though he continued to compose primarily for that theater. The 1860s saw many of his greatest stage successes, including *La belle Hélène* ("The Beautiful Helen," perf. 1864), *Barbe-bleue* ("Bluebeard," perf. 1866), *La vie parisienne* ("The Parisian Life," perf. 1866), *La Grande-Duchesse de Gérolstein* ("The Grand Duchess of Gerolstein," perf. 1867), and *La Périchole* (the name of a gypsy singer, perf. 1868). His works attained widespread popularity abroad, especially in Vienna, where he often visited and where he met Johann Strauss II, "the Waltz King," whom Offenbach encouraged to write operettas of his own. It was, in fact, largely through the success of Offenbach's works that operetta became an established international genre, leading to similar works by such composers as Johann Strauss II in Austria, Arthur Sullivan (of Gilbert and Sullivan) in England, and Victor Herbert in the United States, not to mention the eventual change of the operetta into the twentieth-century musical.

After the civil war of 1870-71, popular taste in the French musical theater began to change. Offenbach spent most of that period abroad (Italy, Spain, England, Austria). When he returned, he found his music on the wane and the more escapist work of Lecocq on the rise.

In 1873 Offenbach took over the management of the Théâtre de la Gaîté in Paris. But he was a poor businessman, and by early 1875 he had gone into personal bankruptcy to pay off the company's debts.

Selling his interest in the Gaîté, Offenbach began once again to concentrate on concerts and composition. In 1876 he toured the United States, and in 1877 he issued a book on his impressions of the New World (published in an English translation as *Offenbach in America*, 1877).

From 1877 on, Offenbach's main preoccupation was his new opera *Les contes d'Hoffmann* ("The Tales of Hoffmann"), his most ambitious, and eventually his most famous, work. At his death he left the opera unorchestrated, and the work was completed, at the family's request, by Ernest Guiraud.

Offenbach died in Paris on October 5, 1880, of heart failure brought on by gout. His prematurely senile brother Jules, who had become a theater conductor in Bordeaux and who had spent his life, without resentment, in his younger brother's shadow, died three days after being informed of Jacques's death. Jacques left five children: Berthe, Mimi, Pepita, Jacqueline, and Auguste. Auguste, a student of the great composer Bizet and an acknowledged authority on Jacques Offenbach's music, died in 1883 at the age of twenty-one.

Offenbach's stage works are often based on comic treatments of familiar subjects, such as Greek mythology *(Orphée aux enfers, La belle Hélène)*, other literary material *(Barbe-bleue; Robinson Crusoé,* perf. 1867), and contemporary society and politics *(La vie parisienne, La Grande-Duchesse de Gérolstein).* Much of his humor is created by quoting familiar melodies in incongruous surroundings, such as Gluck's "Che farò senza Euridice?" ("What Shall I Do without Euridice?" from *Orfeo ed Euridice* ["Orfeo and Euridice"]) in *Orphée aux enfers,* and the patriotic trio from Rossini's *Guillaume Tell* ("William Tell") in *La belle Hélène.* Also humorously incongruous are such elements as the cancan for the gods in *Orphée aux enfers,* and the lilting waltzlike setting of the phrase "Un vile séducteur" ("A Vile Seducer") in *La belle Hélène.* Similarly, he often parodies grand opera (a practice that infuriated serious-minded contemporaries): the finale of *Ba-ta-clan* ("Paraphernalia," the title of a national anthem; perf. 1855) pokes fun at Meyerbeer's opera *Les Huguenots* with ridiculous vocal imitations of trumpet fanfares; and a sketch in *Le carnaval des revues* ("The Carnival of Revues," perf. 1860) parodies Wagner's *Tristan und Isolde* ("Tristan and Isolde") and *Tannhäuser* and satirizes Wagner's own pretentiousness as the Composer of the Future. In *Ba-ta-clan* Offenbach sets gibberish to music, and in *Barkouf* he introduces comic parts for animals.

During his lifetime Offenbach was often criticized by those who disapproved of his use of some of the "naughty" (licentious) aspects of the French popular stage. And high musical circles looked down on his lack of pretense to profound art. After his death, however, his standing was gradually elevated by the powerful dramatic writing found in *Les contes d'Hoffmann,* which portrays three stories by the author E. T. A. Hoffmann. The score contains great melodic appeal, notably in the famous "Barcarolle." Offenbach's lighter stage works received only moderate attention till the middle of the twentieth century, when a renewed interest in classical operetta brought about revivals of his music in the international repertory and reestablished him as a premiere figure in the history of light music.

Selected works:

Stage

Les deux aveugles (known in English as *The Blind Beggars;* libretto, J. Moinaux; perf. 1855)
Ba-ta-clan (libretto, L. Halévy; perf. 1855)
La rose de Saint-Flour (known in English as *The Rose of Auvergne;* libretto, M. Carré, C. Nuitter; perf. 1856)
Orphée aux enfers (libretto, H. Crémieux, L. Halévy; perf. 1858, revised 1874)
Le papillon (ballet, perf. 1860)
Barkouf (libretto, E. Scribe, H. Boisseaux; perf. 1860)
La chanson de Fortunio (known in English as *The Magic Melody;* libretto, H. Crémieux, L. Halévy; perf. 1861)
Le pont des soupirs (known in English as *The Bridge of Sighs;* libretto, H. Crémieux, L. Halévy; perf. 1861, revised 1868)
Die Rheinnixen ("The Rhine Nymphs"; German libretto, A. Wolzogen, from the French of C. Nuitter; perf. 1864)
La belle Hélène (libretto, H. Meilhac, L. Halévy; perf. 1864)
Barbe-bleue (libretto, H. Meilhac, L. Halévy; perf. 1866)
La vie parisienne (libretto, H. Meilhac, L. Halévy; perf. 1866, revised 1873)
La Grande-Duchesse de Gérolstein (libretto, H. Meilhac, L. Halévy; perf. 1867)
Robinson Crusoé (libretto, E. Cormon, H. Crémieux, after D. Defoe; perf. 1867)
La Périchole (libretto, H. Meilhac, L. Halévy; perf. 1868, revised 1874)
Les contes d'Hoffmann (libretto, J. Barbier; perf. 1881)

Others

cello pieces (some with F. von Flotow)
piano pieces
songs

Writings

Histoire d'une valse (c. 1872; English, as "The Story of a Waltz," in *The Theatre,* October 1, 1878)
Offenbach en Amérique: Notes d'un musicien en voyage (1877; English, as *Offenbach in America: Notes of a Travelling Musician,* 1877 in the United States; as *America and the Americans,* 1877 in England; as *Orpheus in America: Offenbach's Diary of His Journey to the New World,* 1957 in the United States, 1958 in England)

David Oistrakh

Dean of Soviet Violinists

(1908-1974)

David Oistrakh, violinist, was born in Odessa, the Ukraine (now in the Soviet Union), on September 30, 1908. His father was an enthusiastic amateur violinist, and his mother sang in the chorus of the Odessa Opera. David's first and only violin instructor was Peter Stolyarsky, with whom the five-year-old Oistrakh began lessons at the teacher's own music school. Later Oistrakh followed Stolyarsky to the Odessa Conservatory.

After graduating from the Odessa Conservatory in 1926, Oistrakh began to concertize wherever he could in the Soviet Union, at first only in minor places and at minor events. His first major appearance came in 1927 when the famed composer Alexander Glazunov invited the young violinist to play Glazunov's *Violin Concerto* under the composer's own direction in Kiev. Glazunov highly praised the teenager's performance.

In 1928 Oistrakh made his Leningrad debut. Also in 1928 he settled in Moscow, where he debuted in 1929.

In the 1930s Oistrakh won a series of important violin

contests that brought him great prominence. Most significant of all was his first prize in the newly established Eugène Ysaÿe International Competition (later known as the Queen Elisabeth International Competition) in Brussels, Belgium, in 1937. That victory marked the beginning of his extremely successful international career (though he had earlier made some minor appearances outside Russia).

During World War II Oistrakh played at the front, in besieged Leningrad, and in hospitals and factories. In 1942 he was awarded the Stalin Prize, the Soviet Union's highest honor. In that same year he became a member of the Communist Party.

In 1945 in Moscow, Oistrakh and the brilliant American violinist Yehudi Menuhin (the first American artist to visit the Soviet Union after the war) gave a memorable performance of J. S. Bach's *Concerto* for two violins. Oistrakh and Menuhin developed a close friendship that lasted for the rest of the Russian's life.

After World War II Oistrakh continued to concertize both inside and outside the Soviet Union, his foreign tours becoming increasingly extensive. He gave concerts in Europe, South America, and the Far East. In 1955 he made the first of several trips to the United States, where he won tremendous praise.

Relaxed and undemonstrative on the stage, Oistrakh let his seemingly effortless musicianship speak for itself. He came to be known throughout the world as one of the greatest violinists of his day, and he was widely regarded as the most characteristic representative of the Soviet school. His early playing emphasized elegance, but later he developed a complete range of stylistic mastery supported by a warm, powerful tone. His playing was a perfect fusion of virtuosity and musicianship.

Oistrakh was willing to perform new music, and many Soviet composers wrote works especially for him. Among such compositions were violin concertos by Khachaturian, Prokofiev, and Shostakovich.

Besides his solo concertizing, Oistrakh was active in playing chamber music and in conducting. He played sonatas with the pianist Lev Oborin, and trios with Oborin and the cellist Sviatoslav Knushevitsky. Oistrakh was a gifted conductor, wielding the baton not only in the Soviet Union but also during his foreign tours. Sometimes on the same program he would play one piece on the violin and then conduct another.

Teaching was an important activity for Oistrakh. In 1934 he became a lecturer at the Moscow Conservatory, and in 1939 he was appointed full professor there. One of his best pupils was Igor Oistrakh, David's own son. (David's wife, the former Tamara Ivanova, who had been a graduate student in piano at the Moscow Conservatory before she married, gave up her career to devote herself to her family.) David and Igor played together in two-violin recitals, and the father conducted violin concertos with his son as soloist.

After suffering a heart attack in 1964, Oistrakh reduced, but did not cease, his concertizing. In 1974 he went to the Netherlands to perform as violinist and conductor in an all-Brahms series of seven concerts. He appeared in the first six, but just before the seventh he died in his Amsterdam hotel room, apparently of a heart attack, on October 24, 1974.

Eugene Ormandy
Creator of
"the Philadelphia Sound"
(1899-1985)

Eugene Ormandy, conductor, was born in Budapest, Hungary, on November 18, 1899. His original name was Jenö (the Hungarian form of Eugene) Blau, being named after the famous Hungarian violinist Jenö Hubay. At the age of three Jenö Blau began to receive violin lessons from his father, a dentist and amateur violinist.

The boy was a true prodigy, and at five he was enrolled as the youngest pupil at the Budapest Royal Academy of Music. Just two years later he began to give public concerts throughout Hungary. At the academy, he studied violin with Jenö Hubay and composition with Zoltán Kodály. He graduated from the academy at fourteen, earned his state artist's diploma at sixteen, and received his diploma as a music professor at seventeen, whereupon the teenager was appointed professor of violin at the academy.

By his late teens he had begun to make concert tours throughout central Europe. At twenty he succeeded Hubay as head of violin master classes at the Budapest Royal Academy of Music, but after two years he was forced to resign because students objected to studying under one so young.

In 1921 he was given a lucrative offer to concertize in the United States. He sold all of his belongings and went to America, but the tour never materialized. Stranded and broke, he happened to meet an old Budapest acquaintance, Erno Rapee, music director at one of New York City's largest movie palaces, the Capitol Theater. Rapee offered the young man a job playing in the second-violin section of the theater's orchestra, which not only accompanied the silent films shown there but also performed musical interludes consisting of works from the standard symphonic repertory. Within a week Eugene Ormandy (as he came to be known in America) had advanced to the concertmaster's chair.

One day in 1924 the scheduled conductor at the Capitol Theater, David Mendoza, became ill, and Rapee asked Ormandy to fill in. Ormandy did so well that he was promoted to the conducting staff as an assistant in 1925, soon afterward becoming the principal conductor. During his conducting years at the Capitol Theater, Ormandy became well grounded in the orchestral repertory through sheer repetition at the theater's numerous shows.

In 1927 he became a naturalized American citizen, and at about the same time he began to broaden his experience by conducting light classics for the new medium of radio, as well as for recordings. In 1929 he resigned from the Capitol Theater to devote himself to a more serious career.

Ormandy soon began to rise to prominence in the role of guest conductor, notably with the prestigious Philadelphia Orchestra in the summers of 1930 and 1931. In late 1931, during the regular concert season, he substituted at the last minute for the famed Arturo Toscanini in three programs with the Philadelphia Orchestra.

Largely on the basis of his fine showing at Philadelphia, Ormandy was appointed principal conductor of the Minneapolis Symphony Orchestra, where he stayed for

with them. Where Stokowski (an organist) had produced a swelling organlike sound from the orchestra, Ormandy (a violinist) produced a mellow but voluptuous stringlike sound now known in music circles as "the Philadelphia sound." Under Ormandy the Philadelphia Orchestra came to be widely regarded as the greatest virtuoso orchestra in the world.

Ormandy concentrated on late nineteenth-century and early twentieth-century scores characterized by rich orchestral colors and by opportunities for technical display, such as works by Tchaikovsky, Mahler, Richard Strauss, Debussy, Ravel, and the young Stravinsky. Those same qualities are also generally evident in the vast number of contemporary compositions that Ormandy conducted. Among his numerous world premieres with the Philadelphia Orchestra were those of Rachmaninoff's *Symphonic Dances* in 1941, Samuel Barber's *Violin Concerto* in 1941, Bartók's *Third Piano Concerto* in 1946, George Antheil's *Fifth Symphony* in 1948, Hindemith's *Clarinet Concerto* in 1950, Paul Creston's *Third Symphony* in 1950, Howard Hanson's *Fifth Symphony* in 1955, Walter Piston's *Seventh Symphony* in 1961, David Diamond's *Seventh Symphony* in 1962, Roy Harris's *Ninth Symphony* in 1963, Roger Sessions's *Fifth Symphony* in 1964, and William Schuman's *Ninth Symphony* in 1969. In addition, Ormandy conducted the American premieres of numerous works by European composers, such as several symphonies by Shostakovich.

He also guest-conducted extensively, notably with the Boston Symphony Orchestra. Ormandy worked very little in opera. One important performance was his Metropolitan Opera debut in a production of Johann Strauss II's *Die Fledermaus* ("The Bat") in 1950.

Ormandy led the Philadelphia Orchestra in many important functions transcending the world of music. On March 20, 1948, he led it in the first televised broadcast, over the Columbia Broadcasting System (CBS) network, by a major symphony orchestra. (Toscanini's National Broadcasting Company [NBC] Symphony Orchestra telecast a concert later the same evening.) On November 22, 1963, Ormandy conducted the Philadelphia Orchestra in a special televised performance of Mozart's *Requiem* because of President Kennedy's assassination earlier that day. In 1973 Ormandy and the Philadelphia Orchestra gave a series of concerts in Communist China, an important early step in thawing the relations between that country and the United States.

Ormandy held his Philadelphia post for an incredible length of time, more than forty years, finally retiring in 1980. After that, he held the title of conductor laureate.

Ormandy was married twice. In 1922 he wedded Steffy Goldner, a harpist with the New York Philharmonic, whom he had met during his tenure at the Capitol Theater. They were divorced in 1947. In 1950 he married Margaret Hitsch.

After a long battle with a cardiac problem, Ormandy died of pneumonia in Philadelphia, Pennsylvania, on March 12, 1985.

five years (1931-36). He built the orchestra into one of the country's finest and expanded its repertory to include twentieth-century works. Through his Minneapolis recordings he attained national renown.

In 1936 he was invited to join the Philadelphia Orchestra, where he shared the conductorship with Leopold Stokowski for two seasons. When Stokowski resigned in 1938, Ormandy succeeded him as music director of the orchestra and simultaneously became sole principal conductor.

The new conductor deliberately strove to create an image different from that of his predecessor. Where Stokowski had been flamboyant and temperamental, Ormandy was unostentatious and reserved. Where Stokowski had acted aloof and superior to his musicians, Ormandy developed warm and personal relationships

Jan Peerce

Opera Singer Identified with "The Bluebird of Happiness"
(1904-1984)

Jan Peerce, tenor, was born of Russian immigrants in New York City, New York, on June 3, 1904. His original name was Jacob Pincus Perelmuth. In his youth he was called Pinky by his friends and Pinye (the Yiddish diminutive of Pincus) by his Orthodox parents.

As a child he sang in local synagogue choirs and took violin lessons, which his parents paid for by taking in boarders. On the day of his bar mitzvah in June 1917, he performed the morning cantorial service himself.

Not long after his bar mitzvah, his parents opened Green Mansion, a catering hall for wedding receptions. Young Perelmuth formed his own music ensemble, called Pinky Pearl and His Society Dance Band, and performed for a fee at the weddings (not only Jewish but also Spanish and Italian). The following summer, in 1918, he altered his group, called it Jack ("Pinky") Pearl and His Society Dance Orchestra, and performed on the borscht circuit (summer theaters and nightclubs associated with Jewish hotels in the Catskills). Pinky led the ensemble while playing his violin, occasionally singing while one of his partners conducted. He continued to perform in various kinds of show-business outlets (theaters, cabarets, dance halls) through the early 1930s.

Meanwhile he attended, but did not graduate from, DeWitt Clinton High School in New York City. Later he participated in the Columbia University Extension Studies because his parents wanted him to become a doctor. But he took such courses for only a couple of years and then dropped them to concentrate on his music career.

In 1932 Perelmuth met the impresario Samuel L. ("Roxy") Rothafel, who convinced the young man to give up the violin in favor of the voice and paid for his vocal lessons with Eleanor McClellan. (Perelmuth earlier had studied with Emilio Roxas, and later would study with Giuseppe Boghetti.) Rothafel also arranged for him to join the new Radio City Music Hall and the *Radio City Music Hall of the Air* radio program. Furthermore, it was Rothafel who changed Jacob Pincus Perelmuth's name first to John Pierce and then to Jan Peerce.

Throughout the 1930s Peerce performed regularly at the Radio City Music Hall and at the Paramount Theater. But he earned his reputation primarily on radio. Besides singing on the *Radio City Music Hall of the Air,* he often performed on a number of other shows, such as *The Chevrolet Hour.* On the *Forverts* program he sang Yiddish, Hebrew, and cantorial music under the name Jascha Pearl.

He was best known, however, for his work on the *Radio City Music Hall of the Air,* where he sang mostly popular ballads. The song with which he became most closely identified was "The Bluebird of Happiness," written especially for him by the composer Sandor Harmati (a violinist at the Radio City Music Hall) and the lyricist Edward Heyman. Peerce recorded the song for a low-paying company called World Broadcasting. To protect his market value as a serious singer, he issued the song under the names Paul Robinson and Randolph Joyce.

An important turning point in his career came in 1938. On a *Radio City Music Hall of the Air* broadcast, Peerce sang the first act of Wagner's *Die Walküre* ("The Valkyrie") in the role of Siegmund. The famed conductor Arturo Toscanini heard the performance and, after an audition, hired Peerce to sing the tenor solo in a radio broadcast of Beethoven's *Ninth Symphony* with Toscanini conducting the National Broadcasting Company (NBC) Symphony Orchestra. Peerce and Toscanini thereafter worked together in numerous performances over the next fifteen years.

In 1939 Peerce came under the management of the impresario Sol Hurok (with whom he stayed till Hurok's death in 1974). Soon Peerce was giving concerts of serious music. His first significant opera appearance came when he sang the Duke of Mantua in Verdi's *Rigoletto* with the San Francisco Opera in October 1941.

Jan Peerce (left) as the Duke of Mantua
in Verdi's *Rigoletto* with Lawrence Tibbett (right)

The next major step in his career came in November 1941 when he won a position with the Metropolitan Opera in New York City. He immediately quit his job at the Radio City Music Hall. Later that month he made his Met debut, singing Alfredo in Verdi's *La traviata* ("The Wayward Woman"). Thereafter, he was a fixture at the Met for over twenty-five years.

Another Met star, Richard Tucker, was married to Sara Perelmuth, Peerce's sister. But the two brothers-in-law were never close.

Besides singing at the Met, Peerce performed as a guest with other major opera companies. He also gave concerts and recitals throughout the United States and Europe, as well as Israel (first in 1950) and the Soviet Union (first in 1956, when he also became the first American since World War II to sing with the Bolshoi Opera). While on tour, he often entered local synagogues on the Sabbath or a holiday to donate his services as cantor (having taken cantorial lessons from Israel Alter), appearing in that function even in the Soviet Union.

Peerce frequently appeared on TV (such as the Johnny Carson and Merv Griffin shows) and recorded, besides serious vocal works, many popular songs and much liturgical music. He sang in the movies *Carnegie Hall* (1947), *Something in the Wind* (1947), and *Of Men and Music* (1951). His singing voice was on the soundtrack of *Tonight We Sing* (1953), though he did not appear on the screen.

In 1966 Peerce celebrated his twenty-fifth anniversary with the Met. But in 1967 he became blind in his right eye as a result of an unsuccessful operation for a cataract. He continued to perform at the Met; but he found it difficult to get around on the stage, especially since his left eye, too, was weak. He retired from the Met at the end of the 1967-68 season.

Peerce, however, still gave recitals, made concert appearances with major orchestras, and performed in operas with other companies, debuting with the Vienna Opera, for example, in 1970. In 1971 he made his Broadway debut, as Tevye in *Fiddler on the Roof*.

Peerce sang with a strong technical command and was capable of producing remarkably even scale passages. His middle register had a dark vibrancy, and his upper tones a metallic ring. His small size (5′5″) worked against his projection of the romantic illusion in opera, but he overcame that liability with acting that was restrained and dignified.

Peerce was most comfortable in Italian spinto roles (expressive, emotional opera parts requiring a high voice), wisely rejecting the heavier tenor roles that were unsuitable for him. Among his best roles were Alfredo in Verdi's *La traviata*, Cavaradossi in Puccini's *Tosca*, the Duke of Mantua in Verdi's *Rigoletto*, Riccardo in Verdi's *Un ballo in maschera* ("A Masked Ball"), and Turiddu in Mascagni's *Cavalleria rusticana* ("Rustic Chivalry"). He was also a popular Don José in Bizet's *Carmen*.

155

Jan Peerce (left) as Alfredo
in Verdi's *La traviata* with Bidú Sayão (right)

In the autumn of 1928 he married Alice Kalmanowitz in a secret civil ceremony (his parents being against the marriage because they wanted him to concentrate on becoming a doctor, and hers opposing it because they wanted a son-in-law with a brighter future than a fiddler could offer). But they did not live together till eight months later, in the late spring of 1929, when they eloped and had a religious wedding with an Orthodox rabbi.

Alice became the most important adviser and manager of his career. For example, in the 1930s she was one of the most powerful voices encouraging him to concentrate on opera rather than popular music. Once, about the year 1940, Peerce was offered a contract to sing on a radio program. Unwisely, and without consulting Alice, he signed the contract, an action that violated three other contracts (with Hurok, with Peerce's popular-music representative, and with the Radio City Music Hall). Alice led the fight—a very difficult one—to get the radio people to cancel the contract. "Since then," Peerce later said, "I've never signed a piece of paper without telling Alice."

The Peerces had three children: Larry, Joyce, and Susan. Larry became a motion-picture director of such films as *Ash Wednesday* (1973) and *The Other Side of the Mountain* (1975). He directed his father in a straight dramatic role in *Goodbye, Columbus* (1969).

In 1974 Peerce had an operation for a cataract on his left eye. This time the operation was a success, and he continued to concertize. In 1976 his memoirs were published as *The Bluebird of Happiness* (with Alan Levy).

In 1981 he helped to dedicate a new Jewish center in New York City, singing opera arias and Yiddish songs. Over the years, in fact, he had personally raised millions of dollars for Jewish and refugee causes.

In 1982 Peerce became ill and went into a coma. Two years later he died at his New Rochelle, New York, home on December 15, 1984.

Itzhak Perlman

Gifted Violinist

(1945-   )

Itzhak Perlman, violinist, was born in Tel Aviv, Palestine (now Israel), on August 31, 1945. His parents were natives of Poland; but they had independently migrated in the mid-1930s to Palestine, where they met and married.

When Itzhak was three years old, he heard the sound of a violin over the radio and immediately expressed a desire to play the instrument himself. His parents bought him a toy violin (whose horrible sound repulsed him so much that he threw it under the bed and refused to play it) and soon afterward a real instrument. At the age of four he was stricken with poliomyelitis, which left him permanently deprived of the use of his legs. (He still walks with leg braces and crutches, and plays seated.)

After a one-year convalescence, during which he continued to practice his violin, little Perlman received a

scholarship from the America-Israel Cultural Foundation and enrolled at the Tel Aviv Academy of Music, where he studied under Rivka Goldgart. He gave his first solo recital at the age of ten, by which time he had already appeared in numerous public concerts and performed over the radio.

In 1958, at the age of thirteen, Perlman won a talent contest, as a result of which he was taken to America for two highly successful appearances on Ed Sullivan's TV variety show. Deciding to remain in the United States, Perlman was soon joined by his parents. The following year he made an American concert tour under the sponsorship of the Zionist Organization of America, which also helped Perlman to obtain scholarships enabling him to enter the Juilliard School of Music in New York City, where he studied with Ivan Galamian and Dorothy DeLay.

Perlman made his official concert debut in a performance at Carnegie Hall in New York City in 1963. The following year, in the same city, he won the Leventritt Award, one of the most prestigious prizes in international music competition. As a result, he was soon engaged for solo appearances with the New York Philharmonic and other major American orchestras.

In 1965 Perlman returned to Israel for the first time since he had left in 1958, making an extremely successful concert tour. During the 1965-66 season he made his first major American tour, covering the nation from coast to coast. A highlight of 1966-67 was his performance in Honolulu of Stravinsky's *Violin Concerto* with the composer conducting. Since the mid-1970s, he has toured extensively in the United States, Canada, South America, Europe, Israel, the Far East, and Australia—usually giving about one hundred concerts a year.

Perlman enjoys the challenge of chamber music. He has, for example, played violin sonatas with the pianist Vladimir Ashkenazy. Among his other chamber-music partners have been the violinist Isaac Stern, the violinist-violist Pinchas Zukerman, and the cellist Lynn Harrell. Perlman is a member of an intimate circle of internationally renowned musical friends known as the Barenboim Gang, led by the pianist-conductor Daniel Barenboim and consisting of the cellist Jacqueline du Pré (Barenboim's wife), the conductor Zubin Mehta, Ashkenazy, Zukerman, and others.

Perhaps the most gifted violinist of his generation, Perlman plays with an instinctive directness of musical expression. Yet he also brings out intellectually derived refinements of detail through the use of his brilliant technique.

Perlman's repertory covers not only Bach and the standard nineteenth-century romantics but also such twentieth-century composers as Bartók, Berg, Prokofiev, and Stravinsky. In 1975 at Carnegie Hall he introduced Robert Mann's *Chiaroscuro*, composed especially for Perlman. A relaxed man with an acute sense of humor and a booming laugh, he also enjoys light music and has performed, for example, violin transcriptions of ragtime piano pieces by Scott Joplin.

In his TV appearances with Stern and Zukerman, Perlman often supplies comic commentaries between numbers. He has been a regular performer at the White House, being especially popular with President Reagan, who appreciates the violinist's show-business instincts.

In early 1967, in a ceremony at the America-Israel Culture House in New York City, Perlman married Toby Friedlander, a violinist and graduate of Juilliard. They had met in 1964 at a summer-camp concert in which he was appearing. The Perlmans have five children: Noah, Navah (a pianist), Leora, Rami, and Ariella.

Roberta Peters
One of the Great Coloratura Sopranos of Her Time
(1930-   )

Roberta Peters, soprano, was born in New York City, New York, on May 4, 1930. Her original name was Roberta Peterman. At the age of twelve, after a couple of years of lessons with a local teacher, she sang for the great opera star Jan Peerce. Soon afterward he sent her to William Herman, Patrice Munsel's voice teacher. At fourteen Roberta left school to intensify her training with Herman (including the careful study of twenty operas), as well as to take lessons in dramatics, languages, and other disciplines—all designed to lead to a career as an opera singer.

She continued that rigorous regimen till, at the age of nineteen, she auditioned for the famed impresario Sol Hurok and, through him, for the Metropolitan Opera in New York City. Her Met debut was scheduled for January 1951, as the Queen of the Night in Mozart's opera *Die Zauberflöte* ("The Magic Flute"). But on November 17, 1950, she went on as a last-minute replacement for the ailing Nadine Conner, in the role of Zerlina in Mozart's *Don Giovanni*. It was a triumphant and incredible performance, especially considering that she had never before sung any opera in public and that she had had absolutely no rehearsals with the orchestra or the company. The years of hard work and preparation had paid off.

In 1952 Peters married the baritone Robert Merrill, another young Met star. Their huge, heavily publicized

wedding took place at the Park Avenue Synagogue in New York City. However, it was a short-lived marriage, and they divorced later that year. But they remained good friends and have often performed together since then.

In 1955 she married Bertram Fields, an investor in hotels and real estate. They had two children: Paul and Bruce.

Besides holding her post at the Met, Peters has given performances with numerous opera companies elsewhere. She sang at the Royal Opera House of Covent Garden in London during the summers of 1951-60 and performed with the Cincinnati Opera during the summers of 1952-53 and 1958. In 1963 she debuted at the Vienna State Opera and at the festivals in Vienna and Salzburg. The following year she made her first appearance at the festival in Munich. In 1972 she debuted at the Kirov Opera in Leningrad and the Bolshoi Opera in Moscow. Her Russian appearances were tremendous successes.

One of the great coloraturas of her time, renowned for her clarity and accuracy, she has been particularly successful as Depina in Mozart's *Così fan tutte* ("Thus Do All Women"), Gilda in Verdi's *Rigoletto,* Lucia in Donizetti's *Lucia di Lammermoor,* Rosina in Rossini's *Il barbiere di Siviglia* ("The Barber of Seville"), and similar roles. In later years she has broadened her repertory to include such lyric soprano parts as Mimi in Puccini's *La bohème* ("The Bohemian Girl") and Violetta in Verdi's *La traviata* ("The Wayward Woman").

Peters has also performed on radio and TV. A versatile recitalist, she regularly programs opera and operetta arias, as well as art, popular, and Jewish songs. Her concert tours have covered the United States, the Soviet Union, Israel, and elsewhere.

She wrote the autobiographical book *A Debut at the Met* (with Louis Biancolli, 1967). At the Hebrew University in Jerusalem, she established the Roberta Peters Scholarship.

Gregor Piatigorsky
Romantic Cellist
(1903-1976)

Sometimes called "the Russian Casals," Gregor Piatigorsky was one of the most renowned cellists of the twentieth century. He was born in Ekaterinoslav, the Ukraine (now Dnepropetrovsk, the Soviet Union), on April 17, 1903. When he was very young, his father took him to a symphony concert, where the boy saw a cello for the first time. From that night on, little Gregor pretended to play the cello, using a long stick for the cello and a short one for the bow. On his seventh birthday, he was given a real cello.

His first teacher was his father, who was a violinist. Soon, however, he began taking lessons from local cellists. One well-known visiting cellist consented to listen to Gregor. After the boy finished, the man said, "Keep away from the cello. You have no talent whatsoever." For a while Gregor stopped playing, but he could not stay away from the instrument. He loved to play it so much that he would often get up at four in the morning to practice, using, he has said, a "soundless system I devised—my fingers on the fingerboard and the bow in the air."

One day the elder Piatigorsky left his family and went to Saint Petersburg to study the violin with Leopold Auer. Gregor, at the tender age of eight, went to work with his cello, getting a job first in a nightclub-brothel and then in a movie theater. He gave his earnings to his mother.

Then his father returned and moved the family to Moscow. There Gregor attended the Moscow Conservatory (1911-16), studying the cello with Alfred von Glehn.

Soon after leaving the conservatory, Piatigorsky won the chair of first cellist at the Bolshoi Theater. He was also invited to become the cellist for the prestigious Lenin String Quartet. Attaining such positions was an incredible achievement for a boy in his middle teens.

But it was the early period after the Russian Revolution of 1917. Piatigorsky, like others, had to face many new political and material hardships. Those difficulties, coupled with painful memories of the bloody pogroms in the czarist Russia of his childhood, finally made him decide to escape.

In 1921 he joined a small group of musicians who went on a concert tour. At a village near Poland, they hired some smugglers to get the troupe across the border. During the escape, they were fired at by guards. Piatigorsky jumped into a nearby river and waded into Poland, holding his cello above his head. He was immediately arrested by Polish border guards, the leader of whom gave orders to deliver Piatigorsky back to the Russians. But some music-loving guards secretly let Piatigorsky go free.

He soon got a job as cellist with the Warsaw Philharmonic. Later he went to Leipzig, where he studied with Julius Klengel. In 1924 he was hired by the conductor Wilhelm Furtwängler as first cellist of the great Berlin Philharmonic Orchestra. During his Berlin years he began to establish himself in solo and trio (with the pianist Artur Schnabel and the violinist Carl Flesch) concerts. In 1928 he resigned from the Berlin Philharmonic to devote himself to a solo career.

He soon developed an international reputation, making his first American tour in 1929. During this period he formed a trio with two other great Russian exiles, the pianist Vladimir Horowitz and the violinist Nathan Milstein.

At the outbreak of World War II, Piatigorsky moved to the United States, where he became a naturalized citizen in 1942. In the same year, he was appointed head of the cello department at the Curtis Institute of Music in Philadelphia. He was there for two years.

His reputation as a concert artist continued to grow. He reached a large audience with his performance in the movie *Carnegie Hall* (1947).

In 1949 he formed another famous trio, this time with the pianist Arthur Rubinstein and the violinist Jascha Heifetz. *Life* magazine called it "the Million Dollar Trio."

He made frequent concert tours throughout the world, including Israel in 1954 with the Israel Philharmonic Orchestra and again in 1970 with Heifetz. Piatigorsky gave the world premieres of cello concertos by Mario Castelnuovo-Tedesco in 1935, Paul Hindemith in 1941, and William Walton in 1957. In 1965 he published his autobiography, *Cellist,* in which he displays a gift for vivid recollections of his tours and friends.

After settling in Los Angeles, he participated in a celebrated series called the Heifetz-Piatigorsky Concerts (1961-76). From 1962 on he was a professor at the University of Southern California (USC), where his cello master classes became famous. In 1975 a chair of music was established in Piatigorsky's name at USC.

Piatigorsky was at his best in romantic music and was particularly well known for his performances of Richard Strauss's *Don Quixote,* Strauss himself referring to the cellist as "mein Don Quixote" ("my Don Quixote"). Though he had a flair for virtuosity, he never set technical perfection as a goal in itself. His objective was to

Gregor Piatigorsky

attain a close rapport with his audience, which he achieved through his eloquence, his sense of grandeur, and his tone of infinite shadings.

Tall (6'3"), dark eyed, and sharp featured, Piatigorsky was referred to by the sculptor Katharine Ward Lane as one of the ten most handsome men in the United States. He was a frequent subject for artists.

He met and married his first wife, Lydia Antik, during his Berlin years (1924-28). She was beautiful and worldly; he was young and shy. After nine childless years they divorced.

In 1937 he married the fine amateur pianist and bassoonist Jacqueline de Rothschild, daughter of Baron Edouard de Rothschild of Paris. Gregor and Jacqueline had a successful marriage that produced two children: Joram and Jephta.

Piatigorsky was noted among his friends for his sense of humor. Once, for example, when his booking agency advised its artists to travel light on their next tour because of wartime restrictions, the cellist wrote to his manager and announced that he had switched to the piccolo.

Piatigorsky continued to teach and perform till late in life. He played, for example, at several concerts given to celebrate his seventieth birthday in 1973. He died at his Los Angeles home on August 6, 1976.

André Previn

Multitalented Musician

(1929-   )

André Previn, who worked his way up from a teenage musical hack in movies to a conductor of the world's greatest orchestras, was born in Berlin, Germany, on April 6, 1929. His original name was Andreas Ludwig Priwin, alternatively, during his early youth in Europe, André Ludwig Prewin.

His father, Jacob, was a lawyer and an excellent amateur pianist whose home was always filled with music played by family and friends. When André turned five, Jacob began to give the boy piano lessons. André later credited his father with having instilled in him "a love for music and, along with that love, a passion for sight-reading." André's musical sight-reading ability would be of tremendous help to him in his later career as a pianist and conductor.

At six André entered the Berlin Academy of Music, where he studied piano with Rudolf Breithaupt. But time was running out for Jews in Berlin, where signs reading *Juden verboten* ("Jews Keep Out") were beginning to appear in public places. In the autumn of 1937 André was expelled from the academy, Breithaupt explaining that he could no longer afford to have a Jewish pupil, especially such a talented one, who would "be noticed" by the Nazi authorities.

In early 1938 the family left Berlin for France, where André studied for a while at the Paris Conservatory. One of his teachers there was the well-known organist Marcel Dupré.

In 1939 the family set sail for their real goal—the United States. One of their relatives, Charles Previn, was head of the music department at Universal Studios in the Hollywood section of Los Angeles, California. When he learned that the family was heading for America, he advised Jacob to change his name from Priwin/Prewin to Previn, especially for the sake of André's professional career. Otherwise, Charles predicted, Americans would "be calling the boy 'André Prune.' Take my word for it; he'll never get rich and famous as André Prune." Encountering Americans on the ship to the United States and realizing that Charles was right, the Prewins became the Previns, Jacob himself Americanizing his name to Jack, while André Ludwig Prewin became André George Previn.

They settled in the Los Angeles area after a brief stay in New York City, and Jack became a piano teacher (because continuing his law practice would have required a prohibitive amount of time to learn English and study American law). André, besides entering public school, privately studied piano with Max Rabinowitsch (whose hands were substituted for those of actors supposedly playing the piano in numerous movies), theory mainly with Joseph Achron and briefly with Ernst Toch, and composition with Mario Castelnuovo-Tedesco.

By the time he was in his early teens, young Previn had already experienced the lure of American popular music. In 1942 he entered Beverly Hills High School, where, during his first year, he organized his own dance band for playing at school dances. He also formed a special band for the annual Beverly Hills High School Variety Show, in which he made his first ventures into arranging and conducting. Previn earned money through many other popular-music outlets during his high-school years, such as playing the piano for a dance academy and a radio program.

Meanwhile, Previn did not lose touch with the world of classical music. In 1945 he began to perform concertos with the California Youth Orchestra, and at about the same time he began to play new and obscure classical music in the Monday Evening Concerts.

But increasingly he was pulled into the world of popular music, specifically music for the movies. In 1945, while still a sixteen-year-old senior in high school, he was hired by Metro-Goldwyn-Mayer (MGM) to write and orchestrate jazzlike variations on "Three Blind Mice" for the pianist José Iturbi, accompanied by an orchestra, to play in the film *Holiday in Mexico* (1946). Previn continued to perform part-time miscellaneous musical chores (including arranging and piano playing) for the studio till his graduation from high school, soon after which he became a full-time arranger for MGM.

Years later Previn explained what made him choose to work in Hollywood: "I stayed because I had a great deal of fun and because the work, in a cheap way, was glamorous and thrilling. I suppose I should also mention greed and stupidity."

In 1948 Previn was finally given a chance to compose an original movie score of his own, *The Sun Comes Up* (1949), a forgettable film starring Jeanette MacDonald and Lassie (who was actually a laddie). Since Previn himself supervised the recording of the music track, *The Sun Comes Up* also marked his debut on any recording stage as a conductor.

In 1949 Previn's career reached its first peak with his highly praised work as arranger of the movie musical *Three Little Words* (1950), in which he skillfully integrated into the score more than a dozen songs by Bert Kalmar and Harry Ruby (whose lives are the subject of the film). One of the stars of *Three Little Words* was Gloria De Haven, who became the first in a long line of famous females with whom Previn would be romantically linked.

161

In 1950 his life took a dramatic turn when he was drafted into the army. Part of his two-year hitch was spent stationed in San Francisco, where Previn met, and studied the classical repertory with, the great conductor Pierre Monteux.

During the same period and in the same city, Previn met the jazz singer Betty Bennett, about whom he later said, "I was crazy about her singing and then I was crazy about her." She introduced him to the city's important jazz musicians, from whom he began to learn that serious jazz was infinitely richer than the watered-down version of it that he had been exposed to in Hollywood. He soon became an accomplished jazz pianist.

When his army service was over, Previn had three career options: jazz pianist, classical conductor, and Hollywood hack. Having decided to marry Betty Bennett, he opted for financial security and returned to MGM in 1952 (later, in 1959, turning to freelance film work).

Also in 1952 André and Betty were married. They had two children: Claudia and Alicia. But the marriage lasted only about five years before André and Betty separated.

During the 1950s and early 1960s, Previn issued a number of successful recordings as a jazz pianist, notably those for Contemporary Records.

But the bulk of his time was spent on Hollywood films. He specialized in arranging the scores of musicals written by other composers, such as Frederick Loewe's *Gigi* (1958), George Gershwin's *Porgy and Bess* (1959), and Loewe's *My Fair Lady* (1964). But Previn also showed compositional skill in his original background scores for such dramatic films as *Bad Day at Black Rock* (1955) and *Elmer Gantry* (1960).

In 1959 Previn married Dory Langdon (originally Dorothy Langan), a lyricist with whom he wrote a number of songs for films, including "The Faraway Part of Town" *(Pepe,* 1960), "Second Chance" *(Two for the Seesaw,* 1962), and "You're Gonna Hear from Me" *(Inside Daisy Clover,* 1965). But the marriage was strained by Dory's increasingly frequent confinements in mental hospitals. After eleven childless years they divorced in 1970.

In the early 1960s Previn began to break away from Hollywood and to establish himself on the concert stage as a pianist and conductor. However, at first he was engaged only for pops concerts that featured mostly Broadway and film music, and he was regularly referred to as "Hollywood's André Previn." Such appearances included performances as pianist and conductor at pops concerts with the Saint Louis Symphony Orchestra on February 10, 1961; January 26, 1962; and March 16, 1963. On March 23, 1963, he made his debut as a conductor of a major orchestra in a classical program, again with the Saint Louis Symphony.

An important step forward came when he was asked to make some recordings with the prestigious London Symphony Orchestra in 1965 and 1966. Then, finally, came the breakthrough that he had been hoping for: in 1967 he was given his own orchestra, being appointed principal conductor of the Houston Symphony Orchestra, where he stayed till 1969.

Soon, however, Previn made the enormous leap to serving as principal conductor of the London Symphony Orchestra (1969-79), a historic association because it was the first of its kind between a major British orchestra and an American conductor. Besides playing the piano and conducting at concerts, Previn began to appear on British TV as a conductor and musical commentator. His versatile musicality and captivating personality made him an English equivalent of America's Leonard Bernstein, who virtually symbolizes classical music to the general public in the United States.

Previn toured with the London Symphony in Europe, the United States, and the Far East. During his London years he also guest-conducted most of the major orchestras in Europe and America. From 1976 to 1984 he led the Pittsburgh Symphony Orchestra, where he attained high visibility on TV through the Public Broadcasting System (PBS) series *Previn and the Pittsburgh.*

He prefers to conduct the repertory from Mozart to moderate twentieth-century composers, such as Benjamin Britten and Dmitri Shostakovich, generally avoiding baroque music and the avant-garde.

André Previn

Previn himself has composed moderate contemporary music, such as the *Symphony* for strings (1962); the concertos for cello (1968), guitar (1971), and piano (1984); and the *Four Outings* for brass quintet (1974). He also composed the musical *Coco* (perf. 1969) for Broadway and the hit *Every Good Boy Deserves Favour* (perf. 1977) for the London stage.

In recent years he has become involved in literary activities. Besides answering questions posed by Anthony Hopkins for *Music Face to Face* (1971), he served as editor for *André Previn's Guide to Music* (1983) and *André Previn's Guide to the Orchestra* (1983).

In 1970, soon after divorcing Dory Langdon, Previn married the actress Mia Farrow. They had twin boys (Matthew and Sascha) and then another boy (Fletcher). In addition, they adopted two Vietnamese girls (Kym Lark [or Lark Song] and Summer [or Daisy]) as well as a Korean girl (Soon-Yi).

Mia, however, eventually decided to resume her film career full time, having reduced her professional activity during the early stages of her marriage with André. Soon it became evident that their careers were pulling them apart, and they divorced in 1979.

In 1982 he married Heather Hales. They have a son (Lukas).

Previn has worked long and hard to earn the respect of music critics, many of whom for years dismissed him as "Hollywood's André Previn." His accomplishments in Houston, London, and Pittsburgh, as well as his recordings with a number of major orchestras, amply testify to the fact that he has long since proven himself as a serious musician and a conductor of major stature.

And now, ironically, he has triumphantly returned to Hollywood—this time as music director and principal conductor of the Los Angeles Philharmonic Orchestra. Named to the post in April 1984 and assuming some administrative duties later that year, he took the podium in his new role in 1985. Also since 1985 he has headed the Royal Philharmonic Orchestra of London.

Selected works:

Stage

Coco (musical; lyrics, A. J. Lerner; perf. 1969)
Every Good Boy Deserves Favour (piece for actors and orchestra; text, T. Stoppard; perf. 1977)

Films
(background scores)

Bad Day at Black Rock (1955)
Elmer Gantry (1960)
Long Day's Journey into Night (1962)
Inside Daisy Clover (1965)
The Fortune Cookie (1966)

Orchestral

Symphony (strings, 1962)
Cello Concerto (1968)
Guitar Concerto (1971)
Principals (1980)
Reflections (1981)
Divertimento (1982)
Piano Concerto (1984)

Songs

"The Faraway Part of Town" (lyrics, D. Langdon; for the film *Pepe,* 1960)
"Second Chance" (lyrics, D. Langdon; for the film *Two for the Seesaw,* 1962)
"You're Gonna Hear from Me" (lyrics, D. Langdon; for the film *Inside Daisy Clover,* 1965)

Chamber

Violin Sonata (1964)
Flute Quartet (1964)
Woodwind Quintet (1973)
Four Outings (brass quintet, 1974)

Piano

Suite for Piano (1967)
Piano Preludes (1972)

Fritz Reiner

Baton Technician

(1888-1963)

Fritz Reiner, conductor, was born in Budapest, Hungary, on December 19, 1888. At the age of six he began to study the piano, and within a few years he was playing four-hand piano music with Leó Weiner, a local boy (three years Reiner's senior) who later became an important composer-teacher. It was Weiner who first encouraged Reiner to become a conductor. They remained close friends till Weiner's death in 1960.

Reiner attended the Budapest Academy of Music from 1898 to 1908, studying piano with István Thomán and composition with Hans Koessler and Béla Bartók. Reiner's mother encouraged his interest in music, but his father, a practical businessman, wanted the boy to become a lawyer. For his father's sake, Fritz Reiner studied law at the University of Budapest even while he was attending the Academy of Music. After he graduated from the music school in 1908, he continued his law studies till 1909, when his father died. He then turned to music full time.

Reiner began his professional music career in 1909 as a vocal coach at the Budapest Opera, where he made his conducting debut in 1910 when he was called on at the last moment to direct a performance of Bizet's *Carmen*. Later in 1910 he became conductor at the National Theater in Laibach. He then conducted at the Budapest People's Opera (1911-14), where he gave the Budapest premiere of Wagner's *Parsifal* in 1914.

Reiner's decision to move to Dresden in 1914 ushered in one of the most crucial periods in his career. As principal conductor of the Saxton State Orchestra symphony concerts and of the Dresden Opera, he became a leading figure in the musical life of Europe. During his Dresden years (1914-21) he conducted his first *Ring* cycle (that is, *Der Ring des Nibelungen* ["The Ring of the Nibelung"], four operas by Wagner) and met Gustav Mahler, Arthur Nikisch (the celebrated conductor who greatly influenced Reiner's conducting style), and Richard Strauss (with whose works Reiner later became closely identified).

After leaving Dresden and making brief appearances in Barcelona, Rome, Buenos Aires, and other cities, Reiner settled in the United States and served in the post of principal conductor of the Cincinnati Symphony Orchestra (1922-31). Conflicts soon developed, the orchestra members rebelling against his dictatorial manner and the directors resenting his programming of modern music. Nevertheless, Reiner successfully rebuilt the orchestra and gave it a previously lacking prestige. While in Cincinnati he promoted contemporary scores by such composers as Bartók, Maurice Ravel, Ottorino Respighi, Roger Sessions, and Igor Stravinsky.

In 1928 Reiner became an American citizen. In 1930, shortly after divorcing his wife, Berta Gardini Gerster (with whom Reiner had two children, Tussy and Eva), he married Carlotta Irwin, a Cincinnati actress. In 1931 the Institute of Fine Arts took control of the Cincinnati Symphony Orchestra and demanded that the conductor present a higher percentage of conservative fare. Reiner soon resigned.

Beginning in 1931 he taught for a number of years at the Curtis Institute of Music in Philadelphia, where in 1937 he conducted the world premiere of Gian Carlo Menotti's opera *Amelia Goes to the Ball* and where his conducting pupils included Leonard Bernstein, Lukas Foss, and Vincent Persichetti. Also during the 1930s Reiner made numerous guest appearances, notably his conducting of the world premiere of Joseph Achron's *Golem* in Venice, Italy, in 1932, and his leading of soprano Kirsten Flagstad and tenor Lauritz Melchoir in Wagner works at the San Francisco Opera during the 1936-38 seasons.

Reiner then spent ten years as conductor and music director of the Pittsburgh Symphony Orchestra (1938-48). Among the highlights of his work in Pittsburgh were his premieres of works by the American composers Paul Creston, Norman Dello Joio, and Walter Piston. In 1943 Reiner guest-conducted the New York Philharmonic in the first American performance of Bartók's *Concerto for Two Pianos, Percussion, and Orchestra*. He resigned from the Pittsburgh Symphony when his superiors reduced the number of musicians in his orchestra and the number of concerts per season.

Reiner's next regular post was at the Metropolitan Opera in New York City (1948-53). He made a spectacular debut in a February 1949 performance of Richard Strauss's *Salome*. Also highly praised were some of his performances of Wagner's *Tristan und Isolde* ("Tristan and Isolde") and Richard Strauss's *Der Rosenkavalier* ("The Knight of the Rose"). In 1950 he guest-conducted the National Broadcasting Company (NBC) Symphony Orchestra in the world premiere of Aaron Copland's *Clarinet Concerto*, with Benny Goodman as soloist. And in 1953, at the Metropolitan, he led the American premiere of Stravinsky's *The Rake's Progress*.

Reiner gained his greatest fame as conductor of the Chicago Symphony Orchestra (1953-62). As previously in Cincinnati and Pittsburgh, Reiner took a company in artistic decline and rebuilt it into a quality orchestra, programming both traditional and modern works. Under Reiner the Chicago Symphony became, in Stravinsky's opinion, "the most precise and flexible orchestra in the world."

Reiner was widely regarded as the greatest baton technician of his time. Expending minimum effort to attain maximum effects, Reiner used small gestures with the baton but through them conveyed infinite nuances. From Nikisch he learned to use eye contact, not flailing arms, to control the orchestra. He believed that with the proper use of baton and eyes, speaking to the orchestra was unnecessary: "When students have completed a course under my direction, any one of them can stand up before an orchestra he has never seen before and conduct a new piece at first sight without verbal explanation, by means of only manual technique."

Reiner, however, was an impatient, irritable man who often burst into fits of temper during rehearsals. He would never have won a popularity contest among orchestra members. But his emphasis on rhythmic precision and clarity of texture created performances that were consistently elegant and unsentimental, though he did not fail to bring out emotion and drama as well. His method was very effective for modern music, and he regularly conducted the works of such contemporary Europeans as Béla Bartók, Paul Hindemith, Zoltán Kodály, Darius Milhaud, Sergei Prokofiev, Arnold Schoenberg, and Igor Stravinsky, as well as the Americans Leonard Bernstein, Aaron Copland, George Gershwin, Morton Gould, Gian Carlo Menotti, Walter Piston, William Schuman, Roger Sessions, and others.

In October 1960 Reiner suffered a heart attack in Chicago. In March 1961 he returned to his conducting podium, but a few months later he was hospitalized again. He finally resigned from the Chicago Symphony in 1962 and retired to his Westport, Connecticut, home, where he lived with his wife, Carlotta. In November 1963 Reiner was rehearsing for a performance with the Metropolitan Opera when he developed pneumonia. He died in New York City on November 15, 1963.

Regina Resnik
Versatile Opera Star
(1922-   )

Regina Resnik, mezzo-soprano (formerly soprano), was born of Ukrainian immigrants in New York City, New York, on August 30, 1922. While attending James Monroe High School, she began to take voice lessons from Rosalie Miller, with whom Resnik continued to study even after achieving professional success. She graduated from high school in 1938 and then enrolled in Hunter College of the City University of New York, where she earned a B.A. in 1942.

That autumn, at the Brooklyn Academy of Music, Resnik made her concert debut. Shortly thereafter Fritz Busch (whom she had met through Rosalie Miller), director of the New Opera Company in New York City, hired her as an understudy for the part of Lady Macbeth in Verdi's *Macbeth*. When the soprano scheduled to sing the role became ill, Resnik took over and in December 1942 made her opera debut.

In 1943 she was engaged by the National Opera of Mexico City. There she performed Leonore in Beethoven's *Fidelio* and Micaëla in Bizet's *Carmen*.

The following year Resnik earned a contract at the Metropolitan Opera by being one (and the only female) of four winners of the company's annual auditions. In December 1944 she made her Met debut, singing Leonora in Verdi's *Il trovatore* ("The Troubadour"), a role that she performed with particular brilliance considering that she had had only a few days' notice, the scheduled singer having become ill.

For the next ten years Resnik continued to sing leading soprano roles at the Met. Among her memorable parts were Alice Ford in Verdi's *Falstaff*, Donna Anna and Donna Elvira in Mozart's *Don Giovanni*, Leonore in Beethoven's *Fidelio*, Musetta in Puccini's *La bohème* ("The Bohemian Girl"), Rosalinda in Johann Strauss II's *Die Fledermaus* ("The Bat"), and Sieglinde in Wagner's *Die Walküre* ("The Valkyrie").

During that period Resnik also participated in some important premieres. In early 1947 she created the role of Delilah in the world premiere of Bernard Rogers's opera *The Warrior*. Later that year, with the Chicago Opera, she sang the part of the Female Chorus in the first American production of Benjamin Britten's *The Rape of Lucretia*. In 1948 she introduced the role of Ellen Orford to New York City in a Metropolitan Opera presentation of Britten's *Peter Grimes*.

Regina Resnik as Klytämnestra in Richard Strauss's *Elektra*

166

In 1946 Resnik married Harry W. Davis, a New York City lawyer who had been her first date. They had one child, Michael, before the marriage ended in divorce.

In 1953 she made her first appearance at the famous Bayreuth Festival in West Germany, singing Sieglinde in Wagner's *Die Walküre*. Shortly thereafter she began to experience difficulty while singing in the normal soprano range. But by cultivating the deeper part of her voice, she soon became a comfortable mezzo-soprano.

Resnik then began a new career, singing mezzo-soprano and alto roles. Her first performance with her new voice was as Amneris in a Cincinnati Summer Opera production of Verdi's *Aïda* in 1955. Early the following year she appeared as Marina in Mussorgsky's *Boris Godunov* at the Met, her first performance there as a mezzo-soprano.

After her voice changed, Resnik became most famous for her title role in Bizet's *Carmen*. Donald Henahan, in the *New York Times,* described her Carmen as "a combination of alley cat and Mae West." Other parts in which she excelled with her lower voice included Dame Quickly in Verdi's *Falstaff,* Herodias in Richard Strauss's *Salome,* Klytämnestra in the same composer's *Elektra,* and Laura in Ponchielli's *La Gioconda* (literally, "The Joyful Girl"; here, the heroine's name).

In 1958 Resnik created the role of the Baroness in the world premiere of Samuel Barber's *Vanessa.* And in the 1972 San Francisco Opera's first American production of Gottfried von Einem's *Der Besuch der alten Dame* ("The Visit of the Old Lady"), she played Claire (the Old Lady).

Beginning in the late 1950s Resnik appeared regularly with the world's leading opera companies: London (at Covent Garden), Milan (at La Scala), Vienna, San Francisco, and elsewhere. Though she continued her association with the Metropolitan Opera, she actually received more acclaim in Europe, particularly in Vienna.

In her prime, Resnik had a rich, resonant voice and a firm upper register. Her acting was always subtle.

Resnik's excellent musicianship and general intelligence led her to expand her activities to include stage direction. In 1971 she directed, and sang the title role in, a Hamburg Opera production of Bizet's *Carmen*. She collaborated in that effort with the painter-sculptor and scenic designer Arbit Blatas, who designed the costumes and scenery. The same pair worked together to direct and design a production of Strauss's *Elektra* (with Resnik also singing Klytämnestra) in Venice, Italy, later that year.

In 1975 Resnik and Blatas directed and designed a new presentation of Verdi's *Falstaff* for the National Opera of Poland in Warsaw. Resnik sang Dame Quickly in that production. By then, the collaborators' professional relationship had blossomed into a personal one as well, and they were married in 1975.

Among the other operas that Resnik has directed in recent years are Menotti's *The Medium* and *The Telephone,* Tchaikovsky's *The Queen of Spades,* and Weill's *Aufstieg und Fall der Stadt Mahagonny* ("Rise and Fall of the City of Mahagonny").

Regina Resnik as the Countess in Tchaikovsky's *The Queen of Spades*

George Rochberg
Leader of Postmodernism
(1918-   )

George Rochberg, composer, was born in Paterson, New Jersey, on July 5, 1918. He studied piano as a child, and in his teens he played in jazz groups and wrote popular songs with lyrics by Bob Russell. While attending the state college in Montclair, New Jersey, from which he graduated with a B.A. in 1939, Rochberg began to extend his composing to art songs and piano pieces. He then attended the David Mannes School of Music (1939-42), where he studied composition with Leopold Mannes, George Szell, and Hans Weisse.

In 1941 Rochberg married Gene Rosenfeld, whom he had met while they were both students in Montclair. They had two children: Paul and Frances.

But the Rochbergs had barely settled into married life before he was drafted by the army for World War II action. Serving from 1942 to 1945, he became a second lieutenant in the infantry, was wounded in Europe, and received the Purple Heart with cluster.

After leaving the army in 1945, Rochberg enrolled at the Curtis Institute of Music in Philadelphia, where he studied theory and composition with Rosario Scalero and Gian Carlo Menotti. He earned his B.Mus. from the Curtis Institute in 1948 and immediately joined the faculty there, where he remained till 1954. In 1949 he obtained an M.A. from the University of Pennsylvania.

In 1951 Rochberg was appointed director of publications for the Theodore Presser Company, a position that he held till he was named chairman of the music department at the University of Pennsylvania in 1960. He left the chairmanship in 1968 but remained as a professor of composition. From 1979 till he retired in 1983, he served as Annenberg Professor of the Humanities.

Rochberg's development as a composer has been marked by a series of stages during which he has produced a number of important compositions and essays that explore major aesthetic issues of his time. His early music reveals a lyricized version of the neoclassical idioms of Hindemith and Stravinsky, as in the *Songs of Solomon* for voice and piano (1946). Even more evident is the exotic influence of Bartók, as in the *First String Quartet* (1952).

Rochberg's deep desire for expressiveness in music led him, beginning in 1948, to an intensive study of Schoenbergian serialism. He became a master of the twelve-tone technique and produced a series of works that reflected his personal conception of serialism, as in the *Twelve Bagatelles* for piano (1952), *David the Psalmist* for tenor and orchestra (1954), and the *Second Symphony* (1956). Under the influence of Webern, Rochberg also created a more refined, economical kind of serialism in the *Cheltenham Concerto* for small orchestra (1958).

After the death of his twenty-year-old son, Paul, from a brain tumor in 1964, Rochberg almost lost the will to create. But soon he found a new meaning in music: "Right now composing is also a way of achieving integration and the means with which I can face existence." Rochberg's discovery of a personal integration with existence led him to search for a more universal musical language, one designed to communicate humanistic ideas to a thoughtful but general audience, not to display technical ingenuity for small groups of cognoscenti.

Feeling constrained by serialism, he sought to expand his gestural possibilities. His first step toward greater inclusivity and flexibility was to incorporate quotations from the music of other composers into his original materials, as in *Contra mortem et tempus* ("Against Time and Death") for four instruments (1965), with quotations from the modernists Berio, Boulez, Ives, and Varèse; *Music for the Magic Theater* for chamber orchestra (1965), with inclusions from the old masters Mozart, Beethoven, and Mahler, as well as the modernists Stockhausen, Varèse, Webern, and Rochberg himself; and *Nach Bach* ("After Bach") for harpsichord or piano (1966), written for the outstanding harpsichordist Igor Kipnis.

Rochberg's gradual assimilation of more and more quotations from the tonal repertory finally led to his complete adoption of traditional elements of style as part of his own aesthetic, even without the use of quotation. His later works show a remarkable coalescence of the past and the present—diatonic elements existing side by side, even simultaneously, with atonal, twelve-tone, and other modern materials. Perhaps more than any other major composer of his time, Rochberg has reclaimed tonality as a means for powerfully original expression. Among his most significant late works are the *Third Symphony* (1969) and the *Third* (1972) through *Sixth* (1978) string quartets.

Since the death of his son, Rochberg has drawn on the literary talents of his family for numerous texts. Material left by his son, Paul, supplied the words for *Tableaux* (1968), *Eleven Songs* (1969), and *Fantasies* (1971). Gene Rochberg helped her husband with the texts for the monodrama *Phaedra* (from Robert Lowell's version of Racine's play, 1974) and the opera *The Confidence Man* (based on Herman Melville's novel, perf. 1982).

Rochberg is the leading spokesman for, and exponent of, postmodernism in music. He has brilliantly and

Selected works:

Stage

Phaedra (monodrama; libretto, Gene Rochberg, after R. Lowell; comp. 1974, perf. 1976)
The Confidence Man (opera; libretto, Gene Rochberg, after H. Melville; perf. 1982)

Orchestral

Chamber Symphony (chamber orchestra, 1953)
Second Symphony (1956)
First Symphony (1957, revised 1977)
Cheltenham Concerto (small orchestra, 1958)
Time-Span I (1960, revised as *Time-Span II*, 1962)
Music for the Magic Theater (chamber orchestra, 1965)
Third Symphony (1969)
Violin Concerto (1974)
Fourth Symphony (1976)
Oboe Concerto (1984)

Band

Apocalyptica (1964)
Black Sounds (1965)

Vocal

Songs of Solomon (voice, piano; texts, Bible; 1946)
David the Psalmist (tenor, orchestra; text, Bible; 1954)
Three Psalms (chorus; texts, Bible; 1954)
Blake Songs (soprano, chamber ensemble; texts, W. Blake; 1961)
Tableaux (soprano, two actors' voices, men's chorus, twelve instrumentalists; texts, P. Rochberg; 1968)
Eleven Songs (voice, piano; texts, P. Rochberg; 1969)
Sacred Song of Reconciliation: Mizmor l'piyus (bass-baritone, chamber orchestra; 1970)
Fantasies (four songs; voice, piano; texts, P. Rochberg; 1971)
Behold, My Servant (chorus, 1973)

Chamber

seven string quartets (1952-79)
Dialogues (clarinet, piano; 1956)
Piano Trio (1963)
Contra mortem et tempus (four instruments, 1965)
Fifty Caprice Variations (violin, after Paganini, 1970)
Electrikaleidoscope (amplified instrumental ensemble, 1972)
Ricordanza ("Remembrance"; cello, piano; 1972)
Ukiyo-E: Pictures of the Floating World (harp, 1973)
Piano Quintet (1975)
Slow Fires of Autumn: Ukiyo-II (flute, harp; 1978)
Viola Sonata (1979)
Duo (oboe, bassoon; 1979)
Octet: A Grand Fantasia (winds, piano, strings; 1980)
Trio (clarinet, horn, piano; 1980)
String Quintet (1982)

Piano

Two Preludes and Fughettas (1946)
Twelve Bagatelles (1952)
Sonata-Fantasia (1956)
Nach Bach (1966)
Carnival Music (1969)
Partita-Variations (1976)

Writings

The Hexachord and Its Relation to the Twelve-Tone Row (1955)
The Aesthetics of Survival: A Composer's View of Twentieth-Century Music (a collection of essays, 1984)

lucidly explained his philosophy in a series of essays, many of them collected in *The Aesthetics of Survival: A Composer's View of Twentieth-Century Music* (1984). "Modernism," he says, "has done little to satisfy the hunger for experience of the marvelous, which is timeless and ahistorical."

His work since the late 1960s has challenged many of the basic tenets of modern art music, such as the belief that significant music can now be written only by using up-to-the-minute fashionable procedures, and the belief that reason (in the form of various preconceived theories, systems, and formulas) must predominate over expression. Rochberg's brilliant use of tonality has effectively destroyed the first notion. And regarding the second, he believes that the purpose of music should be to express mankind's noblest, deepest feelings and that those feelings are rooted in "a moral order in the universe which underlies all real existence." Thus—unlike most of his contemporaries—he strives for balance between reason and feeling: "Music is the sound of the human heart," he says, "shaped and guided by the mind. It is the sounding of the human consciousness in all of its possible states of being."

Richard Rodgers
Dean of American
Musical-Theater Composers
(1902-1979)

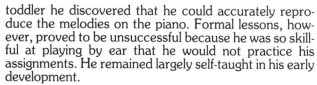

Richard Rodgers, composer, was born in Hammels Station, Long Island, New York, on June 28, 1902. His parents loved the musical theater, and at home they often sang songs from Broadway shows, his mother providing the piano accompaniment. Soon little Richard knew all the songs by heart, and while still a

toddler he discovered that he could accurately reproduce the melodies on the piano. Formal lessons, however, proved to be unsuccessful because he was so skillful at playing by ear that he would not practice his assignments. He remained largely self-taught in his early development.

At the age of seven Richard began to attend the theater in person. He immediately fell in love with it, and over the next several years he was particularly attracted to Broadway by the operettas of Victor Herbert and the early musical comedies of Jerome Kern. Later, in his teens, he was stunned by the magnificence of classical music (as when he heard Enrico Caruso sing in Bizet's *Carmen* at the Metropolitan Opera and Josef Hofmann play the Tchaikovsky *First Piano Concerto* at Carnegie Hall), and he might easily have developed in that direction. But the musical theater, because of its early influence on him, always remained his primary goal.

Richard began to improvise his own melodies at the piano when he was nine. At fourteen, in June 1916, he wrote his first real song, "Camp-fire Days" (lyrics, Nathan Caleb House), while spending a summer vacation at Camp Wigwam in Harrison, Maine.

In early 1917 his older brother, Morty (Mortimer), a student at Columbia University, took him to see Columbia's annual Varsity Show. When Richard expressed admiration for the show's lyrics, Morty introduced him to the lyricist, the prelaw student Oscar Hammerstein II. Richard was inspired by that meeting to attend Columbia so that he, too, could write for the Varsity Show.

He also decided then and there not to waste any more time before making a serious start on what he had already chosen as his profession: songwriting. With a young would-be lyricist named David Dyrenforth, Rodgers created "Auto Show Girl," his first copyrighted song (June 30, 1917).

In the autumn of 1917 Rodgers wrote his first complete musical-comedy score, an amateur production staged by Morty's social-athletic group called the Akron Club for the benefit of America's World War I effort. The show was called *One Minute, Please* and had lyrics mostly by Morty's friend Ralph Engelsman and by Richard Rodgers himself. At its single performance (December 29, 1917), Rodgers conducted the five-person orchestra and played the piano simultaneously.

In March 1919 Rodgers put on another musical comedy for amateurs: *Up Stage and Down,* with lyrics mostly by Rodgers, though others contributed, notably Oscar Hammerstein II. Rodgers (with money from his father, a doctor) published several of the songs from the show, his first works to appear in print.

At about that time, Rodgers began to work with the lyricist Lorenz Hart, seven years older than the composer and already a Columbia University graduate. Hart, who met Rodgers through a mutual friend at Columbia, had previously been limited to translating the texts of German operettas. But he had strong opinions about how to write for the American musical theater, in particular about the need for good poetry in place of the childish lyrics then common on the popular stage. The sixteen-year-old Rodgers was as impressed by the older man's theories as Hart was by the younger man's musicianship.

They collaborated on a number of songs in the spring and summer of 1919. But their professional career together was launched when their song "Any Old Place with You" was purchased by Lew Fields and, on August 26, 1919, interpolated into his production of the Broadway show *A Lonely Romeo*. Later that year "Any Old Place with You" became Rodgers's first professionally published song.

Meanwhile, his academic work was not going well. In 1917 he dropped out, to avoid flunking out, of the Townsend Harris Hall school for advanced students. That autumn he entered the easier DeWitt Clinton High School, but he was unhappy there because it had little cultural activity. In the autumn of 1919 he was able, through special extension courses, to enroll in Columbia University even though he had not finished high school.

While at Columbia (1919-21), Rodgers continued to write musical comedies for amateur production, including the Columbia Varsity Shows *Fly with Me* (perf. 1920) and *You'll Never Know* (perf. 1921). Lew Fields attended *Fly with Me,* with the eventual result that Rodgers and Hart supplied about half the score for Fields's next Broadway show: *Poor Little Ritz Girl* (perf. 1920).

Having fulfilled his major Columbia goal by writing two Varsity Shows, Rodgers transferred in 1921 to the Institute of Musical Art (now known as the Juilliard School of Music) in New York City so that he could concentrate entirely on music. He remained there till 1923 and studied with, among others, Franklin W. Robinson (theory) and Percy Goetschius (harmony). While at the institute, Rodgers continued to write music for amateur shows.

After leaving the institute in 1923, Rodgers, with Hart, began the serious pursuit of success on Broadway. They worked on *The Melody Man* (perf. 1924), but their first major hit was the revue *The Garrick Gaieties* (perf. 1925). In *Dearest Enemy* (perf. 1925) they made their first, and one of the theater's earliest, tentative ventures away from the song-and-dance format of the traditional musical comedy and toward the musical play, in which they attempted to make the songs an integral part of the storytelling and character-revealing process in the context of serious subject matter.

Over the next several years Rodgers and Hart rose to great prominence in American popular music. They wrote many successful musical comedies for the stage, including *The Girl Friend* (perf. 1926), *Peggy-Ann* (notable for being almost entirely a dream sequence, perf.

1926), and *A Connecticut Yankee* (perf. 1927). One of their most memorable songs was created during that early period: "With a Song in My Heart" from *Spring Is Here* (perf. 1929).

In several of their shows, Rodgers and Hart continued to experiment with the musical play. In *Present Arms* (perf. 1928), for example, Rodgers added transitional passages of music to help tie together the stage action. *Chee-Chee* (perf. 1928) was perhaps the team's first true musical play. To keep the story moving, they used a number of short pieces of from four to sixteen measures each, with only six songs of traditional length. The audience's attention was deliberately drawn to the new procedure in a special program note: "The musical numbers, some of them very short, are so interwoven with the story that it would be confusing for the audience to peruse a complete list."

In 1930 Rodgers and Hart went to the Hollywood section of Los Angeles, California. There they created song scores and background music to spoken lines for several movies over the next few years. They attempted, and to a great extent succeeded, in applying their innovations in music-and-story integration to the movie musical. *Love Me Tonight* (1932) established their reputation and supplied them with their first film hits: "Lover," "Isn't It Romantic?" and "Mimi" (the last two written specifically for the special delivery characteristic of the film's star, Maurice Chevalier).

However, their work went for naught when, in 1933, *Forty-second Street* (music, Harry Warren; lyrics, Al Dubin) was released. After that movie's great success, Hollywood turned away from the Rodgers and Hart kind of musical and toward the now famous lavish spectacles of the period, which consisted primarily of a series of dazzling song-and-dance numbers unrelated to plot or character development.

The team's later Hollywood work was highlighted by a song that became a classic. The melody was originally set to a Hart text entitled "Prayer," which was written for, but not used in, the movie *Hollywood Party* (1934). With new lyrics and a new title, "The Bad in Every Man," it was sung in the nonmusical picture *Manhattan Melodrama* (1934). A music publisher convinced Hart to come up with a third, more commercial, set of words for the melody. The lyricist did so, and the result was the only successful Rodgers and Hart song not associated with a stage or screen musical: "Blue Moon."

They returned to Broadway with a circus musical, *Jumbo* (perf. 1935), including the song "The Most Beautiful Girl in the World." In several of the following musicals, Rodgers and Hart reverted to the standard musical comedy, but in a more sophisticated form. Their first effort along those lines was *On Your Toes* (perf. 1936), in which for the first time ballet ("Slaughter on Tenth Avenue," choreographed by George Balanchine) was an integral part of the story line in a musical.

Babes in Arms (perf. 1937) is notable for the variety of its songs, with rhythmic interest in "Johnny One Note," sophistication in "The Lady Is a Tramp," and lyricism in "My Funny Valentine." *Pal Joey* (perf. 1940), with its cynical story (by John O'Hara) and suggestive lyrics (as in "Bewitched, Bothered, and Bewildered"), shocked audiences used to escapist musical comedy, so that the original failed, though a revival (1952) and a film version (1957) were hits.

By the early 1940s Hart's excessive drinking had caused a rift in the partnership, and Rodgers teamed up with Oscar Hammerstein II, who could supply not only the lyrics but also the books to their shows. Rodgers and Hammerstein proceeded to create a series of musicals that achieved unprecedented artistic, critical, and financial success.

Their first effort was *Oklahoma!* (perf. 1943), now widely acclaimed as one of the masterpieces of the American musical theater. More than any earlier musical play, *Oklahoma!* integrated song and dance (actually more like ballet, choreographed by Agnes de Mille) with story and characterization. Perhaps the most famous of several memorable songs in the show is "Oh, What a Beautiful Mornin'."

After writing *Oklahoma!*, Rodgers attempted to supplement his partnership with Hammerstein by temporarily reuniting with Hart, for whom Rodgers still had a deep personal fondness. But other than some minor revisions for a revival of *A Connecticut Yankee*, they were unable to produce anything before Hart's death, at forty-eight, in late 1943. (A film biography of Rodgers and Hart, *Words and Music*, was released in 1948.)

In 1944 Rodgers and Hammerstein founded their own publishing company: Williamson Music (a subsidiary of Chappell). The following year the film *State Fair* was released with a Rodgers and Hammerstein song score, including "It Might As Well Be Spring" and "It's a Grand Night for Singing."

Back on Broadway they wrote *Carousel* (perf. 1945), famed for its unusual operatic soliloquy by the leading character, Billy Bigelow. Rodgers further experimented by opening the show not with the traditional medley type of overture but with a single instrumental piece, the rousing but lovely "Carousel Waltz," which set the mood for the entire play. The score has several hit songs, including "If I Loved You" and "You'll Never Walk Alone," the latter of which has attained the status of a universally accepted hymn. For the rest of his life, Rodgers maintained that his favorite of all of his musicals was *Carousel*.

Allegro (perf. 1947), an experimental psychological drama, was less popular than *Oklahoma!* and *Carousel*. But *South Pacific* (perf. 1949) was another tremendous success. Several of its songs became hits, notably "Some Enchanted Evening."

Rodgers and Hammerstein capped their work together with *The King and I* and *The Sound of Music*, both of which furthered the integration of music and story, and both of which stand as perhaps the summits of artistic achievement in American popular musical theater. In *The King and I* (perf. 1951) Rodgers showed his sensitivity and craftsmanship by deliberately composing songs with a limited range for the female lead, Gertrude Lawrence, because she was not a trained singer. Yet despite his self-imposed restriction, he wrote three of his most successful songs for her: "Hello, Young Lovers," "I

Whistle a Happy Tune," and "Shall We Dance?" Another highlight of the score is the instrumental "March of the Royal Siamese Children." And a stunning effect is created in "The Small House of Uncle Thomas," a narrated ballet that is both humorous and touching.

The Sound of Music (perf. 1959) was Rodgers and Hammerstein's last musical. It contains some of their most memorable songs. The opening "Preludium," sung by the nuns, is a skillfully composed substitute for a conventional overture. "The Sound of Music," the first real song in the work, sets the tone for the whole play by being a tribute to nature and music. "My Favorite Things" is a catalog of simple pleasures. Maria, the governess, offers "Do-Re-Mi" as an elementary music lesson (brilliantly developed and counterpointed by Rodgers) to ingratiate herself with the Von Trapp children. "The Lonely Goatherd," with its rollicking imitations of yodeling, and the instrumental "Laendler," with its gentle rustic-waltz swaying, both evoke the atmosphere of the Austrian Alps. "Climb Ev'ry Mountain" (which has an emotional, hymnlike quality reminiscent of "You'll Never Walk Alone") is the mother superior's exhortation to Maria to face the challenges of life. "Edelweiss" (the last song that Rodgers and Hammerstein ever wrote together) is a lovely folklike song that Von Trapp sings as an expression of his love for his homeland, Austria.

After Hammerstein's death in 1960 Rodgers continued to compose, sometimes to his own lyrics, but with less success. In 1969 he had a heart attack, but he recovered and wrote *Two by Two* (perf. 1970), a recounting of the biblical story of Noah. His last musical was *Rex* (perf. 1976).

Besides writing musicals, Rodgers composed several instrumental works, most notably the incidental music (later formed into a suite) for the TV documentary series *Victory at Sea* (1952). As with his Broadway work, he relied on orchestrators to prepare his nontheatrical compositions for orchestral performance.

Rodgers married Dorothy Feiner in 1930. They had two children who survived (a third died a few minutes after birth): Mary and Linda. While the children were growing up, Rodgers never pushed them into music; but he did provide a musical atmosphere and made ear-training exercises into a pleasant game. Later both daughters composed music for musicals, Mary eventually getting all the way to Broadway with her music for *Once upon a Mattress* (perf. 1959), *Hot Spot* (perf. 1963), and *Working* (to which she contributed a few songs, perf. 1978).

In his late years Rodgers continued to be active, both helping with revivals of his old works and creating new ones, even after his 1969 heart attack and a 1974 laryngectomy. He died in his New York City home on December 30, 1979.

In his career, Rodgers displayed perhaps a higher degree of consistent excellence than any other composer in the history of Broadway. With the sophisticated lyrics of Hart and then the more emotional, sentimental texts of Hammerstein, Rodgers, largely motivated by his own belief in the vital necessity of theatrical experimentation, helped to develop the simple musical comedy into the complex indigenous American art form of the musical play.

His music has that special quality of all superior artists: individuality. Yet in his musicals he was able to create a sense of local color without ever giving up his individuality or slavishly imitating local technique. Examples include Chinese in *Chee-Chee*, French in *Love Me Tonight*, American Southwest in *Oklahoma!*, Siamese in *The King and I*, and Austrian in *The Sound of Music*.

Rodgers's early songs, with Hart, generally kept to the Tin Pan Alley model of four phrases (musically AABA) in thirty-two measures, with little ornamentation and with simple harmonies, but with an uncommon grace and imagination and with a rhythmic interest derived from popular dances influenced by jazz. His later songs, with Hammerstein, showed a richer variety of form, often expanding beyond thirty-two measures.

However, Rodgers's real forte was not so much form as melody. He was unsurpassed among American popular-song composers in his melodic inventiveness and sophistication. Many of his most successful songs (such as "Bewitched, Bothered, and Bewildered" and "The Most Beautiful Girl in the World") are characterized by a graceful lyricism skillfully propelled by placing longer notes and colorful chord progressions on the offbeats of the measure. Some of his more energetic songs (such as "Oklahoma" and "Johnny One Note") build up excitement by using long-held notes on the first beat, followed by an explosive series of shorter notes.

However much the techniques varied from song to song or from show to show, one thing seldom varied in his output: its high quality. Richard Rodgers can justifiably be called the dean of American musical-theater composers.

Selected works:

Stage

Poor Little Ritz Girl (lyrics, L. Hart; perf. 1920)
The Melody Man (lyrics, H. Fields, L. Hart, R. Rodgers; perf. 1924)
The Garrick Gaieties (lyrics, L. Hart, others; perf. 1925)
Dearest Enemy (lyrics, L. Hart; perf. 1925), including:
  "Here in My Arms"
The Girl Friend (lyrics, L. Hart; perf. 1926), including:
  "Blue Room"
Peggy-Ann (lyrics, L. Hart; perf. 1926)
Betsy (lyrics, L. Hart, others; perf. 1926)
A Connecticut Yankee (lyrics, L. Hart; perf. 1927)
Present Arms (lyrics, L. Hart; perf. 1928)
Chee-Chee (lyrics, L. Hart; perf. 1928)
Spring Is Here (lyrics, L. Hart; perf. 1929), including:
  "With a Song in My Heart"
Jumbo (lyrics, L. Hart; perf. 1935), including:
  "Little Girl Blue"
  "The Most Beautiful Girl in the World"
On Your Toes (lyrics, L. Hart; perf. 1936), including:
  "Slaughter on Tenth Avenue" (instrumental)
  "There's a Small Hotel"
Babes in Arms (lyrics, L. Hart; perf. 1937), including:
  "Johnny One Note"

  "The Lady Is a Tramp"
  "My Funny Valentine"
I'd Rather Be Right (lyrics, L. Hart; perf. 1937)
I Married an Angel (lyrics, L. Hart; perf. 1938)
The Boys from Syracuse (lyrics, L. Hart; perf. 1938), including:
  "Falling in Love with Love"
Too Many Girls (lyrics, L. Hart; perf. 1939)
Pal Joey (lyrics, L. Hart; perf. 1940), including:
  "Bewitched, Bothered, and Bewildered"
By Jupiter (lyrics, L. Hart; perf. 1942)
Oklahoma! (lyrics, O. Hammerstein II; perf. 1943), including:
  "Oh, What a Beautiful Mornin'"
  "Oklahoma"
  "People Will Say We're in Love"
  "The Surrey with the Fringe on Top"
Carousel (lyrics, O. Hammerstein II; perf. 1945), including:
  "Carousel Waltz" (instrumental)
  "If I Loved You"
  "June Is Bustin' Out All Over"
  "Soliloquy"
  "What's the Use of Wond'rin'?"
  "You'll Never Walk Alone"
Allegro (lyrics, O. Hammerstein II; perf. 1947)
South Pacific (lyrics, O. Hammerstein II; perf. 1949), including:
  "Bali Ha'i"
  "I'm Gonna Wash That Man Right Outa My Hair"
  "Some Enchanted Evening"
  "There Is Nothin' like a Dame"
  "Younger Than Springtime"
The King and I (lyrics, O. Hammerstein II; perf. 1951), including:
  "Getting to Know You"
  "Hello, Young Lovers"
  "I Whistle a Happy Tune"
  "March of the Royal Siamese Children" (instrumental)
  "The Small House of Uncle Thomas" (narrated ballet, instrumental)
  "Shall We Dance?"
  "We Kiss in a Shadow"
Me and Juliet (lyrics, O. Hammerstein II; perf. 1953), including:
  "No Other Love" (melody originally in *Victory at Sea*)
Flower Drum Song (lyrics, O. Hammerstein II; perf. 1958)
The Sound of Music (lyrics, O. Hammerstein II; perf. 1959), including:
  "Climb Ev'ry Mountain"
  "Do-Re-Mi"
  "Edelweiss"
  "Laendler" (instrumental)
  "The Lonely Goatherd"
  "My Favorite Things"
  "Sixteen Going on Seventeen"
  "The Sound of Music"
No Strings (lyrics, R. Rodgers; perf. 1962), including:
  "The Sweetest Sounds"
Do I Hear a Waltz? (lyrics, S. Sondheim; perf. 1965)
Two by Two (lyrics, M. Charnin; perf. 1970)
Rex (lyrics, S. Harnick; perf. 1976)

Films
(song scores)

The Hot Heiress (lyrics, L. Hart; 1931)
Love Me Tonight (lyrics, L. Hart; 1932), including:
  "Isn't It Romantic?"
  "Lover"
  "Mimi"
The Phantom President (lyrics, L. Hart; 1932)
Hallelujah, I'm a Bum (lyrics, L. Hart; 1933)
Hollywood Party (lyrics, L. Hart; 1934)
Mississippi (lyrics, L. Hart; 1935)
They Met in Argentina (lyrics, L. Hart; 1941)
State Fair (lyrics, O. Hammerstein II; 1945), including:
  "It Might As Well Be Spring"
  "It's a Grand Night for Singing"
Words and Music (lyrics, L. Hart; 1948)

TV Musicals

Cinderella (lyrics, O. Hammerstein II; 1957)
Androcles and the Lion (lyrics, R. Rodgers; 1967)

Songs
(other than those for the above stage, film, and TV works)

"Any Old Place with You" (lyrics, L. Hart; written as an independent song, 1919, and then interpolated into the Broadway show *A Lonely Romeo,* perf. 1919)
"Blue Moon" (lyrics, L. Hart; originally, as "Prayer," written for, but not used in, the film *Hollywood Party,* 1934; then, as "The Bad in Every Man," used in the film *Manhattan Melodrama,* 1934; finally, issued as the independent song "Blue Moon," 1934)

Others

All Points West (solo vocalist-narrator, orchestra; orchestration, A. Deutsch; text, L. Hart; 1936)
Nursery Ballet (orchestra; orchestration, R. Bargy; 1938)
Ghost Town (ballet; orchestration, H. Spialek; 1939)
Victory at Sea (TV documentary series; orchestration, R. R. Bennett; 1952)
Winston Churchill: The Valiant Years (TV documentary series; orchestration, R. E. Dolan, H. Kay, E. Sauter; 1960)

Artur Rodzinski
Builder of Orchestras
(1892-1958)

Artur Rodzinski, conductor, was born in Spalato, Dalmatia (now Split, Yugoslavia), on January 1, 1892. In 1897 his father, a Polish-born physician in the Austrian army, was transferred to Lvov, Poland. There Artur began to study the piano. However, in his teens and early twenties, Artur, at his father's insistence, spent most of his time in the formal study of law.

When World War I broke out in 1914, the elder Rodzinski sent his wife and the twenty-two-year-old Artur to Vienna, where they would be safe. Now beyond the reach of his father, Artur concentrated on music, studying piano with Emil Sauer and Georg von Lalewicz, composition with Joseph Marx and Franz Schreker, and conducting with Franz Schalk.

In 1917 Rodzinski married Ilse Reinesch, a fellow pianist. They had one child: Witold (later a Polish diplomat).

In 1918 Rodzinski returned to Lvov. After several months as a cabaret pianist, he became an accompanist-coach at the Lvov Opera, where he made his conducting debut in 1919 in a performance of Verdi's *Ernani.*

In 1920 Rodzinski became principal conductor at Warsaw's Grand Theater Opera House, where he remained for the next five years. While there he also guest-conducted the Warsaw Philharmonic Orchestra.

At a Rodzinski performance of Wagner's *Die Meistersinger* ("The Mastersingers") in 1925, one member of the audience was the Philadelphia Orchestra conductor Leopold Stokowski, who was vacationing in Poland. Stokowski engaged Rodzinski as guest conductor of the Philadelphia Orchestra in 1925 and then as assistant conductor in the autumn of 1926. Rodzinski held his position as assistant for three seasons, during which he learned a great deal about conducting from Stokowski. While in Philadelphia, Rodzinski also headed the orchestra and opera departments at the Curtis Institute of Music and sometimes conducted the city's Grand Opera Company.

In 1929 Rodzinski was named conductor of the Los Angeles Philharmonic Orchestra, where he remained for four seasons. In 1933 he became a naturalized American citizen.

Also in 1933 Rodzinski took over the Cleveland Orchestra. It was during his ten years there that the Cleveland Orchestra first attained its status as one of the world's most highly regarded virtuoso ensembles. The highlight of his tenure came when he led the Cleveland Orchestra and a cast of Russian singers in the American premiere of Shostakovich's controversial opera *Lady Macbeth of Mtsensk* in early 1935. After a spectacular repeat performance in New York City a few days later, Rodzinski became a musical celebrity.

During his Cleveland years he also made many impressive guest appearances elsewhere, notably with the New York Philharmonic in 1934 and 1937, and at the Salzburg Festival in 1936 and 1937 (the first American to conduct there). His prestige was further enhanced in

1937 when, at the request of Arturo Toscanini, the National Broadcasting Company (NBC) engaged Rodzinski to assemble and train the new NBC Symphony Orchestra, which Toscanini would then take over.

The Cleveland years were also notable ones for Rodzinski's personal life. In 1934, having earlier divorced his first wife, he married Halina Lilpop in Warsaw. Her mother was a niece of the famous violinist Henryk Wieniawski. Artur and Halina had one child: Richard (later an administrator with the San Francisco and Metropolitan opera companies). Life with the complex (warm yet egotistical, generous yet grudge-filled) personality of Rodzinski was not easy for Halina, as she movingly told in her biography-autobiography *Our Two Lives* (1976). But there was fun, too. In December 1935 they presented a mock opera in the dining room of their Cleveland home. The performers were colleagues, and the members of the audience were friends. Entitled *The Secret of Lady Carmen of Seville,* the opera had such characters as Lady Carmen; Tristan, the Barber of Nuremberg and Lady Carmen's lover; and Escamillo, the toreador of Mtsensk and husband of La Tosca.

Rodzinski became dissatisfied with his Cleveland post because of the economy-minded administration of the orchestra by his superiors. When Toscanini left the New York Philharmonic in 1936, Rodzinski became a serious contender to replace him. But when John Barbirolli was appointed to the post, Rodzinski developed a bitter resentment against the Philharmonic's manager, Arthur Judson, a feeling that would publicly explode a decade later.

In December 1942 Barbirolli left the New York Philharmonic, and it was announced that Rodzinski would replace him, beginning with the 1943-44 season. The new conductor began by dismissing fourteen players, including several first-desk musicians. In addition to thus creating tension within the orchestra, he still carried a grudge against the orchestra's manager, Arthur Judson, who Rodzinski thought interfered too much with musical aspects that belonged in the domain of the conductor.

Despite such internal tensions, the orchestra flourished and rose to a new brilliance in performance. Rodzinski's nearly four seasons in New York were probably the high point of his career.

Nevertheless, in February 1947 he demanded that the board of administrators choose between Judson and himself. The board reluctantly accepted Rodzinski's resignation but then discovered that he had long been secretly negotiating to become director of the Chicago Symphony Orchestra.

He went to Chicago for the 1947-48 season and soon had difficulty with the board there as well. Rodzinski and the board quarreled over the budget, his programs, and his contract. In early 1948 the board abruptly announced, along with a public litany of his transgressions, that he would not be rehired for the following season.

Rodzinski then closed his career with ten years of guest-conducting in the United States, Europe, South America, and Cuba (where he headed the Philharmonic Orchestra of Havana during the 1949-50 season). In 1952 he established his residence in Italy, where he conducted concerts and operas, including a 1953 performance in Florence of the first production outside the Soviet Union of Prokofiev's opera *War and Peace.*

Rodzinski was renowned primarily as a builder of orchestras. A strict disciplinarian, he virtually molded the Cleveland Orchestra into the great ensemble that it still is today. He built the NBC Symphony Orchestra and restored the New York Philharmonic and the Chicago Symphony, both of which he had inherited in very poor artistic condition. His interpretations were energetic, though seldom poetic.

He favored the operas of Wagner and the orchestral scores of Brahms, Tchaikovsky, Richard Strauss, and modern composers. Rodzinski conducted the world premieres of numerous works, including, with the Cleveland Orchestra, William Walton's *Violin Concerto* in 1939 and William Schuman's *Fourth Symphony* in 1942; and, with the New York Philharmonic, Paul Hindemith's *Symphonic Metamorphoses on Themes of Carl Maria von Weber* in 1944, Paul Creston's *Second Symphony* in 1945, and Darius Milhaud's *Second Cello Concerto* in 1946.

Colleagues found Rodzinski to be one of the most bizarre characters in the world of serious music. He followed the teachings of the American evangelist Frank Buchman and held many superstitions, such as needing to receive a good-luck kick backstage before going out to conduct a concert. Once, according to Halina in *Our Two Lives,* Rodzinski purchased a revolver to shoot the husband of a woman whom he loved. Fortunately another lover came into Rodzinski's life before he had a chance to use the gun; but thereafter he kept it, loaded,

in his right rear pocket as a good-luck token at concerts. Another time, in a fit of jealousy, he attacked, and attempted to strangle, his assistant conductor at the New York Philharmonic, Leonard Bernstein.

In the autumn of 1958 Rodzinski returned to the United States and conducted two performances of Wagner's *Tristan und Isolde* ("Tristan and Isolde") at the Chicago Lyric Opera, his last public appearances. He had had a decade of recurrent heart attacks and finally died in Boston on November 27, 1958.

Leonard Rose

Outstanding American Cellist
(1918-84)

Leonard Rose, cellist, was born in Washington, D.C., on July 27, 1918. His father, a Russian immigrant whose original name was Rozofsky, earned his living as a tailor (designing clothes for such eminent people as the wives of presidents Coolidge and Harding) but also played as an amateur cellist in symphony orchestras in Washington and Baltimore. Shortly after Leonard's birth, the family moved to Miami, Florida, in the hope that the climate would mitigate the effects of the elder Rose's asthma.

Leonard began to receive piano lessons when he was eight. At ten he changed to the cello, and after a brief period on his own he entered the Miami Conservatory of Music, where he studied with Walter Grassman. At thirteen young Rose won first prize in the cello division of an all-Florida high-school music contest. As a result he was engaged for several concert appearances in Florida.

In 1933 Rose went to New York City to study with Frank Miller (Rose's cousin), who later became principal cellist of the National Broadcasting Company (NBC) Symphony Orchestra. In 1934 Rose won a scholarship to the Curtis Institute of Music in Philadelphia, where he studied with Felix Salmond. While at the Curtis Institute, Rose was placed in the first chair of the cello section of the Curtis Symphony by its conductor, Fritz Reiner. Rose also began to play chamber music at the institute, and in his third year he became Salmond's assistant in cello instruction.

In 1938 Rose graduated from the Curtis Institute and

became assistant principal cellist of the NBC Symphony Orchestra under Arturo Toscanini. After one season with the NBC Symphony, Rose became principal cellist of the Cleveland Orchestra under Artur Rodzinski. While he was in Cleveland, Rose also headed the cello departments of the Cleveland Institute of Music and Oberlin College.

When Rodzinski moved to the New York Philharmonic in 1943, Rose went with him. The following year Rose, the orchestra's principal cellist, made his concerto debut, performing with the Philharmonic at Carnegie Hall. He continued to perform as soloist with the orchestra numerous times over the next several years, his last being at the 1951 Edinburgh Festival, which was simultaneously his first solo appearance in Great Britain.

After leaving the New York Philharmonic in 1951, Rose began to tour widely as a soloist, both in recital and in concert with leading orchestras. Beginning in the early 1950s he toured the United States, adding Europe and Latin America to his schedule in the late 1950s, the Middle East in the early 1960s, and the Far East in the early 1970s. He regularly gave more than one hundred concerts a year during that period. In the early 1960s he was invited by the Kennedy Administration to perform at the White House.

Rose was an excellent chamber-music player. He performed cello sonatas with a number of pianists, especially Gary Graffman. In the late 1950s Rose formed a trio with the violinist Isaac Stern and the pianist Eugene

Istomin. At first they played only for their own pleasure, but soon they realized that their blend was working so well that they could, and should, share it. They made their official public debut at the first International Chamber Music Festival in Israel in 1961, followed by their New York City debut in 1962. The trio immediately won universal praise, and in subsequent years the ensemble spent part of each season on a world tour. A highlight of the trio's existence came in 1970, the Beethoven bicentennial, when they made extra appearances performing Beethoven in the United States, Brazil, Europe, and Israel.

Rose played in a grandiose manner, with a superb technique and a resonant tone in all registers. He was heard to best advantage in the romantic repertory, and he edited performing editions of numerous works.

Rose was enormously successful as a teacher on the staffs of the Curtis Institute (1951-62) and the Juilliard School of Music in New York City (1947-84). His students included Lynn Harrell, Ronald Leonard, and the principal cellists of many leading American orchestras. At one time, seven of the Boston Symphony Orchestra cellists were Rose protégés; Erich Leinsdorf, then the orchestra's conductor, dubbed the cellists the "Rose section."

In 1938 Rose married the violist Minnie Knopow, with whom he had two children: Barbara and Arthur. Minnie died in 1964, and in 1965 Rose married Xenia Petschek, an elementary schoolteacher who formerly wrote news for NBC-TV.

Rose died of leukemia in White Plains, New York, on November 16, 1984.

Josef Rosenblatt
King of Cantors
(1882-1933)

Josef (or Yosef) Rosenblatt, famed cantor affectionately nicknamed Yossele, was born in Belaya Tserkov, near Kiev, the Ukraine (now in the Soviet Union), on May 9, 1882. He evidenced remarkable talent at the age of four, when he began to chant passages of the liturgy in the local synagogue. Receiving very little formal instruction in singing, he was deeply influenced by the ecstatic music of the Hasidic mystics. He absorbed the jubilant character of that music and later expressed it both in the flavor of his performances of traditional tunes and in the animated nature of his original compositions.

At the age of eight, Rosenblatt began ten years of traveling throughout the Austro-Hungarian Empire, performing as a wunderkind cantor at numerous synagogues. At twelve he appeared in the village of Brzesko, near Cracow. There he met a twelve-year-old girl, Taubele Kaufman, whom, though they did not meet again for the next five years, he could not get out of his mind: "Wherever I went I saw Taubele standing before me."

Finally, in 1900, at the age of eighteen, he married Taubele and settled down as the regular cantor at Munkacs (1900-1901), Pressburg (1901-1906), and Hamburg (1906-1912). As an adult he still practiced singing for many hours at a time; and Taubele, a striking beauty, once uttered the wish that she could be transformed into a book of musical notes so that her husband would pay more attention to her.

The Rosenblatts had eight children. The oldest boy, Samuel, served for many years as rabbi of the Beth Tfiloh Congregation in Baltimore and wrote the definitive biography of his father, *Yossele Rosenblatt* (1954). Their second son, Leo, became Josef Rosenblatt's business manager and personal representative. Their other sons were Henry, Marcus, and Ralph, while their daughters were Nettie, Gertrude, and Sylvia.

In 1912 Rosenblatt and his family left Hamburg and settled in the United States, where he became a naturalized citizen in 1917. He worked for many years (1912-26) as cantor of the First Hungarian Congregation Ohab Zedek in New York City. During World War I he began to earn a wider reputation through his concerts of Jewish music. He donated the proceeds from many of his performances then and in the future to various charities.

In 1918 the Chicago Opera Association offered to pay him the enormous fee of $1,000 for each performance of Eléazar in Halévy's opera *La juive* ("The Jewess"). But Rosenblatt refused because he felt that acting in opera would be inappropriate for a synagogue cantor. His refusal stirred a national sensation and brought him to the attention of the general public.

A few weeks later Rosenblatt made his Carnegie Hall debut, in which he publicly sang non-Jewish music for the first time. His recital included opera arias from works by Bizet, Halévy, and Meyerbeer. The performance was a great success, and soon he was giving tours throughout the United States and Europe, singing Jewish liturgical and secular music, as well as non-Jewish works.

He performed in a wide variety of surroundings: in entirely Christian communities, for the wealthy, for the poor on New York City's East Side, and even jointly with the John Philip Sousa band. At the same time his fame greatly spread through his recordings of liturgical chant and Jewish folksong. He gained legendary status in American Jewish life and became the first to reveal to the outside world the beauties of traditional synagogal music. Rosenblatt was often referred to by Jews and non-Jews alike as the King of Cantors.

He had a remarkably uniform control over tones from the low baritone register to the high tenor. And his falsetto sent the masses into ecstasy. Perhaps his greatest quality as a singer was his ability to create entirely original liturgical improvisations that simultaneously amazed musicians and aroused the deepest religious feelings in the devout.

Rosenblatt was beloved for his gentle character as much as he was admired for his art. However, it was his trusting, idealistic nature that led him to invest in an unwise business venture that caused him to declare bankruptcy in 1925 (though he was the highest paid cantor in history and one of the most successful concert and recording artists of his time).

In an attempt to pay off his enormous debts, Rosenblatt began to perform on the vaudeville stage in 1925. The following year he resigned his post with the Ohab Zedek Congregation so that he could spend more time on moneymaking appearances. One such project was his performance of nonliturgical Jewish music in *The Jazz Singer* (1927), the first successful motion picture with sound.

In 1927 Rosenblatt returned to cantorial service, obtaining a post with the Anshei Sfard Congregation of Borough Park in the Brooklyn section of New York City. When Anshei Sfard ran out of funds in 1930, he returned to service at Ohab Zedek, which in turn had to break its contract with him in 1932 because it, too, could no longer afford to pay him. Meanwhile, he continued to give concerts to earn money to pay off his lingering debts.

Deeply interested in the rebirth of Israel, Rosenblatt had a lifelong dream of going to the Holy Land. His opportunity finally came in 1933 when he was asked to go there to help make the film *The Dream of My People,* in which he would be seen and heard chanting prayers of longing for Zion.

But while filming in the heat near the Dead Sea, Rosenblatt became ill, his heart weakened from years of financial stress. He was taken back to Jerusalem, where he died on June 19, 1933, at the age of fifty-one.

Josef Rosenblatt

Anton Rubinstein

Legendary Russian Musician
(1829-94)

Anton Rubinstein, pianist and composer, was born in Vikhvatinetz, Russia, on November 28, 1829. He was one of the greatest pianists of the nineteenth century (as was Nikolay Rubinstein, his brother), his playing being widely regarded as the equal of Franz Liszt's. He was also a prolific composer and an influential, though controversial, figure in Russian music life.

In 1831 baby Anton and the entire Rubinstein family were baptized into the Russian Orthodox church. The conversion was for practical purposes—to avoid excessive taxation and other forms of harassment, as well as to open the children's opportunities in law, teaching, medicine, and other professions closed to Jews. (In spite of his baptism, Rubinstein faced prejudice throughout his life. For example, when he was forty and world famous, he gave a concert in Frankfort on the Main, Germany, afterward going to the city's library and signing the register to get in. An official looked at the name, shook his head, and said, "Jews are not permitted in the building.")

He moved with his parents to Moscow, and at the age of six he began to take piano lessons from his mother. The following year his lessons were taken over by Alexander Villoing, the only professional piano teacher he ever had.

Anton gave his first public performance in 1839, and from 1840 to 1843 Villoing took him on an extended tour of Europe, cashing in on the fashion at that time for child virtuosos. While in Paris, young Rubinstein met Chopin and Liszt. In the Netherlands he was introduced to the Russian imperial family, and in London he was received by Queen Victoria. Traveling through Norway and Sweden, they reached Germany, where they toured in many areas.

Villoing and his protégé returned to Russia in 1843. But soon afterward, in 1844, the Rubinstein family went to Germany and settled in Berlin. There Anton studied counterpoint and harmony with Siegfried Dehn, who had earlier taught the great Russian composer Mikhail Glinka. Young Rubinstein also associated with Mendelssohn and Meyerbeer.

After Anton's father died in 1846, most of the family returned to Russia. Anton, however, spent the next two years in Vienna, where he barely kept himself alive by giving piano lessons.

Returning to Russia in the winter of 1848-49, Rubinstein met the Grand Duchess Elena Pavlovna, sister-in-law of the czar. She found the sophisticated young pianist amusing and allowed him to live in one of her palaces. He became what he jokingly called her "musical stoker," playing at her parties, often in the presence of the czar.

Rubinstein's adult concert career began in 1854, when he toured Europe with tremendous success. During the winter of 1856-57 he stayed with the grand duchess in Nice, France, and they made plans for radical changes in Russian music education. In 1859 they founded the Russian Musical Society, whose concerts Rubinstein conducted. And in 1862 they established the Saint Petersburg Conservatory, of which he became the first director. One of his pupils there was Peter Tchaikovsky. In 1867 Rubinstein resigned both posts and made another triumphant European tour.

By then he was a married man. In 1865 he had wedded Vera Chekuanov, daughter of a member of the czar's guard. Attractive and aristocratic, she was not a true music lover.

The oldest of their three children was Anna, whom her father adored. Rubinstein encouraged Anna to invite her friends over for parties, at which he would play waltzes while the children danced. Their first son, Alexander, always had frail health. Jacob, the younger boy, attempted to be a singer, but he lacked the talent. In fact, none of the children displayed any significant musical aptitude, and Rubinstein made no effort to force or encourage them into music.

Meanwhile, his career flourished. During 1871-72 he conducted the Philharmonic Concerts in Vienna. Also in 1872 he began a tour of the United States with the violinist Henryk Wieniawski, and for the next fifteen years he performed widely as one of the most lionized pianists and conductors of his time.

Rubinstein's pianistic style was characterized by its virility, vitality, rich sonorities, and grandiose effects. He did not care that he played many wrong notes or that he sometimes ignored subtleties in the music of others.

In its power and breadth his piano playing suggested the pianistic manner of Beethoven. Indeed, Beethoven's sonatas were a primary part of Rubinstein's repertory. In fact, Rubinstein, because of his physical resemblance to Beethoven and because of his family's Teutonic background, was for many years rumored to be an illegitimate offspring of the German master.

In 1887 Rubinstein resumed the directorship of the Saint Petersburg Conservatory, after a twenty-year hiatus. In 1889 his fiftieth jubilee as a public performer was lavishly celebrated. The following year he added to his already enormous prestige by establishing an international competition for the Rubinstein Prize, periodically awarded to the winner in each of two categories—composition and piano playing.

Rubinstein was not, however, without enemies in his

homeland. His earliest operas, based on Russian nationalist subjects, failed to impress Russian audiences. As a result of those failures, Rubinstein, in the 1850s and 1860s, developed the idea that Russian nationalist music was not worth writing, and he publicly disdained the work of Russian nationalist composers as "ignorant dilettantism." In fact, one of the reasons that he founded the Saint Petersburg Conservatory was to create a formal mechanism for opposing and eliminating the "mischievous amateurishness" of the nationalists. In turn, the nationalists, led by Mily Balakirev, regarded him as a Teutonic dogmatist.

However, by the 1870s Rubinstein, swept up by the feeling of nationalism and the folk-music boom that followed the freeing of the serfs, began to adopt a nationalist flavor in his own compositions, as in parts of the opera *The Demon* (comp. 1871, perf. 1875) and especially in the opera *Kalashnikov the Merchant* (comp. 1879, perf. 1880) and the *Fifth Symphony* (1880). But perhaps because of his cosmopolitan childhood and his innate Jewish sense of universality born of homelessness, Rubinstein could never completely absorb the nationalist idiom, and it remained only a superficial element in his music.

More important than the nationalist element in his music was the Jewish spirit. After Richard Wagner published the first edition of his anti-Semitic pamphlet *Das Judenthum in der Musik* ("Judaism in Music," 1850), Rubinstein deliberately turned his attention to Jewish subject matter and musical motives, notably in a series of sacred operas. His first such work was *Das verlorene Paradies* ("Paradise Lost"; comp. 1856, perf. 1875), based on a poem by John Milton. His later sacred operas include *Der Thurm zu Babel* ("The Tower of Babel"; comp. 1869, perf. 1870), *Die Makkabäer* ("The Maccabees"; comp. 1874, perf. 1875), *Sulamith* (comp. 1883, perf. 1883), and *Moses* (comp. 1891, perf. 1892).

The sacred operas, with German texts and most often premiered in Germany, were modeled on the oratorios of the German composer Felix Mendelssohn. In keeping with the spirit of assimilation with Western culture, characteristic of many Jews of that time, Rubinstein strove to incorporate elements of the Jewish tradition into a basically Western art-music context.

However, his entire life was shaped precisely by the fact that he had no spiritual or cultural home base. He once confessed, "For Jews I am a Christian, for Christians a Jew, for Russians a German, for Germans a Russian, for classicists an innovator, for innovators a retrograde."

Actually he produced music in the tradition of the early romantics, along the lines of Mendelssohn, Meyerbeer, Schumann, and Chopin; some elements were borrowed from his former student Tchaikovsky. He was strongly opposed to the hyperromanticism of Wagner's wing of the music world.

Rubinstein composed prolifically during his entire career, and many of his works were the rages of the day, his *Second Symphony: Ocean* (1851, revised 1863 and 1880) being probably the most popular orchestral composition in Europe during the second half of the nine-

Anton Rubinstein

teenth century. Indeed, some passages in his music reveal a rich creative impulse. But overall his works show signs of haste and are marred by features designed for immediate appeal, not for enduring significance. Today only a few of his works are still played with any regularity, notably the "Melody in F" for piano (1852). It was undoubtedly his early and enormous success as a performer that induced him to reach out for the same kind of rapidly achieved popularity as a composer.

His work as a teacher and administrator, however, had far-reaching effects. He helped to improve the standard of playing in Russia, and he raised the social status of Russian musicians. His ideas about putting music into schools and about having a state conservatory and a state opera in every important city became the basis of the music system in the present-day Soviet Union.

In 1891 Rubinstein once again resigned his post at the Saint Petersburg Conservatory. For the next three years he made his headquarters in Dresden, Germany. There he taught the young man who would become his most famous pupil: Josef Hofmann.

In the spring of 1893 Rubinstein's elder son, Alexander, became ill with tuberculosis. The other children helped to keep up the boy's spirits. But Rubinstein feared that his high-strung wife, Vera, would break under the strain of seeing Alexander's, or Sasha's, suffering. "Had it not been for music," Rubinstein said, "I myself would have lost hope in everything." Sasha died in September 1893.

Rubinstein survived his son by only one year, returning to Russia just before his own death, in Peterhof (now Petrodvorets), on November 20, 1894. He was then, and remained well into the twentieth century, a legendary figure in the history of music.

Selected works:

Operas

Das verlorene Paradies (libretto, A. Schlönbach, after J. Milton; comp. 1856, perf. 1875)
Der Thurm zu Babel (libretto, J. Rodenberg; comp. 1869, perf. 1870)

The Demon (libretto, P. A. Viskovatov, after M. Lermontov; comp. 1871, perf. 1875)
Die Makkabäer (libretto, S. H. Mosenthal, after O. Ludwig; comp. 1874, perf. 1875)
Kalashnikov the Merchant (libretto, N. Kulikov, after M. Lermontov; comp. 1879, perf. 1880)
Sulamith (libretto, J. Rodenberg, after the Bible; comp. 1883, perf. 1883)
Moses (libretto, S. H. Mosenthal; comp. 1891, perf. 1892)

Orchestral

five piano concertos (1850-74)
six symphonies (1850-86)

Piano

four sonatas (1854-77)
"Melody in F" (from *Two Melodies,* 1852)
Rocky Island (also well known in English by its Russian title, *Kamennïy-ostrov* or *Kamennoi ostrow,* 1854)
many other piano pieces

Others

chamber works
songs

Writings

Autobiography of Anton Rubinstein, 1829-1889 (English, 1890; originally pub. in Russian, 1889)
Music and Its Masters (English, 1892; originally pub. in Russian, 1891)

Arthur Rubinstein
Romantic Pianist
(1887-1982)

Arthur Rubinstein, pianist, was born in Łódź, Poland, on January 28, 1887. (In later years the American impresario Sol Hurok used the *h*-less "Artur" for publicity, but Rubinstein signed himself "Arthur" in countries where it is common practice, "Arturo" in Spain and Italy, and "Artur" in the Slav countries.) By the age of three he was able to play the piano by ear. His father, however, gave Arthur a small violin, feeling that it was a more "distinguished" instrument. The boy promptly smashed the fiddle to pieces (for which he was spanked) and returned to the fuller sounds of the piano.

Arthur displayed such natural talent at the keyboard that the family wrote a letter to the great violinist and pedagogue Joseph Joachim, who offered to see the boy in Berlin. Joachim tested the three-year-old Arthur, confirmed the child's musical aptitude, and offered to supervise the boy's education when Arthur was a little older.

Arthur returned to Łódź and continued to play by ear till an important event took place. Coming home from a symphony concert at which he had been thrilled by Edvard Grieg's *First Peer Gynt Suite,* Arthur sat down and played almost all of it from memory. The conductor of the orchestra at the concert, Julius Kwast, was invited to the house to hear the boy play. Kwast immediately suggested that it was time for Arthur to have formal piano lessons.

His first teacher, a Mrs. Pawlowska, belonged to the old school of piano teaching (elbows close, playing with a coin on the back of the hand); she lasted only a few months. Longer lasting were the lessons from Adolf Prechner. In 1894, at the age of seven, Arthur gave his first public performance, in Łódź, at a charity concert.

After a brief period of study in Warsaw with Alexander Rózycki (an elderly man who often slept through his student's lessons), young Rubinstein was taken back to Joachim in Berlin in 1897. Joachim, as he had promised, began to supervise the boy's musical education. Rubinstein studied piano privately with Heinrich Barth (who accepted the boy on Joachim's recommendation) and theory at the Imperial and Royal Academy in Berlin (where Joachim was president). He studied general subjects privately under Theodor Altmann, who guided Rubinstein, already showing signs of his great love of books, into such fields as history, philosophy, and literature.

In 1899 Rubinstein played Mozart's *Piano Concerto in A Major* (K. 488) at a public concert in Potsdam as a sort of rehearsal for his Berlin debut, two weeks later, playing the same work at the Berlin Academy. In December 1900 Rubinstein was allowed an entire concert to himself at Berlin's Beethoven Hall, performing two concertos with the prestigious Berlin Philharmonic Orchestra: the Mozart concerto from the preceding year and the *Second Piano Concerto* by Saint-Saëns, which became an important vehicle for his virtuosity for the rest of his career. At the same concert, he also played solo pieces by Schumann and Chopin. The concert was a huge success, and he was soon given opportunities to perform at other concerts in Germany and Poland.

In 1902 Rubinstein visited, and received musical advice from, the famous Polish pianist Ignace Paderewski. The following year Rubinstein, anxious to begin his professional career as a pianist, ceased his Berlin studies and went to Warsaw to give concerts. In 1904 he gave his Paris debut and in 1906 made his first tour of the United States.

Returning to Europe, Rubinstein had difficulty in getting engagements. In Berlin in 1908, his career at its lowest ebb, he tried to commit suicide by hanging himself with the belt from his old worn-out robe. His life was spared when the belt broke and he fell to the floor. "I staggered to the piano," he later recalled, "and cried myself out in music. Music . . . brought me back to life." Out of that experience he developed his own secret of happiness: "Love life for better or for worse, without conditions."

Rubinstein soon began to give concerts again on the Continent. He made his London debut in 1912, not only giving solo recitals but also making chamber-music appearances, one partner being the famous Spanish cellist Pablo Casals.

Rubinstein spent the early days of World War I in Paris, working as a civilian translator of letters or documents found on prisoners of war. During that time, he became so horrified at German atrocities that he vowed never again to perform in Germany.

In early 1915 Rubinstein returned to London, where he lived during most of World War I. He gave many concerts there with the Belgian violinist Eugène Ysaÿe, often for various war-related charities. In 1916 he made his debut in Spain, followed in 1917 by his first appearance in South America. In his 1916-17 tours he developed a lifelong enthusiasm for the music of the Spanish composers Isaac Albéniz, Enrique Granados, and especially Manuel de Falla, as well as the Brazilian composer Heitor Villa-Lobos.

His career progressed fairly smoothly, though unspectacularly, till 1932. In that year he married Aniela (known as Nela) Mlynarska, daughter of Emil Mlynarski, a Polish conductor with whom Rubinstein had performed. The marriage proved to be a turning point in his professional as well as his personal life. In his earlier career he had been, by his own admission, a lazy pianist, relying on his natural facility and wonderful memory. He had devoted much of his time to the pleasures of food, wine, and women. Rubinstein explained his early success by saying that the Latin countries (France, Italy, Spain, South American nations) loved him because of his romantic temperament, and Russian audiences had been conditioned to his technical errors by their beloved Anton Rubinstein (no relation). However, he found that English and American audiences felt cheated because, as Rubinstein admitted, he "dropped many notes."

Taking on the responsibilities of a wife and family made him reconsider his approach to his career. He began to practice more diligently, adding a strong sense of discipline to balance his already brilliant temperament. When he made his next tour of the United States, in 1937, the improvement in his performance was immediately evident and highly praised.

When World War II came, Rubinstein escaped to the United States, where he became a naturalized citizen in 1946. After the war he resumed his international tours with an energy that became increasingly amazing with his advancing years. He frequently gave in excess of one hundred concerts a year, many for a wide variety of charities. In his seventies and eighties it was not unusual for him to play in one evening both Brahms concertos or three by Beethoven.

He also continued his interest in chamber music. In 1949, for example, he was part of what *Life* magazine called "the Million Dollar Trio," with the violinist Jascha Heifetz and the cellist Gregor Piatigorsky. In the 1960s and 1970s Rubinstein performed with the Guarneri String Quartet.

By the mid-1970s his failing eyesight was bringing his career to a close. In 1976 he gave a series of farewell concerts in Europe, Israel, and the United States. A Carnegie Hall recital in New York City commemorated the seventieth anniversary of his debut in the same auditorium. His final concert was given in Wigmore Hall in London.

Much of Rubinstein's stay in the United States was spent in the Hollywood section of Los Angeles, Califor-

Arthur Rubinstein

nia, where he became involved in motion pictures. His work included appearing as himself in *Carnegie Hall* (1947) and recording soundtrack music for *I've Always Loved You* (1946) and *Song of Love* (1947), the latter being particularly enjoyable to him because he had to contribute all of the piano music later to be performed on the screen by actors portraying Robert and Clara Schumann, Johannes Brahms, and Franz Liszt. Rubinstein was also the subject of numerous film documentaries.

He was deeply committed to the existence and interests of Israel. Immediately after World War II, when English authorities turned Jewish refugees away from the shores of Palestine and toward camps in Hamburg, Germany, an infuriated Rubinstein refused to perform at his scheduled London concerts unless the appearances were clearly advertised "For the Jewish victims in Hamburg." Having won that concession, he gave the concerts and donated the proceeds to that cause. Soon after the state of Israel was created in 1948, he began to give regular concert tours there. Later, with proceeds from his concerts in Israel (for which he refused payment), the Israel Philharmonic Orchestra established the Rubinstein Chair of Musicology at the Hebrew University of Jerusalem. In 1974 the triennial Arthur Rubinstein International Piano Master Competition was established in Israel.

As a young man Rubinstein championed the works of such modern composers as Debussy, Falla, Poulenc, Prokofiev, and Stravinsky. But in his later years he concentrated on the nineteenth-century romantics. At first Brahms, and later Chopin, aroused his deepest artistic instincts. He was the modern romantic pianist par excellence, retaining the poetic exuberance of the romantic tradition but rejecting the distortions and exaggerations fashionable among players in Rubinstein's youth. Though aided by an incredible hand span of a twelfth, his technique was not necessarily flawless in virtuoso passages. But his unique, memorable style was like the man: witty, intelligent, urbane.

His approach was best heard in his interpretations of Chopin, to most observers the primary vehicle by which Rubinstein came to be regarded as one of the greatest players of the twentieth century. As a child he had heard Chopin played with gross sentimentality. When, as a teenager, he began to play Chopin without traditional affectation, people accused him of being "dry" or "severe." Only much later did his approach come to be generally appreciated as the ideal standard of Chopin interpretation: an outgoing lyricism and a rich tone color, presented in a spirit of aristocratic, yet passionately eloquent, poetry.

Arthur and Nela had four children: Eva, who was a dancer and actress who appeared in the original Broadway production of *The Diary of Anne Frank* (1955) before marrying a Presbyterian minister; Paul, who became a businessman; Alina, who showed early talent at the piano but later entered the field of medicine; and John, who has composed music in a modernistic American idiom but has become better known as an actor, notably in the movies *The Boys from Brazil* (1978) and *Skokie* (TV, 1981) and in the TV series *Crazy like a Fox*. Rubinstein was very close to his children, often taking them on his travels and attending their school and professional activities.

Much of the last part of Rubinstein's life was devoted to writing his autobiography, published in two volumes: *My Young Years* (1973) and *My Many Years* (1980).

He died in Geneva, Switzerland, on December 20, 1982, at the age of ninety-five.

Artur Schnabel
Interpreter of Beethoven
(1882-1951)

Artur Schnabel, pianist, was born in Lipnik, Moravia (now in Czechoslovakia), on April 17, 1882. When he was four years old, his parents acquired a piano for his sister. But it was soon discovered that little Artur was able to play by ear the piano exercises and pieces that he had heard his sister practicing. Her teacher, Minka Patzau, began to give him lessons.

The prodigy showed his musical abilities in other ways as well. Born with the gift of absolute pitch, Artur liked to play a game in which he would turn his back to the keyboard and call out the pitches as his sister struck the keys. He also liked to improvise at the piano, including one opus entitled "Funeral March of a Frog."

At seven he was taken to Vienna to audition for Hans Schmitt, head of the Vienna Conservatory's senior piano class. Though much too young to be admitted to the conservatory, Artur was so impressive that Schmitt gave the boy private lessons for two years. When Artur was eight, he gave a private concert, as a result of which he received financial support from local music lovers for a number of years.

The following year, 1891, Artur was taken to Theodor Leschetizky, the most celebrated piano teacher in Vienna and perhaps in the world at that time. Leschetizky arranged for Artur to have a year of preliminary instruction from assistants, one of whom would place a coin on the back of one of Artur's hands; and if he played an exercise through without dropping the coin, she would give him the money as a present. Artur, of course, appreciated her generosity, but he later discovered that such a "static" technique of playing obstructed true expression in music.

His lessons with Leschetizky himself lasted till 1897. The great teacher, recognizing the boy's extraordinary talent, often said to him, "You will never be a pianist. You are a musician," by which Leschetizky meant that young Schnabel's temperament was more suited to deep musical expression than to mechanical virtuosity. Hence, the teacher encouraged the student to resurrect the musically rich but neglected sonatas of Franz Schubert, but to ignore the flashy *Hungarian Rhapsodies* of Franz Liszt (extremely rare advice from Leschetizky, "the Maker of Virtuosos"). Indeed, in later years Schnabel

would more and more limit his work to Beethoven, Schubert, and Mozart because he wanted to spend time only on music that "was better than it could be performed."

Shortly after starting with Leschetizky, Schnabel began to study theory and composition with Eusebius Mandyczewski. Also during his student years in Vienna, Schnabel made many important musical acquaintances, among them Anton Rubinstein (on whose knee Artur once sat while the older man played a game of cards) and Johannes Brahms (whom Artur socially met many times), as well as literary figures, such as Mark Twain (whose two daughters were members of Leschetizky's piano class).

In early 1897 in Vienna, Schnabel made his official public debut as a soloist. But Vienna, still largely controlled by the old aristocracy, had already entered a period of artistic, moral, and social decadence. For example, when Schnabel was thirteen, Karl Lueger was reelected mayor of Vienna on an openly anti-Semitic program. Strutting young "patriots" commonly stalked the streets bullying and beating children presumed to be Jewish.

In 1898 Schnabel visited Berlin, where he soon settled. There he found a more energetic, optimistic atmosphere; and he gave his Berlin debut in the autumn of that year.

In 1899 Schnabel began to serve as accompanist for Therese Behr, a tall (6', as opposed to his 5'4") and attractive young alto singer. Soon they were appearing regularly together, their most important early concert being in Königsberg on March 26, 1901. The program consisted of a Bach fugue, a set of six songs by Beethoven, Schubert's posthumous *B-flat Sonata,* and Schumann's entire song cycle *Dichterliebe* ("Poet's Love"). The success of the concert was so great that the news spread far and wide. For years Schnabel and Behr performed "the Königsberg program," as it came to be called, by popular demand.

The Königsberg concert was also important in the personal lives of the performers. That night they became secretly engaged to be married, and the date was engraved on what was later to be Therese's wedding ring. In 1905 they were married in Berlin.

Therese, five years Artur's senior and already a famous interpreter of Schubert, Schumann, and Brahms, played an important role in Schnabel's artistic development by joining him in his struggle to express spiritual elevation and depth of meaning through music. They performed in numerous concerts together for many years, culminating in a historic series of Schubert recitals in Berlin in 1928, which commemorated the centennial of the composer's death and included both well-known and unfamiliar Schubert works.

The Schnabels had two children: Karl, who became a pianist-composer and who often performed two-piano music with his father, and Stefan, who became an actor. In addition, Artur had a daughter, Elisabeth, from a liaison that he had had with the Viennese violinist Rosa Hochmann when he was only seventeen. Artur did not know of Elisabeth's existence till she showed up at his front door one day when she was in her early twenties, along with her own two-year-old boy. Elisabeth, too, was musically gifted, and the Schnabels (including the gracious Therese) immediately welcomed her into their home as the daughter of the family.

During his Berlin years (1898-1933) Schnabel often took part in ensemble playing. He was the key figure in the Schnabel Trio, of which there were several different sets of constituent members, among them the violinists Alfred Wittenberg and Carl Flesch, and the cellists Hugo Becker and Gregor Piatigorsky. Schnabel also played chamber music with other outstanding musicians, including the violinist Joseph Szigeti, the violinist-violist Paul Hindemith, and the cellist Pablo Casals.

Schnabel regarded the years 1919 to 1924 as the most musically stimulating and perhaps the happiest period of his life. During that time he met such young modernists as Ernst Krenek and Eduard Erdmann, composed a number of works of his own, and evolved an original manner of performing Beethoven (for which he would become most famous).

In 1925 Schnabel entered a new phase in his career. Previously he had taught many students, but only privately. However, in 1925, with increasing economic trouble in Germany, he finally accepted an offer to teach at the Berlin Academy of Music. He raised the academy's quality of piano teaching to legendary standards. In 1930, having won tremendous success on the international concert stage, he could afford to quit the academy, though he continued to teach privately. Among his pupils were Clifford Curzon and Claude Frank.

In 1927, for the centennial of Beethoven's death, Schnabel played all thirty-two of the composer's piano sonatas in a series of seven concerts in Berlin. In the early 1930s he repeated the Beethoven sonata cycle in Berlin and London. During that time he also began to record all of the Beethoven piano sonatas and piano concertos— an unprecedented project.

In 1933, after Hitler came to power in Germany, the Schnabels left Berlin and spent much of the next five years traveling to various engagements on the Continent, in England, and in the United States (where Schnabel had debuted in 1921). Summers were spent in

Tremezzo, on the shore of Italy's Lake Como, where he held famous master classes.

In 1939 the Schnabels settled in the United States, becoming naturalized American citizens in 1944. Throughout the Second World War, Schnabel remained in America to give concerts, to compose, and to teach in his home and, during the summers, at the University of Michigan. But he was never as widely appreciated in the United States as he was in Europe, and he complained that American managers acted more like salesmen than like music lovers.

Schnabel was one of the first "modern" musicians in that he was not, in the romantic tradition, a showman who lifted his hands needlessly high and shook his head with feigned passion. His performances were concerned with musical substance.

In his early years he played a large repertory, including Chopin, Schumann, Liszt, and moderns, especially modern chamber music. But later he specialized in older music. He played excellent Mozart and Brahms, and he was probably the finest twentieth-century player of Schubert's piano works. However, he attained his greatest renown as the preeminent Beethoven interpreter of his time. In his Beethoven performances, Schnabel, contrary to tradition, did not make a great distinction between melodic and nonmelodic elements (scale passages, accompaniments, figurations). On the contrary, Schnabel articulated each strand of the texture with clarity and vitality. But he did it in such a way that, rather than diminishing the stature of the melody, he infused the whole with an unparalleled eloquence.

As a composer, Schnabel wrote in an uncompromisingly modernistic idiom, heavily laden with dissonance and atonal inclinations. Among his works are three symphonies, five string quartets, numerous piano pieces (which he never performed in public), and songs. He also wrote the books *Reflections on Music* (1933), *Music and the Line of Most Resistance* (1942), and *My Life and Music* (posthumously, 1961; first pub. in Swedish, 1960).

In April 1946 Schnabel began to make return trips to Europe. On one such journey he died in Axenstein, Switzerland, on August 15, 1951.

Alexander Schneider

Musician of Incredible Energy

(1908-   )

Alexander Schneider (full name, Abraham Alexander Schneider), violinist and conductor, was born in Vilnius, Lithuania (now in the Soviet Union), on October 21, 1908. When he was ten years old, he entered the local conservatory, earning money for his lessons by playing waltzes and gypsy tunes in cafés and restaurants.

At sixteen Schneider went to Germany, where he studied in Frankfort on the Main under Adolph Rebner and in Berlin under Carl Flesch. He soon gained success in Germany as a solo violinist, concertmaster, assistant conductor, and leader of his own string quartet.

In 1932 he joined the Budapest String Quartet as second violinist. With that famed ensemble he traveled throughout the world and, with the rest of its members, settled in the United States in the late 1930s, eventually becoming a naturalized American citizen. In 1944 he left the Budapest String Quartet, though he rejoined it for a later tenure (1955-64, when the group disbanded).

In America Schneider, a man of incredible energy, has been involved with a wide variety of music activities. He helped to found the Albeneri Trio (1941), the Schneider String Quartet (1952), and the Brandenburg Players (1972), serving as conductor of the last-named group, a chamber orchestra. He has also guest-conducted many major American symphony orchestras.

It was Schneider who, in 1950, persuaded the great cellist Pablo Casals to come out of retirement for the first Casals Festival, which took place in Prades, France, to mark the bicentenary of Bach's death. Schneider continued to work closely with the cellist for many years, notably in organizing the annual Casals Festivals, first in Prades and then in San Juan, Puerto Rico. Schneider also helped to organize the Israel Music Festival (1960-61) and the New York City concerts (1966) that later came to be known as the recurring Mostly Mozart Festival.

In New York City Schneider was responsible for some highly regarded innovations in concert programming and presentation, many of which initiated long-running concert series. He organized the summer outdoor concerts in Washington Square (1953), the Christmas Eve midnight baroque concerts at Carnegie Hall (1955), the New School Concerts (in conjunction with the New School for Social Research, 1956), and the chamber-music performances called A Weekend of Brahms (1973). Schneider tried to make as many of the concerts as possible available at popular prices, especially for young people, often providing his own services for no fee.

He has been active as a teacher at several institutions, including the University of Washington, Mills College, and the Royal Conservatory in Toronto; and he maintains a close association with the New School for Social Research in New York City. "My purpose," he has explained, "is to get young people to learn how to make music. When you make music, it has to come from your heart, from your soul, or it has no meaning. It's an extraordinary experience when I see the results. They produce a sound a professional orchestra couldn't—a love of music."

A warmhearted, gregarious man known to his friends as Sascha, he plays the violin with an energy and an enthusiasm that reflect his extrovert personality.

Schneider has been wedded and divorced three times, including a marriage to the actress Geraldine Page from 1954 to 1957.

Arnold Schoenberg

A Seminal Figure in Twentieth-Century Music

(1874-1951)

Arnold Schoenberg (originally Schönberg), composer, was born in Vienna, Austria, on September 13, 1874. His parents were not particularly musical, though his father (who owned a shoe store) used to sing folksongs in the home, while his mother's family had produced synagogue cantors for generations. Arnold's younger brother, Heinrich, became a successful opera singer in Prague.

At the age of eight or nine Schoenberg began to study the violin and almost immediately started to compose violin duets, which he played with his local teacher. In 1885, when he was eleven, he entered a Vienna secondary school, where he met a fellow student named Oskar Adler, who was to become a lifelong friend. Adler, a violinist, gave Schoenberg lessons in harmony and ear training. With one of Schoenberg's cousins they formed a trio of two violins and viola, for which Schoenberg composed many marches and dances in the popular style of the day. Later the trio became a quartet, Schoenberg himself moving first to the viola and then to his permanent principal instrument, the cello, on which he was self-taught. After reading an encyclopedia article about how to write sonata forms, he composed quartets for the group. His playing in, and writing for, that amateur ensemble gave him valuable experience on which to draw while composing his numerous chamber works later in life.

In early 1891, shortly after his father died, Schoenberg, to help support the family, left school and started work as a clerk in a small private bank. He hated the job, but he spent his evenings happily involved with music, literature, and philosophy. One of his musical friends was David Josef Bach (later a linguist and mathematician), who inspired Schoenberg to maintain high artistic ideals, an important characteristic throughout the composer's career.

In 1893 Schoenberg began to play the cello in an amateur orchestra. There he met the conductor-composer Alexander von Zemlinsky, who became Schoenberg's only regular teacher of composition. Through Zemlinsky, Schoenberg, previously a follower of Brahms, became a dedicated Wagnerite.

In 1895 Schoenberg left the bank and thereafter devoted himself entirely to music. To earn a living, he conducted small choral societies and did hack work for other composers, such as orchestrating operettas and making piano arrangements.

At the same time, he composed his first significant works. The unnumbered *String Quartet* in D major (1897), the string sextet *Verklärte Nacht* ("Transfigured Night," 1899), and many songs of the period are characterized by Wagnerian chromaticism and postromanticism. The climax of his early style came in the huge symphonic cantata *Gurre-Lieder,* sometimes spelled *Gurrelieder* ("Songs of Gurre," comp. 1901, orchestrated 1911), which recalls not only Wagner but also the postromantic styles of Mahler and Richard Strauss.

Under the influence of a friend, the singer Walter Piean, Schoenberg was converted from Judaism to Protestantism (specifically Lutheranism) and was baptized in 1898. The conversion turned out to be merely the first important outward sign of a spiritual restlessness and searching that haunted Schoenberg throughout his life.

In 1901 Schoenberg married Mathilde von Zemlinsky, his teacher's sister. They had two children: Gertrud (or Trudi, who married Schoenberg's pupil Felix Greissle) and Georg.

The young couple soon moved to Berlin, where he had been offered a job at a cabaret that formed part of Ernst von Wolzogen's Buntes Theater. Again he worked primarily as an arranger of others' music. In mid-1902 he left the cabaret and began to orchestrate operettas. He was saved from such drudgery by Richard Strauss, who used his influence to obtain for Schoenberg a cash award from the Liszt Foundation, as well as a post as a composition teacher at the Stern Conservatory in Berlin. His most important composition of the period was the symphonic poem *Pelleas und Melisande* ("Pelleas and Melisande," 1903), in which he extended the Wagnerian idiom to include many unresolved dissonances, thus hinting at his future direction.

In 1903 Schoenberg returned to Vienna and divided his time between teaching and composing. As a teacher he became the head of a loyal group of young musicians, notably the composers Anton von Webern and Alban Berg, both of whom rose to prominence through acceptance, and individual use, of principles formulated by Schoenberg.

In the early 1900s Schoenberg began to show a new direction in his music, away from postromanticism in general and Wagnerism in particular. His compositions became more compact, objective, dissonant, clear textured, contrapuntally oriented, and rapidly fluctuating in key centers. He displayed those tendencies in his *Eight Songs* (1905), *First String Quartet* (1905), *First Chamber Symphony* (1906), and *Second String Quartet* (1908). In the *Eight Songs* he began to experiment with wide inter-vallic leaps, which later characterized most of his vocal writing. Such works provoked outrage among most listeners of the time, though the great Mahler publicly stood up for the young composer.

During that period of compositional crisis, when he was uncertain of his new goals, Schoenberg also had to face an upheaval in his personal life. He turned to painting as an outlet for some of his ideas, and in 1907 he began to take lessons from the painter Richard Gerstl. Schoenberg's wife, Mathilde, also had lessons with Gerstl, and in 1908 she deserted her husband and went to live with the young artist. The separation affected Schoenberg deeply. In the scherzo movement of his *Second String Quartet,* he incorporated a street song containing the sentiment "it's all over," as well as musical anagrams representing the people involved. Later that year Mathilde, persuaded by Webern, returned to Schoenberg, apparently mostly for the sake of their two children. In November Gerstl committed suicide.

The events of 1908 provoked an intensely emotional surge of creative energy in Schoenberg. His music became increasingly remote from traditional harmonic and tonal practices. Schoenberg's approach paralleled that of some painters and writers (later known as expressionists) who sought to reach deep levels of experience by bypassing the techniques of artistic tradition and obeying inner promptings.

From 1908 through the 1910s, the second of his four major stylistic periods, Schoenberg composed what is usually called *atonal* music (though he preferred the term *pantonal* and still others *totally chromatic),* in which a sense of key is deliberately avoided. The last movement of his *Second String Quartet* is often referred to as the first piece of atonal music (though some feel that the finale is centered, however vaguely, on F-sharp). But his atonal idiom became truly established, and his dissonances fully emancipated from the traditional need of resolution to consonances, in the song cycle *Das Buch der hängenden Gärten* ("The Book of the Hanging Gardens," 1909). He further crystallized his new style in the *Three Piano Pieces* (1909) and *Five Orchestral Pieces* (1909).

In 1910 Schoenberg became an off-campus lecturer in theory and composition for the Vienna Academy of Music. Subjected to many verbal attacks because of his racial background, he finally left Vienna in 1911 and moved to Berlin, where he lectured at the Stern Conservatory. In 1912 he composed *Pierrot lunaire* ("Pierrot in the Moonlight"), a song cycle in which he perfected a vocal style known as *Sprechstimme* (literally, "speaking voice") or *Sprechgesang* (literally, "speaking song"), a kind of voice production halfway between speaking and singing (introduced by Engelbert Humperdinck in 1897).

From 1912 to 1915 Schoenberg spent much of his time touring as a conductor, mostly of his own music. Shortly after the outbreak of World War I, he returned to Vienna and served in the Austrian army from 1915 to 1917.

After the war, Schoenberg founded the Society for Private Musical Performances, whose purpose was to

play modern works for sympathetic audiences. Critics were barred from the concerts. He was prompted to form the society, which lasted only a few years, by the violent hostility displayed by critics and audiences toward most of his compositions. His bitterness toward the music establishment remained with him for the rest of his life.

Meanwhile, Schoenberg found composition to be increasingly difficult, and he produced little between 1912 and 1920. Feeling that he had created chaos in his freely atonal works, he sought organizing principles that would replace the traditional ones that he had abandoned. The result was the system known as dodecaphony, or the twelve-tone technique. Though, unknown to Schoenberg, a similar method of composition had previously been devised by Josef Matthias Hauer, it was Schoenberg who perfected the system as it is known today.

A composition in the dodecaphonic system is based on a series, or row, of all twelve tones of the chromatic scale, arranged in any order that the composer chooses. The series is then permutated and combined in various ways to form a sort of continuous variation throughout the work.

Schoenberg began to experiment with the system in 1920. His first completed work using the twelve-tone technique was the last of his *Five Piano Pieces* (1923), the other four in the set using different serial procedures. The same was true of the *Serenade* for chamber ensemble (1923), in which the fourth movement was written using the dodecaphonic system. The *Piano Sonata* (1923) became the first work built entirely on a twelve-tone series.

Having established serialism as his basic procedure, Schoenberg entered his third stylistic period and produced many of his most important works through the mid-1930s. Among them were the *Third String Quartet* (1927), the *Variations for Orchestra* (1928), the unfinished opera *Moses und Aron* ("Moses and Aaron," 1932), the *Fourth String Quartet* (1936), and the *Violin Concerto* (1936).

In 1923 Schoenberg's wife died. The following year he married Gertrud Kolisch, sister of his pupil Rudolf Kolisch (who was a violinist and the leader of a string quartet that performed many of Schoenberg's chamber works in the 1920s and 1930s). There were three children born of the marriage: Nuria (who married the Italian composer Luigi Nono), Rudolf (sometimes referred to by his middle name, Ronald), and Lawrence (also sometimes referred to by his middle name, Adam).

From 1918 to 1923 Schoenberg divided most of his time between Vienna and Berlin, with some time spent abroad conducting his own music. In 1925 he was appointed professor of composition at the Prussian Academy of Arts in Berlin, and he subsequently moved to that city.

Though he had experienced some incidents of anti-Semitism in Germany and Austria throughout his life, such prejudice increased in virulence in the 1920s because of Hitler's agitations. When the Nazis took over Germany in 1933, Schoenberg was dismissed from his post in Berlin, not only because he was of Jewish background but also because he was a composer of avant-garde music, which was frowned on by the Nazi regime.

For some years Schoenberg had been drifting back to Judaism from his brief interest in the Lutheran church. His dismissal in Berlin awakened him to the need to declare his solidarity with his race and to fulfill his own spiritual development. After fleeing to Paris, he formally returned to the Jewish faith in July 1933. In October of that year he arrived in the United States, where he himself Americanized the spelling of his name from Schönberg to Schoenberg.

After teaching at the Malkin Conservatory in Boston

for several months, he moved to the West Coast and lectured during the 1935-36 academic year at the University of Southern California (USC). He taught at the University of California in Los Angeles (UCLA) from 1936 to 1944. In 1941 he became a naturalized American citizen. His UCLA retirement was forced, by statute, because he had reached the age of seventy. After that, he had a few private pupils.

Schoenberg had little peace of mind during most of his years in America. Besides finding it difficult to adjust to the American music scene, he was deeply distressed at news from Europe. His brother, Heinrich, was murdered by a poison injection in a Nazi hospital. And other relatives and friends were killed in World War II action and Nazi concentration camps.

Schoenberg's composing changed in the United States. His fourth and last period was marked by greater stylistic diversity, sometimes using the twelve-tone system more sparingly and sometimes not at all. In fact, he had never completely abandoned tonal music, having written such tonal works in the 1920s and early 1930s as the beautiful chamber work *Weihnachtsmusik* ("Christmas Music," 1921); two of the choral *Six Pieces* (1930); the *Cello Concerto* (1933), based on music of Georg Matthias Monn; and the *String Quartet Concerto* (1933),

Arnold Schoenberg (self-portrait)

based on music of Handel. The last two pieces led to the *Suite* in G major for string orchestra (1934) in a similar style but with original material.

In his fourth stylistic period Schoenberg often combined tonal and serial elements. For example, the *Variations on a Recitative* for organ (1941) is clearly in D minor but includes serial features. On the other hand, the *Ode to Napoleon* for reciter, piano, and string orchestra (1942) is a dodecaphonic work that ends with a tonic of E-flat. However, after the *Piano Concerto* (1942), which also combines tonal and twelve-tone elements, Schoenberg once again reduced the tonal influence in his music and moved closer to his earlier serial style, as in the *String Trio* (1946).

The expression of human feelings became an important factor in Schoenberg's late music. Influenced by events in Europe and by his own spiritual development, he began to draw his subject matter and inspiration from his ethnic awareness. *Kol nidre* ("All the Vows") for speaker, chorus, and orchestra (1938) is a tonal work that draws on motives from the traditional liturgical melody for the prayer. One of his most profoundly moving works is the twelve-tone composition *A Survivor from Warsaw* for narrator, men's chorus, and orchestra (1947), recounting the true story of Polish Jews who, while being prepared for the gas chamber, asserted their human dignity by singing the ancient Hebrew song *Shema Yisrael* ("Hear, O Israel"). *De profundis* ("Out of the Depths"), a Hebrew setting of Psalm 130 for unaccompanied chorus (1950), is dodecaphonic but with significant relaxations of earlier serial rules. He also sketched the unfinished *Israel Exists Again* for chorus and orchestra (1949) and attempted to complete the 1932 opera *Moses und Aron*.

In his last years he was pleased to see a new interest in his works, especially among young composers. But after a serious heart attack in 1946, he was constantly troubled by ill health, living mostly as a withdrawn invalid.

Schoenberg enthusiastically supported the new state of Israel, and in April 1951 he was elected honorary president of the Israel Academy of Music in Jerusalem. In a letter of gratitude he stated his hope that Israeli musicians would become "priests of art," setting others "an example of the old kind that can make our souls function again as they must if mankind is to evolve any higher."

All his life Schoenberg had been fascinated by number symbolism, and he had a special dread of the number 13, including the 13th day of the month (particularly if a Friday). Becoming convinced that he would not live past the age of 76 (7 + 6 = 13), he fell into a state of deep depression in the summer of 1951. He died in the Brentwood section of Los Angeles, California, about 13 minutes before midnight on Friday, July 13, 1951, at the age of 76.

He was buried in California, but in 1974, the centenary of his birth, his remains were interred in Vienna, Austria, near the memorials to Mozart, Beethoven, and Schubert. In the same year, the Schoenberg Institute was founded in Los Angeles, housing his literary and musical manuscripts.

Schoenberg is now widely recognized as a seminal figure in twentieth-century music, his twelve-tone technique and its further developments having profoundly affected the course of modern music. Ultimately, however, his strong position in music history will rest not merely on his perfection of that technique but on his idealism, intellectual honesty, dedication to craftsmanship, and projection of human feelings.

Selected works:

Stage

Erwartung ("Expectation"; monodrama; text, M. Pappenheim; comp. 1909, perf. 1924)
Die glückliche Hand ("The Lucky Hand"; drama with music; text, A. Schoenberg; comp. 1913, perf. 1924)
Von Heute auf Morgen ("From Today Till Tomorrow"; opera; libretto, M. Blonda [pseudonym of Gertrud Schoenberg]; comp. 1929, perf. 1930)
Moses und Aron (unfinished opera; libretto, A. Schoenberg; comp. 1932, acts 1-2 in concert 1954, perf. 1957)

Orchestral

Pelleas und Melisande (symphonic poem, 1903)
Five Orchestral Pieces (1909)
Variations for Orchestra (1928)
Cello Concerto (after G. M. Monn, 1933)
String Quartet Concerto (after G. F. Handel, 1933)
Suite (string orchestra, 1934)
Violin Concerto (1936)
Second Chamber Symphony (full orchestra, comp. 1906-1916 and 1939)
Piano Concerto (1942)

Choral

Gurre-Lieder (cantata; vocal soloists, choruses, orchestra; text, J. P. Jacobsen; comp. 1901, orchestrated 1911)
Die Jakobsleiter ("Jacob's Ladder"; unfinished oratorio; vocal soloists, choruses, orchestra; text, A. Schoenberg; comp. 1922, revised 1944)
Six Pieces (men's chorus; texts, A. Schoenberg; 1930)
Kol nidre (speaker, chorus, orchestra; text, Jewish liturgy in English with alterations; 1938)
A Survivor from Warsaw (narrator, men's chorus, orchestra; text, A. Schoenberg; 1947)
Israel Exists Again (unfinished; chorus, orchestra; text, A. Schoenberg; 1949)
De profundis (unaccompanied chorus; text, Psalm 130 in Hebrew; 1950)

Solo Vocal

Eight Songs (voice, piano; texts, various authors; 1905)
Das Buch der hängenden Gärten (song cycle; voice, piano; texts, S. George; 1909)
Pierrot lunaire (song cycle; speaker, instrumental chamber ensemble; texts, A. Giraud; 1912)
Ode to Napoleon (reciter, piano, string orchestra; text, L. Byron; 1942)

Chamber

String Quartet (unnumbered, 1897)
Verklärte Nacht (two violins, two violas, two cellos; 1899)
First String Quartet (1905)
First Chamber Symphony (fifteen instruments, 1906)
Second String Quartet (with soprano in movements three and four; text, S. George; 1908)
Weihnachtsmusik (instrumental chamber ensemble, 1921)

Serenade (instrumental chamber ensemble, bass [or baritone] in movement four; text, Petrarch; 1923)
Third String Quartet (1927)
Fourth String Quartet (1936)
String Trio (1946)
Phantasy (violin, piano; 1949)

Keyboard

Three Piano Pieces (1909)
Six Little Piano Pieces (1911)
Five Piano Pieces (1923)
Piano Suite (1923)
Variations on a Recitative (organ, 1941)

Writings

Harmonielehre (written 1911, pub. 1911, revised 1922; English, as *Theory of Harmony*, abridged 1948, complete 1978)
Models for Beginners in Composition (written 1942, pub. 1942, enlarged 1943, revised 1972 by L. Stein)
Structural Functions of Harmony (written 1948, edited by H. Searle and pub. 1954, revised 1969 by L. Stein)
Preliminary Exercises in Counterpoint (written 1950, edited by L. Stein and pub. 1963)
Fundamentals of Musical Composition (written 1948, edited by L. Stein and pub. 1967)
Style and Idea (15 essays, 1950; 104 essays, edited by L. Stein, 1975)

Gunther Schuller
Composer of Third-Stream Music
(1925-   )

Gunther Schuller, composer, was born in New York City, New York, on November 22, 1925. His paternal grandfather was a conductor, bandmaster, and music teacher in Germany, while Gunther's father, Arthur E. Schuller, was a longtime violinist and violist in the New York Philharmonic.

At the age of twelve Gunther entered the Saint Thomas Choir School in New York City, where he appeared as a boy soprano for several years and showed signs of remarkable musical aptitude. During that time he also studied at the Manhattan School of Music and continued his general academic education at Jamaica High School on Long Island. In his early teens he began to learn the flute, his first instrument. But at fourteen he switched to the French horn, encouraged by his father, who realized that there was a current shortage of players on that instrument.

Young Schuller made rapid progress on the French horn; and before he was sixteen he made his professional debut when he played in the horn section of the New York Philharmonic under Arturo Toscanini, who needed extra horn players for a performance of Shostakovich's *Seventh Symphony*. Shortly thereafter the United States entered World War II. Because there soon developed a wartime shortage of professional horn players, Schuller found himself repeatedly called on as an extra horn player for the New York Philharmonic. To concentrate

on his music career, Schuller left high school in 1942 and has never completed his formal academic education.

His ensuing rise as a horn player was meteoric. In early 1943 he joined the horn section of the Ballet Theater Orchestra. He then served as principal horn player of the Cincinnati Symphony Orchestra (1943-45), followed by a long tenure in the same capacity with the Metropolitan Opera Orchestra (1945-59).

In 1959 Schuller gave up the horn to devote himself to a wide variety of other musical activities, some of which he had already begun before 1959. He has been an important teacher, administrator, conductor, broadcaster, editor, publisher, writer, and composer.

While he was with the Cincinnati Symphony Orchestra, he briefly taught the French horn at the Cincinnati College of Music. And during his stay with the Metropolitan Opera Orchestra, he began to teach the instrument at the Manhattan School of Music, where he remained till 1963. He then taught composition at the Yale School of Music (1964-67) and served as president of the New England Conservatory of Music (1967-77). At the latter institution he created a system and atmosphere that led to the training of teachers, composers, and performers who were well grounded not only in the standard repertory but also in contemporary music, ragtime, and jazz. He has also had a long association in various capacities with the summer sessions of the Berkshire Music Center at Tanglewood, near Lenox, Massachusetts.

Schuller conducted a concert series entitled Twentieth-Century Innovations at Carnegie Hall (1962-65). He has also guest-conducted many major orchestras in North America—notably the Boston Symphony Orchestra—and Europe.

A skilled speaker, Schuller has hosted numerous radio and TV programs on twentieth-century music. He has edited works by Charles Ives, Scott Joplin, and Kurt Weill for publication. And in 1975 he became founder and president of Margun Music, Inc., which was set up to publish not only contemporary concert works but also ragtime, jazz, and other vernacular or ethnic music.

Schuller's writings include numerous articles on contemporary music, as well as the books *Horn Technique* (1962) and the much acclaimed *Early Jazz: Its Roots and Musical Development* (1968). As a child he was exposed only to classical music. But while he was with the Cincinnati Symphony Orchestra during World War II, he became enthralled by jazz when he happened to hear Duke Ellington perform. After that, he studied jazz intently and became one of its most important spokesmen and developers. Besides incorporating jazz into his teaching activities, he has promoted it in many other ways, highlighted by the book *Early Jazz*.

However significant Schuller's other achievements have been, his most enduring work lies in his own compositions. Entirely self-taught as a composer, he has an extraordinary ability to absorb a wide variety of influences and then to syncretize them into a unified style of his own. He has, for example, drawn technical ideas from Milton Babbitt, Arnold Schoenberg, Igor Stravinsky, Edgar Varèse, and Anton von Webern.

Jazz, of course, has provided a powerful source of stimulation. In the 1950s he associated with jazz musicians who were beginning to adopt instruments (such as the French horn) and formal compositional procedures (such as fugue) not previously linked with jazz. In the early 1950s he played the French horn in the Miles Davis-led ensemble that established a new style called cool jazz. Later in that decade he worked especially closely with John Lewis of the Modern Jazz Quartet and wrote several works with that group in mind, such as the *Conversations* for jazz quartet and string quartet (1959).

With the Modern Jazz Quartet, Schuller consciously attempted to fuse elements of jazz and contemporary art music. In 1957, during one of his lectures at Tanglewood, Schuller spontaneously invented the term *third stream* to describe such an amalgamation. The expression quickly gained wide currency and is now a well-established term in every literate musician's lexicon. Schuller's works in that direction show a particular concern with establishing the twelve-tone technique in jazz. The wide range in his jazz-related music can be heard in the early *Atonal Jazz Study* for twelve instruments (1948), the *Symphonic Tribute to Duke Ellington* (1955), the *Transformation* for eleven instruments (1957), the *Conversations* previously mentioned, the *Variants on a Theme of John Lewis* for eleven instruments (1960), the *Journey into Jazz* for narrator, jazz quintet, and orchestra (1962), the *Concerto for Orchestra: Gala Music* (1966), and the

opera *The Visitation* (perf. 1966).

Schuller has also shown a fascination for translating visual images into music. *American Triptych* for orchestra (1965), for example, explores literal transfers of three art works into musical terms. The first movement portrays an Alexander Calder mobile by means of four musical lines that rotate through four different orchestral "orbits" at different tempos; thus, like a mobile, the music "moves" without going anywhere. The second movement is a pointillistic evocation of Jackson Pollock's *Out of the West;* the third, a jazz parallel of Stuart Davis's *Swing Landscape.* A similar interest is reflected in the orchestral works *Spectra* (1958), *Seven Studies on Themes of Paul Klee* (1959), and *Shapes and Designs* (1969).

Schuller's works from the 1970s and 1980s show a continuing refinement of his syncretic approach to composition. Among his important recent works are *Four Soundscapes* for orchestra (1975), *Sonata serenata* ("Serenade Sonata") for four instruments (1978), *In Praise of Winds: Symphony for Large Wind Orchestra* (1981), and *Saxophone Concerto* (1983). His *Double-Bassoon Concerto* (1978) was the first ever written.

Schuller married Marjorie Black in 1948. They had met several years earlier when she was a student of voice and piano at the Cincinnati College of Music and he was a member of the faculty there. Two children came of the marriage: Edwin and George.

Selected works:

Opera

The Visitation (libretto, G. Schuller, after F. Kafka; perf. 1966)

Orchestral

First Horn Concerto (1944)
Symphony (brass, percussion; 1950)
Symphonic Tribute to Duke Ellington (1955)
Spectra (1958)
Seven Studies on Themes of Paul Klee (1959)
Variants (jazz quartet, orchestra; 1960)
Journey into Jazz (narrator, jazz quintet, orchestra; 1962)
American Triptych (1965)
Symphony (1965)
First Concerto for Orchestra: Gala Music (1966)
Shapes and Designs (1969)
Four Soundscapes (1975)
Second Concerto for Orchestra (1976)
Violin Concerto (1976)
Second Horn Concerto (1977)
Double-Bassoon Concerto (1978)
Trumpet Concerto (1979)

In Praise of Winds: Symphony for Large Wind Orchestra (1981)
Saxophone Concerto (1983)

Vocal

Sacred Cantata (chorus, orchestra; text, Bible; 1966)
Poems of Time and Eternity (chorus, nine instruments; texts, E. Dickinson; 1972)

Chamber

Atonal Jazz Study (twelve instruments, 1948)
Five Pieces (five horns, 1952)
two string quartets (1957, 1966)
Transformation (eleven instruments, 1957)
Wind Quintet (1958)
Conversations (jazz quartet, string quartet; 1959)
Variants on a Theme of John Lewis (eleven instruments, 1960)
Variants on a Theme of Thelonious Monk (thirteen instruments, 1960)
Double Quintet (wind quintet, brass quintet; 1961)
Concerto da camera ("Chamber Concerto," nine instruments, 1971)
Sonata serenata (four instruments, 1978)

Writings

Horn Technique (1962)
Early Jazz: Its Roots and Musical Development (1968)

William Schuman

One of America's
Most Influential Musicians
(1910-   )

William Schuman, composer, was born in New York City, New York, on August 4, 1910. His father, a businessman, had changed the family name from Schuhmann to Schuman. In his youth, William spent most of his time and energy on sports, especially baseball. But at New York City's George Washington High School, he did organize his own jazz band, called Billy Schuman and His Alamo Society Orchestra, in which he himself sang and played the violin and banjo. The ensemble performed at parties, weddings, bar mitzvahs, and the like. At the same time, he wrote a number of commercial tunes to lyrics by his friend Edward B. Marks, Jr.

After graduating from high school, he began to study business at New York University's School of Commerce. However, he continued his interest in music by spending his spare time writing popular songs, with lyrics mostly by Frank Loesser (who later won fame as a Broadway composer-lyricist). Their songs were performed in vaudeville and nightclub acts. Between 1926 and 1934, Schuman composed tunes for about one hundred popular songs.

An important change took place in Schuman's life in April 1930 when his sister took him to a New York Philharmonic concert conducted by Arturo Toscanini. Schuman became so excited by the concert that he decided to abandon business and to study music seriously.

He immediately began to take harmony lessons from Max Persin, followed the next year by counterpoint lessons with Charles Haubiel. In addition, he took summer courses at the Juilliard School of Music in 1932 and 1933. In 1933 Schuman enrolled at the Teachers College of Columbia University, where he earned the B.S. in 1935 and the M.A. in 1937. He studied conducting during the summer of 1935 at the Salzburg Mozarteum, and from 1936 to 1938 he studied composition under Roy Harris at the Juilliard School and privately.

Meanwhile, in 1935 Schuman had found his first teaching post, at Sarah Lawrence College, located in Bronxville, New York. The financial security that he derived from that job allowed him to marry Frances Prince, whom he had known since 1931. He had heard about Frances (known as Frankie) through their mutual friend Frank Loesser, who had told her, "You must meet Bill Schuman because he's the man you're going to marry." Ironically, the two eventually met quite by accident, without Loesser's help. However, Loesser's prediction did come true when William and Frances married in 1936. They had two children: Anthony and Andrea.

Schuman soon came to the attention of such influential figures as Aaron Copland and Serge Koussevitzky. The latter, head of the Boston Symphony Orchestra, conducted the world premieres of Schuman's *American Festival Overture* in 1939, *Third Symphony* in 1941, cantata *A Free Song* in 1943, and *Symphony for Strings* in 1943. The popular and critical success of the *Third*

Symphony, in particular, established Schuman as a leading American composer.

He also proved to be one of the country's most important teachers and administrators. At Sarah Lawrence College (1935-45) he developed nondogmatic teaching techniques that considered individual interests without sacrificing the cohesiveness of the class as a whole. And from 1939 to 1945 he served as director of the school's chorus, which under his guidance developed into an outstanding ensemble known for its wide-ranging repertory.

Then, after serving briefly as director of publications for G. Schirmer, Inc. (where he remained a special publications consultant till 1952), he was appointed president of the Juilliard School of Music in 1945. At the Juilliard School, Schuman displayed a remarkable gift for organization and innovation. He balanced the school's curriculum, previously performance oriented, by introducing academic studies. He broadened the range of styles studied by including modern music. And, most important of all, he fused the usually separate subjects of music performance, history, theory, and composition into a single program entitled Literature and Materials of Music. Schuman's approach to music education was outlined in *The Juilliard Report on Teaching the Literature and Materials of Music* (edited by Richard Franko Goldman, 1953).

Schuman left the Juilliard School in 1962 to become president of the Lincoln Center for the Performing Arts in New York City. He used that powerful administrative position to encourage the commissioning and performing of American works as well as to institute a student program for young listeners and performers, a chamber-music society, and a summer program of concerts and opera performances.

In 1969 Schuman left his post at the Lincoln Center, and since then he has been active as a consultant and administrator for a number of cultural organizations. He has also been able to devote more time to composition.

The teaching that he received from Roy Harris instilled in Schuman a propensity for expansive gestures, long-breathed melodic lines, and harmonies based on simple triads used in fresh ways. But Schuman early displayed his own characteristics as well: powerfully driving asymmetric rhythms, complex counterpoint, and clear tonalities overlaid with dissonance. His favored medium is the large orchestra, which he often uses in homogeneous groups, with similar material passed from one choir to another. Also common is the device of superimposing up to three distinct layers of orchestral music moving at different speeds.

Schuman's early concert works were composed in a basically neoclassical spirit, with a melodic-rhythmic propulsion that seemed to fit comfortably into the traditional patterns of the symphony, the concerto, and the string quartet. And he has often cast his ideas in the baroque-associated procedures of fugue and passacaglia. At first he seemed to be extremely reticent to express personal emotion. But gradually a characteristic emotional tension began to make itself felt beneath the bright surface of his music.

That emotional development can probably be best heard in his *Third* (1941) through *Sixth* (1948) symphonies (the first two symphonies having been withdrawn by the composer). The *Fourth* (1941) is most clearly neoclassical in spirit, while the *Sixth* is one of his most mature achievements.

A central work in Schuman's output is *Credendum: Article of Faith* (1955). Written for the United Nations Educational, Scientific, and Cultural Organization (UNESCO) through the Department of State, it was the first musical composition commissioned directly by the United States government. Its leaping melodies, energetic rhythms, and orchestral brightness summarize the early and middle stages of his career.

Many of Schuman's works from that period are explorations of Americana. For example, the *American Festival Overture* (1939) opens with a three-note motive that imitates the "wee-awk-eem" call of children on the New York City streets. *A Free Song* (1942) is a secular cantata based on a text by the American poet Walt Whitman. *The Mighty Casey* (1953) is a short opera based on Ernest L. Thayer's poem "Casey at the Bat." Among Schuman's other Americana works, the popular *New England Triptych* for orchestra (1956) stands out for its instilling a modern spirit into three anthems by the eighteenth-century American tunesmith William Billings.

Schuman's late works have become increasingly expressive, and he has openly declared himself to be a romantic. A new direction can be heard in his *Carols of Death* for chorus (1958), in which a rhetorical, dramatic, and profoundly melancholy manner emerges. That outlook continues in the *Seventh Symphony* (1960), which also begins to use stylistic gestures reminiscent of Gustav Mahler.

To Thee, Old Cause for a small orchestra (1968) is a somber "evocation" in memory of Martin Luther King, Jr., and Robert Kennedy. The moving *Ninth Symphony: Le fosse ardeatine* ("The Ardeatine Caves," 1968) was written under the impression received by Schuman when he visited the Roman caves where Germans in 1944 murdered over three hundred Italians (Christian and Jewish) in reprisal for the killing of thirty-two German soldiers by Italian resistance forces.

In Praise of Shahn for orchestra (1969), a portrait of the American artist Ben Shahn commissioned by his friends, introduces Jewish music because of Shahn's affection for it. Among the other works of Schuman's late, rhetorical period are the *Tenth Symphony: American Muse* (1976) and the *Three Colloquies for French Horn and Orchestra* (1979).

His friend Leonard Bernstein has said that what he treasures most about Schuman's music are its qualities of compassion and honesty, which reflect the character of Schuman himself.

Selected works:

Stage

Undertow (ballet, 1945)
Night Journey (ballet, 1947)
Judith (ballet, 1949)
The Mighty Casey (opera; libretto, J. Gury, after E. L. Thayer; perf. 1953; revised as cantata, 1976)
The Witch of Endor (ballet, 1965)

Orchestral

American Festival Overture (1939)
Third Symphony (1941)
Fourth Symphony (1941)
Piano Concerto (1942)
Prayer in Time of War (1943)
Symphony for Strings (or *Fifth Symphony*, 1943)
Circus Overture: Side Show (1944)
Violin Concerto (1947, revised 1954 and 1959)
Sixth Symphony (1948)
Credendum: Article of Faith (1955)
New England Triptych (1956)
Seventh Symphony (1960)
Eighth Symphony (1962)
To Thee, Old Cause: Evocation (oboe, brass, timpani, piano, strings; 1968)
Ninth Symphony: Le fosse ardeatine (1968)
In Praise of Shahn (1969)
Voyage: Cycle of Five Pieces (1972)
Amaryllis (1976)
Tenth Symphony: American Muse (1976)
Three Colloquies for French Horn and Orchestra (1979)

Concert Band

George Washington Bridge (1950)

Vocal

Pioneers! (small vocal ensemble; text, W. Whitman; 1938)
A Free Song (cantata; quartet of vocal soloists, orchestra; text, W. Whitman; 1942)
Carols of Death (chorus; text, W. Whitman; 1958)
The Young Dead Soldiers (soprano, horn, woodwinds, strings; text, A. MacLeish; 1976)
In Sweet Music (mezzo-soprano, flute, viola, harp; text, W. Shakespeare; 1978)

Chamber

Second String Quartet (1937)
Third String Quartet (1939)
Fourth String Quartet (1950)
Amaryllis Variations (string trio, 1964)
Prelude for a Great Occasion (brass, percussion; 1974)

Piano

Three-Score Set (1943)
Voyage (1953)
Three Piano Moods (1958)

Rudolf Serkin

Poet of the Keyboard

(1903-   )

Rudolf Serkin, pianist, was born of Russian parents in Eger, Bohemia (now Cheb, Czechoslovakia), on March 28, 1903. He learned music even before he could read or write, receiving early piano lessons from his father, a bass singer, before being turned over, at the age of four, to a local piano teacher. At five Rudolf made his first public appearance when he played in a concert at a local spa.

At nine he was taken by his father to Vienna for further study. Before returning to Bohemia, the elder Serkin left his son in the care of the piano teacher Richard Robert, who found lodgings for the boy with a local family. Quite naturally lonely at being away from home at such a tender age, Rudolf soon developed a close, lifelong friendship with an older fellow student, George Szell (later a famous conductor).

In 1915, at the age of twelve, Rudolf made his Viennese debut, as the soloist in Mendelssohn's *First Piano Concerto* with Oskar Nedbal conducting the Vienna Symphony Orchestra. Before the concert, family friends had convinced Rudolf's mother to dress him in the Fauntleroy manner, with his hair arranged in curls. He dutifully went to the hairdresser's establishment; but when he saw the result in a mirror, he rushed home in horror and washed the curls out of his hair.

Besides having his piano lessons with Robert, he studied composition with Joseph Marx and later with Arnold Schoenberg. Serkin received no formal academic education, but he enriched himself by extensive reading and personal associations with artists (such as Oskar Kokoschka) and poets (such as Rainer Maria Rilke).

In 1920, his own studies over, young Serkin began to give piano lessons to the children of wealthy Viennese families. Soon, however, he met the concert violinist Adolf Busch, who invited Serkin to live with the Busch family in Berlin and to make a concert tour playing sonatas for violin and piano. In the autumn of 1920 Serkin made his Berlin debut in an all-Bach program as soloist with the Busch Chamber Orchestra conducted by Busch. When the audience asked for an encore at the end of the concert, Busch jokingly suggested that Serkin play Bach's lengthy *Goldberg Variations*. Serkin, to everyone's surprise, did play the nearly hour-long work, and as he later recalled, "When I finished, there were only four people left in the hall. They were Adolf Busch, Artur Schnabel, Alfred Einstein, and myself."

Serkin then began to tour Europe. Besides playing unaccompanied piano pieces, he performed violin sonatas with Busch, chamber works with the Busch Quartet, and solo parts with the Busch Chamber Orchestra. Bach was a favored composer in those concerts, and Serkin's performance of Bach—with a clean attack and an unsentimental sonority—was a revelation to audiences of the time.

Serkin continued to perform with Busch and to live with the Busch family, first in Berlin, then in Darmstadt and, from the late 1920s, in Switzerland.

In 1933 Serkin made his American debut, playing a violin-sonata recital with Busch at the Coolidge Festival in Washington, D.C. Serkin's solo debut in the United States occurred when he played Mozart's *Piano Concerto in B-flat Major* (K. 595) with the New York Philharmonic under the baton of Arturo Toscanini in 1936.

Serkin made numerous appearances in the United States in the late 1930s. In 1939, when World War II began in Europe, he settled in America and soon became a naturalized citizen.

Serkin has had an important impact on American music education. In 1939 he was appointed head of the piano department at the Curtis Institute of Music in Philadelphia, where he became director of the entire school in 1968, serving in that capacity for nearly a decade. In 1949 he helped to found the Marlboro School of Music near his summer home in Guilford, Vermont. He became president and artistic director of the summer school, and one year later he helped to organize the annual Marlboro Music Festival, where his early excellence in chamber music again manifested itself in the programs that he arranged and participated in.

Meanwhile, however, Serkin has continued to concertize extensively. Besides making his American tours, he has regularly appeared in Europe and South America, and he has also concertized in Australia, Iceland, India, Israel, the Far East, and elsewhere.

Possessing an inspired sensibility, Serkin has been called the Poet of the Keyboard. However, the intellect, too, is evident in his playing: he is a master of detail, every effect being carefully planned and boldly articulated; at the same time, he clearly grasps and conveys the overall designs of the works that he plays. Serkin is widely recognized as one of the most profound interpreters of the German tradition from Bach through Richard Strauss.

In 1935 Serkin married Adolf Busch's daughter, Irene. They had six children: Ursula, Elisabeth, John, Peter, Judith, and Marguerite. John is a horn player, while Peter is a well-known concert pianist who, before turning to avant-garde music, appeared with his father in performances of two-piano works.

Artie Shaw
Intellectual Swing-Band Maestro
(1910-   )

Artie Shaw, jazz clarinetist and bandleader, was born in New York City, New York, on May 23, 1910. His original name was Abraham Isaac Arshawsky, but from early childhood he was known as Arthur Arshawsky. When he was seven, he moved with his parents to New Haven, Connecticut, where at thirteen he learned to play the saxophone. Soon he was getting jobs playing in dance bands in his home city and elsewhere.

In 1925 he taught himself to play the clarinet so that he could expand his opportunities for getting jobs. At about that time he decided to change his name. A sensitive boy, he had been deeply hurt many times by anti-Semitism. To a certain extent, he even felt ashamed of being a Jew (a feeling that later, with maturity, he overcame). Therefore, he tried to hide his Jewishness by shortening his name from Arthur Arshawsky to Art Shaw.

In 1929 he was playing with a band in Cleveland when he entered and won an essay contest sponsored by a local newspaper. He had, in fact, long had thoughts about becoming a writer (an ambition that he would later fulfill more completely), but he stayed with music because the money came so easily. The contest prize was a round-trip ticket to California. But he used it only one way, staying in Los Angeles to join Irving Aaronson's band. Later Shaw returned to the East with the band and then left it to do freelance radio work and to play in various spots in the Harlem section of New York City. During that time he was playing both the saxophone and the clarinet, but he gradually shifted to an emphasis on the latter instrument.

Meanwhile, he had learned the hot (complex, improvised) style of jazz playing from his friend Bix Beiderbecke, the cornetist. Shaw first appeared as a hot soloist in May 1936 at the Imperial Theater in New York City. In an extremely unusual move, he backed himself with a string quartet. For some time after that, he led a larger ensemble featuring his clarinet against a string background.

When that group failed to attract sufficient attention, he formed a conventional dance band. In the spring of 1938 he hired the black singer Billie Holiday and thereupon had his first major success, at the Roseland State Ballroom in Boston. By that summer he had already become well known through radio, recordings (especially of Cole Porter's "Begin the Beguine"), and live appearances. His work in New York City the following autumn led to movie offers.

Shaw performed in the films *Dancing Co-ed* (1939) and *Second Chorus* (1940). For the latter film he also served as arranger of the score, consisting of songs by various composers, including his own "Love of My Life" (lyrics, Johnny Mercer). But the musical highlight of that movie and the single performance that more than any other skyrocketed him to lasting fame was his rendition of his own *Clarinet Concerto,* which contains elements of blues, boogie-woogie, and hot jazz.

The year 1939 saw not only Shaw's entry into movies but also another name change. The Victor Recording Company wanted to make his first name Artie, and Shaw accepted the new appellation.

Soon after that, Shaw surprised everyone by beginning to use a very large ensemble with violins, violas, and cellos. Thus he broadened his appeal to include not only hot-jazz lovers but also those who enjoyed sweet (simpler, more smoothly arranged) jazz. His group rapidly became one of the top swing bands of the big-band era; and his Gramercy Five, originally formed from his 1940 band, was a highly regarded chamber ensemble.

Shaw led a navy orchestra (1942-43) in the South Pacific during World War II. After the war he returned to leading groups built around a string sound. And in 1953-54 he developed a revised version of his Gramercy Five.

In 1955 Shaw retired from clarinet playing and entered various businesses, including film production and distribution. He also lectured at colleges and fulfilled his lifelong ambition to be a writer. Perhaps the most intellectual of the swing bandleaders, Shaw wrote the semiautobiographical novel *The Trouble with Cinderella* (1952), as well as other books.

Shaw has gained much notoriety for his many marriages, several to well-known film actresses. His first marriage was to Margaret Allen. His second, for a brief time during 1940, was to the actress Lana Turner, with whom he had worked on the movie *Dancing Co-ed.* Later in the 1940s he wedded, in succession, Elizabeth Kern (the composer Jerome Kern's daughter), with whom Shaw had a son, Steven; the actress Ava Gardner; and Kathleen Winsor. His sixth marriage (1952-56) was to the actress Doris Dowling, with whom he had a son, Jonathan. In 1957 he married the actress Evelyn Keyes.

Shaw's clarinet playing was characterized by an extraordinary control of tone color and by a wide variety of articulation, especially in the high register. Though he

has refrained from publicly playing the clarinet since his 1955 retirement, he has returned to music by conducting his old standards throughout the country; and in the 1980s he formed a new Artie Shaw Orchestra.

A fierce opponent of the recent decline in professional standards in popular music, Shaw fearlessly and lucidly speaks out in public against the visual orientation (such as physical contortions, glitter makeup, and bizarre costumes) of many of today's performers, whose sole musical ability is to repeatedly howl a few "agonized" high pitches. In contrast, Shaw's work as clarinetist, composer, and bandleader continues to stand as evidence that music for the masses can be, when sociological conditions allow it, both popular and musically substantial.

Dinah Shore

Queen of the Juke Boxes

(1917-   )

Dinah Shore, singer and TV personality, was born in Winchester, Tennessee, on March 1, 1917. Her original name was Frances Rose Shore. At the age of eighteen months she was stricken with poliomyelitis, which caused a paralysis in her right leg and foot. She went through six years of rigid physical therapy, and her mother encouraged her to participate in ballet and in vigorous outdoor exercise. The illness made the girl shy yet ambitious to prove her worth despite her infirmity. Besides excelling in many sports, she sang, danced, and showed off to get attention. Even before she could talk plainly, she had performed in public by singing to the customers in her father's department store.

The Shores were the only Jewish family in Winchester, and they had to face the usual anti-Semitic prejudices of the time and place. Little Frances Shore once saw a Ku Klux Klan parade going down the street, the Klansmen hiding behind hoods and sheets. She began to realize that she, as a "different" person, had to work harder than others for success. That feeling was underscored then and later by her sensitivity about her illness and about what she regarded as her physical unattractiveness at the time.

At six she moved with her family to Nashville. Her mother, Anna, who was an aspiring opera singer, encouraged Frances to sing, though the child's devotion to popular music was contrary to Anna's classical tastes. Frances took ukulele lessons and accompanied herself on that instrument while she sang everywhere she went, including the public swimming pool, where she serenaded the lifeguards. She also sang for her eighth-grade class and for her mother's Ladies' Aid Society.

Frances began to take vocal lessons from John A. Lewis, who put her into the First Presbyterian church choir. But after so much solo singing, she found it difficult to harmonize with others. At fourteen she talked her way into a singing job at a local nightclub. After only one performance, however, her parents convinced her to get an education before attempting a music career.

At Hume-Fogg High School in Nashville, she participated in cheerleading, drama, and singing (in a Gilbert and Sullivan operetta). She graduated as the Best All-around Girl of her class.

On the advice of her family (except her mother, who had died when Frances was in high school), young Shore enrolled at Vanderbilt University as a sociology major. However, she continued her interest in music, singing at school assemblies and in student musicals.

In her sophomore year at Vanderbilt, she won a job singing on a local radio show called *Rhythm and Romance*, billing herself as Fannye Rose Shore. The theme song of the show was "Dinah," which she sang not in the usual fast tempo but in a slow, personal manner that she herself has said was an imitation of the black singer Ethel Waters. Radio was a perfect medium for Shore, who could sing her heart out without worrying about her physical imperfections. She began to experiment with using different distances from, and qualities conveyed over, the microphone. She became one of the pioneers in modern microphone techniques.

After her junior year she went to New York City for a college sorority convention. While there, she auditioned for various radio programs, but nothing materialized for her. She went back to Vanderbilt for her senior year.

After graduating in 1938, Shore returned to New York City. She began to sing at WNEW, a local radio station. With her were the young unknowns Dennis Day, Frankie Laine, and Frank Sinatra, with the last of whom Shore had a sometimes bitter rivalry. From her first appearances at WNEW, she called herself Dinah Shore because she had sung "Dinah" at her audition and the people at the station had referred to her as "the 'Dinah' girl." (In 1944 she changed her legal first name from Frances to Dinah.)

Her big break came in January 1939 when she was hired to sing with Leo Reisman's popular orchestra at the Strand Theater. Soon thereafter she made her first recordings, with Xavier Cugat's orchestra. She was so nervous, and the recording studio was so noisy, that when the sound engineer asked her if her name was Dinah Shaw, she said yes; thus, her first records were issued with labels reading "Vocal by Dinah Shaw."

Also in 1939 she was given her own radio series, *The Dinah Shore Show,* which ran for the next three years at fifteen minutes per program. But she first began to earn a national following when she spent two months on the radio show *The Chamber Music Society of Lower Basin Street* in 1940.

She left that series for an even better position: a regular spot on Eddie Cantor's weekly radio show *Time to Smile,* which shot her to stardom and lasting fame. Cantor taught Shore to relax and enjoy singing, which in turn brought more enjoyment vicariously to the audience.

By then her singing style had been firmly established. Shore, who has called herself basically a blues singer, learned much from her childhood black nursemaid, Yah-Yah. "It was Yah-Yah who taught me to swing," Shore has said. From Yah-Yah, Shore learned to imitate Ella

Fitzgerald and other black singers by playfully sliding up and down the scale. The nursemaid also took the child to hear black congregations sing spirituals. Out of those experiences Shore developed her unique throaty, dramatic way of singing in which each word was made meaningful to the listener. Her style has been called "sentimental" and even "gushy," but her phenomenal success in the 1940s and 1950s proved that her approach resonated in some significant way deep within the American psyche.

She rapidly became the top female blues singer in the country and the undisputed queen of the juke boxes. Among her early recording hits were "Yes, My Darling Daughter" (1940), "Memphis Blues" (1940), "Jim" (1941), "Body and Soul" (1941), and "Blues in the Night" (1942).

In 1942 her own radio series, *The Dinah Shore Show*, was lengthened from fifteen to thirty minutes per program. The show continued to run for another five years.

In the summer of 1943 she also hosted *Paul Whiteman Presents*, yet another radio show. During World War II she became a favorite with troops, for whom she traveled many thousands of miles to entertain at camps and hospitals.

During that time she was also signed by Warner Bros. to begin her movie career. First, however, the studio completely remade her appearance. Her black hair was bleached honey-blonde. She had plastic surgery to shorten and reconstruct her nose. Massive dental work was done. And the studio's makeup department did the rest.

Soon after that, in 1943, she married the actor George Montgomery. They both had all-American images, and both lived quieter lives than most of the Hollywood elite. Theirs was called "Hollywood's most successful marriage." They had one child of their own (Melissa) and adopted another (John, usually referred to as Jody). After the birth of her daughter, in 1948, Shore had no desire to return to work, but Montgomery prodded her into picking up her career again.

Shore made her film debut in *Thank Your Lucky Stars* (1943). She also appeared in *Up in Arms* (1944), *Follow the Boys* (1944), *Belle of the Yukon* (1945), *Till the Clouds Roll By* (1946), and *Aaron Slick from Punkin Crick* (1952). Her voice was featured in two Disney feature-length animated films: *Make Mine Music* (1946) and *Fun and Fancy Free* (1947).

But Shore was never comfortable or particularly successful in movies, largely because of the poor roles that she was given. Meanwhile, however, she continued to sparkle in radio and recordings. After the war, her radio work focused on her *Ford Radio Show* appearances. Among her recording hits were "Shoofly Pie and Apple Pan Dowdy" (1946), "Buttons and Bows" (1948), "Dear Hearts and Gentle People" (1949), "Whatever Lola Wants" (1955), "Love and Marriage" (1955), "Chantez-Chantez" (1957), and "Fascination" (1957).

Her career found its culminating point with the rise of television. She hosted her own musical-variety series, known successively as *The Dinah Shore Chevy Show* (1951-56) and *The Dinah Shore Show* (1956-62).

While her career was skyrocketing in the 1950s, Montgomery's was plummeting. In 1958 he, too, entered TV, in a series called *Cimarron City*. Shore allowed him to tout the series on her own show, but *Cimarron City* failed anyway. The different states of their respective careers caused tension in the family. Shore and Montgomery drifted apart for a few more years and then divorced in 1962.

In 1963 she married Maurice Smith, a building contractor whom she had met as a tennis partner in Palm Springs, California. They divorced the following year.

Having left her TV series in 1962, she spent the rest of the 1960s performing at benefits, in nightclubs, and on TV specials. Then she returned to TV on a regular basis, with a variety-talk series entitled *Dinah's Place* (1970-74).

On one of her TV shows in 1971 she met the actor Burt Reynolds. They soon developed one of the most talked-about love affairs in entertainment history. The alliance ended in 1975.

Recently she has hosted a TV talk show known successively as *Dinah!* (1974), *Dinah* (1975-79), and *Dinah and Friends* (since 1979).

Selected recordings:

Singles

"The Thrill of a New Romance" (1939, Victor)
"Yes, My Darling Daughter" (1940, Bluebird)
"Dinah's Blues" (1940, Victor)
"Memphis Blues" (1940, Bluebird)
"Somebody Loves Me" (1940, Bluebird)
"Honeysuckle Rose" (1941, Bluebird)
"Jim" (1941, Bluebird)
"Stardust" (1941, Victor)
"Body and Soul" (1941, Victor)
"Blues in the Night" (1942, Bluebird)
"Why Don't You Fall in Love with Me?" (1942, Victor)
"I'll Walk Alone" (1944, Victor)
"Candy" (1945, Victor)
"Shoofly Pie and Apple Pan Dowdy" (1946, Columbia)
"Laughing on the Outside, Crying on the Inside" (1946, Columbia)
"The Gypsy" (1946, Columbia)
"Doin' What Comes Natur'lly" (1946, Columbia)
"For Sentimental Reasons" (1946, Columbia)
"Anniversary Song" (1947, Columbia)
"Buttons and Bows" (1948, Columbia)
"Lavender Blue" (1948, Columbia)
"Baby, It's Cold Outside" (1949, Columbia)
"Dear Hearts and Gentle People" (1949, Columbia)
"Sweet Violets" (1951, Victor)
"Whatever Lola Wants" (1955, Victor)
"Love and Marriage" (1955, Victor)
"I Could Have Danced All Night" (1956, Victor)
"Chantez-Chantez" (1957, Victor)
"Fascination" (1957, Victor)

with Tony Martin:
"A Penny a Kiss" (1951, Victor)

Albums

Gershwin Show Hits (1945, Victor)
Musical Orchids (1945, Victor)

Beverly Sills
Bubbles
(1929-)

Beverly Sills, coloratura soprano, was born in New York City, New York, on May 25, 1929. Her original name was Belle Silverman; and because she was born with a huge bubble of saliva in her mouth, she was immediately nicknamed Bubbles, a name by which she is still affectionately known to millions of opera lovers. At the age of three Belle won a contest that named her the Most Beautiful Baby of 1932 in the borough of Brooklyn. She won not only the Body category but also the Talent, singing "The Wedding of Jack and Jill."

**Beverly Sills
in the title role
of Donizetti's
*Lucia di Lammermoor***

Her mother, an opera devotee, played Amelita Galli-Curci (an Italian coloratura soprano) phonograph records all day long. By the age of seven Belle had memorized, and could sing, all twenty-two arias on the recordings. At four, as Bubbles Silverman, she began to sing regularly on a local radio show, the *Uncle Bob Rainbow Hour.* Her big song was still "The Wedding of Jack and Jill," which ended with the words "ding, dong, ding." Once, the live audience applauded too soon and drowned out the ending. "Wait a minute!" Bubbles yelled at the audience and into the radio microphone. "I haven't finished my ding-dong!" During that period of time Uncle Bob Emory, the host of the radio show, rented Town Hall in New York City to present some of his little stars. One of them was Bubbles Silverman, who sang a coloratura aria that she had learned from the Galli-Curci records. One impressed columnist jested that Bubbles must have been not a seven-year-old but a midget!

It was also at the age of seven that she was given the stage name Beverly Sills because a friend of her mother's thought that it would look better than Belle Silverman on a marquee. As Beverly Sills she sang in a movie called *Uncle Sol Solves It* for Twentieth Century-Fox, but that job was not followed up by further movie offers.

It was at that time, 1936, that she began her first singing lessons, with Estelle Liebling. She progressed so well that two years later Liebling arranged for her to enter a contest on the *Major Bowes' Amateur Hour* radio show. Beverly sang "Caro nome" ("Dear Name") from Verdi's *Rigoletto,* another aria that she had learned from a Galli-Curci record, and won the contest. As a result of that victory, she became a regular member of the *Major Bowes' Capitol Family Hour* nationwide radio show, where she worked from 1938 to 1941. That series led to her being signed, at the age of eleven, for the radio soap opera *Our Gal Sunday,* on which she sang and acted for nine months (1940-41).

In 1941 the twelve-year-old veteran performer was forced into retirement because her parents wanted her to live a more normal childhood. But she continued her vocal work with Liebling, including the study of many opera roles. She also studied piano with Paolo Gallico (father of the writer Paul Gallico). Her first experience with live opera had come when she was eight, her mother taking her to see Delibes's *Lakmé* at the Metropolitan Opera, with Lily Pons in the title role. The child had instantly become a fan of both Pons and opera. During her forced retirement she continued to attend numerous operas.

In 1944, at fifteen, Sills came out of retirement, made

some Broadway auditions (she was offered chorus jobs, but she refused them), and finally, in 1945, went on tour as a performer in Gilbert and Sullivan operettas. By then she had transferred from regular high school in Brooklyn to the Professional Children's School in the borough of Manhattan, whose course she completed by correspondence while on the tour. During the tour she also became a redhead when her chaperone made a mistake with the hair-coloring recipe invented by Sills's mother to keep the girl's locks a golden blonde. Sills, however, liked the new color and has been a redhead ever since.

In 1946 she made another operetta tour. But then, deciding that the light musical theater was not the correct route to opera, she settled down to more serious study with Liebling. In 1947, through the influence of Liebling, she made her opera debut by playing Frasquita in a production of Bizet's *Carmen* by the Philadelphia Civic Opera Company. But from 1948 to 1950 she found only minor, nonoperatic engagements.

Then Liebling introduced Sills to the stage director Désiré Defrère, who arranged an audition for her with Charles Wagner, an impresario who controlled a touring opera company. Wagner hired her to play Violetta in Verdi's *La traviata* ("The Wayward Woman"), thus beginning her opera career at the age of twenty-two with the Wagner tour in 1951. On that tour she began her most important stagecraft studies, with Defrère, having earlier studied briefly under Armando Annini in Philadelphia in 1947 and Max de Rieux in Paris in 1950.

During the next few years she gave recitals and appeared with various opera companies, including the Wagner touring unit in 1952 (as Micaëla in Bizet's *Carmen),* the Baltimore Opera in 1953 (her first Manon in Massenet's *Manon),* and the San Francisco Opera in 1953 (several roles). In 1954 she worked on a New York City TV series called *Opera Cameo,* singing opera arias and doing commercials for Italian foods and wines.

Sills then took a major step forward by becoming a permanent member of the New York City Opera, debuting as Rosalinda in Johann Strauss II's *Die Fledermaus* ("The Bat") in October 1955. She soon became the company's diva.

In 1956 she married Peter Greenough, a wealthy newspaper editor. She became the stepmother of three daughters: Lindley, Nancy, and Diana, the last of whom was mentally retarded and was living in a special school. In 1959 Sills herself gave birth to a daughter: Meredith, known as Muffy. In 1961 there followed a son: Peter, nicknamed Bucky. Shortly after Bucky was born it was discovered that Muffy was deaf and that Bucky was mentally retarded. At the age of six Bucky was put into the same school attended by Diana, where both children received the necessary special teaching and therapy. Muffy responded well to training for the deaf, and in 1971 she appeared onstage as one of the candle bearers in a New York City Opera production of Donizetti's *Lucia di*

**Beverly Sills in the title role
of Donizetti's *La fille du régiment***

Lammermoor starring her mother in the title role. Later Muffy attended regular schooling. Because of her personal experiences, Sills has long been active on behalf of the Mothers' March on Birth Defects.

Meanwhile, after 1955 she continued to perform at the New York City Opera and to make numerous guest appearances elsewhere. But the turning point of her career, according to Sills herself, was her electric performance of Cleopatra in Handel's *Giulio Cesare* ("Julius Caesar") at the New York City Opera in 1966. She, as well as the public, noticed something new in her work: "My voice had not changed," she later explained; "*I* had." Previously she had sung to win approval, to build a career. Now, she admitted, she sang because she "needed to sing—desperately." Freed from pretensions, her voice simply poured out with the spontaneous ease of a master performer. In addition, she sensed within herself a new serenity and maturity resulting from her struggles to face her children's problems.

After the well-publicized success of her Cleopatra, offers began to come in from all over the world. In 1967 she sang the Queen of the Night in Mozart's *Die Zauberflöte* ("The Magic Flute") for her first performance with the Vienna Opera. In 1969 she debuted at La Scala in Milan, as Pamira in Rossini's *Le siège de Corinthe* ("The Siege of Corinth"). She made her first visit to Israel in late 1970 to give a series of concerts with the Israel Philharmonic Orchestra. Sills returned to the San Francisco Opera for many appearances during 1971-77. And in 1975 she made her long-awaited debut at the Metropolitan Opera in New York City, again as Rossini's Pamira. (She had been kept out of the Met by Rudolf Bing, general manager of the company from 1950 to 1972, who preferred not to hire singers born and trained in America.)

Sills had a secure, often brilliant, vocal technique. And she was among the best of her time as an operatic actress. Her particular qualities were revealed better in light, bel-canto (lyrical, virtuosic) roles than in weighty, dramatic ones. Besides singing the parts already mentioned, she earned fame for her title role in Donizetti's *La fille du régiment* ("The Daughter of the Regiment"), her trio of Tudor queens in Donizetti's *Roberto Devereux* (as Elizabeth I), *Maria Stuarda,* and *Anna Bolena,* as well as her Elvira in Bellini's *I puritani* ("The Puritans"). Sills herself regards her Queen Elizabeth I in *Roberto Devereux* as her finest artistic achievement. There are three other roles in which she feels she was particularly successful: Baby in Douglas Moore's *The Ballad of Baby Doe,* Manon in Massenet's *Manon,* and Cleopatra in Handel's *Giulio Cesare.*

Sills has become a well-known personality outside the opera house, appearing frequently on TV as singer and as conversationalist on talk shows (such as those of Johnny Carson and Dick Cavett).

In 1976 Sills published her autobiography, entitled *Bubbles: A Self-Portrait,* revised as *Bubbles: An Encore* (1981). Since 1979 she has been general director of the New York City Opera. In 1980 she retired from the opera and concert stages, her last opera appearance being as Rosalinda in Johann Strauss II's *Die Fledermaus,* produced by the New York City Opera at Lincoln Center.

**Beverly Sills (right) as Elvira
in Bellini's *I puritani*
with Cesar Antonio Suarez (left)**

Paul Simon and
Art Garfunkel
Famed Singing Duo
(1941-)   (1941-)

Paul Simon and Art Garfunkel formed one of the most significant singing teams in the history of American popular music, their gentle folk-rock style bridging the generation gap in the 1960s. Though they have had basically separate careers since 1970, they still occasionally perform together; and their reputation as a duo continues to overshadow their successes as individuals.

Their association together goes back to their childhoods. Paul Simon was born in Newark, New Jersey, on October 13, 1941. He grew up, however, in the Forest Hills section of the borough of Queens in New York City, where Art(hur) Garfunkel was born on November 5, 1941. They met and became friends when they were both in the sixth grade.

They soon discovered a mutual interest in music. Garfunkel sang in the choir of the local synagogue and served as cantor at his own bar mitzvah. Accompanied by Simon's acoustic guitar, they sang together in the mid-1950s at private parties and school dances. Then, billing themselves as Tom and Jerry (that is, Tom Graph and Jerry Landis—Garfunkel and Simon respectively), they gave concerts, appeared on TV's *American Bandstand,* and recorded songs. They sang in a fairly typical early-rock style, and in the late 1950s they had moderate success with their recording of Simon's "Hey, Schoolgirl." But their follow-up did not fare well, and the team split up soon afterward.

Each continued to sing, but without much success. In the early 1960s Simon performed with the Mystics, Tico and the Triumphs, and others. Garfunkel, during the same period, recorded a few poorly received songs under the name Arty Garr. Several years later they met again while they were in New York City colleges. (Simon earned a B.A. in English literature at Queen's College of the City University of New York, following which he studied law for six months at the Brooklyn Law School. Garfunkel studied architecture and earned a B.A. in art history at Columbia University and then an M.A. in math education at the same institution.)

They decided to team up again. Now, however, both of them were devoted to the new folk-music movement. Simon was the songwriting member of the duo, while many of their performances featured the beautiful tenor voice of Garfunkel. They began to appear at New York City cafés, notably Gerde's Folk City in Greenwich Village. Among the Simon songs in their act was "He Was My Brother," which commemorated the death of his

college classmate Andrew Goodman, a civil-rights worker slain in Mississippi in 1964.

Their first album was *Wednesday Morning, 3 A.M.* (1964). It consists of traditional folk material, some Bob Dylan songs, and a few Simon originals. One of the Simon songs is "The Sounds of Silence," which had attracted little attention when performed with Simon's acoustic guitar; but after producer Tom Wilson grafted, without the previous knowledge of the performers, an electric guitar background to the recording, the song went on to become a major hit (being released as a single in 1965) and to establish Simon and Garfunkel in the forefront of the folk-rock fusion.

Their next album, *Sounds of Silence* (1966), includes the title song and "I Am a Rock," the latter being about a determined withdrawal from emotional commitments. *Parsley, Sage, Rosemary, and Thyme* (1966) contains a number of successes, such as "The Fifty-ninth Street Bridge: Feelin' Groovy," Simon's most relaxed song up to that time; the beautiful "Homeward Bound"; and "Scarborough Fair," an adaptation of a traditional song.

In 1968 they issued an album created from their music track for the 1967 movie *The Graduate,* the project that made Simon and Garfunkel superstars. One of the songs in the album, "Mrs. Robinson" (1968), became a major hit when it was released as a single.

In their fifth album, *Bookends* (1968), Simon moved away from his earlier introspection and created vivid images of American life in the late 1960s, as in "America," "At the Zoo," and "Fakin' It."

Their next album, *Bridge over Troubled Water* (1970), became one of the most successful recordings in the history of popular music. Besides containing the extremely influential title song, the album includes the hits "Cecilia" and "El Condor Pasa."

During the 1960s Simon and Garfunkel gave numerous concerts (especially on college campuses), which were notable for their cool sophistication in contrast to the wild acrobatics of many rock groups, such as the Rolling Stones. The duo also appeared on the Ed Sullivan and Red Skelton TV shows, as well as on a few TV specials of their own.

But after *Bridge over Troubled Water,* Simon and Garfunkel experienced a conflict in tastes. They gave a series of farewell concerts in 1970 and then parted once again.

Simon went on to write and record a number of

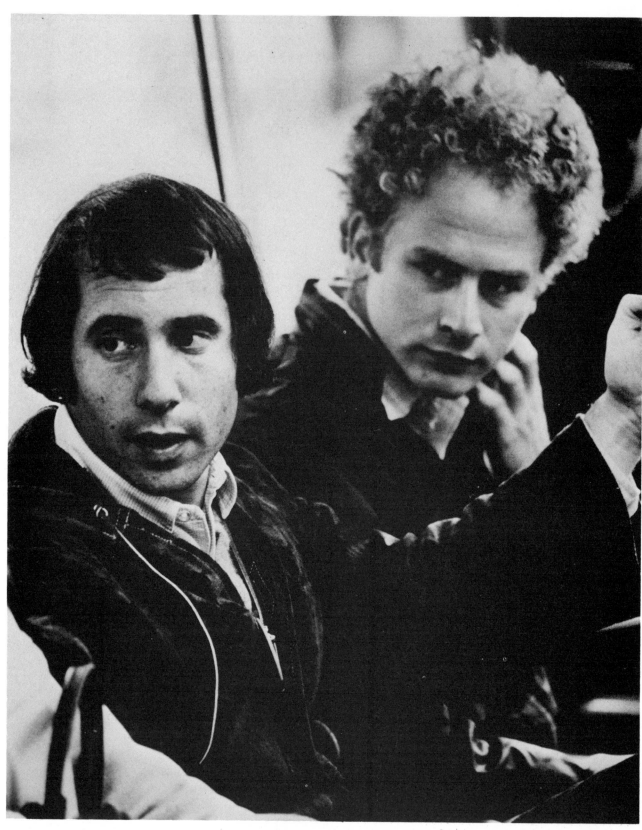

Paul Simon (left) and Art Garfunkel (right)

successful songs, drawing not only on his folk-rock base but also on blues, gospel, New Orleans jazz, reggae, and salsa. His leaning in those new directions could already be heard in the black-gospel roots underlying "Bridge over Troubled Water." His first solo album, *Paul Simon* (1972), which combines jazz, reggae, and rock, includes "Me and Julio down by the Schoolyard." *There Goes Rhymin' Simon* (1973) draws especially from the blues and gospel traditions. It contains such hits as "American Tune," a solemn assessment of America in the early 1960s; "Kodachrome"; the gospel-rock "Loves Me like a Rock"; and the unusual "Take Me to the Mardi Gras," which combines Dixieland jazz and reggae.

Simon's *Still Crazy after All These Years* (1975) displays his most sophisticated music, as in the title song, "Fifty Ways to Leave Your Lover," and several others. Since 1975 he has given concerts, appeared on TV, and played a small nonsinging role in Woody Allen's film *Annie Hall* (1977). Simon also scripted, starred in, and composed and performed the music for the movie *One-Trick Pony* (1980), the music track of which was released as an album.

Meanwhile, Garfunkel turned to acting, notably in the films *Catch-22* (1970) and *Carnal Knowledge* (1971). He then returned to singing and recorded several albums, including *Angel Clare* (1973), *Breakaway* (1975), *Watermark* (1978), and *Scissors Cut* (1981).

However, Simon and Garfunkel have never completely severed their ties. For example, in 1972 they performed together at a fund-raising concert for the George McGovern presidential campaign. Since then they have appeared together onstage a number of times, climaxed by a free concert in front of an audience of about half a million at New York City's Central Park in 1981.

Simon and Garfunkel have also recorded together since 1970. In 1975 they cut the single "My Little Town," which also appeared (as a duet) in Simon's album *Still Crazy after All These Years* and Garfunkel's album *Breakaway*. Simon, with James Taylor, provided background harmonies for Garfunkel's performance of "Wonderful World" in the *Watermark* album. In 1982 they came out with *The Concert in Central Park*, a recording of their 1981 reunion concert. Also in 1982 they issued the single "Wake Up, Little Susie." A highly publicized reunion album tentatively entitled *Think Too Much* was recorded in 1983. But late that year it was reported that Simon had erased Garfunkel from the recording and issued it as a solo album called *Hearts and Bones*.

Simon has written some of the greatest popular music of his era, but he has a healthy humility about his role. "Beethoven is a little better than us," he has said. "He works with more than a rhythm section."

In the early 1970s Simon married Peggy Harper, with whom he had a son, Harper. At about the same time, Garfunkel married Linda Grossman, an architect. Simon's marriage, however, did not last, and in 1983 he married the actress Carrie Fisher, daughter of the actress Debbie Reynolds and the singer Eddie Fisher.

Selected recordings:

Singles

Simon and Garfunkel:

"The Sounds of Silence" (1965, Columbia)
"Homeward Bound" (1966, Columbia)
"I Am a Rock" (1966, Columbia)
"The Dangling Conversation" (1966, Columbia)
"A Hazy Shade of Winter" (1966, Columbia)
"At the Zoo" (1967, Columbia)
"Fakin' It" (1967, Columbia)
"Scarborough Fair" (1968, Columbia)
"Mrs. Robinson" (1968, Columbia)
"The Boxer" (1969, Columbia)
"Bridge over Troubled Water" (1970, Columbia)
"Cecilia" (1970, Columbia)
"El Condor Pasa" (1970, Columbia)
"My Little Town" (1975, Columbia)
"Wake Up, Little Susie" (1982, Warner)

Simon:

"Mother and Child Reunion" (1972, Columbia)
"Me and Julio down by the Schoolyard" (1972, Columbia)
"Kodachrome" (1973, Columbia)
"Loves Me like a Rock" (1973, Columbia)
"American Tune" (1974, Columbia)
"Fifty Ways to Leave Your Lover" (1975, Columbia)
"Still Crazy after All These Years" (1976, Columbia)
"Slip Slidin' Away" (1977, Columbia)
"Late in the Evening" (1980, Warner)
"One-Trick Pony" (1980, Warner)

Garfunkel:

"All I Know" (1973, Columbia)
"I Shall Sing" (1974, Columbia)
"Second Avenue" (1974, Columbia)
"I Only Have Eyes for You" (1975, Columbia)
"Breakway" (1976, Columbia)

Albums

Simon and Garfunkel:

Wednesday Morning, 3 A.M. (1964, Columbia)
Sounds of Silence (1966, Columbia)
Parsley, Sage, Rosemary, and Thyme (1966, Columbia)
The Graduate (1968, Columbia)
Bookends (1968, Columbia)
Bridge over Troubled Water (1970, Columbia)
Simon and Garfunkel's Greatest Hits (1972, Columbia)
The Concert in Central Park (1982, Warner)

Simon:

Paul Simon (1972, Columbia)
There Goes Rhymin' Simon (1973, Columbia)
Still Crazy after All These Years (1975, Columbia)
Greatest Hits, Etc. (1977, Columbia)
One-Trick Pony (1980, Warner)
Hearts and Bones (1983, Warner)

Garfunkel:

Angel Clare (1973, Columbia)
Breakaway (1975, Columbia)
Watermark (1978, Columbia)
Fate for Breakfast (1979, Columbia)
Scissors Cut (1981, Columbia)

Georg Solti
Decisive Conductor
(1912-   )

Georg (originally György) Solti, conductor, was born in Budapest, Hungary, on October 21, 1912. At the age of five he began to take piano lessons, and by the time he was twelve he was already giving public recitals. At thirteen he enrolled at the Franz Liszt Academy of Music in Budapest, where his teachers included Béla Bartók, Ernst von Dohnányi, and Zoltán Kodály. About a year after entering the academy Solti attended a concert conducted by Erich Kleiber, and it was that experience that made the youth decide to become a conductor himself.

In 1930 Solti graduated from the Liszt Academy and joined the Budapest Opera as a coach. There he made his conducting debut in 1938, a performance of Mozart's *Le nozze di Figaro* ("The Marriage of Figaro"). But before he could get his conducting career under way, World War II intervened.

He spent the war years in Switzerland as a coach and piano accompanist. Unable to conduct, he dedicated himself to the piano and won the 1942 Geneva International Piano Competition.

While in Switzerland he met Hedi Oechsli, whom he married in 1946. However, as the years went by, they grew increasingly apart. They had no children.

After the war, Solti was invited by the American military authorities to conduct Beethoven's *Fidelio* in Munich. On the strength of that performance he was appointed music director of the Munich State Opera in 1946. Under his leadership the company developed an excellent international reputation.

In 1952 he left Munich and took up a similar post in Frankfort on the Main, where he also served as principal conductor of the Museum Concerts. During his tenure there he made many guest appearances elsewhere, notably his Covent Garden (London) debut in 1959, in a performance of Richard Strauss's *Der Rosenkavalier* ("The Knight of the Rose"). Subsequently he left Frankfort to serve as director at Covent Garden (1961-71),

where he developed perhaps the best opera company in the world.

During his Covent Garden years Solti met Anne Valerie Pitts, a young reporter sent to interview him for the TV wing of the British Broadcasting Corporation (BBC). They began a romantic liaison in 1964 and, after both got divorces from their spouses, married in 1967. She has been credited with transforming him from a sometimes abrasive and explosive maestro into a more relaxed and even-tempered man. He also became more domesticated, spending a great deal of time with his two daughters.

In 1969, while still at Covent Garden, Solti became music director of the Chicago Symphony Orchestra, a post that he still holds with distinction. And in the early 1970s he spent several years as music director of the Orchestra of Paris.

Nevertheless, influenced partly by his British-born wife, Solti has kept London as the base of his activities. He has been principal guest conductor at Covent Garden since 1971, and from 1979 to 1983 he was principal conductor of the London Philharmonic Orchestra.

Solti's performances are marked by decisiveness and excitement. He is particularly effective with the music of Beethoven, Mahler, and Elgar. But he is primarily renowned as one of the greatest recent interpreters of Wagner. In his recordings, Solti pioneered the use of stereo techniques to simulate the theatrical dimensions of opera performances. His efforts in that direction peaked with the 1966 release of his recording of Wagner's complete *Der Ring des Nibelungen* ("The Ring of the Nibelung," a cycle of four operas).

Stephen Sondheim

Leader of Contemporary American Musical Theater

(1930-)

Stephen Sondheim, composer, was born in New York City, New York, on March 22, 1930. At the age of four he began to pick out tunes on the piano, but for many years he had only sporadic musical training. When he was ten, his parents divorced and he went with his mother to live in Doylestown, Pennsylvania. One of the family friends there was the great musical-theater lyricist Oscar Hammerstein II. With Hammerstein's encouragement young Sondheim developed a fascination for the musical theater.

After spending some time at a military school (which he enjoyed because of the order it put into his life after the confusion of his parents' divorce), Sondheim attended the Quaker-run George School. There, at the age of fifteen, he and two classmates wrote *By George,* a musical about campus life. He showed the manuscript to Hammerstein, who gave the work a thorough critique and immediately began to teach Sondheim the art of writing for the musical theater.

After graduating from George School in 1946, Sondheim enrolled at Williams College in Williamstown, Massachusetts, where he became a music major and where he continued to write words and music for apprentice musicals. When he graduated from college in 1950, he won the Hutchinson Prize, a two-year fellowship that enabled him to study composition privately with the avant-garde composer Milton Babbitt in New York City. But Sondheim never seriously considered writing art music. His goal remained the popular musical theater.

Sondheim's first major project in show business was coscriptwriting for the *Topper* TV series in 1953, a job offered to him by George Oppenheimer, whom Sondheim had met at dinner one evening in Hammerstein's home. Soon after leaving that work, Sondheim was hired to write the songs (music and lyrics) for a proposed Broadway musical, *Saturday Night;* but the show never reached the stage.

His next major effort was to compose the incidental

Stephen Sondheim

music for the play *The Girls of Summer* (1956). He then made the big breakthrough in his career when Leonard Bernstein asked him to write the lyrics to Bernstein's music for *West Side Story* (perf. 1957). The tremendous success of that Broadway musical catapulted Sondheim into the front ranks of theatrical figures. He followed up by writing the lyrics to Jule Styne's music for *Gypsy* (perf. 1959), another Broadway blockbuster.

But Sondheim was not content to limit himself to words. Though he subsequently occasionally wrote lyrics for others, notably for Richard Rodgers in *Do I Hear a Waltz?* (perf. 1965), Sondheim, from the early 1960s on, wrote both music and lyrics for a succession of Broadway musicals that have shown him to be the leading creative figure in the recent history of the American musical theater.

The first Broadway show for which Sondheim supplied both music and lyrics was *A Funny Thing Happened on the Way to the Forum* (perf. 1962), a farce set in a suburb of ancient Rome and based on plays by Plautus. It was a direct antithesis to the prevailing Rodgers and Hammerstein type of musical in that the songs were deliberately nonintegral to the play's plot and characterizations. Sondheim's remarkable musical and verbal wit sparkles throughout the score, as in "That Dirty Old Man."

Anyone Can Whistle (perf. 1964), his next musical, was unsuccessful commercially (running only nine performances). But it was important for establishing Sondheim's future direction. First, it was an experimental musical in that it dealt satirically with a serious subject (the vague line between sane and insane people). Second, he developed a technique that he used many times in the future, namely, the use of traditional musical-comedy style in songs that delineate characters who deal "in attitudes instead of emotions." Third, it was his first chance to compose the highly romantic kind of music that he most enjoys, as in the title song.

However, it was several years before he could follow up with *Company* (perf. 1970), a plotless, antimarriage musical in which the songs serve as a sardonic commentary on a series of vignettes. According to Sondheim, *Company* explores "the increasing difficulty of making one-to-one relationships in an increasingly dehumanized society."

Follies (perf. 1971), another plotless musical, focuses on the loss of American optimism. It is centered on a reunion of former Ziegfeld girls, now disillusioned middle-aged women, in the old rundown theater where they used to perform. To re-create the era of the 1920s and 1930s, Sondheim deliberately imitates, and simultaneously attempts to comment on, the styles of various songwriters of the time, such as Irving Berlin in "Beautiful Girls" and George Gershwin (music) and Dorothy Fields (lyrics) in the torch song "Losing My Mind." Other songs reflect present-day styles, such as "Who's That Woman?"

A Little Night Music (perf. 1973), based on the 1955 Ingmar Bergman comedy film *Smiles of a Summer Night*, is a love story that combines cynicism and sentimentality. All of the songs are characterized by a waltzlike lilt, and the musical style evokes aural memories of Brahms, Rachmaninoff, and Ravel. Sondheim, who regarded the work as an operetta rather than a musical, composed a number of recondite contrapuntal passages but without letting technique get in the way of expression. Most of the songs function as interior monologues in which the characters reveal their deepest thoughts, seldom actually singing to one another. The score contains Sondheim's best-known song: "Send in the Clowns."

While *Company, Follies,* and *A Little Night Music* are eclectic in their musical styles and procedures, Sondheim's next two major theatrical works reach out even more boldly into regions seldom if ever explored in the American musical theater. *Pacific Overtures* (perf. 1976), an attempt to portray Commodore Perry's opening of Japan from a Japanese point of view, skillfully marries Japanese and Western musical sounds. The lyrics suggest haiku, and the staging draws on elements of the traditional Japanese theater, Kabuki.

Sweeney Todd: The Demon Barber of Fleet Street

(perf. 1979), also subtitled *A Musical Thriller,* is a tale of injustice, revenge, and murder. The vocal lines, especially those for the secondary characters, are virtually operatic in conception. The musical idioms range from seventeenth-century baroque patterns to modern bitonality and dissonances reminiscent of Weill and Stravinsky.

Sondheim's recent work includes the stage musical *Merrily We Roll Along* (perf. 1981), a story dealing with idealism and compromise; the background music for the film *Reds* (1981); and the stage musical *Sunday in the Park with George* (perf. 1984), inspired by the painter Georges Seurat and his divisionist art.

Sondheim, more than any other individual, has revitalized the American musical theater with highly intelligent works in the spirit of contemporary realities. While his music is still controversial in its supposed lack of tunefulness and in its wedding of Tin Pan Alley and modern classical techniques, his lyrics are universally admired for their lucidity, economy, and brilliant use of language. More difficult to achieve and more difficult for most listeners to grasp is his linking of the structure of the musical phrase with the rhythms of the verbal cadence.

Unmarried, Sondheim has been romantically associated with many women, including the actress Lee Remick, who starred in his *Anyone Can Whistle.*

He seldom listens to popular music, preferring mostly Ravel and Rachmaninoff, secondarily Prokofiev, Copland, and Britten. His nonmusical activities also center on the entertainment world. With the actor Anthony Perkins (of *Psycho* fame), he coauthored the screenplay for the murder-mystery film *The Last of Sheila* (1973). In 1974 Sondheim made his acting debut, in a TV revival of the George S. Kaufman and Ring Lardner play *June Moon.* Sondheim's compulsion for order and economy can be seen in his love for, and vast collection of, various puzzles, games, and machines dating from the nineteenth century to the present. (His New York City town house is said to have inspired Anthony Shaffer's game-dominated play *Sleuth.*) He has published numerous word games and, in fact, has called lyric writing "an elegant kind of puzzle."

Selected works:

Stage
(music and lyrics by Sondheim unless otherwise stated)

West Side Story (music, Leonard Bernstein; perf. 1957)
Gypsy (music, Jule Styne; perf. 1959)
A Funny Thing Happened on the Way to the Forum (perf. 1962), including:
  "Comedy Tonight"
  "Love, I Hear"
  "Lovely"
  "That Dirty Old Man"
Anyone Can Whistle (perf. 1964), including:
  "Anyone Can Whistle"
  "With So Little to Be Sure Of"
Do I Hear a Waltz? (music, Richard Rodgers; perf. 1965)
Company (perf. 1970), including:
  "Being Alive"
  "Poor Baby"
  "Side by Side by Side"
  "Someone Is Waiting"
Follies (perf. 1971), including:
  "Beautiful Girls"
  "Broadway Baby"
  "The God-Why-Don't-You-Love-Me Blues"
  "I'm Still Here"
  "Losing My Mind"
  "Who's That Woman?"
A Little Night Music (perf. 1973), including:
  "Liaisons"
  "Send in the Clowns"
Pacific Overtures (perf. 1976)
Sweeney Todd: The Demon Barber of Fleet Street (perf. 1979), including:
  "The Ballad of Sweeney Todd"
Merrily We Roll Along (perf. 1981)
Sunday in the Park with George (perf. 1984), including:
  "Beautiful"
  "Move On"
  "Sunday"
  "We Do Not Belong Together"

Other Dramatic

The Girls of Summer (incidental music, 1956)
Invitation to a March (incidental music, 1961)
Stavisky (film, background score; 1974)
Reds (film, background score; 1981)

William Steinberg

Antiromantic Conductor

(1899-1978)

William Steinberg, conductor, was born in Cologne, Germany, on August 1, 1899. His original name was Hans Wilhelm Steinberg. Music was an integral part of his early family life, and he received his first piano lessons, when he was five, from his mother. At nine he also began to learn the violin. When he was thirteen he conducted an amateur performance of his own *Metamorphoses,* a piece for chorus and orchestra based on Ovid's text.

Steinberg's most important teachers were Lazzaro Uzielli in piano, Franz Bölsche in theory and composition, and Hermann Abendroth in conducting. He graduated from the Cologne Conservatory in 1920.

Immediately after graduation, he was engaged at the Cologne Opera as Otto Klemperer's assistant, rising to principal conductor there in 1924. Shortly thereafter he went to the German Opera in Prague, first as a conductor and then, after two years, as music director.

In 1929 Steinberg became music director of the opera in Frankfort on the Main. There he gained a wide reputation for presenting new music, including the world premieres of George Antheil's *Transatlantic,* Arnold Schoenberg's *Von Heute auf Morgen* ("From Today Till Tomorrow"), and Kurt Weill's *Aufstieg und Fall der Stadt Mahagonny* ("Rise and Fall of the City of Mahagonny," simultaneous with a performance in Leipzig), all in 1930.

With the rise of Nazi power in Germany, Steinberg's post at Frankfort became increasingly difficult, not only because of his Jewish background but also because of his reputation for conducting modern "decadent" music. He resisted pressure put on him to program works that fit into the Nazi propaganda scheme. One day in 1933 he arrived at the opera house and found a notice on the bulletin board dismissing him from his post.

Early in their regime the Nazis planned to separate the Jewish community as much as possible from the non-Jewish. Jews were forced to form their own organizations, one of which was the Jewish Cultural Association. From 1933 to 1936 Steinberg was restricted to musical activities in conjunction with that organization. He conducted all-Jewish orchestras for (officially, at least) all-Jewish audiences. However, the standards of performance in those concerts were so high that the Nazis' own ensembles suffered by comparison. Therefore, the Nazis issued another proclamation, banning Jewish concerts except in secluded synagogues. At that point it became obvious that Jewish musicians had no future in Germany.

In 1936 Steinberg, at the invitation of Bronislaw Huberman, went to Palestine and prepared the Palestine Symphony Orchestra (since 1948 called the Israel Philharmonic Orchestra) for performance. After the inaugural concerts, conducted by Arturo Toscanini, Steinberg became the orchestra's principal conductor.

Toscanini was favorably impressed by the way that Steinberg had prepared the Palestine Symphony Orchestra. Thus, in 1937 Toscanini invited Steinberg to the

United States; and by early 1938 Steinberg had settled in New York City, where he became Toscanini's associate conductor of the National Broadcasting Company (NBC) Symphony Orchestra. In addition, Steinberg began to guest-conduct many other symphony orchestras. In 1944 he became a naturalized American citizen, and from that time forward he was known as William, as opposed to his original Hans Wilhelm, Steinberg.

After conducting at the San Francisco Opera (1944-52) and serving as music director of the Buffalo Philharmonic Orchestra (1945-52), he was appointed to the post by which he is chiefly remembered today: music director of the Pittsburgh Symphony Orchestra (1952-76). Concurrently with his Pittsburgh post he was music director of the London Philharmonic (1958-60), principal guest conductor of the New York Philharmonic (1966-68), and music director of the Boston Symphony Orchestra (1969-72). He also guest-conducted leading symphony orchestras, as well as the orchestra and company at the Metropolitan Opera.

Steinberg approached conducting with the selflessness and fidelity to the music characteristic of Toscanini and Klemperer, the two major influences in his career. Antiromantic and undemonstrative, he concentrated his attention on a literal, precise re-creation of the music. His baton technique was unsurpassed for cleanness and clarity; and in his later years his always economical conducting gestures became absolutely minimal.

In his youth Steinberg was sympathetic to new music, particularly during his tenure at the Frankfort Opera. But after he left Frankfort he conducted fewer modern compositions, and his performances of such works tended to be mechanical. He did, however, conduct a few notable world premieres, including Ernst Toch's *Second Piano Concerto* with the Jewish Cultural Association in 1935, Walter Piston's *Second Violin Concerto* with the Pittsburgh Symphony in 1960, and Roger Sessions's *Eighth Symphony* with the New York Philharmonic in 1968. Steinberg's touch was rather heavy for music of the classical period, but he excelled with Beethoven, Wagner, Bruckner, Mahler, Elgar, and especially Richard Strauss. However, it was only late in his career that he finally ceased to disfigure much of his favorite music (Bruckner, Mahler, Elgar) with cuts.

Steinberg had two marriages. In 1927, while working at the German Opera in Prague, he wedded the company's leading female singer, Susanne Jicha. She died in 1932. Two years later he married Lotti Stern, with whom he had three children: Sylvia, Arthur (or Arturo, named after Toscanini), and Richard. Lotti went with him from Germany to Palestine and then to America.

After several years of ill health, Steinberg resigned from his Pittsburgh post in 1976, whereupon he was designated the orchestra's conductor emeritus. He returned to conduct the orchestra in a Beethoven cycle during the 1976-77 season. But his time was nearing its end, and he died in New York City on May 16, 1978.

Isaac Stern

Master Violinist
and Cultural Activist
(1920-   )

Isaac Stern, violinist, was born in Kremenets, the Soviet Union, on July 21, 1920. The following year he moved with his parents to the United States and settled in San Francisco, California. When he was six, his mother began to give him piano lessons, but at eight he switched to the violin.

The first major violinist to be wholly a product of American training, Stern received his entire musical education in California, mainly at the San Francisco Conservatory, where he completed his studies in 1937. He studied briefly with Louis Persinger, but his principal teacher was Naoum Blinder, concertmaster of the San Francisco Symphony Orchestra.

Stern also began his performing career in San Francisco, where he made his recital debut in 1934. Two years later came his first major public appearance: a performance as soloist with the San Francisco Symphony under the baton of Pierre Monteux. In 1937 he made his New York City debut, a successful Town Hall recital.

However, he returned to San Francisco for two more years of study before launching his adult career with another New York City recital. He was immediately acclaimed as one of the top young American violinists.

The progress of Stern's career in its early stages was slowed somewhat by World War II. But during that conflict, besides performing for Allied troops in Greenland, Iceland, and the South Pacific, he gave his first Carnegie Hall recital in New York City (1943) and made his debut as soloist with the New York Philharmonic (1944), under Artur Rodzinski. (Stern has subsequently performed with the New York Philharmonic over eighty times, more than any other violinist in its history.)

Stern's European career began in 1948 at the Lucerne Festival. Since then he has returned to Europe every year and has also played in Australia, Japan, South America, and the Soviet Union. However, as a protest against the atrocities of the Nazi era, he refuses to play in Germany.

Stern has a special relationship with Israel. Perhaps more than any other single artist, he has aided the cultural growth of the young state. One of his most memorable appearances there was his performance of the Mendelssohn *Violin Concerto* with the Israel Philharmonic Orchestra under Leonard Bernstein at the famous Mount Scopus concert celebrating Israel's victory in the Six-Day War of 1967. He also helped to establish the Mishkenot in Jerusalem, a center for scholars and creative artists; helped to found the Jerusalem Music Center, an archive of the past and a place of exposure for musicians of the present; and has long served as the chairman of the board of, and the driving force behind, the

America-Israel Cultural Foundation, which aids the careers of gifted young Israeli artists. Moreover, though he does not teach individual students, he has personally guided and advised many young Israeli violinists both in Israel and in the United States, including Itzhak Perlman and Pinchas Zukerman.

His concern for larger cultural and social issues has also extended beyond Israel. In 1960, when Carnegie Hall was close to demolition, he led the Save Carnegie Hall campaign, and he now serves as president of the Carnegie Hall Foundation. For many years he has fervently advocated government recognition of the importance of the arts, and he has campaigned for political candidates dedicated to helping that cause. He has also actively supported human-rights causes at every opportunity. In 1975 he received the first Albert Schweitzer Music Award for "a life dedicated to music and devoted to humanity."

Stern's playing reflects his vibrant personality. Subordinating technique to the musical concept, he performs with a total emotional involvement and predicates his approach on a desire for intense communication with his audience. He has the rare ability to mold each musical passage into an inevitable whole.

Stern was one of the first violinists to move away from the standard solo-recital program by regularly including a variety of chamber music in his performances. His concerts, billed as "Isaac Stern and Friends," present genres from solos to octets. In 1960 he founded a highly regarded trio with the pianist Eugene Istomin and the cellist Leonard Rose. During the Beethoven bicentennial in 1970 they gave numerous recorded and televised performances of Beethoven works in Paris, London, New York City, and elsewhere. Among his other musical partners through the years have been the cellist Pablo Casals, the violinist-violist Pinchas Zukerman, and the Russian pianist Alexander Zakin, who served as Stern's accompanist for decades.

Stern's repertory of solo and chamber music is vast, and he has recorded nearly every piece in the standard violin literature. Twentieth-century music is heavily represented in his performances, including works by Bartók, Berg, Bloch, Copland, Hindemith, Prokofiev, and Stravinsky. Stern has given several world premieres, including those of William Schuman's *Violin Concerto* in 1950 and Leonard Bernstein's *Serenade* in 1954. In the mid-1970s he premiered violin concertos by George Rochberg and Krzysztof Penderecki.

Stern has also worked in commercial films. He recorded the violin music for the soundtracks of *Humoresque* (1946), in which his brilliant playing helped to offset the embarrassingly strained attempts to portray John Garfield as a violinist on the screen, and *Fiddler on the Roof* (1971), in which his profound understanding of the Jewish tradition helped to create an appropriate atmosphere for the story. In *Tonight We Sing* (1953) Stern appeared in the movie itself, playing the violin and portraying the late violinist Eugène Ysaÿe.

Now universally regarded as one of the greatest violinists in the world, Stern continues to amaze audiences

with his enthusiasm and communicativeness. Music lovers in many countries gave an outpouring of affection and admiration in celebrating his sixtieth birthday in 1980. He responded with numerous concerts, including a memorable one at Avery Fisher Hall in New York City on September 24, 1980.

Another recent highlight of his career was the documentary film *From Mao to Mozart: Isaac Stern in China* (1981), a report on his 1979 trip to China, whose government had invited him to advise the country on the integration of its music life with that of the West. On January 12, 1983, he performed at a Carnegie Hall recital to observe the fortieth anniversary of his debut there.

Stern has been married twice. In 1948 he wedded the ballerina Nora Kaye, but the marriage was short-lived. During a 1951 visit to Israel he met and fell in love with an Israeli, Vera Lindenblit, whom he married later that year. They had three children: Shira, Michael, and David.

Risë Stevens

Famed Carmen

(1913-   )

Risë Stevens, mezzo-soprano, was born in New York City, New York, on June 11, 1913. Daughter of a Lutheran father and Jewish mother, she was originally named Risë Steenberg and was raised a Methodist. Later she took an aunt's married name: Stevens.

As a child she sang regularly on radio. And in her teens she spent two years with the New York Opéra-Comique, mostly performing in the chorus and ballet but occasionally playing a role, such as Prince Orlofsky in Johann Strauss II's *Die Fledermaus* ("The Bat").

Then she began to study with the most important teacher of her career, Anna Schoen-René, at first privately and later through the Juilliard School of Music. Simultaneously Stevens earned her living by singing opera on the *Palmolive Beauty Box Theater* radio show, again mostly in the chorus but occasionally in a role, such as Suzuki in Puccini's *Madama Butterfly* ("Madame Butterfly").

Encouraged and financially aided by Schoen-René, Stevens went to Europe for further study and experience. In 1936, in Prague, she gave her first major opera performance, in the title role of Ambroise Thomas's *Mignon*.

While in Prague, she met the young Hungarian actor Walter Surovy, a handsome matinee idol who was also performing in the city. They soon fell in love but were separated when she had to return to America in 1938.

In December of that year she made her Metropolitan Opera debut. Again her role was Thomas's Mignon.

A few days later Surovy arrived in America, and they were married in 1939. They had one child: Nicky.

Surovy drew on his personal experience to help Stevens battle against the inevitable behind-the-scenes theatrical intrigues that she encountered throughout the following years. He also encouraged her to expand her career. "We have to stretch you," the impish Surovy told her. He proceeded to stretch, or prod, her into concerts, movies, radio, and eventually TV, making Stevens one of the world's best-known singers. She made strong impressions with her singing in the films *The Chocolate Soldier* (1941) and *Carnegie Hall* (1947); and she contributed greatly to the success of *Going My Way* (1944), in which she sang a *Carmen* aria, Schubert's "Ave Maria," and the title song, in addition to having an extended speaking role. In 1945 she headed her own radio series: *The Risë Stevens Show*.

The opera stage, however, remained her base. She continued at the Met till 1962 and also sang with major opera companies in San Francisco, Paris, and elsewhere.

In 1954 she created the title role in the La Scala (Milan, Italy) world premiere of Virgilio Mortari's opera *La figlia del diavolo* ("The Devil's Daughter").

Risë Stevens as Cherubino in Mozart's *Le nozze di Figaro*

Her warm but light lyric voice was unsuited for Wagner or the heavier Verdi parts, but she excelled in such roles as Thomas's Mignon, Cherubino in Mozart's *Le nozze di Figaro* ("The Marriage of Figaro"), Dalila in Saint-Saëns's *Samson et Dalila* ("Samson and Delilah"), Marina in Mussorgsky's *Boris Godunov*, Octavian in Richard Strauss's *Der Rosenkavalier* ("The Knight of the Rose"), and Orfeo (her favorite role) in Gluck's *Orfeo ed Euridice* ("Orfeo and Euridice"). But the role for which Stevens won her greatest fame was the title part in Bizet's *Carmen*. As fine as her Carmen singing was, it was her acting that proved to have the most enduring effect on audiences. The passionate intensity that she put into the role created a more lifelike Carmen than had ever been seen or heard before.

After leaving the Met stage, Stevens continued to broaden her music activities. For example, she helped to open the Music Theater of Lincoln Center in New York City by starring in *The King and I* in 1964. She also did some teaching at the New School for Social Research and at Juilliard.

One of the first women to become involved with music administration, Stevens comanaged (with Michael Manuel) the Metropolitan Opera National (1964-66), a touring company. Later she served as president of the Mannes College of Music (1975-78). She has also been executive director of the Metropolitan Opera National regional auditions and served as adviser for a development program for young artists.

Barbra Streisand

The Most Versatile Personality in Show Business Today

(1942-   )

Barbra Streisand has been successful at singing, composing, acting, and motion-picture producing and directing. She is best known for her singing, in which she displays not only remarkable vocal resources but also extremely original song interpretations, each performance clearly being conceived as a deeply felt personal experience.

She was born in New York City, New York, on April 24, 1942. Her name was Barbara Joan Streisand, but she dropped the middle *a* from her first name soon after beginning her professional career.

The death of her father, when she was only fifteen months old, had an extremely important effect on the formation of her personality. She felt deprived yet special: "It's like someone being blind; they hear better. With me, I felt more, I sensed more—I wanted more."

She was also self-conscious about being awkward and not particularly attractive. She had few close friends. At home, in the Brooklyn section of New York City, she had a tense relationship with her stepfather (who married into the household when she was seven and who left at about the time that she started high school); and her practical mother had little sympathy for the girl's restless nature and impractical dreams of future glory in show business.

To escape her unhappy life, young Streisand spent as much time as she could in the local movie theater. Sometimes she hid under her seat or in the ladies' room to avoid being shooed out with the other children after each Saturday matinee. She watched the pictures over and over again and dreamed of becoming an actress.

In her early teens she made the big plunge into real acting by going to the Malden Bridge Playhouse in upstate New York to try out for work in summer stock. She managed to appear onstage a few times.

After her Malden Bridge experiences, she was totally committed to a career in show business. Eager to get her career under way, she studied extra hard and graduated six months early, in January 1959, from Erasmus Hall High School, where one of her classmates had been Neil Diamond (with whom she later recorded a duet of Diamond's "You Don't Bring Me Flowers," 1978). Streisand soon moved from Brooklyn to the Manhattan section of New York City, where she enrolled in acting classes and went to theater auditions, without much success.

Some of her friends heard her sing, and they encouraged her to turn her attention away from acting and toward singing. Thus, she entered, as a singer, a talent contest held at the Lion, a Greenwich Village nightclub. She won the contest by singing "A Sleepin' Bee." The prize was a short-term job at the club for fifty dollars a week and free meals. It was during that time, June 1960, that she decided to drop the middle *a* from her first name.

She then became a regular performer at another New York City nightclub, the Bon Soir. While performing at the Lion and the Bon Soir, she began to conceive of singing as a form of acting. That insight led her to select unusual or seldom-heard songs and to perform them with unique interpretations that displayed an incredible range and depth of emotion. One of her selections was a song from a Disney cartoon of the 1930s: "Who's Afraid of the Big Bad Wolf?" Usually performed as a light and playful ditty, the song was transformed by Streisand into a surrealistic yet childlike lament. Her performances at the Bon Soir made a tremendous impact on audiences, and her stint there has become legendary.

In 1961 Streisand's star began to rise. She became a regular on *PM East*, Mike Wallace's late-night TV show. She also performed in the off-Broadway revue *Another Evening with Harry Stoones* and moved up from the Bon Soir to the Blue Angel nightclub.

In late 1961 came the major breakthrough in her career: she landed her first significant role in a Broadway play. The show, which opened in New York City in March 1962, was a musical entitled *I Can Get It for You Wholesale*. Streisand's acting (a comedic role as a shy secretary) and singing (especially her self-revealing solo, "Miss Marmelstein") stole the show.

The male lead in *I Can Get It for You Wholesale* was Elliott Gould, who later became a well-known dramatic actor. Streisand and Gould married in 1963, had one child (Jason), and then, after a long separation, divorced in 1971.

After her success in *I Can Get It for You Wholesale*, Streisand got calls to work for major nightclubs and TV shows. A memorable and truly historic TV program resulted from Streisand's appearance on one of Judy Garland's TV shows in 1963, during which the two stars sang together and praised each other's gifts. In May 1963 Streisand was invited to the White House to perform for President Kennedy.

In 1963 she also issued her first album: *The Barbra Streisand Album*. Notable for its wide variety of vocal stylings (such as her ironic rendition of "Happy Days Are Here Again" as a hysterical lament), it became an instant success. The album is not, however, light party music, which most listeners were then accustomed to. People tended to listen to this album when they were alone, with their private feelings. Streisand admitted that she took her auditors' emotions "through the wringer." And they loved it. A cult of Streisand followers immediately developed.

She quickly came out with two more very successful albums: *The Second Barbra Streisand Album* (1963) and *Barbra Streisand: The Third Album* (1964). Among her many other albums in the 1960s was *My Name Is Barbra* (1965), a recording derived from the first of her many TV specials. Perhaps the most memorable of those specials was the admission-free concert taped in the summer of 1967 in New York City's Central Park before an audience of nearly 150,000 people. The taped concert was also released as an album: *A Happening in Central Park* (1967).

Streisand's most famous performance undoubtedly remains her role as the legendary entertainer Fanny Brice in *Funny Girl*, a Broadway musical of 1964. Streisand will forever be identified with her rendition of the song "People" in *Funny Girl*. In 1968 the musical came out as a movie. For her sensitive portrayal of the tragedienne behind Brice's mask of comedy, Streisand won an Academy Award as best actress of the year (actually tying for first place with Katharine Hepburn, who won for her performance in *The Lion in Winter*).

During the next decade, Streisand appeared in many films, both musicals and nonmusicals. Her movie musicals were *Hello, Dolly!* (1969), *On a Clear Day You Can See Forever* (1970), *Funny Lady* (1975, a sequel to *Funny Girl)*, and *A Star Is Born* (1976), for which she wrote the music to the song "Evergreen" (lyrics by Paul Williams), which she sang in the movie. Among her nonmusicals were *The Owl and the Pussycat* (1970), *What's Up, Doc?* (1972), *The Way We Were* (1973), and *The Main Event* (1979).

Meanwhile, her singing career, which somewhat declined in the late 1960s, took new life beginning in the early 1970s. An important turning point in her resurgence was an engagement in Las Vegas. Tense at first because she knew that everyone's expectations were high, Streisand soon relaxed and fulfilled all possible hopes. Overflow crowds gave numerous standing ovations.

Also during the early 1970s, Streisand broadened her stylistic range. Formerly, concentrating on a nonrock ballad style and singing standards and special material, she had succeeded Judy Garland as the queen of theatrical and torch songs, in the tradition of Fanny Brice and Helen Morgan. Even Streisand's performances of three Beatles songs in her first youth-oriented album, *What about Today* (1967), had been done in a theatrical manner.

Now, however, she expanded her repertory and stylistic versatility by performing soft-rock arrangements and songs by such contemporary musicians as Randy Newman, Harry Nilsson, and Laura Nyro. Streisand displayed her new style in the single of Laura Nyro's "Stoney End" (1970) and in the subsequent album *Stoney End* (1971). The "new" Streisand became the inspiration for such 1970s cabaret-rock performers as Peter Allen, Melissa Manchester, Barry Manilow, and Bette Midler.

Streisand did not, of course, completely abandon her earlier manner. Since 1970 she has continued to use both her older and her newer styles in a long list of successful recordings. Among them are the albums *Barbra Streisand's Greatest Hits* (1970), a compendium of her 1960s triumphs; *Barbra Joan Streisand* (1972), which features a medley of ballads by Burt Bacharach (music) and Hal David (lyrics); *The Way We Were* (1974), containing rock and nonrock ballads; *Lazy Afternoon* (1975), a throwback to her prerock style; *Classical Barbra* (1976), an effective presentation of art songs; *Streisand Superman* (1977), one of her most thoroughly contemporary pop-rock albums; *Songbird* (1978), highlighted by her powerful rendition of "Tomorrow" from the musical *Annie*; *Barbra Streisand's Greatest Hits, Vol. 2* (1978), a compendium of her 1970s material; *Wet* (1979), which consists entirely of songs having images of water, including "No More Tears: Enough Is Enough" (a duet with Donna Summer); *Guilty* (1980), a collaboration with the Bee Gees' Barry Gibb, who wrote all of the songs and sang on two cuts; and *Memories* (1981), which contains many of the songs from the second *Greatest Hits* album, plus some new material.

Streisand spent much of her time during the late 1970s and early 1980s on the movie *Yentl* (1983). Based on a short story (whose movie rights she purchased in 1968) by Isaac Bashevis Singer, the film is set in a turn-of-the-century Polish ghetto and focuses on a young woman (Yentl, played by Streisand) who masquerades as a male so that she can study to become a rabbi. When she falls in love with a young man, she cannot reveal her feelings without exposing her true identity. Thus, she expresses her deepest emotions only to herself, by singing dramatic songs as interior monologues. Besides starring and singing in *Yentl*, Streisand coscripted, produced, and directed the movie—an unprecedented accomplishment for a woman in the history of major films.

Yentl was a very deep personal experience for Streisand. She has said, "I made the commitment to *Yentl* when I read the first four words of the story, 'After her father's death . . .'" Those four words brought back memories of the death of Streisand's own father, Emanuel Streisand, who held a Ph.D. in education and who taught English, history, and psychology at a Brooklyn high school. Because she had had an unhappy relationship with her stepfather, Streisand developed through the years an obsession with putting her real father back into her life.

In the movie, Yentl's father secretly teaches her the Talmud, a study traditionally forbidden to women. When her father dies, she disguises herself as a man so that she can continue her studies in honor of her father. Streisand saw her own father in Yentl's, since both men were intellectual and religious Jews. She also saw herself in Yentl, since each had lost her father, had tried to keep him spiritually involved in her life, and had become enmeshed in a battle with the male establishment while trying to find her own identity. Streisand made the film as a memorial to her father: "*Yentl* gave me the chance to create the father I never had."

While researching for *Yentl*, Streisand sought the advice of rabbis. The rabbi of a Venice, California, synagogue refused her offer of payment for his help, but he said that he would be glad to teach her son, Jason Emanuel (named after her father) Gould, for his bar mitzvah. In gratitude, she has given much financial support to the Pacific Jewish Center's new day school. When the rabbi asked how he could repay such generosity, Streisand said that she would be honored to have the new center named the Emanuel Streisand School, in memory of her father.

In preparation for *Yentl*, Streisand studied Hebrew and the Talmud (studies that also made her feel closer to her devout father). During the same period, she donated a large sum to an institute for Jewish intellectual research and, in 1981, gave $500,000 to the cardiology department at the University of California in Los Angeles (UCLA), which thereupon established a cardiology chair in Emanuel Streisand's name.

Since breaking up with Gould, Streisand has been romantically linked with many well-known personalities.

In the early 1970s her escorts included Pierre Trudeau (the prime minister of Canada) and Ryan O'Neal (the rising young actor). She then lived for nearly ten years with Jon Peters, a hairdresser who became a film producer. Now separated from Peters, Streisand has recently dated such prominent men as the actor Richard Gere and the film director George Lucas.

Selected recordings:

Singles

"People" (1964, Columbia)
"Second Hand Rose" (1966, Columbia)
"Stoney End" (1970, Columbia)
"Where You Lead" (1971, Columbia)
"Sweet Inspiration" (1972, Columbia)
"The Way We Were" (1973, Columbia)
"Evergreen" (1977, Columbia)
"My Heart Belongs to Me" (1977, Columbia)
"Songbird" (1978, Columbia)
"Love Theme from *Eyes of Laura Mars:* Prisoner" (1978, Columbia)
"The Main Event" (1979, Columbia)
"Kiss Me in the Rain" (1980, Columbia)
"Woman in Love" (1980, Columbia)
"Comin' in and out of Your Life" (1981, Columbia)

with Neil Diamond:

"You Don't Bring Me Flowers" (1978, Columbia)

with Barry Gibb:

"Guilty" (1980, Columbia)
"What Kind of Fool" (1981, Columbia)

with Donna Summer:

"No More Tears: Enough Is Enough" (1979, Columbia)

Albums

The Barbra Streisand Album (1963, Columbia)
The Second Barbra Streisand Album (1963, Columbia)
Barbra Streisand: The Third Album (1964, Columbia)
Funny Girl (Broadway cast, 1964, Capitol)
People (1965, Columbia)
My Name Is Barbra (1965, Columbia)
My Name Is Barbra, Two (1966, Columbia)
Color Me Barbra (1966, Columbia)
Je m'appelle Barbra ("My Name Is Barbra," 1966, Columbia)
Simply Streisand (1967, Columbia)
A Happening in Central Park (1967, Columbia)
What about Today (1967, Columbia)
Funny Girl (music track from film, 1968, Columbia)
Barbra Streisand's Greatest Hits (1970, Columbia)
Stoney End (1971, Columbia)
Barbra Joan Streisand (1972, Columbia)
The Way We Were (1974, Columbia)
Lazy Afternoon (1975, Columbia)
Classical Barbra (1976, Columbia)
A Star Is Born (1976, Columbia)
Streisand Superman (1977, Columbia)
Songbird (1978, Columbia)
Barbra Streisand's Greatest Hits, Vol. 2 (1978, Columbia)
Wet (1979, Columbia)
Guilty (1980, Columbia)
Memories (1981, Columbia)
Yentl (1983, Columbia)
Emotion (1984, Columbia)
The Broadway Album (1985, Columbia)

Jule Styne
Composer of
Memorable Popular Songs
(1905-   )

Jule Styne, composer, was born in London, England, on December 31, 1905. His original name was Julius Stein. At the age of six he began to take piano lessons. In 1912 he moved with his parents to the United States, where he became a naturalized citizen in 1916.

The family settled in Chicago, and when Jule was eight he entered the Chicago College of Music. Just seven months later he performed as piano soloist with the Chicago Symphony, soon afterward also appearing with the Detroit and Saint Louis symphony orchestras. He dreamed of becoming a professional concert pianist.

During that time he also took harmony and composition lessons and sang in synagogue choirs under various cantors, including Josef Rosenblatt.

However, his dream of becoming a pianist was shattered one day when he was informed (by the pianist Harold Bauer) that his hands were too small and weak for him ever to achieve concert-level status.

Disheartened by that news and anxious to ingratiate himself with his peers, Jule turned to popular music. From the late 1910s to the mid-1930s, he worked with dance bands and jazz groups in Chicago, performing with such jazz greats as the cornetist Bix Beiderbecke and the clarinetist Benny Goodman. Chicago was then one of the nation's most important jazz centers, and his musical experiences there influenced much of his later creative work. During that time he also attended Northwestern University (1927-31).

In 1927 he married Ethel Rubenstein, daughter of an affluent kosher caterer. They had two children: Stanley and Norton.

In 1932 he changed the spelling of his surname from Stein to Styne to avoid confusion with Jules Stein, a medical doctor and head of the Music Corporation of America.

In the mid-1930s Styne moved to New York City to work as a vocal coach. Two years later he went to the Hollywood section of Los Angeles as a vocal coach for film singers, including Alice Faye and the temperamental moppet Shirley Temple.

Soon he began to compose for the movies. Among his song scores were those for the film musicals *Hit Parade of 1941* (1940), *Anchors Aweigh* (1945), and *The Kid from Brooklyn* (1946). One of filmdom's most successful tunesmiths, he wrote the music for such hits as "I'll Walk Alone" (lyrics, Sammy Cahn) for *Follow the Boys* (1944) and "Three Coins in the Fountain" (lyrics, Sammy Cahn) for the movie of the same name (1954).

However, Styne won even greater renown when he turned to Broadway, beginning with the stage musical *High Button Shoes* (perf. 1947). Later shows included *Gentlemen Prefer Blondes* (perf. 1949), with "Diamonds Are a Girl's Best Friend" (lyrics, Leo Robin); *Bells Are Ringing* (perf. 1956), with "The Party's Over" (lyrics, Betty Comden and Adolph Green); *Gypsy* (perf. 1959), with "Let Me Entertain You" (lyrics, Stephen Sondheim); and *Funny Girl* (perf. 1964), with "People" (lyrics, Bob Merrill).

In 1963 Ethel died, and later that year he married Margaret Brown, a British-born international cover girl. Jule and Margaret Styne had two children: Nicholas and Katherine.

In January 1977 Styne began a whole new aspect to his career, publicly singing his own songs in a husky voice and accompanying himself on the piano. His performances are characterized by a relaxed atmosphere (created in part by his informal chatter) and by a remarkable degree of rapport between him and his audiences.

Margaret Styne has described her husband, one of the most rambunctious personalities in show business, as "irresponsible and illogical" yet "irreplaceable and never ever boring. He calls himself Peter Pan—he must be right because he's never grown up enough to forget where dreams are born. I'm glad."

Selected works:

Stage

High Button Shoes (lyrics, S. Cahn; perf. 1947)
Gentlemen Prefer Blondes (lyrics, L. Robin; perf. 1949), including:
  "Diamond's Are a Girl's Best Friend"
  "Gentlemen Prefer Blondes"
Two on the Aisle (lyrics, B. Comden, A. Green; perf. 1951), including:
  "Give a Little, Get a Little"
Hazel Flagg (lyrics, B. Hilliard; perf. 1953)
Bells Are Ringing (lyrics, B. Comden, A. Green; perf. 1956), including:
  "The Party's Over"
Say, Darling (lyrics, B. Comden, A. Green; perf. 1958)
Gypsy (lyrics, S. Sondheim; perf. 1959), including:
  "Everything's Coming Up Roses"
  "Let Me Entertain You"
  "Small World"
Funny Girl (lyrics, B. Merrill; perf. 1964), including:
  "Don't Rain on My Parade"
  "People"
  "You Are Woman"
Hallelujah, Baby! (lyrics, B. Comden, A. Green; perf. 1967)
Sugar (lyrics, B. Merrill; perf. 1972)

Films
(song scores)

Hit Parade of 1941 (lyrics, W. Bullock; 1940), including:
  "Who Am I?"
The Powers Girl (lyrics, K. Gannon; 1943)
Step Lively (lyrics, S. Cahn; 1944)
Anchors Aweigh (lyrics, S. Cahn; 1945), including:
  "I Fall in Love Too Easily"
The Kid from Brooklyn (lyrics, S. Cahn; 1946)
It Happened in Brooklyn (lyrics, S. Cahn; 1947), including:
  "Time after Time"
Romance on the High Seas (lyrics, S. Cahn; 1948), including:
  "It's Magic"
It's a Great Feeling (lyrics, S. Cahn; 1949), including:
  "It's a Great Feeling"

Songs
(other than those for the above shows and films)

"I'll Walk Alone" (lyrics, S. Cahn; for the film *Follow the Boys*, 1944)
"Three Coins in the Fountain" (lyrics, S. Cahn; for the film *Three Coins in the Fountain*, 1954)

George Szell
Conductor Dedicated to the
Composer's Intention
(1897-1970)

George (originally Georg) Szell, conductor, was born in Budapest, Hungary, on June 7, 1897. His parents were music lovers, his father being an avid opera-goer and his mother being an amateur pianist. In his sixth year the family moved to Vienna, where soon afterward his mother began to give him piano lessons.

He showed such great promise that his parents quickly decided to provide him with a complete musical education. He was removed from public schools and given private tutoring at home in general subjects, while receiving music instruction both at the Vienna Academy of Music and in private lessons. His principal teachers were Richard Robert in piano, Eusebius Mandyczewski in theory, and J. B. Foerster and Max Reger in composition. Young Szell's parents also broadened his musical knowledge by taking him to many concerts and operas; for example, when he was seven, he attended a Vienna Opera performance of Mozart's *Don Giovanni* conducted by the famed Gustav Mahler.

In 1908 Szell made his debut as a pianist and composer when he performed a piece of his own, as well as works by Mozart and Mendelssohn, with the Vienna Symphony Orchestra under the baton of Oskar Nedbal. In the summer of 1913 Szell substituted for an ill conductor in the resort town of Bad Kissingen, and thereafter conducting became the main interest in his career.

In 1914 he appeared as pianist, conductor, and composer with the prestigious Berlin Philharmonic Orchestra, performing as soloist in Beethoven's *Fifth Piano Concerto,* conducting Richard Strauss's *Till Eulenspiegels lustige Streiche* ("Till Eulenspiegel's Merry Pranks"), and conducting a symphony of his own. As a result of that concert, he was engaged as assistant conductor to Richard Strauss at the Royal Opera in Berlin, where he worked from 1915 to 1917.

On Strauss's recommendation Szell was named principal conductor at the Municipal Theater in Strasbourg in 1917. But after one season the theater was closed during the French occupation resulting from World War I.

After two seasons conducting at the German Opera in Prague (1919-21), Szell held principal conductorships at opera theaters in Darmstadt (1921-22), Düsseldorf (1922-24), and Berlin (1924-29). In Berlin he also taught at the Academy of Music (1927-30). He then returned to Prague as music director of the German Opera and the Philharmonic (1929-37).

Meanwhile, Szell had been guest-conducting orchestras and opera companies for many years in Europe, the Soviet Union, and the United States. He made his American debut in 1930, conducting the Saint Louis Symphony Orchestra.

In the late 1930s Nazism forced Szell to look for posts outside its sphere of influence. For example, he served as principal conductor of the Scottish Orchestra in Glasgow from 1937 to 1939.

In 1939, while Szell was on his way back to Europe from an Australian tour, World War II broke out and he decided to remain in New York City. With him was his wife, the former Helene Schulz, a young Czech whom he married in Glasgow in 1938. (It was his second marriage, his first ending when his young wife deserted him for the concertmaster of an orchestra that Szell was conducting.) In America he anglicized his first name to George from the original Georg.

During the war, Szell guest-conducted a number of major American orchestras, such as the National Broadcasting Company (NBC) Symphony, the Chicago Symphony, and the Los Angeles Philharmonic, in addition to doing some teaching, piano playing, and orchestral transcribing. His major occupation during those years was as principal conductor of the German repertory at the Metropolitan Opera in New York City, debuting there in 1942 and remaining for five seasons.

In 1946 Szell became a naturalized American citizen. In the same year, he was engaged as music director of the Cleveland Orchestra, where he remained till 1970 and where he gained his greatest renown. The Cleveland

Orchestra had been without a permanent conductor for a few years, and it was going through a period of severe artistic decline. But Szell immediately began to replace musicians and to institute a system of grinding rehearsals and iron discipline. Eventually he also established a system of apprentice conductors and organized a large chorus as an adjunct to the orchestra, placing it under the direction of Robert Shaw.

Szell developed the Cleveland Orchestra into one of the most highly regarded ensembles in the world. He said that his aim was to combine American virtuosity and beauty of sound with European expressivity and style. His orchestra was especially noted for producing sound having the superb clarity and balance usually associated with fine performances by chamber ensembles.

Like Arturo Toscanini, his idol, Szell was a precisionist dedicated to re-creating the composer's explicit intention, minimizing the imposition of his own personality on the music. He strictly avoided sentimental interpretations and flamboyant methods on the podium. Once, when criticized for a reserved performance of Mozart, he defended himself by saying, "I cannot pour chocolate sauce over asparagus."

With his musicians he was a severe taskmaster, frequently behaving in an abrasive and bullying manner. They called him Cyclops because of the way he fixed his bulging eyes (emphasized by being framed in thick glasses) at them.

Szell's regular conducting repertory extended from Bach to Debussy, with his special forte being the Austro-German tradition from Haydn to Richard Strauss. He promoted only a small amount of twentieth-century music, notably works by Béla Bartók, Leoš Janáček, and William Walton. He did, however, conduct some world premieres with the Cleveland Orchestra, such as Paul Hindemith's *Piano Concerto* in 1947, George Rochberg's *Second Symphony* in 1959, Walter Piston's *Symphonic Prelude* in 1961, and Peter Mennin's *Seventh Symphony* in 1964.

In his later years Szell continued to guest-conduct extensively with orchestras and opera companies around the world, being especially associated with the Amsterdam Concertgebouw Orchestra and the Salzburg Festival. And he toured with the Cleveland Orchestra throughout the United States, Canada, Europe, and the Far East.

In 1970 he returned from the Far East with a fever. Soon it was discovered that he had a heart ailment and bone cancer. Szell died in Cleveland on July 30, 1970.

Henryk Szeryng
"Musician's Musician"
(1918-   )

Henryk Szeryng, violinist, was born in Żelazowa Wola (the birthplace of Chopin), near Warsaw, Poland, on September 22, 1918. At the age of five he began to study piano and harmony with his mother. When he was seven he switched to the violin, taking lessons from Maurice Frenkel, who had been Leopold Auer's assistant in Saint Petersburg before World War I.

After studying for a few years, young Szeryng played the Mendelssohn *Violin Concerto* for the famed musician Bronislaw Huberman, and on the latter's advice the boy was sent to Berlin to study with Carl Flesch. In his early teens Szeryng made his first concert tour, playing in several major European cities. But his parents decided that the life of a wandering child prodigy might do him more harm than good. Therefore, they moved to France

so that he could attend the Paris Conservatory and the Sorbonne. While studying in Paris he was greatly influenced by several musicians, including Jacques Thibaud (violin) and Nadia Boulanger (composition).

Immediately after the Nazi invasion of Poland in 1939, Szeryng volunteered for service in the Polish army. His fluent command of several languages secured for him a position as translator and liaison officer for General Wladyslaw Sikorski, prime minister of the Polish government-in-exile. In that capacity Szeryng went to Mexico in 1942 to find homes for thousands of Polish refugees. During the war, he also gave over three hundred concerts in Allied military camps and hospitals around the world, in addition to making his Carnegie Hall debut in New York City in 1943.

After the war he settled in Mexico, where he became a naturalized citizen in 1946. At about the same time, he began to teach at the National University in Mexico City, abandoning his concert career.

In 1954 the pianist Arthur Rubinstein, during a visit to Mexico, heard Szeryng play and was moved to tears. "He is a musician's musician," Rubinstein said of the young violinist. "Real music lovers want emotion—great

moments—which Szeryng's playing gives them."

Encouraged by Rubinstein, Szeryng resumed his concertizing on an international scale. Since then he has regularly appeared throughout the world as recitalist, chamber musician, and soloist with major orchestras.

He has performed many times in, and has developed a special fondness for, Israel. During the Six-Day War (1967) he gave several special concerts in the United States and Europe, donating the proceeds to the Israel Emergency Fund. In 1972 he donated to the Israel Philharmonic Orchestra a valuable Stradivarius violin, famed as the Hercules but renamed by Szeryng as the Kinor David, or Lyre of David. And he has continued in many other ways to support Israeli institutions, young Israeli talent, and the international quest for lasting peace in the Middle East.

Mexico, however, has continued to be Szeryng's home base. For many years he has been Mexico's official goodwill and cultural ambassador to the world, traveling on a diplomatic passport. He also serves as cultural adviser for the Mexican Foreign Ministry and for the Mexican delegation to the United Nations Educational, Scientific, and Cultural Organization (UNESCO). His

225

efforts in those capacities exemplify his fervent concern for the human condition and his belief in the ability of music to bind peoples together, regardless of their social and cultural differences.

His repertory embraces the whole violin literature from Vivaldi to the present day. Many contemporary works have been dedicated to him by Carlos Chávez, Roman Haubenstock-Ramati, Benjamin Lees, and other composers. Szeryng himself reconstructed Paganini's *Third Violin Concerto* and at a London concert in 1971 gave the first modern performance of the work. His playing is marked by great technical command, stylistic versatility, and elegance.

Szeryng still regularly holds master classes in Mexico and at the Geneva Conservatory. He has dozens of pupils from many countries. In recent years he has made a number of appearances as a conductor.

As great a man as he is a violinist, Szeryng is well known in music circles for his kindly nature and for his generosity. He devotes two months each year to helping young colleagues and students. And besides donating the Stradivarius violin to the Israel Philharmonic Orchestra, he has given valuable violins to the National Symphony Orchestra of Mexico, to his former student Shlomo Mintz, and to his former assistant Espin Yepez.

Szeryng has enjoyed the close friendships of many outstanding musicians, including Arthur Rubinstein and Carlos Chávez. In 1984 he married Waltraud Neu von Neviges.

Michael Tilson Thomas
The New Leonard Bernstein
(1944-   )

Michael Tilson Thomas, conductor, was born in the Hollywood section of Los Angeles, California, on December 21, 1944. He sprang from a family with a tradition in the performing arts. His paternal grandparents, Boris and Bessie Thomashefsky, were among the founders of the Yiddish theater in America. His father, Ted Thomas (who took piano lessons from George Gershwin), scripted, produced, and directed Hollywood films, while his mother, Roberta Thomas, headed research for Columbia Pictures. The great actor Paul Muni was related to the family by virtue of marrying Ted's cousin Bella.

Michael was playing the piano by ear at the age of five, and by the time he was eight he could read music. He began the formal study of piano when he was ten. During his teens he studied piano with John Crown and Muriel Kerr, and harpsichord with Alice Ehlers.

Thomas graduated from North Hollywood High School in 1962 and then entered the University of Southern California (USC) with advanced standing, having already attended classes there during his last two years of high school. At USC his principal teacher in theory and conducting was the composer Ingolf Dahl.

Thomas's USC years (1962-68) were filled with valu-

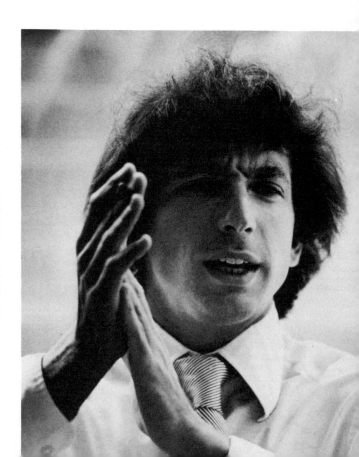

able musical experiences in the Los Angeles area. At the age of nineteen he was named music director of the Young Musicians Foundation Debut Orchestra, a group of student musicians. He also performed as pianist and conductor at the Monday Evening Concerts, which were principally dedicated to presenting modern music; assisted two famous USC teachers, Jascha Heifetz and Gregor Piatigorsky, as a piano accompanist; and conducted the orchestra at the Heifetz-Piatigorsky Concerts.

Invited to the Bayreuth Festival in 1965, Thomas assisted in the preparation for a performance of Wagner's *Parsifal*. In 1967 he conducted at the Ojai Festival in California.

After graduating from USC with a master's degree in 1968, Thomas quickly advanced in the world of music. That summer, on a fellowship, he studied conducting at the Berkshire Music Center at Tanglewood, near Lenox, Massachusetts. While there, he won the Koussevitzky Conducting Prize and conducted the world premiere of Stanley Silverman's *Elephant Steps,* a multimedia "occult" opera.

In 1968 and 1969 Thomas conducted the Youth Concerts of the Los Angeles Philharmonic Orchestra. During that period of time he also guest-conducted the Boston Philharmonia, having earned that privilege by virtue of his winning the Koussevitzky Prize.

In the spring of 1969 William Steinberg heard Thomas guest-conduct the Boston Philharmonia and offered the young man the job of assistant conductor with the immensely prestigious Boston Symphony Orchestra, of which Steinberg was music director. That autumn Thomas made his debut with the orchestra soon after the season opened. Shortly thereafter, on October 22, 1969, Steinberg was conducting the Boston Symphony at the Lincoln Center for the Performing Arts in New York City when he suddenly became ill at intermission. He handed the baton to Thomas, who, with no rehearsal, conducted works by Richard Strauss and Robert Starer so well that he became an instant celebrity. When Steinberg discovered that his illness had been a heart attack, he curtailed his activities, thus providing Thomas with the opportunity to conduct the orchestra more than thirty times during the rest of the 1969-70 season. Thomas was so impressive that at the end of the season he was promoted to associate conductor for the 1970-72 seasons. Becoming increasingly busy with other assignments, Thomas let go of his associate conductorship and accepted an appointment (along with Colin Davis) as principal guest conductor of the Boston Symphony, a post that he held from 1972 to 1974.

During the rest of the 1970s Thomas held two major posts: music director of the Buffalo Philharmonic Orchestra (1971-79), and conductor-commentator for the nationally televised New York Philharmonic Young People's Concerts (1971-77). The latter activity introduced him to millions of viewers and made him one of the most widely known and respected music figures of his time.

Thomas has also conducted at the Berkshire Music Festival (1970 and 1974), directed the Ojai Festival (1972-76), and guest-conducted many leading orchestras in the United States, Europe, and Japan, establishing himself as one of the few American-born conductors with an international following.

In 1975 he made his opera-conducting debut by leading a performance of Gounod's *Faust* with the Cincinnati Opera, and he conducted the American premiere of Berg's *Lulu* with the Sante Fe Opera in 1979. The following year he led the widely praised production of Janáček's *Příhody lišky Bystroušky* (literally, "The Adventures of the Vixen Bystrouška"; known in English as *The Cunning Little Vixen*) at the New York City Opera. During 1981-85 he was a principal guest conductor of the Los Angeles Philharmonic.

Nearly as gifted with words as he is with music, Thomas is a dynamic teacher for both musicians and general audiences. He has directed the Los Angeles Philharmonic Institute and has delivered music lecture-demonstrations at Carnegie Hall in New York City. He now directs the Great Woods Center for the Performing Arts in Massachusetts.

Thomas has a broad range of intellectual and musical interests. Since childhood he has been deeply involved in the physical sciences and in Asiatic studies. His conducting repertory extends from such neglected composers as Perotin (of the medieval period), Josquin des Prez (of the Renaissance period), and Heinrich Schütz (of the baroque period), through the well-known classical and romantic composers, and up to such contemporary experimental composers as Karlheinz Stockhausen and Steve Reich. Deeply committed to winning a larger audience for the entire range of musical expression, he has conducted numerous first performances, including more than a score of world premieres; and in April 1983 at Alice Tully Hall he conducted a program of five New York City premieres in one evening.

Thomas has been referred to as the New Leonard Bernstein because each man had an early career triumph through substituting for an ill colleague and because each gained renown through appearances as conductor-commentator with the New York Philharmonic on TV. In addition, Thomas shares with Bernstein an outgoing personality and a flamboyant podium manner in which his whole body seems to exude music, notably in his version of the "Bernstein bounce."

Richard Tucker
The American Caruso
(1913-75)

Richard Tucker began his career as a cantor and eventually became one of the most highly regarded opera tenors since Caruso. He was born in New York City, New York, on August 28, 1913. His original name was Rubin Ticker. Israel Ticker, his father, was an eastern European immigrant who changed his first name to Samuel in the New World, though he never used the surname Tucker, which the other members of the family adopted.

Richard Tucker in the title role of Giordano's *Andrea Chénier*

Rubin learned traditional Jewish melodies at home from his Orthodox father. Beginning at the age of six, Rubin sang for seven years as a boy alto in the choir under the direction of Samuel Weisser at Tifereth Israel Synagogue on Allen Street in the Lower East Side of the borough of Manhattan in New York City. The boy also studied cantorial singing for many years under Weisser, later taking lessons from the cantorial teacher Zavel Zilberts.

In 1934 he met Sara Perelmuth, sister of the great tenor Jan Peerce. (Later both men were members of the Metropolitan Opera for many years together, but their relationship was never close.) When he wedded Sara in 1936, he was still named Rubin Tucker, and he worked as a fur salesman and as a part-time cantor at Temple Emanuel in Passaic, New Jersey.

In 1937 Tucker began to develop a secular reputation by frequently singing on the *Jewish Daily Forward Hour* radio show in Manhattan. During that year he also changed his first name to Richard, though privately Sara and other members of the family always called him Ruby.

In 1938 he became full cantor at Temple Adath Israel in the Bronx section of New York City, a post that he held till 1943. But Tucker, with Sara's encouragement, was also aiming at an opera career.

Consequently Peerce introduced him to the voice teacher Paul Althouse in 1940. Althouse, a tenor, had become, in 1913, the first native-born and native-trained singer to debut at the Metropolitan Opera with no prior European experience. It was Althouse, Tucker's only secular voice teacher, who perfected the future star's operatic technique.

By 1942 Tucker felt secure enough to enter the Metropolitan Opera Auditions of the Air, but he lost the competition. During that year he also opened his own fur business, which lasted for only a brief time.

His career as a cantor, however, was progressing well. In 1943 he moved up from Temple Adath Israel to the Brooklyn Jewish Center, an immensely prestigious and enjoyable post. There he received spiritual guidance from Rabbi Israel Levinthal, while the music director, the famed Sholom Secunda, wrote many cantorial works for him.

Early in 1944 Tucker rose to national prominence through his performances on the *Chicago Theater of the Air* radio series, which presented capsuled operas and operettas in English translation. He also sang on other network radio shows.

As a result of that exposure Tucker was signed at the

Met later in 1944. He made his Met debut, as Enzo in Ponchielli's *La Gioconda* (literally, "The Joyful Girl"; here, the heroine's name), on January 25, 1945.

Though heavily involved with establishing an opera career, Tucker wanted to remain as cantor at the Brooklyn Jewish Center. But on the recommendation of a panel of five rabbis (by a vote of three to two), he resigned his post there.

Nevertheless, for the rest of his life he continued to offer his services as cantor in many places throughout the world. He himself regarded his greatest single performance, secular or liturgical, as a Sabbath service that he sang in the old synagogue of Vienna, where the famed cantor Salomon Sulzer had officiated in the nineteenth century. Coming only a few years after the horrors of World War II, the occasion had deep significance for Tucker, and his supreme art poured out of him as never before. The worshipers, stunned by what they heard, wept.

On another occasion, a few years later, he officiated at a Sabbath service in a Tel Aviv synagogue. Afterward he led hundreds of worshipers through the city while singing religious hymns.

He also made cantorial recordings, which have affected generations of cantors. In addition, at least one American popular-song performer was strongly influenced by repeatedly listening to Tucker's recorded cantorial music. His name was Elvis Presley.

To Tucker, there was no essential difference between

Richard Tucker (right) as the Duke of Mantua in Verdi's *Rigoletto* with Mado Robin (center) and Elinor Warren (left)

his Jewish cantorial singing and his Italian operatic singing: "They both demand blood and guts," he explained.

But his fame rests primarily on his work in opera. Renowned for his projection of Italian passions, he began his Met career as a lyric tenor, as in his Duke of Mantua in Verdi's *Rigoletto*. However, Tucker's art continued to grow through the years, and he later added dramatic qualities and roles to his vocal resources, excelling, for example, as Canio in Leoncavallo's *I pagliacci* ("The Clowns").

He was praised for the purity and brilliance of his high tones, the evenness of his vocal production, and the combination of sweetness and strength in his voice. Many observers likened him to the great Italian tenor Enrico Caruso (1873-1921).

Tucker and his wife, Sara, had a long-standing ritual that they went through whenever he performed an opera role. While he was onstage, she waited for him in the wing. And when he exited at the end of an act or even in the middle of a scene, they walked arm in arm to his dressing room.

Tucker lived with his wife and three sons—Barry, David, and Henry—in Great Neck, on Long Island, New York. "Every time I sing a role, I sing it twice," he said. "Once on the stage, and then in the car on the way back to Great Neck. My wife and three sons always want to know, Why did you do this, or why did you do that?"

Beginning in the 1950s he made numerous important opera appearances outside the Met, both in America, notably at the San Francisco Opera, and in Europe, being received in such cities as London, Paris, and Milan with acclaim unprecedented for an American-born tenor.

He also gave many concert performances in Israel, including one on the eve of the Six-Day War in 1967, when he broke down with emotion on the stage because he wanted to stay with the Israelis during the coming conflict but had already been convinced that he should leave. Tucker was the recipient of Israel's first Artistic and Cultural Award, and he was given a gold plaque by the National Interfaith Council for his "distinguished service to Israel in its formative years." In addition, he received the Justice Louis D. Brandeis medal for "service to humanity."

In December 1974 he performed the role of Eléazar in Halévy's *La juive* ("The Jewess") in Barcelona, Spain. After many years of ignoring the work, the Met, because of Tucker's vigorous lobbying, was planning to revive the opera in his honor in 1975. But Tucker's last opera appearance was in Barcelona as Don José in Bizet's *Carmen* on Christmas Day of 1974.

Shortly thereafter he returned to the United States for a brief concert tour with Robert Merrill, the great Met baritone. While on that tour, Tucker suddenly died of a heart attack in Kalamazoo, Michigan, on January 8, 1975.

The funeral service was held on the stage of the Metropolitan Opera House, an extremely rare honor. At the end of the service, the stage bare but for the casket and catafalque, the great gold curtain closed on Tucker for the last time.

Sophie Tucker

Last of the Red-hot Mamas
(1884-1966)

Sophie Tucker, singer, was born somewhere in Russia on January 13, 1884. Her mother was en route to the United States when she gave birth to Sophie. The family's name at that time was Kalish. Earlier, however, Sophie's father had run away from his military service and had gone to the United States. Along the way, he made friends with an Italian, Charles Abuza. When Abuza died, Kalish, in fear of being caught by the Russian police, took the dead man's name and papers. Arriving in Boston, he got a job and sent for his pregnant wife. Thus, when the baby girl reached America, she became Sophie, or Sophia (originally Sonia), Abuza.

In 1892 the Abuzas moved from Boston to Hartford, Connecticut, and opened a restaurant. Sophie hated to work in the family business. But one day she began to sing popular songs to bring more customers into the restaurant, and patrons often tipped her for the performances. Theater people who frequented the restaurant inspired and encouraged Sophie to enter show business.

She also appeared in local amateur shows. At first, however, she was shy because of her bulk (145 pounds at the age of thirteen), and she restricted herself to playing the piano accompaniment (with one finger) for the singing of her younger sister, Anna. "Gradually," Sophie later wrote in her autobiography, *Some of These Days* (1945), "at the concerts I began to hear calls for 'the fat girl.' . . . Then I would jump up from the piano stool, forgetting all about my size, and work to get all the laughs I could get." She concluded that "maybe in show business size didn't matter if you could sing and could make people laugh."

Sophie begged her parents to let her leave town so that she could begin a career in show business, but they refused. After graduating from high school, she stayed with the restaurant till 1903, when she married Louis Tuck, a local beer-wagon driver. Louis, however, could not support Sophie and their son, Bert, and the Tucks soon separated.

In 1906, not long after her separation from Tuck, Sophie left her son, Bert, to be raised by her family, with her financial support, while she went to New York City to enter show business under the name Sophie Tucker. She found jobs scarce and often had to literally sing for her supper at restaurants.

Late in 1906 she entered an amateur show, and when the manager saw her he told an associate, according to Tucker's autobiography, "This one's so big and ugly the crowd out front will razz her. Better get some cork and black her up." At that time the use of blackface was still common among white entertainers, but it was usually a matter of choice. Tucker, already insecure about her own appearance, was led to believe that she needed blackface as a disguise. Though she hated blackface, she put it on for her performance in the amateur show, where her robust singing style was very successful.

In December 1906 Tucker made her professional New York City debut, again in blackface, at the Music Hall. She played in various vaudeville theaters for the next couple of years, including Tony Pastor's famed theater in New York City. In 1908 she joined a traveling burlesque show. One day the luggage with her makeup failed to arrive, and she had to perform without blackface. Initially worried, she soon discovered to her pleasant surprise that the audience loved her just as she was. She never used blackface again.

While on tour in 1909, Tucker was spotted by a talent scout and subsequently signed to appear on Broadway in Florenz Ziegfeld's annual *Follies*. During the out-of-town opening night, Tucker stopped the show with her singing. But when the female star, Nora Bayes, objected to competing with the newcomer, Tucker's songs were reduced to one. Then the show opened in New York City, and Bayes's replacement, Eva Tanguay, took Tucker's last song. Tucker, of course, was soon fired. During that unhappy experience, though, she met a black maid, Mollie Elkins, who became a lifelong friend.

Badly shaken by the *Follies* episode, Tucker temporarily lost her voice. But with Elkins's patient help and encouragement, the voice returned after a brief rest. To avoid another *Follies*-type disaster in the future, Tucker engaged the William Morris Agency to manage her career, which thereafter flourished.

Returning to vaudeville, Tucker soon became a major star, specializing in belting out ragtime songs. She also developed a distinctive stage personality in which her large dimensions became an asset, as in her humorous double-entendre singing of such songs as "Nobody Loves a Fat Girl, but Oh, How a Fat Girl Can Love."

In 1911 Tucker appeared in two musical comedies in Chicago, and while she was there she introduced "Some of These Days," which came to be her trademark song. The first peak of her career came in 1914 when she appeared at the Palace Theater in New York City, the most prestigious house in vaudeville.

In 1914 she also married her pianist, Frank Westphal, in Chicago. At the party after the ceremony, the wedding march from Wagner's *Lohengrin* was played by the celebrated concert pianist Ignace Paderewski, who happened to be in the restaurant at the time. However, the marriage soon began to fail. After setting Frank up in a garage business, Sophie went on with her career alone. They were divorced in 1919.

During World War I the fashion in popular music changed from ragtime to jazz. Tucker, getting in on the ground floor of the new music, organized her own jazz band, called the Five Kings of Syncopation, and billed herself as the Queen of Jazz.

After her father's death in 1915, Tucker suddenly began to incorporate sad, sentimental ballads into her performances. She also began to dramatize songs by introducing them with skits and monologues that intensified the emotional impact. By 1920 she had polished her act into its final form: a booming voice, a dramatic and emotional presentation, a suggestive kind of humor, and a repertory of songs ranging from lively jazz to tear-jerking ballads.

After five years at Reisenweber's restaurant in New York City, Tucker and the Five Kings of Syncopation broke up their act and went their separate ways. Soon thereafter, in 1922, Tucker made the first of many tours in England, where she immediately became a huge success and where she remained extremely popular throughout the rest of her career.

Back in the United States, she made a two-year vaudeville tour that began at the Palace. In 1925 she introduced "My Yiddishe Momme" (or "My Yiddisha Mama"), which became one of the songs with which she was most closely identified.

Also in 1925 she returned to England, where she was acclaimed at London's famed Kit-Kat Klub and at various music halls. On the trip home she learned of the death of her mother, and for three months she could not bring herself to sing.

It was in 1928, at the Palace, that Tucker introduced the song "I'm the Last of the Red-hot Mamas." From that time forward she was billed as the Last of the Red-hot Mamas, an epithet by which she became permanently known to audiences everywhere she performed.

In 1928 she also married Al Lackey, a fan who had become her personal manager. It was another short-lived marriage, and they were divorced in 1933.

Though successful in England, Tucker had difficulty on the Continent because of the language barrier. But her rendition of "My Yiddishe Momme" became very popular in Vienna, and she was invited to broadcast the song over the Berlin radio in 1931. However, after Hitler came to power in 1933, her existing records were smashed and further sales of her recordings were banned.

In the early 1930s, when American vaudeville was rapidly dying out, Tucker successfully made the transition to nightclubs. In England, however, music halls continued the tradition of live variety shows, in which Tucker was always most comfortable and effective. In 1934 she went back to England on a tour that was climaxed by her command performance for King George V.

In America Tucker worked not only in nightclubs but also in other major forums for variety stars. She appeared on Broadway in the *Earl Carroll Vanities of 1924*, as well as in the shows *Leave It to Me* (1938) and *High Kickers* (1941). Her musical films included *Honky Tonk* (1929), *Broadway Melody of 1938* (1937), and *Follow the Boys* (1944). She also performed regularly on radio and later on TV, notably on Ed Sullivan's TV show.

By the late 1930s Tucker was already being referred to as a national "institution." Particularly with her explosive live performances, she maintained her popularity for over fifty years. Besides "Some of These Days" and "My Yiddishe Momme," songs with which Tucker was closely identified included the ragtime classic "The Darktown

Strutters' Ball," as well as "Honey Boy" and "How Ya Gonna Keep 'Em down on the Farm after They've Seen Paree?"

Tucker's personal life, however, was troubled by the fact that though she always wanted to be home with her family, her career frequently required her to travel. In marriage, she had to face the inner conflict of simultaneously wanting a strong man and wanting independence. She became the provider and leader in each of her three marriages.

Tucker was a giving person, being involved with much fund raising and philanthropy. In 1945 she established the Sophie Tucker Foundation, and ten years later she endowed a chair in the theater arts at Brandeis University. Also an activist, she helped to organize the American Federation of Actors (later absorbed into the American Guild of Variety Artists, a division of Actors' Equity), which elected her president in 1938.

Even late in life Tucker held her audiences. In the 1950s she appealed to the new generation with her self-effacing humor: "I'm the 3-D Mama with the Big Wide Screen." In 1962 she gave another command performance in London. And in late 1965, at nearly eighty-two years of age, she made a successful appearance in the Latin Quarter of New York City. Tucker died a few months later in the same city on February 9, 1966.

Selected recordings:

Singles

"That Lovin' Rag" (1910, Edison)
"Reuben Rag" (1911, Edison)
"Some of These Days" (1911, Edison)
"You Can't Remember What I Can't Forget" (1919, Aeolian Vocalion)
"Mama Goes Where Papa Goes" (in Yiddish, 1924, Okeh)
"After You've Gone" (1927, Okeh)
"My Yiddishe Momme" (English and Yiddish versions, 1928, Columbia)
"I'm the Last of the Red-hot Mamas" (1929, Victor)
"Sophisticated Lady" (1934, Parlophone)
"The Lady Is a Tramp" (1937, Decca)

Rosalyn Tureck
High Priestess of Bach
(1914-)

Rosalyn Tureck, pianist, was born in Chicago, Illinois, on December 14, 1914. Her parents came to the United States from Russia with the surname Turk (her father being of Turkish origin), which was inadvertently changed to Tureck by an American immigration official. Both parents were descendants of numerous rabbis and cantors, and Rosalyn's mother herself was a fine singer.

At the age of four Rosalyn began to improvise at the piano with both hands. When she was eight, she had her first formal lessons, with a local teacher. The following year she won a contest for young pianists. The prize was a debut recital, which she soon gave with such success that it was followed by another a few months later.

She then began to study with her second teacher, Sophia Brilliant-Liven, who had been an assistant teacher to Anton Rubinstein at the Saint Petersburg Conservatory in Russia. After four years (1925-29) with Brilliant-

Liven, Tureck studied for two years (1929-31) with the concert pianist Jan Chiapusso, who encouraged her to concentrate on the music of J. S. Bach. Under Chiapusso's guidance she also began her musicological studies and learned the characteristics of the harpsichord, the clavichord, and the organ. At the age of fifteen she began to give all-Bach recitals in Chicago.

Then, after a brief period of study with Gavin Williamson, Tureck entered the Juilliard School of Music in New York City in the autumn of 1931. Her piano teacher there was Olga Samaroff, a world-famous pianist.

But the most influential experience of Tureck's stay at the Juilliard School was an incident that occurred just before her seventeenth birthday, in early December 1931. She was practicing Bach's "Prelude and Fugue in A Minor" from the first book of the *Well-tempered Clavier* when she suddenly lost consciousness. She awoke to a sort of epiphany—a sense of having an immediate and intuitive insight into the structure, psychology, and form of Bach's music. It was a new concept of Bach and required an entirely new technique for playing his music.

Tureck had to create the new technique herself, helped by the foundation that she had received from her earlier musicological and instrumental studies of Bach begun under Chiapusso. Her new method involved, for one thing, an intellectual process that grasped the structures and forms in Bach's music as being based on procedures quite different from those found in classical and romantic music, which emphasize harmony, as opposed to Bach's emphasis on counterpoint. She also changed her fingering apparatus, particularly by making each finger as independent as possible. Tureck pulled away from the modern piano technique that strives for lush sonorities and virtuoso display. Instead, her Bach performances came to be characterized by a fidelity to Bach's own scores. "I do what Bach tells me to do," she explained. "I never tell the music what to do." Because of her studies in quest of being as accurate as possible in her performances, Tureck eventually became a highly regarded musical scholar.

Meanwhile, her work with Samaroff continued for four years. Tureck graduated from the Juilliard School in 1935, the same year in which she made her major debut by playing the Brahms *Second Piano Concerto* with Eugene Ormandy conducting the Philadelphia Orchestra at Carnegie Hall in New York City.

In 1937 she gave a highly praised series of six all-Bach recitals at Town Hall in New York City, in which she played the forty-eight preludes and fugues from the *Well-tempered Clavier*, as well as the *Goldberg Variations* and other works. Since then Tureck has made numerous American and Canadian tours, playing not only Bach but

also standard classical and romantic fare.

She made her European debut in 1947 and was astounded at the reception that she was given. "People would run after my car and throw flowers in the window," she said. For many years, in fact, her reputation was much greater in Europe than in the United States. She has also toured in South Africa, South America, Israel, the Far East, and India.

The beginning of Tureck's wide recognition in America came in December 1958 when she performed simultaneously as soloist and conductor of two Bach concertos with the New York Philharmonic, thus becoming the first woman ever to conduct that prestigious orchestra. She has also appeared as soloist-conductor with many other major orchestras, including the London Philharmonia (1958), the Israel Philharmonic (1963), and the Kol Israel Orchestra (1963).

In 1977 she celebrated the fortieth anniversary of her famed 1937 all-Bach recitals by repeating the series in Carnegie Hall. One of the 1977 concerts consisted of the remarkable feat of playing the lengthy *Goldberg Variations* twice, once on the harpsichord and once on the piano.

Tureck is the only pianist who regularly plays the harpsichord and the clavichord in public. She has also performed on the organ, the fortepiano (an eighteenth-century piano), and the Moog synthesizer. And to demonstrate the universality of Bach's ornamentation, she has given concerts of his compositions juxtaposed with Chinese and Indian music.

Tureck has been extremely active as an organizer. In 1951 she founded, and till 1955 directed, the Composers of Today, a society for the performance of international contemporary music. She also established the Tureck Bach Players (1957); the International Bach Society (1966), since 1981 known as the Tureck Bach Institute; and the Institute for Bach Studies (1968).

She has taught at the Philadelphia Conservatory of Music (1935-42), the Juilliard School (1943-55), the University of California at San Diego (1966-72), and several other institutions.

In 1964 she married George Wallingford Downs, a scientist. But he died later that year.

Tureck, dubbed the High Priestess of Bach by the press, has written the book *An Introduction to the Performance of Bach* (1960), as well as many articles on the same subject. She has recorded all of Bach's major keyboard works, has edited pieces by Bach and other composers for publication, and has appeared on TV series (such as *Today* and *Camera Three)* and in special films (such as *Bach on the Frontier of the Future,* 1980).

Alfred Wallenstein
First Great American-born Conductor
(1898-1983)

Alfred Wallenstein, conductor and cellist, was born in Chicago, Illinois, on October 7, 1898. He was a descendant of Albrecht von Wallenstein, a hero of the Thirty Years' War and the inspiration for a famous trilogy of plays by Schiller.

When Alfred was seven he moved to Los Angeles with his parents, whose contractor's supply house in Chicago had burned down. He began to take piano lessons but soon changed to the cello, which he studied with Elsa Johanna Bierlich von Grofé, mother of the composer Ferde Grofé.

From the age of nine young Wallenstein played the cello in public, appearing with his school orchestra and with other amateur groups in the Los Angeles area. Soon he was fulfilling professional engagements in hotels, restaurants, and theaters. For a time he also provided "inspirational music" during the filming of silent movies. At fifteen he was billed as the Wonder-Boy Cellist when he toured the nation on the Orpheum vaudeville circuit, appearing in shows that featured such stars as Vernon and Irene Castle, Will Rogers, and Sophie Tucker.

Just before turning eighteen, Wallenstein joined the cello section of the San Francisco Symphony Orchestra, his first important post in serious music. He spent one season (1916-17) there, after which he toured South and Central America as solo cellist with the famed ballerina Anna Pavlova.

In 1919 he became a cellist with the Los Angeles Philharmonic Orchestra. During his one season (1919-20) there he decided to turn to the field of medicine. Consequently he went back to vaudeville for a time to earn enough for his medical studies. Later in 1920 he went to Europe to study medicine at the University of Leipzig, meanwhile studying cello with Julius Klengel in the same city. Fortunately for the world of music, Wallenstein finally determined to drop medicine and to pursue his career as a cellist.

In 1922 he returned to the United States and joined the cello section of the Chicago Symphony Orchestra, where he soon became principal cellist, often performed as soloist, and remained till 1929. During that time he also gave recitals and served as head of the cello department at the Chicago Musical College (1927-29).

Wallenstein then became principal cellist with the New York Philharmonic under the legendary maestro Arturo Toscanini. The conductor appreciated Wallenstein's ability and made certain that the young cellist performed as soloist at least once each season with the orchestra under Toscanini's own direction. During his

years with the New York Philharmonic (1929-36), Wallenstein continued to give recitals and to appear as guest soloist with other orchestras.

It was Toscanini himself who suggested that Wallenstein take up the baton. In 1931 Wallenstein made his conducting debut by leading a small orchestra in a radio

broadcast out of New York City, thus becoming one of the pioneers in presenting classical music over the air. In the summer of 1932 he conducted at the Hollywood Bowl.

In 1933 he became the founder and director of the Wallenstein Sinfonietta, which he organized for the purpose of playing serious music over radio station WOR. Two years later he was appointed music director of the station, where he remained till 1945. While there, he set very high standards for programming, including such unusual features as all of the Mozart piano concertos and many Bach cantatas. In 1936 he left his first-desk chair at the New York Philharmonic to concentrate on his WOR work, as well as to guest-conduct many orchestras.

Having earned a distinguished reputation by his work in New York City, Wallenstein was then appointed music director and principal conductor of the Los Angeles Philharmonic in 1943, thus becoming the first American-born musician to head a major American symphonic organization. He found the orchestra in a state of artistic deterioration and built it into its present status as one of the premiere orchestras in the world.

During his tenure in Los Angeles (1943-56), Wallenstein created an annual series of programs called Symphonies for Youth, in which the Los Angeles Philhar-monic gave both concerts and nationwide radio broadcasts specifically designed for audiences of children. It was his wife, Virginia Wilson (an accomplished concert pianist whom he had married in 1924), who encouraged him to develop the programs. Her idea and his fulfillment of it produced a wonderfully successful series that exposed countless young listeners to the joys of classical music.

After leaving the Los Angeles Philharmonic in 1956, Wallenstein guest-conducted extensively for five years. He then conducted the Symphony of the Air in New York City (1961-63), headed the Ford Foundation project for young American conductors (1962-64), and spent his final years teaching at the Juilliard School of Music in New York City.

In 1929 Wallenstein performed the solo part in the world premiere of Frederick Stock's *Cello Concerto,* with the Chicago Symphony under the composer. As a conductor he led the National Broadcasting Company (NBC) Symphony in the world premiere of Oscar Levant's *Piano Concerto in One Movement* in 1942 and the Los Angeles Philharmonic in the first performance of Ernst Krenek's *Cello Concerto* in 1954.

Wallenstein died in New York City on February 7 (not, as first reported, February 8), 1983.

Bruno Walter
Articulate Conductor
(1876-1962)

Bruno Walter, conductor, was born in Berlin, Germany, on September 15, 1876. His original name was Bruno Schlesinger. His father, a bookkeeper, often hummed melodies from operas and operettas to the boy. Bruno's mother was a talented amateur pianist and liked to sing Schubert songs. The boy also had memorable early musical experiences at the local Reform synagogue, where the choral chants and organ music had a profound effect on him.

Beginning at the age of six, Bruno received piano lessons, first from his mother and then from the local teacher Konrad Kaiser. At eight Bruno entered the Stern Conservatory in Berlin, where he studied piano with Heinrich Ehrlich, theory with Ludwig Bussler, and composition and conducting with Robert Radeke. Bruno's original intention was to become a concert pianist, and at nine he made his first public appearance by playing the piano at one of the school's recitals. At twelve, in February 1889, he made his public off-campus debut by playing a concerto with the famed Berlin Philharmonic Orchestra.

But a few months after that debut, his career focus suddenly began to change. Previously he had paid little attention to conductors. But one evening he happened to take a seat on a high platform behind the kettledrums at a Berlin Philharmonic concert conducted by Hans von

Bülow. From his vantage point, Bruno "saw in Bülow's face the glow of inspiration and the concentration of energy." It seemed to him that Bülow "had transformed those hundred performers into his instrument, and that he was playing it as a pianist played the piano." Bruno now decided to become a conductor himself.

In 1893 he left the Stern Conservatory to become a coach at the Cologne Opera, where the following year he made his conducting debut in a performance of Albert Lortzing's *Der Waffenschmied* ("The Armorer"). In 1894 he went to the Hamburg Opera to be assistant conductor under Gustav Mahler, who by example inspired Bruno with a sense of dedication to hard work and high ideals. When Mahler decided to leave Hamburg, he encouraged Bruno to do the same, even finding a job for the younger man at Breslau, where Bruno went in 1896.

Theodor Loewe, director of the Breslau Opera, advised the new conductor to change his family name of Schlesinger (derived from the German word meaning "Silesian") because of its frequent occurrence in Breslau, capital of the region of Silesia. It was then that he adopted the surname Walter (which became legal when he took Austrian citizenship in 1911). He chose the name because of its use for characters in Wagner's *Tannhäuser* and *Die Meistersinger* ("The Mastersingers").

After conducting for one season in Breslau and one in Pressburg, Walter was scheduled in 1898 to go to the

highly regarded theater in Riga. On his way to Riga, Walter took a boat across the Baltic Sea. One of the passengers was Elsa Wirthschaft (whose stage name was Elsa Korneck), a lyric-dramatic soprano of the Riga Opera, who sat in a corner, pale with seasickness. "But no matter," Walter later recalled, "one look was enough to convince me that there sat my future wife." Their engagement was announced on Christmas Eve in 1898, and they were married in May 1901. They had two daughters: Lotte and Gretel.

Walter went from Riga to Berlin in 1900, and then, just after his marriage in 1901, he joined Mahler, at the latter's request, at the Vienna Opera. Walter's reputation grew rapidly while he was in Vienna, though he had a brief period during which he lost his confidence because of verbal attacks on him by the anti-Mahler faction in the city. He guest-conducted widely, notably in London, Moscow, and Rome. Mahler left Vienna in 1907 (and was replaced by Felix Weingartner), but Walter stayed till 1912. After Mahler's death in 1911, Walter had the immense distinction of conducting the world premieres of the great conductor-composer's *Das Lied von der Erde* ("The Song of the Earth") in Munich in 1911 and the *Ninth Symphony* in Vienna in 1912.

In 1913 Walter became music director of the Munich Opera, where he stayed till 1922. In 1923 he made his American debut by conducting the New York Symphony Orchestra. He returned to the United States in 1924 and in the same year began regular assignments at London's Covent Garden (1924-31), followed in 1925 by the beginning of his long association with the Salzburg Festival. He also held posts at the Municipal Opera in the Charlottenburg district of Berlin (1925-29) and at the Gewandhaus Concerts in Leipzig (1929-33).

In the late 1920s and early 1930s, Walter made many more guest-conducting appearances in America; and in 1932 he began his long association with the New York Philharmonic. In March 1933 he returned to Germany from an American tour to find that Hitler had been made chancellor and that "the gates of hell had opened." According to Walter, he was officially informed that if he gave his next scheduled concert in Germany, the hall would be smashed to pieces.

He left Germany, served as associate conductor of the Amsterdam Concertgebouw Orchestra (1934-39), and continued his guest appearances with the New York Philharmonic. In 1936 he returned to the Vienna Opera as music director. But in 1938 the Nazis took Austria, and Walter was uprooted again. His elder daughter, Lotte, was arrested in Vienna in March 1938 for her anti-Nazi activities. After some tense days, she was released unharmed in April. Later that year Walter was granted French citizenship. However, in 1939, after his younger daughter, Gretel, had died and World War II had begun, Walter, along with his wife and elder daughter, settled in the United States.

Walter guest-conducted a number of American symphony orchestras during World War II, notably the Los Angeles Philharmonic and the New York Philharmonic. He also began to conduct at the Metropolitan Opera, with which he was associated for several seasons between 1941 and 1957. His first opera at the Metropolitan was *Fidelio,* Beethoven's paean to liberty, a poignant reminder of Walter's own loss of liberty in his homeland. The audience understood the significance of the work and gave Walter a tremendous ovation. In 1945 his wife died, and in 1946 he became an American citizen.

After the war, Walter began to make conducting visits to Europe, including Edinburgh, Salzburg, Vienna, and Munich. At the same time, he continued to perform in the United States, most frequently with the New York Philharmonic. He also appeared on the podium in the film *Carnegie Hall* (1947).

Walter was an intelligent, articulate conductor who got what he wanted from an orchestra by explaining and encouraging, not by shouting and berating. He used a moderate range of gesture, though he was a thorough romantic in an antiromantic age. He believed in music as a moral force and tried to present music that was "informed by a universal spiritual presence."

Walter composed some works of his own, mostly between 1900 and 1910, including symphonies, chamber works, choral pieces, and songs. He also wrote five books, including *Gustav Mahler* (German, 1936; second German edition, 1957; English, 1937; second English edition, 1941; new English translation, with additions, 1958), *Theme and Variations: An Autobiography* (English, 1946), and *Von der Music und vom Musizieren* (German, 1957; English, as *Of Music and Music-Making,* 1961).

In 1957 Walter had a heart attack, and thereafter he limited his apperances. For the next few years he concentrated on making recordings, particularly of the Austro-German romantic giants Beethoven, Brahms, Bruckner, and Mahler. His recordings of Mahler helped in the belated general acceptance of the works of that composer, Walter's old mentor and friend.

Walter spent his last years in his Beverly Hills, California, home. He died there of a heart attack on February 17, 1962.

Leonard Warren

Great Verdi Baritone
(1911-60)

Leonard Warren, baritone, was born of Russian immigrants in New York City, New York, on April 21, 1911. His original surname was Warenoff (or Varenov), but the family later Americanized the name to Warren.

After graduating from Evander Childs High School, he went to work for his father, a wholesale fur dealer. A few years later, with no prior musical training and with little encouragement from his parents, Warren began to study voice with Will J. Stone at the Greenwich House Music School. He took his music lessons in the evenings, while the daytime hours were still devoted to the fur trade.

However, during the early 1930s the Great Depression severely hurt his father's business, and young Warren left to take a series of other jobs, including one as a grease monkey in a service station. In 1935 his prospects brightened when he earned a job in the Radio City Music Hall Glee Club. In the same year, he began serious vocal studies with Sidney Dietch.

In 1938 Warren was a cowinner of the Metropolitan Opera Auditions of the Air. As a consequence, he was given five thousand dollars by George A. Martin, president of the Sherwin-Williams Company, sponsor of the auditions. With that award Warren was able to quit the Radio City Music Hall and go to Italy.

In Milan he studied opera roles with Giuseppe Pais and Riccardo Picozzi. During his stay there he met, and fell in love with, Agatha Leifflen, who also had studied voice in New York City. They wedded in 1941. The marriage led Warren to convert to Catholicism, his wife's religion.

In the autumn of 1938 he returned from Italy to New York City, and in November he gave his first Metropolitan Opera House performance, a Sunday-evening concert consisting of opera excerpts. At that time Warren, still extremely inexperienced, had actually witnessed only one opera production. The following January he made his official Met debut in a complete role, singing Paolo in Verdi's *Simon Boccanegra*.

For several years he sang a variety of roles, but eventually he became renowned primarily as one of the world's foremost Verdi baritones, especially for his title part in *Rigoletto*. Among his other outstanding Verdi roles were Amonasro in *Aïda,* Iago in *Otello,* and the title parts in *Falstaff* and *Simon Boccanegra*. However, he was also skilled at portraying such roles as Barnaba in Ponchielli's *La Gioconda* (literally, "The Joyful Girl"; here, the heroine's name), Scarpia in Puccini's *Tosca,* and Tonio in Leoncavallo's *I pagliacci* ("The Clowns").

Warren had to work hard to overcome two handicaps: a lack of dramatic experience and an inability to learn new music quickly. He solved the first problem by observing fellow performers and by absorbing three years of coaching from Giuseppe de Luca. To attain confidence with new music, he devoted nine to twelve months of preparation to each new role.

Besides performing with the Met, Warren appeared a number of times with other major American opera companies, notably the San Francisco Opera. His foreign work included opera performances in Buenos Aires (1942, 1943, 1946), Rio de Janeiro (summers, 1942-45), Mexico City (1948), Milan (at La Scala, 1953), and Moscow (at the Bolshoi Theater, 1958).

In addition, he made many concert tours of North America, both in recitals and as soloist with major symphony orchestras. He also sang on radio shows and TV programs, including the first operatic concert ever televised (March 10, 1940).

Warren's voice was large, smooth, expressive, rich in timbre, and beautifully controlled from low G up nearly 2½ octaves to the tenor's high C. No one could equal his ability to crescendo and decrescendo in the upper register. And his enunciation of English and Italian was excellent.

Warren pushed his nervous system so hard to reach

Leonard Warren in the title role of Verdi's *Simon Boccanegra*

his goals that, like many other perfectionists, he was often intolerant of opinions that differed from his own. Consequently he created many needless tensions with coworkers by telling them how to do their jobs, including singers, conductors, and directors.

Nevertheless, he led an unpretentious lifestyle. He liked model railroading, tinkering with mechanical objects, and cruising the waters of Long Island Sound.

On March 4, 1960, Warren was onstage at the Met, portraying Don Carlo in Verdi's *La forza del destino* ("The Force of Destiny"), when he suddenly collapsed of a massive cerebral hemorrhage. The curtain was immediately lowered, and backstage a short time later he was pronounced dead.

Leonard Warren in the title role
of Verdi's *Falstaff*

Kurt Weill
Innovative Theater Composer
(1900-1950)

Kurt Weill, composer, was born in Dessau, Germany, on March 2, 1900. His father, Albert Weill, was chief cantor at the synagogue in Dessau from 1899 to 1919 and a composer of liturgical music. Kurt's mother was an amateur pianist. His parents taught him music and gave him many opportunities to attend operas and concerts. At twelve he showed an interest in composition, and at fourteen he began to take piano lessons from Albert Bing (conductor at the local opera), who encouraged young Weill's composing.

In 1918, after a few years with Bing, Weill went to the Berlin Academy of Music, where he studied counterpoint with Friedrich Koch, conducting with Rudolf Krasselt, and composition with Engelbert Humperdinck. In less than a year Weill left the academy, partly because of his financial difficulty and partly because of the school's conservative attitude.

Returning to Dessau in 1919, Weill, through Bing's efforts, took a post as coach at the local opera. Three months later he became conductor of a municipal opera company in Lüdenscheid, where he stayed till the summer of 1920.

Then, feeling the need for more study, Weill spent three years in Berlin with Ferruccio Busoni's master class in composition at the Prussian Academy of Arts. From the classicist Busoni, Weill derived his lifelong musical characteristics of economy of means, directness of statement, and clarity of texture. He also privately studied counterpoint with Philipp Jarnach from 1921 to 1922. While in Berlin, he composed his first large works in a severely modernistic, dissonant idiom, such as the *First Symphony* (1921) and the *Sinfonia sacra* ("Sacred Symphony," 1922).

However, Weill himself soon became dissatisfied with his own musical style. He began to rethink the role of a composer in modern society. While he witnessed the political and moral collapse of the old Germany, he also saw the rise of the new mass-oriented jazz-age pop culture. Weill gradually absorbed the blues, Charlestons, foxtrots, and so on that he heard in the cabarets of post-World War I Berlin. He would eventually apply transformations of such material to his stage music and become one of the most successful and important theater composers of the twentieth century.

In 1922 he hinted at his future direction when he composed his first commissioned work: *Zaubernacht* ("Magic Night," perf. 1922), a children's ballet with singing. The public success of that work encouraged Weill to aim at communicating with a mass audience instead of with the limited number of connoisseurs who had understood his earlier music.

In 1923 he left Busoni's master class and began to give private lessons in theory and composition. Among his pupils were at least two future greats: the pianist Claudio Arrau and the conductor Maurice Abravanel. In 1924 he wrote the first of many published articles that supplemented his income during the next several years.

Also in 1924 Weill developed associations with two people who would profoundly affect his life and career: Georg Kaiser and Lotte Lenya. Ready to embark on his first major theatrical work, Weill became a frequent house guest of the expressionist playwright Kaiser at the latter's home in Grünheide, a Berlin suburb. There they worked on the libretto for the opera *Der Protagonist* ("The Protagonist").

On one such visit Weill met another guest, the young Viennese dancer Karoline Blamauer, who went by the stage name Lotte Lenya. They had been introduced two years earlier, when Lenya auditioned for a part in Weill's *Zaubernacht*. But on that occasion Lenya, standing on the stage, could not see Weill, seated in the darkened theater. She won the part but decided not to take it, and their paths did not cross again till they met accidentally at Kaiser's.

Soon falling in love, Weill and Lenya married in 1926, and she thereafter turned to singing and starred in many of his theatrical successes. "Whatever melody comes to me," he once said, "I first hear it as sung by Lenya."

With Kaiser, Weill forged a close creative partnership that lasted till Weill left Germany ten years later. Their first cooperative effort, *Der Protagonist* (1925), was produced to wide acclaim in 1926.

Weill's next stage work, *Royal Palace* (a ballet-opera with a libretto by Ivan Goll, 1926), was produced in 1927 with much less success, probably because of its experimental character. It combined pantomime with film, and play with opera.

Back with Kaiser again, Weill then composed the music for the comic opera *Der Zar lässt sich photographieren* ("The Czar Has Himself Photographed," 1927). Here, for the first time, Weill openly adopted elements of jazz and other popular idioms. When it was produced with great success in 1928, some serious musicians accused him of "betraying" art. Weill responded by saying, "I write for today. I don't care for posterity."

Thus, he identified himself with the movement known as *Zeitkunst* ("art of the present"), in which contemporary topics were presented in a popular mode of expression. One musical offshoot of the movement was known as *Gebrauchsmusik* ("music for use"), that is, music understandable by the masses and intended for practical use by amateurs or professionals. Such music, however, did not exclude the use of dissonant counterpoint and other modernistic devices. With Paul Hindemith, Weill helped to shape the concept of *Gebrauchsmusik*.

Weill teamed up with the German playwright Bertolt Brecht to create some of the most notable musical stage works of the twentieth century. They began with what is traditionally known in Germany as a *Singspiel* (literally, "sing-play"), a comic opera with spoken dialogue. But to emphasize the songlike, rather than operalike, nature of what they were trying to do, they coined a new word to describe the work: *Songspiel*, drawing on the English word *song* because German *Lied* had concert-hall associations and German *Gesang* was too lofty. They called the work *Mahagonny Songspiel* (comp. and perf. 1927), which established the model for their future efforts: satirical, ideologically motivated, and artistically sophisticated, including a musical fusion of popular elements and modern concert techniques. Two years later they prepared an expanded version, entitled *Aufstieg und Fall der Stadt Mahagonny* ("Rise and Fall of the City of Mahagonny"; comp. 1929, perf. 1930). The work is a satire on capitalistic corruption and is set in a fictitious city in the southern part of the United States.

In 1928 Weill, with Brecht, created his most famous work: *Die Dreigroschenoper,* known to American audiences, through a 1954 version with English lyrics by Marc Blitzstein, as *The Threepenny Opera*. Variously referred to as a ballad opera or a *Stücke mit Musik* ("play with music"), the work is based on the plot of *The Beggar's Opera* (perf. 1728) by John Gay, adapted in such a way as to be a political satire of 1920s Germany. At the historic premiere in Berlin on August 31, 1928, Lotte Lenya starred as Jenny.

The Threepenny Opera is one of the most original and influential works in the modern musical theater. Its sophisticated, jazz-inflected score contains the celebrated song "Mack the Knife." In a perfect collaboration of composer and librettist, Weill and Brecht not only captured the mood of despair in 1920s Germany (a nation nearing a spiritual breakdown) but also endowed the ambience of that locale and moment with a meaning of universal and timeless significance.

The financial success of *The Threepenny Opera* allowed Weill to drop his teaching and writing. From 1929 on he earned his living entirely by composing.

Happy End (comp. and perf. 1929), a Weill-Brecht comedy, is set in 1919 Chicago and focuses on mock gangsters.

Der Jasager ("The Yes-Sayer," comp. and perf. 1930) is a school opera by Weill and Brecht. Based on an old Japanese legend, it once again shows Weill's interest in *Gebrauchsmusik* in that it was written in an idiom simple enough to be performed by children.

Weill's last opera in Germany was *Der Silbersee* ("The Silver Lake," comp. and perf. 1933), with a libretto by Kaiser. But by then the Nazis had taken over in Germany, and Weill was a marked man, not only as a Jew but also as a composer of "decadent" modernism. Taking only a few personal possessions, Weill and his wife fled to France, where they remained from 1933 to 1935.

In 1933 Weill composed *Die sieben Todsünden der Kleinbürger* ("The Seven Deadly Sins of the Petty Bourgeoisie," perf. 1933), the most important work of his French stay. Based on a Brecht libretto, the work is a ballet with singing in which twin sisters (played by Lotte Lenya and the dancer Tilly Losch in the first production) try to earn enough money to build a house for their parents and brothers in Louisiana. The music is in the style of the popular songs of the day.

In 1934 and 1935 Weill composed the music for the biblical drama *Der Weg der Verheissung* ("The Promised Way"). Based on a libretto by Franz Werfel, the work recounts the history of the Jewish people as told by a rabbi to his community at a time of persecution. Though he had abandoned his parents' Orthodox faith in his early adulthood, Weill retained an interest in his Jewish heritage. For *Der Weg der Verheissung* he studied authentic Jewish melodies and tried to evoke their spirit in his own original music.

At the invitation of the theatrical producer-director Max Reinhardt, Weill went to New York City in late 1935 to supervise the preparations for the projected first performance of *Der Weg der Verheissung,* scheduled for early 1936. However, financial problems and other factors caused a long postponement of the premiere.

While waiting for the problems to be resolved, Weill tried his hand at an American musical: *Johnny Johnson* (1936), an antiwar fable by Paul Green. It was produced in New York City in late 1936. Then, in early 1937, came the Broadway production of *Der Weg der Verheissung,* now revised and retitled *The Eternal Road.*

The music of *Johnny Johnson* had too much European sophistication for the tastes of Broadway audiences, and *The Eternal Road* was a disaster. Nevertheless, Weill decided to stay in the United States, determined to adapt himself to American tastes. Indeed, in a remarkably short period of time he did absorb the styles and fashions of American music. Of course, for years he had been injecting elements of American jazz and popular song into his scores, but he still had to remove a characteristic European flavor from his work. Weill did so, yet somehow he managed to retain his sophisticated individuality.

His next effort was the political satire *Knickerbocker Holiday* (comp. and perf. 1938), containing the lovely "September Song" (lyrics, Maxwell Anderson). Weill's music for the show gained a wider audience than his earlier American works had, though the score still reflects his European background.

Then, during World War II, he wrote the scores for two enormously successful Broadway musicals: *Lady in the Dark* (comp. 1940, perf. 1941) and *One Touch of Venus* (comp. and perf. 1943). The first is an early and highly regarded example of the American musical play, in which the songs, instead of being mere appendages, carry the play forward dramatically and psychologically. The second, a more traditional musical comedy, is enriched by a delightfully tuneful score, including the haunting "Speak Low" (lyrics, Odgen Nash).

During his years in the United States, Weill experienced a heightened awareness of his ethnic origin, largely because of the Holocaust in Europe. As reports of the Nazi horrors poured into America, outcries demanding action arose. One such call for action was voiced by Ben Hecht in his 1943 pageant *We Will Never Die,* with incidental music supplied by Weill. The program comprised three parts: "The Roll Call," a recitation of great Jewish names in the arts and sciences from ancient times to the modern era; "Jews in the War," a dramatization of the contributions of American Jewish war heroes; and "Remember Us," a presentation of reports about the slaughters in Nazi Europe. The pageant was directed by Moss Hart, and its stars included Luther Adler, Paul Muni, and Edward G. Robinson. The huge chorus consisted of about two hundred rabbis and about two hundred cantors.

Another manifestation of Weill's Jewish awareness was his composition of a *Kiddush* ("Sanctification") for cantor, chorus, and organ (1946).

Weill also became a dedicated Zionist. To aid and explain the cause of Zionism, Ben Hecht wrote his 1946 drama-pageant *A Flag Is Born,* again with incidental music by Weill. The proceeds of its staging went to the American League for a Free Palestine. Luther Adler directed, while the leading roles were played by Paul Muni, Celia Adler, and the non-Jew Marlon Brando, then virtually unknown, who played the part of a young Jew.

In 1943 Weill became a naturalized American citizen. But the following year, apparently because of a feeling of nostalgia, he wrote a European-style operetta, *The Firebrand of Florence,* based on the memoirs of Benvenuto Cellini. Produced on Broadway in 1945, it was a box-office failure.

However, his last three New York shows were successful. *Street Scene* (comp. 1946, perf. 1947) is based on Elmer Rice's play about lower middle-class life in New York City. *Down in the Valley* (comp. and perf. 1948) is a folk opera. And *Lost in the Stars* (comp. and perf. 1949), with a Maxwell Anderson book based on Alan Paton's novel *Cry, the Beloved Country,* focuses on racial injustice in South Africa.

Weill's Broadway musicals of the late 1940s enhanced his reputation with the public and with the New York theater critics, but not with the music critics or with the intellectually oriented musicians in general. Many such musicians resented Weill's belief that the Western world's tradition of art music had lost touch with the realities and needs of society and had therefore reached its end, regardless of the efforts of conservationists and experimentalists.

Weill suffered much stress from the many nonmusical problems associated with the mechanics of staging Broadway shows. He spent about two-thirds of his time on such matters. While working on a musical adaptation of Mark Twain's *Huckleberry Finn,* Weill died of a long-standing heart ailment in New York City on April 3, 1950.

Among the mourners at his funeral, only one (Marc Blitzstein) came from the world of serious music, which Weill had deliberately abandoned ten years earlier. After Weill's death, his wife, Lotte Lenya, promoted his music in recitals, on TV, in recordings, and in the theater, especially in revivals of *The Threepenny Opera.*

In retrospect Weill can be seen as a key figure in the development of modern forms of musical theater. During his German years he created thoroughly modern forms of the play with music, in which a substantial musical score was an essential part of a spoken drama. The scores themselves were innovative in that they combined popular-music elements with modern techniques (such as atonality, polytonality, and polyrhythm) to produce music that had broad appeal yet sophistication. Finally, he transferred his innovations to Broadway, where he developed Americanized, popularized versions of his earlier forms and style.

Synthesis, then, is the key word for Weill: synthesis of play and music, of popular materials and advanced techniques, and of German innovations and American popularizations.

Selected works:

Stage

Zaubernacht (ballet with singing; libretto, V. Boritch; comp. and perf. 1922)

Der Protagonist (opera; libretto, G. Kaiser; comp. 1925, perf. 1926)

Royal Palace (ballet-opera; libretto, I. Groll; comp. 1926, perf. 1927)

Der Zar lässt sich photographieren (opera; libretto, G. Kaiser; comp. 1927, perf. 1928)

Mahagonny Songspiel (libretto, B. Brecht; comp. and perf. 1927)

Die Dreigroschenoper (play with music; German libretto, B. Brecht; comp. and perf. 1928) (English libretto, M. Blitzstein; perf. 1954), including:
"Mack the Knife"

Aufstieg und Fall der Stadt Mahagonny (opera; libretto, B. Brecht; comp. 1929, perf. 1930)

Happy End (comedy in music; lyrics, B. Brecht; comp. and perf. 1929)

Der Jasager (school opera; libretto, B. Brecht; comp. and perf. 1930)

Der Silbersee (opera; libretto, G. Kaiser; comp. and perf. 1933)

Die sieben Todsünden der Kleinbürger (ballet with singing; libretto, B. Brecht; comp. and perf. 1933)

Der Weg der Verheissung (biblical drama; libretto, F. Werfel; comp. 1935, unperf.) (revised by L. Lewisohn as *The Eternal Road;* perf. 1937)

Johnny Johnson (fable with music; lyrics, P. Green; comp. and perf. 1936)

Knickerbocker Holiday (operetta; lyrics, M. Anderson; comp. and perf. 1938), including:
"September Song"

Lady in the Dark (musical play; lyrics, I. Gershwin; comp. 1940, perf. 1941), including:
"My Ship"

One Touch of Venus (musical comedy; lyrics, O. Nash; comp. and perf. 1943), including:
"Speak Low"

We Will Never Die (pageant, incidental music; text, B. Hecht; perf. 1943)

The Firebrand of Florence (operetta; lyrics, I. Gershwin; comp. 1944, perf. 1945)

A Flag Is Born (drama-pageant, incidental music; text, B. Hecht; perf. 1946)

Street Scene (Broadway opera; lyrics, L. Hughes; comp. 1946, perf. 1947)

Down in the Valley (folk opera; libretto, A. Sundgaard; comp. and perf. 1948)

Lost in the Stars (musical tragedy; lyrics, M. Anderson; comp. and perf. 1949)

Orchestral

First Symphony (1921)
Sinfonia sacra (1922)
Second Symphony (1933)

Vocal

Das Berliner Requiem ("The Berlin Requiem"; cantata; vocal soloists, chorus, instrumental ensemble; text, B. Brecht; 1928)

Kiddush (cantor, chorus, organ; text, Hebrew prayer; 1946)

Chamber

String Quartet (1919)

Lazar Weiner
America's Greatest Yiddish Composer
(1897-1982)

Lazar Weiner, composer, was born in Cherkassy, near Kiev, the Ukraine (now in the Soviet Union), on October 24, 1897. There were no professional musicians in his immediate family, but his mother loved to sing old Jewish melodies. At the age of seven he began to sing in choirs, and at ten he was invited to become a member of the choir at Brodsky Synagogue in Kiev. He was also among a group of Jewish youths who sang children's choruses in productions (such as Mussorgsky's *Boris Godunov)* at the Kiev Opera.

After his voice changed, his attention shifted to the piano. In 1910, at the age of thirteen, he entered the Kiev Conservatory, where he studied piano, theory, and composition. He remained there till 1914, when he immigrated to the United States.

Settling in New York City, he soon began to work as a vocal coach, accompanist, and piano teacher. One of his piano pupils was Sarah Shumiatcher, whom he married in 1921.

His work as a vocal coach and accompanist (for Josef Rosenblatt, Rosa Raisa, and other major Jewish singers) gave him a good understanding of the human voice.

Lazar Weiner

cle Chorus in concerts of Jewish liturgical and secular music, and music director of the weekly radio show *The Message of Israel.* At Central Synagogue he led the world premieres of liturgical works by Ernest Bloch, Darius Milhaud, and others.

In 1939 Weiner helped to found the Jewish Music Forum, which presented the works of leading Jewish musicians and scholars. After the organization dissolved in 1960, he helped to found the Jewish Liturgical Music Society of America.

Weiner lectured on Jewish music at synagogues and community centers in many cities in Canada and the United States. In New York City he lectured on the same subject at the Juilliard School of Music, and beginning in 1953 he was a longtime member of the faculty at the School of Sacred Music of the Hebrew Union College— Jewish Institute of Religion.

Weiner was probably the most significant composer yet produced by the Yiddish milieu in the United States. He drew inspiration from his studies of Yiddish folksong and traditional biblical cantillation, as well as from his analysis of the works of Joel Engel, Alexander Krein, Moses Milner, and other early twentieth-century pioneers active in the Society for Jewish Folk Music (a Russian organization, 1908-1918). From the works of one of those musicians, Joseph Achron, Weiner learned to enrich his music through harmonic and contrapuntal experimentation.

He composed numerous liturgical works, including several complete services. His style for such compositions ranged from simple chantlike melodies to complex contemporary techniques. Always, however, the music was structured for practical synagogue use and served to help convey the meanings of the texts.

Weiner's secular compositions include a variety of instrumental works. But his forte was vocal music. He wrote a successful opera, *The Golem* (perf. 1957), and several significant cantatas, such as *The Last Judgment* (1966).

Weiner was unquestionably the greatest composer of Yiddish art songs of his time. In fact, he was one of the finest art-song composers in any language in the twentieth century. With his remarkable sensitivity to the sound and structure of Yiddish, he was able to mold masterful outpourings of the soul in his songs.

He would fly into a rage if Yiddish was not represented on programs of Jewish music or if Yiddish words were mispronounced by singers. He also railed against what he regarded as the vulgarization of Yiddish culture in show tunes. "Yet," according to his friend Judith K. Eisenstein, "he had the saving grace of humor, which prevented him from becoming an unpleasant fanatic."

Weiner had a great affection for, and closeness with, his family. His wife, Sarah (a gracious, intelligent lady and an excellent musician in her own right), gave piano lessons to their sons, Yehudi and David. With the solid foundation supplied by her teaching and their father's encouragement, Yehudi and David have become outstanding successes in music. Yehudi is a gifted composer. David, who graduated from Juilliard with a major in piano and who earned master's degrees in music (from

Taking advantage of that experience, he composed settings of three Yiddish poems in 1920. He sent the songs to Joel Engel, a pioneer in modern Jewish music. Engel replied that the music was well made but that Weiner, whose style at that time was based almost entirely on Western art music, should "write *Jewish* music to Yiddish texts!"

Weiner thereupon set out to study Jewish melos, especially in Yiddish folksongs and in biblical cantillation and traditional prayer chants. He also continued his formal composition studies, taking lessons from Robert Russell Bennett during 1920-21, Frederick Jacobi during 1923-24, and Joseph Schillinger during 1935-40.

In the early 1920s Weiner began to conduct Jewish choral groups, especially Yiddish amateur singing societies. He also contributed to the repertory for such groups by collecting and arranging Jewish folksongs, as well as by composing works of his own.

In 1926 Weiner became a naturalized American citizen. Soon thereafter he settled into several long-term positions in his new homeland, specifically in New York City, where he served for many years as music director of Central Synagogue, conductor of the Workmen's Cir-

Queen's College of the City University of New York) and psychology (from New York University), now teaches piano and practices psychotherapy. Because the family name was commonly mispronounced, both Yehudi and David changed the spelling of their surname to Wyner to approximate the phonetically correct pronunciation.

In his late years Lazar Weiner came to be widely recognized and honored as one of America's most distinguished contributors to Jewish culture. He died in New York City on January 10, 1982.

Selected works:

Stage

Lag b'Omer ("Thirty-third Day of the Omer," ballet, 1929)
A maise fun amol ("Once upon a Time"; musical comedy; lyrics, P. Hirshbein; perf. 1932)
Fight for Freedom (choral ballet, 1943)
The Golem (opera; libretto, R. Smolover; perf. 1957)
The Marred Passover (ballet, 1958)

Orchestral

Fugue and Postlude (1938)

Cantatas and Services

Amol in a tsayt ("Legend of Toil"; cantata; text, J. Goichberg; 1933)

Mensh in der velt ("Man in the World"; cantata; text, A. Nissenson; 1939)
To Thee, America (cantata; text, A. Leveless; pub. 1944)
Shir l'Shabat ("Song of the Sabbath"; Friday evening service; cantor, chorus, organ; text, Jewish liturgy; 1963)
The Last Judgment (cantata; text, S. Rosenbaum; 1966)
many other services

Solo Songs
(voice and piano)

"Dos gold fun dayne oygn" ("The Gold of Your Eyes"; text, S. Imber; comp. 1923, pub. 1929)
"A gebet" ("A Prayer"; text, J. Rolnik; pub. 1925)
"Shtile tener" ("Hushed, Still Accents"; Yiddish text, N. B. Minkoff; English text, C. Cooperman; pub. 1929)
"Di maisse mit der velt" ("The Story of the World"; text, M. L. Halperin; pub. 1936)
"A maysele" ("A Tale"; text, P. Hirshbein; pub. 1941)
many other songs

Chamber

Chanson hébraïque ("Hebraic Song"; cello, piano; 1922)
Suite (violin, cello, piano; 1929)
String Quartet (1937)

Piano

Three Pieces (pub. 1933)
Five Calculations (1938)

Stefan Wolpe

Composer with a
Profoundly Original Musical Vision
(1902-1972)

Stefan Wolpe, composer, was born in Berlin, Germany, on August 25, 1902. He began piano and theory studies at the age of fifteen. Then, from 1919 to 1924, he attended the Berlin Academy of Music, where he studied under Paul Juon and Franz Schreker. During that period Wolpe also received important private advice from the composer Ferruccio Busoni and was influenced by the music of Alexander Scriabin and Erik Satie.

While still at the Berlin Academy, Wolpe became music director for the Berlin dadaists and began a decade-long involvement with radical socialism. He appeared as composer and pianist at concerts dedicated to furthering the socialist revolution of November 1918. After leaving the Berlin Academy in 1924, he conducted music at demonstrations and rallies, and composed many songs, choral works, and piano pieces on populist and other political subjects. In 1931 he became composer and pianist for Troupe 31, a theater collective directed by Gustav von Wangenheim. Their first production, Wangenheim's play *Die Mausefalle* ("The Mousetrap," 1931), with incidental music by Wolpe, received many successful performances in Germany and Switzerland.

In his proletarian revolutionary music Wolpe used a simple but vigorous tonal idiom. However, he also wrote more serious works in a complex, dissonant style leading progressively toward atonality. Among them were cantatas, chamber operas, and a marvelous set of five songs to poems by Johann Hölderlin. After hearing Paul Whiteman's band in 1926, Wolpe also incorporated jazz elements into many compositions, such as *Blues and Tango* for piano (1926).

In 1927 Wolpe married the painter Ola Okuniewska. Their daughter, Katharina Wolpe, became a well-known pianist.

In March 1933 Wolpe, in company with the Romanian pianist Irma Schoenberg (whom he married in 1934), fled Nazi Germany and went to Vienna, where he studied for a time with Anton von Webern. The following year Wolpe traveled to Palestine. There he taught theory and composition at the Palestine (or Jerusalem) Conservatory of Music till 1938, greatly influencing the first generation of locally educated composers.

Having been pushed out of German society, Wolpe naturally lost interest in composing for German socialistic causes. While in Palestine, he began to explore his Jewish heritage, including the local folk music. Thus inspired, he composed settings of texts from the Hebrew Bible and from contemporary Hebrew and Yiddish poets.

At the same time he also continued to write complex works in which he experimented with remarkably original techniques to achieve atonality. In his *Duo im Hexa-chord* ("Duet in the Hexachord") for oboe and clarinet (1936) and *Four Studies on Basic Rows* for piano (1936), he proved that he could create a wide range of expression even with limited resources.

Wolpe left Palestine in 1938 and settled in the United States, where he became a naturalized citizen in 1944. In 1948 he married the poet Hilda Morley, his third and final wife.

Wolpe taught at a number of American institutions, including the Philadelphia Academy of Music (1949-52), Black Mountain College in North Carolina (1952-56), and C. W. Post College of Long Island University (1957-68), where he also served as chairman of the music department. Among his students were Elmer Bernstein, Morton Feldman, Ezra Laderman, Ralph Shapey, and David Tudor.

Wolpe was an individualist, as unique as Bartók, Schoenberg, Stravinsky, or Webern in the attempt to achieve coherence and communication in modern music. The basis of Wolpe's mature technique is a sort of continuous variation in which focal pitches and small groups of other pitches are combined to form motives, which are then varied to create lines and harmonies. The most important factor is that in his motivic combinations all twelve tones are used in close juxtaposition, producing atonality with a greater degree of freshness than Wolpe felt was possible with Schoenberg's stricter twelve-tone technique. Also, while he retained some of Schoenberg's romantic gestures, Wolpe moved further than Schoenberg did into modern music by employing leaner textures, more rugged lines, and more complex rhythms. And instead of following traditional forms based on repetition and contrast, Wolpe's forms tend to be cumulative. Notable early American-period works in which he explored those procedures include the *Oboe Sonata* (1941), the ballet (on the life of Moses) *The Man from Midian* (1942), the cantata *Yigdal* ("May He Be Magnified," 1945), *Encouragements: The Good Spirit of a Right Cause* for piano (1947), and the *Violin Sonata* (1949).

Later he added other factors to his continuous-variation technique. Most significant were his experiments with presenting two or more widely differing musical events simultaneously or in close juxtaposition. His first outstanding work in that manner was the *Enactments* for three pianos (1953). He refined and expanded his musical language in the *Symphony* (1956, revised 1964) and in many chamber works of the 1950s and 1960s.

From 1964 to 1972 Wolpe suffered increasingly from Parkinson's disease. Struggling against the encroaching symptoms, he wrote several important works (such as the *String Quartet,* 1969) in which his profoundly original musical vision is summarized. He died in New York City on April 4, 1972.

Stefan Wolpe

Selected works:

Stage

chamber operas (1928-29)
Die Mausefalle (incidental music, 1931)
The Man from Midian (ballet, 1942)

Orchestral

Symphony (1956, revised 1964)

Vocal

Hölderlin Lieder ("Hölderlin Songs"; five songs; mezzo-soprano [or alto], piano; texts, J. Hölderlin; 1924, revised 1935)
Politische Satiren ("Political Satires"; four songs; mezzo-soprano [or baritone], piano; texts, T. Ring, F. Bönsch; 1930)
Two Songs from the Song of Songs (alto, piano; texts, Bible; 1936)
Songs from the Hebrew (seven songs; mezzo-soprano [or baritone], piano; texts, mostly Bible; 1938)
Yigdal (cantata; baritone, chorus, organ; text, liturgical hymn, after Maimonides; 1945)

Chamber

Duo im Hexachord (oboe, clarinet; 1936)
Oboe Sonata (1941)
Violin Sonata (1949)
Quintet with Voice (baritone, five instruments; 1957)
Piece in Two Parts (flute, piano; 1960)
Piece for Two Instrumental Units (seven instruments, 1963)
Trio in Two Parts (flute, cello, piano; 1964)
String Quartet (1969)

Piano

Blues and Tango (1926)
Four Pieces (1929)
Four Studies on Basic Rows (1936)
Dance in the Form of a Chaconne (1938)
Zemach Suite (1939)
Encouragements: The Good Spirit of a Right Cause (1947)
Enactments (three pianos, 1953)
Form (1959)
Form IV (1969)

Yehudi Wyner
Rhapsodic Composer
(1929-   )

Yehudi Wyner, composer and pianist, was born in Calgary, Canada, on June 1, 1929. He is the son of the composer Lazar Weiner and the pianist Sarah Naomi Weiner (née Shumiatcher). Since Lazar (a native of the Ukraine) and Sarah (a native of Canada) were naturalized American citizens, Yehudi was born an American despite the fact that his birth took place in Canada. Sarah had gone to Calgary to be with her mother and family just before giving birth to Yehudi. When he was two months old, his parents returned with him to the United States.

The family was constantly annoyed by the fact that many people mispronounced the name Weiner. Yehudi eventually changed the spelling to Wyner to clarify the proper pronunciation.

Sarah supervised all of Yehudi's early musical training, though Lazar, too, encouraged the boy's artistic development. Later Yehudi studied at the Juilliard School of Music, from which he graduated in 1946. He went on to attend Yale University, where he studied composition with Paul Hindemith. At Yale he earned his B.A. (1950), B.Mus. (1951), and M.Mus. (1953), also receiving an M.A. (1952) from Harvard University, where one of his composition teachers was Walter Piston.

Soon after completing his studies at Yale, Wyner, on a fellowship, went to Rome, where he stayed for three years. He then returned to the United States and appeared in many concerts with his father, both men functioning in the roles of pianist and composer.

Wyner has held numerous positions, including instructor at Hebrew Union College in New York City (1957-59), music director of the Westchester Reform Temple in New York City (1959-68), theory teacher at Yale (assistant professor, 1963-69; associate professor, 1969-77), and music director of the New Haven Opera Society (1968-77). Since 1976 he has been on the faculty of the Berkshire Music Center at Tanglewood, near Lenox, Massachusetts, and since 1978 he has been a professor of music at the State University of New York in Purchase.

Wyner composed his early works in a neoclassical idiom, influenced largely by Hindemith and Igor Stravinsky. Among such works are the *Short Sonata* for clarinet and piano (1950) and the *Partita* for piano (1952).

But since the late 1950s his music has become more chromatic, expressive, rhapsodic, and improvisatory, often with a Jewish flavor. His important mature works include the *Da camera* ("For the Chamber") for piano and orchestra (1967), the *Dances of Atonement* for violin and piano (1976), and the *Wind Quintet* (1984).

Wyner's many religious works, usually based on traditional Jewish chant, are generally practical and unpretentious. His *Friday Evening Service* (1963) and *Torah Service* (1966) are especially effective liturgical compositions.

Wyner has been married twice. In 1951 he wedded Nancy Joan Braverman, with whom he had three children: Isaiah, Adam, and Cassia. In 1967 he divorced her and married the soprano Susan M. Davenny, who, as Susan Davenny Wyner, has become one of America's most outstanding recital, concert, and opera artists.

Selected works:

Orchestral

Da camera (piano, orchestra; 1967)

Choral

Psalm 143 (chorus; text, Bible; 1952)
Friday Evening Service (cantor, chorus, organ; text, Jewish liturgy; 1963)
Torah Service (chorus, instruments; text, Jewish liturgy; 1966)

Yehudi Wyner

Solo Vocal

Songs (1950-71)
Intermedio ("Intermezzo"; soprano, string orchestra; wordless vocalizing; 1974)

Chamber

Short Sonata (clarinet, piano; 1950)
Dance Variations (eight instruments; 1953, revised 1959)
Concert Duo (violin, piano; 1957)
Serenade (seven instruments, 1958)
Passover Offering (four instruments, 1959)
Three Informal Pieces (violin, piano; 1961, revised 1969)
Cadenza! (clarinet, piano [or harpsichord]; 1969)
Dances of Atonement (violin, piano; 1976)
Piano Quartet (1980)
All the Rage (flute, piano; 1980)
Passage (seven instruments, 1983)
Wind Quintet (1984)

Piano

Easy Suite (1949)
Partita (1952)
Sonata (1954)
Three Short Fantasies (1971)

Lazar Weiner (left) and Yehudi Wyner (right)

Pinchas Zukerman

Brilliant Violinist-
Violist-Conductor
(1948-   )

Pinchas Zukerman, violinist, was born in Tel Aviv, Israel, on July 16, 1948. His parents were concentration-camp survivors from Poland. Jehuda Zukerman, Pinchas's father, was a professional violinist who had formerly played in the Warsaw Philharmonic; after World War II, in Israel, he taught during the days and played in his own nightclub band during the evenings.

At the age of five Pinchas learned to play a recorder. At seven he began to receive violin lessons from his father. One year later Pinchas entered the Academy of Music in Tel Aviv, where he studied violin with Ilona Feher. Soon young Zukerman was playing the violin publicly at bar mitzvahs and other events.

During a visit to Israel in 1961, the violinist Isaac Stern and the cellist Pablo Casals heard Zukerman perform. On their recommendations he received scholarships (including one from the America-Israel Cultural Foundation) enabling him to enroll at the Juilliard School of Music in New York City.

In 1962 Zukerman arrived in the United States and, because his parents had to move to Montreal to find work, began to live with the pianist Eugene Istomin's family. Stern himself became young Zukerman's legal guardian in America.

At the Juilliard School, Zukerman took violin lessons from Ivan Galamian and studied the viola for use in chamber music. He also attended the Professional Children's School, as well as the High School of Performing Arts.

However, Zukerman did not immediately adjust well to his new surroundings. By his own admission spoiled by early adulation in Israel, he could not cope with being merely another prodigy among many prodigies at the Juilliard School. And it rankled him to be told to do exercises that he felt he had already mastered. Soon he started playing hooky. When Stern found out about Zukerman's attitude and conduct, the older man cornered the younger one and forcefully explained, as later recalled by Zukerman, "that music isn't a profession; it's a way of life."

After being straightened out by Stern, Zukerman diligently applied himself to his studies and progressed rapidly. In October 1963 he made his New York City debut at Town Hall, performing with the New York Orchestral Society for the United Nations Children's Fund. In 1966 he appeared at the Spoleto Festival in Italy.

But the event that skyrocketed Zukerman to prominence was his being named the joint winner (with Kyung-Wha Chung of Korea) of the Leventritt International Competition in New York City in 1967. He soon received a recording contract, as well as a contract with the impresario Sol Hurok to tour the United States and Canada.

In 1969 Zukerman made his first major New York City appearance when he played the Mendelssohn *Violin Concerto* with the New York Philharmonic under Leonard Bernstein. In 1971 Zukerman gave his first New York City solo recital, which was filmed in its entirety as a British Broadcasting Corporaton (BBC) documentary. He has also been featured in various American TV specials and has appeared as a guest on many TV talk-variety shows.

Pinchas Zukerman

Zukerman has concertized extensively in the United States and Europe. Besides playing the violin, he has appeared as a viola soloist, his handling of the larger instrument being aided by his six-foot muscular physique. Zukerman has gained special renown for his ability to perform expertly with both instruments in a single concert, a difficult feat that he has tossed off many times with seeming ease.

He has been particularly active and successful in chamber music, performing two-violin music with Stern, violin sonatas with the pianist Daniel Barenboim, and piano trios with Barenboim and the cellist Jacqueline du Pré. Zukerman has also joined forces with the flutist Jean-Pierre Rampal, the Guarneri String Quartet, and others.

Since the 1960s Zukerman, Barenboim, and du Pré, along with the pianist Vladimir Ashkenazy, the conductor Zubin Mehta, and the violinist Itzhak Perlman have formed an intimate circle of friends, among whom Zukerman is known as Pinky.

His playing is noted for its rich melodic line, expressive phrasing, and brilliant technique, highlighted by a delicate spiccato (a style of bowing in which the bow is allowed to drop on the string and rebound after each note).

However, in recent years he has turned increasingly to conducting. His role as conductor began in 1970 with the English Chamber Orchestra, and he has since guest-conducted such major orchestras as the New York Philharmonic, the Boston Symphony, and the London New Philharmonia. At first he conducted Bach, Vivaldi, and Mozart concertos with himself as soloist, later turning to straight conducting. Since 1980 he has served as music director of the Saint Paul Chamber Orchestra in Minnesota.

Zukerman's move to the United States in 1962 proved to be permanent. In 1976 he became a naturalized American citizen.

While attending the Juilliard School, he met Eugenia Rich, first flutist of the Juilliard Orchestra. Married in 1968 in a Jewish religious ceremony, they had two children: Arianna and Natalia. The Zukermans also formed a professional partnership, making some recordings and giving numerous joint concerts in America and abroad till their separation in late 1983.

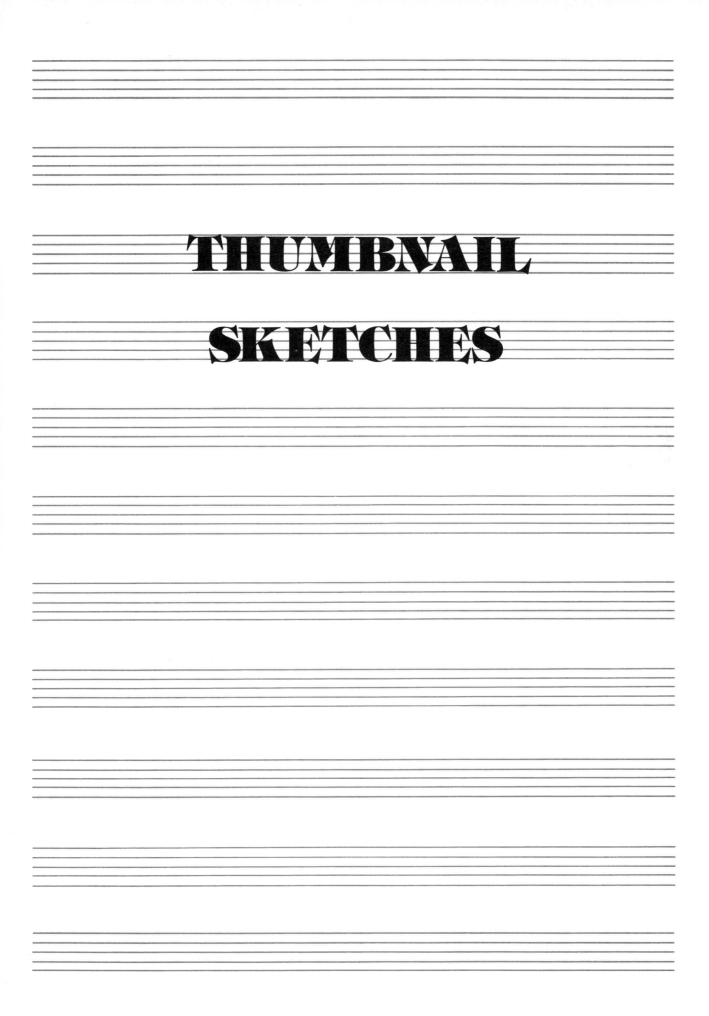

THUMBNAIL

SKETCHES

A

ABRAVANEL, MAURICE (born January 6, 1903, in Turkish-ruled Salonika, Greece). Conductor. Raised in Switzerland, he began his career in Germany, where he conducted at various theaters till the rise of Hitler in 1933. He then conducted ballet in Paris, including, in 1933, the world premiere of *Die sieben Todsünden der Kleinbürger* ("The Seven Deadly Sins of the Petty Bourgeoisie") by Kurt Weill, under whom Abravanel had studied in Germany. In 1936 he immigrated to the United States, where, after two years with the Metropolitan Opera (1936–38), he turned to Broadway and specialized in leading the premieres of Weill's American stage works, such as *Knickerbocker Holiday* in 1938, *Lady in the Dark* in 1941, and *One Touch of Venus* in 1943. However, Abravanel's fame rests primarily on his tenure as conductor of the Utah Symphony Orchestra (1947–79), which he built from scratch into one of the finest ensembles in America.

ACHRON, ISIDOR (born November 24, 1892, in Warsaw, Poland; died May 12, 1948, in New York City, New York). Composer and pianist. Brother of the composer Joseph Achron. Immigrating to the United States in 1922, Isidor settled in New York City, accompanied the violinist Jascha Heifetz in 1922–23, and performed as a concert pianist. His compositions, basically in the romantic tradition, include many solo piano works, two piano concertos (1937, 1942), and the *Suite grotesque* for orchestra (perf. 1942).

ACHRON, JOSEPH (born May 13, 1886, in Losdseje, Poland; died April 29, 1943, in Los Angeles, California). Composer and violinist. Brother of the composer Isidor Achron. Joseph became a child prodigy and moved to Russia, where he toured as a violinist, helped the Society for Jewish Folk Music (1908–1918), and composed for the Hebrew Chamber Theater in Petrograd (1919–21). After a visit to Palestine (1924) he settled in the United States (1925). In New York City he wrote music for Yiddish plays and composed his *Evening Service for the Sabbath* (1932). From 1934 on he lived in Los Angeles, California, where he continued his concert career. Achron used a traditional romantic style in his early music, colored with Jewish inflections, but later he adopted atonality and polytonality. He is best known for his three violin concertos (1925, 1933, and 1937) and *Golem* (1932), a chamber-orchestra work in which the first section is exactly retrograded in the last section to symbolize the undoing of the monster Golem.

ADLER, GUIDO (born November 1, 1855, in Eibenschütz, Moravia [now Ivančice, Czechoslovakia]; died February 15, 1941, in Vienna, Austria). Musicologist. One of the founders of modern musicology, he wrote the pioneering essay "Umfang, Methode, und Ziel der Musikwissenschaft" ("Scope, Method, and Aim of the Science of Music," 1885). He was the first to emphasize the importance of style criticism in music research, as in his book *Der Stil in der Musik* ("Style in Music," 1911, revised 1929). The musicological institute that he founded at the University of Vienna became the model for similar institutes elsewhere. He helped to initiate the famous collection *Denkmäler der Tonkunst in Österreich* ("Monuments of Music in Austria") and served as its editor from its inception in 1894 till 1938, when he was removed from the post by the Nazis.

ADLER, LARRY (originally LAWRENCE ADLER; born February 10, 1914, in Baltimore, Maryland). Harmonica player. Generally acknowledged to be the world's greatest harmonica player and the first to raise the instrument to concert status. He began his professional career in his early teens, soon after winning the Maryland Harmonica Championship in 1927. At first Adler played only popular tunes, but in the late 1930s he added classical pieces to his repertory and began to appear with symphony orchestras. He played by ear (as explained in his book *How I Play*, 1937) till the early 1940s, when he learned how to read music, notably through lessons with Ernst Toch. Concert works for harmonica and orchestra were written for him by Ralph Vaughan Williams, Darius Milhaud, and others. Adler himself has composed music, including background scores for the films *Genevieve* (1953) and *A High Wind in Jamaica* (1965). In the late 1940s right-wing fanatics drove him out of the United States, accusing him of having un-American thoughts. He settled in England, but by the 1970s he had gradually returned to active concertizing in his native land. Adler gave war tours in Israel in 1967 (Six-Day War) and 1973 (Yom Kippur War).

ADLER, SAMUEL (born March 4, 1928, in Mannheim, Germany). Composer and conductor. He immigrated with his family to the United States in 1939. Entering the military service in 1950, he organized the Seventh Army Symphony Orchestra, which he conducted in numerous concerts in Germany and Austria. After leaving the army, he served as music director of Temple Emanu-El in Dallas (1953-56). He has also conducted concerts and operas in Europe and America. His music follows midstream modernism, with basically tonal harmony frequently interrupted by atonal episodes. Many passages evoke the liturgical cantillation of traditional Jewish music. Adler has composed operas, orchestral works, chamber music, and vocal pieces, including synagogal services.

ADORNO, THEODOR W(IESENGRUND) (originally THEODOR WIESENGRUND; born September 11, 1903, in Frankfort on the Main, Germany; died August 6, 1969, in

Visp, Switzerland). Sociologist of music. In his early writings he used the name Theodor Wiesengrund-Adorno. He left Nazi Germany in 1934, spent several years in England, and then moved to the United States in 1938. In 1940 he settled in Los Angeles, where he advised Thomas Mann in the musical aspects of the latter's novel *Doktor Faustus* ("Doctor Faustus"), in which the central character is a composer whose musical ideas parallel those of Arnold Schoenberg. In 1949 Adorno returned to Frankfort. Many of his writings are in the field of social philosophy. As a musicologist he drew on Freudian and Marxist ideologies to support his contention that avant-garde music is an outlet for the free individual repressed by the modern world's "managed societies," both East and West. He believed that serious music has had to become abstruse and unpleasant because simplicity and pleasure have become tools for molding uncritical consumers. He was the first to name and analyze the "culture industry." Among his principal works are the books *Philosophie der neuen Musik* (1949; third edition, 1967; English, as *Philosophy of Modern Music*, 1973) and *Einleitung in die Musiksoziologie* (1962; second edition, 1968; English, as *Introduction to the Sociology of Music*, 1976).

AGUILAR, EMANUEL ABRAHAM (born August 23, 1824, in London, England; died February 18, 1904, in London, England). Pianist and composer. He was especially praised for his playing of Beethoven. Aguilar's own works cover a variety of genres, including operas, cantatas, symphonies, chamber pieces, songs, and harmonizations for the collection entitled *The Ancient Melodies of the Liturgy of the Spanish and Portuguese Jews* (1857).

ALKAN, CHARLES (originally CHARLES MORHANGE; born November 30, 1813, in Paris, France; died March 29, 1888, in Paris, France). Composer and pianist. Early in life he replaced his original surname, Morhange, with his father's first name, Alkan. His few concert appearances proved him to be one of the leading piano virtuosos of the nineteenth century. However, his innate shyness and misanthropy grew into his dominant characteristics, and he not only avoided company but also concertized and published only at intervals, so that long periods of his life were undocumented. Unlike many great Jewish-born musicians of his time, he remained a strict adherent of Judaism, a decision that may have contributed to his withdrawal from the Christian-dominated musical mainstream. His compositions, mostly for the piano, show some influence by Beethoven, Berlioz, and especially Chopin. But Alkan stands alone in his pioneering exploitations of piano sonorities, especially in the extreme registers, and in his harmonic innovations, as in his clashing simultaneities and in his unconventional habit of beginning a piece in one key and ending it in another. His most ambitious work is the *Douze études* ("Twelve Studies") for piano (pub. 1857). Largely ignored during his lifetime, the mysterious Alkan remains a major figure who has yet to be fully recognized.

ALPERT, HERB (born March 31, 1935, in Los Angeles, California). Trumpeter. In 1962 he founded the Tijuana Brass, and as its leader and arranger he created an "Ameriachi" sound that blended rock 'n' roll, jazz, and Mexican mariachi. "The Lonely Bull" (1962) and "A Taste of Honey" (1965) were early hits. In "This Guy's in Love with You" (1968) Alpert performed a vocal, a rare departure from his usual trumpet solos. He withdrew from performing for about a decade and then returned with one of his most successful

recordings: "Rise" (1979). His recent albums include *Rise* (1979), *Beyond* (1980), *Magic Man* (1981), and *Fandango* (1982).

ALTSCHULER, MODEST (born February 15, 1873, in Mogilev, Russia; died September 12, 1963, in Los Angeles, California). Conductor. He immigrated to the United States, where he organized the Russian Symphony Orchestra (1904) and conducted it for many years. Altschuler led the orchestra in the world premiere of Scriabin's *Fourth Symphony: Le poème de l'extase* ("The Poem of Ecstasy") in 1908.

AMAR, LICCO (born December 4, 1891, in Budapest, Hungary; died July 19, 1959, in Freiburg, West Germany). Violinist. Moving to Germany, Amar served as concertmaster of the Berlin Philharmonic (1915–20) and the National Theater Orchestra of Mannheim (1920–23). In 1921 he formed the Amar String Quartet, which held a high reputation throughout the 1920s for its performances of new music. Compelled to leave Germany in 1933, Amar spent many years in Turkey before returning to his adopted homeland in 1957.

ANCONA, MARIO (born February 28, 1860, in Leghorn, Italy; died February 22, 1931, in Florence, Italy). Baritone. His first opera appearance was in Trieste (1889), followed by debuts at La Scala in Milan (1890), Covent Garden in London (1893), and the Metropolitan Opera in New York City (1893). Extremely versatile, he sang a wide variety of roles in the operas of Mozart, Wagner, Verdi, Puccini, Bizet, Gounod, and others. Ancona retired in 1916.

APEL, WILLI (born October 10, 1893, in Konitz, Germany [now Chojnice, Poland]). Musicologist. In 1936 he immigrated to the United States, where his writings have had a profound effect on higher music education. His *Harvard Dictionary of Music* (1944, revised 1969) was the first American general reference book to give as much attention to early and exotic music as to the more familiar repertory. The *Historical Anthology of Music* (with Archibald T. Davison; volume 1, 1946, revised 1949; volume 2, 1950) follows the same approach. Among his other outstanding contributions are *The Notation of Polyphonic Music, 900–1600* (1942; revised fifth edition, 1961), *Masters of the Keyboard* (1947), *Gregorian Chant* (1958; third edition, 1966), and *Geschichte der Orgel- und Klaviermusik bis 1700* (1967; revised, in English, as *The History of Keyboard Music to 1700*, 1972).

APPLEBAUM, LOUIS (born April 3, 1918, in Toronto, Canada). Composer. He has composed background scores for movies in Canada and the United States, including the American film *The Story of GI Joe* (1945). His concert works, which show the influence of Stravinsky, include *Three Stratford Fanfares* (1953), *Suite of Miniature Dances* (1958), and *Concertante* (1967), all for orchestra.

ARKIN, ALAN (born March 26, 1934, in New York City, New York). Singer. Now a well-known actor, he actually achieved his first success in show business as a folksinger in the mid-1950s, accompanying himself on the guitar. From 1957 to 1959 he performed in nightclubs as part of a folk trio, the Tarriers. He has written some songs, including "Cuddle Bug" and "That's Me," and made recordings of children's music, such as *The Babysitters* (1958) and *The Family*

Album (1965). Arkin also wrote the allegorical children's book *The Lemming Conditon* (1976).

ARPA, GIOVANNI LEONARDO DELL' (or GIAN LEONARDO DELL' ARPA; original surname, MOLLICA; born c. 1525 in Naples, Italy; died January 1602 in Naples, Italy). Harpist and composer. Performing in aristocratic circles, he acquired the Italian words *dell' Arpa* ("of the Harp") as a new surname because of his outstanding ability to play the double harp. He composed some effective vocal works.

AUER, LEOPOLD (born June 7, 1845, in Veszprém, Hungary; died July 15, 1930, in Loschwitz, near Dresden, Germany). Violinist. In his youth he performed as a concert artist in Europe. But he earned his greatest fame as a teacher at the Saint Petersburg Conservatory in Russia (1868–1917), producing such masters as Mischa Elman, Jascha Heifetz, and Efrem Zimbalist. He also continued to perform, and many works were dedicated to him, notably Tchaikovsky's *Sérénade mélancolique,* ("Melancholy Serenade"). Yet Auer refused the dedication and first performance of Tchaikovsky's now famous *Violin Concerto,* declaring the work to be too long and technically awkward. (Tchaikovsky then gave the concerto to another Jewish violinist, Adolph Brodsky.) Later, however, Auer changed his mind; the work became one of his favorites and one of the staples in the repertories of his pupils. In 1917 he left strife-torn Russia and in 1918 settled in the United States, where he spent the rest of his life. He died during a vacation in Germany. Auer was the principal early propagator of the Russian bow grip, which consists of pressing the bow stick with the center joint of the index finger, resulting in a richer tone than that produced by other grips. He explained his method in his book *Violin Playing As I Teach It* (1921). He also wrote the autobiography *My Long Life in Music* (1923).

AVSHALOMOV, AARON (born November 11, 1894, in Nikolayevsk, Russia; died April 26, 1965, in New York City, New York). Composer. He spent many years in China, where he composed works that integrated Chinese melodies and rhythms with Western forms and instruments, as in the ballet *The Soul of the Ch'in* (1933) and the opera *The Great Wall* (perf. 1945). In 1947 he immigrated to the United States, where he continued to specialize in large forms, particularly symphonies. Jacob Avshalomov, Aaron's son, is an active conductor and composer in the United States.

AX, EMANUEL (born June 8, 1949, in Lvov, the Soviet Union). Pianist. His parents lost their first spouses in the Holocaust, and they themselves survived internment in Nazi concentration camps. The family moved to Warsaw when Emanuel was eight and to Canada two years later, finally settling in New York City in 1961. His career skyrocketed after he won the Arthur Rubinstein International Piano Master Competition in Tel Aviv in 1974, and he added the Avery Fisher Prize in 1979. He has appeared with major American orchestras, has toured Central and South America, and has given joint recitals with the violinist Nathan Milstein in Europe and Japan. Ax plays with a sonorous tone and with a greater sense of color than is characteristic of other pianists of his generation. He thrives on Mozart and Chopin, though he also excels with Schumann, Ravel, and contemporary composers.

B

BABIN, VICTOR (born December 13, 1908, in Moscow, Russia; died March 1, 1972, in Cleveland, Ohio). Pianist and composer. He moved to Berlin and in 1933 married the pianist Vitya (later Victoria) Vronsky, with whom he performed throughout his career in the famous piano duo known as Vronsky and Babin. In 1937 he immigrated to the United States, where he spent his late years as director of the Cleveland Institute of Music (1961–72). Babin's compositions are in a conservative, postromantic idiom and include two concertos for two pianos and orchestra, other works for two pianos, and solo piano pieces.

BAER, ABRAHAM (born December 26, 1834, in Filehne, near Posen, Germany [now Wieleń, near Poznań, Poland]; died 1894 in Gotëborg, Sweden). Cantor and earliest important collector of Jewish liturgical melodies. In his youth he moved to Gotëborg, where he became assistant cantor in 1857 and chief cantor in 1860. His *Baal tefillah; oder, Der practische Vorbeter* ("Master of Prayer; or, The Practical Cantor"; 1877, with many later editions), a collection of traditional synagogal melodies and recitatives in new arrangements for the Polish, German, and Sephardic rituals, became the basic manual for many European cantors. It includes material by Salomon Sulzer, Samuel Naumbourg, Louis Lewandowski, and Baer himself.

BARNETT, JOHN (born July 15, 1802, in Bedford, England; died April 16, 1890, in Leckhampton, England). Composer. Uncle of the composer John Francis Barnett. John Barnett's father was Bernhard Beer, a Prussian diamond merchant said to have been a cousin of the composer Giacomo Meyerbeer. After settling in England, Beer changed his name to Barnett. John Barnett composed music for numerous farces, melodramas, and burlesques. But his reputation rests almost entirely on one opera, *The Mountain Sylph* (perf. 1834), in which he reintroduced recitative into English opera, replacing the spoken dialogue that had been customary since the 1760s.

BARNETT, JOHN FRANCIS (born October 16, 1837, in London, England; died November 24, 1916, in London, England). Composer. Nephew of the composer John Barnett. John Francis Barnett's most popular compositions were his cantatas, such as *The Ancient Mariner* (1867) and *The Eve of St. Agnes* (1913). He also wrote orchestral works, delightful salon piano pieces, and the book *Musical Reminiscences and Impressions* (1906).

BARRY, JEFF (originally JEFF ADELBERG; born April 3, 1939, in New York City, New York). Composer. He collaborated on the music and lyrics for the popular songs "Tell Laura I Love Her" (with Ben Raleigh, 1960), "The Kind of Boy You Can't Forget" (with Ellie Greenwich, 1963), "Sugar, Sugar" (with Andy Kim, 1969), and "I Honestly Love You" (with Peter Allen, 1974). Barry also worked on the theme songs for TV's *The Jeffersons* ("Movin' On Up," with Ja'net DuBois, written 1974, first aired 1975) and *One Day at a Time* ("One Day at a Time," with Nancy Barry, 1975).

BEAUX ARTS TRIO, consisting of pianist MENAHEM PRESSLER (born December 16, 1923, in Magdeburg, Ger-

Beaux Arts Trio

many), violinist ISIDORE COHEN (born December 16, 1922, in New York City, New York), and cellist BERNARD GREENHOUSE (born January 3, 1916, in Newark, New Jersey). Piano trio formed in 1955. Pressler and Greenhouse have remained since its founding, Cohen joining the group a few years later when the original violinist, Daniel Guilet, retired. While concertizing throughout the world and recording much of the standard repertory, the Beaux Arts Trio has elevated the status of the previously neglected piano trio to the level of that of the string quartet. It has become one of the most admired ensembles of any kind on the current scene and has been praised for its emotional fire, its grasp of stylistic nuances, and its precision as an artistic unit. Each of its members has also developed a distinguished career as a solo concert artist.

BEKKER, PAUL (originally MAX PAUL EUGEN BEKKER; born September 11, 1882, in Berlin, Germany; died March 7, 1937, in New York City, New York). Writer. A powerful music critic in Germany, he helped to advocate the music of such moderns as Mahler, Schoenberg, and Hindemith. To escape the Nazis, he left Germany in 1934 and settled in New York City. Shortly before his death, he completed his only book written in English: *The Story of the Orchestra* (1936). Among his important books in German were *Beethoven* (1911; English, 1925; second English edition, 1939) and *Richard Wagner* (1924; English, 1931). Bekker pioneered the use of sociological factors to help understand musical creation and performance.

BELLISON, SIMEON (born December 4, 1883, in Moscow, Russia; died May 4, 1953, in New York City, New York). Clarinetist. He served as first clarinetist for the opera orchestras in Moscow (1904–1914) and Saint Petersburg (1915) and then toured the Far East and America with a chamber ensemble (1917-20). In 1920 he defected to the United States and soon began a long tenure as first clarinetist of the New York Philharmonic (1920-48). Bellison's

papers and instruments are stored at the Rubin Academy of Music in Jerusalem.

BELY, VICTOR (born January 14, 1904, in Berdichev, Russia). Composer. Writing in a popular style for the masses, he has produced many songs and choral works on revolutionary and socialist subjects. But he gained his greatest fame for his World War II songs, which were widely sung by Soviet troops.

BENATZKY, RALPH (originally RUDOLF BENATZKY; born June 5, 1884, in Mährisch-Budweis, Moravia [now Moravske Budejovice, Czechoslovakia]; died October 17, 1957, in Zurich, Switzerland). Composer. Working mostly in Vienna and Berlin, he composed many cabaret songs and stage works, winning worldwide fame with his operetta *Im weissen Rössl* (known in English as *White Horse Inn,* perf. 1930). In 1933 he left Germany and lived successively in Paris, Vienna, Los Angeles, and Zurich. A prolific composer, he wrote nearly 100 stage works, about 250 film scores, and approximately 5,000 songs.

BENEDICT, JULIUS (born November 27, 1804, in Stuttgart, Germany; died June 5, 1885, in London, England). Composer, conductor, and pianist. As a teenager he was introduced to Beethoven, and he was present at the famous meeting between Carl Maria von Weber and Beethoven in Baden on October 5, 1823. Benedict held several conducting posts in Europe, notably in London, where he arrived in 1835. He composed mostly vocal works, including the opera *The Lily of Killarney* (perf., 1862) and the choral piece *The Legent of St. Cecilia* (1866). One of the finest pianists of his day, he performed with a pre-Lisztian clarity and wrote two piano concertos.

BERGER, ARTHUR (born May 15, 1912, in New York City, New York). Composer. He wrote his early works in a neoclassical, Stravinskian fashion. Later he turned to post-Webernian serialism. However, throughout his career he has demonstrated personal characteristics, notably his clear textures and large, nervous melodic leaps. His most widely played early work is the *Woodwind Quartet* (1941). A transitional period, during which Berger wrote what he himself called "neoclassical twelve-tone" music, is represented by his *Chamber Music* for thirteen instruments (1956). His later style, generally serial but by no means strictly so, has yielded such outstanding works as the *Movement* for orchestra (1969); the *Trio* for guitar, violin, and piano (1972); and the *Improvisation for A.C. for piano* (1981).

BERGSON, MICHAEL (originally MICHAL SONNENBERG, took surname BERGSON, derived from BERKSON ["son of Berek"], his father being named Berek Sonnenberg [né Zbitkower]; born May 20, 1820, in Warsaw, Poland; died March 9, 1898, in London, England). Pianist and composer. He concertized in Italy (1846-50), Austria-Germany (1850-53), and Paris (1853-63). In 1863 he turned to teaching in Geneva, and late in life he settled in London. His piano music is patterned after Chopin's. Bergson also composed operas, songs, and a variety of instrumental works. He was the father of the great French philosopher Henri Bergson.

BERLIJN, ANTON (originally ARON WOLF; born May 2, 1817, in Amsterdam, the Netherlands; died January 18, 1870, in Amsterdam, the Netherlands). Composer and conductor. In Amsterdam he conducted several singing societies and directed synagogal music. His compositions include a wide variety of secular and liturgical music. Berlijn's archives, including correspondence with such eminent musicians as Mendelssohn and Meyerbeer, are stored at the National and University Library in Jerusalem.

BERLINSKI, HERMAN (born August 18, 1910, in Leipzig, Germany). Composer. During World War II he immigrated to the United States, where he eventually worked as music director of the Washington, D.C., Hebrew Congregation. His music echoes elements of traditional Jewish cantillation, yet it is often cast in a modernistic idiom, including the use of the twelve-tone technique. His secular works include the *Flute Sonata* (1941) and several sinfonias for organ. Among his liturgical works are the *Kaddish* ("Holy," 1953) and the *Avodat Shabbat* ("Sabbath Service," 1957).

BERNSTEIN, ELMER (born April 4, 1922, in New York City, New York). Composer. After a few years as a concert pianist in the late 1940s, he turned to composing background scores for movies. His second film score, *Sudden Fear* (1952), attracted favorable attention. But it was with his jazz score for *The Man with the Golden Arm* (1955) that he rose to great prominence. Since then he has been one of the film industry's most successful composers. He has a distinctive style, sometimes including jazz elements, as in *Walk on the Wild Side* (1962), but more often characterized by a fresh lyricism, an economical orchestral texture, and a penchant for thematic metamorphosis, notably in *The Great Escape* (1963). Among his other memorable film scores are those for *The Ten Commandments* (1956), *The Magnificent Seven* (1960), *Summer and Smoke* (1961), *Birdman of Alcatraz* (1962), *To Kill a Mockingbird* (1962), *The World of Henry Orient* (1964), *True Grit* (1969), *The Shootist* (1976), *Airplane!* (1980), *The Chosen* (1982), and *The Black Cauldron* (1985).

BIKEL, THEODORE (born May 2, 1924, in Vienna, Austria). Singer. He settled in Palestine in 1938 and the United States in 1954. A well-known actor, he is also a remarkable scholar, linguist, and singer. He collected folksongs in various languages and published some of them with comments in the book *Folksongs and Footnotes* (1960). Bikel has appeared as a concert folksinger, accompanying himself on the guitar, in America and elsewhere since 1955, and he has sung many times on radio and TV. His albums include *Bravo Bikel* (1959), *Folk Songs from Just About Everywhere* (1959), and *From Bondage to Freedom* (1961). Bikel was the original Captain Georg Von Trapp in Rodgers and Hammerstein's Broadway musical *The Sound of Music* in 1959. He has starred as Tevye in numerous productions of Bock and Harnick's *Fiddler on the Roof* and as Mayer Rothschild in Bock and Harnick's *The Rothschilds*.

BINDER, ABRAHAM WOLFE (born January 13, 1895, in New York City, New York; died October 10, 1966, in New York City, New York). Composer and conductor. Son and grandson of cantors, he began to lead choirs in 1909, at the age of fourteen. In 1917 he organized the first music department ever established for a YMHA, at the Ninety-second Street branch in New York City. In 1922 he became music director at the Stephen Wise Free Synagogue, where he reintroduced the traditional chanting of the Bible yet retained the Reform spirit. Binder composed a number of effective instrumental works, such as *Holy Land Impres-*

sions for orchestra (1932) and *Dybbuk Suite* for chamber ensemble (1956), as well as the opera *A Goat from Chelm* (perf. 1960). He also wrote cantatas, oratorios, and synagogal services.

BIRNBAUM, EDUARD (born 1855 in Cracow, Poland; died 1920 in Königsberg, Germany [now Kaliningrad, the Soviet Union]). Cantor, musicologist, liturgiologist, and composer. Besides serving as chief cantor in Königsberg from 1879 to 1920, he composed liturgical works, collected old Hebrew music manuscripts, published many studies on Jewish music and liturgy, and compiled a thematic catalog of Ashkenazic synagogal melodies covering the entire oral and written tradition to 1910. Many of his papers are now in the Birnbaum Collection at Hebrew Union College in Cincinnati, Ohio.

BLANTER, MATVEY (born February 10, 1903, in Potshep, Chernigov region, Russia). Composer. He is known primarily for his songs, including "Katyusha" (1938), which attained international popularity during World War II. Composer of light, lyrical, Russian-flavored music, Blanter is regarded in his native land as a creator of the modern Soviet song style.

BLECH, LEO (born April 21, 1871, in Aachen, Germany; died August 24, 1958, in Berlin, Germany). Conductor and composer. He conducted opera in Aachen (1893–99) and Prague (1899–1906), after which he spent most of his time in Berlin. In 1937 the Nazis would not let him return from a guest appearance in Riga. He lived in Riga for four years, moved to Stockholm in 1941, and finally returned to Berlin in 1949. Blech, whose conducting style was clear and elegant, focused on the operas of Wagner, Verdi, and Bizet. He composed his own operas in the tradition of Engelbert Humperdinck.

BLOCH, ANDRÉ (born January 18, 1873, in Wissembourg, Germany [now Wissembourg, France]; died August 7, 1960, in Paris, France). Composer. In 1893 he won the Prix de Rome. Bloch composed operas and symphonic works, the best being the *Suite palestinienne* ("Palestinian Suite") for cello and orchestra (1948).

BLUMENFELD, FELIX (born April 19, 1863, in Kovalyovka, near Kherson, Russia; died January 21, 1931, in Moscow, the Soviet Union). Pianist and composer. His piano playing was influenced by the brilliant, lyric manner of Anton Rubinstein. In turn, Blumenfeld developed a method of piano teaching that influenced Heinrich Neuhaus (Blumenfeld's nephew) and other great Soviet pianists. One of Blumenfeld's own pupils was Vladimir Horowitz. As a composer Blumenfeld was influenced by Chopin and was most effective in his piano variations and preludes.

BLUMENTHAL, JACOB (or JACQUES BLUMENTHAL; born October 4, 1829, in Hamburg, Germany; died May 17, 1908, in London, England). Pianist and composer. In 1848 he settled in London, where he served as court pianist to Queen Victoria and composed piano pieces in a fashionable salon style. However, he gained his greatest fame among the English, most of whom knew him as Jacques Blumenthal (being so listed in the *Dictionary of National Biography),* as a composer of sentimental songs, such as "The Days That Are No More" (lyrics, Alfred Tennyson; pub. probably 1861), "The Day Is Past" (lyrics, Felicia Hemans; pub. probably 1871), and "Come Not, When I Am Dead" (lyrics, Alfred Tennyson; pub. 1894).

BOCK, JERRY (originally JERROLD BOCK; born November 23, 1928, in New Haven, Connecticut). Composer. After contributing songs to TV programs in the early 1950s, he turned to Broadway, where he composed the song scores for the musicals *Fiorello!* (perf. 1959), *The Rothschilds* (perf. 1970), and many others. His greatest hit was the musical *Fiddler on the Roof* (perf. 1964), a story about Jews in a 1905 Russian village. *Fiddler*'s songs—including "*If I Were a Rich Man,*" "*Sunrise, Sunset,*" and "*Tradition*" (lyrics, Sheldon Harnick)—are essentially in a Broadway idiom, but some have a Jewish flavor.

BODANZKY, ARTUR (born December 16, 1877, in Vienna, Austria; died November 23, 1939, in New York City, New York). Conductor. He became Gustav Mahler's assistant at the Vienna Opera in 1902, and there soon followed conducting engagements at theaters and concert halls in major European cities. From 1915 on, New York City was his center of activity, particularly at the Metropolitan Opera. He had a large repertory, but he was best known for his Wagner. Bodanzky's conducting style followed the Mahlerian tradition of emphasizing climactic effects and color contrasts.

BODKY, ERWIN (born March 7, 1896, in Ragnit, Germany [now Neman, the Soviet Union]; died December 6, 1958, in Lucerne, Switzerland). Keyboardist and musicologist. He was active as a pianist and teacher in Berlin during the 1920s and in Amsterdam from 1933 to 1938, when he settled in the United States. In 1942 he founded the Cambridge Collegium Musicum (later the Cambridge Society for Early Music), an organization that stimulated him to perform on the harpsichord and clavichord and to do scholarly research, as in his book *The Interpretation of Bach's Keyboard Works* (1960).

BONOFF, KARLA (born 1952 in Los Angeles, California). Singer and composer. She came to prominence when her friend Linda Ronstadt recorded three Bonoff songs, including "Lose Again," for the album *Hasten Down the Wind* (1976). Bonoff's music and lyrics mix folk and folk-rock elements. Her own albums include *Karla Bonoff* (1977) and *Wild Heart of the Young* (1981).

BORGE, VICTOR (originally BORGE ROSENBAUM; born January 3, 1909, in Copenhagen, Denmark). Pianist and comedian. After appearing as a youthful concert pianist for a number of years (1922–34), he turned to a unique kind of sophisticated musical humor and became one of Denmark's leading personalities on stage, screen, and radio. In 1940 he left Nazi-dominated Europe and immigrated to the United States, where he performed frequently on radio and in nightclubs during the 1940s, later giving numerous one-man shows in theaters and on TV specials. His one-man Broadway show *Comedy in Music* was an outstanding success, running from 1953 to 1956. Borge, however, is still a first-rate musician, and he has continued to appear as soloist with major symphony orchestras.

BOROVSKY, ALEXANDER (born March 18, 1889, in Mitau, Latvia [now Jelgava, the Soviet Union]; died April 27, 1968, in Waban, Massachusetts). Pianist. After touring for many years as a concert pianist throughout Europe, he settled in the United States in 1941. Borovsky made numerous recordings in his late years, especially of Bach and Liszt.

BRAHAM, JOHN (originally JOHN ABRAHAM; born March 20, 1774, in London, England; died February 17, 1856, in London, England). Tenor and composer. His surname was a clipped form of his father's name, Abraham, a choir singer at the Great Synagogue in London, where John Braham himself sang as a child. Later he sang English and Italian operas in England, Italy, and elsewhere. Soon he began to collaborate with composers by writing music for his own, and sometimes other, roles in new operas. His most popular interpolation was "The Death of Nelson" in Matthew Peter King's opera *The Americans* (perf. 1811). Braham was the singer who introduced (and helped to edit) Isaac Nathan's work *A Selection of Hebrew Melodies, Ancient and Modern* in the late 1810s. He had a remarkable voice, with an even scale throughout an extremely wide vocal range. In his late years he became a baritone, making his last appearance in 1852, at the age of seventy-eight.

BRANT, HENRY (born September 15, 1913, in Montreal, Canada). Composer. He is a pioneer in spatial-antiphonal music, in which widely separated groups of performers are placed at specified points in the auditorium. Each group plays, simultaneously and/or antiphonally, music that is entirely different from that of the other groups. His stated purpose is to evoke the "new stresses, layered insanities, and multidirectional assaults of contemporary life on the spirit." Such works include *Antiphony I* (1953), *The Grand Universal Circus* (a theater piece, with musical and dramatic incidents, 1956), *Voyage Four* (with performers positioned on the walls and beneath the floor, 1963), *Antiphonal Responses* (1977), *The Secret Calendar* (1980), and *Meteor Farm* (1982).

BRECHER, GUSTAV (born February 5, 1879, in Eichwald, near Teplitz [now Teplice], Bohemia [now in Czechoslovakia]; died May 1940 in Ostend, Belgium). Conductor. He conducted in several German cities, notably Frankfort on the Main (1916–24) and Leipzig (1924–33). While attempting to flee from pursuing Nazis, he and his wife committed suicide aboard a boat off the Belgian coast when their vessel was intercepted by the Germans.

BRÉVAL, LUCIENNE (originally BERTHA SCHILLING; born November 4, 1869, in Männedorf, Switzerland; died August 15, 1935, in Neuilly-sur-Seine, near Paris, France). Soprano. In 1892 she joined the Paris Opéra, which she dominated for the next thirty years. An outstanding dramatic soprano, she was most famous for her Brünnhilde in Wagner's *Die Walküre* ("The Valkyrie") and her Carmen in Bizet's *Carmen*. She also sang in the world premieres of many operas by French composers, including Dukas, Fauré, and Massenet. In classical grand opera, Bréval set the standard for her time.

BRODSKY, ADOLPH (originally ADOLF BRODSKY; born April 2, 1851, in Taganrog, Russia; died January 22, 1929, in Manchester, England). Violinist. In 1881 in Vienna he gave the world premiere of Tchaikovsky's *Violin Concerto*, which had previously been declared unplayable by Leopold Auer. Brodsky served as concertmaster of the New York Symphony Orchestra (1890–94) and then directed the Manchester College of Music (1895–1929). He also led his own string quartet in Manchester for almost thirty years. While in England he anglicized the spelling of his first name from Adolf to Adolph.

BROOKS, ELKIE (born February 25, 1945, in Manchester,

England). Singer. She is noted for her blues inflections and jazz-rock fusions. Her albums include *Rich Man's Woman* (1975) and *Live and Learn* (1979).

BROWNING, JOHN (born May 23, 1933, in Denver, Colorado). Pianist. He won the Leventritt Award in 1955 and took second place in the 1956 Queen Elisabeth International Piano Competition in Brussels. Since then he has concertized internationally, concentrating on Mozart, nineteenth-century romantics, Prokofiev, and Samuel Barber, whose *Piano Concerto* Browning introduced in 1962.

BRÜLL, IGNAZ (born November 7, 1846, in Prossnitz, Moravia [now Prostĕjov, Czechoslovakia]; died September 17, 1907, in Vienna, Austria). Pianist and composer. Early in his career Brüll made many concert tours, but gradually he became more involved with composing. He developed a close friendship with Johannes Brahms, who highly valued Brüll's musicianship and judgment. Brahms and Brüll often played four-hand arrangements of Brahms's new works. The most successful composition from Brüll's own pen was the opera *Das goldene Kreuz* ("The Golden Cross," perf. 1875). He also wrote many piano works.

BUKOFZER, MANFRED F(RITZ) (born March 17, 1910, in Oldenburg, Germany; died December 7, 1955, in Berkeley, California). Musicologist. He immigrated to the United States in 1939. His *Music in the Baroque Era* (1947) has become a standard text. Among his other works are *Studies in Medieval and Renaissance Music* (1950) and *The Place of Musicology in American Institutions of Higher Learning* (1957).

C

CASTELNUOVO-TEDESCO, MARIO (born April 3, 1895, in Florence, Italy; died March 16, 1968, in Los Angeles, California). Composer. He earned an international reputation in Italy before Mussolini's anti-Semitic policies drove him out in 1939. Immigrating to the United States, he soon settled in southern California, where he composed background scores for films, such as *And Then There Were None* (1945). He blended Italian, Spanish, and French sources into a mild but sophisticated style of modernism that can be characterized as a personal brand of impressionism. Though he wrote concert works of many kinds and lengths, he was at his best in small forms: songs, piano pieces, guitar solos. His Jewish-related works include *Le danze del re David* ("The Dances of King David") for piano (1925), a rhapsody on traditional Hebrew themes; *Second Violin Concerto: I profeti* ("The Prophets," 1931), partly based on Jewish Italian melodies; *Sacred Service* (1943, enlarged 1950), one of the great monuments of art music for the synagogue; and *Memorial Service for the Departed* (1960).

CERVETTO, GIACOBBE BASEVI (originally GIACOBBE [or JACOB] BASEVI; born c. 1682 in Italy; died January 14, 1783, in London, England). Cellist and composer. By the 1740s he had settled in England and had begun to give concerts in London. He was one of a group of Italians who first brought the cello, previously used only for accompaniment, into favor as a solo instrument in England. Cervetto

composed many chamber pieces involving the cello. He lived to be more than one hundred years old. James Cervetto, his son, was also a cellist and composer.

CHAGRIN, FRANCIS (born November 15, 1905, in Bucharest, Romania; died November 10, 1972, in London, England). Composer and conductor. In 1936 he immigrated to England, where he founded and directed the Committee (later the Society) for the Promotion of New Music (1943-72), for many years the only English organization to help young or unknown composers obtain performances of their works. Chagrin himself composed much theater and movie music, his film scores including those for *Last Holiday* (1950) and *Marriage of Convenience* (1961). His concert works are highlighted by two completed symphonies (1959, 1970).

CHAGY, BERYL (or BERELE CHAGY; born 1892 in Dagda, Latvia [now in the Soviet Union]; died April 25, 1954, in Newark, New Jersey). Cantor. At the age of eighteen he became a cantor in Smolensk, Russia. Three years later (1913) he immigrated to the United States, where he held cantorial posts in Detroit, Boston, and Newark before spending several years in Johannesburg, South Africa. Returning to America, he worked as a cantor in New York City, gave many concerts, and made numerous recordings. One of the most popular cantorial performers of his time, Chagy sang with a clear tenor voice capable of unusually graceful coloratura. His *Tefillot Chagy* ("Chagy Prayers," pub. 1937) consists of eighty-seven recitatives for use by cantors during Sabbath services. He retired in 1952, two years before he died of a heart attack while attending services at Young Israel Synagogue in Newark.

CHAJES, JULIUS (born December 21, 1910, in Lemberg, Galicia [now Lvov, the Soviet Union]). Composer and pianist. In 1933 he won the piano prize at an international competition in Vienna. The following year found him in Tel Aviv, teaching piano. In 1937 he immigrated to the United States, where in 1940 he became music director of the Jewish Community Center in Detroit. His compositions strongly reflect the flavor of Jewish melos, and he frequently quotes actual folksongs or religious melodies. Chajes has written a wide variety of instrumental pieces and vocal works, including liturgical music. Among his best-known compositions are several cantatas on biblical subjects, notably *The Promised Land* (pub. 1951).

CHASINS, ABRAM (born August 17, 1903, in New York

City, New York). Pianist, composer, and writer. He toured as a concert pianist from the mid-1920s to the mid-1940s. His compositions are colorfully neoromantic in style, as in the two piano concertos (1928, 1931), the popular *Three Chinese Pieces* for piano (1928), and the *Parade* for orchestra (1930). In 1931 an orchestral version of *Three Chinese Pieces* (1929) became the first work by an American composer ever conducted by Arturo Toscanini. Chasins has written several popular books on music, notably *Speaking of Pianists* (1957; third edition, 1982), *Music at the Crossroads* (1972), and *Leopold Stokowski: A Profile* (1979).

CHERKASSKY, SHURA (born October 7, 1911, in Odessa,

the Ukraine [now in the Soviet Union]). Pianist. He immigrated to the United States when he was a child and debuted, in Baltimore, at the age of eleven. Since then he has made many worldwide tours. One of the last great pianists of the romantic tradition, Cherkassky has a brilliant technique, a wide range of tone color, and an imaginative sense of interpretation. He is especially effective with Liszt's operatic paraphrases and Tchaikovsky's *First Piano Concerto*.

COHEN, HARRIET (born December 2, 1895, in London,

England; died November 13, 1967, in London, England). Pianist. Her small hands limited her repertory, but she became an excellent performer of Bach and the contemporary English school. She gave the world premiere of Ralph Vaughan Williams's *Piano Concerto* in 1933, and most of Arnold Bax's piano pieces were written for her. During a London benefit concert for refugee scientists in 1934, she was accompanied on the violin by Albert Einstein. Cohen also supported Jewish, especially Israeli, causes. After she injured her right hand in 1948, she played with only her left hand till she resumed two-handed playing in 1951. But the injury never properly healed, and in 1960 she had to retire. She presented her ideas on piano playing in the book *Music's Handmaid* (1936, revised 1950) and also wrote *A Bundle of Time: The Memoirs of Harriet Cohen* (1969).

COHEN, LEONARD (born September 21, 1934, in Montreal, Canada). Singer and composer. His lyrics characteristically center on existential despair, while his music is in a folk or folk-rock idiom. At least two of his songs, "Suzanne" and "Bird on a Wire," have been widely sung by other performers. His own recordings include the albums *The Songs of Leonard Cohen* (1967), with "Suzanne" and "Sisters of Mercy"; *Songs from a Room* (1969), with "Bird on a Wire"; and *Recent Songs* (1979).

COHN, AL(VIN) (born November 24, 1925, in New York City, New York). Jazz saxophonist and arranger. He played the saxophone in bands led by Woody Herman, Buddy Rich, and Artie Shaw. Cohn has written material for TV shows hosted by Steve Allen, Pat Boone, and Andy Williams, and has orchestrated several Broadway musicals.

COLEMAN, CY (originally SEYMOUR KAUFMAN; born June 14, 1929, in New York City, New York). Composer and pianist. At the age of six he began to give piano recitals, and in his late teens he started to play in New York City nightclubs. In the 1950s he composed music for radio and TV shows. His reputation began to grow when he wrote the songs "Witchcraft" (lyrics, Carolyn Leigh; for an unproduced revue, then for the nightclub revue *Take Five*, perf. 1957) and "Firefly" (lyrics, Carolyn Leigh; 1958). He went on to compose complete song scores for a number of Broadway musicals, including *Wildcat* (perf. 1960), with "Hey, Look Me Over" (lyrics, Carolyn Leigh); *Sweet Charity* (perf. 1966), with "Big Spender" (lyrics, Dorothy Fields); and *I Love My Wife* (perf. 1977), with "Hey There, Good Times" (lyrics, Michael Stewart). Coleman has also composed for films, including background scores for *Father Goose* (1964), *The Troublemaker* (1964), and *The Art of Love* (1965). He supplied *Father Goose* with the lighthearted "Pass Me By" (lyrics, Carolyn Leigh).

COLONNE, EDOUARD (originally JUDAS COLONNE; born July 23, 1838, in Bordeaux, France; died March 28, 1910, in Paris, France). Conductor. In 1873 he founded an orchestral association that later became famous as the Colonne Concerts. He took the orchestra on many tours to other countries, including Russia and the United States. Colonne built the group's reputation mainly through performances of Berlioz and new works. Among his world premieres were those of Georges Enesco's *First Symphony* in 1906 and Maurice Ravel's *Rapsodie espagnole* ("Spanish Rhapsody") in 1908.

CONSOLO, FEDERICO (or JEHIEL NAHMANY SEFARDI;

born April 8, 1841, in Ancona, Italy; died December 14, 1906, in Florence, Italy). Violinist, researcher, and composer. He was a successful violin virtuoso till his early forties, when a nerve injury ended his career. Consolo then turned to composition and research, his most important publication being *Sefer shire Yisrael* ("Book of the Songs of Israel," 1892), a collection of traditional Sephardic synagogal songs for unaccompanied voice.

COOPER, EMIL (born December 20, 1877, in Kherson, Russia; died November 16, 1960, in New York City, New York). Conductor. He made his conducting debut, in Odessa, in 1896. After conducting opera in Kiev (1900-1904), he went to Moscow, where he led the world premiere of Rimsky-Korsakov's *The Golden Cockerel* in 1909 and the first performances of works by Rachmaninoff, Scriabin, and others. Cooper periodically conducted Sergei Diaghilev's ballet and opera troupe in Paris. After 1922 he conducted internationally, having especially strong connections with the Chicago Civic Opera, the Metropolitan Opera in New York City, and the Montreal Opera Guild.

COSTA, MICHAEL (originally MICHELE COSTA; born February 4, 1808, in Naples, Italy; died April 29, 1884, in Hove, England). Conductor and composer. In 1829 he went to England, and over the next fifty years he was a dominant personality there, directing London's leading symphonic and choral ensembles. He also founded the Royal Italian Opera (1847), with which he earned a reputation as one of the outstanding opera conductors of his time. His compositions include operas, ballets, and oratorios.

COWEN, FREDERIC HYMEN (originally HYMEN FREDERICK COWEN; born January 29, 1852, in Kingston, Jamaica; died October 6, 1935, in London, England). Composer, writer, conductor, and pianist. At the age of four he was taken to England. After working for a time as a pianist and composer, he conducted the London Philharmonic (1888-92, 1900-1907) and several other orchestras. His best-known compositions are his light orchestral pieces, such as *In the Olden Time* (1883) and *The Butterfly's Ball* (1901). Cowen also wrote biographies of Haydn, Mendelssohn, and Mozart (all three, 1912); *My Art and My Friends* (1913), his memoirs; and *Music As She Is Wrote* (1915), an amusing glossary of musical terms.

D

DAMROSCH, LEOPOLD (born October 22, 1832, in Posen, Germany [now Poznań, Poland]; died February 15, 1885, in New York City, New York). Violinist and conductor. In 1857 Franz Liszt appointed Damrosch principal violinist of the court orchestra in Weimar. From 1858 to 1871 Damrosch was active, especially in Breslau, as a violinist and conductor. In 1871 he immigrated to the United States and settled in New York City, where he founded the Oratorio Society (1873) and the Symphony Society (1878), both of which he conducted for the rest of his life. He also helped to establish a German repertory at the Metropolitan Opera during the 1884-85 season, conducting the American premieres of several Wagner works. Before his 1857 marriage

to the singer Helene von Heimburg, he was baptized into her Lutheran faith. Three of their children became famous in music: Frank, a choral conductor and music educator; Walter, a symphony and opera conductor; and Clara, a pianist and the wife of the musician-educator David Mannes.

DAVID, FERDINAND (born probably June 19 [sometimes listed as January 19], 1810, in Hamburg, Germany; died July 18, 1873, near Klosters, Switzerland). Violinist. In his childhood he gave recitals with piano accompaniment by Louise David, his sister (who later gained fame as Madame Dulcken), and developed a friendship with Felix Mendelssohn, with whom he often played chamber music. In 1836 he was appointed concertmaster of the Leipzig Gewandhaus Orchestra under Mendelssohn, a post that David held with special distinction for the rest of his life. In 1843 he became

the first head of the violin department of the new Leipzig Conservatory (founded by Mendelssohn), where he guided many of the nineteenth century's finest violinists, including Joseph Joachim. In 1845 David gave the world premiere of Mendelssohn's *Violin Concerto,* which owed some of its success to the invaluable advice that David had given Mendelssohn during the composition of the work. Though he continued to appear as a soloist, David earned renown primarily as a concertmaster and, increasingly in his later years, as a conductor. He played with great technical command, musicianship, and intelligence. David edited many works, notably the first practical edition of Bach's unaccompanied violin pieces. His *Violinschule* ("Violin Method," 1863) and studies were widely used till the end of the nineteenth century.

DAVID, SAMUEL (born November 12, 1836, in Paris,

France; died October 3, 1895, in Paris, France). Composer. He won the Prix de Rome in 1858. In 1872 he became music director of the Paris synagogues, a post that he held for the rest of his life. David composed operas, symphonies, and a variety of vocal pieces, including synagogal works.

DAVIDOV, KARL (originally KARL DAVIDHOFF; born March 15, 1838, in Goldingen, Courland [now Kuldiga, the Soviet Union]; died February 26, 1889, in Moscow, Russia). Cellist. In his youth he left his native Russia and spent three years (1859-62) in Leipzig, where he performed as a soloist, chamber-music player, and principal cellist of the Gewandhaus Orchestra. In 1862 he returned to Russia, eventually serving as director of the Saint Petersburg Conservatory (1876-87). He also made European concert tours, during which he sometimes performed with such musical giants as Franz Liszt, Anton Rubinstein, and Camille Saint-Saëns.

DESSAU, PAUL (born December 19, 1894, in Hamburg, Germany; died June 28, 1979, in East Berlin, East Germany). Composer and conductor. Early in his career he coached and conducted at opera houses in several cities, notably Berlin (1925-33). In 1933 he went to Paris and then, during World War II, to America. In 1948 he returned to Germany and settled in East Berlin. A devoted Marxist, Dessau wrote many politically slanted vocal and stage works in collaboration with the writer Bertolt Brecht. He composed prolifically in most of the established genres, especially those favored by socialist realists: operas, incidental music to plays, film scores, choral works, and songs. His style is based in Viennese expressionism, with some traces of Jewish folk elements. One of his best late works, the opera *Einstein* (perf. 1973), contains a vast array of diverse material, including the twelve-tone technique, aleatoric passages, jazz, popular styles, and Bach quotations.

DEUTSCH, OTTO ERICH (born September 5, 1883, in Vienna, Austria; died November 23, 1967, in Vienna, Austria). Biographer and bibliographer. With the rise of Nazism he left his native Vienna and spent the years 1939-51 in England, where he proposed and edited (1946-50) a union catalog of all music printed before 1801 and held in British libraries. In 1951 he returned to Vienna. Deutsch's great contribution to music was to raise the documentary biography to a new level of meticulous scholarship. His studies of Handel and Mozart are important, but he is best known for his work on Schubert. His Schubert biography was published in German in 1914; part of it was published in English in London as *Schubert: A Documentary Biography* (1946), the American version being *The Schubert Reader: A Life of Franz Schubert in Letters and Documents* (1947). In 1951 Deutsch (with Donald R. Wakeling) published a thematic catalog of Schubert's works, which are now routinely identified by the numbers attached to them by Deutsch.

DRESDEN, SEM (born April 20, 1881, in Amsterdam, the Netherlands; died July 30, 1957, in The Hague, the Netherlands). Composer. His works are in a German neoromantic style, with some harmonic traits characteristic of French impressionism and some melodic rhythms derived from Dutch music. Before 1935 he concentrated on chamber and vocal music, notably the choral work *Chorus tragicus* ("Tragic Chorus," 1927), whose subject is the fall of Jerusalem. During the period 1935-50 he wrote a series of solo concertos. After that, he composed a variety of works, including the *Dansflitsen* ("Dance Flashes") for orchestra

(1951) and the *Chorus symphonicus* ("Symphonic Chorus") for vocal soloists, chorus, and orchestra (1955).

DUKAS, PAUL (born October 1, 1865, in Paris, France; died May 17, 1935, in Paris, France). Composer. Some of his compositions are classical in spirit, while others are romantic with an overlay of impressionistic devices borrowed from his friend Claude Debussy. The classically oriented *Symphony in C Major* (1896) is a joyful work recalling the extrovert manner of Georges Bizet. The tone poem *L'apprenti sorcier* ("The Sorcerer's Apprentice," 1897), Dukas's most famous work, was inspired by a Goethe ballad (in turn derived from a tale by the ancient Roman author Lucian) that tells how a sorcerer's apprentice gets into difficulties when he tries to apply his master's magic. The work succeeds in at least three ways: its effective illustration of the program; its brilliant orchestration; and its taut, almost Beethovenian, construction, which gives the piece a classical shape despite its romantic-impressionistic thematic and harmonic contents. Dukas contributed two important works to the French piano repertory with his *Piano Sonata in E-flat Minor* (1901) and his *Variations, interlude, et final sur un thème de Rameau* ("Variations, Interlude, and Finale on a Theme by Rameau," 1902). Both works can be termed classical in spirit, though the monumental sonata shows some of the fire of Beethoven, and the variations cover a wide range of rapidly shifting moods, including a rare hint of his Judaic heritage in a bass passage reminiscent of solemn synagogal chant. More overtly romantic in conception are the opera *Ariane et Barbe-bleue* ("Ariadne and Bluebeard"; comp. 1906, perf. 1907) and the ballet *La péri* ("The Peri," 1912). A meticulous craftsman, Dukas always wrote slowly. In his late years his enthusiasm for composition almost completely ceased. Finally, in his last lucid moments before his death, the perfectionist Dukas destroyed all of his unpublished manuscripts.

DU PRÉ, JACQUELINE (born January 26, 1945, in Oxford, England). Cellist. Born of non-Jewish parents, she converted to Judaism when she married the pianist-conductor Daniel Barenboim in 1967. Though commanding an impeccable technique, du Pré played instinctively, in a passionate, broadly conceived manner. Her trademark work was Elgar's *Cello Concerto*. In 1973 she developed multiple sclerosis, which ended her career.

DUSHKIN, SAMUEL (born December 13, 1891, in Suwalki, Poland; died June 24, 1976, in New York City, New York). Violinist. He immigrated to the United States when he was a child. Dushkin toured Europe from 1918 and the United States from 1924. Especially identified with contemporary music, Dushkin performed the world premieres of Stravinsky's *Violin Concerto* in 1931 and *Duo concertante* ("Concertante for Two") in 1932. And with Stravinsky he toured Europe (1932-34) and made recordings.

E

EDWARDS, GUS (originally GUSTAVE EDWARD SIMON; born August 18, 1879, in Inowrazlaw [now Inowrocław; German, Hohensalza], Poland; died November 7, 1945, in Los Angeles, California). Composer and singer. At the age of eight he immigrated with his family to the United States. He became a vaudeville singer and then began to compose his own songs. His "Tammany" (lyrics, Vincent P. Bryan; 1905) became the official theme song of the New York Democratic political machine. "In My Merry Oldsmobile" (lyrics, Vincent P. Bryan; 1905) was the first hit on the subject of automobiles. He also composed the popular "If a Girl like You Loved a Boy like Me" (lyrics, Will D. Cobb; 1905). In 1907 he created a vaudeville act in which he starred as a schoolmaster, supported by a number of child performers. The show was a huge success and lasted for about twenty-five years. He had one of the sharpest eyes for talent in the history of show business, discovering, and putting into his act, many future celebrities, such as Ray Bolger, Eddie Cantor, George Jessel, Groucho Marx, Eleanor Powell, and Walter Winchell. Edwards came to be known as the Star Maker. He composed most of the songs for the show, including the well-known "School Days" (lyrics, Will D. Cobb; 1907) and the classic "By the Light of the Silvery Moon" (lyrics, Edward Madden; 1909).

EDWARDS, SHERMAN (born April 3, 1919, in New York City, New York; died March 30, 1981, in New York City, New York). Composer. He wrote the music for such popular songs as "Broken-hearted Melody" (lyrics, Hal David; 1959) and "See You in September " (lyrics, Sid Wayne; 1959). One of his major efforts was the Broadway musical *1776* (perf. 1969).

EINSTEIN, ALFRED (born December 30, 1880, in Munich, Germany; died February 13, 1952, in El Cerrito, California). Musicologist. Cousin of the scientist Albert Einstein. After the Nazis came to power in 1933, he went to England and Italy before arriving in the United States in the late 1930s. His most important work is *The Italian Madrigal* (1949), the first comprehensive study of that subject in any language. He edited the ninth through eleventh editions (1910-29) of Hugo Riemann's *Musik Lexikon* ("Music Dictionary"). His essays, on an extremely wide variety of music topics, are consistently brilliant. His work as a music critic led him to write the fine survey for general readers *Geschichte der Musik* (1917; revised sixth edition, 1953; English, 1936; Fifth English edition, as *A Short History of Music,* 1948). Less highly regarded by many musicologists are Einstein's *Mozart: His Character, His Work* (1945; fourth edition, 1959) and *Music in the Romantic Era* (1947; second edition, 1949).

EISLER, HANNS (born July 6, 1898, in Leipzig, Germany; died September 6, 1962, in East Berlin, East Germany). Composer. His early works, such as the first two piano sonatas (1923, 1924), reflect the complex modernism of Arnold Schoenberg, his teacher. Joining the German Communist party in 1926, Eisler began to write simpler, politically slanted music, mostly vocal works with texts often supplied by Bertolt Brecht. In 1933 Eisler left Nazi-dominated Germany, finally settling in the United States in 1938. There he composed background scores for such

movies as *Hangmen Also Die* (1943) and *None but the Lonely Heart* (1944) and wrote (assisted by Theodor W. Adorno) the book *Composing for the Films* (1947). After being attacked by the Committee on Un-American Activities in 1947, he was deported in 1948. Eisler went to East Berlin and composed music in a popular style that reflected the spirit of the revolutionary socialist movement, as in his film scores, incidental music to plays, and vocal works, one of which was the national anthem of East Germany. He did, however, continue to write some concert works, such as the *Rhapsodie* for soprano and orchestra (1949). Eisler used a wide variety of techniques in his music. His songs, aimed at the masses, tend to be simple and diatonic; but they have a freshness created by avoiding conventional patterns. At the other pole are some of his orchestral and chamber pieces written in an advanced, dissonant, chromatic style. Many of his works combine the two approaches.

ELLIOT, CASS(ANDRA) (originally ELLEN NAOMI COHEN; born September 19, 1943, in Baltimore, Maryland; died July 29, 1974, in London, England). Singer. In 1965, coming out of the Greenwich Village folk scene, she helped to form the Mamas and the Papas, a folk-rock group. After the group broke up in 1968, Mama Cass, as she billed herself, went solo, recording the hit single "Dream a Little Dream of Me" (1968), as well as the albums *Make Your Own Kind of Music* (1969) and *Mama's Big Ones* (1971).

ELLIOTT, RAMBLIN' JACK (originally ELLIOTT CHARLES ADNOPOZ; born August 1, 1931, in New York City, New York). Singer. He went to Greenwich Village, became a protégé of Woody Guthrie, and made an impact during the urban folk movement of the 1950s and 1960s. His repertory consists largely of Guthrie songs, with Bob Dylan material also heavily represented. Elliott's principal work is the album *The Essential Ramblin' Jack Elliott* (1976).

ELLIS, VIVIAN (born October 29, 1903, in Hampstead, England). Composer. In the mid-1920s he began to supply music for English musical comedies and revues. His first big success was *Mr. Cinders* (perf. 1928). After World War II he turned to light operas, notably *Bless the Bride* (perf. 1947). Ellis became a director of the Performing Right Society in 1955, rising to the presidency in 1983.

ELMAN, MISCHA (born January 20, 1891, in Talnoye, near Kiev, the Ukraine [now in the Soviet Union]; died April 5, 1967, in New York City, New York). Violinist. At thirteen Elman began his meteoric rise with his debut, in Saint Petersburg, followed by spectacular appearances in Berlin (1904), London (1905), and New York City (1908). In 1911 he settled in the United States. He made many world tours, founded the Elman String Quartet (1926), and in 1943 gave the world premiere of Bohuslav Martinu's *Violin Concerto.* At his peak he and Jascha Heifetz were synonymous with violinistic prowess. But while Heifetz gained fame especially for his technique, Elman earned renown primarily for his rich, sensuous, expressive tone, which entered into music legends as "the Elman tone." His passionate temperament found its best outlet in the romantic concertos of Mendelssohn, Tchaikovsky, and Wieniawski, though he also effectively interpreted Beethoven and Mozart.

ELMAN, ZIGGY (originally HARRY FINKELMAN; born May 26, 1914, in Philadelphia, Pennsylvania; died June 26, 1968, in Van Nuys, California). Jazz trumpeter. He was best known as the featured trumpeter with Benny Goodman's band (1936-40), especially in the group's rendition of "And the Angels Sing." After a stint with Tommy Dorsey (1940-47, except for military service, 1943-46), he went to Los Angeles and led his own band at the Palladium. Later he did commercial TV work for Dinah Shore, Bing Crosby, and others. Elman had a florid style and often wove elements of frailachs (lively Jewish folk-dance tunes) into his solos.

ENGEL, JOEL (originally YULY [or JULIUS] ENGEL; born April 16, 1868, in Berdyansk, the Ukraine [now in the Soviet Union]; died February 11, 1927, in Tel Aviv, Palestine [now Israel]). Composer. In the 1890s he began to collect, arrange, perform, and publish Jewish folksongs. When the Society for Jewish Folk Music was founded in 1908 in Russia, Engel became one of its most active members. He gained international recognition with his incidental music to the play *Ha-dybbuk* ("The Dybbuk," 1922), his score reflecting his belief that folksongs express the Jewish spirit. After two years (1922-24) in Berlin, he settled in Tel Aviv and composed Hebrew-Palestinian songs. Now regarded as the earliest pioneer of modern Jewish music, he has had his name attached to a prestigious award for composition in Israel: the Engel Prize.

ERLANGER, CAMILLE (born May 25, 1863, in Paris, France; died April 24, 1919, in Paris, France). Composer. He won the Prix de Rome in 1888 and gained fame with his opera *Le juif polonais* ("The Polish Jew," perf. 1900), which is still active in the repertories of many opera houses.

ETTINGER, MAX (born December 27, 1874, in Lemberg, Galicia [now Lvov, the Soviet Union]; died July 19, 1951, in Basel, Switzerland). Composer and conductor. He worked as a conductor in Munich (1900-1920), Leipzig (1920-29), and Berlin (1929-33). But constant ill health led him to spend more and more time on composition. In 1933 he fled to Switzerland, where he remained for the rest of his life. Ettinger composed several significant operas, as well as instrumental works, choral pieces, and songs. While his earlier music follows German romantic lines, his later music is heavily influenced by Jewish tradition, notably in the choral work *Jiddisch Requiem* ("Jewish Requiem," 1947).

EULENBURG. Family of music publishers. ERNST EULENBURG (born November 30, 1847, in Berlin, Germany; died September 11, 1926, in Leipzig, Germany) established a publishing house in his own name in Leipzig in 1874. At first he published mostly educational and choral material. Then, in the early 1890s, he acquired the miniature-score series previously published by Payne in Leipzig. More than one thousand works, including large orchestral pieces, were subsequently issued through Eulenburg's series of miniature scores. KURT EULENBURG (born February 22, 1879, in Berlin, Germany; died April 10, 1982 [at the age of 103], in London England), Ernst's son, entered the firm in 1911 and became sole owner in 1926. Besides extending the miniature-score department, he published the original text ("Urtext") of much of Mozart's music. Kurt moved the company to London in 1939 and opened branches in Zurich (1947) and Stuttgart (1950). He retired in 1968.

EWEN, DAVID (born November 26, 1907, in Lemberg, Galicia [now Lvov, the Soviet Union]; died December 28, 1985, in Miami, Florida). Writer. In America since his early childhood. He wrote much about Jewish music, notably in the

book *Hebrew Music: A Study and an Interpretation* (1931). But he is best known as the world's most prolific writer of general-audience books (about one hundred of them) covering all areas of Western serious and popular music. Many of his works deal with the classical sphere, such as *Mainstreams of Music* (four volumes, 1972-75). But he has won his greatest fame for his books on American musical theater, such as *Composers for the American Musical Theatre* (1968), and on American popular music, such as *All the Years of American Popular Music* (1977). A major recent achievement is his *American Composers: A Biographical Dictionary* (1982).

F

FALL, LEO(POLD) (born February 2, 1873, in Olmütz, Moravia [now Olomouc, Czechoslovakia]; died September 16, 1925, in Vienna, Austria). Composer. He performed as a violinist and conductor in numerous theaters till 1906, when he settled in Vienna to compose operettas. He joined Emmerich Kálmán, Franz Lehár, and Oscar Straus as one of the preeminent light composers of his time. His operettas, which are characterized by their abundance of memorable tunes, include *Die Dollarprinzessin* ("The Dollar Princess," perf. 1907), *The Eternal Waltz* (perf. 1911 in English during a visit to London), *Die Rose von Stambul* ("The Rose of Stamboul," perf. 1916), and *Madame Pompadour* (perf. 1922).

FELDMAN, MORTON (born January 12, 1926, in New York City, New York). Composer. His artistic inclinations were profoundly influenced by the work of abstract expressionist painters. The new painting inspired him to seek "a sound world more direct, more immediate, more physical than anything that had existed before. To me my score is my canvas, my space. What I do is try to sensitize this area—this time-space." He is well known for his pointillistic scoring (isolated pitches being common in his work) and his subdued dynamic range. His conception of music as a "timespace" led him to invent a new means of notation to give certain freedoms in performance. Called graphic notation, the method involves the use of drawn visual analogues (lines, boxes, numbers, and so on) to indicate pitches, rhythms, and other musical events in general terms only. His first such work was a set called *Projections I-V* for instrumental ensembles (1950-51). In 1953 he returned to conventional notation of pitches but continued to experiment with various levels of freedom for performers, especially in matters of time, as in *Piece* for four pianos (1957), *Durations I-V* for instrumental ensembles (1960-62), and *Last Pieces* for piano (1963). After 1970 he returned completely to conventional notation of fixed works, retaining, however, his unique, unsystematic style, as in *Three Clarinets, Cello, and Piano* (1971), *Piano and Orchestra* (1975), and *Why Patterns* for violin, piano, and percussion (1978).

FEUERMANN, EMANUEL (born November 22, 1902, in Kolomea, Galicia [now Kolomyya, the Soviet Union]; died May 25, 1942, in New York City, New York). Cellist. In 1909 he moved with his family to Vienna, where he debuted in 1912. In 1935 he made his American debut, and from 1938 he lived in the United States. Besides concertizing as a soloist, he became a renowned chamber-music player, notably in trios with Bronislaw Huberman (violin) and Artur Schnabel (piano), and Jascha Heifetz (violin) and Arthur Rubinstein (piano). Feuermann possessed a sure technique, warm tone, and lucid style. Some musicians regarded him as the greatest cellist of the twentieth century. But he died before he could fully establish his reputation or influence.

FISHER, AVERY (born March 4, 1906, in New York City, New York). Pioneer in audio equipment and patron of music. In 1937 he founded the company that came to be known as Fisher Radio, one of the foremost manufacturers of audio equipment. He sold the firm in 1969. Four years later he gave the New York Philharmonic $10 million to renovate the interior of Philharmonic Hall. In 1976 the auditorium was inaugurated with a gala concert at which the structure was officially renamed Avery Fisher Hall. He also created the Avery Fisher Prize, awarded periodically to outstanding musicians.

FISHER, EDDIE (originally EDWIN FISHER; born August 10, 1928, in Philadelphia, Pennsylvania). Singer. He sang on local radio shows as a child in Philadelphia, and he appeared at the famous Copacabana nightclub in New York City when he was only eighteen. But the major breakthrough in his career came when Eddie Cantor asked him to join the Cantor tour in 1949. Fisher's success on that tour led to a recording contract with RCA Victor, which in turn led to his stardom. In the early 1950s he enjoyed the same preeminent status in American popular music that Frank Sinatra had commanded in the 1940s and that Elvis Presley would win in the late 1950s. Fisher's first hit record was "Thinking of You" (1950), followed by "Turn Back the Hands of Time" (1951), "I'm Yours" (1952), "Even Now" (1953), "Oh, My Papa" (1953), "I'm Always Hearing Wedding Bells" (1955), "On the Street Where You Live" (1956), and many others. His great popularity led to his own TV show: *Coke Time* (1953-56). However, the shift in popular taste to rock music hurt his career, and his last commercially successful recording was "Games That Lovers Play" (1966). Nevertheless, he has remained a significant figure in nightclub work, especially in Las Vegas. Fisher has had a tumultuous personal life; since the late 1950s his fame has rested less on his musical achievements than on his stormy first three marriages, to the actresses Debbie Reynolds, Elizabeth Taylor, and Connie Stevens. He wrote the remarkably candid autobiography *Eddie: My Life, My Loves* (1981).

FITELBERG, GRZEGORZ (or GREGOR FITELBERG; born October 18, 1879, in Dvinsk, Latvia [now Daugavpils, the Soviet Union]; died June 10, 1953, in Katowice, Poland). Conductor and composer. Father of the composer Jerzy Fitelberg. In 1908 he became chief conductor of the Warsaw Philharmonic. After a period in Russia (1914-21), he conducted for Sergei Diaghilev's company in Paris (1921-24), where he led the world premiere of Stravinsky's opera *Mavra* in 1922. Returning to Poland, he again served as chief conductor of the Warsaw Philharmonic (1923-34) and then founded the Polish Radio Symphony Orchestra, which he conducted, except for a few years abroad, for the rest of his life. He conducted much new Polish music, notably works by Karol Szymanowski. Fitelberg's own music, based on German and Russian late romanticism, includes orchestral works, chamber music, and songs.

FITELBERG, JERZY (born May 20, 1903, in Warsaw, Poland; died April 25, 1951, in New York City, New York). Composer. Son of the conductor Grzegorz Fitelberg. Jerzy left Poland in his teens, living in Berlin (1922-32), Paris (1933-39), and New York City (1940-51). He composed in a personal, romantically tinged neoclassical style. In his late years he began to infuse elements of Polish folk music into his works. His best music is in his concertos and chamber pieces, especially the five string quartets (1926-45).

FLESCH, CARL (born October 9, 1873, in Moson, Hungary; died November 14, 1944, in Lucerne, Switzerland). Violinist. He debuted in Vienna in 1895 and Berlin in 1896, but he gained his first wide recognition when, in 1905, he gave a series of five Berlin concerts illustrating the historical development of violin literature from the seventeenth to the twentieth centuries. He developed into a soloist of international acclaim and played in a famous trio with the pianist Artur Schnabel and the cellist Hugo Becker. Flesch's playing was characterized by its flawless technique, purity of approach, and intellectual grasp of styles. His gift was not instinctive but analytical, a quality that gave him a wonderful diagnostic ability in teaching. His pupils included Ida Haendel, Henryk Szeryng, and Henri Temianka. Flesch wrote an important method: *Die Kunst des Violinspiels* (volume 1, 1923; volume 2, 1928), later published in English as *The Art of Violin Playing* (volume 1, 1924; volume 2, 1930). His book *The Memoirs of Carl Flesch* (English, 1957; third edition, 1974) was published posthumously.

FRANKEL, BENJAMIN (born January 31, 1906, in London, England; died February 12, 1973, in London, England). Composer. He earned his greatest fame for his background scores for movies, many of which are notable for their skillful musical characterizations. His more than one hundred film scores include those for *The Seventh Veil* (1945), *Mine Own Executioner* (1947), *The Man in the White Suit* (1951), and *The Night of the Iguana* (1964). But Frankel also composed serious concert works, notably eight symphonies (1958-71) that combine serial techniques and tonal elements.

FREED, ISADORE (born March 26, 1900, in Brest-Litovsk, Russia [now Brest, the Soviet Union]; died November 10, 1960, in New York City, New York). Composer. As a small child he was taken to the United States. His music, in a pandiatonic neoclassical style, includes operas, symphonies, other orchestral works, and chamber pieces. Among his Jewish works are the oratorio *Prophecy of Micah* (1957), Sabbath services, organ pieces, and songs.

FRIEDLAENDER, MAX (or MAX FRIEDLÄNDER; born October 12, 1852, in Brieg, Silesia [now Brzeg, Poland]; died May 2, 1934, in Berlin, Germany). Musicologist and bass-baritone. After a brief but successful career as a lieder and oratorio singer, he turned to musicology in 1884. His great contribution was to collect, publish, and study German lieder and folksongs. He discovered more than one hundred previously lost manuscripts of Schubert songs.

FRIEDMANN, ARON (born August 22, 1855, in Schaki [or Szaki], Lithuania [now in the Soviet Union]; died June 9, 1936, in Berlin, Germany). Cantor. He served as chief cantor in Berlin (1882-1923) and published *Shir li-Schelomo* ("The Song of Solomon"; 1901; second edition, 1930), a collection of traditional cantorial melodies. Friedmann also composed a variety of vocal pieces and published the literary works *Der synagogale Gesang* ("Synagogal Song"; 1904; second editon, 1908) and *Lebensbilder berühmter Kantoren* ("Life Stories of Famous Cantors"; three volumes, 1918-27).

FROMM, HERBERT (born February 23, 1905, in Kitzingen, Germany). Composer and conductor. In 1937 he immigrated to the United States, where he served as organist and music director at Temple Beth Zion in Buffalo (1937-41) and at Temple Israel in Boston (1941-73). Fromm has composed a wide range of instrumental works. But he is best known for his sacred choral music, such as *The Song of Miriam* (1945), and his cantatas, such as *The Stranger* (perf. 1957) and *Memorial Cantata* (1973).

G

GABRILOWITSCH, OSSIP (born February 7, 1878, in Saint Petersburg, Russia [now Leningrad, the Soviet Union]; died September 14, 1936, in Detroit, Michigan). Pianist and conductor. In his late teens he began to tour Europe and America as a pianist and conductor. He gained particular fame for giving a series of historical concerts (Europe, 1912-13; America, 1914-15) illustrating the development of various piano genres. In 1909 he married the American singer Clara Clemens, daughter of the writer Samuel L. Clemens (better known by his pen name, Mark Twain). Immigrating to the United States, Gabrilowitsch served as principal conductor of the Detroit Symphony Orchestra (1918-35), raising it to a position of international respect, and coconducted (with Leopold Stokowski) the Philadelphia Orchestra (1928-31). His pianism was noted for its poetic qualities, with brilliance being a secondary consideration. He often appeared in joint recital with his wife, who wrote a biography of him: *My Husband Gabrilowitsch* (1938).

GÉDALGE, ANDRÉ (born December 27, 1856, in Paris, France; died February 5, 1926, in Chessy, France). Theorist and composer. His *Traité de la fugue* (1901; English, as *Treatise on Fugue*, 1964) is still regarded by many as an unsurpassed study of the subject. He composed in the French nineteenth-century romantic tradition and produced a wide variety of works featuring brilliant counterpoint.

GEIRINGER, KARL (born April 26, 1899, in Vienna, Austria). Musicologist. Since 1940 he has lived in the United States. His books include *The Bach Family: Seven Generations of Creative Genius* (1954) and *Johann Sebastian Bach: The Culmination of an Era* (with his wife, Irene Geiringer, 1966). In 1943 he issued an important study of musical instruments, later revised as *Instruments in the History of Western Music* (1978).

GERNSHEIM, FRIEDRICH (born July 17, 1839, in Worms, Germany; died September 10/11, 1916, in Berlin, Germany). Composer. His music shows the influence of his friend Johannes Brahms. Gernsheim wrote a wide variety of works, but his most effective compositions are his chamber pieces, particularly his string quartets. In 1966 most of his papers were given to the Jewish National and University Library in Jerusalem.

GETZ, STAN(LEY) (born February 2, 1927, in Philadelphia, Pennsylvania). Jazz saxophonist. After playing in bands led by Jack Teagarden, Stan Kenton, Jimmy Dorsey, and Benny Goodman, Getz performed with Woody Herman's band (1947-49), with which he first rose to prominence through this work in Herman's recording of "Early Autumn" (1949). In 1949 Getz formed an ensemble and has led his own group ever since. He was featured in the biopic *The Benny Goodman Story* (1956). In the 1960s he became closely identified with a new style called the bossa nova, a blend of Brazilian melodies and rhythms with American jazz harmonies and improvisations. One of the top tenor saxophonists of his time, Getz retains hs eminent position among young listeners even though he has made no concessions to such recent developments as electronics and jazz-rock fusion.

GILELS, EMIL (born October 19, 1916, in Odessa, the Ukraine [now in the Soviet Union]; died October 14, 1985, in Moscow). Pianist. He gained wide recognition by winning the prestigious Ysaÿe (later the Queen Elisabeth) International Competition in Brussels in 1938. In 1955 he became the first prominent Soviet artist to appear in the United States after World War II, and after that he toured in America more than a dozen times to enthusiastic response. One of the most highly regarded pianists of the new Russian school, Gilels had a flawless technique and an extraordinary ability to delineate gradations of sound from the most delicate to the most powerful. His large repertory extended from Bach to Bartok. The violinist Elivaveta Gilels, his sister, married the violinist Leonid Kogan.

GIMPEL, BRONISLAW (born January 29, 1911, in Lemberg, Galicia [now Lvov, the Soviet Union]; died May 1, 1979, in Los Angeles, California). Violinist. Brother of the pianist Jakob Gimpel. Bronislaw served as concertmaster of orchestras in Königsberg (1929-31) and Göteborg (1931-36) before immigrating to the United States, where he held a similar post with the Los Angeles Philharmonic (1937-42). After World War II he concertized throughout the United States and Europe and played in several chamber ensembles, including the Mannes Piano Trio (1950-56) and the New England String Quartet (1967-73). He was especially effective in his interpretations of Bach.

GIMPEL, JAKOB (born April 16, 1906, in Lemberg, Galicia [now Lvov, the Soviet Union]). Pianist. Brother of the violinist Bronislaw Gimpel. Jakob made his concert debut in 1923, in Vienna, where he had gone to finish his studies. He soon developed a brilliant career as a recitalist and as an orchestral soloist, especially in Germany. However, when the Nazis took over that country, Gimpel moved to Palestine. (He later received the Ben-Gurion Award of Israel.) In 1938 he immigrated to the United States, settling in Los Angeles. After World War II he concertized in America and Europe. He is a masterful interpreter of the romantic literature, especially Beethoven, Schumann, and Chopin. Jakob and Bronislaw were scheduled to play a joint recital in Los Angeles on May 9, 1979, but Bronislaw died on May 1. Jakob thereupon changed the concert to a solo recital in his brother's memory.

GLIÉRE, REINHOLD (born January 11, 1875, in Kiev, the Ukraine [now in the Soviet Union]; died June 23, 1956, in Moscow, the Soviet Union). Composer. He adopted the Russian romantic style prevalent in Moscow at the turn of the century and later incorporated elements of Russian folk music into his scores. Favoring large forms and grand gestures, he wrote operas and many colorful orchestral works, including tone poems and symphonies, notably the *Third Symphony: Ilya Murometz* (1911), which evokes the story of a legendary Russian hero. He is widely regarded as the founder of Soviet ballet, and he made his greatest impact in that genre, as in *The Red Poppy* (1927; revised as *The Red Flower*, 1949), which made him world famous, and *The Bronze Horseman* (1949).

GLUCK, ALMA (originally REBA FIERSOHN; born May 11, 1884, in Bucharest, Romania; died October 27, 1938, in New York City, New York). Soprano. As a small child she was brought to the United States, where she married the businessman Bernard Gluck in 1902. She took the stage name Alma Gluck for her Metropolitan Opera debut in 1909. In 1912 she left the company, divorced Gluck, and went to Europe. After her return to the United States in 1913, she devoted herself almost exclusively to concert appearances, singing mostly popular ballads but also arias and art songs. In 1914 she married the violinist Efrem Zimbalist, who often appeared with her in joint recital. Among the two or three best-loved opera and concert singers of her time, she was also one of the first successful recording artists. Gluck, a lyric soprano with coloratura abilities, gained renown for the purity of her tone and her musical line. She had two famous children. By Gluck, she had Abigail, who, under the name Marcia Davenport (Davenport being the surname of her second husband), became a well-known music critic and novelist, her novel *Of Lena Geyer* (1936) being based on incidents in her mother's professional life. By Zimbalist, Alma Gluck had Efrem Zimbalist, Jr., who became an actor.

GNESSIN, MIKHAIL (or MIKHAIL [or MICHAEL] GNIESSIN; born February 2, 1883, in Rostov-on-Don, Russia; died May 5, 1957, in Moscow, the Soviet Union). Composer. He wrote his early works in the traditional Russian romantic vein, especially in a number of instrumental and vocal pieces inspired by the writings of Poe and Shelley. But his attention soon shifted to Jewish musical materials and subject matter; and he became active in the early development of the Society for Jewish Folk Music, founded in Saint Petersburg in 1908 (and disbanded by the Soviet authorities in 1918). Among his many Jewish-related compositions are the *Variations on a Jewish Theme* for string quartet (1916), the opera *Abraham's Youth* (1923), and the selection "The Jewish Orchestra at the Ball" from the incidental music to Gogol's play *The Inspector General* (1926). In 1929 the Soviet authorities stopped the publication of Gnessin's Jewish works. However, a socialist at heart, he had already adapted himself to the new order and had begun to write music acceptable to the Communist regime, as in the pro-Revolution symphonic work *1905-1917* (1925). Later in life he often used folk materials of various peoples in the Soviet Union. His sisters Jelena (a well-known pianist), Jewgenija, and Marija opened their own music school in Moscow in 1895.

GODOWSKY, LEOPOLD (born February 13, 1870, in Soshly, near Vilnius, Lithuania [now in the Soviet Union]; died November 21, 1938, in New York City, New York). Pianist and composer. He debuted at the age of nine and began to tour at eleven. Godowsky spent most of 1890-1900 in the United States. Following another period in Europe (1900-1914), he returned to America for permanent domi-

cile. His concert career came to a sudden end when he suffered a stroke and consequent partial paralysis in 1930. Godowsky developed the pianistic method of "weight and relaxation," in which the pianist's power comes not from muscular force but from the relaxed use of arm weight. He was also concerned with developing the often overlooked left-hand technique. By applying his ideas to his own performances, he became one of the great virtuosos of his time, renowned as a powerful, intellectual pianist, especially in his ability to bring out inner parts and to delineate artistically conceived left-hand playing. Godowsky composed and transcribed numerous virtuoso piano pieces. He published most of his original music in sets of short compositions, the best known being "Alt Wien" ("Old Vienna," 1920). Leopold Godowsky, Jr., his son, married George Gershwin's sister, Frances. The son was a violinist, but he earned fame primarily as the coinventor, with Leopold Mannes, of the Kodachrome process used in color photography.

GOLD, ERNEST (originally ERNEST GOLDNER; born July 13, 1921, in Vienna, Austria). Composer. In 1938 he fled the Nazis and immigrated to the United States. Early in his career he composed some concert pieces but had more success with his popular songs, notably "Practice Makes Perfect" (lyrics, Don Roberts; 1940). In 1945 he began to work in the Hollywood section of Los Angeles, California, where he became one of the world's greatest composers of background scores for films. He rose to prominence with his music for *On the Beach* (1959), a stark film showing the end of human life after a nuclear war. Soon afterward he produced his classic score for *Exodus* (1960), a story about the birth of modern Israel. In fact, several of his best scores are for films dealing with Jews or anti-Semitism, including *Judgment at Nuremberg* (1961), *Pressure Point* (1962), *Ship of Fools* (1965), and *Wallenberg: A Hero's Story* (TV mini-series, 1985). Among his other movie scores are those for *The Defiant Ones* (1958), *Inherit the Wind* (1960), *It's a Mad, Mad, Mad, Mad World* (1963), *The Secret of Santa Vittoria* (1969), and *Cross of Iron* (1977). In 1975 Gold became the first screen composer to have a star with his name placed in the pavement of Hollywood's Walk of Fame. From 1950 to 1969 he was married to the singer Marni Nixon, best known for her ghostsinging on movie soundtracks, as for Audrey Hepburn in *My Fair Lady* (1964).

GOLDFADEN, ABRAHAM (originally ABRAHAM GOLDENFODIM; born July 1840 in Starokonstantinov, the Ukraine [now in the Soviet Union]; died January 1908 in New York City, New York). Playwright who supplied music to his own plays. Famed as the founder of the modern Yiddish theater (in Iaşi, Romania, in 1876), Goldfaden also had a musical impact. He could not write music, but he adapted tunes from such sources as synagogal chants, Jewish folksongs, non-Jewish folk and popular music of eastern Europe, and French and Italian opera arias. By touring Europe with his troupe, he popularized the tunes in their new garb. His plays include *The Witch* (1879), *Shulamit* (1880), and *Son of My People* (1908). Goldfaden visited New York City in 1887-89 and returned to settle there in 1903.

GOLDMAN, EDWIN FRANKO (born January 1, 1878, in Louisville, Kentucky; died February 21, 1956, in New York City, New York). Bandmaster and composer. Father of the bandmaster Richard Franko Goldman. After serving as solo cornetist at the Metropolitan Opera (1899-1909), Edwin formed his own band (1911) and championed new and unjustly forgotten band music. He himself composed over one hundred marches, and he wrote books on how to train bands. The Goldman Band, which he conducted for the rest of his life, set a high standard for bands in both musical proficiency and breadth of repertory.

GOLDMAN, RICHARD FRANKO (born December 7, 1910, in New York City, New York; died January 19, 1980, in Baltimore, Maryland). Bandmaster and composer. Son of the bandmaster Edwin Franko Goldman. Richard assisted his father with the Goldman Band till the elder man's death, after which the son conducted the band for the rest of his life (1956-80). He composed band music and works for various other ensembles in which he experimented with applying modern harmonies to pieces that could be performed by average players. Goldman also wrote books on bands, band music, and harmony.

GOLDMARK, KARL (born May 18, 1830, in Keszthely, Hungary; died January 2, 1915, in Vienna, Austria). Composer. Uncle of the composer Rubin Goldmark. He belonged to no particular school of composition, and he absorbed influences from such diverse sources as Hungarian folk music, synagogal chant, and the German romantics. His best-known works are the opera *Die Königin von Saba* ("The Queen of Sheba," perf. 1875) and the symphony *Ländliche Hochzeit* ("Rustic Wedding," 1876), both of which show the influence of Wagner's chromaticism.

GOLDMARK, RUBIN (born August 15, 1872, in New York City, New York; died March 16, 1936, in New York City, New York). Composer. Nephew of the composer Karl Goldmark. His *Negro Rhapsody* for orchestra (1923) became popular. But today he is remembered chiefly as the private teacher of Aaron Copland and George Gershwin.

GOLDOVSKY, BORIS (born June 7, 1908, in Moscow, Russia). Pianist, conductor, and opera producer. Son of the violinist Léa Luboshutz and nephew of the pianist Pierre Luboshutz. His debut as a pianist came in Berlin in 1921. In 1930 he immigrated to the United States, where he gave many concerts. Soon, however, he turned to conducting and producing operas. He was responsible for introducing to the American stage many European operas, such as Britten's *Peter Grimes*. Since 1946 he has been a regular commentator on the Metropolitan Opera radio broadcasts. He wrote the books *Accents on Opera* (1953) and *Bringing Opera to Life* (1968).

GOLDSCHMIDT, OTTO (born August 21, 1829, in Hamburg, Germany; died February 24, 1907, in London, England). Pianist and composer. In 1851-52 he served as piano accompanist to the Swedish soprano Jenny Lind on an American tour. Soon they fell in love with each other. Lind stood as sponsor for his baptism (1851), a prerequisite to their marriage, which took place in an Episcopal ceremony in Boston (1852). Thereafter, they gave many joint recitals together. In 1858 they settled in England. Goldschmidt composed songs and instrumental works, but he is best remembered for the oratorio *Ruth* (1867), written for his wife and her famous high F-sharp.

GOLSCHMANN, VLADIMIR (born December 16, 1893, in Paris, France; died March 1, 1972, in New York City, New York). Conductor. In 1919 he founded (with the help of a wealthy patron) the Golschmann Concerts, which he con-

ducted for several years. He concentrated on the music of contemporary French composers, including Honegger, Milhaud, and Poulenc. Throughout the 1920s Golschmann guest-conducted major orchestras in Europe and the United States. After one such appearance with the Saint Louis Symphony Orchestra in the early 1930s, he was appointed the orchestra's principal conductor. He remained there for more than twenty-five years, after which he served as music director of the symphony orchestras in Tulsa (1958-61) and Denver (1964-70). Among the world premieres that he conducted were those of Antheil's *Ballet mécanique* ("Mechanical Ballet") in 1926 and Korngold's *Violin Concerto* in 1947. Golschmann was noted for his dependable technique, romantic temperament, and breadth of taste. Boris Golschmann, Vladimir's brother, was a concert pianist of great promise before he was arrested by the Nazis during their occupation of France; he never reappeared.

GOODMAN, STEVE (born July 25, 1948, in Chicago, Illinois; died September 20, 1984, in Seattle, Washington). Singer and composer. He became the center of the 1970s urban folk scene when his "City of New Orleans" (music and lyrics by Goodman) was recorded and released by Arlo Guthrie in 1972. The song had already appeared on Goodman's own album *Steve Goodman* (1971). His other albums include *High and Outside* (1979) and *Artistic Hair* (1983).

GORE, LESLEY (born May 2, 1946, in New York City, New York). Singer and composer. Writing her own music and lyrics, she rose to prominence with "It's My Party" (1963) and "You Don't Own Me" (1963). Her later work includes the album *Love Me by Name* (1978).

GORME, EYDIE. *See* LAWRENCE, STEVE and GORME, EYDIE.

GRAFFMAN, GARY (born October 14, 1928, in New York City, New York). Pianist. His father, Vladimir Graffman, had been a violinist in Russia till the Revolution of 1917, after which he immigrated to the United States, where he played and taught the violin. At the age of three Gary began to take violin lessons from his father but soon switched to the piano. Making rapid progress, he appeared as soloist with the Philadelphia String Simfonietta under Fabien Sevitzky in 1936 and the Indianapolis Symphony under the same conductor in 1938. Also in 1938 he gave a solo recital at Town Hall in New York City. In 1947 he won the Rachmaninoff Prize, as a result of which he made his official debut as a mature concert soloist, a performance with the Philadelphia Orchestra conducted by Eugene Ormandy. The following year he made his official recital debut, at Carnegie Hall in New York City. When Graffman won the prestigious Leventritt Award in 1949, he gained wide renown and was offered engagements with America's leading orchestras. He made the first of his many annual American concert tours in 1951. In 1955 he began his international career with his first South American tour, followed in 1956 by his first European season. His initial tour of the Soviet Union came in 1968. He has also appeared in Africa, Asia, and Australia. One of the few concert pianists able to tune a piano, Graffman carried his own piano-tuning tools with him on his travels. In 1964 he canceled a scheduled appearance in Jackson, Mississippi, because he refused to play before a segregated audience. He was the first established concert artist to make such a gesture. Graffman was most comfortable with music from the nineteenth and early twentieth centuries. He had the ability to re-create musical structure with logic and with a sense of the cumulative interrelatedness of all of the musical elements involved. He possessed an easy virtuosity, but he depended on musicianship, not pyrotechnic pianism or flamboyant personality to achieve his effects. In about 1979 he began to lose the use of his right hand because of an ailment that some doctors have called carpal-tunnel syndrome, a kind of strain that affects overtaxed instrumentalists. But the prognosis for his condition is good (particularly considering recent successes with similarly disabled artists, notably Leon Fleisher), and he is currently undergoing therapy to effect his cure. Graffman published his autobiography as *I Really Should Be Practicing* (1981).

GREENBERG, NOAH (born April 9, 1919, in New York City, New York; died January 9, 1966, in New York City, New York). Conductor and musicologist. In 1952 he founded the Pro Musica Antiqua (later the New York Pro Musica), an ensemble for the performance of medieval and Renaissance music. Guided by Greenberg's scholarly investigations, the Pro Musica performed with authentic styles on copies of original instruments. In 1958 he created a great stir in the music community through his revival of the medieval liturgical drama *The Play of Daniel*, followed in 1963 by *The Play of Herod*. Greenberg sparked a general interest in early music and inspired the formation of other ensembles for its performance.

GREY, JOEL (originally JOEL KATZ; born April 11, 1932, in Cleveland, Ohio). Singer. Son of Mickey Katz, a dance-band clarinetist and a comic musician in the American Yiddish musical theater. As a child Joel performed various comedy and musical acts onstage, with and without his father. In 1956 he made his Broadway debut in *The Littlest Revue*. He was propelled to stardom by playing the master of ceremonies in the Broadway musical *Cabaret* in 1966, a role that he repeated with great success in the film version (1972). Grey also distinguished himself in a production of Gilbert and Sullivan's operetta *The Yeoman of the Guard* (TV, 1984).

GRUENBERG, LOUIS (born August 3, 1884, near Brest-Litovsk, Russia [now Brest, the Soviet Union]; died June 10, 1964, in Beverly Hills, California). Composer. His parents brought him to the United States when he was two years old. He incorporated jazz elements into many of his best pieces, as in *Jazzberries* for piano (pub. 1925), *Jazz Suite* for orchestra (1925), and *Jazzettes* for violin and piano (pub. 1926). His most successful dramatic work is the opera *The Emperor Jones* (comp. 1931, perf. 1933), which draws inspiration from black spirituals, as does his *Violin Concerto* (1944), which was commissioned by Jascha Heifetz. Gruenberg composed many background scores for films, such as *The Fight for Life* (1940) and *So Ends Our Night* (1941).

GUTHRIE, ARLO (born July 10, 1947, in New York City, New York). Singer and composer. Son of the folksinger Woody Guthrie and his Jewish wife, Marjorie Mazia Greenblatt. Writing his own music and lyrics, he launched his career with the folk-based "Alice's Restaurant" (1967), still his best-known song. Later he moved in the direction of folk-rock. Guthrie has recorded songs by his father and other songwriters, as well as originals. His albums include *Alice's Restaurant* (1967), *Hobo's Lullaby* (1972), *Amigo* (1976), *Outlasting the Blues* (1979), and *Power of Love* (1981).

H

HAENDEL, IDA (born December 15, variously reported from 1923 to 1928, in Chelm, Poland). Violinist. She moved to London in 1938 and Canada in 1952. Haendel has toured extensively in Europe, America, and the Middle East. She was honored by being one of the great violinists invited to perform at the Huberman Centenary in Tel Aviv, Israel, in 1982. Haendel plays with an assured technique and in a generally classical manner, with a certain emotional reserve that has tended to limit her popularity with general audiences. She has written her own story in *Woman with Violin: An Autobiography* (1970).

HAHN, REYNALDO (born August 9, 1875, in Caracas, Venezuela; died January 28, 1947, in Paris, France). Composer. He composed mostly for the stage, including operas, ballets, and musical comedies. But his favorite genre was operetta, his finest work being *Ciboulette* (perf. 1923), followed by *Brummel* (perf. 1931) and *Malvina* (per. 1935).

HALÉVY, JACQUES (or FROMENTAL HALÉVY, originally JACQUES-FRANÇOIS-FROMENTAL-ELIE LÉVY; born May 27, 1799, in Paris, France; died March 17, 1862, in Nice, France). Composer. The family changed its name from Lévy to Halévy in 1807. In 1819 he won the Prix de Rome.

Halévy composed a wide variety of operas, but his reputation today rests principally on one grand opera: *La juive* ("The Jewess," perf. 1835). His style was influenced by the operas of Cherubini and Meyerbeer. Halévy's daughter Genevieve married the composer Georges Bizet.

HAMBOURG, MARK (born June 12, 1879, in Boguchar, Russia; died August 26, 1960, in Cambridge, England). Pianist and composer. He debuted in Moscow in 1888 and in London the following year. In 1896 he settled in England. Hambourg performed in the grand romantic tradition. One of his best-known piano works is the *Variations on a Theme by Paganini* (1902). His books include *How to Play the Piano* (1922) and *The Eighth Octave* (1951), the latter being his memoirs. He formed a trio with his brothers, Jan (violin) and Boris (cello). Later Mark played piano duets with one of his four daughters, Michal. His father, the pianist Michael (originally Mikhail) Hambourg, founded, with Jan and Boris, the Hambourg Conservatory of Music in Toronto in 1911.

HAMLISCH, MARVIN (born June 2, 1944, in New York City, New York). Composer and pianist. A child prodigy, he had already given piano recitals at Town Hall and elsewhere in New York City before reaching his teens. However, he tired of the nervous strain of concertizing and turned to writing popular music. His adaptation of Scott Joplin rags for the movie *The Sting* (1973) helped to initiate the ragtime revival of the 1970s. Hamlisch's original background scores for films include those for *Kotch* (1971), with the song "Life Is What You Make It" (lyrics, Johnny Mercer); *The Way We Were* (1973), with the title song (lyrics, Alan and Marilyn Bergman); *The Spy Who Loved Me* (1977), with the song "Nobody Does It Better" (lyrics, Carole Bayer Sager); and *Ordinary People* (1980). He also composed music for the Broadway shows *A Chorus Line* (perf. 1975) and *They're Playing Our Song* (perf. 1979). Hamlisch, having shaken off the nerves of his youth, made his major concert debut as a pianist, accompanied by the Minnesota Orchestra, in 1975.

HANSLICK, EDUARD (born September 11, 1825, in Prague, Bohemia [now in Czechoslovakia]; died August 6, 1904, in Baden, near Vienna, Austria). The first great professional music critic.

HASKIL, CLARA (born January 7, 1895, in Bucharest, Romania; died December 7, 1960, in Brussels, Belgium). Pianist. Small and frail, she was hampered throughout her career by a muscular disease. But with remarkable courage and determination, she continued to be active during periods of remission from her ailment. Haskil possessed a profound musicianship. She was extremely effective with Beethoven and Schubert, but she achieved her greatest renown for her clean, strong performances of Mozart.

HAUBENSTOCK-RAMATI, ROMAN (born February 27, 1919, in Cracow, Poland). Composer. His early compositions were written in an intensely expressive form of serialism. But later he experimented with pieces that he called "mobiles," in which the components can be joined in various ways during performance, in a sort of collage, as in the *Petite musique de nuit* ("Little Night Music") for orchestra (1959). He also developed an interest in graphic notation, as in his *Poetics* cycle for various ensembles (1972).

HELFMAN, MAX (born May 25, 1901, in Radzyń, Poland; died August 9, 1963, in Dallas, Texas). Choral conductor and composer. He was brought to the United States in 1909. Helfman conducted choral groups at Temple Emanuel in Paterson, New Jersey (1926-39), at Temple B'nai Abraham in Newark, New Jersey (1940-53), at Temple Sinai in Los Angeles (1954-57), and at the Washington Hebrew Congregation (1958-62). He composed much liturgical music.

HELLER, STEPHEN (originally JACOB HELLER, then, on childhood conversion to Roman Catholicism, ISTVÁN HELLER; born May 15, 1813, in Pest [now Budapest], Hungary; died January 14, 1888, in Paris, France). Pianist and composer. He made his debut in 1828. In 1838 he moved to Paris, where he spent the rest of his life. In his late years a nervous ailment curtailed his piano playing. Heller composed several hundred piano works, including sonatas, dances, and character pieces. He was a key transitional figure between German romanticism and French impressionism, the latter style pointed to in his late works. But Heller remains an underrated composer, and he is known today chiefly through his piano studies.

HEMSI, ALBERTO (full name, ALBERTO HEMSI CHICUREL; born December 23, 1896, in Kasaba [now Turgutlu], Turkey; died October 8, 1975, in Aubervilliers, near Paris, France). Composer, conductor, ethnomusicologist, and music publisher. He spent much of his youth in Italy and Rhodes before moving to Alexandria, Egypt, where he served as music director at the Grand Synagogue (1927-57) and established and conducted the Alexandria Philharmonic Orchestra (1928-40). In Alexandria he also founded the Edition orientale de musique (Oriental Edition of Music), the first Egyptian house to publish the music of composers familiar with Middle Eastern culture. In 1957 he moved to Paris to serve as professor of music at the Jewish Seminary. The following year he became music director of the Berith Shalom Synagogue. Among his ethnomusicological writings is the book *La musique de la Torah* ("The Music of the Torah," 1929). Hemsi believed that the Western tonal system would eventually replace the Eastern. His own compositions—orchestral, chamber, vocal, piano—show a compromise between Western techniques and Oriental tradition.

HENSCHEL, GEORGE (originally ISIDOR GEORG HENSCHEL; born February 18, 1850, in Breslau, Silesia [now Wrocław, Poland]; died September 10, 1934, in Aviemore, Scotland). Conductor. Converting to Christianity as a youth, he never made professional use of his original first name, Isidor. He conducted the newly founded Boston Symphony Orchestra (1881-84) and then settled in Great Britain, where he founded and conducted the London Symphony Concerts (1886-97), led the Handel Society of London (1912-14), and guest-conducted elsewhere. He wrote the books *Personal Recollections of Johannes Brahms* (1907) and *Musings and Memoirs of a Musician* (1918).

HERRMANN, BERNARD (born June 19, 1911, in New York City, New York; died December 24, 1975, in Los Angeles, California). Composer and conductor. He served as staff conductor (1938-42) and then as principal conductor (1942-59) of the Columbia Broadcasting System (CBS) Symphony Orchestra. He also guest-conducted other major orchestras in Europe and America. Herrmann's concert works reflect a neoromantic but highly individual style, as in the cantata *Moby Dick* (1938) and the string-quartet piece *Echoes* (1965). But his fame rests primarily on his film music, which includes some of the subtlest and most emotionally compelling background scores in the history of movies. His first film score was for the Orson Welles classic *Citizen Kane* (1941), followed by *All That Money Can Buy* (also known as *The Devil and Daniel Webster*, 1941) and another Welles picture, *The Magnificent Ambersons* (1942). Later he had great success in scoring a series of Alfred Hitchcock suspense thrillers, such as *Vertigo* (1958), *Psycho* (1960), and *Marnie* (1964). Other movies for which Herrmann supplied background music include *Anna and the King of Siam* (1946), *The Ghost and Mrs. Muir* (1947), *The Day the Earth Stood Still* (1951), *Journey to the Center of the Earth* (1959), *Fahrenheit 451* (1966), *Obsession* (1976), and *Taxi Driver* (1976).

HERTZKA, EMIL (born August 3, 1869, in what is now Budapest, Hungary; died May 9, 1932, in Vienna, Austria). Music publisher. In 1901 he joined the staff at the newly founded Universal Edition, which he subsequently directed from 1907 till his death. Hertzka championed and published the works of many modern composers, including Bartók, Schoenberg, and Weill.

HERZ, HENRI (originally HEINRICH HERZ; born January 6, 1803, in Vienna, Austria; died January 5, 1888, in Paris, France). Pianist and composer. One of the most popular virtuosos in the second quarter of the nineteenth century, he performed frequently throughout Europe, and from 1845 to 1851 he made extended concert tours in the New World. As a composer Herz deliberately cultivated popularity by writing over two hundred piano pieces in the light, elegant style fashionable at the time. Salon pieces (especially dances) and variations predominate. He also wrote some still valuable finger exercises.

HILLER, FERDINAND (born October 24, 1811, in Frankfort on the Main, Germany; died May 11, 1885, in Cologne, Germany). Pianist, conductor, and composer. His father's original surname was Hildesheim. Hiller spent seven years (1828-35) as a pianist in Paris. Returning to Germany, he became one of the first representatives of the modern conductor (that is, an authoritative person independent of the performance group). He conducted the Leipzig Gewandhaus Concerts (1843-44) and then controlled the music activities in Cologne (1850-84). His best compositions are his songs and piano pieces. Among his other works are the oratorio *Die Zerstörung Jerusalems* ("The Destruction of Jerusalem," pub. 1840) and the cantata *Israels Siegesgesang* ("Victory Song of Israel," pub. 1872).

HINRICHSEN. Family of music publishers. HEINRICH HINRICHSEN (or HENRI HINRICHSEN; born February 5, 1868, in Hamburg, Germany; died September 30, 1942, in the concentration camp at Oświęcim [German, Auschwitz], Poland) took over the C. F. Peters music-publishing company in Leipzig in 1900. Under his leadership the firm issued works by such composers as Mahler, Schoenberg, Richard Strauss, and Hugo Wolf. Later he was joined in the company by his three sons: MAX (born July 6, 1901, in Leipzig, Germany; died December 17, 1965, in London, England), WALTER (born September 23, 1907, in Leipzig, Germany; died July 21, 1969, in New York City, New York), and HANS (born August 22, 1909, in Leipzig, Germany; died September 18, 1940, in the concentration camp at Perpignan, France). Max left the firm in 1937 and founded the Hinrichsen Edition in London in 1938, renamed the Peters Edition in 1975; it now publishes mostly English music.

Walter immigrated to the United States in 1936 and established the C. F. Peters Corporation in New York City in 1948; his great interest was in issuing works by contemporary composers, such as Cage, Feldman, Ligeti, and Penderecki.

HODES, ART(HUR) (born November 14, 1904, in Nikolayev, the Ukraine [now in the Soviet Union]). Jazz pianist.

HOLDE, ARTUR (born October 16, 1885, in Rendsburg, Germany; died June 23, 1962, in New York City, New York). Writer and conductor. He directed music at a synagogue in Frankfurt on the Main (1910-36) before immigrating in 1937 to the United States, where he served as choirmaster of the Hebrew Tabernacle in New York City (1937-43). In both Germany and America he also worked as a music critic and wrote many articles. His book *Jews in Music* (1959) covers the contributions of Jews to Jewish music and to music in general.

HOLLAENDER, FRIEDRICH (or, in English-speaking countries, FREDERICK HOLLANDER; born October 18, 1896, in London, England; died January 18, 1976, in Munich, Germany). Composer. Son of the composer Victor Hollaender and nephew of the violinist Gustav Hollaender. Friedrich is best known for his film music, especially for the German picture *Der blaue Engel* (1930), for which he wrote the background score and the song "Ich bin von Kopf bis Fuss auf Liebe eingestellt" (lyrics, Robert Liebmann); the movie was released the same year, in English, as *The Blue Angel*, the song being retitled as "Falling in Love Again" (lyrics, Sammy Lerner). Original English-language films to which he contributed songs and/or background scores include *Destry Rides Again* (1939), *A Foreign Affair* (1948), *Androcles and the Lion* (1952), and *We're No Angels* (1955).

HOLLAENDER, GUSTAV (born February 15, 1855, in Leobschütz, Upper Silesia [now Głubczyce, Poland]; died December 4, 1915, in Berlin, Germany). Violinist and composer. Brother of the composer Victor Hollaender and uncle of the composer Friedrich Hollaender. Gustav toured as a concert violinist and performed in chamber ensembles. He composed many violin works, including violin concertos.

HOLLAENDER, VICTOR (sometimes used the pseudonym ARRICHA DEL TOLVENO; born April 20, 1866, in Loebschütz, Upper Silesia [now Głubczyce, Poland]; died October 24, 1940, in Los Angeles, California). Composer and conductor. Brother of the violinist Gustav Hollaender and father of the composer Friedrich Hollaender. Victor worked as a theater conductor in Berlin and London. He composed a number of successful operettas, including the English works *The Bey of Morocco* (perf. 1894) and *Double Dealings* (perf. 1898). In 1934 he fled Nazi Germany and moved to the United States.

HORENSTEIN, JASCHA (born May 6, 1898, in Kiev, the Ukraine [now in the Soviet Union]; died April 2, 1973, in London, England). Conductor. He guest-conducted the Berlin Philharmonic (1925-28) and served as chief conductor of the Düsseldorf Opera (1928-33) till the Nazis forced him out. Horenstein wandered for several years, visited Palestine in 1938, and settled in the United States in 1940. After World War II he conducted internationally. He performed many modern works, but he was best known for his Bruckner and Mahler.

HORNBOSTEL, ERICH M(ORITZ) VON (born February 25, 1877, in Vienna, Austria; died November 29, 1935, in Cambridge, England). Musicologist. As a specialist in studying non-European music (including fieldwork with the Pawnee Indians as early as 1906), Hornbostel was one of the pioneers in comparative musicology (later called ethnomusicology). He also investigated the psychology of music perception.

HUBERMAN, BRONISLAW (born December 19, 1882, in Częstochowa, Poland; died June 15, 1947, in Corsier-sur-Vevey, Switzerland). Violinist. As a preteenager he gave concerts that caused a sensation. In 1896 he played the Brahms *Violin Concerto* in the presence of the composer, who was deeply moved by the performance. There followed many years of concertizing in Europe and America. In 1936 Huberman assembled some Jewish refugee musicians in Palestine and organized the Palestine (or Palestine Symphony) Orchestra (since 1948 called the Israel Philharmonic Orchestra). He invited Hans Wilhelm Steinberg (later called William Steinberg) to Palestine to prepare the orchestra for its first concerts, which were conducted by Arturo Toscanini later in 1936. Huberman's violin playing was noted for its beautiful and unique tone quality, especially for its many shades of pianissimo. An impetuous player, he could rise to extraordinary levels of expression, though his impulsiveness sometimes caused him to lose control of his technique. His library and papers are housed at the Central Music Library in Tel Aviv.

I

IAN, JANIS (originally JANIS FINK; born April 7, 1951, in New York City, New York). Singer and composer. In her midteens she wrote the music and lyrics for her own recording of the hit "Society's Child" (1967), a protest song concerning interracial romance. The song was then included in her first album, *Janis Ian* (1967). After a slump she came back with the album *Between the Lines* (1975), including "At Seventeen." Among her later albums is *Restless Eyes* (1981).

IDELSOHN, ABRAHAM ZVI (born July 13, 1882, in Filzburg, near Libava [now Liepāja], Latvia [now in the Soviet Union]; died August 14, 1938, in Johannesburg, South Africa). Musicologist, cantor, and composer. Possessing a powerful baritone voice, he served as a cantor in Regensburg (1903-1905) and Johannesburg (1905-1906). Then, in Jerusalem (1906-1921), he worked as a cantor and pioneered music education in the region. He also composed much cantorial music, including several complete synagogal services. During his years in Palestine he intensely researched the oral tradition of music in the Jewish community, resulting in his ten-volume *Thesaurus of Hebrew-Oriental Melodies* (1914-32). In 1921 he went to Europe, and in 1922 he settled in the United States, where he helped the Hebrew Union College of Cincinnati to become a center of Jewish-music research. Near the end of his life he moved back to Johannesburg. Idelsohn, the founder of modern Jewish musicology, wrote the important book *Jewish Music in Its Historical Development* (1929).

J

JACOBI, FREDERICK (born May 4, 1891, in San Francisco, California; died October 24, 1952, in New York City, New York). Composer. Early in his career his field studies of Pueblo Indian music led to his *String Quartet on Indian Themes* (1924), *Indian Dances* for orchestra (1928), and similar works. Later he synthesized classical, romantic, and modern elements in such works as the *Second String Quartet* (1933) and the *Concertino* for piano and strings (1946). Many of his later works are on Jewish subjects or for synagogal use, including sacred services and *Six Pieces for Use in the Synagogue* for organ (1933).

JACOBI, GEORG (or GEORGES JACOBY; born February 13, 1840, in Berlin, Germany; died September 13, 1906, in London, England). Conductor and composer. Moving to France, he conducted Offenbach stage works at the Bouffes-Parisiens and composed some operettas. In 1871 Jacobi settled in London as a conductor and composer of comic operas, ballets, and other works.

JACOBS, ARTHUR (born June 14, 1922, in Manchester, England). Writer. He wrote music criticism for a number of periodicals, including the *Jewish Chronicle* (1963-75). A strong advocate of performing opera in English, he has translated many librettos into his native tongue. His original writings include the books *Gilbert and Sullivan* (1951) and *A Short History of Western Music* (1972). Famed for its compact precision is his little lexicon *A New Dictionary of Music* (1958; revised fourth edition, *The New Penguin Dictionary of Music,* 1978).

JADASSOHN, SALOMON (born August 13, 1831, in Breslau, Silesia [now Wrocław, Poland]; died February 1, 1902, in Leipzig, Germany). Theorist. He wrote a set of five theory textbooks that codified the traditional views of harmony (1883), counterpoint (1884), canon and fugue (1884), form (1885), and instrumentation (1889). The books were translated into many languages, and Jadassohn's conservative approach had a profound influence on music teaching for many years.

JADLOWKER, HERMANN (born July 1877 in Riga, Latvia [now in the Soviet Union]; died May 13, 1953, in Tel Aviv, Israel). Tenor. He began his opera career in Germany, attracting international attention in Karlsruhe (1906-1909) and singing in Berlin off and on from 1909 to 1921. At the Metropolitan Opera in New York City he created the Prince in the world premiere of Humperdinck's *Die Königskinder* ("The King's Children") in 1910. In 1912 he created Bacchus in the first performance, in Stuttgart, of Richard Strauss's *Ariadne auf Naxos* ("Ariadne at Naxos"). In 1929 he returned to Riga and served as cantor in the synagogue. In 1938 he settled in Palestine. Essentially a lyric tenor, he hurt his voice late in life when he tried to sing Wagnerian roles.

JOACHIM, JOSEPH (born June 28, 1831, in Kitsee, near Pressburg, Slovakia [now Köpcsény, near Bratislava, Czechoslovakia]; died August 15, 1907, in Berlin, Germany). Violinist and composer. In November 1843 he made his major debut, as soloist at one of the Leipzig Gewandhaus Concerts conducted by Felix Mendelssohn. Soon coming to the forefront of young violinists, Joachim was invited by

Franz Liszt to become concertmaster in Weimar in 1850. Later Joachim served as music director in Hanover (1853-65) but resigned that post in protest against his employers' anti-Jewish attitude toward one of his colleagues (a problem that Joachim avoided by his early conversion to Protestantism). In 1868 he became head of the newly established school that later became known as the Berlin Academy of Music, where he remained for the rest of his life. Among his pupils were the violinists Leopold Auer, Jenö Hubay, and Bronislaw Huberman. A staunch proponent of the classical line in German music (as opposed to the Liszt-Wagner hyperromantic line), Joachim was an intimate friend and musical partner of Schumann and Brahms; in fact, it was Joachim who wrote the now famous letter of introduction that young Brahms carried to Schumann's door in 1853. Joachim also served as technical adviser for Brahms's great *Violin Concerto*, which the violinist premiered under the composer's baton in 1879. He was the first great violinist willing to submerge his own personality into the works and intentions of other composers, thus helping to create the modern art of interpretative playing. Recordings that he made late in life reveal the integrity and nobility of his style. A gifted composer, he wrote a variety of works, including the *Hebräische Melodien* ("Hebrew Melodies") for viola and piano (pub. 1855) and the *Konzert in ungarischer Weise* ("Concerto in Hungarian Style") for violin and orchestra (pub. 1861). With Andreas Moser he published the *Violinschule* ("Violin Method," 1905).

JOEL, BILLY (originally WILLIAM JOEL; born May 9, 1949, in Hicksville, Long Island, New York). Singer and composer. His albums include *The Stranger* (1977), *Fifty-second Street* (1978), and *An Innocent Man* (1983).

JONAS, EMILE (born March 5, 1827, in Paris, France; died May 22, 1905, in Saint-Germain-en-Laye, France). Composer. He served as music director of, and published collections of Hebrew tunes for, the Portuguese synagogue in Paris. Jonas also composed many French operettas in the style of Offenbach, as well as the English-language stage work *Cinderella the Younger* (perf. 1871 in London).

JOSEFFY, RAFAEL (born July 3, 1852, in Hunfalu, Hungary; died June 25, 1915, in New York City, New York). Pianist. After several years of successful concertizing in Europe, he debuted in the United States (1879), where he then settled for the rest of his life. Joseffy was among the first pianists to play Brahms regularly, especially in America. His publications include his famous editions of Chopin's works, his *School of Advanced Piano Playing* (1902), and his numerous piano pieces.

K

KAHN, ERICH ITOR (born July 23, 1905, in Rimbach, Germany; died March 5, 1956, in New York City, New York). Composer and pianist. Moving to the United States in 1941, he organized, with the violinist Alexander Schneider and the cellist Benar Heifetz, the Albeneri Trio (the name being an acronym of the players' first names). He also appeared in piano recitals and other music activities. Kahn composed highly personal music in which he married the twelve-tone technique to a warm, expressive lyricism. His works include *Rhapsodie hassidique* ("Hasidic Rhapsody") for chorus (1938), *Nenia Judaeis qui hoc aetate perierunt* ("Lament for the Jews Who Perished in This Age") for cello and piano (1943), *Ciaccona dei tempi di guerra* ("Chaconne in Time of War") for piano (1943), and *Actus tragicus* ("Tragic Deed") for ten instruments (1947).

KÁLMÁN, EMMERICH (originally IMRE KÁLMÁN; born October 24, 1882, in Siófok, Hungary; died October 30, 1953, in Paris, France). Composer. When chronic neuritis put an end to his early ambition to be a concert pianist, he turned to composition. He wrote a series of operettas that combined Viennese elements (especially the waltz) with a Hungarian flavor. A superb craftsman, Kálmán was noted for his well-made finales, which bear comparison with those in many serious operas. His operettas include *Tatárjárás* (known in English as *The Gay Hussars*, perf. 1908), and *Die Csárdásfürstin* (known in English as *The Gypsy Princess*, perf. 1915), and *Gräfin Mariza* ("Countess Mariza," perf. 1924). In the late 1930s he moved to Paris and then to the United States. He retained his Hungarian nationality till 1942, when the Hungarian government completely aligned itself with Hitler; soon afterward Kálmán took American citizenship. After World War II he returned to Europe. His final work, the stage show *Arizona Lady* (perf. 1954), was completed after his death by Charles Emmerich Kálmán, Emmerich's son and a fine composer of musicals and other light pieces.

KAREL, RUDOLF (born November 9, 1880, in Pilsen, Bohemia [now Plzeň, Czechoslovakia]; died March 6, 1945, in Terezín, Czechoslovakia). Composer. His music is based in the romantic tradition of Dvořák and Tchaikovsky, though his mature work sometimes shows the modern traits of modal harmonies, complex counterpoint, and irregular rhythms. He composed many operas, cantatas, and programmatic orchestral works, such as the *Jarni symfonie* ("Spring Symphony," 1938). During World War II he joined the Czech resistance movement, and in 1943 the Gestapo arrested him. He died in the Terezín (German, Theresienstadt) ghetto.

KATZ, ISRAEL J(OSEPH) (born July 21, 1930, in New York City, New York). Ethnomusicologist. His researches have centered on the music of ethnic groups in the Mediterranean region, especially the Sephardic and Oriental Jewish communities. He has published many articles, as well as the book *Judeo-Spanish Traditional Ballads from Jerusalem: An Ethnomusicological Study* (doctoral dissertation, University of California in Los Angeles, 1967; pub. 1972 and 1975). Katz has served for many years on the editorial staff of *Musica judaica: Journal of the American Society for Jewish Music*.

KAYLAN, HOWARD (born June 22, 1945, in New York City, New York) and **VOLMAN, MARK** (born April 19, 1944, in Los Angeles, California). Singers. They were among the original Turtles, whose biggest hit was "Happy Together" (1967). Later they formed a duet and called themselves the Phlorescent Leech and Eddie, soon shortened to Flo and Eddie. Their albums include *The Phlorescent Leech and Eddie* (1972) and *Rock Steady with Flo and Eddie* (1981).

KENTNER, LOUIS (originally LAJOS KENTNER; born July 19, 1905, in Karwin, Silesia [now Karviná, Czechoslovakia]). Pianist and composer. His bravura and grandeur have won him special renown for his Liszt interpretations, but he is also highly regarded for his delicate Chopin and for his Mozart, Beethoven, Schubert, Bartók, and Kodály. In 1935 he settled in England. Kentner has written a number of compositions, notably the *Three Sonatinas for Piano* (pub. 1939), as well as the valuable book *Piano* (1976).

KERTÉSZ, ISTVÁN (born August 28, 1929, in Budapest, Hungary; died April 16, 1973, near Tel Aviv, Israel). Conductor. He conducted the Györ Philharmonic (1953-55) and the Budapest Opera (1955-57) before leaving Hungary soon after the 1956 uprising. Settling in Germany, he led the Augsburg Opera (1958-63), the Cologne Opera (1964-73), and the London Symphony (1965-68). He also established close ties with other orchestras, notably the Chicago Symphony. His work was characterized by an intense but unexaggerated expressiveness and by a warm sound emphasizing the lower strings. He had a special fondness for Mozart, Brahms, and such moderns as Bartók and Stravinsky. Kertész toured Israel many times with the Israel Philharmonic. During his final visit to Israel, he drowned when he was

caught in a current while swimming in the Mediterranean Sea.

KING, CAROLE (original surname, KLEIN; born February 9, 1942, in New York City, New York). Composer and singer. She went to high school in the Brooklyn section of New York City with Neil Sedaka, whose song "Oh, Carol" refers to her. With her first husband, Gerry Goffin, as lyricist, King composed many of the most successful pop and rock songs of the 1960s, including "Will You Love Me Tomorrow?" (1960), "Go Away, Little Girl" (1962), and "Up on the Roof" (1962). After King and Goffin divorced in 1968, she took some time off and then returned to music in 1970 as both a composer and a singer. Since then she has used lyrics by Goffin and others, including herself. Among her albums are *Tapestry* (with her and Goffin's "It's Too Late," 1971), *Thoroughbred* (1976), and *One to One* (1982). The singer Louise Goffin, daughter of King and Goffin, issued her first album, *Kid Blue*, in 1979.

KINSKY, GEORG LUDWIG (born September 29, 1882, in Marienwerder, Germany [now Kwidzyn, Poland]; died April 7, 1951, in Berlin, Germany). Musicologist. A pioneer in music iconography, Kinsky published (with Robert Haas and Hans Schnoor) *Geschichte der Musik in Bildern* (1929; English, as *A History of Music in Pictures*, 1930). He also prepared an important thematic catalog of Beethoven's music (completed by Hans Halm and published in 1955).

KIRCHNER, LEON (born January 24, 1919, in New York City, New York). Composer. He began by composing under the various influences of Mahler, Bartók, Hindemith, and Stravinsky. One of his most important early works is the *First String Quartet* (1949), which shows the influence of Bartók. Soon, however, he entered the aesthetic orbit of Schoenberg and Berg, though he never adopted their twelve-tone technique. His music is, in fact, remarkably free of preconceived notions. He opposes those who embrace "the superficial security of current style and fad worship and make a fetish of complexity." "Idea," he continues, "the precious ore of art, is lost in the jungle of graphs, prepared tapes, feedbacks, and cold minutiae." Kirchner's own highly personal style is characterized by its powerful expressivity. Composed in a freely chromatic idiom, his music fluctuates between tonal and atonal implications. His forms are created not by obvious surface oppositions but by evolutions from one emotional state to another, his purpose being, as he says, to "involve the listener very directly with the organic growth of a work." His most famous composition is the intense *First Piano Concerto* (1953). Among his other works are the profoundly moving *Third String Quartet* (1966), the sublime *Music for Orchestra* (1969), and the wrenchingly expressive opera *Lily* (perf. 1977).

KLETZKI, PAUL (originally PAWEL KLECKI; born March 21, 1900, in Łódź, Poland; died March 5, 1973, in Liverpool, England). Conductor. He conducted in Berlin (1923-33) till the Hitler era, during which he worked in Italy, the Soviet Union, and Switzerland. After 1945 he appeared widely as a guest conductor on the international scene. He also served as principal conductor of the Liverpool Philharmonic (1954-55) and music director of the Dallas Symphony (1960-63), the Bern Symphony (1964-66), and the Orchestre de la Suisse Romande (of Geneva, 1967-69). He had an accomplished technique, and his interpretations were clear and fresh. Though he had a special fondness for the romantics, he also conducted contemporary music.

KOFFLER, JÓZEF (born November 28, 1896, in Stryj, Poland [now Stry, the Soviet Union]; died 1943 in Wieliczka, near Cracow, Poland). Composer. He was the first Polish composer to adopt Arnold Schoenberg's twelve-tone technique of composition. Koffler was also probably the first composer anywhere to incorporate folk materials into twelve-tone serialism. Furthermore, unlike most serialists, he aligned himself with neoclassicism. Among his most effective works are the *String Trio* (1929), the *Piano Sonatina* (1931), and the *Third Symphony* (1938). Koffler, with his wife and child, was killed during a street roundup of Jews.

KOGAN, LEONID (born November 14, 1924, in Ekaterinoslav [now Dnepropetrovsk], the Soviet Union; died December 17, 1982, in Mytishchi, the Soviet Union). Violinist. In 1951 he established his international reputation by winning the prestigious Queen Elisabeth Competition in Brussels. Later in the 1950s he began to tour Europe and the United States. Next to David Oistrakh, Kogan was the foremost Soviet violinist. But Kogan's style was more objective and contemporary than the older master's was. Kogan had a broad repertory, from Bach to Paganini to modern composers; many Soviets wrote works for him. Married to the violinist Elizaveta Gilels (sister of the pianist Emil Gilels), Kogan often publicly performed duets with her. Pavel Kogan, their son, sometimes joined them for three-violin music. Leonid died on a train in a railroad station while on his way to a concert engagement.

KOLISCH, RUDOLF (born July 20, 1896, in Klamm on the Semmering, Austria; died August 1, 1978, in Watertown, Massachusetts). Violinist. Because of a childhood injury to his left hand, Kolisch, throughout his career, held the violin with his right hand, the bow with his left. He performed as a virtuoso and then, in 1922, formed the Kolisch String Quartet, which soon became internationally famous as the first string quartet to play the standard repertory from memory and as a propagator of new music, especially that of Schoenberg (who married Gertrud Kolisch, Rudolf's sister), Berg, and Webern. In 1935 Kolisch settled in the United States, disbanding the quartet four years later. He then led the Pro Arte String Quartet from 1942 on.

KOSAKOFF, REUVEN (born January 8, 1898, in New Haven, Connecticut). Pianist and composer. After settling in New York City, he appeared frequently as a concert pianist. His compositions include several biblical cantatas, two Sabbath services, a piano concerto based on Hebrew themes, and a number of smaller piano pieces. He made many effective arrangements of Jewish folksongs.

KOSHETZ, NINA (born December 30, 1894, in Kiev, the Ukraine [now in the Soviet Union]; died May 14, 1965, in Santa Ana, California). Soprano. She toured Russia with the pianist-composer Sergei Rachmaninoff, of whose songs she became a famous interpreter. After the Russian Revolution of 1917, Koshetz immigrated to the United States, where she gave recitals and performed as soloist with major orchestras, specializing in Russian songs.

KOUGUELL, ARKADIE (born December 25, 1898, in Simferopol, the Ukraine [now in the Soviet Union]). Composer and pianist. He lived in Beirut (1928-48) and Paris (1948-52) before settling in the United States in 1952. He has composed much instrumental music, including *Impressions of Damascus* for orchestra (1930), *Piano Concerto* (1930), *Piano Concerto for Left Hand* (1934), chamber pieces, and piano sonatas.

KREIN, ALEXANDER (born October 20, 1883, in Nizhni Novgorod, Russia [now Gorki, the Soviet Union]; died April 21, 1951, in Staraya Russa, the Soviet Union). Composer. Brother of the composer Grigory Krein and uncle of the composer Julian Krein. Alexander became active in the Moscow branch of the Society for Jewish Folk Music and later wrote music for many Jewish plays, such as *Ghetto* (1924). He also composed operas, orchestral works, vocal music, and chamber pieces, such as the *Hebrew Sketches* for clarinet and string quartet (1910). His style reflects elements from Debussy, Scriabin, and authentic Jewish music.

KREIN, GRIGORY (born March 18, 1879, in Nizhni Novgorod, Russia [now Gorki, the Soviet Union]; died January 6, 1955, in Komarovo, near Leningrad, the Soviet Union). Composer. Brother of the composer Alexander Krein and father of the composer Julian Krein. Grigory composed instrumental works for a variety of ensembles, sometimes incorporating Jewish themes.

KREIN, JULIAN (born March 5, 1913, in Moscow, Russia). Composer. Son of the composer Grigory Krein and nephew of the composer Alexander Krein. Julian, who has occasionally utilized Jewish motives, is a composer of great lyric gifts. His music is characterized by advanced harmonic techniques, intense emotionalism, and programmatic intentions, as in the symphonic prelude *Destruction* (1929), which tries to express pacifist ideals, and in the *Spring Symphony* (1938).

KURTH, ERNST (born June 1, 1886, in Vienna, Austria; died August 2, 1946, in Bern, Switzerland). Musicologist. His writings are important to both musicology and philosophy. In *Grundlagen des linearen Kontrapunkts* ("Foundations of Linear Counterpoint," 1917; fifth edition, 1956), he introduced the term *linear counterpoint. Romantische Harmonik und ihre Krise in Wagners "Tristan"* ("Romantic Harmony and Its Crisis in Wagner's *Tristan*," 1920; third edition, 1923) is both an advanced harmony text and a psychological analysis of romantic music. Other important books are *Bruckner* (1925) and *Musikpsychologie* ("Psychology of Music," 1931; second edition, 1947). The central thought in all of his works is that music comes from psychic energy, an idea derived from Schopenhauer and Freud.

KURZ, SELMA (born November 15, 1874, in Bielitz, Silesia [now Bielsko-Biała, Poland]; died May 10, 1933, in Vienna, Austria). Soprano. She was a leading figure at the Vienna Opera for nearly thirty years (1899-1927). At first she sang lyric, dramatic soprano roles, such as the title character in Puccini's *Tosca*. Later she gained her greatest fame for coloratura soprano roles, such as Gilda in Verdi's *Rigoletto*. Kurz was renowned for the purity and ease of her vocal production, especially for the remarkable perfection and duration of her trill.

L

LACHMANN, ROBERT (born November 28, 1892, in Berlin, Germany; died May 8, 1939, in Jerusalem, Palestine [now Israel]). Ethnomusicologist. In 1935 the Hebrew University of Jerusalem asked him to establish its Phonogram Archive for Oriental Music, which became the starting point for modern ethnomusicology in Israel. Lachmann made numerous recordings of authentic Jewish and Arab music. Among his many important writings is the book *Jewish Cantillation and Song in the Isle of Djerba* (1940).

LADERMAN, EZRA (born June 29, 1924, in New York City, New York). Composer. Though technically based in traditional romanticism, his style is marked by intensity and individuality of expression. Many of his most important works are on Jewish topics, such as the cantata *And David Wept* (1971), the *Third Symphony: Jerusalem* (1973), and the *Meditations on Isaiah* for cello (1973). He also composed the background score for the documentary film *The Eleanor Roosevelt Story* (1965), the *Concerto for Flute, Bassoon, and Orchestra* (perf. 1983), numerous preludes for organ, and a wide variety of other works.

LANE, BURTON (originally BURTON LEVY; born February 12, 1912, in New York City, New York). Composer. He contributed songs to New York City revues before going to the Hollywood section of Los Angeles to compose for movies. One of his best-known film songs is "Stop! You're Breaking My Heart" (lyrics, Ted Koehler) for *Artists and Models* (1937). However, his greatest successes have

resulted from his occasional returns to stage work, including *Hold On to Your Hats* (perf. 1940), Al Jolson's last Broadway musical; *Finian's Rainbow* (perf. 1947), with "How Are Things in Glocca Morra?" (lyrics, E. Y. Harburg); and *On a Clear Day You Can See Forever* (perf. 1965), with the title song (lyrics, Alan J. Lerner).

LAREDO, RUTH (originally RUTH MECKLER; born November 20, 1937, in Detroit, Michigan). Pianist. In 1960 she married the American violinist of Bolivian birth Jaime Laredo, with whom she performed in many joint recitals. (They separated and divorced in the mid-1970s.) The first American woman pianist to win international recognition, Ruth Laredo is a successful recitalist, orchestral soloist, and chamber musician. She is the first pianist to have recorded the complete solo works of Rachmaninoff and is also an

expert performer of Tchaikovsky, Scriabin, Barber, and Ravel, her signature piece being Ravel's *La Valse* ("The Waltz").

LAWRENCE, STEVE (originally SIDNEY LEIBOWITZ; born

July 8, 1935, in New York City, New York) and **GORME, EYDIE** (originally EDITH GORME; born August 16, 1932, in New York City, New York). Singers. They worked together on Steve Allen's TV variety show *Tonight!* from 1954 to 1957, and in the latter year they married. Since then they have sung together in nightclubs, on recordings, on their own TV specials, and in the Broadway musical *Golden Rainbow* (1968). They also had some hit solo records, including Lawrence's "Go Away, Little Girl" (1962) and Gorme's "Blame It on the Bossa Nova" (1963).

LEIBOWITZ, RENÉ (born February 17, 1913, in Warsaw, Poland; died August 28, 1972, in Paris, France). Musicologist, composer, and conductor. His major contribution to music was his promotion of the Second Viennese School (Schoenberg, Berg, Webern) through conducting their works, writing about their music, and privately teaching their serial techniques. One of his pupils was Pierre Boulez. Leibowitz's own compositions adhere closely to the techniques and aesthetics of Schoenberg and Berg.

LEICHTENTRITT, HUGO (born January 1, 1874, in Pleschen, near Posen, Germany [now Pleszow, near Poznań, Poland]; died November 13, 1951, in Cambridge, Massachusetts). Musicologist. He immigrated to the United States in the early 1930s. His writings are noted for their thoroughness, as in the monumental *Geschichte der Motette* ("History of the Motet," 1908). His thoughts culminated in *Music, History, and Ideas* (1938; fourth edition, 1954), which examines music as part of general culture, and *Music of the Western Nations* (edited by Nicolas Slonimsky, 1956), which views music as an expression of the cultural status of various countries.

LENYA, LOTTE (originally KAROLINE BLAMAUER; born October 18, 1898, in Vienna, Austria; died November 27, 1981, in New York City, New York). Singing actress. For her professional career she took the surname Lenya, which she derived from her childhood nickname, Lenja. At the age of four she learned acrobatics and performed in a small

neighborhood circus. Later she became a dancer and gained experience by performing in ballet sequences in operas. In 1926 she married the composer Kurt Weill, and the following year she made her singing debut by appearing in the world premiere of his stage work *Mahagonny Songspiel*. In 1928 she created the role of Jenny in the first performance of Weill's masterpiece, *Die Dreigroschenoper* ("The Threepenny Opera"). They fled Nazi Germany in 1933, spent about two years in Paris, and then settled in the United States. Lenya developed an international reputation by performing both in Weill's musical works and as a straight actress. After his early death, in 1950, she devoted much of the rest of her life to promoting his works through such means as TV performances and stage revivals of his German-period compositions. She was widely regarded as the world's leading interpreter of his music. Lenya's forte was not her singing voice, which was not highly trained, but rather her dramatic insight and her musical instinct in presenting the half-spoken, half-sung lines in Weill's works.

LEVANT, OSCAR (born December 27, 1906, in Pittsburgh, Pennsylvania; died August 14, 1972, in Beverly Hills, California). Pianist and composer. He became most famous for his piano interpretations of music by his good friend George Gershwin. Levant composed music for many popular songs, including those for several movies, such as *Street Girl* (lyrics, Sidney Clare; 1929) and *Music Is Magic* (lyrics, Sidney Clare; 1935). He also appeared in a number of films as a wisecracking actor, sometimes playing the piano, as in *Rhapsody in Blue* (1945) and *An American in Paris* (1951). His concert compositions are in a complex, modern vein and include the *Nocturne* for orchestra (1937) and the *Piano Concerto in One Movement* (perf. 1942). His books of reminiscences display a caustic wit: *A Smattering of Ignorance* (1940), *The Memoirs of an Amnesiac* (1965), and *The Unimportance of Being Oscar* (1968).

LEVI, HERMANN (born November 7, 1839, in Giessen, Germany; died May 13, 1900, in Munich, Germany). Conductor. He conducted in Saarbrücken (1859-61) and at the German Opera in Rotterdam (1861-64), followed by tenures as court conductor in Karlsruhe (1864-72) and Munich (1872-90; music director, 1894-96). In Munich he also served as unofficial musical adviser to the synagogue. He developed a close working relationship with Richard Wagner, who somewhat restrained his anti-Semitism out of respect for Levi's musical talent. However, in 1882 Wagner made a clumsy effort to convert Levi, son of a rabbi, to Christianity before Levi's scheduled conducting of the first performance of Wagner's *Parsifal*, a Christian music drama. Levi nearly withdrew from the assignment; but Wagner and others smoothed things over, and Levi conducted the world premiere of the work in Bayreuth. Ironically it was the Jew Levi who conducted the music program at the funeral of the anti-Semite Wagner the following year. Levi's conducting was renowned for its solid technique and economy of gesture.

LEVITZKI, MISCHA (born May 25, 1898, in Kremenchug, Russia; died January 2, 1941, in Avon-by-the-Sea, New Jersey). Pianist and composer. When he was eight years old, he came to the United States with his parents. He had a successful career as a concert pianist and composed some charming piano pieces.

LEVY, MARVIN DAVID (born August 2, 1932, in Passaic,

New Jersey). Composer. His music is in an expressionistic atonal idiom. Levy's most important work is *Mourning Becomes Electra* (perf. 1967), one of the few American operas commissioned for the Metropolitan Opera. He has also composed other operas, various instrumental pieces, and choral music, including the *Sacred Service* (1964) for the Park Avenue Synagogue in New York City.

LEWANDOWSKI, LOUIS (originally LAZARUS LEWANDOWSKI; born April 3, 1821, in Wreschen, near Posen, Germany [now near Poznań, Poland]; died February 3, 1894, in Berlin, Germany). Composer and conductor. Granduncle of the cantor Manfred Lewandowski. From 1840 on he served as conductor of the synagogue choir in Berlin. Adopting the style of German romanticism, particularly that of Mendelssohn, Lewandowski composed liturgical music and made simplified arrangements of traditional synagogal melodies. Among his chief compilations are *Kol rinah u'tefillah* ("The Voice of Praise and Prayer") for one and two voices (1871) and *Todah w'simrah* ("Praise and Song") for four voices, soloists, and optional organ accompaniment (two volumes, 1876-82). Though he failed to keep the true spirit of Jewish cantillation, he succeeded in his main aim: to appeal to a broad spectrum of listeners. For half a century after his death, Lewandowski's work was the single greatest influence on Western Ashkenazic synagogal music.

LEWANDOWSKI, MANFRED (born September 1, 1895, in Hamburg, Germany; died September 8, 1970, in Philadelphia, Pennsylvania). Cantor. Grandnephew of the composer Louis Lewandowski. Manfred studied with Josef Rosenblatt. He rose to prominence as a cantor in Berlin and made numerous recordings, many of which were destroyed by the Nazis in 1933. In 1938 he went to Paris, and in 1939 he immigrated to the United States, where he performed widely as one of the finest cantorial artists of his time.

LEWENTHAL, RAYMOND (born August 29, 1926, in San Antonio, Texas). Pianist. After a promising beginning to his concert career, he was attacked by thugs in New York City in 1953 and received arm and hand fractures. In 1961 he successfully resumed his public appearances. Though he has performed works by major composers, especially Liszt, Lewenthal has built his reputation primarily by concentrating on such neglected nineteenth-century composers as Adolph von Henselt, Johann Hummel, and Sigismond Thalberg. He is closely identified with, and largely responsible for the recent interest in, the music of Charles Alkan.

LHEVINNE, ROSINA (originally ROSINA BESSIE; born March 28, 1880, in Kiev, the Ukraine [now in the Soviet Union]; died November 9, 1976, in Glendale, California). Pianist. Shortly after graduating from the Moscow Conservatory in 1898 she married the pianist Josef Lhevinne. Thereafter she devoted most of her energy to supervising her husband's career, assisting him with his teaching, and appearing with him in two-piano works. In 1919 the Lhevinnes immigrated to the United States. Soon after her husband's death Rosina was given his position at the Juilliard School of Music in New York City, where she remained for many years (1945-76) and came to be regarded as one of the great teachers of her time. Her pupils included John Browning, Van Cliburn, and James Levine. In her later years she performed publicly as a soloist on occasion. Her manner was that of the old-style romanticist, with an emphasis on the sensuous aspects of her art.

LIEBERMANN, ROLF (born September 14, 1910, in Zurich, Switzerland). Composer. His *Concerto for Jazzband and Symphony Orchestra* (1954) was an early attempt to bring jazz players and conventional performers together, as well as to combine jazz and the twelve-tone technique. But he built his reputation primarily as a composer of partly twelve-tone operas, notably *Penelope* (perf. 1954). He has done little composing since becoming involved with opera administration in the late 1950s.

LIEBERSON, GODDARD (born April 5, 1911, in Hanley, Staffordshire, England; died May 29, 1977, in New York City, New York). Music executive and composer. He was brought to the United States as a child. In 1939 he joined the staff at Columbia Records, where he later served as president (1955-66, 1973-75). Lieberson was an important catalyst in promoting long-playing records, and he established the liberal policy at Columbia Records regarding the recording of modern works. He composed a number of pieces himself, such as the orchestral *Five Modern Painters* (1929).

LIST, EMANUEL (originally EMANUEL FLEISSIG; born March 22, 1888, in Vienna, Austria; died June 21, 1967, in Vienna, Austria). Bass. In 1914 he arrived in the United States and began to perform in burlesque, vaudeville, minstrel shows, and movie theaters. Returning to Vienna in 1920, he began to sing opera there in 1922, followed by ten years in Berlin (1923-33). Removed from his Berlin post by the Nazis, he sang at the Metropolitan Opera in New York City (1933-50) and then returned to Europe. With his deep, rich voice and imposing presence, he made an excellent Baron Ochs in Richard Strauss's *Der Rosenkavalier* ("The Knight of the Rose"), and he was particularly renowned for his Wagner villains. List also sang lieder, especially Schubert.

LIUZZI, FERDINANDO (or FERNANDO LIUZZI; born December 19, 1884, in Senigallia, Italy; died October 6, 1940, in Florence, Italy). His essays on Palestrina, early Christian hymnody, and the interaction of Italian and Flemish music are fundamental to the knowledge of early Italian music.

LOCKSPEISER, EDWARD (born May 21, 1905, in London, England; died February 3, 1973, in Alfriston, Sussex, England). Musicologist. His special interest was French music, as seen in his books *Berlioz* (1939) and *Bizet* (1951). His masterpiece, written after thirty years of intense research, is *Debussy: His Life and Music* (volume 1, 1962; volume 2, 1965). Another important work is *Music and Painting: A Study in Comparative Ideas from Turner to Schoenberg* (1973).

LOESSER, ARTHUR (born August 26, 1894, in New York City, New York; died January 4, 1969, in Cleveland, Ohio). Pianist and writer. Brother of the composer Frank Loesser. He began his fine concert career in 1913. But he is remembered today chiefly for his imaginative writings on music, notably *Men, Women, and Pianos: A Social History* (1954).

LONDON, GEORGE (originally GEORGE BURNSTEIN; born May 30, 1920, in Montreal, Canada; died March 24, 1985, in Armonk, New York). Bass-baritone. His international career began with an engagement at the Vienna Opera (1949), followed by his debuts at Bayreuth (1951), the Metropolitan Opera in New York City (1951), and La Scala in Milan (1952). In 1960 he performed the lead in Mussorgsky's *Boris Godunov* at the Bolshoi in Moscow, the first non-Russian invited to sing the role there. His other notable roles included Mephistopheles in Gounod's *Faust* and the title character in Mozart's *Don Giovanni*. In 1967 a problem with his vocal cords caused him to retire. He then devoted himself to arts administration till he had a heart attack in 1977, after which he was permanently incapacitated.

LOURIÉ, ARTHUR VINCENT (born May 14, 1892, in Saint Petersburg, Russia [now Leningrad, the Soviet Union]; died October 13, 1966, in Princeton, New Jersey). Composer. He moved to Berlin in 1921, Paris in 1924, and America in 1941. His early music was influenced by the hyperchromatic, quasi-atonal style of Scriabin, as in Lourié's *Préludes fragiles* ("Fragile Preludes") for piano (1915). Later he preferred a modal style influenced by Stravinsky, as in Lourié's *Sonata liturgica* ("Liturgical Sonata") for alto voices and chamber orchestra (1928), which is based on melodic ideas having a kinship to plainsong (Lourié having converted to Roman Catholicism in his youth).

LOWINSKY, EDWARD E(LIAS) (born January 12, 1908, in Stuttgart, Germany; died October 11, 1985, in Chicago, Illinois). Musicologist. He immigrated to the United States in 1940. Lowinsky has become one of the major figures in post-World War II musicology, gaining special fame for his controversial book *Secret Chromatic Art in the Netherlands Motet* (1946), which sparked a continuing debate about the nature of chromatic alterations intended for performance, but not written out, by some Renaissance composers. Another provocative work is his *Tonality and Atonality in Sixteenth-Century Music* (1961, revised 1962).

LUBOSHUTZ, LÉA (originally LÉA LUBOSHITS; born February 22, 1885, in Odessa, the Ukraine [now in the Soviet Union]; died March 18, 1965, in Philadelphia, Pennsylvania). Violinist. Sister of the pianist Pierre Luboshutz and mother of the pianist Boris Goldovsky. Soon after the Russian Revolution of 1917, Léa left Russia and lived for several years in Europe before settling in the United States in 1925. In that year she gave the American premiere of Prokofiev's *First Violin Concerto*. She gave many joint recitals with Boris Goldovsky.

LUBOSHUTZ, PIERRE (originally PIERRE LUBOSHITS; born June 17, 1891, in Odessa, the Ukraine [now in the Soviet Union]; died April 17, 1971, in Rockport, Maine). Pianist. Brother of the violinist Léa Luboshutz and uncle of the pianist Boris Goldovsky. In 1926 he came to the United States and served as piano accompanist for the violinist Efrem Zimbalist, the cellist Gregor Piatigorsky, and others. He married the pianist Genia Nemenoff, with whom he formed a piano duet for public concerts.

LUCCA, PAULINE (born April 25, 1841, in Vienna, Austria; died February 28, 1908, in Vienna, Austria). Soprano. She debuted, in Olmütz, in 1859 as Elvira in Verdi's *Ernani*. While singing in Prague in 1860, she attracted the attention of Meyerbeer, on whose recommendation she was engaged at the Berlin Opera, where she remained from 1861 to 1872. Lucca made her American debut in 1872 and then sang at the Vienna Opera (1874-89). Possessor of a 2½-octave range, she was one of the greatest sopranos of her time, renowned for such dramatic roles as Selika in Meyerbeer's *L'africaine* ("The African Woman") and the title part in Bizet's *Carmen*.

M

MACIAS, ENRICO (born December 11, 1938, in Constantine, Algeria). Singer and composer. He settled in France, where his singing of his own light songs has made him one of that nation's most popular entertainers. In 1967 he visited Israel and sang for the troops; Arab countries thereupon barred him from performing in their lands.

MANN, HERBIE (originally HERBERT SOLOMON; born April 16, 1930, in New York City, New York). Jazz flutist. Since 1959 he has led his own group. Among his many tours have been visits to Africa (1960), Brazil (1961-62), Japan (1964), and Scandinavia, Cyprus, and Turkey (1971). His music has at various times incorporated Afro-Latin, Brazilian, and Middle Eastern elements, as well as rock.

MANN, MANFRED (originally MICHAEL LUBOWITZ; born October 21, 1940, in Johannesburg, South Africa). Keyboardist. Fronting several different ensembles named after him, he has recorded material in various blends of jazz, rock, and other popular idioms. His best-known recordings are "Do Wah Diddy Diddy" (1964) and "Blinded by the Light" (1976). His albums include *Manfred Mann's Earth Band* (1972), *Angel Station* (1979), and *Somewhere in Afrika* (1983).

MANNES, DAVID (born February 16, 1866, in New York City, New York; died April 25, 1959, in New York City, New York). Violinist and educator. He played violin with the New York Symphony Orchestra from 1891 to 1912, serving as concertmaster from 1898 on. Also in 1898 he married the pianist Clara Damrosch, sister of the orchestra's conductor, Walter Damrosch. Mannes founded two important music institutions in New York City: in 1912 the Music School Settlement for Colored Children, and in 1916 the David Mannes School of Music, which in 1953 became the degree-granting Mannes College of Music. He wrote the autobiography *Music Is My Faith* (1938). David and Clara (who was born into the Lutheran faith) had a son, Leopold Damrosch Mannes, who was a pianist and composer, as well as the director of the family's school when it became a college; but he gained his greatest fame as coinventor, with Leopold Godowsky, Jr., of the Kodachrome process of color photography.

MARTIN, TONY (originally ALVIN MORRIS; born December 25, 1913, in Oakland, California). Singer. He began in show business as a dance-band saxophonist and later became a singer as well. In 1935 he entered the movies, for which his name was changed from Al Morris to Anthony Martin, soon shortened to Tony Martin (the legal change taking place in 1936). His first significant singing role was in *Sing, Baby, Sing* (1936), in which he met the actress Alice Faye. They married in 1936 and then appeared together in the films *You Can't Have Everything* (1937) and *Sally, Irene, and Mary* (1938). Shortly afterward they were divorced. He later sang in the movies *Ziegfeld Girl* (1941), *The Big Store* (1941), *Till the Clouds Roll By* (1946), *Casbah* (1948), *Here Come the Girls* (1953), and others. Martin was also one of the most successful recording artists from the late 1930s through the early 1950s, with such hits as "All the Things You Are" (1939), "Fools Rush In Where Angels Fear to Tread" (1940), "The Last Time I Saw Paris" (1940), "You Stepped out of a

Dream" (1941), "Sleepy Lagoon" (1942), "Hooray for Love" (1948), "Kiss of Fire" (1952), and "Stranger in Paradise" (1953). In 1951 he had a major hit when he sang a duet with Dinah Shore in "A Penny a Kiss." In 1948 he married the dancer Cyd Charisse. They appeared together in the films *Deep in My Heart* (1954) and *Meet Me in Las Vegas* (1956). Since 1964 they have performed extensively together in nightclubs and theaters. They are known as the Man with the Golden Voice and the Girl with the Golden Legs.

MARX, ADOLF BERNHARD (born 1795 in Halle, Germany; died May 17, 1866, in Berlin, Germany). Theorist. He was a close friend of the Mendelssohn family in Berlin, and he often advised Felix Mendelssohn in musical matters. Marx wrote the influential book *Die Lehre von der musikalischen Komposition* ("The Theory of Musical Composition," four volumes, 1837-47, with many later editions; English, volume 1 in 1852, volume 4 in 1910), which simplified the techniques of composition. Marx was apparently the first theorist to use the term *Sonatenform* ("sonata form") to describe a type of one-movement structure.

MARX BROTHERS. Family of musicians and comedians. Because the births of most of the brothers were not recorded—Groucho's and Zeppo's were—many different birth dates have been published. The following dates are based on the best recent evidence. CHICO (originally LEONARD; born August 21, 1887, in New York City, New York; died October 11, 1961, in Beverly Hills, California) played the piano and feigned an Italian accent. HARPO (originally ADOLPH, later ARTHUR; born November 23, 1888, in New York City, New York; died September 28, 1964, in Los Angeles, California) had the role of the childlike mute who played the harp. GROUCHO (originally JULIUS; born October 2, 1890, in New York City, New York; died August 19, 1977, in Los Angeles, California) was the wisecracker who sang—with a nasal twang and an outrageous, inimitable, lovable mockery—a variety of comic songs. ZEPPO (originally HERBERT; born February 25, 1901, in New York City, New York; died November 30, 1979, in Palm Springs, California) acted as the straight man, especially for Groucho, and crooned romantic songs. The boys began in vaudeville, where another brother, GUMMO (originally MILTON; born October 23, 1892, in New York City, New York; died April 21, 1977, in Palm Springs, California), appeared briefly with the team. The other four went on to great success in three Broadway shows: *I'll Say She Is!* (1924), *The Cocoanuts* (1925), and *Animal Crackers* (1928). But they gained their greatest fame in movies, beginning with filmed versions of *The Cocoanuts* (1929) and *Animal Crackers* (1930). The next three films with the four Marx Brothers were *Monkey Business* (1931), *Horse Feathers* (1932), and *Duck Soup* (1933). Then Zeppo left the team, and Chico, Harpo, and Groucho went on to make *A Night at the Opera* (1935), *A Day at the Races* (1937), *At the Circus* (1939), *A Night in Casablanca* (1946), *Love Happy* (1950), and a few other movies. Chico's and Harpo's zany antics tended to overshadow the fact that they were excellent instinctive musicians. A highlight of Groucho's adventures in singing was his rendition of "Lydia, the Tattooed Lady" in *At the Circus*. The biography *Growing Up with Chico* (1980) was written by Maxine Marx, Chico's daughter. Autobiographical books by the brothers themselves include Harpo's *Harpo Speaks!* (1961) and Groucho's *Groucho and Me* (1959) and *Memoirs of a Mangy Lover* (1963).

MASSARY, FRITZI (originally FRIEDERIKE MASSARYK; born March 21, 1882, in Vienna, Austria; died January 30, 1969, in Los Angeles, California). Soprano. Based in Berlin (1904-1933), she reigned as the greatest operetta diva of her time and raised the art of operetta singing to a new artistic level. Leo Fall, Emmerich Kálmán, Franz Lehár, and Oscar Straus wrote operettas especially for her. After the Nazi takeover of Germany, Massary moved to London and then to California.

MATZENAUER, MARGARETE (born June 1, 1881, in Temesvár, Hungary [now Timişoara, Romania]; died May 19, 1963, in Van Nuys, California). Singer. After singing opera in Strasbourg (1901-1904) and Munich (1904-1911), she immigrated to the United States. In America she performed at the Metropolitan Opera in New York City (1911-30) till her retirement from opera, after which she gave recitals for a few years. Matzenauer had an exceptional vocal range, being able to perform soprano and alto parts with equal richness and power. Her repertory, too, was wide, ranging from Gluck to Dukas.

MENDEL, ARTHUR (born June 6, 1905, in Boston, Massachusetts; died October 14, 1979, in Newark, New Jersey). Musicologist. The foremost Bach scholar of his generation, he prepared *The Bach Reader* (with Hans T. David; 1945, revised 1966), a documentary biography. Mendel also did research in the history of musical pitch, rhythmic structures in the Renaissance and the baroque, and Josquin des Prez's music.

MENDEL, HERMANN (born August 6, 1834, in Halle, Germany; died October 26, 1876, in Berlin, Germany). Music lexicographer. He published two little books (1868-69) on Meyerbeer. His great work was a multivolume music encyclopedia, which he began to publish in 1870. But he died in the middle of the project, and it was completed by August Reissmann, the final volume being issued in 1883.

MENDELSSOHN, FANNY (born November 14, 1805, in Hamburg, Germany; died May 14, 1847, in Berlin, Germany). Pianist and composer. Sister of the composer Felix Mendelssohn. In 1829 Fanny married the painter Wilhelm Hensel, but throughout her life she remained a close personal and musical adviser to her brother Felix. An excellent musician, she occasionally played the piano in public. Her compositions, which follow a style remarkably similar to that of her brother, include songs, choruses, chamber music, and piano pieces.

MENUHIN, HEPHZIBAH (born May 20, 1920, in San Francisco, California; died January 1, 1981, in London, England). Pianist. Sister of the pianist Yaltah Menuhin and the violinist Yehudi Menuhin. Hephzibah gave sonata recitals with Yehudi from 1934 on. A well-known soloist in her own right, she was especially active in Australia.

MENUHIN, YALTAH (born October 7, 1922, in San Francisco, California). Pianist. Sister of the pianist Hephzibah Menuhin and the violinist Yehudi Menuhin. Though a fine soloist, she has gained her reputation primarily as an outstanding chamber-music player.

MEYER, ERNST HERMANN (born December 8, 1905, in Berlin, Germany). Composer and musicologist. In 1933, to escape the Nazis, he went to England, where he made pioneer researches into old English chamber music and summarized his findings in the book *English Chamber Music: The History of a Great Art from the Middle Ages to Purcell* (1946; second edition, 1951). A devoted Marxist-Leninist, Meyer moved to East Germany in 1948 and composed a variety of instrumental works and vocal music according to the ideals of socialist realism.

MILNER, MOSES (originally MIKHAIL MELNIKOFF; born December 29, 1886, in Rakitno, near Kiev, the Ukraine [now in the Soviet Union]; died October 25, 1953, in Leningrad, the Soviet Union). Composer and conductor. He was one of the principal figures in the activities of the Society for Jewish Folk Music, which existed in Russia from 1908 to 1918. Milner conducted the choir in the Great Synagogue of Saint Petersburg (1912-19) and then composed and conducted music for various Jewish and non-Jewish theaters in Russia. Much of his music, secular and liturgical, is based on Jewish folk or folk-inspired tunes, as well as on traditional Jewish religious motives. A few of his works, notably the song "In Cheder" (1914), have retained great popularity. He composed the first Yiddish opera ever staged in Russia: *Die himlen brenen* ("The Heavens Aflame," perf. 1923). In Milner's later years Jewish art was repressed in the Soviet Union, and he turned to general subjects.

MOISEIWITSCH, BENNO (born February 22, 1890, in Odessa, the Ukraine [now in the Soviet Union]; died April 9, 1963, in London, England). Pianist. Moving with his family to England, Moiseiwitsch made his official debut, in Reading, in 1908. In 1909 he gave his first London performance, and from 1919 on he toured Europe and America regularly. His playing was brilliant yet poetic, and he favored the romantic composers.

MOSCHELES, IGNAZ (born May 23, 1794, in Prague, Bohemia [now in Czechoslovakia]; died March 10, 1870, in Leipzig, Germany). Pianist and composer. He had close personal and professional relationships with Beethoven, Mendelssohn, and other musical giants of his time. One of the last great representatives of the classical school of pianists, Moscheles played with clarity and precision; yet he also began a new era through the sheer brilliance of his technique. He composed for a wide variety of forces; but only his piano pieces remain important, especially his early, Beethoven-influenced sonatas, such as the *Sonate mélancolique* ("Melancholy Sonata," 1814). Many of his piano studies are still used.

MOSZKOWSKI, MORITZ (born August 23, 1854, in Breslau, Silesia [now Wrocław, Poland]; died March 4, 1925, in Paris, France). Pianist and composer. While still in his teens, he began a long and successful career as a pianist, concertizing throughout Europe. In 1897 he retired to Paris. Moszkowski's large, serious works were less successful than his light pieces were. Still popular are his many Spanish dances for piano.

MOTTL, FELIX (born August 24, 1856, in Unter-Saint Veit, near Vienna; died July 2, 1911, in Munich, Germany). Conductor. In 1876 he assisted at the first Bayreuth Festival of Wagner's music, and in 1886 he made his initial appearance there as a conductor. During his tenure as opera and symphony conductor in Karlsruhe (1881-1903), Mottl raised the city's musical standards to the highest in Germany. His last years were spent conducting in Munich. Mottl was best known for his performances of Wagner.

N

NACHEZ, TIVADAR (or THEODOR NASCHITZ; born May 1, 1859, in Pest [now Budapest], Hungary; died May 29, 1930, in Lausanne, Switzerland). Violinist and composer. As a boy he performed with Franz Liszt and won the great pianist's approval. Nachez concertized internationally but lived most of his adult life in London. He composed many violin pieces derived from Hungarian folksongs.

NADEL, ARNO (born October 3, 1878, in Vilnius, Lithuania [now in the Soviet Union]; died March 1943 in Oświęcim, Poland). Musicologist and conductor. In 1916 he began to conduct synagogal choral music in Berlin, and later he became music supervisor of the city's entire Jewish community. He restored old vocal traditions in the synagogues and raised the musical standards of the choirs. He also published several anthologies of eastern European Jewish folksongs. Nadel was murdered at the Oświęcim (German, Auschwitz) concentration camp.

NATHAN, ISAAC (born 1790 in Canterbury, England; died January 15, 1864, in Sydney, Australia). Composer. Granduncle of the pianist Harold Samuel. In 1814 he was introduced to Lord Byron, whom Nathan induced to write the set of poems entitled *Hebrew Melodies*. Nathan drew on the poems for texts to go with his adaptations of Jewish chants, issuing his work as *A Selection of Hebrew Melodies, Ancient and Modern* (pub. 1815-22, revised 1840). He also gained fame for his comic opera *Sweethearts and Wives* (perf. 1823). In 1841 financial trouble caused him to move to Australia, where, as the first resident professional musician, he earned the title of Father of Australian Music by founding choral societies, establishing a music periodical, and pioneering in the production of operas. The conductor Charles Mackerras is Nathan's great-great-great-grandson.

NAUMBOURG, SAMUEL (born March 15, 1817, in Dennenlohe, near Ansbach, Germany; died May 1, 1880, in Saint-Mandé, near Paris, France). Cantor and composer. A descendant of many generations of south German cantors, he served as a senior cantor in Paris (1845-80). Drawing on the styles of French and Italian opera, he composed original liturgical music and arranged traditional Jewish melodies. His multivolume *Zemirot Yisrael* ("Songs of Israel"; 1847-64; second edition, 1874) contains original and traditional pieces (including a few each by Halévy and Meyerbeer) set for cantor and choir, some with organ accompaniment. It became popular not only in France but also among North African Sephardic Jews, through whom the book's influence spread to Israel.

NETTL, BRUNO (born March 14, 1930, in Prague, Czechoslovakia). Ethnomusicologist. Son of the musicologist Paul Nettl. He came with his father to the United States in 1939. His studies, basic to the field of ethnomusicology, include

North American Indian Musical Styles (1954), *Music in Primitive Culture* (1956), *Folk and Traditional Music of the Western Continents* (1965; second edition, 1973), and *The Study of Ethnomusicology* (1983).

NETTL, PAUL (born January 10, 1889, in Hohenelbe, Bohemia [now Vrchlabí, Czechoslovakia]; died January 8, 1972, in Bloomington, Indiana). Musicologist. Father of the ethnomusicologist Bruno Nettl. He immigrated to the United States in 1939. One of his favorite topics of study was dance music, as in *The Story of Dance Music* (1947) and *The Dance in Classical Music* (1963). His other works include *National Anthems* (1952, enlarged 1967), *Beethoven Encyclopedia* (1956; revised, as *Beethoven Handbook,* 1967), and *Mozart and Masonry* (1957).

NEWMAN, ALFRED (born March 17, 1901, in New Haven, Connecticut; died February 17, 1970, in Los Angeles, California). Composer. Uncle of the composer Randy Newman. Alfred wrote lush romantic background scores for many films, including *Wuthering Heights* (1939), *Captain from Castile* (1947), *The Robe* (1953), and *Airport* (1970). His brothers Emil and Lionel also composed film music.

NEWMAN, RANDY (born November 28, 1943, in Los Angeles, California). Composer and singer. In the late 1960s, writing his own words and music, he helped to introduce a new kind of popular song, called soft rock or salon rock, characterized by subtle lyrics and sophisticated melodies. Among his albums are *Randy Newman* (1968); *Twelve Songs* (1970); *Sail Away* (1972); *Little Criminals* (1977), with "Short People"; and *Trouble in Paradise* (1983). He also composed the background music for the movie *Ragtime* (1981). The film composers Alfred, Emil, and Lionel Newman were Randy's uncles.

NYRO, LAURA (born October 18, 1947, in New York City, New York). Composer and singer. She made an impact through her soft-rock style that linked poetic lyrics with a musical fusion of folk, jazz, and soul. Her biggest successes have come from performances of her songs by others, such as the Fifth Dimension's recording of "Wedding Bell Blues" (1969) and Barbra Streisand's rendition of "Stoney End" (1970). Nyro's own albums include *Eli and the Thirteenth Confession* (1968), *Gonna Take a Miracle* (1971), and *Nested* (1978).

O

OBADIAH THE PROSELYTE (real name, JEAN DROCOS [or DREUX]; flourished early twelfth century in Oppido, Apulia, Italy). A Norman-Italian baronet who converted to Judaism, he wrote, under the assumed name Obadiah the Proselyte, the earliest surviving manuscript sources of Jewish music. Written in Beneventan neumes (medieval notional signs characteristic of the Monastery of Benevent in southern Italy), the manuscripts consist of four compositions: a piece of art music, a hymn on the death of Moses, and two works based on scriptural verses.

OCHS, PHIL (born December 19, 1940, in El Paso, Texas;

died April 9, 1976, in Far Rockaway, New York). Composer and singer. He wrote his own music (based in the American folk tradition) and lyrics (often with topical, especially politically related, subjects). His albums include *All the News That's Fit to Sing* (1964) and *Pleasures of the Harbor* (1967). With *Tape from California* (1968) he began to incorporate elements of rock music into his work, an idiom that he continued to exploit in *Rehearsals for Retirement* (1969). Creatively exhausted, he committed suicide at the age of thirty-five.

OISTRAKH, IGOR (born April 27, 1931, in Odessa, the Soviet Union). Violinist. Son of the violinist David Oistrakh. While still a student, he won first prize in the International Festival of Democratic Youth in Budapest (1949) and the Wieniawski Contest in Poznań (1952). Compared with his father, Igor has a leaner, more modern tone, and his interpretations are more objective. He is particularly effective in performing Bartók. Father and son often appeared in violin duets and double concertos. And sometimes David conducted while Igor played solo works. In recital Igor is regularly accompanied on the piano by his wife, the former Natalya Sertsalova.

ORNSTEIN, LEO (born December 1892 in Kremenchug, the Ukraine [now in the Soviet Union]). Composer and pianist. His father, a cantor, led the family away from the anti-Semitic disturbances in Russia, and in 1907 they settled in the United States. Leo Ornstein became a successful concert pianist in America and Europe. But his major reputation came as a result of his composing some wildly dissonant, polyrhythmic, and polytonal piano pieces that set off a battle between radical and conservative factions in the world of music. Through such works as *Dwarf Suite* (1913) and *Wild Men's Dance* (pub. c. 1915), Ornstein became known as the world's leading futurist composer. His later works, fairly conservative for their time, include *Nocturne and Dance of the Fates* for orchestra (c. 1937), *Biography in Sonata Form* for piano (1974), and *Hebraic Fantasy* for violin and piano (1975).

P

PASTA, GIUDITTA (originally GIUDITTA NEGRI; born October 28, 1797, in Saronno, near Milan, Italy; died April 1, 1865 in Blevio, Como, Italy). Soprano. Created title roles in Donizetti's *Anna Bolena* (1830) and Bellini's *Norma* (1831). Married a tenor named Pasta.

PAULY, ROSE (or ROSA PAULY, originally ROSE POLLAK; born March 15, 1894, in Eperjes, Hungary [now Prešov, Czechoslovakia]; died December 14, 1975, near Tel Aviv, Israel). Soprano. She sang in Germany (1918-31), Vienna (1929-35), Italy (1935-39), and elsewhere, including San Francisco and New York City. Pauly was renowned for her title roles in Richard Strauss's *Elektra* and *Salome*. In 1946 she settled in Palestine.

PERAHIA, MURRAY (born April 19, 1947, in New York City, New York). Pianist. He rose to prominence by winning the 1972 Leeds International Pianoforte Competition in England. Perahia has toured extensively as a concert pianist and has occasionally performed as pianist-conductor in Mozart concertos. He is renowned for his delicate tones in the softer dynamic ranges and for his lyric phrasing. He favors the romantic literature of Chopin, Mendelssohn, and Schumann.

PERGAMENT, MOSES (born September 21, 1893, in Helsinki, Finland; died March 5, 1977, in Gustavsberg, near Stockholm, Sweden). Composer. His music shows the influence of many sources, including Sibelius, Russian music, French impressionism, German expressionism, and Jewish cantillation. Pergament's most important work is the choral symphony *Den judiska sången* ("Jewish Songs," 1944).

PIMSLEUR, SOLOMON (born September 19, 1900, in Paris, France; died April 22, 1962, in New York City, New York).

Pianist and composer. He was brought to the United States in 1903. Besides giving many successful piano recitals in America, he composed romantic orchestral works, chamber music, and piano pieces. *The Diary of Anne Frank,* a projected opera, was unfinished at his death.

PINCHERLE, MARC (born June 13, 1888, in Constantine, Algeria; died June 20, 1974, in Paris, France). Musicologist. His researches centered on the early history of violin music, notably in the books *Antonio Vivaldi et la musique instrumentale* ("Antonio Vivaldi and Instrumental Music," 1948) and *Vivaldi* (1955; English, as *Vivaldi: Genius of the Baroque,* 1957). He also wrote books on Corelli and Kreisler.

PISK, PAUL (born May 16, 1893, in Vienna, Austria). Composer and musicologist. In 1936 he settled in the United States. His articles focus on Schoenberg and the Second

Rose Pauly (bottom left) in the title role of Richard Strauss's *Elektra*

Viennese School. He also wrote the book *A History of Music and Musical Style* (with Homer Ulrich, 1963). Pisk's compositions, which combine the freely atonal idiom of Viennese postromanticism with classical and baroque forms, include a variety of instrumental and vocal genres.

POLLACK, EGON (born May 3, 1879, in Prague, Bohemia [now in Czechoslovakia]; died June 14, 1933, in Prague, Czechoslovakia). Conductor. He conducted opera in Bremen (1905-1910), Leipzig (1910-12), Frankfort on the Main (1912-17), and Hamburg (1922-31). Pollack was widely regarded as the foremost interpreter of Richard Strauss. He died of a heart attack while conducting a performance of Beethoven's *Fidelio*.

POPPER, DAVID (born December 9, 1843, in Prague, Bohemia [now in Czechoslovakia]; died August 7, 1913, in Baden, near Vienna, Austria). Cellist and composer. He played with a finished technique, a full tone, and a classical approach. Popper composed many melodious, idiomatic cello pieces and studies.

Q

QUELER, EVE (originally EVE RABIN; born January 1, 1936, in New York City, New York). Conductor. In 1956 she married Stanley N. Queler. Impatient with the lack of opportunities for a woman conductor, she founded the Opera Orchestra of New York in the late 1960s. That ensemble, which specializes in concert performances of opera, has not only given Queler herself a vehicle for expression but also provided young performers with a chance to be heard. She has guest-conducted many orchestras. Queler has done much to pioneer the acceptance of women on the podium.

R

RAISA, ROSA (original surname, BURCHSTEIN; born May 23, 1893, in Białystok, Poland; died September 28, 1963, in Los Angeles, California). Soprano. At the age of fourteen she fled Poland to escape a pogrom and settled in Naples, Italy. She made her concert debut, in Rome, in 1912. A year later came her opera debut, in Parma. Raisa sang regularly with the Chicago Opera Company (1913-14, 1916-32, 1933-36) and gave many American premieres of Italian operas. She also created the title role in the world premiere of Puccini's *Turandot,* at La Scala in Milan (1926). Other companies throughout the world engaged her for many years. She was known as a thrilling dramatic soprano, especially admired for her title roles in Bellini's *Norma,* Puccini's *Tosca,* and Verdi's *Aïda.* In 1929 Raisa married the baritone Giacomo Rimini, whom she had met when both were members of the Chicago Opera Company. She sang with him in many opera productions, and in 1937 they retired to open a singing school in Chicago.

RASKIN, JUDITH (born June 21, 1928, in New York City, New York; died December 21, 1984, in New York City, New York). Soprano. At the Met from 1962 to 1972.

RATHAUS, KAROL (born September 16, 1895, in Ternopol, the Ukraine [now in the Soviet Union]; died November 21, 1954, in New York City, New York). Composer. He immigrated to the United States in 1938. His music shows many influences, but three predominate: Polish folk elements, Jewish rhapsodic lyricism, and the gestures of Austro-German postromanticism infused with the vitality of modern rhythmic patterns, melodic angularity, and dissonance. His *Third Symphony* (1943) stands out in a varied list that includes operas, ballets, film scores, chamber music, piano pieces, and miscellaneous vocal works.

RAVAN, GENYA (originally GOLDIE ZELKOWITZ; born 1942 in Łódź, Poland). Singer and composer. She grew up in New York City. In 1962 she formed Goldie and the Gingerbreads, one of the earliest all-female rock bands. After she changed her name to Genya Ravan in 1969, she formed several new groups, including Baby (1971). In her early recordings she interpreted the songs of others, but later she wrote much of her own material. Her albums include *Genya Ravan with Baby* (1972) and *And I Mean It* (1979).

REDDY, HELEN (born October 25, 1941, in Melbourne, Australia). Singer. Born a non-Jew. She came to the United States in 1966, soon met the talent agent Jeff Wald, and, after formally converting to Judaism, married him later that year. (She filed for divorce in 1981.) Her first major success was her recording of "I Am Woman" (1972), for which she wrote the lyrics (music, Ray Burton). Among her albums are *I Am Woman* (1972), *Ear Candy* (1977), and *Reddy* (1980).

REDLICH, HANS F(ERDINAND) (born February 11, 1903, in Vienna, Austria; died November 27, 1968, in Manchester, England). He settled in England in 1939. His writings include *Claudio Monteverdi* (German, 1949; English, 1952), *Bruckner and Mahler* (1955, revised 1963), *Alban Berg: The Man and His Music* (1957), and articles on the Second Viennese School (a designation that he invented).

REMÉNYI, EDE (or EDUARD REMÉNYI, originally EDUARD HOFFMANN; born January 17, 1828, in Miskolc, Hungary; died May 15, 1898, in San Francisco, California). Violinist. He began his career in Hungary in 1846. In 1848 he was exiled from his native land for his involvement in the Hungarian uprising against Austria. He then performed in America, toured Germany with Brahms, and served as solo violinist to Queen Victoria in England (1854-59). In 1860, after receiving amnesty, he returned to Hungary but continued his international career, finally settling in America in 1878. He died while playing at a concert. Reményi had a masterful technique, but his playing was especially marked by his fiery temperament and his showmanship. It was through his influence that Brahms's Hungarian dances owed more to the gypsy tradition than to true Magyar music.

RETI, RUDOLPH (originally RUDOLF RÉTI; born November 27, 1885, in Užice, Serbia [now Titovo Užice, Yugoslavia]; died February 7, 1957, in Montclair, New Jersey). Writer and composer. His book *The Thematic Process in Music* (1951) examines motivic cells as the basis of composition. *Tonality, Atonality, Pantonality* (1958) explores early atonal music. Reti's compositions, noted for their precise structures and stylistic unity, include orchestral works, vocal music, and piano pieces.

RIETI, VITTORIO (born January 28, 1898, in Alexandria, Egypt). Composer. He worked in Europe till World War II came, when he fled to the United States. His works, noted for their sophisticated, graceful neoclassicism, include many ballets and operas, as well as miscellaneous instrumental music and vocal pieces.

RIFKIN, JOSHUA (born April 22, 1944, in New York City, New York). Musicologist, pianist, conductor, and composer. His research has centered on Renaissance and baroque music. As a pianist and conductor he was influential in the 1970s ragtime revival. He has composed chamber music and songs.

ROGERS, BERNARD (born February 4, 1893, in New York City, New York; died May 24, 1968, in Rochester, New York). Composer. His music is in a modern romantic style focusing on intense personal expression. Author of the standard textbook *The Art of Orchestration* (1951) and a master of practical orchestral writing, he found the large ensemble to be his most congenial medium, as in his five symphonies (1920-59). Japanese prints influenced some of his subject matter and orchestral color, as in *Fuji in the Sunset Glow* (1925) and *New Japanese Dances* (1961). Some of his vocal works are based on biblical subjects, including the cantata *The Prophet Isaiah* (1950) and several choral psalms.

ROITMAN, DAVID (born 1884 in the Ukraine [now in the Soviet Union]; died April 4, 1943, in New York City, New York). Cantor and composer. He served as cantor in Elisavetgrad (1904-1909), Vilna (1909-1912), and Saint Petersburg (1912-17; the city was renamed Petrograd in 1914). In 1918 he fled Elisavetgrad during a pogrom, and in 1919 he founded the Hebrew Music School in Odessa. He also made numerous concert tours during his years in Russia. In the early 1920s he immigrated to the United States, where he continued his concert tours and served as cantor at Congregation Shaare Zedek in New York City (1924-43). Roitman, who made many recordings, was famed for his flexible lyric tenor voice, in particular for his exceptional falsetto. He composed the popular liturgical lament *Rachel mevakah al baneha* ("Rachel Weeps for Her Children," arranged for voice and piano by Abraham Wolfe Binder, pub. 1930).

ROLAND-MANUEL, ALEXIS (originally ROLAND ALEXIS MANUEL LÉVY; born March 22, 1891, in Paris, France; died November 2, 1966, in Paris, France). Composer and writer. He composed in a French neoclassical manner, drawing on many characteristics of his teacher and idol Maurice Ravel. Roland-Manuel was most effective in ballet and chamber music. His books include three on Ravel, notably *Maurice Ravel* (1938; English, 1947).

ROMANOS (or ROMANOS MELODOS; born late fifth century, probably in Emesa [now Homs], Syria; died after 555 in Constantinople, capital of the Byzantine Empire [now İstanbul, Turkey]). Byzantine hymn writer and composer. Evidence suggests that he was of Jewish descent, though it is not known if his parents had converted to Christianity before his birth or if he converted himself in his early youth. Legend has it that the Virgin Mary gave Romanos a scroll on which he was divinely inspired to write an example of a Byzantine liturgical form that later came to be known by the Greek word *kontakion* ("scroll"; plural, *kontakia*). He became the greatest master of the form, which was the first important kind of Byzantine hymnography. Romanos, however, never used the word *kontakion*; he called his works songs, praises, prayers, and so on. His reputation was so great that the word *Melodos* ("Maker of Songs") became part of his name. Of the roughly thousand hymns attributed to him, only eighty-five texts survive, of which sixty are probably genuine. None of his music is extant. The earliest melodies now associated with his texts come from the thirteenth century.

ROMBERG, SIGMUND (born July 29, 1887, in Nagykanizsa, Hungary; died November 9, 1951, in New York City, New York). Composer. In 1909 he immigrated to the United States, where he composed a string of European-style operettas that proved to be among the last popular works in that genre in America, including *The Student Prince* (perf. 1924), *The Desert Song* (perf. 1926), and *Rosalie* (perf. 1928). Later he successfully made the transition to American-style musical comedies, notably in *Up in Central Park* (perf. 1945).

RONALD, LANDON (originally LANDON RONALD RUSSELL; born June 7, 1873, in London, England; died August 14, 1938, in London, England). Conductor and composer. Son of the composer Henry Russell. After making his Covent Garden debut in 1896, he conducted musical comedy in London (1898-1902), held posts with the New Symphony Orchestra (1909-1914) and the Scottish Orchestra (1916-20), and guest-conducted extensively. Ronald was especially known for interpreting the works of his friend Edward Elgar and for performing with the violinist Fritz Kreisler, another close friend. Among Ronald's compositions are stage works, orchestral pieces, and about three hundred songs. He wrote two books of reminiscences, including *Myself and Others* (1931).

ROSÉ, ARNOLD (born October 24, 1863, in Iaşi, Romania; died August 25, 1946, in London, England). Violinist. For many years (1881-1938) he was first violinist of both the Vienna Opera and the Vienna Philharmonic orchestras. In 1882 he founded the Rosé String Quartet; the original cellist of the group was Eduard Rosé, Arnold's brother (who later died in a concentration camp). The quartet became one of the finest of the period and gave world premieres of works by Brahms, Schoenberg, and others. Rosé worked closely with Gustav Mahler during the latter's direction of the Vienna Opera (1897-1907) and in 1902 married Justine Mahler, the maestro's sister. In 1938 Rosé went to England, where he continued to play publicly as late as 1945. He was especially renowned for his sure left-hand technique and purity of intonation.

ROSEN, CHARLES (born May 5, 1927, in New York City, New York). Pianist and writer. He made his concert debut in New York City's Town Hall in 1951, and in the same year he made the first complete recording of Debussy's études. Since then he has toured widely in the United States and Europe. His playing is marked by a profoundly intellectual approach, and he favors nonromantic composers, such as Bach, Beethoven, Schoenberg, Webern, Elliott Carter, and Boulez. He participated in the world premiere of Carter's *Concerto for Piano and Harpsichord* in 1961. Rosen is a brilliant writer on music, notably in his highly acclaimed book *The Classical Style: Haydn, Mozart, Beethoven* (1971; second edition, 1972), as well as in *Arnold Schoenberg* (1975) and *Sonata Forms* (1980).

ROSEN, NATHANIEL (born June 9, 1948, in Altadena, California). Cellist. He was principal cellist of the Los Angeles

Chamber Orchestra (1970-76) and the Pittsburgh Symphony (1977-79). In 1977 Rosen gained instant recognition in America when he became the first cellist to win the prestigious Naumburg Competition. The following year his international career blossomed when he won the Tchaikovsky Competition in Moscow, the first American cellist to win that award and the first American gold medalist of any kind there since the pianist Van Cliburn in 1958. He now tours extensively throughout the world in recital and as soloist with major orchestras. His repertory covers not only standard works but also new music, giving, for example, the world premieres of compositions by William Kraft and Robert Linn. Possessing a dazzling technique and a richness of expressive powers, Rosen is widely regarded as one of the world's preeminent cellists of his generation.

ROSENFELD, PAUL (born May 4, 1890, in New York City, New York; died July 21, 1946, in New York City, New York). Writer. As a music critic he championed new music and was among the first to recognize the talents of several outstanding young composers, notably Aaron Copland. His books include *Modern Tendencies in Music* (1927).

ROSENSTOCK, JOSEPH (born January 27, 1895, in Cracow, Poland; died October 17, 1985, in New York City). Conductor. He conducted opera in various German cities before the Nazis took over in 1933, after which he served as music director for the Jewish Cultural Association in Berlin till 1936. He then left Germany and conducted the Nippon Philharmonic Orchestra in Tokyo till 1941. Immigrating to the United States, he worked with the New York City Opera (1948-55).

ROSENTHAL, HAROLD (born September 30, 1917, in London, England). Writer. He has been on the staff of *Opera* magazine for many years (assistant editor, 1950-53; editor, since 1953). Under his guidance it has become the most influential publication in the opera world. Among his books are *Sopranos of Today* (1956), *The Concise Oxford Dictionary of Opera* (with John Warrack; 1964, revised 1979), *Great Singers of Today* (1966), and *My Mad World of Opera: The Autobiography of the Editor of "Opera" Magazine* (1982).

ROSENTHAL, MANUEL (originally EMMANUEL ROSENTHAL; born June 18, 1904, in Paris, France). Conductor and composer. After leading the French Radio National Orchestra (1944-47) and the Seattle Symphony (1948-51), he embarked on an international conducting career, specializing in twentieth-century French music. Rosenthal arranged and orchestrated Jacques Offenbach tunes to form the score for the ballet *Gaîté parisienne* (1938), also known in English as *The Gay Parisian*, the title under which it was issued as a film (1941); the music has come to be an immensely popular concert piece. Rosenthal's own music is cast in an august neoclassical style, as in the *Symphony in C* (1949).

ROSENTHAL, MORITZ (born December 18, 1862, in Lemberg, Galicia [now Lvov, the Soviet Union]; died September 3, 1946, in New York City, New York). Pianist. Cousin of the pianist Fannie Zeisler. In 1875 he moved with his parents to Vienna. In 1876 he gave his first full recital, following which he made a concert tour of eastern Europe. In the late 1870s he was befriended by Franz Liszt, who not only gave Rosenthal lessons but also supervised the young man's career. But in the early 1880s Rosenthal suddenly abandoned the concert stage and entered the University of Vienna as a philosophy student. When he resumed concertizing several years later, he surprised everyone by emerging as a fully matured artist with a dazzling pianistic virtuosity. He made his first American tour in 1888. Over the next fifty years he triumphantly performed throughout the United States and much of the rest of the world. He was admired by such composers as Johannes Brahms (a close personal friend), Johann Strauss II, and Peter Tchaikovsky. Driven out of Vienna by the Nazis in 1938, Rosenthal immigrated to the United States and settled in New York City. Later that year the golden jubilee of his American debut was celebrated in a Carnegie Hall concert. Rosenthal himself, nearly seventy-six years old and revered as the last of the great pianists trained by Liszt, performed impressively at the event. In the early part of his career he was regarded primarily as a virtuoso technician. But as he grew older he added rich musicianly qualities to his playing, gaining renown especially for his ability to sustain long phrases and for his incredibly sensitive tonal control in all registers. His favorite composers were Chopin and Beethoven. He was also famed for his numerous witticisms, which he uttered with a twinkle in his eye. Once, for example, he said of the famous pianist Ignace Paderewski (whose name sparked much more respect among lay audiences than among professional musicians): "He plays well, but he's no Paderewski." Of a "child prodigy," Rosenthal asked: "Tell me, how old are you *still*?" Poking fun at the overemphasized aspect of early development in musicians, he said of himself: "I was born at an early age and sang a chromatic scale when I was one hour old." Because he was small in size but great in musical powers, Rosenthal was nicknamed the Little Giant of the Piano.

ROSOWSKY, SOLOMON (born 1878 in Riga, Latvia [now in the Soviet Union]; died July 31, 1962, in New York City, New York). Composer and musicologist. He helped to organize the Society for Jewish Folk Music (1908), founded the Riga Jewish Conservatory of Music (1920), and then lived in Palestine (1925-47), where he composed incidental music for the Hebrew theater. In 1947 he immigrated to the United States. He composed orchestral works, chamber music, and songs. His scholarly studies focused on Hebrew Bible cantillation, and he summarized his findings in *The Cantillation of the Bible: The Five Books of Moses* (1957).

ROSSI, SALAMONE (or SALOMONE [or SALAMON DE' or SHLOMO] ROSSI; born probably August 19, 1570, probably in Mantua, Italy; died c. 1630, probably in Mantua, Italy). Composer. He always added the epithet *il Ebreo* ("the Jew") after his name. An important pioneer in baroque musical techniques, Rossi helped to develop the vocal duet, the trio sonata, the application of sets of variations to instrumental ensembles, and the idiomatic use of the violin. He published several sets of vocal works and several sets of instrumental works. Rossi's great contribution to Jewish music was *Hashirim asher li-Shelomo ("The Songs of Solomon,"* pub. 1622-23), a collection of contrapuntal settings of Hebrew psalms, hymns, and synagogal songs. Madama Europa, the famous virtuoso singer, was his sister.

ROTHMÜLLER, ARON MARKO (sometimes used the pseudonym JEHUDA KINOR; born December 31, 1908, in Trnjani, near Brod [now Slavonski Brod], Croatia [now in Yugoslavia]). Baritone, composer, and writer. He sang at the Zurich Opera (1935-48) before moving to the United States (1948), where he performed with the Metropolitan Opera (1958-61, 1964-65). One of the finest singing actors of his time, he was particularly admired for his Wagner roles and for his lead in Berg's *Wozzeck*. Rothmüller's works include Sephardic religious songs, chamber music, orchestral pieces, and the book *Die Musik der Juden* (1951; English, as *The Music of the Jews,* 1953, revised 1967). Since 1981 he has taught in Jerusalem.

RÓZSAVÖLGYI, MÁRK (originally MARK MORDECAI ROSENTHAL; born 1789 in Balassagyarmat, Hungary; died January 23, 1848, in Pest, Hungary). Composer and violinist. He became a well-known violinist and led his own orchestra in the 1820s and 1830s. In the 1840s, while living in Pest, he formed a gypsy band. As a composer he was the last important master of the verbunkos (a soldiers' dance) and the first of the csárdás (a ballroom dance). Some of Rózsavölgyi's tunes were borrowed by Franz Liszt for use in a few of the latter's Hungarian rhapsodies.

RUBINSTEIN, NIKOLAY (born June 14, 1835, in Moscow, Russia; died March 23, 1881, in Paris, France). Pianist, conductor, and educator. Brother of the pianist Anton Rubinstein. A child prodigy, Nikolay soon developed into one of the great virtuoso pianists of his time. During the 1859-60 season he founded the Moscow branch of the Russian Musical Society, whose concerts he conducted. In 1866 he founded the Moscow Conservatory, which he headed till his death. As a pianist Nikolay was more analytical than his brother was, more inclined to emphasize important points of structure and to focus on clarity of detail. Tchaikovsky, whom Nikolay hired at the conservatory and encouraged as a composer, rated Nikolay even above Anton as a pianist.

RUDEL, JULIUS (born March 6, 1921, in Vienna, Austria). Conductor. In 1938 he immigrated to the United States. In 1943 he joined the New York City Opera as a rehearsal pianist, became a conductor there the following year, and

from 1957 to 1979 served as director of the company. He has also guest-conducted many major orchestras, such as the Chicago Symphony. Rudel made his Metropolitan Opera debut in 1978, and since 1979 he has been music director of the Buffalo Philharmonic Orchestra.

RUDOLF, MAX (born June 15, 1902, in Frankfort on the Main, Germany). Conductor. He conducted in Darmstadt

(1923-29), Prague (1929-35), and Sweden (1935-40) before immigrating to the United States in 1940. In America he conducted at the Metropolitan Opera (1945-58), where he was especially admired for his Mozart performances. He then served as music director of the Cincinnati Symphony Orchestra (1958-69) and conducted again at the Met (1973-75). Rudolf, author of the widely used textbook *The Grammar of Conducting* (1950), gained renown for his excellent technique, particularly his ability to subdivide the beat without impairing the basic pulse.

RUSSELL, HENRY (born December 24, 1812, in Sheerness, England; died December 8, 1900, in London, England). Composer and singer. He spent most of the 1830s and early 1840s in Canada and the United States, thereafter returning to England. On his concert tours he sang dramatic, topical, and sentimental ballads, many of his own composition. He was the most influential composer of American songs before Stephen Foster (who began to publish in 1844), and he was the most popular songwriter in Great Britain during the first half of the nineteenth century. His most famous work was the sentimental American ballad "Woodman, Spare That Tree" (lyrics, George P. Morris; 1837). Racial intolerance was the topic of Russell's "The Indian Hunter"

(lyrics, Eliza Cook; 1837), the first American popular song to demand equal justice for the Indian. "The Old Arm Chair" (lyrics, Eliza Cook; 1840) initiated America's flood of mother (or "mammy") songs. Reflecting his English background were "The Ivy Green" (lyrics, Charles Dickens; c. 1837); "A Life on the Ocean Wave" (lyrics, Epes Sargent; 1838), which was adopted as the official march of the British Royal Marines in 1889; "The Maniac" (lyrics, Matthew G. Lewis; pub. 1848), a dramatic exposition of the horrors of mental institutions; and "Cheer! Boys, Cheer!" (lyrics, Charles Mackay; c. 1850), his most popular song in the English ballad style. He published his autobiography as *Cheer! Boys, Cheer!* (1895). With his first wife, who was non-Jewish, he had his sons William Russell, who became an author, and Henry Russell, who became an opera manager. With his second wife, a Jewess, he had his son Landon Russell, who became the conductor Landon Ronald.

S

SACHS, CURT (born June 29, 1881, in Berlin, Germany; died February 5, 1959, in New York City, New York). He immigrated to the United States in 1937. One of the true giants in musicology, Sachs mastered many areas and presented his views with comprehensiveness. His works include *Real-Lexikon der Musikinstrumente* ("Dictionary of Musical Instruments," 1913), *The History of Musical Instruments* (1940), *The Rise of Music in the Ancient World, East and West* (1943), *Our Musical Heritage* (1948; second edition, 1955), *Rhythm and Tempo: A Study in Music History* (1953), and *The Wellsprings of Music: An Introduction to Ethnomusicology* (edited by Jaap Kunst, 1962).

SADIE, STANLEY (born October 30, 1930, in London, England). Musicologist. His writings include the biographies *Mozart* (1966), *Beethoven* (1967; second edition, 1974), and *Handel* (1968; second edition, 1976). He is also an outstanding editor, notably of *The New Grove Dictionary of Music and Musicians* (1980) and *The New Grove Dictionary of Musical Instruments* (1984).

SALESKI, GDAL (born February 11, 1888, in Kiev, the Ukraine [now in the Soviet Union]; died October 8, 1966, in Los Angeles, California). Cellist and writer. In his youth he sang in a Kiev synagogue. Moving to Germany, he studied cello and played in the Leipzig Gewandhaus Orchestra. He then lived in Scandinavia for several years (1915-21) before immigrating to the United States, where he served as a cellist in the National Broadcasting Company (NBC) Symphony Orchestra (1937-48) under the legendary conductor Arturo Toscanini. Saleski wrote the book *Famous Musicians of a Wandering Race* (1927), revised and enlarged as *Famous Musicians of Jewish Origin* (1949), which includes a number of people who actually had no traceable Jewish blood, such as Georges Bizet, Maurice Ravel, and Camille Saint-Saëns.

SAMINSKY, LAZARE (born November 8, 1882, in Vale-Hotzulovo, near Odessa, the Ukraine [now in the Soviet Union]; died June 30, 1959, in Port Chester, New York). Composer and writer. In 1908 he helped to found the

Society for Jewish Folk Music. He settled in the United States in 1920. His music, based in the romantic tradition, incorporates elements from Jewish folk and liturgical music. Saminsky's output includes stage works, Sabbath and holiday services, choral music, a variety of instrumental pieces, and the book *Music of the Ghetto and the Bible* (1934).

SAMUEL, ADOLPHE (originally ADOLPHE-ABRAHAM SAMUEL; born July 11, 1824, in Liège, United Kingdom of Netherlands [now Liège, Belgium]; died September 11, 1898, in Ghent, Belgium). Composer and writer. He won the Belgian Prix de Rome (1845), founded the Brussels Popular Concerts (1865), and established the first annual music festival in Brussels (1869). He associated with the greatest musicians of his day, studying for a time with Mendelssohn and Meyerbeer and maintaining a correspondence with Berlioz. Samuel was a respected music critic, and he published, among other books, his *Cours d'harmonie pratique* ("Practical Harmony Textbook," 1861). His compositions include operas, seven symphonies (influenced by Berlioz), and a wide variety of smaller works.

SAMUEL, HAROLD (born May 23, 1879, in London, England; died January 15, 1937, in London, England). Pianist. Grandnephew of the composer Isaac Nathan. For many years he was known only as an accompanist. Then, in 1921, he gave a daily series of Bach recitals for a week in London. His performances helped to spark the modern demand to hear Bach's original scores, not the nineteenth-century arrangements still commonly played in the 1920s. Subsequently he became known as a Bach specialist, but his repertory was actually broad, including the Brahms concertos and a variety of chamber works.

SANDERLING, KURT (born September 19, 1912, in Arys, Germany [now Orzysz, Poland]). Conductor. In 1936 he fled Nazi Germany and went to the Soviet Union, where he conducted the Moscow Radio Symphony Orchestra (1936-41) and coconducted the Leningrad Philharmonic Orchestra (1941-60). He then returned to Germany and served as chief conductor of the East Berlin Symphony Orchestra (1960-77). He has also guest-conducted in Western Europe and the United States. Sanderling's interpretations are marked by a blend of intellect and expression, of clarity and shading. He favors the late romantics (Tchaikovsky, Mahler) and their followers (Sibelius, Prokofiev).

SCHILLINGER, JOSEPH (born August 31, 1895, in Kharkov, the Ukraine [now in the Soviet Union]; died March 23, 1943, in New York City, New York). Theorist and composer. In 1927 he organized the first jazz orchestra in the Soviet Union, and the following year he immigrated to the United Sates. He formulated a mathematically based system of music theory, which he privately taught to many (especially commercial) American composers, notably George Gershwin. The principles of the theory are laid out in *The Schillinger System of Musical Composition* (1941; third edition, edited by Lyle Dowling and Arnold Shaw, 1946). Schillinger's own works include *March of the Orient* for orchestra (1924) and *First Airphonic Suite* for theremin and orchestra (1929).

SCHLESINGER. Family of music publishers. ADOLPH SCHLESINGER (originally ABRAHAM SCHLESINGER; born October 4, 1769, in Sülz, Silesia [now in Czechoslovakia]; died November 11, 1838, in Berlin, Germany) founded a publishing house in his own name in Berlin in 1810. He was the original publisher of a number of works by Beethoven and Carl Maria von Weber, and he issued the first edition of Bach's monumental *St. Matthew Passion*. One of Schlesinger's three sons, CARL (born 1808 in Berlin; died 1831 in Berlin), lived only briefly. But the other two became important publishers: MAURICE (or MORITZ, originally MORA; born October 3, 1797, in Berlin, Germany; died February 25, 1871, in Baden-Baden, Germany) and HEINRICH (born 1810 in Berlin, Germany; died December 14, 1879, in Berlin, Germany). It was Maurice who personally established the family's contact with Beethoven in 1819. Also in 1819 Maurice moved to Paris, where in 1821 he founded his own publishing company. One of his employees during the period 1840-42 was Richard Wagner, who made piano (and other) arrangements of opera scores. Maurice was an early publisher of works by Beethoven, Berlioz, Chopin, Donizetti, Liszt, Mendelssohn, and Meyerbeer. He also published the weekly *Gazette musicale de Paris* ("Musical Gazette of Paris," beginning in 1834), later called the *Revue et gazette musicale* ("Musical Review and Gazette," beginning in 1835). The periodical, now an extremely valuable source of information about the music and musicians of the time, attracted such contributors as Berlioz, Liszt, Schumann, and Wagner. Maurice sold his publishing house in 1846. His brother Heinrich inherited control of their father's company, which published works by many of the same composers associated with Maurice's firm. Heinrich also edited and published the influential music periodical *Echo* ("Echo," 1851-65). He sold his publishing company in 1864.

SCHÖNE, LOTTE (originally CHARLOTTE BODENSTEIN; born December 15, 1891, in Vienna, Austria; died December 22, 1977, in Bobigny, near Paris, France). Soprano. She sang opera, especially Mozart, in Vienna and Berlin till the Nazis took over Germany in 1933, after which she went to Paris and remained there till 1938. During World War II she hid in the French Alps. After the war she turned her attention to concerts before retiring in 1953. Schöne was famed for her great physical beauty (*schöne*, in fact, meaning "beautiful" in German) and for her light voice and ease of vocal production.

SCHORR, FRIEDRICH (born September 2, 1888, in Nagyvárad, Hungary [now Oradea, Romania]; died August 14, 1953, in Farmington, Connecticut). Bass-baritone. He sang opera in Graz (1912-16), Prague (1916-18), Cologne (1918-23), and Berlin (1923-31). Then he immigrated to the United States and joined the Metropolitan Opera in New York City, where he closed his career in 1943. Schorr was regarded as the outstanding Wagnerian bass-baritone of his time.

SCHREKER, FRANZ (born March 23, 1878, in Monaco; died March 21, 1934, in Berlin, Germany). Composer and conductor. He founded and conducted the Vienna Philharmonic Chorus (1908-1920), which gave the world premiere of Schoenberg's *Gurre-Lieder* ("Songs of Gurre") in 1913. As a composer Schreker was a leader in the development of late romanticism toward expressionism. He was most effective in his operas, for which he wrote his own librettos and in which he emphasized psychological conflicts.

SCHULHOFF, ERVÍN (or ERWIN SCHULHOFF; born June 8, 1894, in Prague, Bohemia [now in Czechoslovakia]; died August 18, 1942, in Wülzburg, Germany). Composer and pianist. Great-grandnephew of the pianist Julius Schulhoff.

He actively promoted new music in his piano recitals, giving, for example, the first performances of the quarter-tone pieces of Alois Hába. Schulhoff's music is eclectic, drawing on German postromanticism, French impressionism, jazz, neoclassicism, and other styles. His works cover a complete range of musical genres: stage, orchestral, vocal, chamber, and piano. He died in a Nazi concentration camp.

SCHULHOFF, JULIUS (born August 2, 1825, in Prague, Bohemia [now in Czechoslovakia]; died March 13, 1898, in Berlin, Germany). Pianist and composer. Great-granduncle of the composer Ervín Schulhoff. In Paris he gave concerts under the patronage of Chopin. After touring in Austria, England, Spain, and Russia, he settled in Paris. Later he lived in Dresden and then Berlin. Schulhoff published some excellent salon piano pieces.

SCHWARZ, RUDOLF (born April 29, 1905, in Vienna, Austria). Conductor. He conducted opera in Düsseldorf (1923-27) and Karlsruhe (1927-33). Forced by the Nazis to resign the latter post, he served as music director of the Jewish Cultural Association in Berlin (1936-41) before he was interned in German labor camps (1943-45). After World War II he went to England, where he conducted the Bournemouth Municipal Orchestra (1947-51), the City of Birmingham Symphony Orchestra (1951-57), the British Broadcasting Corporation (BBC) Symphony Orchestra (1957-62), and the Northern Sinfonia in Newcastle upon Tyne (principal conductor, 1964-73; principal guest conductor, 1973-82). Schwarz developed a reputation for programming a variety of standard and contemporary works.

SECUNDA, SHOLOM (born August 23, 1894, in Aleksandriya, the Ukraine [now in the Soviet Union]; died June 13, 1974, in New York City, New York). Composer. He came to the United States in 1908. In 1913 he began to work in American Yiddish theaters, where he soon became a dominant force as both composer and music director. He also served for many years as music director of the Brooklyn Jewish Center. Secunda composed dozens of Yiddish operettas and musical plays, as well as many orchestral works, chamber pieces, oratorios, songs, and liturgical works.

SEDAKA, NEIL (born March 13, 1939, in New York City, New York). Composer and singer. After a promising beginning as a classical pianist, he turned to composing tunes for popular songs with lyrics by his high-school friend Howard Greenfield. Their first hit was "Stupid Cupid" (1958). Then Sedaka began to record their songs himself, including "Oh, Carol" (1959), which referred to his high-school friend Carol Klein, later famous as the singer-composer Carole King. That success was followed by "Calendar Girl" (1960), "Stairway to Heaven" (1960), and "Breaking Up Is Hard to Do" (1962). The fashion in popular music changed (largely because of the Beatles), and Sedaka withdrew from sight for several years. But in the 1970s he returned and wrote the music for "Bad Blood" (lyrics, Phil Cody; 1975) and "Love Will Keep Us Together" (lyrics, Greenfield; 1975). His albums include *Sedaka's Back* (1974), *The Hungry Years* (1975), *In the Pocket* (1980), and *Twenty Golden Pieces* (1982).

SEIBER, MÁTYÁS (born May 4, 1905, in Budapest, Hungary; died September 24, 1960, in Kruger National Park, South Africa). Composer. In 1933 he left Germany, and in 1935 he settled in England. In 1960 he was engaged to lecture at universities in South Africa, where he was killed in an automobile accident. Seiber's music shows the influence of jazz, Bartók, Schoenberg, diverse folk elements, and other sources. He composed orchestral works, chamber music, and vocal pieces. His greatest work is the cantata *Ulysses* (1947).

SENDREY, ALBERT (born December 26, 1911, in Chicago, Illinois). Composer. Son of the musicologist Alfred Sendrey. Albert worked as an arranger of film scores for movie companies in Paris (1935-37) and London (1937-44) before moving to the Hollywood section of Los Angeles, California, where he did similar work. He composed an original background score for the film *Father's Little Dividend* (1951). Among his concert works are *Oriental Suite* for orchestra (1935), symphonies, cello pieces, and piano compositions.

SENDREY, ALFRED (originally ALADÁR SZENDREI; born February 29, 1884, in Budapest, Hungary; died March 3, 1976, in Los Angeles, California). Musicologist, conductor, and composer. Father of the composer Albert Sendrey. He conducted opera in Cologne (1905-1907), Mülhausen (1907-1909), Brno (1908-1911), Philadelphia and Chicago (1911-12), Hamburg (1912-13), New York City (1913-14), Berlin (1914-16), Vienna (1916-18), and Leipzig (1918-24). He then conducted the Leipzig Symphony Orchestra (1924-32). After several years as a radio program director in Paris (1933-40), he settled in the United States. In New York City he taught at the Ninety-second Street YMHA (1941-44). Moving to Los Angeles, he served as music director at Fairfax Synagogue (1952-56) and Sinai Temple (1956-64) and as professor of music at the University of Judaism (1962-72). Sendrey composed an opera, a symphony, choral works, and chamber pieces. His writings include *Bibliography of Jewish Music* (1951), *Music in Ancient Israel* (1969), and *The Music of the Jews in the Diaspora (up to 1800)* (1970).

SEVITZKY, FABIEN (originally FABIEN KOUSSEVITZKY; born September 29, 1891, in Vyshni Volochek, Russia; died February 2, 1967, in Athens, Greece). Conductor. Nephew of the conductor Serge Koussevitzky. Fabien entered music as a concert double-bass player under his original surname, Koussevitzky. But on the advice of his famous uncle, who also had started as a double-bass player, Fabien truncated his name to Sevitzky. Under that name he began to conduct in his native land. In 1922 he left the Soviet Union, and in 1923 he arrived in the United States, where he organized the Philadelphia Chamber String Simfonietta (1925) and conducted the Indianapolis Symphony Orchestra (1937-55). Sevitzky died while in Greece as a guest conductor.

SHAPERO, HAROLD (born April 29, 1920, in Lynn, Massachusetts). Composer. His early works were influenced by Schoenberg's aesthetic and twelve-tone technique, but he quickly turned to the neoclassicism of Stravinsky and Copland. In 1968 he began to experiment with electronic composition. His works include the *Trumpet Sonata* (1939), the *First String Quartet* (1940), the *Symphony for Classical Orchestra* (1947), the *Arioso Variations* for piano (1948), and the *Three Improvisations in B-flat* for piano and synthesizer (1968). The American Jewish Tercentenary Committee commissioned his cantata *Until Day and Night Shall Cease* (1954).

SILVERSTEIN, JOSEPH (born March 21, 1932, in Detroit,

Michigan). Violinist and conductor. Beginning at the age of eighteen, he spent three seasons with the Houston Symphony, one with the Philadelphia Orchestra, and one with the Denver Symphony, where he was both concertmaster and assistant conductor. In 1955 he joined the violin section of the Boston Symphony (as its youngest member), where he became concertmaster in 1962 and assistant conductor in 1971. He held both posts till 1983. During his years with the Boston Symphony, he gained international recognition when he took the silver medal in the 1959 Queen Elisabeth Competition in Brussels and then won the 1960 Naumburg Award. He made his New York City concert debut in 1961, organized the Boston Chamber Players in 1962 (directing the group till 1983), and served as principal guest conductor of the Baltimore Symphony during 1981-83. As soloist and/or conductor, Silverstein has appeared with more than one hundred orchestras in the United States, Japan, Europe, and Israel. He is one of the most accomplished violinists of his generation, possessing a rich tone, a solid technique, and an intelligent musicianship. In 1983 he was named music director of the Utah Symphony.

SILVERSTEIN, SHEL(BY) (born 1932 in Chicago, Illinois). Composer and singer. A well-known cartoonist (for *Playboy* magazine) and author (of the children's classic *The Giving Tree,* 1964), Silverstein has also written the words and music for many songs. In his early work, notably "The Unicorn Song" (1961), he evoked the American folk tradition. Later he wrote in a variety of country-music idioms, as in "A Boy Named Sue" (1969), "One's on the Way" (1971), and "Queen of the Silver Dollar" (1972). He wrote the song scores for the movies *Ned Kelly* (1970) and *Who Is Harry Kellerman and Why Is He Saying Those Terrible Things about Me?* (1971). And he recorded the albums *Inside Folk Music* (1961) and *Freakin' at the Freakers Ball* (1972).

SIMON, CARLY (born June 25, 1945, in New York City, New York). Singer and composer. Her albums include *Carly Simon* (1971); *Anticipation* (1971); *No Secrets* (1972), with her most highly regarded song, "You're So Vain" (her own music and lyrics); *Another Passenger* (1976); and *Hello, Big Man* (1983). She was married for a number of years to the singer James Taylor, with whom she sometimes performed. Carly's sister Joanna Simon is a member of the New York City Opera. Their father, Richard Simon, was a cofounder of the publishing firm Simon and Schuster.

SINIGAGLIA, LEONE (born August 14, 1868, in Turin, Italy; died May 16, 1944, in Turin, Italy). Composer. He composed numerous popular concert works based on the flavor, or the actual tunes, of Piedmontese folksongs. Orchestral pieces, chamber music, and vocal works form his output. Sinigaglia died of a stroke while fleeing from Fascist police who were rounding up Jews for deportation.

SIROTA, GERSHON (born 1874 in the Russian province of Podolia [now in the Soviet Union]; died 1943 in Warsaw, Poland). Cantor. While holding posts as a cantor successively in Odessa, Vilna, and Warsaw, he made many concert tours throughout Europe and America. One of the greatest cantor virtuosos in history, Sirota, a tenor, could also produce deeply emotional effects. He was widely compared with the world's leading opera tenors. In 1903 he became the first cantor to make recordings. The only great European cantor of his time not to accept a post in the United States,

Sirota and his family died in the Warsaw ghetto during the Holocaust.

SLONIMSKY, NICOLAS (born April 27, 1894, in Saint Petersburg, Russia [now Leningrad, the Soviet Union]). Lexicographer, conductor, and composer. He immigrated to the United States in 1923. In 1927 he organized the Chamber Orchestra of Boston to present modern works. With that orchestra he gave the world premiere of Charles Ives's *Three Places in New England* in 1931. He also guest-conducted major orchestras in America and Europe. But his modernistic programs so irritated audiences and managements that his conducting career came to a grinding halt in 1933. His own works began under the influence of Russian romanticism, as in the *Russian Prelude* for piano (1914). He adopted impressionism in his *Five Advertising Songs* (1925), which was followed by pieces in various experimental idioms, such as the *Studies in Black and White* for piano (1928), in which the right hand plays on the white keys while the left stays on the black. He continued to compose even at an advanced age, as in his piano *Minitudes* (1977). But it was when he turned to music lexicography that he found his true métier. He helped to edit the fourth edition (1946) and completely edited the fifth through eighth editions (1949-58) of *The International Cyclopedia of Music and Musicians,* and he edited the fifth through seventh editions (1958-84) of *Baker's Biographical Dictionary of Musicians.* Among the books that he has written are *Music Since 1900* (1937; fourth edition, 1971) and *Lexicon of Musical Invective* (1953; second edition, 1965). His reference works are noted for their polysyllabic vocabulary—he coined the term *pandiatonicism* (1937)—and their element of whimsy.

SNOW, PHOEBE (originally PHOEBE LAUB; born July 17, 1952, in New York City, New York). Singer and composer. Quickly showing her ability to sing in a variety of styles, Snow made an immediate impact with her first album, *Phoebe Snow* (1974). Later albums include *Rock Away* (1981).

SOLOMON (full name, SOLOMON CUTNER; born August 9, 1902, in London, England). Pianist. Billed as Solomon—he never used his surname professionally—he began to perform in public at the age of eight. But after several years of hectic concertizing, he retired for a time. Reemerging as a young adult virtuoso, Solomon conquered Europe and America with the clarity, brilliance, and poetry of his playing. Fellow musicians, in particular, admired the depth and genuineness of his talent. A paralytic stroke ended his career in 1956.

SPECTOR, JOHANNA (originally JOHANNA LICHTENBERG; born 1920 in Liepāja, Latvia [now in the Soviet Union]). Ethnomusicologist. In 1939 she married Robert Spector, who was killed by the Nazis in 1941. After spending the war years in concentration camps, she immigrated to the United States in 1947. Since 1954 she has been on the faculty of the Jewish Theological Seminary of America in New York City, where in 1962 she became the founder and director of the department of ethnomusicology. She has collected tape recordings of Jewish music in the Middle East and Europe, as well as Arabic, Indian, Turkish, and other tunes. Among her writings are *Samaritan Chant* (1965), *Musical Tradition and Innovation in Central Asia* (1966), and *Middle Eastern Music* (1973).

SPERRY, PAUL (born April 14 [the year, at Mr. Sperry's request, remains private] in Chicago, Illinois). Lyric tenor. His opera repertory extends from seventeenth-century rarities by Monteverdi to twentieth-century works by Berio, Britten, Stockhausen, and others. Sperry is one of today's leading concert and recital artists, his repertory covering hundreds of songs in a dozen languages. The *New York Times* described one of his performances as a "tour de force of the recitalist's craft." More than twenty-five composers—such as Hans Werner Henze, Martin David Levy, Bruno

Maderna, and Louise Talma—have written works especially for Sperry.

STARER, ROBERT (born January 8, 1924, in Vienna, Austria). Composer. He arrived in the United States in 1947. His music is noted for its direct expression and poignant lyricism, often conveyed through the use of small melodic intervals and motivic repetitions. Some of his works use twelve-tone serialism, notably the beautiful *Trio* for clarinet, cello, and piano (1964). He first gained renown for a series of ballets written for Martha Graham, including *Samson Agonistes* (1961). Starer has also written a *Sabbath Eve Service* (1967), as well as operas, symphonies, and a variety of other works.

STEIN, ERWIN (born November 7, 1885, in Vienna, Austria; died July 17, 1958, in London, England). Writer. He moved to England in 1938. Stein wrote many articles on Schoenberg and the twelve-tone technique. He also edited and published a collection of Schoenberg's letters (German, 1958; English, 1964) and wrote the book *Form and Performance* (1962).

STEINBERG, MAXIMILIAN (born July 4, 1883, in Vilnius, Lithuania [now in the Soviet Union]; died December 6, 1946, in Leningrad, the Soviet Union). Composer. His creative work was strongly influenced by Rimsky-Korsakov, whose daughter Steinberg married. He composed orchestral works (including symphonies), chamber music, and vocal pieces.

STERN, JULIUS (born August 8, 1820, in Breslau, Silesia [now Wrocław, Poland]; died February 27, 1883, in Berlin, Germany). Conductor and educator. In Berlin he conducted his own choral society (1847-74). In 1850, with Theodor Kullak and Adolf Bernhard Marx, he founded the Berlin institution that came to be known as the Stern Conservatory, one of the best music schools in Europe.

STEUERMANN, EDWARD (or EDUARD STEUERMANN; born June 18, 1892, in Sambor, near Lemberg [now Lvov], Galicia [now in the Soviet Union]; died November 11, 1964, in New York City, New York). Pianist and composer. In his teens he went to Germany, where he participated in the world premieres of many works by Schoenberg, Berg, and Webern. In the standard repertory Beethoven was his forte. He settled in the United States in 1936. Steuermann's compositions, some freely atonal and others serial, include orchestral works, chamber music, choruses, songs, and piano pieces.

STIEDRY, FRITZ (born October 11, 1883, in Vienna, Austria; died August 8, 1968, in Zurich, Switzerland). Conductor. He worked principally in Berlin till he was forced out by the Nazis in 1933. After a stay in the Soviet Union, he immigrated to the United States and conducted at the Metropolitan Opera in New York City (1946-58), specializing in Verdi and Wagner. From 1958 on he lived mostly in Zurich. Stiedry conducted the world premieres of Schoenberg's *Die glückliche Hand* ("The Lucky Hand") in 1924 and *Second Chamber Symphony* in 1940.

STOLLER, MIKE (born March 13, 1933, in New York City, New York). Composer. With lyrics provided by Jerry Leiber, Stoller wrote the music for many early rhythm-and-blues and rock-'n'-roll classics, such as "Hound Dog" (1956; original version in collaboration with Johnny Otis, 1953) and "Jailhouse Rock" (1957), both made famous through recordings by Elvis Presley.

STOLYARSKY, PETER (born November 30, 1871, in Lipovets, the Ukraine [now in the Soviet Union]; died April 24, 1944, in Sverdlovsk, the Soviet Union). Violin teacher. In Odessa in 1911 he founded his own private violin school, which in the early 1920s became incorporated into the Odessa Conservatory. He was an inspirational teacher, carefully building the confidence of each young violinist. His pupils included Nathan Milstein and David Oistrakh. Stolyarsky is regarded as one of the founders of the modern Russian school of violin playing.

STRANSKY, JOSEF (born September 9, 1872, in Humpolec, Bohemia [now in Czechoslovakia]; died March 6, 1936, in New York City, New York). Conductor. In 1898 he began to conduct opera in Prague, followed by engagements in Hamburg and Berlin. The peak of his career came as successor to Mahler at the New York Philharmonic (1911-23).

STRAUS, OSCAR (born March 6, 1870, in Vienna, Austria; died January 11, 1954, in Ischl, Austria). Composer. He

gained immense international fame through his operettas, notably *Ein Walzertraum* ("A Waltz Dream," perf. 1907), *Der tapfere Soldat* ("The Chocolate Soldier," perf. 1908), and *Der letzte Walzer* ("The Last Waltz," perf. 1920). Each of his best works has an artistic unity (sometimes achieved through the use of leitmotives) unique in the operettas of his time. During the Nazi period, Straus lived in France and the United States. He returned to Austria after World War II. Besides writing operettas, he composed instrumental works, film scores, and about five hundred cabaret songs.

STROUSE, CHARLES (born June 7, 1928, in New York City, New York). Composer. He wrote the song scores for the stage musicals *Bye, Bye, Birdie* (perf. 1960), *Golden Boy* (perf. 1964), and *Annie* (perf. 1977), with the well-known "Tomorrow" (lyrics, Martin Charnin). Strouse also composed background scores for the movies *Bonnie and Clyde* (1967), *The Night They Raided Minsky's* (1968), *There Was a Crooked Man* (1970), and *Just Tell Me What You Want* (1980). He wrote the theme song for TV's *All in the Family* (first aired 1971): "Those Were the Days" (lyrics, Lee Adams).

SULZER, SALOMON (originally SALOMON LOEWY [or LEVY]; born March 30, 1804, in Hohenems, Austria; died January 17, 1890, in Vienna, Austria). Cantor and composer. In 1809 his parents changed their surname from Loewy to Sulzer, after the Austrian village of Sülz, where their ancestors had settled during an exile from Hohenems, to which they returned in 1748. Chief cantor in Vienna for fifty-five years (1826-81), Sulzer became legendary among the Jews of his time because of his remarkable baritone-tenor voice, his charismatic personality, and his compositions for the moderate Reform synagogue service in Vienna. His outstanding work is the *Shir Zion* ("Song of Zion"; volume 1, 1838-40; volume 2, 1865-66). Adopting a style similar to that of his friend Franz Schubert (who contributed some pieces to *Shir Zion*), Sulzer created, in *Shir Zion*, the earliest complete and thoroughly organized repertory in Hebrew arranged for a cantor and a four-part male choir. In keeping with the moderate spirit of the Viennese Jewish community, he built most of his pieces from traditional synagogal melodies and stressed their original Oriental character, yet he harmonized them in the German romantic manner. His compositions were widely used as models in synagogues throughout Europe. Sulzer's sons, Julius (a violinist) and Joseph (a cellist), were respected musicians.

SWADOS, ELIZABETH (born February 5, 1951, in Buffalo, New York). Composer for avant-garde and popular theater.

SZABOLCSI, BENCE (born August 2, 1899, in Budapest, Hungary; died January 21, 1973, in Budapest, Hungary). Musicologist. He helped to create musicology in his native land through his studies of early and contemporary Hungarian music. Szabolcsi also contributed to the field of general music history, notably with his book *A melódia története* (1950; second edition, 1957; English, as *A History of Melody*, 1965).

SZIGETI, JOSEPH (born September 5, 1892, in Budapest, Hungary; died February 19, 1973, in Lucerne, Switzerland). Violinist. He came from a musical family; for example, one of his uncles, Dezsö Szigeti, was a violinist for many years in the orchestra of the Metropolitan Opera in New York City. At the age of ten Joseph began to appear in public at casinos, summer resorts, and so on. His formal concert debut came in Berlin in 1905. He spent 1907-1913 in Great Britain. Returning to the Continent in 1913, he had his career interrupted by World War I and turned to teaching till 1924, when he resumed extensive concertizing. In 1925 he began to make annual tours of the United States. Throughout the 1930s he toured worldwide, and in 1940 he settled in America, where he concertized during World War II. In early 1942 he narrowly missed death when he left an airplane in Albuquerque, New Mexico, to make room for some ferrying pilots; the plane crashed a short time later, killing all of the pilots as well as another passenger—the famed actress Carole Lombard. After the war Szigeti concertized in Europe and America. In 1960 he moved to Switzerland and gradually withdrew from playing in public. His career was unusual in that even though he began as a child prodigy, his reputation did not flower till he was in his thirties. His early training led him into the trap of mere virtuosic display. But he gradually abandoned that approach in favor of a deeply intelligent musicianship. Believing that dry, harsh sounds were often appropriate in certain musical contexts, he purposely avoided cultivating a tone of consistent sensuous beauty. The resulting austere tone quality was a major reason for the slowness at which he built a personal audience. Holding the bow in the old-fashioned way, with the elbow close to the body, Szigeti produced much power but at the expense of creating extraneous sounds. He was renowned for his ability to make virtuosity seem easy by playing difficult works without the usual violinistic show-

manship. Szigeti was an excellent performer of Bach, Beethoven, and Brahms, but he was particularly famed as an interpreter of contemporary music. One of the pioneers among performers who regularly presented advanced twentieth-century music to the public, he played new music with conviction and persuaded concert managers and recording companies to accept such compositions. He participated in the world premieres of numerous works, including Bloch's *Violin Concerto* in 1938 and Bartók's *Contrasts* for violin, piano, and clarinet in 1939. Szigeti wrote books about the violin and its repertory, notably *Szigeti on the Violin* (1969; second edition, 1979); and he issued his autobiography as *With Strings Attached* (1947, enlarged 1967).

T

TANSMAN, ALEXANDRE (born June 12, 1897, in Łódź, Poland). Composer. In 1919 he moved to Paris, where he developed an individual lyricism and melancholy, as in the orchestral *Danse de la sorcière* ("Dance of the Sorceress," 1923) and the *Flute Sonata* (1925). But his range also extended to the jazz imitations in his popular piano piece *Sonatine transatlantique* ("Transatlantic Sonatina," 1930). During World War II he lived in the United States, where he wrote film scores, including the background music for *Flesh and Fantasy* (1943). In 1946 he returned to France. Like Stravinsky, with whom he had developed a close association when both men were in America, Tansman embraced divergent idioms and techniques to create a moderately modern style. Tansman's moving *Stèle* ("Stele") for voice and instrumental ensemble (1972) commemorates Stravinsky's death. He also wrote a biography of Stravinsky (French, 1948; English, 1949), as well as a variety of instrumental pieces and vocal works, including the oratorio *Isaïe le prophète* ("Isaiah the Prophet," 1951).

TAUSIG, CARL (originally KAROL TAUSIG; born November 4, 1841, in Warsaw, Poland; died July 17, 1871, in Leipzig, Germany). Pianist and composer. In 1858 Tausig began his concert career, at first with mixed success because of his tendency toward excessive showmanship. But by 1865 he had settled into a more dignified style, which received general acclaim. However, his tours weakened his always fragile health, and he died of typhoid at the age of twenty-nine. The most gifted and famous of the first generation of Franz Liszt's pupils, Tausig played in a fiery, grand manner, yet with a controlled tone and touch and with a technique that Liszt himself called "infallible." He had a large and varied repertory, his fantastic memory drawing on works from Domenico Scarlatti to Liszt. Tausig composed many works, but the only ones of continuing interest are some chromatic finger exercises.

TEICHER, LOUIS (born August 24, 1924, in Wilkes Barre, Pennsylvania). Pianist and composer. In 1947 he teamed up with Arthur Ferrante to form the piano duo Ferrante and Teicher. Famed primarily for their arrangements and renditions of light music from films and Broadway musicals, Ferrante and Teicher have made numerous concert tours throughout the United States and Canada, performed frequently on TV and radio, and issued many popular record-

ings. Teicher, in collaboration with Ferrante, has composed some songs and light instrumental works, including the title song (lyrics, Noel Sherman) for the film *A Rage to Live* (1965).

TEMIANKA, HENRI (born November 19, 1906, in Greenrock, Scotland). Violinist and conductor. Besides touring widely as a concert violinist, he founded and led the famous Paganini String Quartet (1946-66). Temianka has also conducted many orchestras, notably the California Chamber Symphony, which he founded in 1960 and which he still directs. His reminiscences are in *Facing the Music: An Irreverent Close-up of the Real Concert World* (1973). Temianka's violin playing is noted for its flawless technique, expressive tone, and well-conceived interpretations in which genuine emotional involvement is conveyed without loss of intellectual control.

TERTIS, LIONEL (born December 29, 1876, in West Hartlepool, England; died February 22, 1975, in London, England). The world's foremost violist. Tertis, more than any other individual, was responsible for the public's acceptance of the viola as a solo instrument. He played with a big, powerful tone, and he designed a large viola to help produce the sound that he wanted. Tertis wrote the method *Beauty of Tone in String Playing* (1938) and the autobiography *Cinderella No More* (1953; revised and enlarged, as *My Viola and I*, 1974). He continued to play occasionally till he was eighty-seven, and he lived to be nearly one hundred.

THALBERG, SIGISMOND (born January 8, 1812, in Pâquis, near Geneva, Switzerland; died April 27, 1871, in Posillipo, near Naples, Italy). Pianist and composer. In 1826, at the age of twelve, he established himself as a successful salon pianist in Vienna. In 1830 he began his international career, and soon he became one of the most lionized pianists of his time, rivaling even Franz Liszt. He retired to Italy in 1864. In the virtuoso tradition of the era, Thalberg played mostly his own works, of which the most effective are the fantasies on opera arias. His basic compositional method was to place the melody in the middle of the keyboard, where the thumbs and the sustaining pedal would come into play, and then to ornament the tune with passage work above and below. That procedure allowed him to display the main characteristic of his pianism: the combination of a singing style and a brilliant technique. His legato was highly praised; Liszt himself said that "Thalberg is the only artist who can play the violin on the keyboard."

TIOMKIN, DIMITRI (born May 10, 1894, in Poltava, the Ukraine [now in the Soviet Union]; died November 11, 1979, in London, England). Composer and pianist. After World War I and the Russian Revolution, he left his homeland to work as a concert pianist in western Europe. In 1928 he performed the European premiere of Gershwin's *Concerto in F*. Tiomkin's first visit to the United States came in 1925, and in 1929 he settled in the Hollywood section of Los Angeles, California, to compose background scores for movies. In 1968 he retired to London. His compositional style, based in nineteenth-century Slavonic romanticism, was perfect for commercial films; and he became one of the movie industry's most respected and versatile craftsmen. He was equally effective with fantasies, such as *Lost Horizon* (1937); westerns, such as *Duel in the Sun* (1946); science-fiction thrillers, such as *The Thing* (1951); melodramas, such as *I Confess* (1953); and adventures, such as *Fifty-five Days at Peking* (1963). His suspenseful background score for *High Noon* (1952) helped to turn a routine western into one of the all-time movie classics. Through his enormously popular, and dramatically integral, title song for *High Noon* (lyrics, Ned Washington), Tiomkin virtually created the modern practice of attempting to link commercially successful songs with nonmusical pictures. Among his many other outstanding film scores are those for *Alice in Wonderland* (1933), *Cyrano de Bergerac* (1950), *The High and the Mighty* (1954), *Friendly Persuasion* (1956), *Giant* (1956), *The Old Man and the Sea* (1958), *The Alamo* (1960), *The Fall of the Roman Empire* (1964), and *Tchaikovsky* (1971). He published his autobiography as *Please Don't Hate Me* (with Prosper Buranelli, 1959).

TISCHLER, HANS (born January 18, 1915, in Vienna, Austria). Musicologist. He immigrated to the United States in 1938. His writings include *Practical Harmony* (1964), *A Structural Analysis of Mozart's Piano Concertos* (1966), and articles on medieval polyphony.

TOCH, ERNST (born December 7, 1887, in Vienna, Austria; died October 1, 1964, in Santa Monica, California). Composer. He immigrated to the United States in 1934. Toch's mature music is in a generally neoclassical style, though a romantic element of expressiveness is often apparent, particularly in some highly chromatic, nearly atonal, passages. His output is dominated by thirteen string quartets (1902-1954) and seven symphonies (1950-64). He composed background music for the films *Peter Ibbetson* (1935) and *The Unseen* (1945), among others. And his vocal music is highlighted by the *Cantata of the Bitter Herbs* (1938), inspired by the traditional texts of the seder ceremony.

TOUREL, JENNIE (originally JENNIE DAVIDSON; born June 22, 1900, in Saint Petersburg, Russia [now Leningrad, the Soviet Union]; died November 23, 1973, in New York City, New York). Mezzo-soprano. She fled Russia soon after the 1917 Revolution and settled in Paris, where she studied with Anna El-Tour, whose surname the student anagrammatized to form her own stage name, Tourel. In 1931 she began to sing opera in Paris, and she made her Metropolitan Opera debut in New York City in 1937. Tourel left Paris just before the Nazi invasion in 1940, eventually settling in the United States. She continued to sing opera, notably as Baba the Turk in the world premiere of Stravinsky's *The Rake's Progress* in 1951. But she devoted most of her career to recitals and concerts, giving the first performances of many songs by Poulenc and Hindemith and participating in the world premieres of Leonard Bernstein's *First Symphony: Jeremiah* in 1942 and his *Third Symphony: Kaddish ("Holy")* in 1963. Under Bernstein's direction she performed as soloist in Mahler's *Second Symphony* at the famous Mount Scopus (near Jerusalem) concert of July 9, 1967, celebrating the Israeli victory in the Six-Day War. Widely regarded as the world's foremost interpreter of French vocal music, she was also renowned for her mastery of the Italian coloratura mezzo-soprano repertory. Her versatility, technique, and control over subtle nuances of style, text, and tone color earned Tourel a special place in the annals of vocal art.

TSFASMAN, ALEXANDER (born December 14, 1906, in Aleksandrovsk, the Ukraine [now Zaporozhye, the Soviet Union]; died January 25, 1971, in Leningrad, the Soviet Union). Pianist, conductor, and composer. In 1926 he organized a jazz band in Moscow and soon became the foremost conductor of jazz in the Soviet Union. In his late years he appeared most frequently as a piano soloist with stage orchestras, playing his own works and arrangements of light music by others. His compositions, which are based in jazz, include a concerto for piano and jazz band, popular songs, theater music, and film scores.

U

UNGER, MAX (originally ERNST MAX UNGER; born May 28, 1883, in Taura, Germany; died December 1, 1959, in Zurich, Switzerland). Musicologist. He wrote more than 150 articles about Beethoven and published a complete edition of Beethoven's letters.

V

VEPRIK, ALEXANDER (born June 23, 1899, in Balta, near Odessa, the Ukraine [now in the Soviet Union]; died October 13, 1958, in Moscow, the Soviet Union). Composer and musicologist. His music combines formal, harmonic, and instrumental-color characteristics of the Russian national school with melodies that reflect the emotional, ornamental, rhapsodic manner of Jewish cantillation.

Among his best compositions are the *Kaddish* ("Holy") for voice and instrumental ensemble (1925) and the *Songs and Dances of the Ghetto* for orchestra (1927). He composed a variety of other works, as well as book-length studies of orchestral style.

VOGEL, WLADIMIR (born February 29, 1896, in Moscow, Russia; died June 19, 1984, in Zurich, Switzerland). Composer. He spent his mature years in Switzerland. His music, beginning with the *Violin Concerto* (1937), is based on a personal use of the twelve-tone technique. Preoccupied with the philosophical and mystical aspects of his art, Vogel became a master of the speaking chorus. His list includes many choral pieces, as well as orchestral works and chamber music.

VOLMAN, MARK. *See* KAYLAN, HOWARD and VOLMAN, MARK.

VOLPE, ARNOLD (born July 9, 1869, in Kaunas, Lithuania [now in the Soviet Union]; died February 2, 1940, in Miami, Florida). Conductor. In 1898 he settled in the United States, where he founded and led the Young Men's Symphony Orchestra of New York (1902-1919) and the Volpe Symphony Orchestra (1904-1914). He also served as music director of the Washington, D.C., Opera Company (1919-22), and in 1926 he organized the University of Miami Symphony Orchestra.

VON TILZER, ALBERT (originally ALBERT GUMM; born March 29, 1878, in Indianapolis, Indiana; died October 1, 1956, in Los Angeles, California). Composer. Brother of the composer Harry Von Tilzer. Albert composed the music to the classic song "Take Me Out to the Ball Game" (lyrics, Jack Norworth; 1908), which he himself introduced by singing it on the vaudeville stage. Strangely, it was not till twenty years later that he actually saw his first baseball game. Among his other well-known songs are "Put Your Arms around Me, Honey" (lyrics, Junie McCree; 1910) and "I'll Be with You in Apple Blossom Time" (lyrics, Neville Fleeson; 1920).

VON TILZER, HARRY (originally HARRY GUMM; born July 8, 1872, in Detroit, Michigan; died January 10, 1946, in New York City, New York). Composer and music publisher. Brother of the composer Albert Von Tilzer. Early in his career Harry adopted his mother's maiden name, Tilzer, and added Von to it for distinction. He worked as a tumbler in a circus and later became a singer, pianist, and composer in vaudeville (from 1892 in New York City). His song "My Old New Hampshire Home" (lyrics, Andrew B. Sterling; 1898) was so successful that he was offered a partnership in the publishing firm of Shapiro, Bernstein, and Company, which also published his hit "A Bird in a Gilded Cage" (lyrics, Arthur J. Lamb; 1900). In 1902 he founded the Harry Von Tilzer Music Company, one of the most important publishers in the history of American popular music. It issued not only Von Tilzer's own works but also those of other composers, including George Gershwin's first published song. Among Von Tilzer's best-known songs are "The Mansion of Aching Hearts" (lyrics, Arthur J. Lamb; 1902), "On a Sunday Afternoon" (lyrics, Andrew B. Sterling; 1902), "Wait 'Til the Sun Shines, Nellie" (lyrics, Andrew B. Sterling; 1905), and "I Want a Girl Just like the Girl That Married Dear Old Dad" (lyrics, William Dillon; 1911). His song "Alexander, Don't You Love Your Baby No More?" (lyrics, Andrew B. Sterling; 1904) was probably the stimulus for Irving Berlin's famous "Alexander's Ragtime Band" (1911). Von Tilzer may also have inspired the name Tin Pan Alley (for the New York City area where popular-music publishers were concentrated) when, in about 1903, a visiting journalist noticed that the composer-publisher had stuffed paper between the strings of the office piano to produce a "tinny" sound. Von Tilzer's sentimental ballads did not fit in well with the jazz age, and his last successful song was "Just around the Corner" (lyrics, Dolph Singer; 1925). Four of his five brothers adopted his pseudonym and entered the music business: Jules (or Julie) Von Tilzer became president of the Harry Von Tilzer Music Company, Will Von Tilzer wrote lyrics and became head of the Broadway Music Company, Jack Von Tilzer cofounded and directed the York Music Company, and Albert Von Tilzer became a popular-song composer.

W

WALDTEUFEL, EMILE (originally CHARLES EMILE LÉVY; born December 9, 1837, in Strasbourg, France; died February 12, 1915, in Paris, France). Composer. Known as the Waltz King of France, he is the world's most popular waltz composer next to the Strauss family. Waldteufel wrote dance music having a poetic, aristocratic distinctiveness. Among his classic waltzes are *Violettes* ("Violets," pub. 1876), *Les sirènes* ("The Sirens," pub. 1878), *Dolorès* ("Dolores," pub. 1880), *Les patineurs* ("The Skaters," pub. 1882), *Estudiantina* ("Students," pub. 1883), *España* ("Spain," pub. 1886), and *Acclamations* ("Acclamations," pub. 1888).

WAXMAN, FRANZ (originally FRANZ WACHSMANN; born December 24, 1906, in Königshütte, Upper Silesia [now Chorzów, Poland]; died February 24, 1967, in Los Angeles, California). Composer. Using a late-romantic style, he wrote many film scores, including *Bride of Frankenstein* (1935), *Rebecca* (1940), and *Sunset Boulevard* (1950). He often composed effective contrapuntal passages, as in *The Spirit of St. Louis* (1957). In his late years he wrote two intensely Jewish art works: the oratorio *Joshua* (1959) and the song cycle *The Song of Terezin* (1965).

WEINBERG, JACOB (born July 7, 1879, in Odessa, the Ukraine [now in the Soviet Union]; died November 2, 1956, in New York City, New York). Composer. He lived in Palestine (1921-26) and then settled in the United States. Among his compositions are the oratorios *Isaiah* (1948) and *The Life of Moses* (1952), liturgical works, instrumental pieces, and songs.

WEINBERGER, JAROMIR (born January 8, 1896, in Prague, Bohemia [now in Czechoslovakia]; died August 8, 1967, in Saint Petersburg, Florida). Composer. He earned international fame with his comic opera *Švanda dudák* ("Schwanda the Bagpiper," perf. 1927), which shows his gift for tuneful melody and his absorption of Czech and Slovak folk music. The polka and fugue from the opera are perennial favorites in orchestral concerts. He also wrote on Jewish subjects, as in the orchestral *Neima Ivrit* ("Hebrew Song," 1936). In 1939 he immigrated to the United States, where he turned to American subject matter and folk-music materials, as in *The Legend of Sleepy Hollow* for orchestra (1940) and *The Lincoln Symphony* (1941). Depressed at feeling left out of the mainstream of American music activity, Weinberger committed suicide through an overdose of sleeping pills. His manuscripts are housed mainly at the Jaromir Weinberger Archives in Jerusalem.

WEINSTOCK, HERBERT (born November 16, 1905, in Milwaukee, Wisconsin; died October 21, 1971, in New York City, New York). Writer. His writings focus on opera and biography, as in *The Opera: A History of Its Creation and Performance* (1941; second edition, as *The World of Opera*, 1962), *Donizetti and the World of Opera in Italy, Paris, and Vienna in the First Half of the Nineteenth Century* (1963), *Rossini: A Biography* (1968), and *Vincenzo Bellini: His Life and Operas* (1971).

WEISGALL, HUGO (born October 13, 1912, in Eibenschütz, Moravia [now Ivančice, Czechoslovakia]). Composer. He immigrated to the United States in 1920. His operas deal with many of the crucial philosophical, social, and moral issues of the twentieth century. His style is generally in an expressionistic atonal, sometimes twelve-tone, idiom. Among his operas are *The Tenor* (comp. 1950, perf. 1952), *The Stronger* (comp. 1952, perf. 1952), *Six Characters in Search of an Author* (comp. 1956, perf. 1959), *Purgatory* (comp. 1958, perf. 1961), and *Jenny; or, The Hundred Nights* (perf. 1976).

WEISMAN, BEN (born November 16, 1921, in Providence, Rhode Island). Composer. He wrote the music for many popular songs of the 1950s and 1960s, such as "Lonely Blue Boy" (lyrics, Fred Wise; 1958) and "The Night Has a Thousand Eyes" (music and lyrics in collaboration with Dottie Wayne and Marilyn Garrett, 1962). Several of his songs were written for, or used by, Elvis Presley, such as the title song for the movie *Follow That Dream* (lyrics, Fred Wise; 1962).

WEISSENBERG, ALEXIS (born July 26, 1929, in Sofia, Bulgaria). Pianist. He went to Palestine as a refugee in 1945 and by 1946 had arrived in New York City. The following year, having won the prestigious Leventritt International Competition, he made his formal debut, in New York City, and began an international career. He is a master of the keyboard music from Bach to Bartók.

WEISSER, ALBERT (born 1918 in New York City, New York; died 1982). Musicologist and composer. His literary works are highlighted by *The Modern Renaissance of Jewish Music* (1954), and his compositions include *Three Popular Songs after Sholom Aleichem* (1959). For many years he served on the editorial staff of *Musica judaica: Journal of the American Society for Jewish Music*.

WELLESZ, EGON (born October 21, 1885, in Vienna, Austria; died November 9, 1974, in Oxford, England). Musicologist and composer. In 1938 he immigrated to England. As a composer he was influenced by Schoenberg's twelve-tone technique, and he became the master's first biographer (German, 1921; English, 1924). But Wellesz used the technique only sparingly, generally preferring chromatic tonality

Egon Wellesz

as a shaping force. His best compositions are the operas and ballets of the 1920s and the nine symphonies that he wrote during his years in England. As a musicologist he reached his peak with *A History of Byzantine Music and Hymnography* (1949; revised third edition, 1963).

WERNER, ERIC (born August 1, 1901, in Lundenberg, Moravia [now Břeclav, Czechoslovakia]). Musicologist. He immigrated to the United States in 1938. Werner's book *The Sacred Bridge* (1959) traces the liturgical and musical parallels between Jewish and early Christian music. His other works include *Hebrew Music* (1961), *Mendelssohn: A New Image of the Composer and His Age* (1963), *A Voice Still Heard: The Sacred Songs of the Ashkenazic Jews* (1976), and articles on the philosophy and aesthetics of music.

WHITEMAN, PAUL (born March 28, 1890, in Denver, Colorado; died December 29, 1967, in Doylestown, Pennsylvania). Jazz bandleader. In 1907 he joined the viola section of the Denver Symphony Orchestra. In 1914 he moved to San Francisco and got a job with the orchestra of the Panama-Pacific Exposition. The following year he became a violist with the San Francisco Symphony Orchestra. In 1917 he discovered jazz when he patronized a San Francisco dance hall, and he immediately began to study the new style. In 1918 he quit the San Francisco Symphony and spent a brief period of time as a navy bandmaster. Released from the navy, Whiteman, in 1919, began to form his own dance

bands for various hotels, nightclubs, theaters, and ships in the United States, Mexico, and Europe. By 1924 he had set up over fifty different groups. Whiteman introduced a mixed style of orchestration and performance that he called symphonic jazz, in which jazz elements were only one of several musical resources used. Orthodox jazz was most evident in the improvised solos by outstanding Whiteman band members, eventually including such performers as the cornetist Bix Beiderbecke, the clarinetist Jimmy Dorsey, and the trombonist Tommy Dorsey. But Whiteman induced his arrangers, notably Ferde Grofé, to create a new style that combined elements of mainstream popular and classical music with jazz. By applying jazz rhythms and inflections to popular tunes and classical melodies, Whiteman emphasized the fact that jazz was not a kind of music but a manner of performance. He helped to establish jazz and related forms as listeners' music, not just dancers' music. Whiteman was soon known as the King of Jazz. On February 12, 1924, he gave the first concert of jazz music presented as a serious art form. The concert was held at Aeolian Hall in New York City and was highlighted by the world premiere of George Gershwin's *Rhapsody in Blue* (which Whiteman had personally commissioned and encouraged), with the composer as piano soloist and Whiteman as conductor. Whiteman later held seven similar concerts (the last in 1938), each, like the first, being labeled an "experiment" in modern music. Among the other world premieres that he conducted were those of Grofé's *Grand Canyon Suite* in 1931 and Igor Stravinsky's *Scherzo à la russe* ("Russian Scherzo") in 1944. Whiteman appeared with his band in a number of movies, beginning with *King of Jazz* (1930), which was also notable for the screen debut of one of his vocalists, Bing Crosby (whom Whiteman had hired in 1926). Among Whiteman's later films were *Thanks a Million* (1935), *Strike Up the Band* (1940), *Rhapsody in Blue* (1945), and *The Fabulous Dorseys* (1947). He often performed on radio; and later he became one of the first to exploit TV, hosting the musical show *TV Teen Club* (1949-54). In his late years he served as music director of the American Broadcasting Company (ABC). Whiteman recorded his thoughts on the new popular music in his book *Jazz* (with Mary Margaret McBride, 1926). He also wrote *How to Be a Bandleader* (with Leslie Lieber, 1941) and *Records for Millions* (1948).

(.)
WIENER, JEAN (born March 19, 1896, in Paris, France; died June 8, 1982, in Paris, France). Composer and pianist. He discovered jazz in his teens and soon became one of the earliest and most important jazzmen in France. His compositions, in a Gershwin-like jazz idiom, include theater music, film scores, and concert pieces.

WIENIAWSKI, HENRYK (or HENRI WIENIAWSKI; born July 10, 1835, in Lublin, Poland; died March 31, 1880, in Moscow, Russia). Violinist and composer. Nephew of the pianist Edouard Wolff and brother of the pianist Józef Wieniawski. He traveled as a virtuoso and, early in his career, played in numerous concerts with Józef. During an extended stay in Saint Petersburg (1860-72), Henryk greatly influenced the development of the Russian violin school. In 1872 he resumed his world travels. Returning to Russia in 1879 for a concert tour, he became gravely ill with a long-standing heart ailment and died there. Perhaps the greatest violinist of the generation after Paganini, Wieniawski played with a French training colored by a Slavonic temperament, with a brilliant technique enriched by a lyricism and fiery emotion heightened by an intensified vibrato. He bowed unconventionally for the time, holding the right elbow high and pressing the bow with the index finger above the second joint. Russian violinists, in particular, adopted his method, and it came to be called the Russian bow grip. As a composer he combined the violinistic virtuosity of Paganini with a mature romanticism. His études are, next only to Paganini's, the most difficult yet musical study pieces for the violin. But his crowning works, and standard items in any violinist's repertory, are his two violin concertos (pub. 1853 and 1870 respectively). His youngest daughter, Irene, became Lady Dean Paul and composed under the pen name Poldowski.

WIENIAWSKI, JÓZEF (or JOSEPH WIENIAWSKI; born May 23, 1837, in Lublin, Poland; died November 11, 1912, in Brussels, Belgium). Pianist. Nephew of the pianist Edouard Wolff and brother of the violinist Henryk Wieniawski. As a youth he toured with Henryk. Later he performed widely on his own before settling in Belgium. He was noted for his fine musicianship and technique, and for his abilities as a sight reader and accompanist. Adam Tadeusz Wieniawski, nephew of Henryk and Józef, was a Polish pianist and composer who helped to organize the Frédéric Chopin International Piano Competition (1927) and the International Henryk Wieniawski Violin Competition (1935), both in Poland.

WOLFF, ALBERT (born January 19, 1884, in Paris, France; died February 20, 1970, in Paris, France). Conductor. He conducted for many years in Paris, at both the Opéra-Comique (beginning in 1911) and the Opéra (beginning in 1949). Wolff was an excellent interpreter of the new French music of his time, and he led the world premieres of many works by Debussy, Milhaud, Poulenc, Ravel, and others.

WOLFF, EDOUARD (born September 15, 1816, in Warsaw, Poland; died October 16, 1880, in Paris, France). Pianist and composer. Uncle of the violinist Henryk Wieniawski and the pianist Józef Wieniawski. In 1835 he settled in Paris. One of his good friends there was his Polish compatriot Frédéric Chopin, whose manner of playing Wolff imitated. Wolff's piano compositions also show the influence of Chopin.

WORMSER, ANDRÉ (born November 1, 1851, in Paris, France; died November 4, 1926, in Paris, France). Composer. In 1875 he won the Prix de Rome. His most successful composition was his score for the pantomime *L'enfant prodigue* ("The Prodigal Son," perf. 1890). He also wrote other stage works, orchestral music, choruses, songs, and piano pieces.

Y

YASSER, JOSEPH (born April 16, 1893, in Łódź, Poland). Musicologist and organist. In 1923 he immigrated to the United States. He has performed as an organist in concerts and in synagogues, notably at New York City's Temple Rodeph Sholom (1929-60), where he also served as choirmaster. His writings include many articles on Jewish music. But the work by which he is most widely known is the controversial book *A Theory of Evolving Tonality* (1932),

which presents a hypothesis of historical scalar evolution, including the origin of the pentatonic (five-tone) scale, its development with its two auxiliary degrees into the familiar heptatonic (seven-tone) scale, and the postulation of an ultimate Western scale of nineteen (twelve main, seven auxiliary) degrees.

Z

ZEISLER, FANNIE (originally FANNIE BLUMENFELD; born July 16, 1863, in Bielitz, Silesia [now Bielsko-Biała, Poland]; died August 20, 1927, in Chicago, Illinois). Pianist. Cousin of the pianist Moritz Rosenthal. Brought to America at the age of five, she settled in Chicago with her parents, who changed their surname from Blumenfeld to Bloomfield. She concertized from 1883 to 1885 as Fannie Bloomfield. In 1885 she married the Chicago lawyer Sigmund Zeisler, and thereafter she appeared as Fannie Zeisler. Her manner of playing was fiery and incisive.

ZEITLIN, ZVI (born February 21, 1923, in Dubrovnik, Yugoslavia). Violinist. While studying at the Hebrew University of Jerusalem, he debuted, with the Palestine Orchestra, in 1940. In 1947 he immigrated to the United States, where he gave his first performance in 1951. He plays both standard and modern works, including pieces written for him by Paul Ben-Haim and others. Zeitlin is one of the few violinists who regularly play Schoenberg's difficult concerto. He has also done research in Hebrew biblical cantillation.

ZEVON, WARREN (born January 24, 1947, in Chicago, Illinois). Singer and composer. He wrote the music and lyrics for "He Quit Me," used in the movie *Midnight Cowboy* (1969), and "Hasten Down the Wind," used as the title song for a 1976 album by Linda Ronstadt. His own albums include *Warren Zevon* (1976) and *The Envoy* (1982).

ZILBERTS, ZAVEL (born 1881 in Karlin, near Pinsk, Russia; died April 25, 1949, in New York City, New York). Composer, conductor, and cantor. As a teenager he became a cantor in Karlin, succeeding his deceased father. Later he conducted the Hazomir chorus in Łódź, Poland (1903-1907), at that time the world's largest Jewish choral group. Returning to Russia, he conducted the Central Synagogue choir in Moscow (1907-1914). After another period with the Hazomir chorus, he immigrated to the United States (1920), where he led various synagogue choirs and other choral groups, including the Zilberts Choral Society of New York City. Zilberts composed many synagogal works, often drawing on motives from biblical cantillation. His setting of the traditional *Havdalah* ("Distinction") for solo singer, chorus, and piano, or for violin and piano (pub. 1923), has become a classic. Among his other well-known compositions are his biblical cantata *Yakob's halom* ("Jacob's Dream," pub. 1934) and his collection *Music for the Synagogue* (pub. 1943).

ZIMBALIST, EFREM (born April 1889 or 1890 in Rostov-on-Don, Russia; died February 22, 1985, in Reno, Nevada). Violinist and composer. He began his concert career in 1907, and in 1911 he debuted in the United States, where he soon settled. In 1914 he married the soprano Alma Gluck, with whom he frequently appeared in joint recital. In 1943 he married Mary Louise Curtis Bok (Gluck having died in 1938), founder of the Curtis Institute of Music, of which he served as director from 1941 to 1968. He continued to perform into the 1950s, giving, for example, the world premiere of Gian Carlo Menotti's *Violin Concerto* in 1952. In 1970 Zimbalist retired to Reno, Nevada, where he practiced the violin every day till he was well into his nineties. Less emotional than Mischa Elman and less perfectionist than Jascha Heifetz, Zimbalist represented, with those violinists, the peak of the Leopold Auer school. His playing was characterized by an unhurried nobility and by a search for deep meaning in each piece. He composed music in many genres, notably the successful musical comedy *Honeydew* (perf.

1920) and the *American Rhapsody* for orchestra (1936, revised 1943). His son, Efrem Zimbalist, Jr., began as a musician but then became an actor, notably in the TV series *The FBI*.

ZUKOFSKY, PAUL (born October 22, 1943, in New York City, New York). Violinist. He performed extensively as a child prodigy, and his father, the poet Louis Zukofsky, wrote a novel, *Little* (1970), about a violin wunderkind. As he grew older Paul developed a special interest in twentieth-century music. Possessing a remarkable command of both traditional and new virtuoso techniques, he has given the world premieres of works by Babbitt, Crumb, Sessions, Wuorinen, and others.

Addenda

RUBY, HARRY (originally HARRY RUBINSTEIN; born January 27, 1895, in New York City, New York; died February 23, 1974, in Woodland Hills, California). Composer of Groucho Marx's theme song, "Hooray for Captain Spaulding" from the stage show *Animal Crackers* (1928), and of "Three Little Words" from the film *Check and Double Check* (1930), both with lyrics by Bert Kalmar.

SCHWARTZ, ARTHUR (born November 25, 1900, in New York City, New York; died September 3, 1984, in Kintnersville, Pennsylvania). Composer of "Dancing in the Dark" from the stage show *The Band Wagon* (1931) and of "You and the Night and the Music" from the stage show *Revenge with Music* (1934), both with lyrics by Howard Dietz.

A

ADLER, ISRAEL (born January 17, 1925, in Berlin, Germany). Musicologist. He moved to Palestine in 1937. His specialty is Jewish music from medieval times to the emancipation of European Jews in the early nineteenth century. Adler wrote the important book *Musical Life and Traditions of the Portuguese Community of Amsterdam* (1974). He served as joint editor of the music department of the *Encyclopaedia Judaica* (1972) and has edited *Juval: Studies of the Jewish Music Research Center* since 1968.

ADNI, DANIEL (born December 6, 1951, in Haifa, Israel). Pianist. At the age of twelve he gave his first public recital, in Haifa. His professional career began in 1970, in London, and his New York City debut came in 1976. He has concertized internationally and has made outstanding recordings of

Mendelssohn and Grieg. In 1973 in Berlin he gave the first performance outside Great Britain of Alexander Goehr's *Piano Concerto*. Adni's playing is characterized by a bright, clear tone and by intelligent phrasing.

ALEXANDER, HAIM (originally HEINZ ALEXANDER; born August 9, 1915, in Berlin, Germany). Composer. He immigrated to Jerusalem in 1936. His early works display a modal chromaticism with a strong Jewish flavor, as in *Six Israeli Dances* for piano (also in several other arrangements, 1950). Later compositions show an increasing interest in serialism, and in *Patterns* for piano (1973) the two approaches are ingeniously combined. He has written for a variety of forces, both vocal and instrumental.

ALOTIN, YARDENA (born October 19, 1930, in Tel Aviv, Palestine [now Israel]). Composer. In much of her music she has attempted to recapture the spirit of biblical times. One of her best-known works is *Al golah dvuyah* ("A Painful Exile") for mezzo-soprano and orchestra (1958). Her instrumental compositions include the *Sonatina* for violin and piano (1970). Alotin has written many youth or educational pieces, which are widely performed.

AMIRAN, EMANUEL (originally EMANUEL POUGATCHOV; born August 8, 1909, in Warsaw, Poland). Composer. He arrived in Jerusalem in his teens. In 1945, with Leo Kestenberg, he helped to found Palestine's first music-teachers' training college, in Tel Aviv. Among Amiran's compositions are many incidental scores to plays, popular solo and choral songs, cantatas, and a variety of instrumental works.

ARIÉ, RAPHAEL (born August 22, 1920, in Sofia, Bulgaria). Bass. He joined the local opera company in Sofia after World War II. In 1946 he won a major competition in Geneva, as a result of which he was hired to sing at the famed La Scala in Milan, where he debuted in 1947. In 1951 he created the role of Trulove in the world premiere of Stravinsky's opera *The Rake's Progress* in Venice. He quickly established himself as a leading bass in the major opera houses in Italy, the rest of Europe, and America. Arié became an Israeli citizen but continued his international career.

ATZMON, MOSHE (originally MOSHE GROSZBERGER; born July 30, 1931, in Budapest, Hungary). Conductor. He settled in Palestine in 1944. In 1963 he won the Dimitri Mitropoulos Competition and the Leonard Bernstein Prize, followed in 1964 by a competition sponsored by the Liverpool Philharmonic. Atzmon soon embarked on a successful career as an international conductor, notably as chief conductor of the North German Radio Symphony Orchestra (1972-76) and the Basel Symphony Orchestra (since 1972).

AVENARY, HANOCH (originally HERBERT LOEWENSTEIN;

born May 25, 1908, in Danzig, Germany [now Gdańsk, Poland]). Musicologist. In 1936 he settled in Palestine, where he became one of the first musicologists in the region. Avenary's writings include *Studies in the Hebrew, Syrian, and Greek Liturgical Recitative* (1963), *Hebrew Hymn Tunes: The Rise and Development of a Musical Tradition* (1971), and *The Ashkenazi Tradition of Biblical Chant between 1500 and 1900* (1976).

AVIDOM, MENAHEM (originally MENAHEM MAHLER-KALKSTEIN; born January 6, 1908, in Stanislau, the Ukraine [now Ivano-Frankovsk, the Soviet Union]). Composer. He went to the Holy Land in 1925, soon left to study abroad, and finally returned to settle in Palestine in 1935. In his earliest mature works he displayed a great command of the Mediterranean style, as in his first five symphonies, notably the *Second Symphony: David* (1949). In the early 1960s Avidom moved away from regionalism and toward various

international styles. He sometimes used the twelve-tone technique, though he retained an Oriental melodic flavor. Among his outstanding late works are the *Enigma* for seven instruments (1962) and the *Tenth Symphony: Sinfonia brevis* ("Short Symphony," 1981).

AVNI, TZVI (born September 2, 1927, in Saarbrücken, Germany). Composer. He settled in Palestine in 1935. His early compositions, such as the *Piano Sonata* (1961), show the influence of the Mediterranean style. The next stage in his music reveals a more radical approach, using serialism, clusters, and some aleatoricism, though Oriental melodic fragments continue to be in evidence, as in the orchestral

work *Al naharot Bavel* ("By the Rivers of Babylon," 1971). Since the early 1970s he has further developed those elements and has made increasing use of electronic sounds and of noise effects on tape, as in *Of Elephants and Mosquitoes* for synthesizer (1971); *Gilgulim* ("Reincarnations") for narrator and tape (1973); and *Synchromotrask*, a theater piece for a tape, a woman, and a door (1976).

B

BARSHAI, RUDOLF (born September 28, 1924, in Labinskaya [now Labinsk], the Soviet Union). Conductor. In the mid-1950s he organized, and began to conduct, the Moscow Chamber Orchestra. Major symphony orchestras in the Soviet Union also engaged him as conductor, starting in 1967. In 1976 he moved to Israel, where he directed the Israel Chamber Orchestra till 1981. He has also guest-conducted extensively in Europe, Japan, and the United States. Since 1982 Barshai has been principal conductor and artistic adviser of the Bournemouth Symphony Orchestra in England, though he still resides principally in Israel.

BEN-HAIM, PAUL (or PAUL BEN HAIM, originally PAUL FRANKENBURGER; born July 5, 1897, in Munich, Germany; died January 15, 1984, in Jerusalem, Israel). Composer. In 1933 he settled in Palestine. He absorbed Jewish folk elements and attempted to synthesize Eastern and Western traditions in his music. His scores are noted for their excellent craftsmanship and their rich, romantic style. Among his outstanding orchestral works are the following: *First Symphony* (1940), *Second Symphony* (1945), *The Sweet Psalmist of Israel* (1953), and *Violin Concerto* (1962). He also wrote an important *String Quartet* (1937) and a number of piano compositions. Perhaps his most original music, where his Oriental lyricism has its greatest effect, is in his vocal music, including songs, miscellaneous choral pieces, and liturgical works.

BERTINI, GARY (born May 1, 1927, in Brichevo, Bessarabia [now in the Soviet Union]). Conductor and composer. Bertini founded the Rinat (later the Israel Chamber) Choir in 1955 and the Israel Chamber Ensemble, comprising both an opera company and an orchestra, in 1965. He was music director of the Jerusalem Symphony Orchestra (1978-81) and music adviser of the Detroit Symphony (1981-83), and he has guest-conducted internationally. Since 1983 he has been chief conductor of the Cologne Symphony Orchestra. He has led the world premieres of numerous works by Israelis, especially Partos and Seter. Bertini's own compositions include incidental music to many plays; the *Concerto for horn, strings, and timpani* (1952); the ballet *Delet aluma* ("The Unfound Door," 1962); and vocal works.

BOSCOVICH, ALEXANDER URIAH (born August 16, 1907, in Kolozsvár, Hungary [now Cluj, Romania]; died November 1964 in Tel Aviv, Israel). Composer. In 1938 he immigrated to Palestine. One of the pioneers of Israeli music, Boscovich tried to synthesize the Jewish tradition with Western art-music practices. During the 1940s he composed in a neoclassical-Mediterranean style, as in the *Oboe Concerto* (1943) and the *Semitic Suite* for piano or orchestra (1947). After a long period of composing little, he began to write music that deliberately juxtaposed advanced (especially twelve-tone) and conservative elements, as in the cantata *Daughter of Israel* (1960) and the *Concerto da camera* ("Chamber Concerto") for violin and instrumental ensemble (1962). Some of his late work shows a preoccupation with translating the Hebrew language into musical terms, even in purely instrumental compositions, especially in *Adayim* ("Ornaments") for flute and orchestra (1964).

BRAUN, YEHEZKIEL (born January 18, 1922, in Breslau, Silesia [now Wrocław, Poland]). Composer. He immigrated to Palestine with his family in 1924. Jewish folk music has inspired the simplicity and eloquence of his original melodies. His works include the *Piano Sonata* (1957), the *Illuminations to the Book of Ruth* for orchestra (1965), and the *Sabbath Evening Service* for cantor, choir, and organ (1962).

BROD, MAX (born May 27, 1884, in Prague, Bohemia [now in Czechoslovakia]; died December 20, 1968, in Tel Aviv, Israel). Writer and composer. In 1939 he settled in Palestine. His book *Die Musik Israels* ("The Music of Israel," 1951) relates the early development of Israeli music and examines the Jewish elements in Mendelssohn and Mahler. In his own compositions Brod helped to evolve the Mediterranean style. His works, which are characterized by their lyricism, include mostly vocal music and piano pieces.

C

COMISSIONA, SERGIU (born June 1928 in Bucharest, Romania). Conductor. After conducting briefly in Romania, he immigrated to Israel, where he was a citizen from 1959 to 1976. He served as music director of the Haifa Symphony Orchestra (1959-64), founded the Israel Chamber Orchestra (1960), and frequently guest-conducted in Europe and the United States. Comissiona began to spend more and more time in America, where he became a naturalized citizen on July 4, 1976. In his new homeland he has been music director of the Baltimore Symphony Orchestra (1969-84), principal conductor of the American Symphony Orchestra in New York City (1978-82), and music director of the Houston Symphony Orchestra (since 1984). With his dramatic conducting gestures, he projects a colorful personality in performance. He favors romantic and impressionistic works.

D

DA-OZ, RAM (originally ABRAHAM [or AVRAHAM] DAUS; born October 17, 1929, in Berlin, Germany). Composer. In 1934 he moved with his parents to Palestine, where he was blinded during the Israeli War for Independence in 1948. His early works are tonal but chromatic and often extremely expressive, as in the orchestral *Metamorphoses of Grief and Consolation* (1959). In the 1960s he experimented with free atonality, as in the *Lea Goldberg Songs* (1962), and with

twelve-tone serialism, as in the *Second String Quartet* (1964). Later Da-Oz evolved a variety of personal approaches for structuring modern music in such works as *Changing Patterns* for chamber orchestra (1967), *Rhapsody on a Jewish Yemenite Song* for piano and strings (1971), and *Mood Ring* for piano (1976).

DAUS, ABRAHAM (or AVRAHAM DAUS; born June 6, 1902, in Berlin, Germany; died 1974 in Tel Aviv, Israel). Composer and conductor. He conducted opera in Germany (1922-33) before moving to Palestine (1936). From 1940 to 1963 he lived in agricultural settlements and worked as a choral conductor. He based his early music in a moderately dissonant tonal idiom, as in *Petach el hayam* ("An Outlet to the Sea") for vocal soloists, small chorus, and small orchestra (1937). Beginning with the *String Quartet* (1954), he turned to the twelve-tone technique. Then, in the 1960s, his style became freer and more individual, as in *Testimony of an Angry Man* for piano (1967).

E

EDEL, YITZHAK (born January 1, 1896, in Warsaw, Poland; died December 14, 1973, in Tel Aviv, Israel). Composer. In 1929 he immigrated to Palestine. Edel's music reflects the influence of the eastern European Jewish tradition. His major work is the folk cantata *Lamitnadvim baam* ("To the Volunteers of the People," 1957). But he also helped to transform Jewish music into unified extended art works in the Western tradition, as in the *Capriccio* for piano (1946), the *Israeli Dance* for piano (1950), and the *Tehilim* ("Psalms") for soprano and string quartet (1963).

EDEN, BRACHA (born July 15, 1928, in Jerusalem, Palestine [now Israel]) and **TAMIR, ALEXANDER** (born April 2, 1931, in Vilnius, Lithuania [now in the Soviet Union]). Pianists who form the Eden-Tamir Duo. Their major debuts were in Israel (1954), New York City (1955), Rome (1956), London (1957), and Paris (1957). They have greatly influenced the piano-duet repertory by playing neglected works by Clementi, Czerny, and Hummel, and by performing transcriptions of such modern masterpieces as Stravinsky's *Le sacre du printemps* ("The Rite of Spring").

EHRLICH, ABEL (born September 3, 1915, in Cranz, Germany). Composer. He settled in Palestine in the late 1930s. Up to the mid-1950s he composed in the Mediterranean style. Then he turned to serialism and other modern resources. One of his most highly regarded works is *Tevicah* ("The Claim"), a group of songs for solo voices, chorus, and instrumental ensemble (1974).

F

FRIED, MIRIAM (born September 9, 1946, in Satu-Mare, Romania). Violinist. At the age of two she was taken to Israel by her parents. She rose to prominence by taking first prize

Miriam Fried

at the Paganini International Competition in Genoa (1968) and by becoming the first woman to win the Queen Elisabeth International Competition in Brussels (1971). Subsequently Fried has toured worldwide. She plays with a brilliant technique, an intelligent musicianship, and a rare depth of humaneness. She is married to the violinist Paul Biss.

G

GELBRUN, ARTUR (born July 11, 1913, in Warsaw, Poland). Composer and conductor. In 1949 he moved to Israel, where he served as chief conductor of the Israel Youth Symphony Orchestra (1950-56) and the Inter-Kibbutz Symphony Orchestra (1950-55). His music is based in the romantic tradition, with some use of modern techniques, such as serialism. Gelbrun's compositions include symphonies, other orchestral works, chamber music, and vocal pieces.

GERSON-KIWI, EDITH (full name, ESTHER EDITH GERSON-KIWI; born May 13, 1908, in Berlin, Germany). Musicologist. She moved to Palestine in 1935. Her writings have covered many topics, but her specialty, on which she is widely regarded as an outstanding authority, is ethnic music of the Middle East. Among her important works is *The Legacy of Jewish Music through the Ages in the Dispersion* (1964).

GILBOA, JACOB (born May 2, 1920, in Košice, Czechoslovakia). Composer. He moved to Palestine in 1938. Gilboa began by composing in the Mediterranean style. But in the 1960s he turned to such modernistic devices as clusters, quarter-tones, and electronic sounds. Among his mature works are *Twelve Glass Windows of Chagall in Jerusalem* for voices and instrumental ensemble (1966) and *Five Red Sea Impressions* for instrumental ensemble and tape (1976).

GITLIS, IVRY (born August 22, 1922, in Haifa, Palestine [now Israel]). Violinist. Since the mid-1950s he has toured widely, especially in Paris, where he eventually settled. Gitlis is admired for his playing of twentieth-century music, notably the violin concertos of Berg, Hindemith, and Stravinsky. His brilliant technique is highlighted by a strong rhythmic sense.

GLANTZ, LEIB (born June 1, 1898, in Kiev, the Ukraine [now in the Soviet Union]; died January 27, 1964, in Tel Aviv, Israel). Cantor and composer. He began his cantorial career at the age of eight, touring Russia with his father, also a cantor. Young Glanz later worked as a cantor at various synagogues in the United States (1926-54) before moving in 1954 to Tel Aviv, Israel, where he performed as a cantor and founded and directed an academy for cantors. He earned a wide reputation as a fine lyric tenor who avoided the "sobbing" style characteristic of many other cantors of his time. Instead, he developed a simple warmth of expression and an original approach to interpretation. He also did research on theoretical aspects of Jewish music, specifically the prayer modes, and regarded the pentatonic (five-tone) scale as the true ancient basis of Jewish music. His own compositions include songs and liturgical works.

GRADENWITZ, PETER (born January 24, 1910, in Berlin, Germany). Musicologist. In 1936 he settled in Palestine, where he founded the Israeli Music Publications (1949). Under his direction it became the first music-publishing house in Israel to attain international stature. His writings include *The Music of Israel: Its Rise and Growth through Five Thousand Years* (1949, revised 1978) and *Johann Stamitz: Leben und Werk* ("Johann Stamitz: Life and Work," 1978).

I

INBAL, ELIAHU (born February 16, 1936, in Jerusalem, Palestine [now Israel]). Conductor. His career began in Italy, notably at La Scala in Milan (1965). He went on to guest-conduct many of the world's great orchestras, such as the London Philharmonic (1965) and the Chicago Symphony (1969). Since 1974 he has been chief conductor of the Frankfort Radio Symphony Orchestra. Inbal prefers the standard repertory, especially Beethoven, and he has been praised for his recordings of Bruckner, Scriabin, and Schumann.

Eliahu Inbal

J

JACOBY, HANOCH (originally HEINRICH JACOBY; born March 2, 1909, in Königsberg, Germany [now Kaliningrad, the Soviet Union]). Composer. He settled in Palestine in 1934. His compositions show the influence of Hindemith's Germanic neoclassicism. Jacoby has often used biblical or Jewish subject matter, as in the Hebrew cantata *Od yom yavo* ("A Day Will Come," 1944) and the *Jewish Oriental Folklore* suite for string orchestra (1977).

K

KALICHSTEIN, JOSEPH (born January 15, 1946, in Tel Aviv, Palestine [now Israel]). Pianist. In 1969 he won the highly coveted Leventritt Award in New York City. Since then he has regularly appeared throughout the world as a recitalist, a soloist with major orchestras, and an outstanding chamber musician. His repertory extends from Mozart, through the romantics, and to such moderns as Bartók, Prokofiev, and Stravinsky. He possesses an extraordinary technique and a superb musical sensibility.

KAMINSKI, JOSEPH (born November 17, 1903, in Odessa, the Ukraine [now in the Soviet Union]; died October 14, 1972, in Tel Aviv, Israel). Violinist and composer. He led the violins of the Palestine (later the Israel Philharmonic) Orchestra from 1937 to 1969. His compositions mix the influences of plainsong, late romanticism, and Israeli folk music. Kaminski's finest works are the *Trumpet Concertino* (1941) and the *Violin Concerto* (1948).

KATZ, MINDRU (born April 3, 1925, in Bucharest, Romania; died January 30, 1978, in İstanbul, Turkey). Pianist. He toured Eastern Europe from 1947 to 1959. In 1959 he settled in Israel, thereafter extending his tours to many parts of the world. Katz's repertory was wide, from Bach to Prokofiev; but he received his greatest acclaim for his Beethoven, Chopin, and Brahms.

KESTENBERG, LEO (born November 27, 1882, in Rosenberg, Hungary [now Ružomberok, Czechoslovakia]; died January 14, 1962, in Tel Aviv, Israel). Educator. He reformed music education in Germany and then, with the rise of Hitler, moved to Prague, where he founded and directed the International Society for Music Education. In 1938 he settled in Palestine. In 1945 he helped to found, and became the first director of, a music-teachers' training college in Tel Aviv, the first such school in Palestine.

Joseph Kalichstein

L

LAKNER, YEHOSHUA (born April 24, 1924, in Bratislava, Czechoslovakia). Composer. He moved to Palestine in 1941. In 1963 he settled in Zurich. His music belongs to the expressionist school and employs free atonality, serialism, electronic sounds, and some jazz elements. Among Lakner's works are the *Flute Sonata* (1948); the electronic incidental music to Bertolt Brecht's *Turandot* (1969); and the *Umläufe* ("Cycles") for flute, bass clarinet, piano, and two tapes (1976).

LAVRY, MARC (born December 22, 1903, in Riga, Latvia [now in the Soviet Union]; died March 1967 in Haifa, Israel). Composer and conductor. In 1935 he settled in Palestine, where he conducted the Palestine Folk Opera (1941-47). His oratorio *Shir ha-shirim* ("The Song of Songs," 1940) draws on Jewish cantillation, and his folk opera *Dan ha-shomer* ("Dan the Guard," perf. 1945) was the first Palestinian opera in Hebrew to receive a stage performance. He also wrote liturgical music, as well as orchestral, chamber, and piano pieces. His style is based on the development of diatonic-modal Oriental melodies.

LEVI, YOEL (born August 16, 1950, in Romania). Conductor, In his early childhood he moved with his family to Israel. He learned to play violin, piano, and various percussion instruments. In 1978 he won first prize in the prestigious interna-

tional conductor's competition held in Besançon, France. Also in 1978 Levi began a six-year tenure on the staff of the Cleveland Orchestra (assistant, 1978-80; resident, 1980-84). In early 1985 he made his first appearances with that orchestra as guest conductor. He has also become increasingly in demand as a guest conductor with other major orchestras throughout the world, including the Berlin Philharmonic, the Boston Symphony, and the London Symphony. One of the most respected conductors of his generation, Levi conducts works ranging from Handel to Penderecki.

LUCA, SERGIU (born April 4, 1943, in Bucharest, Romania). Violinist. In 1950 he moved with his parents to Israel. In 1952, at the tender age of nine, he made his concert debut, as soloist with the Haifa Symphony Orchestra. In 1965 he made his American debut, with the Philadelphia Orchestra. Since then he has toured internationally to great success. His performances have increasingly focused on baroque music, at which he excells.

M

MAAYANI, AMI (born January 13, 1936, in Ramat Gan, Palestine [now Israel]). Composer. His early works draw heavily on various Near Eastern traditional materials. Later compositions combine those elements with European forms and French impressionistic devices. Among his best-known works are the *First Harp Concerto* (1960) and the *Symphony of Psalms* for voices and orchestra (1974).

MINTZ, SHLOMO (born October 30, 1957, in Moscow, the Soviet Union). Violinist. Taken to Israel by his family when he was two years old, he began his violin studies there at the age of three. At nine he gave his first public performance, and at eleven he debuted with the Israel Philharmonic, playing the Mendelssohn *Violin Concerto* while Zubin Mehta conducted. Shortly thereafter the same orchestra called on him to fill in for the ailing violinist Itzhak Perlman, and on only a week's notice Mintz prepared and performed Paganini's *First Violin Concerto*. In 1973, during a period of study in the United States, he made his New York City debut, as soloist in the Bruch *First Violin Concerto* with the Pittsburgh Symphony under William Steinberg. He made his European debut three years later with a recital at the Brighton Festival and immediately became, at the age of only nineteen, a touring soloist. Since the late 1970s he has been playing between 100 and 120 concerts a season, appearing both in recital and as soloist with virtually all of the world's major orchestras. In 1982 he was one of the renowned violinists invited by the Israel Philharmonic to participate in the festival honoring the orchestra's principal founder, Bronislaw Huberman. Mintz performed as a soloist with the New York Philharmonic under Zubin Mehta on the nationally televised New Year's Eve special *Live from Lincoln Center* in 1984.

MIRON, ISSACHAR (born July 5, 1920, in Kutno, Poland). Composer. He settled in Palestine in 1939. Miron has composed concert and liturgical music, but he is most famous for his hundreds of songs in a popular style.

Photo: Jack Mitchell

Shlomo Mintz

N

NATRA, SERGIU (born April 12, 1924, in Bucharest, Romania). Composer. He settled in Israel in 1961. In his early works, Natra composed under the influence of Hindemith, Prokofiev, and Stravinsky. But since his arrival in Israel, he has adopted a generally atonal idiom. Among his outstanding mature works are *Song of Deborah* for mezzo-soprano and chamber orchestra (1967) and *Avodat hakodesh* ("Sacred Service") for tenor, chorus, and organ (1976).

O

ORGAD, BEN-ZION (born August 21, 1926, in Gelsenkirchen, Germany). Composer. In 1933 he moved to Palestine. Many of his works use biblical texts or topics, as in the cantata *Hazon Yeshayahu* ("Isaiah's Vision," 1953). Orgad's vocal works often call for the simultaneous enuncia-

tion of different texts by various soloists or choral groups, as in the cantata *Sippuro shel halil* ("Story of a Pipe," 1972). A similar procedure is used in some purely instrumental compositions, such as *Ashmoret shniya* ("Second Watch") for chamber orchestra (1973).

P

PARTOS, OEDOEN (or ÖDÖN PARTOS; born October 1, 1907, in Budapest, Hungary; died July 6, 1977, in Tel Aviv, Israel). Composer and violist. In the late 1930s, at Bronislaw Huberman's invitation, Partos settled in Palestine to head the viola section of the newly formed Palestine (later the Israel Philharmonic) Orchestra. He played viola in the orchestra till 1956, meanwhile also performing in the Israel String Quartet (1939-54) and as a soloist in Israel and abroad. In his early music, Partos composed in the contemporary European style, with special influence from Bartók and Kodály, as in the *Concertino* for strings (1932, revised 1953). After moving to Palestine he applied Western techniques to eastern European Jewish material, as in *Yiz kor* ("In Memo-

309

riam") for strings (1947), and to Arabic elements, as in *Hezionot* ("Visions") for flute, piano, and strings (1957). In the 1960s he used the twelve-tone technique, as in *Tehilim* ("Psalms") for string quartet or for chamber orchestra (1960). After 1970 Partos composed in a freer, more advanced manner, including the use of clusters, microtones, and some aleatoric passages; among his late works are *Music for Chamber Orchestra* (1972) and *Mizmor* ("Psalm") for harp (1975).

PELLEG, FRANK (originally FRANK POLLAK; born September 24, 1910, in Prague, Bohemia [now in Czechoslovakia]; died September 20, 1968, in Haifa, Israel). Harpsichordist, pianist, and composer. In 1936 he settled in Palestine. He made many piano tours abroad, but he gained distinction especially for his harpsichord performances of Bach and other baroque masters. Pelleg wrote instrumental pieces, vocal works, and music-appreciation books.

R

RODAN, MENDI (born April 17, 1929, in Iaşi, Romania). Conductor. He settled in Israel in 1961, conducted the Israel Philharmonic that year, served as chief conductor of the Israel Broadcasting Symphony (1963-72), founded and conducted the Jerusalem Chamber Orchestra (1965-69), and has guest-conducted many European ensembles. Rodan has led the world premieres of numerous Israeli works.

RONLY-RIKLIS, SHALOM (born January 24, 1922, in Tel Aviv, Palestine [now Israel]). Conductor. He served as chief conductor of the Israel Defense Forces Band (1949-60), directed the Israel Broadcasting Symphony (1961-70), and has conducted other Israeli ensembles. In 1971 he became artistic coordinator of the Israel Philharmonic. Ronly-Riklis has also established an international reputation by guest-conducting many major orchestras abroad.

S

SADAI, YIZHAK (or YIZHAK SIDI; born May 13, 1935, in Sofia, Bulgaria). Composer. He moved with his parents to Israel in 1949. Sadai's mature compositions show little specifically Jewish influence. Instead, they convey an avant-garde European aesthetic, often in a post-Webern impressionistic idiom. Representative works include *Anagram* for chamber orchestra and tape (1973) and *Nine Pieces* for piano (1975).

SALMON, KAREL (originally KARL SALOMON; born November 13, 1897, in Heidelberg, Germany; died January 15, 1974, in Beit Zayit, near Jerusalem, Israel). Composer, conductor, and bass-baritone. He worked in Germany as a singer and conductor from 1919 to 1933, when he moved to Palestine. In 1933 he founded the region's first chamber orchestra, and in 1936 he became the first music director of the Palestine Broadcasting Service (later called Kol Israel). Composing primarily in the Mediterranean style, Salmon wrote his *Second Symphony: Nights of Canaan* (1949) and his *Israeli Youth Symphony* (1950), as well as other orchestral works, operas, piano pieces, and a wide variety of vocal (including liturgical) music.

SALZMAN, PNINA (born February 24, 1924, in Tel Aviv, Palestine [now Israel]). Pianist. While studying in Paris, she began to give public recitals when she was only nine years old. At fifteen she began to appear as soloist with the world's major orchestras. Salzman early displayed a wide repertory and soon became the first Israeli-born pianist to gain international fame.

SCHIDLOWSKY, LEÓN (born July 21, 1931, in Santiago, Chile). Composer. He settled in Israel in 1969. Schidlowsky's music utilizes a full range of twentieth-century resources, including free atonality, the twelve-tone technique, total serialism, aleatoricism, and graphic notation. Jewish topics are prevalent, especially the Holocaust, as in the choral symphony *La noche de cristal* ("The Night of the Crystal," 1961). Other important works include *Kaddish* ("Holy") for cello and orchestra (1967), *Koloth* ("Voices") for harp (1971), and *Golem* for voices and tape (1975).

SEGAL, URI (born March 7, 1944, in Jerusalem, Palestine [now Israel]). Conductor. His official debut occurred when he conducted the Sjaelland Orchestra in Copenhagen (1969). Soon afterward he led the Israel Philharmonic. In 1970 he settled in London and began to appear with many European orchestras. His American debut, with the Chi-

cago Symphony, came in 1972. In 1979 he moved back to Jerusalem. Segal is closely associated with numerous orchestras, especially the Israel Chamber Orchestra and the Philharmonia Hungarica.

SETER, MORDECAI (Russian surname, STAROMINSKY; born February 26, 1916, in Novorossisk, Russia). Composer. In 1926 he moved to Palestine. His mature music falls into three periods. The first consists largely of liturgical vocal music based on eastern Jewish folk traditions, as in the *Sabbath Cantata* (1940). The second applies a similar approach to instruments, as in the *Ricercar* for strings (1956). The third shows a more cosmopolitan manner, sometimes involving a personal application of the twelve-tone technique, as in the *Jerusalem Symphony* (1966, revised 1968). His recent works have intensified his modernistic tendencies, especially in such chamber pieces as his first four string quartets (1975-77) and in such piano music as his *Piano Sonata* (1982).

SHERIFF, NOAM (born January 7, 1935, in Tel Aviv, Palestine [now Israel]). Composer. Sheriff's music combines Jewish folk elements with modern Western tonal and rhythmic complexities. His *Piano Sonata* (1961), for example, alternates those two idioms in successive passages. Among his other outstanding achievements are the *Israel Suite* for orchestra (1965) and the electronic music, on tape, for the ballet *Cain* (1970).

SHLONSKY, VERDINA (born January 22, 1913, in Kremenchug, the Ukraine [now in the Soviet Union]). Composer and pianist. She moved to Palestine in 1929 and has worked as a concert pianist and theater composer. Her compositions include *Poème hébraïque* ("Hebraic Poem") for voice and piano (1931), *Jeremiah* for orchestra (1936), *String Quartet* (1948), and numerous songs and piano pieces. She has written in a variety of styles, from simple diatonic to complex atonal, generally for romantic purposes.

SINGER, GEORGE (born August 6, 1908, in Prague, Bohemia [now in Czechoslovakia]). Conductor and composer. In 1939 he settled in Palestine, where he soon became a successful guest conductor of several symphony and opera orchestras. Since 1947 he has also conducted abroad, debuting in the Soviet Union in 1965, the United States in 1968, and London in 1976. He has led the world premieres of many Israeli works. Singer himself has composed both instrumental music and vocal pieces.

STERNBERG, ERICH WALTER (born May 31, 1891, in Berlin, Germany; died December 15, 1974, in Tel Aviv, Israel). Composer. In 1932 he moved to Palestine. His deep interest in the Bible is reflected in many works on biblical subjects, such as the cantata *David and Goliath* (1927) and the orchestral pieces *The Twelve Tribes of Israel* (1942) and *Noah's Ark* (1960). However, one of his best-known works is *Ha-orev* ("The Raven") for baritone and orchestra (1949), based on Edgar Allan Poe's famous poem.

STUTSCHEWSKY, JOACHIM (or YEHOYACHIN STUTSCHEWSKY; born February 7, 1891, in Romny, the Ukraine [now in the Soviet Union]; died November 14, 1982, in Tel Aviv, Israel). Cellist, composer, and ethnomusicologist. He performed as a concert cellist in Jena (1912-14), Zurich (1914-24), and Vienna (1924-38). One of his most important activities during that time was his work as a

member of the famous Kolisch String Quartet. Settling in Palestine in 1938, Stutschewsky studied Jewish folk music and began to compose works in which folk themes are manipulated with modern Western techniques. A highlight in his output is the symphonic suite *Israel* (1964). Among his writings are a valuable cello method and the book *Musical Folklore of Eastern Jewry* (1959).

T

TAL, JOSEF (originally JOSEF GRUENTHAL; born September

photo © Aliza Auerbach

18, 1910, in Pinne, near Posen, Germany [now near Poznań, Poland]). Composer. He moved to Palestine in 1934. For subject matter, Tal draws on the history and philosophy of the Old Testament; and for rhythms and inflections, he draws on the modern Hebrew language. Nevertheless, he avoids obvious regionalism in his basic musical materials. Much of his music is based on a personal use of the twelve-tone technique, as in the *First Symphony* (1953) and the first two string quartets (1959, 1964). But since the 1960s he has also been Israel's foremost composer of electronic music, as in *Frequencies 440-462* for tape (1973). Tal is particularly renowned for his operas, such as the twelve-tone *Ashmedai* (comp. 1969, perf. 1971) and the electronic *Massada* (comp. 1972, perf. 1973).

TALMI, YOAV (born April 28, 1943, in Kibbutz Merhavia, Palestine [now Israel]). Conductor. In 1969 he won the Koussevitzky Memorial Conducting Prize at the Tanglewood Music Festival in Massachusetts. Since then he has held numerous posts, notably as artistic director and conductor of the Gelders Orchestra in Arnhem, the Netherlands (1974-80), principal guest conductor of the Munich

Philharmonic (1979-81), and music director of the Israel Chamber Orchestra (since 1984). In 1973 he won the Rupert Conductor's Competition in London, subsequently leading all of London's major orchestras. Other Old World orchestras that he regularly conducts include the Berlin Philharmonic, the Israel Philharmonic, and the Munich Philharmonic. He is also rapidly becoming a popular guest conductor in North America, appearing with the Indianapolis

Symphony, the Rochester Philharmonic, the Vancouver Symphony, and others. Talmi is gaining a reputation as one of the most brilliant conductors of his time.

TAMIR, ALEXANDER. *See* EDEN, BRACHA and TAMIR, ALEXANDER.

TAUBE, MICHAEL (born March 13, 1890, in Łódź, Poland; died February 23, 1972, in Tel Aviv, Israel). Conductor and composer. In 1933 he became one of the founders of the Jewish Cultural Association in Germany. He went to Palestine in 1935 and helped to establish the Palestine (later the Israel Philharmonic) Orchestra, serving as one of the orchestra's principal conductors from its inception in 1936. Taube also guest-conducted extensively in Israel and abroad, notably with the Berlin Philharmonic. He composed orchestral works and chamber pieces.

Y

YANNAY, YEHUDA (born May 26, 1937, in Timişoara, Romania). Composer. He settled in Israel in 1951, but since the mid-1960s he has studied and worked in the United States. Yannay's compositions, in a hypermodern idiom, include works in a variety of genres. But he is best known for his theater pieces involving unusual combinations of visual and musical elements. *Houdini's Ninth* (1969), for example, is for double bass, an escape artist straitjacketed to the instrument, two hospital orderlies, and a record-player manipulator who plays a recording of the "Ode to Joy" from Beethoven's *Ninth Symphony*. *American Sonorama* (1976) is a ballet score derived from sounds of speeches by illiterate politicians.

YELLIN, THELMA (originally THELMA BENTWICH; born March 15, 1895, in London, England; died March 21, 1959, in Jerusalem, Israel). Cellist. Daughter of the Zionist leader Herbert Bentwich. She settled in Palestine in 1920 and married Eliezer Yellin in 1921. Thelma Yellin founded the Jerusalem Musical Society (1921); established the Jerusalem String Quartet (1922); helped Huberman to form the Palestine (later the Israel Philharmonic) Orchestra, taking part in the ensemble's first concert, under Toscanini, in 1936; and founded the Israel String Quartet (1951). Through her efforts a secondary school for talented young musicians was established in Tel Aviv; it opened in 1962 as the Thelma Yellin School. One of the foremost cellists of her generation, she followed the Casals tradition of playing with artistic purpose rather than with showmanship.

Glossary

aleatoricism (adjective, **aleatoric**) Any method of composition that includes chance or random elements with regard to the construction and/or performance of the music.

art song A song of serious artistic intent written by a trained musician. (Compare *folksong* and *popular song*.)

atonality (adjective, **atonal**) The absence of tonality (that is, the traditional reference to a tonal center).

baroque period The period of European art music from about 1600 to about 1750. The music is characterized by elaborate ornamentation, contrasting effects, powerful tensions and climaxes, and various contrapuntal devices and styles.

bitonality (adjective, **bitonal**) See *polytonality*.

blues A kind of melancholy song that originated among American blacks. It is characterized by "blue" notes (lowered third and seventh degrees of the scale) and by stereotyped twelve-measure harmonic patterns.

boogie-woogie A percussive style of playing blues on the piano, characterized by persistent repetitions of a bass figure in the left hand and by florid improvisations on a simple melody in the right hand.

bop (short for the original term, **bebop**) A type of 1940s jazz characterized by complex rhythms, dissonant harmony, and long, highly florid melodic lines.

Broadway A street in New York City on or near which are located most of the city's major theaters. Songs from Broadway musicals often differ from those of Tin Pan Alley by being tied to a show's plot and/or by being more musically sophisticated.

cantillation Liturgical chanting in a speechlike manner without accompaniment.

cantor The solo singer in a Jewish service.

chant A song, especially an unaccompanied liturgical melody in free rhythm.

Charleston A lively ballroom dance popular during the 1920s.

chord The simultaneous sounding of three or more tones. The term is sometimes applied to two tones, more properly called an *interval*.

chorus See *refrain*.

chromaticism (adjective, **chromatic**) The frequent use of tones foreign to a standard major or minor scale of a given tonality. (Compare *diatonicism*.)

classical music (1) Music of the classical period (1770-1830). (2) Music having the qualities of order, balance, economy, and objectivity. (3) Any serious music, as opposed to popular music.

classicism (adjective, **classical**) (1) The period of European art music from about 1770 to about 1830. (2) Any style of music having the qualities of order, balance, economy, and objectivity. (Compare *romanticism*.)

cluster (or **tone cluster**) Several consecutive tones of a scale sounded simultaneously, producing a strong dissonance.

coloratura Florid ornamentation (such as trills, arpeggios, and rapid scales) in vocal music designed to display a singer's skill.

consonance (adjective, **consonant**) A combination of two or more tones that create an effect generally felt to be stable or agreeable. (Compare *dissonance*.)

cool jazz A type of 1950s jazz characterized by emotional restraint, use of nontraditional jazz instruments (such as the French horn), and adoption of classical techniques (such as the fugue).

counterpoint (adjective, **contrapuntal**) Music containing two or more simultaneous melodies.

country music Commercial music deriving from or imitating a variety of American rural and cowboy styles. (Sometimes called *hillbilly music*).

country-rock Music having features of both country music and rock music.

diatonicism (adjective, **diatonic**) The use of tones that belong to a standard major or minor scale of a given tonality. (Compare *chromaticism*.)

dissonance (adjective, **dissonant**) A combination of two or more tones that create an effect generally felt to be unstable or disagreeable. (Compare *consonance*.)

dodecaphony (adjective, **dodecaphonic**) Same as *twelve-tone technique*.

ear training A type of instruction designed to teach the student to recognize and write down musical intervals and rhythms.

expressionism (adjective, **expressionistic**) A movement in music from about 1910 to about 1930, represented chiefly by Schoenberg and Berg. The aim is to express the deepest levels of a composer's mind and emotion, often when in a state of great anxiety. Atonality is common in expressionistic music.

figure A short coherent group of notes, especially if nonthematic. (Compare *motive*.)

finale The closing number of an act in an opera.

folk-rock Music having features of both folk music and rock music.

folksong (1) A song that is traditional among the common people of a region. (2) A song that echoes the simple qualities of a true folksong but was written by a known composer. (Compare *art song* and *popular song*.)

foxtrot A ballroom dance, beginning about 1915, comprising a variety of slow and fast steps.

fugato A passage in fugal style.

fugue (adjective, **fugal**) A composition in which (usually) a single short theme is stated in a part, repeated or imitated in turn in each of the other parts, and then contrapuntally developed.

gospel music A style of folksinging originally associated with Protestant evangelistic revival meetings.

gospel-rock Music having features of both gospel music and rock music.

graphic notation The use of drawn visual analogues (lines, boxes, numbers, and so on) to indicate pitches, rhythms, and other musical events in general terms only.

hard rock Rock music marked by loudness and a steady insistent beat.

harmony (adjective, **harmonic**) A single chord, or the whole chordal structure of a composition or a section thereof.

hot jazz Jazz marked by emotional excitement, complex rhythms, and free improvisations. (Compare *sweet jazz*.)

impressionism (adjective, **impressionistic**) A style in the late nineteenth and early twentieth centuries, represented in music chiefly by Debussy. The aim is to hint at momentary moods and impressions. This is achieved by avoiding the usual procedure of presenting well-defined material and dynamically developing it. Instead, the music consists basically of nonfunctional successions of vague melodic fragments and splashes of instrumental and harmonic color.

interval (adjective, **intervallic**) The difference in pitch between two tones, sounded together (harmonic interval) or one after the other (melodic interval).

jazz A broad category of American music developed from blues, ragtime, spirituals, and other popular forms and characterized by improvisation, syncopated rhythms, and "blue" notes (lowered third and seventh degrees of the scale).

key Same as *tonality*.

klezmer (plural, **klezmorim**) A Jewish folk instrumentalist.

late romanticism (adjective, **late romantic**) The last stage of the romantic period, peaking about 1890 to 1910 but extending beyond that time in its influence.

line See *part* sense (1).

linear counterpoint Contrapuntal music as viewed with an emphasis on its linear (or horizontal) aspects, rather than on its harmonic (or vertical) aspects.

measure A group of musical beats (units of musical time).

Mediterranean style A compositional style characterized by Middle Eastern melodic patterns combined with Western elements, such as moderately dissonant harmony and impressionistic orchestration. The style was developed in the 1940s by the Eastern Mediterranean School of composers, including Menahem Avidom, Paul Ben-Haim, Alexander Uriah Boscovich, and Max Brod.

microtone A musical interval smaller than a half tone.

minimalism An artistic movement, developed in the 1960s, that attempts to achieve maximum effects with minimum means, early represented in music chiefly by Philip Glass.

mode (adjective, **modal**) A scale, especially referring to any of the medieval scales associated with Catholic church music, as distinct from the modern major and minor scales.

modulation The act of changing from one tonality to another.

motive A short coherent group of notes used as a thematic building block. (Compare *figure*.)

multimedia (or **mixed media**) The simultaneous presentation of a series of effects in more than two media, as by combining acting, graphic art, tape recordings, and live music.

music track In a film, the tape of the music score before it is combined with other tracks. See *soundtrack*.

neoclassicism (adjective, **neoclassical**) A movement of twentieth-century music, beginning in the 1920s and led by Stravinsky and Hindemith, that is characterized by contemporary stylistic features being fused with elements derived from seventeenth- and eighteenth-century music, such as economy, objectivity, contrapuntal textures, and restricted forms.

neoromanticism (adjective, **neoromantic**) Any twentieth-century attempt to revive nineteenth-century romantic characteristics, often intensified through the use of such contemporary musical devices as free dissonance and dynamic rhythms.

orchestral color (1) In composition, the overall effect produced by the combination of timbres in music for the orchestra. (2) In conducting, the sonic shades produced by choices made about the balancing and articulating of various lines in the texture of music for the orchestra.

pandiatonicism (adjective, **pandiatonic**) The use of a diatonic scale as a tonal basis but with a free use of dissonance and without the traditional harmonic restrictions associated with the scale.

pantonality (adjective, **pantonal**) Literally, the inclusion of all tonalities. The term is used by some as equivalent to *atonality*, by others as synonymous with *twelve-tone technique*.

part (1) The series of tones written for, and executed by, a voice or instrument. Also called *line* or *voice*. (2) A section of a composition.

passacaglia A kind of variation form based on a continually repeated line, usually in the bass.

passage work A section that displays virtuosity (as through scales and arpeggios) rather than important musical ideas.

plainsong The ancient unaccompanied chant of the Roman Catholic church service. More broadly, any ancient liturgical chant.

pointillism (adjective, **pointillistic**) In music, the technique of distributing a melodic line among different instruments so that only one or two successive tones will be heard in the same timbre.

polyrhythm (adjective, **polyrhythmic**) The simultaneous use of strongly contrasting rhythms in different parts of the musical texture.

polytonality (adjective, **polytonal**) The use of two or more tonalities simultaneously. When limited to two tonalities, the effect is sometimes referred to specifically as *bitonality*.

pop-rock Music having features of both light popular music and hard-rock music.

popular song A song that is usually easily memorized and performed and that is designed to have wide appeal. (Compare *art song* and *folksong*.)

postmodernism (adjective, **postmodern**) A movement in reaction against the philosophy and practices of modern music.

postromanticism (adjective, **postromantic**) Same as *late romanticism*.

preclassical Relating to a time before the classical period.

progressive jazz A type of 1950s jazz that developed out of the earlier bop style, characterized by harmonic, contrapuntal, and rhythmic experimentation.

quarter tone A musical interval of one-half a half step.

ragtime An early form of jazz, in fashion from about 1896 to about 1918. It is characterized by strong syncopation in the melody with a regularly accented accompaniment.

refrain In a song, a section that recurs regularly, especially after each verse. Also called *chorus*.

reggae Jamaican popular music that combines indigenous elements with features of rock 'n' roll and soul music.

register In a human voice or a musical instrument, a portion of the range differing in sound quality from the other portions.

resolution The progression of a dissonance to a consonance.

rhythm and blues A type of black, urban popular music influenced by the blues and marked by a strong simple beat. It was an immediate precursor of rock 'n' roll.

rock (short for **rock 'n' roll**) Any of various outgrowths of 1950s rock 'n' roll, now featuring amplified guitars and keyboards.

rock 'n' roll (or **rock and roll**) A kind of American popular music that emerged in the 1950s from the black ethnic style of rhythm and blues. It is characterized by a strong beat and much repetition of simple melodic phrases.

romanticism (adjective, **romantic**) (1) The period of European art music from about 1820 to about 1910. (2) Any style of music having the qualities of unrest, exaggeration, diffusion, and subjectivity. (Compare *classicism*.)

row (short for **tone row** or **twelve-tone row**) See *twelve-tone technique*.

rubato A fluctuation of tempo within a musical phrase, alternately faster and slower according to the requirements of musical expression.

salon music Music of a light character, more suitable for the drawing room than for the concert hall.

salon rock Same as *soft rock*.

salsa Latin American popular music that has absorbed characteristics of jazz, rhythm and blues, and rock.

scale A series of tones rising or falling according to a certain pattern of melodic intervals. A major scale, for example, is found on the white keys of the piano from C to C: C, D, E, F, G, A, B, C. A minor scale on C would use E-flat instead of E, and, under certain conditions, A-flat instead of A and B-flat instead of B. Major and minor scales are diatonic scales. The chromatic scale consists of twelve successive half steps, covering all twelve pitch classes in the standard Western tuning system.

Second Viennese School The Viennese twelve-tone composers of the early twentieth century, led by Schoenberg, Berg, and Webern. The designation presumes the First Viennese School to have been the late eighteenth-century group of classicists led by Haydn, Mozart, and Beethoven.

serialism (adjective, **serial**) A compositional system based on a series of tones in a fixed order without regard to traditional tonality. Especially the *twelve-tone technique*.

series Same as *row*.

socialist realism A theory in the Soviet arts calling for the production of artistic works that develop social consciousness in a socialist state. Soviet music so formulated tends to be in an accessible nationalist idiom. Socialists elsewhere have adopted the ideals of socialist realism without the nationalist element.

soft rock Rock music that is gentler than hard rock.

sonata form (or **sonata-allegro form** or **first-movement form**) A form frequently used for single movements of sonatas, consisting of three principal sections: exposition, development, and recapitulation.

songplugger One who publicizes, or plugs, songs by performing them.

soul A style of music originating with American black gospel singing. It contains elements of rhythm and blues and is characterized by intense feeling.

soundtrack The area on a motion-picture film that carries the sound record, a composite of separate tracks for dialogue, music, and sound effects.

spiritual A type of religious song cultivated by black slaves in the American South.

sweet jazz Jazz marked by emotional restraint, fairly simple rhythms, and smoothly pleasing arrangements (instead of improvisations), often in imitation of symphonic or salon music. (Compare *hot jazz*.)

swing A style of jazz playing popular in the late 1930s, characterized by sophisticated big-band arrangements with interpolated improvisations by soloists.

symphonic jazz Jazz mixed with other styles (especially classical gestures) in arrangements that emphasize jazz as a serious art form beyond its early function as dance music.

syncopation (adjective, **syncopated**) The shifting of an accent from a strong to a weak beat, or from a strong to a weak part of a beat.

texture The general character of a composition created when lines are performed together. Texture may be basically contrapuntal or chordal, light or heavy.

timbre The characteristic quality of a tone produced on a specific instrument or by a human voice.

Tin Pan Alley The New York City area where popular-music publishers were concentrated during much of the twentieth century. The songs issued from Tin Pan Alley were generally simple and frankly commercial. (Compare *Broadway*.)

tonality (adjective, **tonal**) Broadly, the principle of organizing all of the tones of a piece of music in relation to one tone, the tonal center. Some theorists limit the term to music based on a major or minor scale (as opposed to various other kinds of scales).

tone color (1) Same as *timbre*. (2) In pianism, the sonic shades produced by such means as balancing lines and using the pedals to various degrees.

315

total serialism   Serialism applied not only to tones but also to other factors, such as rhythms, dynamics, and timbres.

triad   A traditional kind of three-tone chord.

trill   The rapid alternation of two tones a scale degree apart.

twelve-tone technique   A method of composition, devised by Arnold Schoenberg, in which the twelve tones of the chromatic scale are arranged in any fixed order (*row*), without regard for traditional tonality, and then subjected to permutations and combinations.

verse   In a song, a section preceding the refrain (if any) and excluding the introduction (if any).

vibrato   Slight and rapid variations in the pitch of a vocal or instrumental tone, produced to add warmth and expressiveness to the performance.

voice   (1) The singing voice divided into classes, such as soprano. (2) Same as *part* sense (1).

waltz   A graceful nineteenth-century round dance with three beats per measure.

Index

318

Smith, Melville, 100
Snow, Phoebe, 292
Snyder, Ted, 34
Society for Jewish Folk Music, 244, 264, 267, 275, 281, 287
Solomon, 292
Solti, Georg, 208-209
Sondheim, Stephen, 209-211
Sonnenberg, Berek, 256
Sonnenthal, Adolf von, 104
Sonnenthal, Luise von (Mrs. Erich Wolfgang Korngold), 104
Spector, Johanna, 292
Spector, Robert (Johanna Spector's husband), 292
Sperry, Paul, 292
Spiegelberg, Frances (Mrs. Jascha Heifetz), 82
Stacy, Jess, 78
Starer, Robert, 292
Stein, Erwin, 292
Steinberg, Maximilian, 293
Steinberg, William, 212-213, 227, 272, 308
Steiner, Max, 15
Stengel, Casey, 135
Stern, Isaac, 14, 31, 39, 157, 158, 176-77, 214-15, 249, 250
Stern, Julius, 293
Stern, Lotti (Mrs. William Steinberg), 213
Sternberg, Constantine von, 21
Sternberg, Erich Walter, 311
Steuermann, Edward, 293
Stevens, Connie (Mrs. Eddie Fisher), 265
Stevens, Risë, 15, 216-17
Stewart, Paula (Mrs. Burt Bacharach), 28
Stewart, Thomas (Evelyn Lear's husband), 112
Stiedry, Fritz, 293
Stokowski, Leopold, 30, 146, 153, 174, 266
Stoller, Mike, 293
Stolyarsky, Peter, 144, 151, 293
Stone, Will J., 238
Stransky, Josef, 293
Straus, Oscar, 264, 280, 293
Strauss, Johann, I, 14
Strauss, Johann, II, 148, 149, 286
Strauss, Johann, III, 66
Strauss, Richard, 81, 103, 108, 123, 160, 164, 188, 223
Strauss, Wolf, 14
Stravinsky, Igor, 57, 146, 157, 164, 262, 294
Streisand, Barbra, 14, 48, 59, 217-20, 282
Streisand, Emanuel, 220
Strouse, Charles, 293
Stutschewsky, Joachim, 311
Styne, Jule, 210, 221-22

Sullivan, Arthur, 149
Sullivan, Jo (Mrs. Frank Loesser), 119
Sulzer, Joseph, 294
Sulzer, Julius, 294
Sulzer, Salomon, 13, 230, 293-94
Sumbatian, Anaida, 26
Summer, Donna, 219
Surovy, Walter (Risë Stevens's husband), 216
Swados, Elizabeth, 294
Sylvester, James, 77
Szabolcsi, Bence, 294
Szell, George, 115, 168, 197, 222-24
Szeryng, Henryk, 224-26, 265
Szigeti, Dezsö, 294
Szigeti, Joseph, 78, 186, 294

Tal, Josef, 311
Talmi, Yoav, 312
Tamir, Alexander, 305
Tanguay, Eva, 232
Tansman, Alexandre, 294
Taranda, Anya (Mrs. Harold Arlen), 24
Tarnowski, Sergei, 85
Taube, Michael, 312
Tausig, Carl, 294
Taylor, Deems, 106
Taylor, Elizabeth (Mrs. Eddie Fisher), 265
Taylor, James (Carly Simon's husband), 207, 291
Tchaikovsky, Peter, 117, 123, 179, 180, 255, 286, 287
Teagarden, Jack, 266
Teicher, Louis, 294-95
Temianka, Henri, 265, 295
Temple, Shirley, 221
Tertis, Lionel, 295
Thalberg, Sigismond, 128, 295
Thibaud, Jacques, 225
Thomán, István, 164
Thomas, Dylan, 63
Thomas, Michael Tilson, 226-28
Thomas, Roberta, 226
Thomas, Ted, 226
Thomashefsky, Bessie, 226
Thomashefsky, Boris, 226
Thompson, Randall, 38, 100
Thomson, Sue, 116
Thomson, Virgil, 43, 52
Thuille, Ludwig, 44
Tibbett, Lawrence, 134
Ticker, Samuel, 229
Tiomkin, Dimitri, 295
Tischler, Hans, 295
Tobias, Ida (Mrs. Eddie Cantor), 49, 50, 51
Tobin, Louise (Mrs. Harry James), 88
Toch, Ernst, 161, 253, 295
Toscanini, Arturo, 86, 113, 124, 134-35,

152, 153, 154, 175, 176, 192, 194, 198, 212-13, 224, 235, 260, 272, 288, 312
Toscanini, Wanda (Mrs. Vladimir Horowitz), 86
Tourel, Jennie, 296
Tours, Frank, 96
Trudeau, Pierre, 220
Truman, Harry S, 135
Truman, Margaret, 135
Tsfasman, Alexander, 296
Tuck, Louis (Sophie Tucker's husband), 231
Tucker, Richard, 154, 229-30
Tucker, Sophie, 14, 72, 231-33, 235
Tudor, David, 246
Tureck, Rosalyn, 233-34
Turner, Lana (Mrs. Artie Shaw), 199
Twain, Mark. See Clemens, Samuel L.
Tzerko, Aube, 60

Unger, Max, 296
Urban, Heinrich, 110
Ushkov, Natalya (Mrs. Serge Koussevitzky), 107-108, 109
Uzielli, Lazzaro, 212

Vacano, Wolfgang, 115
Vale, Jerry, 143
Valenti, Fernando, 100
Vanzetti, Bartolomeo, 42
Vengerova, Isabella, 38, 70
Veprik, Alexander, 296
Victoria (queen of England), 179, 284
Vidal, Paul, 52
Vidor, Florence (Mrs. Jascha Heifetz), 82
Villoing, Alexander, 179
Vogel, Wladimir, 296
Vogler, Georg Joseph, Abbé, 136
Volman, Mark, 274
Volpe, Arnold, 296
Von Tilzer, Albert, 296, 297
Von Tilzer, Harry, 72, 296-97
Von Tilzer, Jack, 297
Von Tilzer, Jules, 297
Von Tilzer, Will, 297
Vronsky, Vitya, 255

Wagner, Charles, 203
Wagner, Cosima, 14
Wagner, Richard, 14, 130, 137, 150, 180, 277, 289
Wald, Jeff (Helen Reddy's husband), 284
Waldteufel, Emile, 297
Wallace, Mike, 87
Wallenstein, Albrecht von, 235
Wallenstein, Alfred, 115, 235-36

About the Author

Darryl Lyman coedited *Fifty Golden Years of Oscar* (1979), the official history of the Academy of Motion Picture Arts and Sciences. He is the coauthor (with Marjorie D. Lewis) of the college textbook *Essential English* (1981) and the author of *From Simple Sounds to Symphonies* (1982) and *The Animal Things We Say* (1983).

Mr. Lyman won many awards for clarinet playing in his youth. Later he composed a variety of well-received postmodern works. *Great Jews in Music* reflects his deep love of music and his thirty years of musical study and experience.